**INTERNATIONAL
AND
COMPARATIVE
CRIMINAL
LAW
SERIES**

Editorial Board
Series Editor
M. Cherif Bassiouni
President, International Human Rights Law Institute, DePaul University
President, International Institute of Higher Studies in Criminal Sciences, Siracusa, Italy, President, International Association of Penal Law, DePaul University
Professor of Law, DePaul University, Chicago, IL, USA

Diane Amann
Professor of Law
University of California
School of Law
Davis, CA, USA

Christopher L. Blakesley
J.Y. Sanders Professor of Law
Louisiana State University Law Center
Baton Rouge, LA, USA

Roger S. Clark
Board of Governors Professor
The State University of New Jersey
School of Law
Camden, NJ, USA

John Dugard
Member, International Law Commission, Geneva; Professor of Law, University of Witwatersrand, South Africa and University of Utrecht
Utrecht, The Netherlands

Albin Eser
Professor of Criminal Law, Albert Ludwig University; Director, Max-Planck Institute for International and Comparative Criminal Law
Freiburg, i. B., Germany

Alfredo Etcheberry
Professor of Criminal Law
National University of Chile; President, Chilean Lawyers' Association
Santiago, Chile

Jordan Paust
Professor of Law
University of Houston Law Center
Houston, TX, USA

Mario Pisani
Professor of Criminal Procedure
Faculty of Law, University of Milan
Milan, Italy

William Michael Reisman
Myers S. McDougal Professor of Law and Jurisprudence, Yale Law School
New Haven, CT, USA

Leila Sadat
Professor of Law
Washington University in St. Louis
School of Law
St. Louis, MO, USA

Michael P. Scharf
Professor of Law
New England School of Law
Boston, MA, USA

Kuniji Shibahara
Professor Emeritus
University of Tokyo, Faculty of Law
Tokyo, Japan

Otto Triffterer
Professor of International Criminal Law and Procedure, Faculty of Law, University of Salzburg
Salzburg, Austria

A MANUAL ON INTERNATIONAL HUMANITARIAN LAW AND ARMS CONTROL AGREEMENTS

EDITED BY M. CHERIF BASSIOUNI

Transnational Publishers, Inc.
Ardsley, New York

Published and Distributed by *Transnational Publishers, Inc.*
Ardsley Park Science and Technology Center
410 Saw Mill River Road
Ardsley, NY 10502

_____

Phone: 914-693-5100
Fax: 914-693-4430
E-mail: Info@transnationalpubs.com
Web: www.transnationalpubs.com

Library of Congress Cataloging-in-Publication Data

A manual on international humanitarian law and arms control agreements / edited by M. Cherif Bassiouni.
    p.cm.
    Includes bibliographical references.
    ISBN 1-57105-145-7
    1. Arms control—Sources. 2. Treaties—Collections. I. Bassiouni, M. Cherif

KZ5624.I58 2000
341.7'33'026—dc21

                                             00-059995

Copyright © 2000 by Transnational Publishers, Inc. and M. Cherif Bassiouni

All rights reserved. No part of this publication may be reproduced in any form or by any electronic or mechanical means including information storage and retrieval systems without permission in writing from the publisher.

Manufactured in the United States of America

CONTENTS

Acknowledgements .... *xiii*

Table of Abbreviations .... *xv*

Preface .... *xvii*

The Evolution of International Humanitarian Law and
Arms Control Agreements 1

Methodology and Analysis 47

Chart A: Penal Characteristics 67

Chart B: Contextual Applicability 73

Chart C: Type of Control Regime 79

**CHAPTER I: MULTILATERAL INSTRUMENTS ON THE
REGULATION OF ARMED CONFLICTS AND THE
CONTROL OF WEAPONS**

Introduction 83

I-1. Declaration Renouncing the Use, in Time of War, of Explosive
Projectiles Under 400 Grammes Weight (St. Petersburg Declaration)
11 December, 1868 85

I-2. Project of an International Declaration Concerning the Laws and Customs
of War, 27 August, 1874 87

I-3. Convention (II) with Respect to the Laws and Customs of War on Land
and its annex: Regulation Concerning the Laws and Customs of War on
Land, 29 July, 1899 93

I-4. Declaration Concerning the Prohibition, for the Term of Five Years, the
Launching Of Projectiles and Explosives from Balloons, and Other
Methods of Similar Nature (First Hague, IV, 1) 29 July, 1899 97

I-5. Declaration Concerning the Prohibition of the Use of Projectiles
Diffusing Asphyxiating Gases (First Hague, IV, 2) 29 July, 1899 99

I-6. Declaration Concerning the Prohibition of the Use of Expanding Bullets
(First Hague, IV, 3) 29 July, 1899 101

v

I-7. Convention (IV) Respecting the Laws and Customs of War on Land and Its Annex: Regulation Concerning the Laws and Customs of War on Land, 18 October, 1907 103

I-8. Convention Respecting the Rights and Duties of Neutral Powers And Persons in Case of War on Land (Second Hague, V) 18 October, 1907 .. 107

I-9. Convention (VII) Relating to the Conversion of Merchant Ships into War-Ships, 18 October, 1907 111

I-10. Convention Relative to the Laying of Automatic Submarine Contact Mines (Second Hague, VIII) 18 October, 1907 115

I-11. Convention Concerning Bombardment by Naval Forces in Time of War (Second Hague, IX) 18 October, 1907 119

I-12. Convention (X) for the Adaptation to Maritime Warfare of the Principles of the Geneva Convention, 18 October, 1907 123

I-13. Convention Concerning the Rights and Duties of Neutral Powers in Naval War (Second Hague, XIII) 18 October, 1907 129

I-14. Declaration Relative to Prohibiting the Discharge of Projectiles and Explosives from Balloons (Second Hague, XIV) 18 October, 1907 135

I-15. Declaration Concerning the Laws of Naval War, 26 February, 1909 137

I-16. Convention Relating to the Non-Fortification and Neutralisation of the Aaland Islands, 20 October, 1921 147

I-17. Treaty Relating to the Use of Submarines and Noxious Gases in Warfare, 1922 149

I-18. Rules Concerning the Control of Wireless Telegraphy in Time of War and Air Warfare, February, 1923 151

I-19. Convention on Maritime Neutrality, 20 February, 1928 161

I-20. Treaty for the Limitation and Reduction of Naval Armaments (London Treaty) 22 April, 1930 167

I-21. *Procès-verbal* Relating to the Rules of Submarine Warfare set forth in Part IV of the Treaty of London, 6 November, 1936 169

I-22. The Nyon Agreement, 14 September, 1937 171

vii International Humanitarian Law and Arms Control Agreements

I-23. Agreement Supplementary to the Nyon Agreement, 17 September, 1937 173

I-24. Protocol No. III on the Control of Armaments (Treaty for Collaboration in Economic, Social and Cultural Matters of Collective Self-Defence Control of Armaments), 23 October, 1943 175

I-25. Convention for the Amelioration of the Condition of the Wounded and Sick in Armed Forces in the Field (Geneva Convention I) August 12, 1949 177

I-26. Convention for the Amelioration of the Condition of the Wounded, Sick, and Shipwrecked Members of the Armed Forces at Sea (Geneva Convention II) August 12, 1949 179

I-27. Convention Relative to the Protection of Civilian Persons in Time of War (Geneva Convention IV) August 12, 1949 181

I-28. Convention on the Prohibition of Military or Any Other Hostile Use of Environmental Modification Techniques, 18 May, 1977 183

I-29. Protocol Additional to the Geneva Convention of 12 August, 1949, and Relating to the Protection of Victims of International Armed Conflicts (Protocol I) 8 June, 1977 189

I-30. Protocol Additional to the Geneva Convention of 12 August, 1949, and Relating to the Protection of Victims of Non-International Armed Conflicts (Protocol II) 8 June, 1977 207

I-31. Resolution on Small-Calibre Weapons Systems by the United Nations Conference on Prohibitions or Restrictions on the Use of Certain Conventional Weapons 28 September, 1979 215

I-32. Convention on Prohibitions and Restrictions on the Use of Certain Conventional Weapons Which May be Deemed to be Excessively Injurious or to have Indiscriminate Effects, 10 October, 1980 217

I-32(a). Protocol on Non-Detectable Fragments to the Convention on Prohibitions or Restrictions on the Use of Certain Conventional Weapons (Protocol I) 10 October, 1980 225

I-32(b). Protocol on Prohibitions or Restrictions on the Use of Mines, Booby-Traps, and Other Devices to the Convention on Prohibitions or Restrictions on the Use of Certain Conventional Weapons (Protocol II) 10 October, 1980 227

I-32(c). Protocol on Prohibitions or Restrictions on the Use of Incendiary Weapons to the Convention on Prohibitions or Restrictions on the Use of Certain Conventional Weapons (Protocol III) 10 October, 1980...247

I-32(d). Protocol (IV) on Blinding Laser Weapons, 12 October, 1995 251

I-33. United Nations Convention on Law of the Sea, 1982 253

I-34. United Nations International Convention for the Suppression of Terrorist Bombings[1], 12 January, 1998 259

PRINCIPAL MANUALS ON THE REGULATION OF ARMED CONFLICTS AND WEAPONS CONTROL EVIDENCING CUSTOMARY INTERNATIONAL LAW

I-35. Instructions for the Government of Armies of the United States in the Field (Lieber Code) 24 April, 1863 273

I-36. The Laws of War on Land, (Oxford Manual) 9 September, 1880 291

I-37. Manual of the Laws of Naval War, 9 August, 1913 303

I-38. San Remo Manual on International Law Applicable to Armed Conflicts at Sea, 12 June, 1994 321

CHAPTER II: MULTILATERAL INSTRUMENTS ON THE REGULATION, CONTROL, AND PROHIBITION OF WEAPONS OF MASS DESTRUCTION

Introduction 353

II-1. Protocol for the Prohibition of the Use in War of Asphyxiating, Poisonous or Other Gases, and of Bacteriological Methods of Warfare, 17 June, 1925 357

II-2. Draft Convention for the Protection of Civilian Populations Against New Engines of War, 2 September, 1938 361

II-3. Treaty on the Non-Proliferation of Nuclear Weapons, 1 July, 1968 369

II-4. The Distinction Between Military Objectives and Non-Military Objectives in General and Particularly the Problems Associated with Weapons of Mass Destruction, 9 September 1969 377

---

[1] This is the only instrument in this category that addresses the use of weapons in peace-time.

ix *International Humanitarian Law and Arms Control Agreements*

II-5. Convention on the Prohibition of the Development, Production and Stockpiling of Bacteriological (Biological) and Toxin Weapons and on Their Destruction, 10 April, 1972 379

II-6. Convention on the Prohibition of the Development, Production, Stockpiling and Use of Chemical Weapons and on Their Destruction, 13 January, 1993 385

II-7. Draft Convention on Nuclear Terrorism (1998) 433

II-8. International Court of Justice Advisory Opinion on the Legality of Threat Or Use of Nuclear Weapons (1996) 443

CHAPTER III: MULTILATERAL INSTRUMENTS ON THE PROHIBITION OF EMPLACEMENT OF WEAPONS OF MASS DESTRUCTION IN CERTAIN MEDIA

Introduction 483

III-1. The Antarctic Treaty, 1 December, 1959 485

III-2. Treaty Banning Nuclear Weapon Tests in the Atmosphere, in Outer Space and Under Water, 5 August, 1963 493

III-3. Treaty on Principles Governing the Activities of States in the Exploration of Outer Space, Including the Moon and Other Celestial Bodies, 27 January, 1967 497

III-4. Treaty on the Prohibition of the Emplacement of Nuclear Weapons and Other Weapons of Mass Destruction on the Sea-Bed and the Ocean Floor and in the Subsoil Thereof, 11 February, 1971 505

III-5. Agreement Governing the Activities of States on the Moon and Other Celestial Bodies, 5 December, 1979 511

CHAPTER IV: REGIONAL NUCLEAR FREE ZONES AGREEMENTS

Introduction 513

IV-1(a). Treaty for the Prohibition of Nuclear Weapons in Latin America (Treaty of Tlatelolco) 14 February, 1968 515

IV-1(b). Additional Protocol I to the Treaty for the Prohibition of Nuclear Weapons in Latin America, 14 February, 1967 529

IV-1(c). Additional Protocol II to the Treaty of 14 February, 1967 for the
Prohibition of Nuclear Weapons in Latin America,
14 February, 1967 531

IV-2. South Pacific Nuclear-Free Zone Treaty (Treaty of Raratonga)
6 August, 1985 533

IV-3. Treaty on South-East Asia Nuclear Weapon-Free Zone,
15 December, 1995 547

IV-4(a). African Nuclear-Weapon Free Zone Treaty, 21 June, 1996 559

IV-4(b). The Cairo Declaration, 12 June 1996 567

CHAPTER V: MIDDLE EAST ARMS CONTROL AND SECURITY AGREEMENTS

Introduction 569

V-1. United Nations Security Council Resolution 50, 29 May, 1948 571

V-2. Agreement for the Demilitarization of Mount Scopus Area,
7 July, 1948 573

V-3. Egyptian-Israeli General Armistice Agreement, 24 February, 1949 575

V-4. Separation of Forces Agreement Between Israel and Syria,
31 May, 1974 585

V-5. Separation of Forces Agreement Between Israel and Egypt,
18 January, 1974 587

V-6. Interim Agreement Between Israel and Egypt, 1 September, 1975 589

V-7. Camp David Accords, 17 September, 1978 597

V-8. Peace Treaty Between Israel and Egypt, 26 March, 1979 605

V-9. Treaty of Peace Between the State of Israel and the Hashemite Kingdom
of Jordan, 26 October, 1994 621

V-10. Israeli-Palestinian Interim Agreement on the West Bank and the Gaza
Strip, 28 September, 1995 631

V-11. Israel-Lebanon Cease-Fire Understanding, 26 April, 1996 655

xi *International Humanitarian Law and Arms Control Agreements*

V-12. Protocol Concerning the Redeployment in Hebron, 17 January, 1997 . 657

V-13. The Wye River Memorandum, 23 October, 1998 667

V-14. The Sharm el-Sheikh Memorandum on Implementation Timeline of Outstanding Commitments of Agreements Signed and Resumption of Permanent Status Negotiations, 4 September, 1999 677

V-15. Protocol Concerning Safe Passage Between the West Bank and Gaza Strip, 5 October, 1999 683

V-16. U.N. General Assembly Resolution on Establishment of a Nuclear Weapon Free Zone in the Region of the Middle East, 1999 695

CHAPTER VI: EUROPEAN ARMS CONTROL AND SECURITY AGREEMENTS

Introduction 699

VI-1. Conventional Armed Forces in Europe (CFE) Treaty 701

VI-2. Addendum to the Conventional Armed Forces in Europe Treaty 725

CHAPTER VII: BILATERAL NUCLEAR WEAPONS CONTROL AGREEMENTS- THE UNITED STATES OF AMERICA AND THE UNION OF SOVIET SOCIALIST REPUBLICS

Introduction 739

VII-1. Treaty Between the United States of America and the Union of Soviet Socialist Republics on the Limitation of Anti-Ballistic Missile Systems (ABM Treaty), 3 October, 1972 741

VII-2. Treaty Between the United States of America and the Union of Soviet Socialist Republics on the Limitation of Strategic Offensive Arms (SALT II), 18 June, 1979 747

VII-3. Protocol to the Treaty Between the United States of America and the Union of Soviet Socialist Republics on the Limitation of Strategic Offensive Arms 777

VII-4. Treaty Between the United States of America and the Union of Soviet Socialist Republics on the Elimination of their Intermediate-Range and Short-Range Missiles, 1 June, 1988 781

VII-5. Treaty Between the United States of America and the Union of Soviet Socialist Republics on the Limitation of Underground Nuclear Weapons Tests, 11 December 1990 799

VII-6. Protocol to Treaty Between the United States of America and the Union of Soviet Socialist Republics on the Limitation of Underground Nuclear Weapons Tests 803

CHAPTER VIII: THE MISSILE TECHNOLOGY CONTROL REGIME

Introduction 807

VIII-1. Guidelines for Sensitive Missile-Relevant Transfers, 7 January, 1993 809

VIII-2. Missile Technology Control Regime Equipment And Technology Annex, 11 June, 1996 813

CONCLUSION 837

ACKNOWLEDGEMENTS

This is to gratefully acknowledge the research assistance of Adam A. Quader, the editorial assistance of Lindsay Glauner, and the support of the John D. and Catherine T. MacArthur Foundation for the work of the Group of Experts on Arms Control and Regional Security in the Middle East Including Elimination of Weapons of Mass Destruction, for which this research was done.

TABLE OF ABBREVIATIONS

AM. J. INT'L L.	AMERICAN JOURNAL OF INTERNATIONAL LAW
BASSIOUNI, CRIMES AGAINST HUMANITY	M. CHERIF BASSIOUNI, CRIMES AGAINST HUMANITY IN INTERNATIONAL CRIMINAL LAW (1992)
BASSIOUNI, ICL	M. CHERIF BASSIOUNI, INTERNATIONAL CRIMINAL LAW (3 VOLS. 1999)
BASSIOUNI, ICL CONVENTIONS	M. CHERIF BASSIOUNI, INTERNATIONAL CRIMINAL CONVENTIONS AND THEIR PENAL PROVISIONS (1997)
BEVANS	TREATIES AND OTHER INTERNATIONAL AGREEMENTS OF THE UNITED STATES OF AMERICA, 1776-1949 (C.F. Bevans ed.1970, 13 vols.)
Consol. T.S.	Consolidated Treaty Series
E.A.S.	(U.S.) Executive Agreement Series
Europ. T.S.	European Treaty Series
G.A. (U.N.)	General Assembly
GAOR	(U.N.) General Assembly Official Records
HUDSON	INTERNATIONAL LEGISLATION, 1909-1945 (M. Hudson ed., photo reprint 1972, 9 vols.)
ICJ	International Court of Justice
I.L.M.	INTERNATIONAL LEGAL MATERIALS
ILC	International Law Commission
League of Nations O.J.	League of Nations Official Journal
L.N.T.S.	League of Nations Treaty Series
Malloy	Treaties, Conventions, International Acts, Protocols, and Agreements Between the United States of America and Other Powers, 1776-1909 (W. Malloy ed., photo reprint 1965, 4 vols.)

MARTENS	MARTENS NOUVEAU RECUEIL GENERAL DES TRAITES ET AUTRES ACTES RELATIFS AUX RAPPORTS DE DROIT INTERNATIONAL (three series: 1843-1875, First Series; 1876-1908, Second Series; 1915-1944, Third Series)
Miller	Treaties and Other International Acts of the United States of America (H. Miller ed., 1942, 8 vols.)
OAS	Organization of American States
O.A.S. Treaty Series	Organization of American States Treaty Series
Parry's	THE CONSOLIDATED TREATY SERIES (C. Parry ed., 1969 & Supp., 231 vols.)
S.C.	(U.N.) Security Council
S. Exec.	Senate Executive Documents
Stat.	United States Statutes at Large
T.I.A.S.	(U.S.) Treaties and Other International Acts Series
U.N.	United Nations
U.N.T.S.	United Nations Treaty Series
U.S.T.	United States Treaties and Other International Agreements

PREFACE

Since the origins of humankind, man has consistently developed weapons that kill more people and cause greater devastation. In recent times, an increase in science and technology has allowed for the development of more sophisticated weapons, perversely designed to cause great human pain and suffering. These weapons reveal the negative aspect of human inventiveness and destructiveness. Concurrently, however, and throughout all civilizations, efforts at minimizing the harmful consequences of weapons of war have also been consistent. These efforts derive from humanistic values that have sustained the evolution of international humanitarian law throughout the last 5,000 years of recorded history.

Since the French Revolution in 1789 to the 1999 armed conflict in Kosovo, an estimated 200 million persons have lost their lives. If wars cannot be eradicated, then at least we must strive for a lessening of the harm they cause. More specifically, we must eliminate the use of weapons of mass destruction and other weapons that cause what has come to be known as "unnecessary pain and suffering."

The humanization of armed conflict necessarily means limitations on the use of weapons in time of war and also in time of peace. Wartime limitations on the use of more destructive weapons, in of itself, contradict the traditional doctrine that war is the infliction of the greatest harm on the enemy in order to secure submission. To offset that doctrine with a humanistic argument alone has not proven to be enough. However, in time, that doctrine has gradually given way to another, namely that the aims of war can best be achieved by the least amount of harm inflicted on the enemy in order to gain the most advantages in political outcomes. In other words, the aims of war are no longer to be viewed in terms of the infliction of the greatest harm but in terms of inflicting the least amount of harm to achieve the swiftest political results. That is what Von Clausewitz argued in 1832 when he stated, "war is the continuation of diplomacy but by other means." At present, pragmatic self-interest and mutuality of interests add their weight to humanistic values, supporting elimination, limitation and control of certain types of weapons, both in time of war and later in time of peace.

The making of modern weapons of war does not however reflect the philosophical transformation of the aims of war stated above. One reason is that such weapons give states the deterrence capability inherent in possessing overwhelming destructive military capabilities. Thus, these weapons become the best guarantee for security, as well as the most effective means of exercising subtle influence or even hegemonistic influence over an opposing or enemy state. In part, this was evident after World War II in the Cold War confrontation between the Western and Eastern blocks where nuclear weapons became the essence of the theory of deterrence. The possession of these weapons in great quantities by both sides provided mutually assured destruction and thus lessened the prospects of their use.

During that same period of the Cold War the voices of humanism that called for the ban of nuclear weapons were hardly heard by those who had the power to eliminate such weapons. In fact, their reduction by the United States and Union of Soviet Socialist Republic as of the 1970's was predicated on pragmatic and strategic arguments and not because of humanistic concerns. But the elimination of nuclear, chemical and biological weapons have since then become part of the expectations of a growing multitude throughout the world. Indeed, opposition to weapons of mass destruction of all types and their elimination has been consistently growing throughout the world.

Efforts to eliminate weapons of mass destruction are based on the arguments that such weapons are: 1) indiscriminate in the harm they cause; 2) widespread in their harmful effects; 3) cause great pain and suffering to many non-combatants who could be directly exposed or indirectly affected by them; and 4) affect the environment by causing permanent damage.

Even though the world has conveniently ignored the victims of the atomic bombs that were dropped on the Japanese cities of Hiroshima and Nagasaki, in 1945, the dangerous effects of atomic bombs certainly weigh heavy on the minds of various individuals. Thus, as potential access by states and non-state actors to weapons of mass destruction increases, the threat perception of many people throughout the world also increases.

One of the aims of this book is to compile in a useful manner all instruments that pertain to the regulation of armed conflict and to place them in their own appropriate chapters. These chapters are: Multilateral Instruments on the Regulation of Armed Conflicts and Control of Weapons; Principal Manuals on the Regulation of Armed Conflicts and Weapons Control Evidencing Customary International Law; Multilateral Instruments on the Regulation, Control, and Prohibition of Weapons of Mass Destruction; Multilateral Instruments on the Prohibition of Emplacement of Weapons of Mass Destruction in Certain Media; Regional Nuclear Free Zones Agreements; Middle East Arms Control and Security Agreements; European Arms Control and Security Agreements; Bilateral Nuclear Weapons Control Agreements Between the United States of America and The Union of Soviet Socialist Republics and its Successor States; and a G-7 Voluntary Missile Technology Regime.

While the various legal and control regimes compiled herein strengthen the overall goal of eliminating and controlling weapons, there is no connection between all of these categories of agreements, which contain a variety of norms, regulations and undertakings applicable to weapons. Thus, for the time being, we must rely on whatever synergy can be developed between these various types of norms, regulations and undertakings in order to strengthen the overall framework of weapons control.

There are eighty-four instruments contained in this book whose adoption covers a period from 1863 to May of 2000. To assist the researcher, a detailed methodology is included, as well as three charts dealing with the penal characteristics contained in these instruments, their contextual applicability (time of peace, time of war), and the type of control regime.

Admittedly, the methodology followed reflects the influence of the discipline that I largely contributed in shaping, namely international criminal law. Thus others, particularly political scientists and military strategists, may find that this work does not necessarily reflect their concerns and interests. However, since there is no compilation of all of these legal regimes, this effort will hopefully be a worthwhile contribution to the study of humanitarian law and weapons control.

M. Cherif Bassiouni

Chicago, July 7, 2000

EVOLUTION OF INTERNATIONAL HUMANITARIAN LAW AND ARMS CONTROL AGREEMENTS[1]

Introduction

For over five thousand years, humanitarian principles regulating armed conflicts evolved gradually in different civilizations.[2] In time, these humanitarian principles formed an inter-woven fabric of norms and rules designed to prevent certain forms of physical harm and hardships from befalling non-combatants, as well as certain categories of combatants such as the sick, wounded, shipwrecked and prisoners of war.[3] As the protective scheme of prescriptions and proscriptions contained in conventional and customary international law developed, both qualitatively and quantitatively,[4] more serious breaches of international law were criminalized.[5] But the process of normative development in international criminal law, of which international humanitarian law is such an important part, has never been part of a consistent or cohesive international legal policy.[6] Instead, international crimes, including war crimes and crimes against humanity, have evolved by virtue of a haphazard mixture of conventions, customs, general

---

[1] Parts of this article are based on M. CHERIF BASSIOUNI, CRIMES AGAINST HUMANITY IN INTERNATIONAL CRIMINAL LAW 42-62. (2d. rev. ed. 1999) [hereinafter BASSIOUNI, CRIMES AGAINST HUMANITY] and Leslie C. Green, *International Regulation of Armed Conflicts, in* 1 INTERNATIONAL CRIMINAL LAW 355 (M. C. Bassiouni ed., 2d ed. 1999) [hereinafter BASSIOUNI, ICL].

[2] See generally FRANÇOIS BUGNION, LA COMITÉ INTERNATIONAL DE LA CROIX-ROUGE ET LA PROTECTION DES VICTIMES DE LA GUERRE (1994); HILAIRE MCCOUBREY, *Humanitarianism in the Laws of Armed Conflict, in* INTERNATIONAL HUMANITARIAN LAW 1-21 (1990); Gerald I.A.D. Draper, *The Development of International Humanitarian Law, in* INTERNATIONAL DIMENSIONS OF HUMANITARIAN LAW 67 (UNESCO 1988); INTERNATIONAL DIMENSIONS OF HUMANITARIAN LAW (UNESCO 1988); JEAN S. PICTET, DEVELOPMENT AND PRINCIPLES OF INTERNATIONAL HUMANITARIAN LAW (1985); GEOFFREY BEST, HUMANITY IN WARFARE (1983); Edward F. Sherman, *The Civilianization of Military Law*, 22 ME. L. REV. 3 (1970); Leslie C. Green, THE CONTEMPORARY LAW OF ARMED CONFLICT (1993); Leslie C. Green, ESSAYS ON THE MODERN LAW OF WAR (1985).

[3] See generally HOWARD LEVIE, THE CODE OF INTERNATIONAL ARMED CONFLICT (1986); THE LAWS OF ARMED CONFLICTS (Dietrich Schindler, Jiří Toman eds., 1988); THE LAW OF WAR: A DOCUMENTARY HISTORY (Leon Friedman ed., 1972).

[4] See BASSIOUNI, INTERNATIONAL CRIMINAL LAW CONVENTIONS AND THEIR PENAL PROVISIONS (1997) [hereinafter BASSIOUNI, ICL CONVENTIONS].

[5] Richard B. Lillich, *Can the Criminal Process Be Used to Help Enforce Human Rights Law?, in* INTERNATIONAL HUMAN RIGHTS: PROBLEMS OF LAW, POLICY AND PRACTICE (War Crimes, Genocide, *Apartheid*, Terrorism and Torture) 864 (1991); M. Cherif Bassiouni, *The Proscribing Function of International Criminal Law in the Processes of International Protection of Human Rights*, 9 YALE J. WORLD PUB. ORD. 193, 196-98 (1982); JACK DONNELLY, UNIVERSAL HUMAN RIGHTS IN THEORY AND PRACTICE (1989).

[6] See Richard B. Lillich, *Respect for Human Rights in Armed Conflict, Civil Strife and States of Emergency (Human Rights in Extremes), in* INTERNATIONAL HUMAN RIGHTS: PROBLEMS OF LAW, POLICY, AND PRACTICE 766 (1991).

principles, and the writings of scholars.[7] Among these sources of international law, the writings of the most distinguished publicists have significantly contributed to the shaping and advancement of world community values and expectations.[8]

---

[7] See Art. 38, Charter of the United Nations, Statute of the International Court of Justice, signed at San Francisco, June 26, 1945, 59 Stat. 1031, T.S. No. 993, and PCIJ Statute, art. 38, ¶ 3 (listing the sources of international law).

[8] See, inter alia, the following major texts: M. CHERIF BASSIOUNI, A DRAFT INTERNATIONAL CRIMINAL CODE AND DRAFT STATUTE FOR AN INTERNATIONAL CRIMINAL TRIBUNAL (1987); M. CHERIF BASSIOUNI, INTERNATIONAL CRIMINAL LAW (Vols. I, II, & III, 1986-1987 and 2d. rev. ed., 1999); INTERNATIONAL CRIMINAL LAW: A COLLECTION OF INTERNATIONAL AND EUROPEAN DOCUMENTS (Christine Van den Wyngaert ed., 1996); JORDAN J. PAUST, M. CHERIF BASSIOUNI ET AL., INTERNATIONAL CRIMINAL LAW: CASES AND MATERIALS (1996); ANDRE HUET & RENEE KOERING-JOULIN, DROIT PÉNAL INTERNATIONAL (1994); M. CHERIF BASSIOUNI, CRIMES AGAINST HUMANITY IN INTERNATIONAL CRIMINAL LAW (1992); HAIDONG LI, DIE PRINZIPIEN DES INTERNATIONALEN STRAFRECHT (1991); M. CHERIF BASSIOUNI, INTERNATIONAL CRIMES DIGEST/INDEX (1985); DIETRICH OEHLER, INTERNATIONALEN STRARECHT (1973); AKTUELLE PROBLEME DES INTERNATIONALEN STRARECHTS (Dietrich Oehler & Paul G. Potz eds., 1970); JOSEPH B. KEENAN & BRENDAN F. BROWN, CRIMES AGAINST INTERNATIONAL LAW (1950); ALBERT DE LA PRADELLE, UNE REVOLUTION DANS LE DROIT PÉNAL INTERNATIONAL (1946); ROLANDO QUADRI, DIRITTO PENALE INTERNATIONALE (1944); FRANCESCO COSENTINI, ESSAI D'UN CODE PÉNALE INTERNATIONALE DRESSÉ SUR LA BASE COMPARATIVE DES PROJETS ET TEXTES RECENTS DES CODES PÉNAUX (1937); HELLMUTH VON WEBER, INTERNATIONALE STRAGERRICHTSBARKEIT (1934); ALFRED HEGLER, PRINZIPEN DES INTERNATIONALEN STRAFRECHTS (1906); FRIEDRICH MEILI, LEHRBUCH DES INTERNATIONALEN STRAFRECHTS UND STRAFPROZESSRECHTS (1910); HENRI DONNEDIEU DE VABRES, INTRODUCTION: L'ETUDE DU DROIT PÉNAL INTERNATIONAL (1922); VESPASIEN V. PELLA, LA CODIFICATION DU DROIT PÉNAL INTERNATIONAL (1922); MAURICE TRAVERS, LE DROIT PÉNAL INTERNATIONAL ET SA MISE EN OEUVRE EN TEMPS DE PAIX ET EN TEMPS DE GUERRE (5 vols. 1920-1922); HENRI DONNEDIEU DE VABRES, LES PRINCIPES MODERNES DU DROIT PÉNAL INTERNATIONAL (1928); NINO LEVI, DIRITTO PENALE INTERNAZIONALE (1944); HANS-HEINRICH JESCHECK, DIE VERANTWORTLICHKEIT DER STAATSORGANE NACH VÖLKERSTRAFRECHT (1952); STEFAN GLASER, INTRODUCTION À L'ETUDE DU DROIT PÉNAL INTERNATIONAL (1954); ANTONIO QUINTANO RIPOLLES, TRATADO DE DERECHO PENAL INTERNACIONAL Y INTERNACIONAL PENAL (2 vols. 1955-1957); STEFAN GLASER, L'INFRACTION INTERNATIONALE, SES ELEMENTS CONSTITUTIFS ET SES ASPECTS JURIDIQUE (1957); INTERNATIONAL CRIMINAL LAW (Gerhard O.W. Mueller & Edward M. Wise eds. 1965); OTTO TRIFFTERER, DOGMATISCHE UNTERSUCHUNGEN ZUR ENTWICKLUNG DES MATERIELLEN VOLKERSTRAFRECHTS SEIT NURNBERG (1966); STANISLAW PLAWSKI, ETUDE DES PRINCIPES FONDAMENTAUX DU DROIT INTERNATIONAL PÉNAL (1972); 1 BASSIOUNI AND NANDA TREATISE; LA BELGIQUE ET LE DROIT INTERNATIONAL PÉNAL (Bart B. DeSchutter ed. 1975); STEFAN GLASER, DROIT PÉNAL INTERNATIONAL CONVENTIONNEL (2 vols. 1977-79); G. FIERRO, LA LEY PENAL Y EL DERECHO INTERNACIONAL (1977-79); CLAUDE LOMBOIS, DROIT PÉNAL INTERNATIONAL (2d ed. 1979); HASSANEIN EBEID, AL-GARIMA AL-DAWLIA (THE INTERNATIONAL CRIME) (1979); BASSIOUNI, ICL CONVENTIONS, supra note 4; BASSIOUNI DRAFT CODE; FARHAD MALEKIAN, INTERNATIONAL CRIMINAL LAW (2 vols. 1991). See also inter alia the following major articles: M. Cherif Bassiouni, The Penal Characteristics of Conventional International Criminal Law, 15 CASE W. RES. J. INT'L L. 27 (1983); Leslie C. Green, Is There an International Criminal Law?, 21 ALBERTA L. REV. 251 (1983); Farooq Hassan, The Theoretical Basis of Punishment in International Criminal Law, 15 CASE W. RES. J. INT'L L. 39 (1983); M. Cherif Bassiouni, The Proscribing Function of International Criminal Law in the Process of International Protection of Human Rights, 8 YALE J. WORLD PUB. ORD. 193 (1982); Leslie C. Green, New Trends in International Criminal Law, 1981 ISR. Y.B. HUM. RTS. 9; Hans Heinrich Jescheck, Development, Present State and Future Prospects of International Criminal Law, 52 REVUE INTERNATIONALE DE DROIT PENAL 337 (1981); Leslie C. Green, An International Criminal Code - Now?, 3 DALHOUSIE L.J. 560 (1976); M. Cherif Bassiouni, An Appraisal of the Growth and Developing Trends of International Criminal Law, 45 REVUE INTERNATIONALE DE DROIT PENAL 405 (1974); Robert Legros, Droit Pénal International 1967, 48 REVUE DE DROIT PÉNAL ET DE CRIMINOLOGIE 259 (1968); Hans-Heinrich Jescheck, Etat Actuel et Perspectives d'Avenir des Projets

dans le Domaine du Droit International Pénal, 35 REVUE INTERNATIONALE DE DROIT PENAL 83 (1964); W.I. Ganshof van der Meersch, *Justice et Droit International Pénal*, 42 REVUE DE DROIT PÉNAL ET DE CRIMINOLOGIE 3 (1961); Leslie C. Green, *New Approach to International Criminal Law*, 28 SOLIC. 106 (1961); Jean Y. Dautricourt, *Le Droit International Pénal*, 37 REVUE DE DROIT PÉNAL ET DE CRIMINOLOGIE 243 (1957); Jacques Verhaegen, *Les Impasses du Droit International Pénal*, 38 REVUE DE DROITS PÉNALET DE CRIMINOLOGIE 3 (1957); Stefan Glaser, *Element Moral de l'Infraction Internationale*, 59 REVUE GÉNÈRALE DE DROIT INTERNATIONAL PUBLIC 537 (1955); A.D. Belinante, *Les Principes de Droit Pénal International et les Conventions Internationales*, 2 NEDERLANDS TIJDSCHRIT VOOR INTERNATIONAL RECHT 243 (1955); Guiliano Vassalli, *In tema di Diritto Internazionale Pénale*, 56 GUISTIZIA PENALE (1951); Stefan Glaser, *Les Infractions Internationales et Leurs Sanctions*, 29 REVUE DE DROIT PÉNAL ET DE CRIMINOLOGIE 811 (1949); Henri F. Donnedieu de Vabres, *La Codification du Droit Pénal International*, 19 REVUE INTERNATIONALE DE DROIT PENAL 21 (1948); Stefan Glaser, *Le Principe de la Legalité des Delits et des Peines et les Procés des Criminels de Guerre*, 28 REVUE DE DROIT PÉNAL ET DE CRIMINOLOGIE 230 (1948); Henri F. Donnedieu de Vabres, *Les Procés de Nuremberg et le Principe de la Legalité et des Peines*, 26 REVUE DE DROIT PÉNAL ET DE CRIMINOLOGIE 813 (1947); Henri F. Donnedieu de Vabres, *Le Procés de Nuremberg Devant les Principes Modernes du Droit Pénal International*, 7 RECUEIL DES COURS 481 (1947); Albert de La Pradelle, *Une Revolution Dans le Droit Pénal International*, 13 NOUVELLE REVUE DE DROIT INTERNATIONAL PRIVE 360 (1946); Gerald Abrahams, *Retribution: An Inquiry into the Possibility of an International Criminal Law*, 92 LAW J. 38, 45, 53 (1942); Roberto Ago, *Le Delit International*, 68 RECUEIL DES COURS DE L'ACADEMIE DE DROIT INTERNATIONAL DE LA HAYE 419 (1939); Henri F. Donnedieu de Vabres, *La Repression Internationale des Delits du Droits des Gens*, 2 NOUVELLE REVUE DE DROIT INTERNATIONAL PRIVE 7 (1935); Vespasian P. Vella, *Plan d'un Code Repressi Mondial*, 12 REVUE INTERNATIONALE DE DROIT PENAL 348 (1935); Carlos Alcorta, *La Doctrina del Derecho Pénal Internacional*, 2 REVISTA ARGENTINA DE DERECHO INTERNACIONAL 271 (1931); Guiseppe Sagone, *Pour un Droit Pénal International*, 5 REVUE INTERNATIONALE DE DROIT PENAL 363 (1928); Quintiliano Saldana, *Projet de Code Pénal International*, 1 CONGRÉS INTERNATIONAL DE DROIT PÉNAL (1926); G. Glover Alexander, *International Criminal Law*, 5 J. COMP. LEGIS. & INT'L L. 90 (1923); G. Clover Alexander, *International Criminal Law*, 3 J. COMP. LEGIS. & INT'L L. 237 (1921); Max Radin, *International Crimes*, 32 IOWA L. REV. 33 (1946); Edward M. Wise, *Prolegomenan to the Principles of International Criminal Law*, 16 N.Y. L. F. 562 (1970); Georg Schwarzenberger, *The Problem of an International Criminal Law*, 3 CURRENT LEGAL PROBS. 263 (1950); Yoram Dinstein, *International Criminal Law*, 5 ISR. Y.B. HUM. RTS. 55 (1975); Quincy Wright, *The Scope of International Criminal Law: A Conceptual Framework*, 15 VA. J. INT'L L. 562 (1975); Edward M. Wise, *War Crimes and Criminal Law*, in STUDIES IN COMPARATIVE LAW 35 (Edward M. Wise & Gerhard O W Mueller eds., 1975); Leslie C. Green, *An International Criminal Code Now?*, 3 DALHOUSIE L.J. 560 (1976); Gerhard O.W. Mueller, *International Criminal Law: Civitas Maxima – An Overview*, 15 CASE W. RES. J. INT'L L. 1 (1983); Robert Friedlander, *The Foundations of International Criminal Law: A Present Day Inquiry*, 15 CASE W. RES. J. INT'L L. 13 (1983); Yoram Dinstein, *International Criminal Law*, 20 ISR. L. REV. 206 (1985); Dietrich Schindler, *Crimes Against the Law of Nations*, 8 ENCYCLOPEDIA OF PUB. INT'L L. 109 (1985); Edward M. Wise, *Terrorism and the Problems of an International Criminal Law*, 19 CONN. L. REV. 799 (1987); Leslie C. Green, *International Criminal Law and the Protection of Human Rights*, in CONTEMPORARY PROBLEMS OF INTERNATIONAL LAW. ESSAYS IN HONOR OF GEORG SCHWARZENBERGER 116 (Bin Cheng & Edward D. Brown eds., 1988); Roger S. Clark, *Offenses of International Concern: Multilateral State Treaty Practice in the Forty Years Since Nuremberg*, 57 NORDIC J. INT'L L. 49 (1988); Edward M. Wise, *International Crimes and Domestic Criminal Law*, 38 DEPAUL L. REV. 923 (1989). *See also* 52 REVUE INTERNATIONALE DE DROIT PENAL, Nos. 3-4 (1981), symposium issue on a Draft International Criminal Code: Pierre Bouzat, *Introduction*, 331; Hans-Heinrich Jescheck, *Development, Present State and Future Prospects of International Criminal Law*, 337; John F. Decker, *A Critique of the Draft International Criminal Code*, 373; Reynald Ottenhof, *Considerations sur la Forme, le Style, et la Methode d'Elaboration du Projet de Code Penal International*, 385; Robert Friedlander, *Some Observations on Specific Crimes Relating to the Draft International Criminal Code Project*, 393; Dietrich Oehler, *Perspectives on the Contents of the Special Part of the Draft International Criminal Code*, 407; Ved P. Nanda, *International Crimes under the Draft International Criminal Code*, 427; Symposium Issue on International Criminal Law, 15 NOVA L.

In the area of arms control, various cultures from several time periods have attempted to mitigate the harmful effects of war through some type of regulation. Some have worked in earnest at the eradication of war, unfortunately without much success, while others, instead, have worked in some success toward the humanization of armed conflicts. The latter principle, representing the law of armed conflict (or international humanitarian law), is based on the assumption that:

> States engaged in an armed conflict will necessarily inflict death and injury upon persons and damage to property, and seeks to limit these effects by preventing the infliction of suffering and damage which is unnecessary because it serves no useful military purpose. The law goes beyond that, however, for it requires that, even where destruction does have a military purpose, a balance be struck between the attainment of that purpose and other values, such as the preservation of civilian life; it prohibits the carrying out of an attack when the military benefit which may be expected to ensue is outweighed by the damage to those values.
>
> The principal objective of the law of weaponry [a part of the law of armed conflict] is the protection of these values. Thus, the prohibition of indiscriminate weapons and methods of warfare is designed to serve the objective of distinguishing between civilians and civilian objects, on the one hand, and combatants and military objectives, on the other, and protecting the former. Similarly, the principle that belligerents may not employ weapons or methods of warfare of a nature to cause unnecessary suffering serves the objective of protecting even combatants from suffering and death which is not necessary for the achievement of legitimate military goals. [9]

Because the pursuit of war has invariably been to achieve military success through the fastest means and with the least costs, irrespective of the harm inflicted upon the enemy, the humanization of armed conflict has been difficult. Thus, humanizing alone has never been a sufficient basis to induce nations to altruistically limit the use of their might against their enemies. Instead, pragmatic and policy arguments have greatly aided in the evolution of the modern doctrine on the regulation of armed conflicts. It is therefore feared to say that humanism, mutually of interest, pragmatism and policy considerations all combined to produce a body of law that prohibits certain weapons and restricts the use of others. The prohibitions and restrictions, as discussed below, go from the general to the specific and include broad principles as well as narrow proscriptions.

REV. 343 *et seq.* (1991). *See also* the Draft Code of Offenses and from 1982 to 1996 the various ILC texts of the Draft Code of Crimes in the Yearbook of the International Law Commission.

[9] Christopher Greenwood, *The Law of Weaponry at the Start of the New Millennium in* THE LAW OF ARMED CONFLICT IN THE NEW MILLENNIUM 189 (Schmitt and Green eds., 1998).

Historical Evolution

A historical review of the regulation of armed conflicts reveals that various civilizations, dating back five thousand years, have either specifically prohibited or at least condemned unnecessary use of force and violence against certain categories of persons and against certain targets. This historical process, spanning several millennia, reveals the convergence of basic human values in diverse civilizations. The existence of the same basic values in such diverse civilizations cannot be attributed only to the migration of ideas. Instead, it reflects an intrinsic commonality in the sharing of such values. This is noteworthy because over a span of millenia diverse civilizations geographically not contiguous, have reached the same humanistic conclusions. If anything, this similarity supports the proposition embodied in the Preamble of the 1907 Hague Convention, namely that these commonly shared values make up the "laws of humanity."

In the course of this historical evolution, certain principles emerged that restricted the actions of a combatant during the time of war. This was the beginning of what became known as *jus ad bellum*.

The Chinese scholar Sun Tzu, in the fifth century B.C., asserted that in war it is important to "treat captives well, and care for them."[10] He also wrote that a general should only attack the enemy armies, "for the worst policy is to attack cities."[11] The modern principle that it is not the purpose of war to inflict unnecessary or excessive suffering was clearly illustrated, in the seventh century B.C., by the Chinese aristocratic code of chivalry:

> Chinese charioteers of the Chou period were clearly infected by chivalry.... In a battle between the rival states of Ch'u and Sung in 1638 B.C., the Duke of Sung's minister of war twice asked permission to attack the enemy before he had formed ranks, making the perfectly reasonable point that "they are many but we are few;" he was refused. After the Sung had been defeated and the Duke wounded, he justified himself as follows: "The gentleman does not inflict a second wound, or take the grey-haired prisoner.... Though I am but the unworthy remnant of a fallen dynasty, I would not sound my drums to attack an enemy who has not completed the formation of his ranks." Other practices deemed unchivalrous among Chinese chariot aristocrats were taking advantage of a fleeing enemy who was having trouble with his chariot (he might even be assisted), injuring a ruler, attacking an enemy state when it was mourning a ruler or was divided by internal troubles."[12]

---

[10] SUN TZU, THE ART OF WAR 76 (Samuel B. Griffith trans., 1971).

[11] *Id.* at 78 (III, "Offensive Strategy").

[12] JOHN KEEGAN, A HISTORY OF WARFARE 173 (1994) (citing Herrlee G. Creel, THE ORIGINS OF STATECRAFT IN CHINA 257, 265 (1970)).

In one of India's epic poems, *Ramayana*, in which a mythical weapon that could obliterate an entire enemy nation was expressly forbidden because "such destruction en masse was forbidden by the ancient laws of war, even though [the enemy] was fighting an unjust war with an unrighteous objective."[13] Another famous Hindu epic, the *Mahabaratha*, which some have dated as early as 200 B.C., prohibits the use of so-called "hyperdestructive" weapons. One such mythical weapon was the *pasupathastra*, which was forbidden because "when the fight was restricted to ordinary conventional weapons, the use of extraordinary or unconventional types was not even moral, let alone in conformity with religion or the recognized rules of warfare."[14] Even though the above examples are from mythological stories, they illustrate the basic values with respect to armed conflict. In the fourth century B.C., in India, the BOOK OF MANU upheld the same principles.[15] The Laws of Manu stated that "when a king fights his foes in battle, let him not strike with weapons concealed, nor with barbed, poisoned, or the points of which are blazed with fire . . . [because] these are the weapons of the wicked."[16] The Laws of Manu also prohibited weapons that caused unnecessary, excessive suffering. These included arrows with heated, poisoned, or hooked spikes and tips.[17]

In ancient Greece, an awareness existed that certain acts were contrary "to traditional usages and principles spontaneously enforced by human conscience."[18] Herodotus recounts that as early as the fifth century B.C. certain conduct was prohibited:

[T]he slaughter of the Persian envoys by the Athenians and Spartans was confessedly a transgression of the [laws of men], as a law of the human race generally, and not merely as a law applicable exclusively to the barbarians. And Xerxes recognized and submitted to such general law, when he answered on suggestions being made to him that he should resort to similar retaliation,

---

[13] International Court of Justice Advisory Opinion No. 95, *The Legality of the Threat or Use of Nuclear Weapons*, 35 I.L.M. 809, 897 (July 8, 1996) (Judge Weeramantry in dissent, citing *Ramayana*).

[14] Nagendra Singh, *The Distinguishable Characteristics of the Concept of the Law as it Developed in Ancient India, in* LIBER AMICORUM FOR THE RT. HON. LORD WILBERFORCE 93 (Maarten Bos & Ian Brownline eds., 1987) (citing *The Mahabharatha)*.

[15] *See* THE BOOK OF MANU: MANUSMURTI discussed in detail by Nagendra Singh in *Armed Conflicts and Humanitarian Laws of Ancient India, in* ETUDES ET ESSAIS SUR LE DROIT INTERNATIONAL HUMANITAIRE ET SUR LES PRINCIPES DE LA CROIX-ROUGE EN L'HONNEUR DE JEAN PICTET (Christophe Swinarski ed. 1984); and COMMENTARIES: THE LAWS OF MANU (Georg Bühler trans., 1967).

[16] THE LAWS OF MANU 230, Tit. VII, 90 (Georg Buhler trans. & ed., 1889).

[17] *Id. See* Nagendra Singh, INDIA AND INTERNATIONAL LAW 72 (1973).

[18] COLEMAN PHILLIPSON, 1 THE INTERNATIONAL LAW AND CUSTOM OF ANCIENT GREECE AND ROME 59 (1911) wherein the author states that many rulers of ancient Greece were conscious of the need to observe "traditional usages and principles spontaneously enforced by human conscience," *id.* at 50 [hereinafter PHILLIPSON].

International Humanitarian Law and Arms Control Agreements 7

that he would not be like Lacedaemonians, for they had violated the law of all nations, by murdering his heralds, and that he would not do the very thing which he blamed in them.[19]

In Homer's epic *The Odyssey*, the use of poisoned weapons was considered to be a grave violation to the way of the gods:

Temples and priests and embassies were considered inviolable . . . Mercy . . . was shown to helpless captives. Prisoners were ransomed and exchanged. Safe-conducts were granted and respected. Truces were established and, for the most part, faithfully observed . . . . It was considered wrong to cut off or poison the enemy's water supply, or to make use of poisoned weapons. Treacherous strategems of every description were condemned as being contrary to civilized warfare.[20]

Similarly, with respect to the Romans, it has been written that:

Undoubtedly, the belligerent operations of Rome, from the point of view of introducing various mitigations in the field, and adopting a milder policy after victory, are distinctly of a positive character. They were more regular and disciplined than those of any other ancient nation. They did not as a rule degenerate into indiscriminate slaughter, and unrestrained devastation…The *ius belli* imposed restrictions on barbarism and condemned all acts of treachery.[21]

However, such self-imposed restrictions were not universally applied. For both ancient Greeks and Romans, the rules of war applied only to "civilized sovereign states, properly organized, and enjoying a regular constitution."[22] Hence:

barbarians, savage tribes . . . and the like were debarred from the benefits and relaxations established by international law and custom . . . . In Homer . . . hostilities for the most part assumed the form of indiscriminate brigandage, and were but rarely conducted with a view to achieving regular conquests, and extending the territory of the victorious community. Extermination rather than subjugation of the enemy was the usual practice…Sometimes prisoners were sacrificed to the gods, corpses mutilated, and mercy refused to children, and to the old and sickly.[23]

---

[19] *Id.* at 60 (citing HERODOTUS, HISTORY).

[20] PHILLIPSON, *supra* note 18, at 221 (citing HOMER, THE ODYSSEY Bk. I, 11. 260-3 Richmond Lattimore ed. & trans., 1967)).

[21] PHILLIPSON, *supra* note 18, 227-29, 232; MARCUS TULLIUS CICERO, DE OFFICIIS, Lib. III, cap. Xxii (Walter Miller trans., 1975) (1483).

[22] PHILLIPSON, *supra* note 18, 227-29.

[23] *Id.* at 195, 207-209, 210.

The three monotheistic faiths of Judaism, Christianity and Islam join in the affirmation of the same humanitarian principles. The similarity between the admonitions of the *Qu'ràn* and those of the Old Testament are best expressed in the *Second Book of Kings*:

the King of Israel . . . said to Eli'sha, "My Father shall I slay them?" . . . He answered, "You shall not slay them. Would you slay those whom you have taken captive with your sword and bow? Set bread and water before them, that they may eat and drink and go to their master."[24]

Another relevant text of the Old Testament is found in *Deuteronomy*, in which specific regulations for the conduct of sieges are spelled out:

When thou shalt besiege a city a long time in making war against it to take it, thou shalt not destroy the trees thereof by wielding an axe against them; for thou mayest eat of them, but thou shalt not cut them down; for is the tree of the field man, that it should be besieged of thee? Only the trees of which thou knowest that they are not trees for food, them thou mayest destroy and cut down, that thou mayest build bullwarks against the city that makes war with thee, until it fall.[25]

The destruction of vegetation unessential to human life was justified only by military necessity by traditional Jewish law:

Josephus elaborates that this included not setting fire to their land or destroying beasts of labor. Maimonides flatly states that the destruction of fruit trees for the mere purpose of afflicting the civilian population is prohibited and, finally, we have the broad interpretation of Rabbi Ishmael that 'not only are fruit trees but, by argument, from minor to major, stores of fruit itself may not be destroyed.[26]

Jews honor the Sabbath and other holy days like *Yom Kippur*, wherein no warlike activities can be conducted on those days; the same is true in Islam on the various days of the *Eid*. Similarly, in Medieval times, the Roman Catholic Church specifically proscribed the conduct of war on particular days. In fact, as the Archbishop of Arles exclaimed in 1035, there was to be a "Truce of God" from "vespers on Wednesday to sunrise on Monday."[27]

---

[24] 2 *Kings* 6:21, 22.

[25] *Deuteronomy* 20: 19-20.

[26] Guy B. Roberts, *Judaic Sources of and Views on the Laws of War*, 37 NAVAL L. REV. 221, 231 (1988).

[27] *See* PETER D. TROOBOFF, INTRODUCTION TO LAW AND RESPONSIBILITY IN WARFARE 7 (Peter D. Trooboff ed. 1975). *See also* LESLIE C. GREEN, *International Criminal Law and the*

The Islamic civilization, based on the *Qu'ràn*, set forth specific rules as to the legitimacy of war and its conduct.[28] In 634 A.D., Caliph Abu Bakr gave the Muslim Arab army invading Syria the following instructions:

Do not commit treachery, nor depart from the right path. You must not mutilate, neither kill a child or aged man or woman. Do not destroy a palm tree, nor burn it with fire and do not cut any fruitful tree. You must not slay any of the flock or the herds or the camels, save for your subsistence. You are likely to pass by people who have devoted their lives to monastic services; leave them to that which they have devoted their lives.[29]

Abu Bakr's mandate was based on the *Qu'ràn* and the *Sunna*, the tradition of the Prophet Muhammad and the two principal sources of the *Shari'a*, Islamic law.

Fundamental to the early Islamic values relating to warfare was the reduction of unnecessary or excessive suffering. For example, the Qur'an enjoins on the victor the duty to feed captives.[30] Also, Islamic legal treatises on the law of nations from the ninth century forbade the killing of women, children, elderly, blind, crippled, and the insane.[31] Similarly, in his day, the Prophet Muhammad entered into a peace treaty with the Meccans, the treaty of Hodaibiya, which provided for the protection of civilians. These Muslim principles, rules and practices influenced the development of Western legal thought through Islam's contacts during the Middle Ages with Western civilization, particularly in Spain, Southern France and

---

Protection of Human Rights, in CONTEMPORARY PROBLEMS OF INTERNATIONAL LAW: ESSAYS IN HONOUR OF GEORG SCHWARZENBERGER ON HIS EIGHTIETH BIRTHDAY 116-37 (Bin Cheng & Edward D. Brown eds., 1988) where the author refers to many valuable historical precedents, *id.* at 116-29.

[28] The cases and practices of Muslim conduct in war were taught by Al-Shaybani in the eighth century and were written in a digest by el-Shahristani. The first known publication was in Hyderabad in 1335-1336, translated by Majid Khadduri in WAR AND PEACE IN THE LAW OF ISLAM. *See also* Roger C. Algase, *Protection of Civilian Lives in Warfare: A Comparison between Islamic Law and Modern International Law Concerning the Conduct of Hostilities*, 16 REVUE DE DROIT PÉNAL MILITAIRE ET DE DROIT DE LA GUERRE 246 (1977); M. Cherif Bassiouni, *Islam: Concept, Law and World Habeas Corpus*, 1 RUT.-CAM. L.J. 160 (1969); *see also, e.g.*, SOBHI MAHMASSANI, THE PRINCIPLES OF INTERNATIONAL LAW IN LIGHT OF ISLAMIC DOCTRINE (1966); MAJID KHADDURI, THE ISLAMIC LAW OF NATIONS (1966); SAID RAMADAN, ISLAMIC LAW, ITS SCOPE AND EQUITY (1961); MUHAMMAD HAMIDULLAH, MUSLIM CONDUCT OF STATE (1961); Mohamed Abdallah Draz, *Le Droit International Public de l'Islam*, 5 REV. EGYPTIENNE DE DROIT INT'L 17 (1949), Ahmed Rechid, *L'Islam et le Droit de Gens*, 60 RECUEIL DES COURS DE L'ACADEMIE DE DROIT INTERNATIONAL DE LA HAYE 371 (1937); NAJIB ARMANAZI, L'ISLAM ET LE DROIT INTERNATIONAL (1929); Syed H.R. Abdul Majid, *The Moslem International Law*, 28 LAW Q. REV. 89 (1912).

[29] *Cited in* MAJID KHADDURI, WAR AND PEACE IN THE LAW OF ISLAM 102 (1955), and Waldemar A. Solf, *Protection of Civilians Against the Effects of Hostilities Under Customary International Law and under Protocol I*, 1 AM. U.J. INT'L L. & POL'Y 117, 118 (1986). *See also* MCCOUBREY, *supra* note 2, at 9 referring to the humanitarian practices of Abu Bakr and Salah el-Din el Ayyubi in the fourth Crusade.

30 *Qur'an, Surat al-Baqarah* II:205.

31 THE ISLAMIC LAW OF NATIONS (Shaybani's *Siyar*) 29-31, 47, 81, 110-11 (Majid Khadduri trans., 1966) (1911).

Southern Italy when these areas were under Muslim control, and also as a result of Muslim and Christian contacts during the Crusades. This influence clearly appears in the writings of certain Canonists.[32]

Thus the values embodied in these moral and legal positions were not only found in Western civilization, they also existed in other civilizations such as the Chinese,[33] Hindu,[34] Egyptian and Assyrian-Babylonian, and in Islam, all of which devised principles of legitimacy for resorting to war and particular rules for its conduct.[35] However, after the seventh century it was mostly Western civilization that advanced these values and shaped the norms we now call humanitarian law.

In Western civilization, the writings of Aristotle, Cicero, St. Augustine and St. Thomas Aquinas have set forth the philosophical premises for the conditions of legitimacy of war, so as to distinguish between the just and the unjust war.[36] But Western civilization also developed principles and norms limiting the means and harmful consequences of the conduct of war. St. Thomas Aquinas, in his *Summa Theologica* frequently quoting St. Augustine (who lived in what is now Tunisia), refers to these basic laws of humanity in the treatment of civilian noncombatants, the sick, wounded and prisoners of war as follows, "these rules belong to the *jus gentium* which are deduced from natural law as conclusion principles."[37] He called it "positive human law," not because it was codified, but because citizens of civilized nations agreed to it.[38]

---

[32] See Franciscus de Vitoria (1483-1617), *De Indis et de Jure Belli*, in CLASSICS OF INTERNATIONAL LAW (James B. Scott ed. 1917); Francisco Suárez (1548-1584), *On War*, in 2 CLASSICS OF INTERNATIONAL LAW (James B. Scott ed. 1944); Balthazar Ayala (1548-1584), *Three Books on the Law of War*, in 2 CLASSICS OF INTERNATIONAL LAW (John P. Bate trans., 1912); Alberico Gentili (1552-1608), *De Jure Belli Libri Tres*, in CLASSICS OF INTERNATIONAL LAW (James B. Scott ed., 1933). For a recent account of Islamic influence on canonist writers and consequently on Hugo Grotius who relied on their works, see CHARLES S. RHYNE, INTERNATIONAL LAW 23 (1971). Ayala, Gentili, Suarez, and Grotius all wrote that women and those unable to bear arms should always be spared, although as Ayala reported the practice was seldom followed.

[33] See SUN TZU, *supra* note 10, at 76.

[34] See THE ISLAMIC LAW OF NATIONS, *supra* note 31.

[35] For a description of some of the practices of war in these civilizations see generally ANDRÉ AYMARD & JEANNINE AUBOYER, 1 L'ORIENT ET LA GRÉCE ANTIQUE 293-99 (1953); PIERRE ROUSSEL ET AL., LA GRÉCE ET L'ORIENT: DES GUERRES MEDIQUES À LA CONQUÊTE ROMAINE (2d. ed. 1938); and MICHAEL GRANT, ARMY OF THE CAESARS (1974). *See also* GEOFFREY BEST, WAR AND LAW SINCE 1945 (1945), and JOHN KEEGAN, A HISTORY OF WARFARE, *supra* note 12.

[36] The distillation of these writings is found in GROTIUS, *infra* note 48, which is considered to be one of the foundations of Western international law; *see also* SAMUEL PUFENDORF, DE JURE NATURAE ET GENTIUM LIBRI Octo 8, III (1672), in 2 CLASSICS OF INTERNATIONAL LAW (William A. Oldfather trans., 1934); EMMERICH DE VATTEL, LE DROIT DES GENS (1758), in 2 CLASSICS OF INTERNATIONAL LAW (Charles G. Fenwick trans., 1916). *See also, e.g.*, ARTHUR NUSSBAUM, A CONCISE HISTORY OF THE LAW OF NATIONS (1954); Joachim von Elbe, *The Evolution of the Concept of the Just War in International Law*, 33 AM. J. INT'L L. 665 (1939).

[37] 2 ac, Q. 95 art. 4. For an English translation of ST. THOMAS AQUINAS', SUMMA THEOLOGICA, see the first complete American edition, published by Benziger Bros. Inc. (1947).

[38] *Id.* at Conclusion

This concept of natural law, which Plato and Aristotle posited long before St. Thomas, was also the supreme law of the Romans who divided the *jus positivum* into *jus gentium* and *jus civile*. In this connection, Maurice H. Keen, a scholar on the law of war in the Middle Ages, stated:

> [T]he "Roman people" meant not only the man of the empire but those of the independent *regna* and *civitates* also, and so a law which was common to it, was genuinely a "law of nations." To the *jus gentium* in its broader sense of the natural law of all men, these two laws added for those within Christendom a further series of positive rules, for "beyond doubt the canon and civil laws add something further in the matter of war over and above the dictates of reason." Once again there was no question of any conflict of laws, for the equity of the canon and civil laws was just the same as that of the *jus gentium*. They too derived their ultimate authority from natural reason. The canon law was derived from natural law because it was derived from Holy Writ, and "The divine laws operate in nature." The civil law was founded in natural law, because it was the accepted definition of civil laws that they were derived "from the law of nature, by means of specific rulings on particulars." For the Roman people these two laws expanded the *jus naturale* and the *jus gentium* with a further series of specific rules, binding on all its members, but on them only. In dealings with *extranei*, as Tartars, Greeks and Saracens, only the rules of the *jus gentium* proper were binding.[39]

In the eighteenth century, international law scholar, Georg F. Martens echoed these views:

> [B]ut our right to wound and kill being founded on self-defence, or on the resistance opposed to us, we can, with justice wound or take the life of none except those who take an active part in the war. So that, children, old men, women, and in general all of those who cannot carry arms, or who ought not to do it, are safe under the protection of the law of nations, unless they have exercised violence against the enemy.[40]

As the laws of chivalry developed during the Middle Ages in Western Europe, so did rules limiting the means and manner of conducting war.[41] Heraldic courts

---

[39] MAURICE H. KEEN, THE LAWS OF WAR IN THE LATE MIDDLE AGES 14-15 (1965) wherein he relies upon the medieval work of HONORE BONET, TREE OF BATTLES, *id.* at 21; and *see* AUGUSTINE FITZGERALD, PEACE AND WAR IN ANTIQUITY (1931). For an earlier seminal work see PHILIPPE CONTAMINE, WAR IN THE MIDDLE AGES (Michael Jones trans., 1984). Interestingly the rules of war until well into the 1800's were with respect to Christians applicable only to wars in Christendom.

[40] GEORG F. MARTENS, SUMMARY OF THE LAW OF NATIONS 282 (1788) (William Cobbett trans., 1795).

[41] *See* KEEN, *supra* note 39, and FITZGERALD, *supra* note 39. *See also* Suzanne Bastid, *Le Droit de la Guerre dans des Documents Judiciaires Francais du XIVe Siècle*, 8 ANNUAIRE FRANÇAIS DE DROIT INTERNATIONAL 181 (1962) referring to the records of the Hundred Years' War (1337-1469)

developed a code of chivalry, enforced by the Christian princes that regulated a knight's conduct in battle.[42] The codes of chivalry prohibited the use of long-distance weapons such as the cross-bow, which was expressly forbidden as anathema by the Second Lateran Council in 1139. "To the Church, these weapons were hateful to God. To the knights they were weapons whereby men not of the knightly order could fell a knight . . . . Worse, they were weapons that enabled a man to strike without the risk of being struck."[43] In addition, the Church forbade the faithful from deploying "darts or catapults in order to reduce as far as possible the number of engines of destruction and death."[44]

The goal of all these principles, norms and rules was to protect noncombatants, innocent civilians and those who were *hors de combat* from unnecessary harm. As Keen informs us about the siege of Limoges in 1370:

> Three French knights, who had defended themselves gallantly, seeing at length no alternative to surrender, threw themselves on the mercy of John of Gaunt and the Earl of Cambridge. "My Lords," they cried, "we are yours: you have vanquished us. Act therefore to the law of arms." John of Gaunt acceded to their request, and they were taken prisoner on the understanding that their lives would be protected.[45]

On the march to Agincourt in 1415, Shakespeare quotes Henry V giving his army the following instructions:

> We give express charge that in our marches through the country there be nothing compelled from the villages, nothing taken but paid for, none of the French upbraided or abused in disdainful language; For when levity and cruelty play for a kingdom, the gentler gamester is the soonest winner.[46]

Referring to the battle of Agincourt, when King Henry V of England felt compelled to execute his French prisoners held in his besieged base camp, Shakespeare has the King's Captain Fluellen exclaim: "Kill the poys and the

---

which reveal the existence of rules of warfare protection of noncombatants and prisoners of war, as well as the prosecution of violators of these rules; Giovanni daLegnano, tractabus de bello, de repraesaliis et de duello (1477); HONORÉ BONET, THE TREE OF BATTLES (ca. 1387) (G.W. Coupland ed. 1949) (Ernest Nys trans., 1883) and PEDRO LOPEZ D'AYALA, CRONICLES DE LOS REYES DE CASTILLA TOME I (1779-1780) describing several trials for violations of the laws of war; CHARLES G. FENWICK, DIGEST OF INTERNATIONAL LAW 7 (1965); and HENRY J.S. MAINE, INTERNATIONAL LAW 138-40 (2d ed. 1894).

[42] KEEN, *supra* note 39.

[43] Gerald Irving A. Dare Draper, *The Interaction of Christianity and Chivalry in the Historical Development of the Law of War,* 5 INT'L REV. OF THE RED CROSS 3, 19 (1965).

[44] *Corpus Juris Cononici*, Decretal V, *see* PIERINO BELLI, DE RE MILITARI ET BELLO TRACTATUS Pars VII, cap. III, 29, 186 (Herbert Nutting trans., 1936) (1563).

[45] *Id.* (citing OEUVRES DE FROISSART 43 (Kervyn de Leffenhove ed. 1869)).

[46] WILLIAM SHAKESPEARE, THE LIFE OF HENRY THE FIFTH, Act 3, Scene 6.

luggage! 'tis expressly against the law of arms: 'tis as arrant a piece of knavery . . . as can be offer'd."[47]

In 1625 the famed Hugo Grotius stated:

[Consider] both those who wage war and on what grounds war may be waged. It follows that we should determine what is permissible in war, also to what extent, and in what ways, it is permissible. What is permissible in war is viewed either absolutely or in relation to a previous premise. It is viewed absolutely, first from the standpoint of the law of nature, and then from that of the law of nations.[48]

However, despite the condemnations by the Church and knightly orders, the very existence, utility, and effectiveness of weapons that violated Christian teachings and chivalric codes made it practically impossible to proscribe their use. Commenting on this state of affairs, Pierino Belli wrote:

But today regard is so far lacking for this rule that firearms of a thousand kinds are the most common and popular implements of war; as if too few avenues of death had been discovered in the course of centuries, had not the generations of our fathers, rivaling God with His lightning, invented this means whereby, even at a single discharge, men are sent to perdition by the hundreds.[49]

After the Middle Ages, additional norms and rules were developed, thereby strengthening these basic principles of humanity on which they were based. This historical phase was also founded upon the emerging shared values of the world community to regulate conduct and to limit the resort to war, in order to minimize harmful human consequences. Thereafter, bilateral and multilateral treaties, particularly following the Treaty of Westphalia in 1648, represented a tangible expression of these values and concerns, and thereby sought to regulate relations among states for the prevention and conduct of war.[50] Thus, with regard to the care of wounded in the battlefield, Professor Green states:

---

[47] *Id.* at Act 4, Scene 7, *see* Theodor Meron, *Shakespeare's Henry the Fifth and the Law of War*, 86 AM. J. INT'L L. 1 (1992). *See also* THEODOR MERON, HENRY'S WARS AND SHAKESPEARE'S LAWS (1993).

[48] HUGO GROTIUS, DE JURE BELLI AC PACIS (Libri Tres) (1625), *reported in* 3 CLASSICS OF INTERNATIONAL LAW 599 (Francis W. Kelsey trans., 1925).

[49] BELLI, *supra* note 44.

[50] *See* MAJOR PEACE TREATIES OF MODERN HISTORY 1698-1967 (Fred L. Israel & Emanuel Chill eds., with an introduction by Arnold Toynbee, 1967). *See, e.g.*, Leo Gross, *The Peace of Westphalia*, 1648-1948, 42 AM. J. INT'L L. 20 (1948).

In 1679 a convention was signed between the Elector of Brandenburg, for the League of Augsburg, and the Count of Asfield, who commanded the French forces [providing] for a mutual respect towards both hospitals and wounded . . . [The] convention [of] 1743 between Lord Stair on behalf of the Pragmatic army and the Marshall Noailles for the French during the Dettingen campaign bound both sides to treat hospitals and wounded with consideration. Noailles, when he thought that his operations might cause alarm to the inmates at the hospitals at Tachenheim, went so far as to send word that they should rest tranquil as they would not be disturbed. A fuller, and more highly developed type of agreement, was that signed at L'Ecluse in 1759 by the Marshal de Brail, who commanded the French, and Major General Conway the British general officer commanding. The hospital staff, chaplains, doctors, surgeons and apothecaries were not . . . to be taken prisoners; and, if they should happen to be apprehended within the lines of the enemy, they were to be sent back immediately. The wounded of the enemy who should fall into the hands of their opponents were to be cared for, and their food and medicine should in due course be paid for. They were not to be made prisoner and might stay in hospital safely under guard. Surgeons and servants might be sent to them under the general's passports. Finally, on their discharge, they were themselves to travel under the same authority and were to travel by the shortest route.[51]

During the Age of Enlightenment, the development of norms and rules continued, but the emphasis was on the pragmatism of regulating the conduct of war. As argued by Jean-Jacques Rousseau in his seminal work *Le Contrat Social:*

Since the aim of war is to subdue a hostile State, a combatant has the right to kill the defenders of that state while they are armed; but as soon as they lay down their arms and surrender, they cease to be either enemies or instruments of the enemy; they become simply men once more, and no one has any longer the right to take their lives. It is sometimes possible to destroy a state without killing their lives. It is sometimes possible to destroy a state without killing a single one of its members, and war gives no right to inflict any more destruction than is necessary for victory. These principles were not invented by Grotius, nor are they founded on the authority of the poets; they are derived from the nature of things; they are based on reason.[52]

---

[51] *See* LESLIE C. GREEN, ESSAYS ON THE MODERN LAW OF WAR 86 (1985) (citing GEOFFREY G. BUTLER & SIMON MACCOBY, THE DEVELOPMENT OF INTERNATIONAL LAW 149-50 (1928)). PICTET, *supra* note 2, recounts that prior to the battle of Fontenoy in 1747, Louis XV of France declared in advance of the battle that the wounded be treated like his own men because as wounded they were no longer enemies. They were *hors de combat*.

[52] JEAN-JACQUES ROUSSEAU, THE SOCIAL CONTRACT AND DISCOURSES 171 (G.D.H. Cole trans., 1973). Rousseau also argued that "War then is not a relation between men, but between states, in war individuals are enemies wholly by chance, not as men, not even as citizens, but only as soldiers, not as members of their country, but also as its defenders." *Id.*

In many respects, the evolution of humanitarianism in armed conflicts came to fruition in the middle of the nineteenth century, specifically after the battle of Solferino in June of 1859 where France defeated Austria-Hungary.[53] Henry Dunant, a Swiss businessman who happened to be in the vicinity of the battlefield, was deeply moved by the sight of the many wounded men who were left to suffer and die for the lack of medical attention. After his experience, Dunant organized medical relief in the battlefield. Thereafter, he published a booklet entitled *Souvenirs de Solferino* (1862) in which he proposed the establishment of voluntary relief agencies to aid the battlefield wounded and for an international agreement on the humane treatment of the sick and injured of war.[54] Dunant's proposals became a reality on August 22, 1864 with the Geneva Convention for the Amelioration of the Condition of the Wounded of Armies in the Field.

Between 1854 and 1997, fifty-nine international instruments on the regulation of armed conflicts were developed.[55] These instruments set forth principles to humanize armed conflicts by prohibiting the use of certain weapons that inflict unnecessary pain and suffering. These instruments also set out to protect noncombatants, prisoners of war, the sick, the wounded, the shipwrecked, cultural monuments, property and heritage, and, more recently, Protocol I of the Geneva Conventions added the protection of the environment.

The Regulation, Control, and Prohibition of the Use of Certain Weapons in the Context of War

In the area of weapons control there exists two primary types of weapons: 1) those that are specifically prohibited by a convention or subject to a general prohibition, such as unnecessary pain and suffering, and 2) permissible weapons which are limited in accordance to the principles of discrimination and proportionality, which deal with the use of weapons.

The notion of prohibiting weapons in order to protect combatants from unnecessary pain and suffering was not a product of modern international law. It

---

[53] See HILAIRE MCCOUBREY, INTERNATIONAL HUMANITARIAN LAW 6, 10-11 (1990).

[54] Henry Dunant's proposals stirred great interest and received widespread attention. Following the publication of Dunant's booklet, Gustave Moynier, President of the Geneva Public Welfare Society, organized a committee of five (all Swiss, including Dunant) to examine the practical possibilities for implementing the proposal — that committee was the forerunner of the International Committee of the Red Cross.

[55] See BASSIOUNI, ICL CONVENTIONS, *supra* note 4, at 515-600. There also exist thirty-four other international instruments containing relevant provisions from 1868 to 1997, which are classified under other categories of crimes. Convention on the Prohibition of the Use, Stockpiling, Production and Transfer of Anti-Personnel Mines and on their Destruction, *signed in* Oslo, Sept. 18, 1997, see http:www.vvaf.org/landmine/us/updates/events97/treaty9_29.html. *Id.* at 285-504. *See also* BIBLIOGRAPHY OF INTERNATIONAL HUMANITARIAN LAW APPLICABLE IN ARMED CONFLICTS (2d ed. revised & updated, International Committee of the Red Cross and Henry Dunant Institute, Geneva, 1987); Yves Sandoz, *Penal Aspects of International Humanitarian Law, in* BASSIOUNI, ICL, *supra* note 1, at 209; Howard S. Levie, *Criminality in the Law of War, in* BASSIOUNI, ICL, *supra* note 1, at 233.

was derived from a doctrine developed by the Second Lateran Council of 1139, which prohibited the use of the crossbow and the harquebus. Arguably, this doctrine is the philosophical foundation for the prohibition, *inter alia*, of weapons of mass destruction such as chemical and biological weapons,[56] and in the opinion of this writer, it also extends to nuclear weapons.[57] Weapons of mass destruction that kill and destroy indiscriminately should be banned irrespective of the actual or comparative pain and suffering they generate. This is the case with chemical and biological weapons, but not so, as of now, with nuclear weapons. However, contemporary weapons deemed conventional have been prohibited by multilateral conventions. They include blinding laser weapons, incendiary weapons, and antipersonnel land mines.

The modern doctrine for control and prohibition of certain weapons reflects certain values and embodies certain policy considerations. The modern international instruments inspired by these values and policy considerations include: the Declaration of Paris of 1856;[58] the Geneva (Red Cross) Convention of 1864;[59] the St. Petersburg Declaration of 1868;[60] the Declaration of Brussels of 1874;[61] the Hague Conventions of 1899[62] and 1907[63] (including the Annex on the

---

[56] Contemporary experts seek to distinguish between weapons which cause unnecessary pain and suffering and conventionally prohibited weapons like the Convention on the Prohibition of the Development, Production and Stockpiling of Bacteriological (Biological) and Toxin Weapons and on Their Destruction, 10 April 1972, 26 U.S.T. 583, and the Convention on the Prohibition of the Development, Production, Stockpiling and Use of Chemical Weapons and on Their Destruction, 13 January 1993, S. Treaty Doc. No. 103-21.

[57] The International Court of Justice in a recent advisory opinion did not find that the use of nuclear weapons constitutes a violation of customary international law. *Legality of the Threat or Use of Nuclear Weapons* (Advisory Opinion of International Court of Justice), *supra* note 13, at 809 & 1343 (1996).

[58] Declaration Respecting Maritime Law, Paris, Apr. 16 1856, 15 MARTENS 791; 115 Parry's 1; *reprinted in* 1 AM. J. INT'L L. 89 (1907) (Supp.).

[59] Geneva Convention for the Amelioration of the Condition of the Wounded in Armies in the Field, Geneva, Aug. 22, 1864, 18 MARTENS 440; 22 Stat. 940; T.S. No. 377, 55 Brit. & For. St. Papers 43; *reprinted in* 1 AM. J. INT'L L. 90 (1907) (Supp.).

[60] Declaration Renouncing the Use, in Time of War, of Explosive Projectiles Under 400 Grammes Weight (St. Petersburg Declaration), *signed at St. Petersburg*, Dec. 11, 1868, 18 MARTENS 474; 138 Parry's 297; *reprinted in* 1 AM. J. INT'L L. 95 (1907) (Supp.).

[61] Project of an International Declaration Concerning the Laws and Customs of War (Declaration of Brussels) [Brussels Conference on the Laws and Customs of War, No. 18], *adopted at Brussels*, Aug. 27, 1874, 4 MARTENS (2d) 219 and 226, 148 Parry's 133, *reprinted in* 1 AM. J. INT'L L. 96 (1907) (Supp.).

[62] Convention for the Peaceful Adjustment of International Disputes (First Hague, I), The Hague, July 29, 1899, 26 MARTENS (2d) 920, 32 Stat. 1779, T.S. No. 392, *reprinted in* 1 AM. J. INT'L L. 107 (1907); Convention for the Adaptation to Maritime Warfare of the Principles of the Geneva Convention of Aug. 22, 1864 (First Hague, III), *signed at The Hague*, July 29, 1899, 26 MARTENS (2d) 979, 32 Stat. 1827, T.S. No. 396, *reprinted in* 1 AM. J. INT'L L. 159 (1907); Declaration Concerning the Prohibition, for the Term of Five Years, of the Launching of Projectiles and Explosives from Balloons or Other New Methods of a Similar Nature (First Hague, IV, 1), *signed at The Hague*, July 29, 1899, 26 MARTENS (2d) 994, 32 Stat. 1839, T.S. No. 393, *reprinted in* 1 AM. J. INT'L L. 153 (1907); Declaration Concerning the Prohibition of the Use of Projectiles Diffusing Asphyxiating Gases (First Hague, IV, 2),

Laws and Customs of Land Warfare); the 1925 Protocol for the Prohibition of the Use in War of Asphyxiating, Poisonous or other Gases and Bacteriological Methods of Warfare;[64] the Geneva Convention of 1929;[65] the Four Geneva Conventions of 1949;[66] the two 1977 Protocols to the 1949 Geneva Conventions;[67]

---

signed at The Hague, July 29, 1899, 26 MARTENS (2d) 998, 187 Parry's 453, *reprinted in* 1 AM. J. INT'L L. 157 (1907); Declaration Concerning the Prohibition of the Use of Expanding Bullets (First Hague, IV, 3), *signed at The Hague,* July 29, 1899, 26 MARTENS (2d) 1002, 187 Parry's 459, *reprinted in* 1 AM. J. INT'L L. 155 (1907) (Supp.).

[63] Convention for the Pacific Settlement of International Disputes (Second Hague, I), *signed at The Hague,* Oct. 18, 1907, 3 MARTENS (3d) 360, 36 Stat. 2199, T.S. No. 536, *reprinted in* 2 AM. J. INT'L L. 43 (1908); Convention Respecting the Limitation of the Employment of Force for the Recovery of Contract Debts (Second Hague, II), *signed at The Hague,* Oct. 18, 1907, 3 MARTENS, (3d) 414, 36 Stat. 2259, T.S. No. 537, *reprinted in* 2 AM. J. INT'L L. 81 (1908); Convention Relative to the Opening of Hostilities (Second Hague, III), *signed at The Hague,* Oct. 18, 1907, 3 MARTENS (3d) 437, 36 Stat. 2259, T.S. No. 538, *reprinted in* 2 AM. J. INT'L L.85 (1908); Convention Respecting the Laws and Customs of War on Land (Second Hague, IV) *signed at The Hague,* Oct. 18, 1907, 36 Stat. 2277, 1 Bevans 631; Convention Respecting the Rights and Duties of Neutral Powers and Persons in Case of War on Land (Second Hague, V) *signed at The Hague,* Oct. 18, 1907, 3 MARTENS (3d) 504, 36 Stat. 2310, T.S. No. 540, *reprinted in* 2 AM. J. INT'L L. 117 (1908); Convention Relative to the Status of Enemy Merchant Ships at the Outbreak of Hostilities (Second Hague, VI), *signed at The Hague,* Oct. 18, 1907, 3 MARTENS (3d) 533, *reprinted in* 2 AM. J. INT'L L. 127 (1908); Convention Relative to the Conversion of Merchant Ships into Warships (Second Hague, VII), *signed at The Hague,* Oct. 18, 1907, 3 MARTENS (3d) 557, *reprinted in* 2 AM. J. INT'L L. 133 (1908), Convention Relative to the Laying of Automatic Submarine Contact Mines (Second Hague, VIII), *signed at The Hague,* Oct. 18, 1907, 3 MARTENS (3d) 580, 36 Stat. 2332, T.S. No. 541, *reprinted in* 2 AM. J. INT'L L. 138 (1908); Convention Concerning Bombardment by Naval Forces in Time of War (Second Hague, IX), *signed at The Hague,* Oct. 18, 1907, 3 MARTENS (3d) 604, 36 Stat. 2351, T.S. No. 542, *reprinted in* 2 AM. J. INT'L L. 146 (1908); Convention for the Adaptation of the Principles of the Geneva Convention to Maritime Warfare (Second Hague, X), *signed at The Hague,* Oct. 18, 1907, 3 MARTENS (3d) 630, 36 Stat. 2371, T.S. No. 543, *reprinted in* 2 AM. J. INT'L L. 153 (1908); Convention Relative to Certain Restrictions with Regard to the Exercise of the Right of Capture in Naval War (Second Hague, XI), *signed at The Hague,* Oct. 18, 1907, 3 MARTENS (3d) 663, 36 Stat. 2396, T.S. No. 544, *reprinted in* 2 AM. J. INT'L L. 167 (1908); Convention Relative to the Establishment of an International Prize Court (Second Hague, XII), *signed at The Hague,* Oct. 18, 1907, 3 MARTENS (3d) 688, *reprinted in* 2 AM. J. INT'L L.174 (1908); Convention Concerning the Rights and Duties of Neutral Powers in Naval War (Second Hague, XIII), *signed at The Hague,* Oct. 18, 1907, 3 MARTENS (3d) 713, 36 Stat. 2415, T.S. No. 545, *reprinted in* 2 AM. J. INT'L L. 202 (1908); Declaration Relative to Prohibiting the Discharge of Projectiles and Explosives from Balloons (Second Hague, XIV), *signed at The Hague,* Oct. 18, 1907, 3 MARTENS (3d) 745, 36 Stat. 2439, T.S. No. 546, *reprinted in* 2 AM. J. INT'L L. 216 (1908).

[64] 1925 Protocol for the Prohibition of the Use in War of Asphyxiating, Poisonous, or other Gases and Bacteriological Methods of Warfare, signed at Geneva, June 17, 1925, 94 L.N.T.S. 65, 26 U.S.T. 571, T.I.A.S. No. 8061, *reprinted in* 25 AM. J. INT'L L. 94 (1931).

[65] 1929 Geneva Convention on the Amelioration of the Condition of the Wounded and Sick in Armed Forces in the Field, July 27, 1929, 47 Stat. 2074 *reprinted in* 2 BEVANS 965.

[66] *See* JEAN S. PICTET, COMMENTARIES ON THE FOURTH GENEVA CONVENTION (1956).

[67] *See* COMMENTARY ON THE ADDITIONAL PROTOCOLS 583-1124 (Yves Sandoz et al. eds. 1987); and NEW RULES FOR VICTIMS OF ARMED CONFLICTS 273-489 (Michael Bothe et al. eds. 1982). *See also* Waldemar A. Solf, *Protection of Civilians Against the Effects of Hostilities Under Customary International Law and Under Protocol I,* 1 AM. U. J. INT'L L. & POL'Y 117 (1986); Waldemar A. Solf & Edward R. Cummings, *A Survey of Penal Sanctions Under Protocol I to the Geneva Conventions of August 12, 1949,* 9 CASE W. RES. J. INT'L L. 205 (1977).

the Convention on the Prohibition of Military or Any Hostile Use of Environmental Modification Techniques;[68] and the Convention on Prohibitions and Restrictions on the Use of Certain Conventional Weapons Which May be Deemed to be Excessively Injurious or to have Indiscriminate Effects.[69] In 1997, a new convention on land was developed.[70] This collection of international instruments embodies principles, norms and rules developed over centuries of tragic human experience.

Historically, international regulation, control, or prohibition of the use of certain weapons has been a gradual process. Basically there have been two separate tracks for this development. The first track consists of international conventions signed at the Hague in 1899 and in 1907. The two Hague Conventions codified what is commonly known as customary law of armed conflicts. In time, "Hague Law" was supplemented by the practice of states, as well as by other multilateral conventions dealing specifically with certain weapons. In time, other arms control agreements will become part of customary international law, and as a result they will ban the use of more weapons. The second track is composed of conventional international humanitarian law as reflected in the Geneva Conventions of 1864, 1929, Four Conventions of 1949, and the two Additional Protocols of 1977.

In addition to these two tracks there exists a separate body of multilateral and bilateral arms control agreements, entered into between nations, which either restrict or ban weapons of mass destruction. Within this body, there are essentially three different types of agreements. First are the major arms control agreements that provide for general, wide-scale regulation, control, or prohibition of weapons of mass destruction. These include, for example, the 1968 Treaty on Non-Proliferation of Nuclear Weapons,[71] the 1972 Convention on the Prohibition of the Development, Production and Stockpiling of Bacteriological (Biological) and Toxin Weapons and on Their Destruction,[72] and the 1993 Convention on the

---

[68] Convention on the Prohibition of Military or Any Other Hostile Use of Environmental Modification Techniques, *opened for signature* at Geneva, May 18, 1977, U.N. G.A. Res. 31/721 (XXXI), 31 U.N. GAOR Supp. (No. 39), at 36, U.N. Doc. A/31/39 (1976), 31 U.S.T. 333, 1108 U.N.T.S. 151, 16 I.L.M. 88.

[69] Convention on Prohibitions and Restrictions on the Use of Certain Conventional Weapons Which May be Deemed to be Excessively Injurious or to have Indiscriminate Effects, *concluded at Geneva*, Oct. 10, 1980, U.N. Doc. A/Conf.95/15 (1980), 19 I.L.M. 1523, 1342 U.N.T.S. 7.

[70] Convention on the Prohibition of the Use, Stockpiling, Production and Transfer of Anti-Personnel Mines and on their Destruction, *signed at Oslo*, Sept. 18, 1997, *see* http://www.vvaf.org/landmine/us/updates/events97/treaty9_29.html.

[71] Treaty on the Non-Proliferation of Nuclear Weapons, *signed at Washington, London, Moscow*, 21 U.S.T. 483, 729 U.N.T.S. 161, 7 I.L.M. 809, entered into force 5 March 1970; entered into force with respect to the United States 5 March 1970.

[72] Convention on the Prohibition of the Development, Production and Stockpiling of Bacteriological (Biological) and Toxin Weapons and Their Destruction, *signed at Washington, London, Moscow*, 26 U.S.T. 583, 1015 U.N.T.S. 163, 11 I. L. M. 309, entered into force 26 March 1975; entered into force with respect to the United States 26 March 1975.

International Humanitarian Law and Arms Control Agreements 19

Prohibition of the Development, Production, Stockpiling and Use of Chemical Weapons and on Their Destruction.[73] The second type consists of those arms control agreements that restrict weapons of mass destruction from certain media. These include: the Antarctic Treaty of 1959;[74] the 1963 Treaty Banning Nuclear Weapons Tests in the Atmosphere, in Outer-Space, and Under Water;[75] the 1967 Treaty on Principles Governing the Activities of States in the Exploration of Outer Space, Including the Moon and Other Celestial Bodies;[76] the 1971 Treaty on the Prohibition of the Emplacement of Nuclear Weapons and Other Weapons of Mass Destruction on the Sea-Bed and the Ocean Floor and in the Subsoil Thereof;[77] and the 1979 Agreement Governing the Activities of States on the Moon and Other Celestial Bodies. [78]

The third type of arms control agreements consists of bans on nuclear weapons in specially designated nuclear free zones. Instruments of this type include: the 1967 Treaty for the Prohibition of Nuclear Weapons in Latin America (also called the Treaty of Tlatelolco);[79] the 1985 South Pacific Nuclear Free Zone Treaty (also called the Treaty of Raratonga);[80] the 1995 Treaty on South-East Asia Nuclear

---

[73] Convention on the Prohibition of the Development, Production, Stockpiling and Use of Chemical Weapons and on their Destruction, *signed at Paris*, 13 January 1993, S. TREATY DOC. NO. 103 21, 32 I.L.M. 800, entered into force 29 April 1997.

[74] The Antarctic Treaty, *signed at Washington*, 12 U.S.T. 794, 54 AM. J. INT'L L. 477 (1960), entered into force with respect to the United States 23 June 1961.

[75] Treaty Banning Nuclear Weapon Tests in the Atmoshpere, in Outer Space and Under Water, *signed at Moscow*, 14 U.S.T. 1313, 480 U.N.T.S. 43, 2 I.L.M. 302, entered into force 10 October 1963; entered into force with respect to the United States 10 October 1963.

[76] Treaty on Principles Governing the Activities of States in the Exploration and Use of Outer Space, including the Moon and Other Celestial Bodies, *signed at Washington, London and Moscow*, 18 U.S.T. 2410, 610 U.N.T.S. 205, 6 I.L.M. 386, entered into force 10 October 1967; entered into force with respect to the United States 10 October 1967.

[77] Treaty on the Prohibition of the Emplacement of Nuclear Weapons and Other Weapons of Mass Destruction on the Sea-bed and the Ocean Floor and in the Subsoil Thereof, *signed at Washington, London and Moscow*, 23 U.S.T. 701, T.I.A.S. No. 7337, 955 U.N.T.S. 115, entered into force 18 May 1972; entered into force with respect to the United States 18 May 1972.

[78] Agreement Governing the Activities of States on the Moon and other Celestial Bodies, *opened for signature at New York*, 1363 U.N.T.S. 3, 18 I.L.M. 1434, entered into force 11 July 1984.

[79] Treaty for the Prohibition of Nuclear Weapons in Latin America [Treaty of Tlatelolco] (inter-American), *opened for signature at Mexico City*, 22 U.S.T. 762, 634 U.N.T.S. 281, 6 I.L.M. 521, entered into force 22 April 1968.

[80] South Pacific Nuclear Free Zone Treaty [Treaty of Rarotonga], *signed at Rarotonga, Cook Islands*, 24 I.L.M. 1440, not yet in force (1985).

Weapon Free Zone;[81] and the 1996 African Nuclear Weapon Free Zone Treaty (also called the Treaty of Pelindaba).[82]

As mentioned above, the Geneva track, representing conventional international humanitarian law, embodies many aspects of customary international law; thus in effect conventional international law overlaps significantly with customary international law. However, this overlap is least significant in the area of weapons control since the Four Geneva Conventions of 1949 failed to mention weapons control and the issue was scarcely dealt with in Protocol I of 1977. Thus weapons control remains essentially within the sphere of customary international law, but continues to be subjected to certain general principles of conventional international law (which have also become custom), namely the prohibition of weapons that cause unnecessary pain and suffering, and the limitation of permissible weapons in accordance with the principles of discrimination and proportionality.

As mentioned above and in Chapter I of this book, conventional international law as reflected in the thirty-four instruments dealing with the use of weapons in time of war contain specific prohibitions as well as limitations to the use of certain weapons. Each one of these conventions has different legal regimes, varying degrees of effectiveness and a wide-range of state-parties. Due to these differences, a problem arises as to how to determine when such a convention, either prohibiting or limiting the use of weapons, rises to the level of customary international law in order to be applicable to non-signatory states. [83]

Article 8(2)(b) of the 1998 Rome Statute of the International Criminal Court (ICC) codified the prohibition of the following weapons:

1. Article 8(2)(b)(xvii) includes the employment of poison or poisoned weapons;
2. Article 8(2)(b)(xviii) includes the employment of asphyxiating, poisonous or other gases, and all analogous liquids, materials or devices;
3. Article 8(2)(b)(xix) includes the employment of bullets which expand or flatten easily in the human body, such as bullets with a hard envelope which does not entirely cover the core or is placed with incisions;

---

[81] Treaty on Southeast Asia Nuclear Weapon-Free Zone, *signed at Bangkok*, 35 I.L.M. 635 (1995).

[82] African Nuclear-Weapon-Free Zone Treaty, *signed at Addis Ababa*, 35 I.L.M. 698 (1996).

[83] This problem arose in connection to the drafting of the relevant provisions of Article 8 of the Rome Statute of the International Criminal Court. The United States, the United Kingdom, and France took the lead in the drafting of the article along with Switzerland. The drafters opted to subdivide Article 8 into segments reflecting different sources of law applicable to different contexts. *See* M. Cherif Bassiouni, *Negotiating the Treaty of Rome on the Establishment of an International Criminal Court*, 32 CORNELL INT'L L.J. 462 (1999). *See also* Rome Statute of the International Criminal Court, U.N. GAOR, 53d Sess., U.N. Doc. A/CONF. 183/9 (1998), *reprinted in* 39 I.L.M. 999 (1998) and Michael Cottier, *Preliminary Remarks on subparagraphs (xvii)-(xx): Prohibited Weapons: Drafting History in* COMMENTARY ON THE ROME STATUTE OF THE INTERNATIONAL CRIMINAL COURT 239 (Otto Triffterer ed., 1999).

International Humanitarian Law and Arms Control Agreements 21

4. Article 8(2)(b)(xx) includes the employment of weapons, projectiles and material and methods of warfare which are of a nature to cause superfluous injury or unnecessary suffering or which are inherently indiscriminate in violation of the international law of armed conflict, provided that such weapons, projectiles and material and methods of warfare are the subject of a comprehensive prohibition and are accordance with the relevant provisions set forth in articles 121 and 123.[84]

Significantly, violations of the above sections of Article 8(2)(b) fall under customary international law, not conventional law, and are classified as war crimes.[85]

The Prohibition Against Unnecessary Pain and Suffering

The evolution of international regulations of armed conflicts was also paralleled in national laws and military regulations.[86] Among these national regulations are those which Gustavus Adolphus of Sweden promulgated in 1621 in the *Articles of Military Laws to be Observed in the Wars*. They provided in the general article that "no Colonel or Captain shall command his soldiers to do any unlawful thing; which who so does, shall be punished according to the discretion of

---

[84] Rome Statute of the International Criminal Court, *supra* note 83, at Article 8(2)(b).

[85] Even though the wording of Article 8(2)(b)(xviii) is similar to the wording of the Geneva Protocol of 1925, which reflects conventional international law, all violations of Article 8(2)(b) are founded in customary international law. *See* COMMENTARY ON THE ROME STATUTE OF THE INTERNATIONAL CRIMINAL COURT, *supra* note 83, at 241-44.

[86] For the national military regulations see Lieber Code. Promulgated as *Instruction for the Government of the United States in the Field by Order of the Secretary of War*, in Washington D.C., Apr 24, 1863 and approved by President Lincoln. For other similar rules of the United States of America, see RULES OF LAND WARFARE, War Dept. Doc. No. 467, Office of the Chief of Staff, approved Apr. 25, 1914 (G.P.O. 1917); and Army Field Manual 27-10, RULES OF LAND WARFARE (1956). *See also* GEORGE B. DAVIS, A TREATISE ON THE MILITARY LAW OF THE UNITED STATES (3rd rev. ed. 1918) (which traces the history of the first Articles of War of 1775); and WILLIAM C. DE HART, OBSERVATIONS ON MILITARY LAW, AND THE CONSTITUTION, AND PRACTICE OF COURTS MARTIAL (1846). *See also* WILLIAM W. WINTHROP, MILITARY LAW AND PRECEDENTS (1896); The BRITISH MANUAL OF MILITARY LAW (1929 revised in 1940); GERMAN ARMY REGULATIONS (1902, revised in 1911, revised in 1935) to which the 1907 Hague Convention was appended as Annex II, quoted in Hersch Lauterpacht, *The Law of Nations and the Punishment of War Crimes*, 21 BRIT. Y.B. INT'L L. 58 (1944); the 1935 version; and the OXFORD MANUAL ON THE LAWS AND CUSTOMS OF WAR ON LAND (Institute of International Law, 1880). *See also Regolamento di Servizio in Guera*, in 3 LEGGI E DECRETI DEL REGNO D'ITALIA 3184 (1896). For commentaries on these laws and regulations by distinguished publicists, see JOHANN K. BLUNTSCHLI, DROIT INTERNATIONAL § 531-32 (5th ed. 1895); CARLOS CALVO, 4 LE DROIT INTERNATIONAL THEORIE ET PRATIQUE § 2034-35 (5th ed. 1896); JOHN B. MOORE, 7 DIGEST OF INTERNATIONAL LAW § 1109 (1906); CHARLES C. HYDE, 2 INTERNATIONAL LAW § 653-54 (1922); LASSA OPPENHEIM, 2 INTERNATIONAL LAW § 107 (6th ed. 1940).

the Judge."[87] In the United States, the first Articles of War, promulgated in 1775, contained explicit provisions for the punishment of officers who failed to keep "good order" among the troops, which included a number of prescriptions for the protection of civilians, prisoners of war, and the sick and injured in the field. This provision was retained and strengthened in the *Articles of War of 1806*,[88] and served as the basis for prosecutions for conduct against the law of nations.[89] The most noteworthy national regulations are the United States Lieber Code of 1863,[90] the 1880 *Oxford Manual*,[91] Great Britain's war office *Manual of Military Law of 1929*,[92] and the German General Staff *Kriegsbrauch im Landkriege* (Regulations of War) of 1902.[93] These are only some examples of national military regulations protecting, *inter alia*, civilian populations. Consequently, there can be no question that national laws prohibited the same conduct that was prohibited under international law. Presently, over 188 countries have included in their military laws or military regulations provisions on the protection and treatment of civilians, prisoners of war, the sick, injured and the shipwrecked during armed conflict.[94] These national laws and regulations are the result of the Four Geneva Conventions of 12 August 1949, and Additional Protocols I and II of 1977, which require the introduction of such norms in the national laws of the contracting parties, and which also require the dissemination of these rules to military personnel in order to insure compliance and to avoid claims of ignorance of the law.

As a result of the Lieber Code's explicit condemnation of unnecessary suffering, stating that "military necessity does not admit of cruelty . . . the infliction of suffering for the sake of suffering" is unlawful, numerous similar codes and

---

[87] GUSTAVUS ADOLPHUS, ARTICLES OF MILITARY LAWS TO BE OBSERVED IN THE WARS (1621), cited in Leo Gross, *The Punishment of War Criminals: The Nuremberg Trial*, 11 NETH. INT'L L. REV. 356 (1955). Adolphus' rules served as a source for the British Articles of War, which, in turn, served as the source for the first American Articles of War (1775). *See* Edward F. Sherman, *The Civilization of Military Law*, 22 ME. L. REV. 3 (1970).

[88] Articles of War, Art. IX (1775); re-enacted with modifications, Articles of War, Art. IX (1776); Articles of War, Art. 32 (1806). This provision survives in weakened form in the *Uniform Code of Military Justice*, Art. 138, 10 U.S.C. ¶ 1038. *See also* DAVIS, DE HART and WINTHROP, *supra* note 86.

[89] *Henfield's Case*, 11 F. Cas. 1099 (Case No. 6,360) (C.C. Pa. 1793) (violation of principles of neutrality by civilian).

[90] *See* 1925 Protocol for the Prohibition of the Use in War of Asphyxiating, Poisonous, or other Gases and Bacteriological Methods of Warfare, *supra* note 64.

[91] *See* OXFORD MANUAL ON THE LAWS AND CUSTOMS OF WAR ON LAND, *supra* note 86.

[92] *See* BRITISH MANUAL OF MILITARY LAW, *supra* note 86. The first manual was developed under the title of LAWES AND ORDINANCES OF WARRE, *see* CHARLES M. CLODE, I THE MILITARY FORCES OF THE CROWN, App. VI (1869), *quoted* by Leslie C. Green in *The Law of Armed Conflict and the Enforcement of International Criminal Law*, 27 ANNUAIRE CANADIEN DE DROIT INTERNATIONAL 7 (1984).

[93] *See* GERMAN ARMY REGULATIONS, *supra* note 86. These regulations were amended in 1935 but they preserved the same rules referred to in note 86 and accompanying text.

[94] *See* BASSIOUNI, ICL CONVENTIONS, *supra* note 4, at 284-85, 515-600.

manuals were promulgated by various countries.[95] Between 1870 and 1893, for example, such regulations were adopted by: Prussia, 1870; The Netherlands, 1871; France, 1877; Russia, 1877 and 1904; Serbia, 1878; Argentina, 1881; Great Britain, 1883 and 1904; and Spain, 1893.[96] Even though these codes did not proscribe any particular types of weapons, they did set the framework through which weapons resulting in unnecessary suffering could later be prohibited. Such prohibition came about in 1868 with the adoption of the St. Petersburg Declaration, which prohibited the use of "any projectile of a weight below 400 grammes, which is either explosive or charged with fulminating or inflammable substances."[97] The policy reason for this prohibition was the prevention of unnecessary suffering, although such terminology was not expressly used:

...the only legitimate object which States should endeavor to accomplish during war is to weaken the military forces of the enemy;
...for this purpose it is sufficient to disable the greatest possible number of men;
...this object would be exceeded by the employment of arms which uselessly aggravate the sufferings of disabled men, or render death inevitable.[98]

In the 1874 Brussels Conference, the first explicit use of the phrase "unnecessary suffering" can be found:

...the only legitimate object which States should have in view during war is to weaken the enemy without inflicting upon him *unnecessary suffering* ...
...[T]he Conference...participates in the conviction...that a further step may be taken by revising the laws and general usages of war...whether with the object of defining them with greater precision, or with the view of laying down...certain limits which will restrain, so far as possible, the severities of war.[99]

While the Brussels Conference Project never entered into force, it formed the basis for subsequent laws and manuals on the regulation of war. Specifically, Articles 12 and 13 are important in their establishing a framework for prohibiting poisoned weapons:

Art. 12. The laws of war do not recognize in belligerents an unlimited power in the adoption of means of injuring the enemy.

---

95   Instructions for the Government of Armies of the United States in the Field, Apr. 24, 1863.

96   SIR THOMAS ERSKINE HOLLAND, THE LAWS OF WAR ON LAND 72-3 (1908).

97   Declaration Renouncing the Use, in Time of War, of Explosive Projectiles Under 400 Grammes Weight, *supra* note 60.

98   *Id.*

99   Project of an International Declaration Concerning the Laws and Customs of War, *supra* note 61 (emphasis added).

Art. 13. According to this principle are especially forbidden:
(a) Employment of poison or poisoned weapons;...
(d) The employment of arms, projectiles or material calculated to cause *unnecessary suffering*, as well as the use of projectiles prohibited by the Declaration of St. Petersburg of 1868.[100]

The influence of the Brussels Conference's condemnation of certain weapons in order to limit suffering can be seen in the more comprehensive *Manual on the Laws of War*, drafted in 1880 by the Institut de Droit International at its Oxford Conference. For example, the initial "General Principles" written in the *Manual* provides that:

The state of war does not admit of acts of violence, save between the armed forces of belligerent States...Every belligerent force is bound to conform to the laws of war. The laws of war do not recognize in belligerents an unlimited liberty as to the means of injuring the enemy. They are to abstain especially from all needless severity, as well as from all perfidious, unjust, or tyrannical acts.[101]

In addition, the *Manual* specifically applies the above principles to weapons in Article 8 and Article 9:

8. It is forbidden to make use of poison in any form whatever...
9. It is forbidden:
(a) To employ arms, projectiles, or materials of any kind calculated to cause superfluous suffering, or to aggravate wounds...[102]

It should be borne in mind that the real importance of the *Oxford Manual* is not as a binding form of law, as it was not intended as such, but rather as a guide for subsequent international peace conferences that took place at the Hague Conventions of 1899 and 1907. In particular, various provisions from the *Manual* have been embodied in the preamble to the 1899 Hague Convention and other relevant treaties.[103]

The Preambles of the First Hague Convention of 1899 on the Laws and Customs of War and the Fourth Hague Convention of 1907, as well as their annexed Regulations Respecting the Laws and Customs of War on Land are illustrative of this point. The Preambles of the two conventions used the term "laws

---

[100] *Id.*

[101] OXFORD MANUAL ON THE LAWS AND CUSTOMS OF WAR ON LAND, *supra* note 86.

[102] *Id.*

[103] Leslie Green, *What Is-Why Is There-the Law of War?* in THE LAW OF ARMED CONFLICT INTO THE NEXT MILLENNIUM 161 (Schmitt and Green eds., 1989).

of humanity," and they based their normative prescriptions on these unarticulated values.[104]

Prior to 1945, the words used in the preambles of the two Hague Conventions were the only references in conventional international law which resembled the term "crimes against humanity."[105] Though the Hague Conventions concerned "war crimes" in a narrow and specific sense, they derived from the larger meaning of violations "the laws of humanity."[106] Thus, these words were intended to provide an overarching concept to protect against unspecified violations whose identification in positive international law was left to future normative development.

As the predecessor to the 1907 Hague Convention, the 1899 Hague Convention was the first comprehensive international instrument to develop rules derived from the customary practices of states in time of war.[107] At the time, it went even further when it stated that in cases not covered by specific regulations:

Populations and belligerents remain under the protection and empire of the principles of international law, as they result from the usages established between civilized nations, from the laws of humanity, and the requirements of the public conscience.[108]

The basis for such protection of the principles of international law was then reinforced and expanded in the Preamble to the 1907 Hague Convention which states:

It has not been found possible at present to concert regulations covering all the circumstances which arise in practice. On the other hand, the High Contracting Parties clearly do not intend that unforeseen cases should, in the

---

[104] See 1899 Hague Convention With Respect to the Laws and Customs of War on Land, July 29, 1899, 32 Stat. 1803, T.S. No. 403, 26 MARTENS (ser. 2) 949, *reprinted in* 1 AM. J. INT'L L. 129 (1907) (Supp.); and 1907 Hague Convention Respecting the Laws and Customs of War on Land, Oct. 18, 1907, 36 Stat. 2277, T.S. No. 539, 3 MARTENS (ser. 3) 461, *reprinted in* 2 AM. J. INT'L L. 90 (1908) (Supp.), 1 FRIEDMAN 308, 1 BEVANS 631.

[105] The 1907 Hague Convention provides that:

the inhabitants and the belligerents shall remain under the protection and the rule of principles of the laws of nations, as they result from the usages established among civilized peoples, from the *laws of humanity*, and the dictates of the public conscience. (emphasis added).

1907 Hague Convention, preamble (emphasis added), *supra* note 104, at 92. The preamble of the 1899 Hague Convention employs similar phrasing. See *infra* note 108 and accompanying text.

[106] See Egon Schwelb, *Crimes Against Humanity*, 23 BRIT. Y.B. INT'L L. 178, 180 (1946). Professor Schwelb's article is probably the most reliable scholarly article on the interpretation of Article 6(c); and BASSIOUNI, CRIMES AGAINST HUMANITY, *supra* note 1.

[107] Project of an International Declaration Concerning the Laws and Customs of War, *supra* note 61. The 1874 Declaration of Brussels also developed rules derived from the customary laws of war, but it never entered into force. *Id.*

[108] 1899 Hague Convention, *supra* note 104, at ¶ 9 of the Pmbl (emphasis added).

absence of a written undertaking, be left to the arbitrary judgment of military commanders. Until a more complete code of the laws of war has been issued, the High Contracting Parties deem it expedient to declare that, in cases not included in the Regulations adopted by them, the inhabitants and the belligerents remain under the protection and the rule of the principles of the law of nations, as they result from the usages established among civilized peoples, from the laws of humanity, and the dictates of the public conscience.[109]

This language embodies the well-known Martens clause[110] which permits the resort to "general principles" as a means of interpreting provisions in international instruments and to fill gaps in conventional textual language.[111]

The extension of the "general principle" contained in Preamble of the 1899 and 1907 Conventions is reflected in Article 22 of the Hague Regulations in the 1899 and 1907 Conventions which provides for another general norm that *"the right of belligerents to adopt means of injuring the enemy is not unlimited."* [112]

---

[109] 1907 Hague Convention, *supra* note 104, at ¶¶ 6-8 of the Pmbl (emphasis added).

[110] The Martens Clause is named after Fyodor Martens, the Russian diplomat and jurist who drafted it. A similar formula appears in each of the 1949 Geneva Conventions and in the 1977 Protocols. *See* First Geneva Convention for the Amelioration of the Condition of the Wounded and Sick in Armed Forces in the Field, 75 U.N.T.S. 31, 6 U.S.T. 3114, T.I.A.S. No. 3362 at art. 63(4); Second Geneva Convention of 1949 for the Amelioration of the Condition of Wounded, Sick, and Shipwrecked Members of the Armed Forces at Sea, 75 U.N.T.S. 85, 6 U.S.T. 3217, T.I.A.S. No. 3363 at art. 62(4); Third Geneva Convention of 1949 relative to the Treatment of Prisoners of War, 75 U.N.T.S. 135, 6 U.S.T. 3316, T.I.A.S. No. 3364 at art. 142(4); Fourth Geneva Convention of 1949 relative to the Protection of Civilian Persons in Time of War, U.N.T.S. 287, 6 U.S.T. 3516, T.I.A.S. No. 3365 at art. 158(4); Protocol Additional to the Geneva Conventions of August 12, 1949 and Relating to the Protection of Victims of International Armed Conflict, June 8, 1977, para. 4, Art. 51.4(b-c), U.N. Doc. A/32/144, Annex I (1977), *reprinted in* 16 I.L.M. 1391, 1413 (1977), at art. 1(2) [hereinafter Protocol I]; Protocol Additional to Geneva Convention of Aug. 12, 1949, and Relating to the Protection of Victims of Non-International Armed Conflicts, *opened for signature*, Dec. 12, 1977, U.N. Doc. A/32/144 AnnexII, *reprinted in* 16 I.L.M. 1391 at pmbl. [hereinafter Protocol II]; PABLO BENVENUTI, *La Clausola MARTENS e la Tradizione Classica del Diritto Naturale nella Codificazione del Conflicts Armati, in* SCRITTI DEGLI ALLIEVI IN MEMORIA DI GUISEPPE BARILE 173 (1995).

[111] *See* M. Cherif Bassiouni, *A Functional Approach to "General Principles of International Law,"* 11 MICH J. INT'L L. 768 (1990). The same formulation of the Hague Conventions has been used in the latest international instrument on the humanitarian law of armed conflicts, Protocol I states in Article 1:

In cases not covered by this Protocol or by other international agreements, civilians and combatants remain under the protection and authority of the principles of international law derived from established custom, from the principles of humanity and from the dictates of public conscience. (emphasis added).

1977 Protocol I, *supra* note 110, at art. 1. *See also* Waldemar A. Solf, *Protection of Civilians Against the Effects of Hostilities Under Customary International Law and Under Protocol I*, 1 AM. U.J. INT'L L. & POL'Y 117 (1986).

[112] Protocol I, *supra* note 110, at Article 35(1) which parallels the Hague Conventions' general norm on the implicit limitation on the "methods" of war. That article states *"in any armed conflict, the*

International Humanitarian Law and Arms Control Agreements 27

Some regulations that emerged from these conventions proscribed the use of certain weapons against individual soldiers, as opposed to use against enemy armies in general. For example, Declaration (IV, 2) of the 1899 Hague Convention provides for state parties to "agree to abstain from the use of projectiles the sole object of which is the diffusion of asphyxiating or deleterious gases."[113] Another example is the Declaration (IV, 3) from the same Convention, which prohibited the use of "bullets which expand or flatten easily in the human body, such as bullets with a hard envelope which does not entirely cover the core or is pierced with incisions."[114]

While the 1907 Hague Convention IV with Respect to the Laws and Customs of War on Land prohibited, in much the same manner as previously discussed texts, the use of poisoned weapons and "arms, projectiles or material calculated to cause unnecessary suffering," it makes no mention of any other type of weapon. Though this may seem at first glance to be a failure of the Conference, it should be recalled that it also adopted Declaration (XIV) Prohibiting the Discharge of Projectiles and Explosives from Balloons. The Declaration also prohibited discharge of projectiles and explosives from "other new methods of a similar nature."[115] Prior to this, the only law on this matter was the 1899 Declaration (IV,1), which prohibited such discharges only for a term of five years. As a result, this text reinforced the prohibition of certain types of aerial bombardments and the use of weapons of a non-explosive nature, such as asphyxiating gases.

However, despite both the historic prohibition of poisoned weapons and the 1899 Declaration prohibiting the "use of projectiles diffusing asphyxiating gases," poisoned gas was used as a devastating weapon during World War I. As a result, two instruments were developed to specifically establish the illegality of poisoned gas. First was the 1922 Treaty Relating to the Use of Submarines and Noxious Gases. More comprehensive, however, was the 1925 Geneva Protocol for the Prohibition of the Use in War of Asphyxiating, Poisonous or Other Gases, and of Bacteriological Methods of Warfare:

> Whereas the use of asphyxiating, poisonous or other gases, and of all analogous liquids, materials or devices, has been justly condemned by the general opinion of the civilized world; and Whereas the prohibition of such use has been declared in Treaties to which the majority of the Powers of the world are Parties; and To the end that this prohibition shall be universally

---

right of the parties to the conflict to choose methods or means of warfare is not unlimited." (emphasis added).

113 Declaration Concerning the Prohibition of the Use of Projectiles Diffusing Asphyxiating Gases, *supra* note 62.

114 Declaration Concerning the Prohibition of the Use of Expanding Bullets, *supra* note 62.

115 Declaration Relative to Prohibiting the Discharge of Projectiles and Explosives from Balloons, *supra* note 63.

accepted as part of International Law, binding alike the conscience and the practice of nations.[116]

Significantly, violations of the above provisions have been drafted as war crimes in the Rome Statute of the International Criminal Court:

Article 8(2)(b)(xx) includes the employment of weapons, projectiles and material and methods of warfare which are of a nature to cause superfluous injury or unnecessary suffering or which are inherently indiscriminate in violation of the international law of armed conflict, provided that such weapons, projectiles and material and methods of warfare are the subject of a comprehensive prohibition and are accordance with the relevant provisions set forth in articles 121 and 123.[117]

With respect to the Geneva Conventions of 1949, Leslie C. Green notes that although they are "generally regarded as being the constituent instruments of humanitarian law," they are silent on the "means and methods of warfare."[118] He points out, however, that when these instruments were amended in 1977 "by way of two additional Protocols: I concerning international armed conflicts and II non-international conflicts," a new legal development emerged.[119] Citing Part III, Section I of Protocol I, Green points out Article 35 for its focus on methods and means of warfare:

1. In any armed conflict, the right of the Parties to the conflict to choose methods or means of warfare is not unlimited.
2. It is prohibited to employ weapons, projectiles and material and methods of warfare of a nature to cause superfluous injury or unnecessary suffering.
3. It is prohibited to employ methods or means of warfare which are intended, or may be expected to, cause widespread, long-term and severe damage to the environment.[120]

A significant innovation in the above text is the inclusion of language that protects the environment from long-term damage. In addition, Article 36 places state parties in a more duty-bound position with respect to the manufacture as well as use of certain weapons than ever before:

---

[116] 1925 Geneva Protocol for the Prohibition of the Use in War of Asphyxiating, Poisonous or Other Gases, and of Bacterial Methods of Warfare, *supra* note 64.

[117] Rome Statute of the International Criminal Court, *supra* note 83, at Article 8(2)(b)(xx).

[118] BASSIOUNI, ICL, *supra* note 1, at 478.

[119] *Id.*

[120] Protocol I, *supra* note 110.

...in the study, development, acquisition or adoption of a new weapon, means or method of warfare, a high Contracting Party is under an obligation to determine whether its employment would, in some or all circumstances, be prohibited by this Protocol or by any other rule of international law applicable to the High Contracting Party.[121]

Professor Green observes that an important outgrowth of the above innovation is that "the concept of unnecessary suffering caused to individuals is no longer the criterion for condemnation."[122] Instead of only focusing on the effect actually caused by the use of weapons "which might otherwise be lawful," Green argues, the prohibition "is now extended to ban weapons which are likely to have this effect."[123] Green also points out that despite the well known indiscriminate and harmful effects of nuclear weapons, no prohibition of them was included in Protocol I. At the time of adopting the Protocol, the question of nuclear weapons was considered to be the proper purview of "disarmament discussions." [124] In 1996, the International Court of Justice issued an Advisory Opinion on the Legality of the Threat or Use of Nuclear Weapons, in which it decided that "there was no customary or conventional international law either authorizing or actually prohibiting the threat or use of nuclear weapons...[and] could not make up its mind definitively either in favor or against the legality of the use of the nuclear weapon."[125] It is significant, however, that the Court unanimously did hold that:

A threat or use of nuclear weapons should also be compatible with the requirements of the international law applicable in armed conflict, particularly those of the principles and rules of international humanitarian law [which are directed against the imposition of "unnecessary suffering"], as well as with specific obligations under treaties and other undertakings which expressly deal with nuclear weapons.[126]

The 1972 Convention on the Prohibition of the Development, Production and Stockpiling of Bacteriological (Biological) and Toxin Weapons and on Their Destruction is an example of one of the first instances where a particular weapon was itself banned by international agreement, and not merely its use.[127] The policy reason for such a ban was stated clearly by the drafters, who wrote that the Convention was adopted to affect the "progress towards general disarmament

---

[121] BASSIOUNI, ICL, *supra* note 1, at 478.

[122] *Id.*

[123] *Id.*

[124] *Id.* at 479.

[125] *Id.* at 483-84.

[126] Advisory Opinion of the International Court of Justice on July 8, *Legality of the Threat or Use of Nuclear Weapons, supra* note 13, at 828-30.

[127] BASSIOUNI, ICL, *supra* note 1, at 485.

[including nuclear weapons] under strict international control."[128] A similar Convention, one of the most detailed and comprehensive to date, was adopted in 1993 with respect to chemical weapons. State parties to the Chemical Weapons Convention agreed upon the prohibition on development, production, and retention of chemical weapons, and to destroy such weapons already in existence.[129]

A major breakthrough occurred in 1980 with the adoption of the Convention on Prohibition or Restrictions on the Use of Certain Conventional Weapons Which May be Deemed to be Excessively Injurious or to Have Indiscriminate Effects. The Protocols to this Convention provide it with practical effect. Protocol I on Non-Detectable Fragments, for instance, forbids the use of "any weapon the primary effect of which is to injure by fragments which in the human body escape detection by X-rays."[130] In the Protocol On Prohibitions or Restrictions on the Use of Mines, Booby-Traps and Other Devices (Protocol II), particular attention is paid to proscribing devices that are manually placed, remote controlled operated, or time detonated. Land mines are not declared illegal in all circumstances, and the Protocol only proscribes their use against civilian populations. In addition, the use cannot be so indiscriminate as to create collateral damage that is "excessive in relation to the concrete and direct military advantage anticipated."[131] Protocol III proscribes certain kinds of incendiary weapons specifically defined in Article 2:

> ...any weapon or munition which is primarily designed to set fire to objects or to cause burn injury to persons through the action of flame, heat, or combination thereof, produced by a chemical reaction of a substance delivered on the target...Incendiary weapons do not include:
> (a) Munitions which may have incidental incendiary effects, such as illuminants, tracers, smoke or signalling systems;
> (b) Munitions designed to combine penetration, blast or fragmentation effects with an additional incendiary effect, such as armour-piercing projectiles, fragmentation shells, explosive bombs and similar combined-effects munitions in which the incendiary effect is not specifically designed to cause burn injury to persons, but to be used against military objectives, such as armoured vehicles, aircraft and installations or facilities...[132]

---

[128] *Id.*

[129] Convention on the Prohibition of the Development, Production and Stockpiling and Use of Chemical Weapons and on their Destruction, *supra* note 73

[130] Protocol on Non-Detectable Fragments to Convention on Prohibitions or Restrictions on the Use of Certain Conventional Weapons Which May be Deemed to be Excessively Injurious or to have Indiscriminate Effects [Protocol I], *adopted at Geneva*, U.N. Doc. A/CONF.95/15 (1980), 19 I.L.M. 1529, entered into force 2 December 1983.

[131] *Id.*

[132] Protocol on Prohibitions or Restrictions on the Use of Incendiary Weapons to the Convention on Prohibitions or Restrictions on the Use of Certain Conventional Weapons, Oct. 10, 1980, [Protocol III], *adopted at Geneva*, U.N. Doc. A/CONF.95/15 (1980), 19 I.L.M. 1534, entered into force 2 December 1983 with provisions.

In 1996, Protocol IV was added to the Convention in order to address the more high-tech developments in weaponry. It prohibits the employment of laser weapons "specifically designed, as their sole combat function or as one of their combat functions" to render the enemy permanently blind. Laser weapons themselves are not prohibited, and "blindness as an incidental, or collateral effect of the legitimate military employment of laser systems, including laser systems used against optical equipment, is not covered by the prohibition," regardless of whether or not permanent blindness is incidental to the employment of the weapon.[133]

Limitations on the Use of Permissible Weapons

As discussed earlier, prohibited weapons are specifically restricted by conventional international law or general principles, such as unnecessary pain and suffering; whereas, permissible weapons are only limited in accordance to the principles of discrimination and proportionality, as reflected in both conventional and customary international law.

The Principle of Discrimination in the Use of Weapons

The basic rule of discrimination, which functions to limit the use of certain weapons, bestows in the belligerent forces the "obligation to draw a firm line of demarcation between civilians and civilian objects, on the one hand, and combatants and military objectives, on the other."[134] The U.N. General Assembly in Resolution 2444 of 1969 stated the rule of discrimination as follows:

a. That the right of the parties to a conflict to adopt means of injuring the enemy is not unlimited;

b. That it is prohibited to launch attacks against the civilian population as such; and

c. That a distinction must be made at all times between persons taking part in the hostilities and members of the civilian population to the effect that the latter be spared as much as possible.[135]

The conventional and customary laws of armed conflict prohibit the use of weapons that cause indiscriminate harm and damage. These are contained in the

---

[133] Additional Protocol to the Convention on Prohibitions or Restrictions on the Use of Certain Conventional Weapons which may be Deemed to be Excessively Injurious or to have Indiscriminate Effects (Protocol IV) on Blinding Laser Weapons, *adopted*, 12 October 1995, 90 AM. J. INT'L L. 484 (1996), not yet in force.

[134] H. Levie, II THE CODE OF INTERNATIONAL ARMED CONFLICT 81 (1986).

[135] G.A. Res. 2444 (XXIII), 23 U.N. GAOR, Supp. (No. 18), at 50, U.N. Doc. A/7218 (1969).

provisions of the Geneva Convention of August 12, 1949 and Protocol I of 1977.[136] Article 57(2)(b) of Protocol I provides that:

Among others, the following types of attacks are to be considered as indiscriminate:

An attack which may be expected to cause incidental loss of civilian life, injury to civilians, damage to civilian objects, or a combination thereof, which would be excessive in relation to the concrete and direct military advantage anticipated.[137]

For example, Article 35 of Part III, Section I of Protocol I provides that the means and methods of warfare are "not unlimited," and that it is prohibited to "employ weapons, projectiles and material" that is of a nature to "cause superfluous injury or unnecessary suffering."[138] In its Advisory Opinion, the International Court of Justice affirmatively addressed the question of whether international humanitarian law applies to nuclear weapons:

In the view of the vast majority of States as well as writers there can be no doubt as to the applicability of humanitarian law to nuclear weapons.

Indeed, nuclear weapons were invented after most of the principles and rules of humanitarian law applicable in armed conflict had already come into existence; the Conferences of 1949 and 1974-1977 left these weapons aside, and there is a qualitative as well as quantitative difference between nuclear weapons and all conventional arms. However, it cannot be concluded from this that the established principles and rules of humanitarian law applicable in armed conflict did not apply to nuclear weapons. Such a conclusion would be incompatible with the intrinsically humanitarian character of the legal principles in question which permeates the entire law of armed conflict and applies to all forms of warfare and to all kinds of weapons, those of the past, those of the present and those of the future.

None of the statements made before the Court in any way advocated a freedom to use nuclear weapons without regard to humanitarian constraints. Quite the reverse; it has been explicitly stated,

"Restrictions set by the rules applicable to armed conflicts in respect of means and methods of warfare definitely also extend to nuclear weapons" (Russian Federation, CR 95/29, p. 52);

"So far as the customary law of war is concerned, the United Kingdom has always accepted that the use of nuclear weapons is subject to the general principles of the jus in bello" (United Kingdom, CR 95/34, p. 45); and

---

[136] Protocol I, *supra* note 110.

[137] *Id.*

[138] *Id.* at Article 35.

"The United States has long shared the view that the law of armed conflict governs the use of nuclear weapons -- just as it governs the use of conventional weapons" (United States of America, CR 95/34, p. 85.)

Finally, the Court points to the Martens Clause, whose continuing existence and applicability is not to be doubted, as an affirmation that the principles and rules of humanitarian law apply to nuclear weapons.[139]

One of the cardinal principles of humanitarian law of armed conflict is the protection of civilians and civilian objects during time of war. This presupposes a principle of discrimination. Two separate questions that must be asked when evaluating a military act are those of *jus ad bellum* and *jus in bello*. The first question asks when a state can justly go to war, while the second examines the actual justness of the particular conduct during war. More importantly for our purposes, *jus in bello* doctrinal questions frame the legal way in which international humanitarian law achieves its goal of protecting non-combatants from the indiscriminate effects of war. According to Michael N. Schmitt, classic examples of this type of protection include "the limitations on targeting civilians and civilian objects, the protection of medical personnel and facilities, and norms regarding the treatment of prisoners of war."[140]

The principle of discrimination limits the use of weapons that are by nature indiscriminate, and therefore incapable of discriminating between lawful and unlawful targets, or between combatants and non-combatants.[141] According to Protocol I of the Geneva Convention of 1949,

> Indiscriminate attacks are...(b) those which employ a method or means of combat which cannot be directed at a specific military objective; or (c) those which employ a method or means of combat the effects of which cannot be limited as required by this Protocol; and consequently, in each such case, are of a nature to strike military objectives and civilians or civilian objects without discretion.[142]

In addition, the principle of discrimination proscribes the indiscriminate use of weapons, "regardless of their innate ability to discriminate."[143] Three aspects of discrimination are distinction, proportionality, and minimizing collateral damage

---

[139] Advisory Opinion of the International Court of Justice on July 8, *Legality of the Threat or Use of Nuclear Weapons*, *supra* note 13, at 828.

[140] Michael N. Schmitt, *The Principle of Discrimination in 21st Century Warfare*, 2 YALE HUM. RTS. AND DEV. L. J. 145 (1999).

[140] *Id.* at 147.

[142] Protocol I, *supra* note 110, at 1413.

[143] Schmitt, *supra* note 140, at 148.

and incidental injury.[144] Article 48 of the Protocol states that parties involved in war must "distinguish between the civilian population and combatants and between civilian objects and military objectives and accordingly direct their operations only against military objectives."[145] Article 51.2 also provides for this prohibition, stating that, "the civilian population as such, as well as individual civilians, shall not be the object of attack."[146] Also, Article 52.2 provides that "attacks shall be to strictly military objectives."[147]

Articles 51 and 57 of the Protocol codify the proportionality component of discrimination. Accordingly, attacks "which may be expected to cause incidental loss of civilian life, injury to civilians, damage to civilian objects, or a combination thereof, which would be excessive in relation to the concrete and direct military advantage anticipated" are forbidden.[148] Lastly, discrimination requires the least collateral damage to be sought. This is enshrined in Article 57 of the Protocol, which states that "with respect to attacks, the following precautions shall be taken . . . take all feasible precautions in the choice of means and methods of attack with a view to avoiding, and in any event to minimizing, incidental loss of civilian life, injury to civilians and damage to civilian objects . . . ."[149]

The above discussion of humanitarian law principles provides context for the conclusion in the Advisory Opinion that nuclear weapons fall under the realm of restrictions provided for under Geneva law. Specifically, nuclear weapons that are not used in violation of the above principles of discrimination would have to be guaranteed to produce very limited collateral damage, not harm civilians, and not cause unnecessary pain and suffering.

The Rule of Proportionality

Limitations on the use of weapons also arise from general norms, such as the rule of proportionality inferred from Articles 15 and 22 of the Lieber Code, and later established in Articles 51(5)(b) and 57(2)(b) of the 1977 Protocol I.[150]

Article 57(2)(a)(ii) provides that:
Those who plan or decide upon an attack shall take all feasible precautions in the choice of means and methods of attack with a view to

---

[144] *Id.*

[145] *Id.* at 149 (citing Additional Protocol I, Art. 48.).

[146] *Id.* at 149.

[147] *Id.* at 149.

[148] *Id.* at 150 (citing Additional Protocol I, Article 51.5(b)).

[149] *Id.* at 152 (citing Article 57.2(a)(ii)).

[150] A.P.V. ROGERS, LAW ON THE BATTLEFIELD 16 (1996) [hereinafter ROGERS].

avoiding, and in any event minimizing, incidental loss of civilian life, injury to civilians and damage to civilian objects.[151]

Article 57(2)(b) provides that:
An attack shall be cancelled or suspended if it becomes apparent that the objective is not a military one or is subject to special protection or that the attack may be expected to cause incidental loss of civilian life, injury to civilians, damage to civilian objects, or a combination thereof, which would be excessive in relation to the concrete and direct military advantage anticipated.[152]

According to the United States interpretation of the above provisions, the proportionality rule "prohibits military action in which the negative effects (such as collateral civilian casualties) clearly outweigh the military gain."[153] According to the International Committee for the Red Cross Commentary on the Additional Protocols of June 8, 1977, there are numerous factors to be taken into account. These include the following: the military importance of the target or objective; the density of the civilian population; the likely incidental effects of the attack; possible release of hazardous substances; the types of weapon available to attack the target and their accuracy; whether the defenders are deliberately exposing civilians or civilian objects to risk; and the mode of attack and the timing of the attack.[154]

Thus the general rule of proportionality is that the losses resulting from a military act should not be excessive in relation to the anticipated military advantage.[155] Solf and Grandison have articulated a concise explanation of the proportionality rule:

[I]n directing attacks against military objectives, some incidental injury to civilians...is likely, at times, to result. Accordingly, the law has interposed the further requirement, under what is commonly termed the "Rule of Proportionality," that attacks against military objectives cannot be made when the injury to civilians and damage to civilian property [that] is likely to occur is out of proportion to the military advantage reasonably expected to be gained.[156]

---

[151] Protocol I, *supra* note 110, at 1391.

[152] *Id.*

[153] ROGERS, *supra* note 150.

[154] *Id.* at 19.

[155] EDWARD KWAKWA, THE INTERNATIONAL LAW OF ARMED CONFLICT: PERSONAL AND MATERIAL FIELDS OF APPLICATION 38 (1992).

[156] Solf and Grandison, *International Humanitarian Law Applied in Armed Conflict,* 10 J. Int'l L. and Econ. 567, 583 (1979).

Another facet of warfare, which is related to the proportionality rule, is the protection of the environment. Even though the 1977 Convention on the Prohibition of Military or Any Other Hostile Use of Environmental Modification Techniques[157] does not enforce sanctions, it should be read in the context of Protocol I.[158] In Article 35(2) of Protocol I, "it is prohibited to employ methods or means of warfare which are intended, or may be expected, to cause widespread long-term and severe damage to the natural environment."[159] Moreover, Article 55 of the Protocol provides that:

> Care shall be taken in warfare to protect the natural environment against widespread, long-term and severe damage. This protection includes a prohibition of the use of methods or means of warfare which are intended or may be expected to cause such damage to the natural environment and thereby to prejudice the health or survival of the population [and] attacks against the natural environment by way of reprisals are prohibited.[160]

Arms Control and Disarmament Agreements

Arms control agreements fall into four different categories: 1) multilateral and bilateral treaties on arms control dealing with weapons of mass destruction; 2) the prohibition of emplacement of weapons of mass destruction in certain areas; 3) regional agreements including nuclear weapons free zones, and European and Middle Eastern peace and security agreements; and 4) voluntary regulations concerning the export and transfer of technology. These agreements are distinguishable from international humanitarian law because violations of international humanitarian law can be deemed war crimes, depending upon the type of violation. The degree of criminality for these violations is discussed in Chart A, which can be found on page 63.

As discussed above, the values of international humanitarian law are founded in notions of humanity, whereas these four categories of arms control agreements and peace treaties, which contain arms control agreements, are entirely different. Instead, they are the product of bilateral or multilateral treaties negotiated on the basis of political considerations and the interests of the respective governments, and do not contain penal provisions. Violations of these provisions raise questions of state responsibility for wrongful conduct and eventually the issue of damages. Moreover, legal techniques by which treaties are prepared differ significantly, as

---

[157] Convention on the Prohibition of Military or Any other Hostile Use of Environmental Modification Techniques, *supra* note 68.

[158] LESLIE C. GREEN, THE CONTEMPORARY LAW OF ARMED CONFLICT 137 (2000).

[159] Protocol I, *supra* note 110, at Article 35(2).

[160] Protocol I, *supra* note 110, at Article 55.

well as do the control regimes they establish. For theses reasons arms control agreements are described separately in this book, in Chapters II through VIII.

Emplacement of Weapons of Mass Destruction in Certain Media

This category contains agreements that prohibit the emplacement of nuclear, chemical, and biological weapons in media such as outer space, the moon, and the ocean floor. These agreements span the high point of Cold War activity, starting with the 1959 Antarctic Treaty[161] banning nuclear weapon tests in Antarctica and culminating with the 1979 Agreement Governing the Activities of States on the Moon and Other Celestial Bodies[162].

The rationale behind these prohibitions is to enhance the peace and security of humankind, therefore the agreements are related to the preservation of peace and the prohibition of aggression. They are also intended explicitly or implicitly to protect the environment. For example, they encourage international cooperation for peaceful scientific research in the global commons.

A violation of the obligations contained in these agreements constitutes a violation of international humanitarian law, and may be deemed an emerging customary law violation includable in war crimes. However, these agreements do not contain penal elements, and are therefore, at this time, only the foundation for future criminalization.

The Nuclear Non-Proliferation Regime, Differential Responsibility for International Security, and the International Court of Justice Advisory Opinion on the Legality of the Threat or Use of Nuclear Weapons: A New Era of Customary International Law[163]

The international community through the Nuclear Non-Proliferation Treaty (NPT) has expressed a position favoring the limitation of nuclear weapons to known nuclear states.[164] Presently the nuclear states that have ratified the Non-Proliferation Treaty are the five permanent members of the Security Council: United States of America, England, France, China, and the Russian Federation. The Non-Proliferation Treaty commits signatory states not to develop nuclear weapons. Article I proscribes nuclear powers from transferring nuclear weapons to

---

[161] The Antarctic Treaty, *supra* note 74.

[162] Agreement Governing the Activities of States on the Moon and Other Celestial Bodies, *supra* note 78.

[163] The Treaties in this section are examples of progressive customary international law. They represent the beginning of a new custom and era of non-proliferation of weapons of mass destruction, leading to the prohibition of nuclear weapons, non-first use, regional nuclear free zones, and limits on testing.

[164] Nuclear Non-Proliferation Treaty, 729 U.N.T.S. 161. The Treaty entered into force on March 5, 1970. In 1995 it was extended indefinitely.

non-nuclear countries, and from assisting them in the development of such technology.[165] Article II prevents states from receiving such weapons.[166]

The Non-Proliferation Treaty today obliges the five accepted nuclear powers to refrain from using nuclear weapons against non-nuclear weapons states that are parties to the Treaty.[167] Regarding these nuclear powers, Judge Oda of the International Court of Justice wrote in his dissenting opinion to the Advisory Opinion on the Legality of the Threat or Use of Nuclear Weapons:

> ...they have themselves given security assurances to the non-nuclear-weapon States by certain statements they have made in the Security Council. In addition, those nuclear-weapon States, insofar as they adhere to the Protocols appended to the respective Nuclear Free Zone Treaties, are bound not to use or threaten to use nuclear weapons against States Parties to those respective treaties.[168]

A system of differential security responsibility has evolved by which the five recognized nuclear powers also agree to come to the aid of any non-nuclear weapon state that is party to the Non-Proliferation Treaty, in the event that they come under nuclear weapon attack. It is contemplated that such aid might give rise to an exceptional justification to use a nuclear weapon against an aggressor. Thus the incentive for states to join the Non-Proliferation regime is increased. The guarantee of immediate assistance is clearly stated in Security Council Resolution 984 (1995):

> ...nuclear weapon State Permanent Members will act immediately in accordance with the relevant provisions of the Charter of the United Nations, in the event that such States are the victim of an act of, or object of a threat of, aggression in which nuclear weapons are used...[169]

That the above provision may in fact be an emergency justification for the threat or use of nuclear weapons is suggested by Judge Schwebel in his dissenting opinion to the International Court of Justice's Advisory Opinion:

---

[165] *Id.* at Art I.

[166] *Id.* at Art II.

[167] U.N. Doc S/1995/261, 262, 263 and 264; S/1995/265; W. Michael Reisman, *Towards A Normative Theory Of Differential Responsibility For International Security Functions: Responsibilities of Major Powers, in* JAPAN AND INTERNATIONAL LAW: PAST, PRESENT, AND FUTURE 49 (Nisuki Ando ed., 1999) [hereinafter Reisman].

[168] Advisory Opinion of the International Court of Justice on July 8, *Legality of the Threat or Use of Nuclear Weapons, supra* note 13, at 855, para 41 (Judge Oda, dissenting opinion); Reisman, *supra* note 167.

[169] U.N. Res. 984, Para. 2 (1995), adopted 11 April 1995.

International Humanitarian Law and Arms Control Agreements 39

(The Security Council, in Resolution 984) accepted the possibility of the threat or use of nuclear weapons, particularly to assist a non-nuclear-weapon State that, in the words of paragraph 7 [of Security Council Resolution 984] "is a victim of an act of, or an object of a threat of, aggression in which nuclear weapons are used."[170]

It is now well known that both India, Pakistan and Israel developed nuclear weapons and that other countries are seeking to do so such as North Korea and Iraq. Notwithstanding these few exceptions, the international community has signified its commitment to the Non-Proliferation Treaty, as evidenced by the fact that 182 states have ratified it.[171] This is reinforced by the following regional nuclear-free-zone treaties: Treaty for the Prohibition of Nuclear Weapons in Latin America (Treaty of Tlatelolco),[172] the South Pacific Nuclear-Free-Zone Treaty (Treaty of Raratonga),[173] the Treaty on Southeast Asia Nuclear Weapon-Free Zone,[174] and the African Nuclear-Weapon-Free Zone Treaty (Treaty of Pelindaba).[175]

The above regional nuclear-free-zone treaties cumulatively represent all of the following countries: Argentina; the Bahamas; Barbados; Bolivia; Brazil; Chile; Colombia; Costa Rica; Dominican Republic; Ecuador; El Salvador; Grenada; Guatemala; Haiti; Honduras; Jamaica; Mexico; Nicaragua; Panama; Paraguay; Peru; Suriname; Trinidad & Tobago; Uruguay; Venezuela; Australia; Cook Islands; Fiji; Kiribati; New Zealand; Niue; Papua New Guinea; Brunei; Darussalam; Cambodia; Indonesia; Laos; Malaysia; Philippines; Singapore; Thailand; Vietnam; Algeria; Angola; Benin; Burkina Faso; Burundi; Cameroon; Cape Verde; Central African Republic; Chad; Comoros; Côte D'Ivoire; Djibouti; Egypt; Eritrea; Ethiopia; Gambia; Ghana; Guinea; Guinea-Bissau; Kenya; Lesotho; Libya; Malawi; Mali; Mauritania; Mauritius; Morocco; Mozambique; Namibia; Niger; Nigeria; Rwanda; Senegal; Sierra Leone; South Africa; The Sudan; Swaziland; Tanzania; Togo; Tunisia; Uganda; Zaire; Zambia; and Zimbabwe.

---

[170] Advisory Opinion of International Court of Justice on July 8, *Legality of the Threat or Use of Nuclear Weapons*, *supra* note 13, at 838 (Judge Schwebel, dissenting opinion); Reisman, *supra* note 167, at 51.

[171] Resiman, *supra* note 167, at 48.

[172] Treaty for the Prohibition of Nuclear Weapons in Latin America (Treaty of Tlatelolco), *supra* note 79.

[173] The South Pacific Nuclear-Free-Zone Treaty (Treaty of Raratonga), *supra* note 80.

[174] The Treaty on Southeast Asia Nuclear Weapon-Free Zone, *supra* note 81.

[175] The African Nuclear-Weapon-Free Zone Treaty (Treaty of Pelindaba), *supra* note 82.

The International Court of Justice, in its Advisory Opinion on the Legality of the Threat or Use of Nuclear Weapons[176] also took a strong position against the use of nuclear weapons and more particularly against the first use of nuclear weapons. Unanimously, the Court held the following:

> A threat or use of force by means of nuclear weapons that is contrary to Article 2, paragraph 4, of the United Nations Charter and that fails to meet all the requirements of Article 51, is unlawful;
>
> A threat or use of nuclear weapons should also be compatible with the requirements of the international law applicable in armed conflict, particularly those of the principles and rules of international humanitarian law, as well as with specific obligations under treaties and other undertakings which expressly deal with nuclear weapons;
>
> There exists an obligation to pursue in good faith and bring to a conclusion negotiations leading to nuclear disarmament in all its aspects under strict and effective international control.[177]

Elaborating on the obligation of good faith negotiation for nuclear disarmament, the Court stressed that it was an obligation of result:

> ...the Court appreciates the full importance of the recognition by Article VI of the Treaty on the Non-Proliferation of Nuclear Weapons of an obligation to negotiate in good faith a nuclear disarmament. The legal import of that obligation goes beyond that of a mere obligation of conduct; the obligation involved here is an obligation to achieve a precise result -- nuclear disarmament in all its aspects -- by adopting a particular course of conduct, namely, the pursuit of negotiations on the matter in good faith.

This twofold obligation to pursue and to conclude negotiations formally concerns the 182 States parties to the Treaty on the Non-Proliferation of Nuclear Weapons, or, in other words, the vast majority of the international community.

Virtually the whole of this community appears moreover to have been involved when resolutions of the United Nations General Assembly concerning nuclear disarmament have repeatedly been unanimously adopted. Indeed, any realistic search for general and complete disarmament, especially nuclear disarmament, necessitates the co-operation of all States.

Even the very first General Assembly resolution, unanimously adopted on 24 January 1946 at the London session, set up a commission whose terms of

---

[176] Advisory Opinion of International Court of Justice on July 8, *Legality of the Threat or Use of Nuclear*, *supra* note 13, (Judge Oda, dissenting); Reisman, *supra* note 167, at 49.

[177] *Id* at 831.

reference included making specific proposals for, among other things, "the elimination from national armaments of atomic weapons and of all other major weapons adaptable to mass destruction". In a large number of subsequent resolutions, the General Assembly has reaffirmed the need for nuclear disarmament. Thus, in resolution 808 A (IX) of 4 November 1954, which was likewise unanimously adopted, it concluded that, "a further effort should be made to reach agreement on comprehensive and co-ordinated proposals to be embodied in a draft international disarmament convention providing for: . . . (b) The total prohibition of the use and manufacture of nuclear weapons and weapons of mass destruction of every type, together with the conversion of existing stocks of nuclear weapons for peaceful purposes."

The same conviction has been expressed outside the United Nations context in various instruments.[178]

Middle East Arms Control and Security Agreements

The Middle East has experienced various conflicts since the end of 1947; however, a gradual evolution in the peace process continues to exist. As evidenced in various peace agreements, this evolution represents the impetus toward establishing a regional security regime for eliminating weapons of mass destruction from the Middle East.

The Middle East region has yet to develop a comprehensive arms control legal regime. From the 1948 UN Security Council Resolution on Palestine[179] to the 1999 Protocol Concerning Safe Passage Between the West Bank and Gaza Strip[180], the evolution of arms control has been completely ad hoc. As can be seen in the instruments that are listed below, arms control provisions in Middle Eastern agreements are generally secondary to military, political, and security issues, such as: terrorism, refugees, safe passage, transfer of political authority, and economic issues.

The negotiations between Israel and the Palestinian National Authority have, thus far, primarily addressed issues that are relevant to short term stability in the region. For example, they have focused on small arms, limited explosive devices, police and soldier regulations, and licensing controls for the sale, production, and possession of handguns and rifles by individuals or groups. Thus, more regulations exist which cover internal security rather than international arms control. Examples include the 1995 Israel-Palestinian Interim Agreement on the West Bank

---

[178] *Id.* at 830.

[179] United Nations Security Council Resolution 50, U.N. SCOR, May 29, 1948, U.N. Doc. S/801, 50 (1948).

[180] Protocol Concerning Safe Passage Between the West Bank and the Gaza Strip, October 5, 1999, <http://www.israel.org/mfa/go.asp?MFAH00pq0>.

and Gaza Strip[181], and the 1997 Protocol Concerning the Redeployment in Hebron[182]. The two most sophisticated provisions are found in the 1998 Wye River Memorandum[183] and the 1999 Protocol Concerning Safe Passage Between the West Bank and Gaza Strip[184]. In Wye, an important step was made to endorse the criminalization of violations of licensing schemes for weapons and related materials; in the Protocol, such licensing regulations were extended to the transportation of dangerous substances.

The creation and maintenance of demilitarized zones is one recurring arms control technique, which is evidenced in the above provisions, that may help lay the legal and political groundwork for the realization that a more all inclusive Weapons of Mass Destruction (WMD) free zone is necessary. This technique has early roots in the Middle East security paradigm. As early as 1948, the Agreement for the Demilitarization of Mount Scopus Area[185] preserved the area by ensuring that it would not be used as a staging post for any military activity. A similar provision was drafted in the 1949 Egyptian-Israeli Arimistice Agreement,[186] as was in the 1979 Annex I to the Peace Treaty Between Egypt and Israel[187].

The 1994 Treaty of Peace Between the State of Israel and the Hashemite Kingdom of Jordan[188] contains exceptional provisions dealing with non-conventional weapons. Article 4.3 and Article 4.7(b), which deal with non-conventional weapons, are significant in the following ways:[189]

---

[181] Israeli-Palestinian Interim Agreement on the West Bank and the Gaza Strip, Washington D.C., September 28, 1995, <http://www.israel-mfa.gov.il/peace/iaannex1.html>.

[182] Protocol Concerning the Redeployment in Hebron, January 17, 1997, <http://www.israel-mfa.gov.il/peace.html>.

[183] The Wye River Memorandum, October 23, 1998, <http://www.isreal.org/mfa/go.asp?MFAH00pq0>.

[184] *See* Protocol Concerning Safe Passage Between the West Bank and the Gaza Strip, *supra* note 180.

[185] Agreement for the Demilitarization of Mount Scopus Area, July 7, 1948.

[186] Egyptian-Israel General Armistice Agreement, February 24, 1949, <http://metalab.unc.edu/sullivan/docs?Sinail.html>.

[187] Peace Treaty Between Isreal and Eqypt, March 26, 1979, <http://metalab.unc.edu/sullivan/docs?Sinail.html>.

[188] Treaty of Peace Between The State of Israel and The Hashemite Kingdom of Jordan (1994), <http://metalab.unc.edu/sullivan/docs?Sinail.html>.

[189] *Id* at Article 4, which provides that the Parties undertake to "refrain from the threat or use of force or weapons, conventional, non-conventional or of any other kind, against each other..."(Article 4.3) Article 4.7(b) provides that the Parties undertake to "work as a matter of priority, and as soon as possible in the context of the Multilateral Working Group on Arms Control and Regional Security, and jointly...towards the creation in the Middle East of a region free from hostile alliances and coaltions and the creation of a Middle East free from weapons of mass destruction, both conventional and non-conventional, in the context of a comprehensive, lasting and stable peace, characterized by the renunciation of the use of force, reconciliation, and goodwill."(Article 4.7(b)).

1. Articles 4.3 and 4.7(b) envision and call for the development of a Middle East regional arms control legal regime to make the region free of all weapons of mass destruction.
2. The treaty endorses international cooperation with the Multilateral Working Group on Arms Control and Regional Security.
3. The treaty proscribes not only the use, but also the threat of use of all types of weapons.
4. The treaty also distinguishes between conventional and non-conventional, while proscribing both.
5. The treaty directly imposes arms control obligations on the two national governments of Jordan and Israel with respect to each other, thereby setting a precedent for state responsibility, as opposed to only holding non-state actors criminally liable.

The United Nations General Assembly passed between 1974 and 1999 a total of twenty-five resolutions calling for the establishment of a nuclear weapon free zone in the Middle East. They call for the need for cooperation with the International Atomic Energy Agency (IAEA) safeguards as well as reinforcing the Non-Proliferation Treaty (NPT) regime. The above cooperation is especially important in light of the fact that the documents also generally emphasize that there is an "inalienable right of all States to acquire and develop nuclear energy for peaceful purposes." While the documents call on all States in the region to "declare their support" for a nuclear weapon free zone, "not to develop, produce, test, or otherwise acquire" nuclear weapons, and to "render their assistance" in the establishment of such a zone, there is a recurring emphasis on the "essential role of the United Nations" throughout the entire process.[190]

The language of these resolutions is sometimes shaped by the political climate of the time. For example, in 1981 the resolution directly addressed the Israeli attack on Iraqi nuclear installations. The language emphasized that the "adherence to the Treaty on Non-Proliferation of Nuclear Weapons by all parties of the region will be conducive to a speedy establishment of a nuclear weapon free zone," and pointed out that the General Assembly was "deeply concerned that the future of the Treaty in the region has been gravely endangered by the attack carried out by Israel, which is not a party to the Treaty, on the nuclear installations of Iraq, which is a party to that Treaty."[191] As a result, the subsequent resolutions continually stressed the importance of the NPT and IAEA to the building of international peace and security in the region, as well as the "need for appropriate measures on the question of the prohibition of military attacks on nuclear facilities."[192]

---

[190] U.N. Doc A/RES/54/51, 7 January 2000.

[191] U.N. Doc Resolution 36/87, 9 December 1981.

[192] U.N. Doc A/RES/46/30 65th Plenary Meeting, 6 December 1991.

In the late 1990's, the Middle East Peace Process and international diplomacy were recognized as important tools for the building of consensus and practical mechanisms leading to the nuclear weapon free zone. For example, in 1996 the resolution noted "the importance of the ongoing bilateral Middle East peace negotiations and the activities of the multilateral working group on arms control and regional security in the Middle East."[193] Also, the phraseology calling for a "zone free of weapons of mass destruction, including nuclear weapons" suggests that the emerging threats of chemical and biological weapons were anticipated.[194] Also, the term "mutually verifiable" was added to the term "nuclear weapon free zone," suggesting an awareness of the growing dynamic of inter-state military competition in the Middle East.[195]

European Arms Control and Security Agreements and the Missile Technology Control Regime

The 1990 Conventional Armed Forces in Europe (CFE) Treaty and the Addendum to the Treaty represent a classic arms control agreement.[196] Limitations fall on five categories of weapons: tanks, artillery, armored combat vehicles, combat helicopters, and attack aircraft. The treaty applies among NATO members and former Warsaw Pact members.

The Missile Technology Control Regime (MTCR)[197] is an informal and voluntary association of countries that share the goals of nonproliferation of unmanned delivery systems for weapons of mass destruction, and seek to coordinate national export licensing efforts aimed at preventing their proliferation. However, it should be noted that the MTCR is not actually a treaty. It is a voluntary "regime" consisting of a common export policy (MTCR Guidelines) applied to a common list (MTCR Annex) of controlled items. These controlled items include virtually all equipment and technology needed or missile development, production, and operation. The MTCR is the only multilateral arrangement dealing with ballistic and cruise missile and other WMD delivery vehicle systems or related equipment, material and technology.

The MTCR Guidelines restrict transfers of missiles and technology related to missiles. The original 1987 Guidelines restricted transfers of nuclear-capable missiles and related technology. However, in January 1993, the MTCR Partners extended the Guidelines to cover delivery systems capable of carrying all types of

---

[193] U.N. Doc A/RES/50/66, 9 January 1996.

[194] Id.

[195] U.N. Doc A/RES/54/51, 7 January 2000.

[196] Conventional Armed Forces in Europe (CFE) Treaty, November 10, 1990; done at Paris, November 19, 1990, 30 I.L.M. 6 (1991).

[197] Missile Technology Control Regime (MTCR) Equipment and Technology Annex 11 June 1996, <http://www.state.gov/www/global/arms/treaties/mtcr_anx.html>.

weapons of mass destruction (chemical and biological weapons, as well as nuclear).

The relevance of this voluntary control regime is that it paves the way for a worldwide legal control regime on weapons of mass destruction and the delivery capabilities that can be used in connection with these weapons. Thus, the elimination of weapons of mass destruction must necessarily lead to the control of delivery systems in order to be fully effective.

Conclusion

The cumulative effect of the above historical experiences and precedents demonstrates the universality of humanitarian principles governing the conduct of armed conflicts. Even though these humanitarian principles, norms and rules regulating armed conflict developed over several millennia, spanning various civilizations located continents apart, they have evolved in the same direction. In time, each succeeding generation reinforced values and strengthened norms and rules. The everlasting articulation of the profound meaning of this process is contained in the Preamble of the 1907 Hague Convention, which simply and yet eloquently refers to the "laws of humanity." This evolution can be seen in its spatial and temporal dimensions as part and parcel of the processes of humankind's history.[198] This historical evolution demonstrates that the principles informing international humanitarian law and arms control existed as part of the "general principles of law recognized by civilized nations" long before the promulgation of such instruments.[199]

---

[198] Arnold Toynbee refers to some 34 civilizations between 3500 B.C. and our century whose evolution he chronicles in his 12 volumes entitled A STUDY OF HISTORY (1939-1962); *See also* the abridged one volume version: ARNOLD TOYNBEE, A STUDY OF HISTORY 72 (1972). More specifically in a case involving the law of war *Ex Parte Quirin,* 317 U.S. 1 (1942) the United States Supreme Court held: "The Law of war, like civil law, has a great *lex non scripta*, its own common law. This common law of war is a centuries old body of largely unwritten rules and principles of international law which governs the behavior of both soldiers and civilians during time of war. WILLIAM WINTHROP, MILITARY LAW AND PRECEDENTS (1920), 17, 41, 42, 773. *Id.* at 13-14.

[199] In 1776, Thomas Paine, in his famous book *Common Sense*, urged the new United States of America to follow this principle, stating: "The Laying of a country desolate with fire and sword, declaring war against the national rights of all mankind, and extirpating the defenders from the face of the Earth is the concern of every man . . . ." THOMAS PAINE, COMMON SENSE, Introduction (Feb. 14, 1776), *reprinted in* THE ESSENTIAL THOMAS PAINE 23-24 (Sidney Hook ed. 1969).

METHODOLOGY AND ANALYSIS

I. SCOPE OF STUDY

This manual includes eighty-four international arms control instruments (conventions and protocols annexed to conventions) which were elaborated between 1863 and May 2000. International Criminal Law is identified on the basis of the existence of one or more penal characteristics contained in each of the instruments. These penal characteristics are listed below. All relevant multilateral instruments have been included, even those which have been superceded or which are no longer in effect. They are numbered consecutively by date of signature, and divided into eight categories. The eight categories of arms control instruments are included in the text in the following corresponding chapters.

Chapter I: Multilateral Instruments on the Regulation of Armed Conflicts and Weapons Control

Chapter I is divided into two parts. The first part includes all relevant multilateral instruments on the regulation of armed conflicts and weapons control. The second part includes the principal manuals on the regulation of armed conflicts and weapons control evidencing customary international law. The first category of instruments included in the present volume is the most extensive. While this category includes the greatest number of conventions thirty-eight instruments, it also covers the longest time period. Starting with the earliest instrument, the St. Petersburg Declaration of 1868[1], to the 1995 Protocol on Blinding Laser Weapons (Protocol IV to the Convention on Prohibitions or Restrictions on the Use of Certain Conventional Weapons).[2] These two instruments illustrate the evolution of arms control regulation and prohibition, as well as the growing challenge of sophisticated weaponry that has developed since the ban on explosive projectiles of 400 grammes weight to the ban on the use of blinding lasers.

Many of the instruments in Chapter I embody customary law, but the concept is broader than the specifics contained in these instruments. Some of the norms embodied in these instruments apply in time of war, while others also apply to time of peace. More specifically, some conventions apply to use, while others apply to possession of certain weapons.

Unlawful use of weapons is defined as employment of weapons whose use is prohibited. This is to be distinguished from unauthorized use of permissible weapons, but whose use may be limited or controlled by general or specific norms. Because of the distinction between the contexts of war and peace, the use of certain

---

[1] Declaration Renouncing the Use in Time of War, of Explosive Projectiles Under 400 Grammes Weight (St. Petersberg Declaration), *signed at St. Petersberg*, Dec. 11, 1868, 18 MARTENS 474; 138 Parry's 297; *reprinted in* 1 AM. J. INT'L L. 95 (1907)(Supp.).

[2] Additional Protocol to the Convention on Prohibitions or Restrictions on the Use of Certain Conventional Weapons which may be Deemed to be Excessively Injurious or to have Indiscriminate Effects (Protocol IV) on Blinding Laser Weapons, *adopted* 12 October 1995, 90 AM. J. INT'L L. 484 (1996), not yet in force.

weapons may, paradoxically, be deemed an international crime when used in time of war, but not when used in time of peace. However, this distinction is gradually eroding in contemporary legal doctrine.

Conventions on weapons of mass destruction such as chemical and biological weapons are not included in Chapter I, but are included in Chapter II because of their peculiar nature. So far there is no prohibition on the use of nuclear weapons, though an emerging rule of customary international law makes the "first use" of nuclear weapons a violation.

Chapter I includes relevant provisions of the Geneva Conventions of 12 August 1949. These conventions do not contain a specific prohibition against weapons that cause unnecessary pain and suffering, nor does it have specific provisions that deal with weapons. However, insofar as the use of weapons can cause harm to protected persons such as civilians, prisoners of war, the sick, wounded, and shipwrecked, they constitute violations of the 1949 Geneva Conventions. These violations are reflected in the grave breaches provisions. The 1982 Convention on the Law of the Sea[3] is included because of its relevant provisions to the use of weapons. Lastly, Chapter I ends with the 1998 United Nations International Convention for the Suppression of Terrorist Bombings,[4] which is the only instrument in this chapter that also applies in time of peace, and presumably also in time of war, unless it is a legitimate war-related action, which is doubtful.

Principal Manuals on the Regulation of Armed Conflicts and Weapons Control Evidencing Customary International Law

The second part of Chapter I includes four principal manuals on the international law of war. While this is not an exhaustive list, it is a representative one. Two of the manuals concern the laws of war on land, and the remaining two focus on the laws of war at sea. The first manual included in this section is the Lieber Code of 1863 representing the instructions for the government of United States Army first developed during President Lincoln's term in office. The documents in this second category are not multilateral agreements, but they are included in this volume because of their importance to the development of customary international law. For example, the first document in this category, the Lieber Code, prohibits the use of poisons under Article 16. Subsequent conventions such as the Brussels Conference of 1874,[5] and the Hague Conventions on Land Warfare in 1899 and 1907 followed this example.

---

[3] Convention on the Law of the Sea [Montego Bay Convention], *opened for signature at Montego Bay*, 516 U.N.T.S. 205, 21 I.L.M. 1261, entered into force 16 November 1994.

[4] United Nations International Convention for the Suppression of Terrorist Bombings, January 12, 1998, U.N. Doc A/Res/52/164; <http://www.sipri.se/cbw/docs/terrorism-conv-text.html>.

[5] Project of an International Declaration Concering the Laws and Customs of War [Declaration of Brussels] (Brussels Conference on the Laws and Customs of War, No. 18), *adopted at Brussels*, 4 MARTENS (ser. 2) 219.

Thus, these manuals evidence customary international law. But they have also set the course for future practice as now the armed forces of every country have their separate manuals or military codes that embody the provisions of the Geneva Conventions and customary international law.

Chapter II: Multilateral Instruments on the Regulation, Control, and Prohibition of Weapons of Mass Destruction

Chapter II contains eight multilateral instruments on the regulation, control, and prohibition of weapons of mass destruction. They start with the 1925 Protocol for the Prohibition of the Use in War of Asphyxiating, Poisonous or Other Gases, and of Bacteriological Methods of Warfare[6], to the Draft Convention on Nuclear Terrorism proposed by the Russian Government to the United Nations in 1998,[7] which was still being negotiated at the U.N. in July 2000. The capabilities of these weapons justify the growing concern of the international community with preventing the use of these devices by state and non-State actors.

Chapter II includes the 1996 International Court of Justice Advisory Opinion on the *Legality of Threat or Use of Nuclear Weapons*,[8] which proscribes the first use of nuclear weapons. These instruments that deal with weapons of mass destruction also fall in the category of customary international law. The overall concept derives from the Preamble of the 1907 Hague Convention, which codifies customary international law, as it existed then. It states:

It has not been found possible at present to concert regulations covering all the circumstances which arise in practice. On the other hand, the High Contracting Parties clearly do not intend that unforeseen cases should, in the absence of a written undertaking, be left to the arbitrary judgment of military commanders. Until a more complete code of the laws of war has been issued, the High Contracting Parties deem it expedient to declare that, in cases not included in the Regulations adopted by them, the inhabitants and the belligerents remain under the protection and the rule of the principles of the law of nations, as they result from the usages established among civilized peoples, from the laws of humanity, and the dictates of the public conscience.[9]

---

[6] 1925 Protocol for the Prohibition of the Use in War of Asphyxiating, Poisonous, or other Gases and Bacteriological Methods of Warfare, *signed at Geneva*, June 17, 1925, 94 L.N.T.S. 65, 26 U.S.T. 571, T.I.A.S. No. 8061, *reprinted in* 25 AM. J. INT'L L. 94 (1931).

[7] Draft International Convention for the Suppression of Acts of Nuclear Terrorism; Revised Text Proposed by the Friends of the Chairman (October 1998) United Nations General Assembly, Fifty-third Session, Sixth Committee, A/C.6/53l.4.

[8] Advisory Opinion of the International Court of Justice on July 8, *Legality of Threat or Use of Nuclear Weapons*, U.N. Doc. A/51/218 (1996), *reprinted in* 35 I.L.M. 828.

[9] 1907 Hague Convention Respecting the Laws and Customs of War on Land, Oct. 18, 1907, 36 Stat. 2277, T.s. No. 539, 3 MARTENS NOUCEAU RECUEIL (ser. 3) 461, *reprinted in* 2 AM. J. INT'L L. 90 (1908) (Supp.), 1 FRIEDMAN 308, 1 BEVANS 631 at ¶¶ 6-8 of the Pmbl (emphasis added).

This language embodies the well-known Martens clause[10] which permits the resort to "general principles" as a means of interpreting provisions in international instruments and to fill gaps in conventional textual language.[11]

The extension of the "general principle" contained in Preamble of the 1899 and 1907 Conventions is reflected in Article 22 of the Hague Regulations in the 1899 and 1907 Conventions which provides for another general norm that *"the right of belligerents to adopt means of injuring the enemy is not unlimited."* [12]

Moreover, the 1907 Hague Convention IV with Respect to the Laws and Customs of War on Land expressly prohibited the use of "arms, projectiles, or material calculated to cause unnecessary pain and suffering." The 1907 Hague Convention applies only to states and to armed conflicts between states. The 1949 Geneva Convention extended the protection against unnecessary pain and suffering in Article 35 of Part III, Section I of Protocol I, which applies to international conflicts:

---

[10] The Martens Clause is named after Fyodor Martens, the Russian diplomat and jurist who drafted it. A similar formula appears in each of the 1949 Geneva Conventions and in the 1977 Protocols. *See* First Geneva Convention for the Amelioration of the Condition of the Wounded and Sick in Armed Forces in the Field, 75 U.N.T.S. 31, 6 U.S.T. 3114, T.I.A.s. No. 3362 at art. 63(4); Second Geneva Convention of 1949 for the Amelioration of the Condition of Wounded, Sick, and Shipwrecked Members of the Armed Forces at Sea, 75 U.N.T.S. 85, 6 U.S.T. 3217, T.I.A.S. No. 3363 at art. 62(4); Third Geneva Convention of 1949 relative to the Treatment of Prisoners of War, 75 U.N.T.S. 135, 6 U.S.T. 3316, T.I.A.S. No. 3364 at art. 142(4); Fourth Geneva Convention of 1949 relative to the Protection of Civilian Persons in Time of War, U.N.T.S. 287, 6 U.S.T. 3516, T.I.A.S. No. 3365 at art. 158(4); Protocol Additional to Geneva Conventions of August 12, 1949, and Relating to the Protection of Victims of International Armed Conflicts, *open for signature* Dec. 12, 1977, U.N. Doc. A/32/144 Annex I, *reprinted in* 16 I.L.M. 1391; 72 AM. J. INT'L L. 457 (1977) at art. 1(2) [hereinafter Protocol I]; Protocol Additional to Geneva Convention of Aug 12, 1949, and Relating to the Protection of Victims of Non-International Armed Conflicts, *opened for signature*, Dec. 12, 1977, U.N. Doc. A/32/144 Annex II, *reprinted in* 16 I.L.M. 1391 at pmbl. [hereinafter Protocol II]; PAOLO BENVENUTI, *La Clausola MARTENS e la Tradizione Classica del Diritto Naturale nella Codificazione del Conflicts Armati*, in SCRITTI DEGLI ALLIEVI IN MEMORIA DI GUISEPPE BARILE 173 (1995).

[11] *See* M. Cherif Bassiouni, *A Functional Approach to A General Principles of International Law*, 11 MICH J. INT'L L. 768 (1990). The same formulation of the Hague Conventions has been used in the latest international instrument on the humanitarian law of armed conflicts, Protocol I states in Article 1:

> In cases not covered by this Protocol or by other international agreements, civilians and combatants remain under the protection and authority of the principles of international law derived from established custom, from the principles of humanity and from the dictates of public conscience. (emphasis added).

Protocol I, *supra* note 2, at art. 1. *See also* Waldemar A. Solf, *Protection of Civilians Against the Effects of Hostilities Under Customary International Law and Under Protocol I*, 1 AM. U. J. INT'L & POL'Y 117 (1989).

[12] Protocol I at Article 35(1), which parallels the Hague Conventions' general norm on the implicit limitation on the "methods" of war. That article states *"in any armed conflict, the right of the parties to the conflict to choose methods or means of warfare is not unlimited."* (emphasis added).

International Humanitarian Law and Arms Control Agreements 51

1. In any armed conflict, the right of the Parties to the conflict to choose methods or means of warfare is not unlimited.
2. It is prohibited to employ weapons, projectiles and material and methods of warfare of a nature to cause superfluous injury or unnecessary suffering.[13]

The normative provisions contained in some of these conventions are thus reinforced by the general limitations contained in customary international law.

Chapter III: Multilateral Instruments on the Prohibition of Emplacement of Weapons of Mass Destruction in Certain Media

Chapter III includes five major multilateral treaties on the prohibition of emplacement of weapons of mass destruction in certain media. This category includes specialized arms control agreements that prohibit the emplacement of nuclear, chemical, and biological weapons in media such as outer space, the moon, and the ocean floor. Significantly, the instruments in this section span the high period of Cold War activity, starting with the 1959 Antarctic Treaty[14] banning nuclear weapon tests in Antarctica and culminating with the 1979 Agreement Governing the Activities of States on the Moon and Other Celestial Bodies.[15] Illustrative of the Cold War influence on this period is the fact that three treaties were signed at Moscow, and four were signed in the United States.

A very positive development in these treaties is that in addition to proscribing military activities involving weapons of mass destruction in areas traditionally deemed to be global commons, the treaties also encourage international cooperation for peaceful scientific research in the commons. Chapter III also includes treaties with provisions that proscribe nuclear weapons tests in outer space, under water, or in the atmosphere, as well as emplacement of nuclear weapons on the sea-bed, ocean floor, or sub-soil.

The five instruments included in this section are illustrative of the trend starting in the Cold War of prohibiting the emplacement of certain weapons in particular areas. The rationale for these prohibitions is to enhance the peace and security of humankind, and the instruments are thus related to the preservation of peace and the prohibition of aggression. They are, however, also intended explicitly or implicitly to protect the environment. However, their primary subject matter is weapons and consequently these documents are included here.

A violation of the obligations contained in these instruments constitutes a violation of international law, and may be deemed an emerging customary law violation included in war crimes. These conventions do not however contain penal

---

13. *Id.*

[14] The Antarctic Treaty, *signed at Washington*, 12 U.S.T. 794, 54 AM. J. INT'L L. 477 (1960), entered into force with respect to the United States 26 March 1975.

[15] Agreement Governing the Activities of States on the Moon and other Celestial Bodies, *opened for signature at New York*, 1363 U.N.T.S. 3, 18 I.L.M. 1434 entered into force 11 July 1984.

elements and are therefore at this time only the foundation for future criminalization.

Chapter IV: Regional Nuclear Free Zones Agreements

Chapter IV includes seven regional nuclear free zones agreements. The regions covered are Latin America, Africa, South East Asia, and the South Pacific. The earliest agreement is from 1968 with the Treaty for the Prohibition of Nuclear Weapons in Latin America (Treaty of Tlatelolco)[16], which also has two Additional Protocols included[17]. The most recent regional nuclear free zone agreement is the 1996 African Nuclear Free Zone Treaty (Treaty of Pelindaba),[18] which is accompanied by the Cairo Declaration of 1996.[19] It is significant to note that these were signed after the mid-1960's. The most recent regional nuclear free zone treaty is the African Treaty of Pelindaba, signed in 1996. These dates suggest a continued trend toward a paradigm and strategy of regionalism in the domain of international security.

These instruments are not deemed part of international humanitarian law, and they are not necessarily part of "arms control" agreements. They are therefore in a category of their own. They do not contain penal characteristics and the violation of their terms raises only the prospect of international civil adjudication. It can be said that violations of such agreements constitute a breach of the Principles of State Responsibility elaborated by the ILC.

The relevance of these agreements is that, taken in *pari material* with developments on the use of nuclear weapons (see Chapter II, particularly instrument II-8 at p. 443), leads to the conclusion that an emerging custom bans not only the "first use" of nuclear weapons, but also their possession.

---

[16] Treaty for the Prohibition of Nuclear Weapons in Latin America [Treaty of Tlatelolco] (Inter-American), *opened for signature at Mexico City*,,22 U.S.T. 762, 634 U.N.T.S. 281, 6 I.L.M. 521, entered into force 22 April 1986.

[17] Additional Protocol I to the Treaty for the Prohibition of Nuclear Weapons in Latin America [Treaty of Tlatelolco] (Inter-American), *done at Mexico City*, 14 February 1967, T.I.A.S. No. 10147, 634 U.N.T.S. 362, 28 I.L.M. 1405, entered into force with respect to the United States 23 November 1981; Additional Protocol II to the Treaty for the Prohibition of Nuclear Weapons in Latin America [Treaty of Tlatelolco] (Inter-American), *done at Mexico City*, 14 February 1967, 22 U.S.T. 754, 634 U.N.T.S. 364, 28 I.L.M. 1413, entered into force with respect to the United States 12 May 1971.

[18] African Nuclear-Weapon-Free Zone Treaty, *signed at Addis Ababa*, 35 I.L.M. 698 (1996).

[19] Cairo Declaration, June 1996; adopted on the occasion of the signing of the African Nuclear-Weapon-Free Zone Treaty, Cairo, 11 April 1996.

International Humanitarian Law and Arms Control Agreements 53

Chapter V: Middle East Arms Control and Security Agreements

The Middle East region has yet to develop a comprehensive arms control regime. From the 1948 UN Security Council Resolution on Palestine[20] to the 1999 Protocol Concerning Safe Passage Between the West Bank and Gaza Strip,[21] the evolution of arms control in that region has been ad hoc. But the prospects of generalized peace in the region may still exist, particularly after the completion of bilateral agreements between Israel and all its Arab neighbors. The time for a multilateral regional security regime which also eliminates weapons of mass destruction will have arrived.

As can be seen in the fifteen instruments that are included in this chapter, arms control provisions in Middle Eastern agreements are generally secondary to the primary issues of military, political, and security issues including: terrorism; refugees; safe passage; transfer of political authority; and economic issues. The agreements involving Egypt, Israel, Jordan, and Lebanon deal with the security arrangements. The 1994 Treaty of Peace Between the State of Israel and the Hashemite Kingdom of Jordan[22] has provisions that are exceptional in that they deal with non-conventional weapons, and call for a regional weapons of mass destruction free zone in the Middle East. These bilateral agreements form the basis for a future regional agreement.

Chapter VI: European Arms Control and Security Agreements

Chapter VI pertains to a classic arms control category. It includes the 1990 Conventional Armed Forces in Europe (CFE) Treaty,[23] and the Addendum to the Treaty.[24] The Treaty limits five categories of weapons: tanks, artillery, armored combat vehicles, combat helicopters, and attack aircraft. The agreement applies among NATO members and former Warsaw Pact members. By way of the Tashkent Agreement, the Russian Federation and the Ukraine acknowledged as successor states the responsibilities originally agreed to by the Soviet Union. Also,

---

[20] United Nations Security Council Resolution 50, U.N. SCOR, May 29, 1948, U.N. Doc. S/801, 50 (1948)

[21] Protocol Concerning Safe Passage Between the West Bank and Gaza Strip, October 5, 1999, <http://www.israel.org/mfa/go.asp?MFAH00pq0>.

[22] Treaty of Peace Between The State of Israel and The Hashemite Kingdom of Jordan (1994), <http://metalab.unc.edu/sullivan/docs?Sinail.html.>.

[23] Conventional Armed Forces in Europe (CFE) Treaty, November 10, 1990; done at Paris, November 19, 1990, 30 I.L.M. 6 (1991).

[24] Addendum to the Conventional Armed Forces in Europe (CFE) Treaty, Final Document of the First Conference to Review the Operation of the Treaty on Conventional Armed Forces in Europe and the Concluding Act of the Negotiation on Personnel Strength, Vienna, 15-31 May 1996, <http://www.state.gov/www/global/arms/bureau_np?treaties_np.htm>.

in 1992 the Russian Federation announced that it would be successor state to all treaties formerly binding on the Union of Soviet Socialist Republics.

Chapter VII: Bilateral Nuclear Weapons Control Agreements - United States of America and the Union of Soviet Socialist Republics and its Successor States

Chapter VII includes six bilateral nuclear weapons control agreements between the United States and the Union of Soviet Socialist Republics. The first agreement is the 1972 Treaty Between the United States of America and the Union of Soviet Socialist Republics on the Limitation of Anti-Ballistic Missile Systems (ABM Treaty).[25] The last agreement included is the 1974 Treaty Between the United States of America and the Union of Soviet Socialist Republics on the Limitation of Underground Nuclear Weapon Tests (Threshold Test Ban Treaty, TTBT),[26] and the 1990 Protocol to the Treaty.[27]

On May 23, 1992, Belarus, Kazakhstan, Russian Federation, and Ukraine signed the Lisbon Protocol, which established them as legally bound successor states to the Soviet Union's START I Treaty obligation. In addition Belarus, Kazakhstan, and Ukraine committed in the Lisbon Protocol to accede to the Nuclear Non-Proliferation Treaty (NPT) as non-nuclear weapons states.[28]

The United States, Russian Federation, Belarus, Kazakhstan, and Ukraine signed two sets of strategic arms control agreements on September 26, 1997, advancing commitments made during the March 1997 Clinton-Yeltsin Helsinki Summit. Secretary of State Albright and Foreign Ministers Primakov, Antonovich, Tokayev, and Udovendo of the Russian Federation, Belarus, Kazakhstan, and Ukraine, respectively, signed a Memorandum of Understanding providing for succession to the ABM Treaty. In addition, Representatives of the US and Russian Federation exchanged legally binding letters codifying the Helsinki Summit commitment to the progress of START II agenda.[29] Moreover, in January 1992 the Ministry of Foreign Affairs of the Russian Federation issued a statement by which

---

[25] Treaty Between the United States of America and the Union of Soviet Socialist Republics on the Limitation of Anti-Ballistic Missile Systems (ABM Treaty), 3 October 1972, [signed at Moscow May 26, 1972; ratification advised by U.S. Senate August 3, 1972; ratified by U.S. President September 30, 1972; proclaimed by U.S. President October 3, 1972; instruments on ratification exchanged October 3, 1972; entered into force October 3, 1972].

[26] Treaty Between the United States of America and the Union of Soviet Socialist Republics on the Limitation of Underground Nuclear Weapon Tests (Threshold Test Ban Treaty, TTBT), *signed at Moscow*, 13 I.L.M. 967.

[27] Protocol to the Treaty of July 3, 1974, Between the United States of America and the union of Soviet Socialist Republics on the Limitation of Underground Nuclear Weapons Tests, *signed at Washington*, June 1, 1990; entered into force December 11, 1990.

[28] http://www.state.gov/www/global/ar...ets/wmd/nuclear/start2/abmtmd.html

[29] http://www.state.gov/www/global/ar...ets/wmd/nuclear/start2/abmtmd.html

International Humanitarian Law and Arms Control Agreements 55

the Russian Federation officially accepted all rights and obligations following from international agreements signed by the Union of Soviet Socialist Republics.

As classic arms control agreements, particularly bilateral ones, their breach by any one of the parties only raises the possibility of an action before the ICJ for breach of treaty. Their relevance, however, is that they support the emerging custom applicable to the elimination of nuclear weapons. (See Chapters III, IV, V, and VI.)

Chapter VIII: The Missile Technology Control Regime (MTCR)

Chapter VIII includes the two important instruments of the Missile Technology Control Regime. The first instrument is the Guidelines for Sensitive Missile-Relevant Transfers of 7 January 1993.[30] The second is the Missile Technology Control Regime Equipment and Technology Annex of 11 June 1996.[31]

The MTCR is not a treaty. The "Regime" consists of a common export policy (MTCR Guidelines) applied to a common list (MTCR Annex) of controlled items, including virtually all equipment and technology needed or missile development, production, and operation. These multilateral export controls are implemented by each Partner in accordance with its national legislation. The MTCR is the only multilateral arrangement dealing with ballistic and cruise missile and other WMD delivery vehicle systems or related equipment, material and technology.

The relevance of this voluntary control regime is that it paves the way for a worldwide legal control regime on weapons of mass destruction and the delivery capabilities that can be used in connection with these weapons. Thus, the elimination of weapons of mass destruction must necessarily lead to the control of delivery systems in order to be fully effective.

II. TREATY INFORMATION

Title of Documents

The heading for each convention begins with the *seriatim* Arabic numeral of the instruments which are in a chronological order. The title of each listed document is the one that appears in the most authoritative international source for that document. If a common name exists for the document, it is included in brackets. Also, if the instrument is regional in scope, this is indicated in parentheses. This information is followed by the place and date of the document's signing, as well as its official citation, and where applicable, the citation to U.S. sources. In the case of instruments which predate the inception of the League of

---

[30] Guidelines for Sensitive Missile-Relevant Transfers of 7 January 1993, <http://www.state.gov/www/global/arms/treaties/mter_anx.html>.

[31] Missile Technology Control Regime (MTCR) Equipment and Technology Annex, 11 June 1996, <http://www.state.gov/www/global/arms/treaties/mter_anx.html>.

Nations, the most authoritative source for that period, the *Martens Nouveau Recueil* has been used. In the event that a post-1945 document has not yet been reproduced in the United Nations Treaty Series (U.N.T.S.), the title which appears in the relevant United Nations official publication has been used (i.e., General Assembly Resolution). If an instrument appears in a United States source, this source is cited. This includes: Stat., T.I.A.S., T.S. and U.S.T. When the source cited is T.S., FOR. REL., I.L.M. or Parry's, this indicates that the document has not been published in any primary international or United States source. Following the official and/or semi-official citation, a list of other publications wherein the document was reproduced is provided to refer the reader to the more accessible English language sources containing the text of the document. The official sources appear first, followed by other sources of the document.

The final entries to the title section are the document's date of entry into force, its date of entry into force with respect to the United States, and, finally, its official language or languages.

State Signatories and State Parties

The "State Signatories" entry lists in an alphabetical order all states that signed the convention at the time it was concluded.

The heading "State Parties" lists all parties which ratified, acceded, or succeeded to the document, and which are therefore bound by the convention irrespective of whether they were state signatories.

In some instances instruments are not subject to signature because they were adopted by a United Nations body or by a regional organization. In these cases the instrument in question was directly opened for acceptance by states, or for adherence through a subsequent protocol.

Differences in names of States between "State Signatories" and "State Parties" reflect a name change between the time of the signing and the time of the ratification, accession, or succession.

State party information is sometimes difficult to obtain, and has to be culled from a variety of sources. For early documents, which appear in L.N.T.S. or U.N.T.S., State party information can be found in their respective periodic indices. The L.N.T.S. indices are not complete and the U.N.T.S. is several years in arrears. State party information for these documents may, however, be found in the following U.S. sources: HUDSON, MALLOY, and MILLER. Another useful source is the *British Treaty Index* for those conventions to which Great Britain is a State party. Another source examined, though needing verification, is *World Treaty Index*. The United Nations publishes an index to those instruments for which the Secretary-General acts as a depository, the *Multilateral Treaties Deposited with the Secretary General*. In addition, it is possible to access latest date information on the Internet, UN Home Page, HTTP://WWW.UN.ORG. The United Nations updates this page with the most current states parties, signatories, and reservations.

For those conventions to which the United States is a party, and which are currently in force, the source of State party information is the Department of State's publication *Treaties in Force*.

International Humanitarian Law and Arms Control Agreements 57

Where both *Treaties in Force* and the United Nations Secretary-General's compilation contain State party information for a particular instrument, both sources are used in the State Signatory and State Party sections of the data. *Treaties in Force* gives a more complete listing of successor States, and those territories and areas to which a given treaty is deemed to apply, though, of course, from a U.S. perspective.

In the case of conventions which were originally deposited with the League of Nations and for which depository functions were later assumed by the United Nations by way of an amending protocol, the U.N. Secretary-General's compilation provides State party listings for the original convention, the amending protocol, and the convention as amended. *Treaties in Force* provides one list of State party information which combines all of these separate components. The Secretary-General's compilation is however used for such conventions, since the Secretary-General is their official depository.

Under the heading "Reservations upon signature, accession and ratification" is a listing of those States that have made reservations or declarations at the time of signature, accession or ratification. The same sources relied upon for State parties have been relied upon in this listing.

Penal Characteristics

This author has identified the following ten distinguishing penal characteristics of international crimes:[32]

1. Explicit or implicit recognition of proscribed conduct as constituting an international crime, or a crime under international law, or a crime;
2. Implicit recognition of the penal nature of the act by establishing a duty to prohibit, prevent, prosecute, punish, or the like;
3. Criminalization of the proscribed conduct;
4. Duty or right to prosecute;
5. Duty or right to punish the proscribed conduct;
6. Duty or right to extradite;
7. Duty or right to cooperate in prosecution, punishment (including judicial assistance);
8. Establishment of a criminal jurisdictional basis;
9. Reference to the establishment of an international criminal court or international tribunal with penal characteristics;
10. No defense of superior orders.

---

[32] Penal characteristics that exist in a given instrument have been noted under the heading "Relevant Penal Characteristics & Penal Provisions." Where a document contains no penal provisions, an explanatory note is provided as to the reason for its inclusion notwithstanding the absence of penal characteristics.

The existence of any one of these ten penal characteristics has been deemed sufficient to identify the multilateral instrument as part of international criminal law. The list of penal characteristics pertaining to each document refers the reader to the relevant specific provisions in that document. A given provision in a document may however contain more than one penal characteristic; if this is the case, it will be re-cited under the other characteristic to which it also applies. The convention's provision containing the penal characteristic in question is reproduced after the various data items to facilitate the researcher's task.

Contextual Applicability

In addition to the Penal Characteristics heading before each instrument, there is a heading labeled Applicability. This section indicates whether the instrument is applicable during time of war only, time of peace only, or both times of war and peace.

Control Regime

Another header that is listed before each document is Control, which points out what type of arms control is called for. The options here are those documents that regulate rather than prohibit certain arms activities.

State Succession

Between 1985 and the present, several federal States have broken up into separate States. From the Union of Soviet Socialist Republics emerged the newly independent States of Armenia, Azerbaijan, Belarus, Georgia, Kazakhstan, Kyrgyzstan, Moldova, the Russian Federation, Tajikistan, Turkmenistan, Ukraine, Uzbekistan, Estonia, Latvia and Lithuania. The break-up of the Socialist Federal Republic of Yugoslavia led to the establishment of the Federation of Bosnia and Herzegovina, the Republic of Croatia, the Republic of Slovenia and the Federal Republic of Yugoslavia (Serbia and Montenegro). Out of the dissolution of the Czech and Slovak Federal Republic, the Czech Republic and the Slovak Republic emerged.

State successions resulting from these changes have not always been reflected in the text, except with respect to the Geneva Conventions and their protocols. This is largely due to the peculiarities that State succession to treaties entails.

In 1994, the United Nations issued a report entitled *Summary of Practice of the Secretary-General as Depository of Multilateral Treaties* in which the Treaty Section of the Office of Legal Affairs overviewed the topic of successions to treaties.[33] The *Summary* included, *inter alia*, the following observations which are reproduced here *verbatim*:

---

[33] U.N. Doc. ST/LEG/8 (1994).

International Humanitarian Law and Arms Control Agreements 59

A. Background, Definitions and General Principles[34]

1. Background

When a non-independent Territory becomes an independent State and accordingly attains the full exercise of external sovereignty, the depositary is faced, as a result of that change, with the problem of the status of the new State as concerns treaties and agreements deposited with him the application of which was extended to the previously non-independent Territory concerned by the State that was at the time responsible for its external relations.

At the beginning of the existence of the United Nations the problem of succession arose only with respect to treaties concluded under the auspices of the League of Nations. As time went on, however, an increasing number of United Nations treaties were concluded and were applied or extended to dependent Territories which subsequently became independent States. The United Nations gradually developed the practice described below to determine whether the new States were to be considered as continuing to be bound by treaties applied to their Territories by their predecessors. In the past, "new States" were mostly "non-metropolitan" Territories that had subsequently become independent. However, more recently, a number of new States have come into being as a result of the separation of part of the Territory of another (predecessor) State. It should be noted that the Vienna Convention on Succession of States in respect of Treaties was adopted on 23 August 1978, and although as at 1 June 1994 it was not yet in force, the Convention in many of its aspects codifies established customary law on the matter.

2. Definitions

The terms hereinafter may be defined as follows (see article 2 of the Convention):

- "Succession of States" means the replacement of one State by another in the responsibility for the international relations of the Territory;
- "Predecessor State" means the State that has been replaced by another State on the occurrence of a succession of States;
- "Successor State" means the State that has replaced another State on the occurrence of a succession of States;
- "Date of the succession of States" means the date upon which the successor State replaced the predecessor State in the responsibility for the international relations of the Territory to which the succession of States relates;

---

[34] *Id.* at 86-91 (citations and internal references omitted).

- "Newly independent State" means a successor State the Territory of which immediately before the date of the succession of States was a dependent Territory for the international relations of which the predecessor State was responsible;
- "Notification or instrument of succession" means, in relation to a multilateral treaty, any notification, however phrased or named, made by a successor State expressing its consent to be considered as bound by the treaty.

3. General Principles

When a Territory, whether it was a non-metropolitan Territory or part of a separated State, becomes an independent State, it "succeeds" to the "predecessor" State, i.e., it becomes responsible for its international relations in lieu of the predecessor State, as of the date when it so replaces the predecessor State; this date is normally the date of independence of the successor State. As concerns treaties, the successor State has then the option of: (a) participating in any treaty which is open to it by signing and depositing an instrument of ratification or taking a similar action in order to become bound by the treaty, or (b) succeeding to any treaty the application of which was extended to it by the predecessor State (thus preserving the continuity of the application of the treaty), by depositing an instrument of succession in respect thereof. It is to be noted that, in accordance with the rules of customary succession, there is no time limit for the deposit of such instrument of succession.

New States may not only succeed to treaties in force that had been applied to them by the predecessor State prior to the succession of States, but they may also invoke, as successor, treaty actions taken on their behalf by the predecessor State (for example, signature of a treaty). Thus a newly independent State may ratify a treaty if it had been signed by the predecessor State intending that the treaty should extend to the Territory that subsequently became independent. Similarly, a newly independent State may, by a notification to that effect, establish its status as a contracting State to a multilateral treaty not yet in force if the predecessor State was itself a contracting State and had indicated that its action also applied to the then Territory.

Such successions, however, are possible only when it does not appear from the treaty or otherwise that the participation of the new State would be incompatible with the purpose of the treaty or that it would require the consent of the other parties. In this domain the Secretary-General generally follows the established customary law, as codified by the Vienna Convention on the Succession of States in respect of Treaties.

B. Participation of New States in Treaties

As concerns the participation of new States in treaties, on the basis of prior application of another treaty to the Territory before its independence, the first case in which the Secretary-General, as depositary, was confronted with this question was that of the Protocol of 11 December 1946 amending various agreements, conventions and protocols on narcotic drugs concluded prior to the Second World War. Article V of the Protocol provides that it is "open for signature or acceptance by any of the States Parties to the Agreements, Conventions and Protocols on narcotic drugs" which the Protocol of 11 December 1946 was designed to amend and "to which the Secretary-General of the United Nations has communicated a copy". The Secretary-General had then to decide whether new States that had in the meantime become independent, e.g., Syria and Lebanon, to which France had extended the application of certain agreements amended by the Protocol, should be invited to become parties to the Protocol. The Secretary-General satisfied himself that the Governments of Syria and Lebanon considered themselves bound by the agreements on narcotic drugs previously applied in their territory and invited them to become parties to the Protocol amending those agreements. Syria and Lebanon became parties to the Protocol of 11 December 1946 by signature without reservation as to approval, on 11 and 13 December 1946 respectively. Syria and Lebanon likewise became parties, by definitive signature to the Protocol of 12 November 1947 to amend the Conventions of 1921 and 1933 for the Suppression of the Traffic in Women and Children, although this Protocol was in principle only open, under its article III, to States parties to those Conventions.

This practice became established, albeit with some variations, reflecting the nature of the clauses in the treaties in question relating to the devolution of obligations under multilateral treaties as well as the interpretation placed on those clauses by the parties concerned. Thus, the Hashemite Kingdom of Jordan was invited to become a party to the Protocol of 11 December 1946, amending the Agreements, Conventions and Protocols on Narcotic Drugs, and to the Protocol of 12 November 1947, to amend the Convention for the Suppression of the Traffic in Women and Children, in view of the fact that some of those agreements had previously been applied in the territory of the Hashemite Kingdom of Jordan.

C. Participation by Succession

1. When There Are Provisions Relating to Succession in the Treaty

Some agreements make the exercise of the right of succession subject to restrictive conditions. Thus, the International Cocoa Agreement 1975 provides, in substance, in its article 71, paragraph 4, that notification of succession must be effected within 90 days after the attainment of independence and that it shall take effect as from the date of the Secretary-General's receipt thereof.

The provisions of a treaty may even totally rule out succession. Such would be the case if the treaty was open only to the participation of the members of a regional commission which itself would not be open to the new State. In such cases, the situation is clear and the Secretary-General simply abides by the provisions of the treaty.

The agreements that have established an intergovernmental organization usually contain express rules concerning admission to that organization. These rules may exclude succession if, for example, participation is limited to a regional area. They may also simply have the effect of restricting the possibility of succession. Such is the case for the Convention on the International Maritime Consultative Organization and the Constitution of the World Health Organization, both of which require that non-members of the United Nations first deposit an application for membership, which must be approved by the organization concerned. In such cases, the Secretary-General, as depositary, first consults the intergovernmental organization concerned to make sure that the membership, by way of succession, of the newly independent State has been duly approved.

2. In the Absence of Provisions Relating to Succession

In the absence of provisions which set specific conditions for succession or which otherwise restrict succession, the Secretary-General is guided by the participation clauses of the treaties as well as by the general principles governing the participation of States. The independence of the new successor State, which then exercises its sovereignty on its territory, is without effect on the treaty rights and obligations of the predecessor State in its own (remaining) territory. Thus, after the separation of parts of the territory of the Union of Soviet Socialist Republics (which became independent States), the Russian Federation continued all treaty rights and obligations of the predecessor State.

A different situation occurs when the predecessor State disappears. Such was the case when the Czech Republic and Slovakia were formed upon the agreed dissolution of Czechoslovakia, which consequently ceased to exist. Each of the new States is then in the position of a succeeding State.

The Secretary-General accepts instruments of succession by "new States" on the following two conditions: (a) that the treaty was applied to, or the treaty action taken on behalf of, the territory of the new State by the predecessor State prior to the succession of States; and (b) that the territory has been recognized as a State, within the Vienna formula and the practice of the General Assembly.

The question of whether the treaty had been applied to a Non-Self-Governing Territory before independence raises no difficulty if the treaty had been expressly extended to the Territory by the predecessor State. However, this is not always so. When the treaty was not expressly extended to the Territory, the Secretary-General accepts instruments of succession if the predecessor State was a party to the treaty, if it had not formally excluded the application of the treaty to the Territory and if the succeeding State declares that the treaty was indeed applied in the Territory. If under the provisions of the treaty the participation in the treaty was limited in scope - if, for example, it was only open to States falling within the geographical scope of a regional commission in which the new State could not become a member - the Secretary-General would call the attention of the new State concerned to the apparent inconsistency. As concerns the recognition of the entity as a State, when instruments of succession were transmitted to the Secretary-General by entities which had separated from a predecessor State but which were not yet Members of the United Nations or of a specialized agency, and had not been unequivocally recognized as States, *inter alia*, by the General Assembly, the Secretary-General indicated to those entities that only after they had been recognized as States could he accept their instruments for deposit.

When the instrument is accepted in deposit, the Secretary-General circulates a corresponding depositary notification.

3. Reservations Withdrawn or Made Upon Succession

In extending the application of a treaty to a Territory, the State responsible for that Territory's international relations may have made reservations. When depositing an instrument of succession, a new State finds itself in the position of a State that would deposit an instrument of ratification or of a similar nature. At the time of deposit the succeeding State may, therefore, make any reservations that would be allowed by the treaty, in the same manner as any new participant. It may also withdraw any reservations made by the predecessor State.

D. "General" Declarations of Succession

Frequently, newly independent States will submit to the Secretary-General "general" declarations of succession, usually requesting that the declaration be circulated to all States Members of the United Nations. The Secretary-General duly complies with such a request but does not consider such a declaration as a valid instrument of succession to any of the treaties deposited with him, and he so informs the Government of the new State concerned. In so doing, the Secretary-General is guided by the following considerations.

The deposit of an instrument of succession results in having the succeeding State become bound, in its own name, by the treaty to which the succession applies, with exactly the same rights and obligations as if that State had ratified or acceded to, or otherwise accepted, the treaty. Consequently, it has always been the position of the Secretary-General, in his capacity as depositary, to record a succeeding State as a party to a given treaty solely on the basis of a formal document similar to instruments of ratification, accession, etc., that is, a notification emanating from the Head of State, the Head of Government or the Minister for Foreign Affairs, which should specify the treaty or treaties by which the State concerned recognizes itself to be bound.

General declarations are not sufficiently authoritative to have the States concerned listed as parties in the publication *Multilateral Treaties Deposited with the Secretary-General*. In essence, those declarations usually indicate that a review of the treaties applied to the territory of the State before accession to independence is in progress and that the State concerned would specify in due course which treaties should continue to be considered as binding and which should be considered as having lapsed. Those declarations also mention that pending completion of the review, it should be "presumed" (sometimes "legally presumed") that each treaty had been succeeded to by the State concerned, and that action should be based on that presumption. However, such a presumption, while it could possibly be used by other States as a basis for practical action, can certainly not be taken as a formal and unambiguous acknowledgment of the obligations contained in a given treaty, since it can be unilaterally reversed at any time in respect of any treaty. Finally, it should be emphasized that such "general declarations" are not addressed to the Secretary-General in his capacity as depositary of multilateral treaties, but rather for the purpose of circulation to States Members of the United Nations and of the specialized agencies.

In connection with the above, it is to be noted that, in fact, formal instruments of succession to specifically identified treaties are routinely deposited with the Secretary-General by States that have previously deposited a "general declaration of succession," thus avoiding any uncertainty arising under a different practice. And it is only when such instruments are deposited with the Secretary-General that the State concerned is henceforth officially listed in the records of the treaty as a party thereto. It should be emphasized, however, that the position of the Secretary-General, as depositary, is absolutely not binding on States, which may draw from the general declaration of succession any legal consequences which they may deem fit.

Other depositaries have in fact taken the opposite view of that of the Secretary-General and have considered that such general declarations of succession resulted in having the State concerned become bound to all treaties deposited with them. Those depositaries have accordingly listed those States among the parties. However, as experience has shown, a number of such States have subsequently informed the depositary concerned that upon further review they would not succeed to a given treaty and that the treaty should accordingly be considered as having lapsed as of the day of independence. Such communications were sometimes circulated years after the depositary had listed the State concerned as a party; the depositary then had to cancel the "deposit" of the instrument of succession in respect of the State and the treaty concerned.

E. Devolution Agreements

At the time of independence, the successor and the predecessor States sometimes conclude a "devolution agreement" which regulates the inheritance by the successor State of treaty rights and obligations that may exist by virtue of the previous application of treaties to the Territory by the predecessor State. Such devolution agreements are optional, however, and their absence does not restrict the capacity of the succeeding State, which is based on the principles of self-determination and of sovereign equality of States.

The considerations described above in respect of general declarations of succession also apply to such devolution agreements concluded between new States and the States formerly responsible for their international relations. Here again, the usually very general wording does not allow for a formal action to be taken by the Secretary-General as the depositary of an individual treaty. For example, in the exchange of letters of 20 June 1966 between the United Kingdom and The Gambia: "... it is the understanding of the [two Governments] that the Government of The Gambia are in agreement (i) that all obligations and responsibilities of the Government of the United Kingdom which arose from any valid instrument applying to The Gambia immediately before the 18th of February, 1965, continued to apply to The Gambia and were assumed by the Government of The Gambia as from that date ...".

It should further be stressed that participation in a multilateral treaty is normally the result of procedures specifically provided for by the treaty and effected with the parties to that treaty or with the depositary appointed by them. A change in participation entails a change in the obligations and rights of all parties to the treaty, and it cannot therefore result from the provisions of another treaty, by virtue of the rule *pacta tertiis nec nocent nec prosunt*, which has been codified as article 34 of the Vienna Convention on the Law of Treaties. However, if the devolution agreements unambiguously provide that the successor State shall henceforth assume all obligations and enjoy all rights which would exist by virtue of the application of treaties, the Secretary General, if he were to receive such a devolution agreement, would treat such an agreement as an instrument of succession, but only if the treaties concerned were clearly and specifically identified.

III. HOW TO INTERPRET THE COMPARATIVE CHARTS

Three comparative charts that summarize the empirical data for all relevant arms control agreements is included herein. All instruments are identified by official name as well as the chapter number corresponding to the table of contents in this volume. Seven factors are compared. First, we ask what penal characteristics are found within the treaty, and in what relevant provision. The penal characteristics are assigned numbers 1-10, and correspond with the numbering introduced in the Methodology section. Also, the agreements themselves are numbered in accordance with the Table of Contents list. As an illustration, consider the Declaration Concerning the Prohibition of the Use of Expanding Bullets. It is treaty number I-6 in the Table of Contents. On the comparative chart included in this section, therefore, treaty number I-6 corresponds to the same document. Next to the treaty number there is a column indicating the relevant penal characteristics and penal provisions that apply are in parenthesis. Thus the Declaration Concerning the Prohibition of the Use of Expanding Bullets includes the penal characteristic numbered 2, which stands for: *Implicit recognition of the penal nature of the act by establishing a duty to prohibit, prevent, prosecute, punish, or the like*. Penal characteristic 2 can be found paragraph 1 of the document, as is indicated by the chart.

In addition to the relevant penal characteristics, the charts also have columns that answer the following questions:

> a. Does the agreement provide for the control of certain weapons during time of war only?

b. Does the agreement provide for the control of certain weapons during time of peace only?
c. Does the agreement provide for the control of certain weapons during both time of peace and time of war?
d. Does the agreement explicitly or implicitly *regulate* certain weapons and/or their use?
e. Does the agreement explicitly or implicitly *prohibit* certain weapons and/or their use?

Penal characteristic 2 is by far the most commonly found in the documents examined. This suggests that since the Lieber Code of 1863 to the present, the method of creating international criminal law with respect to arms control has been through the implicit recognition of the penal nature of the given act, based on an agreed upon duty to prohibit, prevent, punish, prosecute, or the like. In total, there are forty-one multilateral instruments that utilize penal characteristic 2 to achieve the particular arms control objective. Moreover, practically all of these agreements include penal characteristic 2 in multiple articles or penal provisions. As a result, criminality can be deduced and developed as a part of customary international law from the duties that these arms control agreements have placed on contracting parties.

CHART A
PENAL CHARACTERISTICS

INSTRUMENT	PEN. CHAR.	CHAPTER
Instructions for the Government of Armies of the United States in the Field (Lieber Code [1863])	2(Art. 16,30)	I-35
Declaration Renouncing the Use, in Time of War, of Explosive Projectiles Under 400 Grammes Weight (St. Petersburg Declaration [1868])	2	I-1
Project of an International Declaration Concerning the Laws and Customs of War (1874)	1(Art.15,16)	I-2
Project of an International Declaration Concerning the Laws and Customs of War (1874)	2(Art.13a,e)	I-2
The Laws of War on Land (Oxford Manual, [1880])	2(Art.8a,9a)	I-36
The Laws of War on Land (Oxford Manual, [1880])	5(Art.32c.84)	I-36
Convention (II) Respecting the Laws and Customs of War on Land and Its Annex: Regulation Concerning the Laws and Customs of War on Land (1899)	1(Art.25,26)	I-3
Convention (II) Respecting the Laws and Customs of War on Land and Its Annex: Regulation Concerning the Laws and Customs of War on Land (1899)	2(Art.23a,e)	I-3
Declaration Concerning the Prohibition, for the Term of Five Years, the Launching of Projectiles and Explosives from Balloons, and Other Methods of a Similar Nature (First Hague, IV, 1 [1899])	1	I-4
Declaration Concerning the Prohibition of the Use of Projectiles Diffusing Asphyxiating Gases (First Hague, IV, 2 [1899])	2 (Para.1)	I-5
Declaration Concerning the Prohibition of the Use of Expanding Bullets (First Hague, IV, 3 [1899])	2 (Para.1)	I-6
Convention (IV) Respecting the Laws and Customs of War on Land and Its Annex: Regulation Concerning the Laws and Customs of War on Land (1907)	1(Art.25,26)	I-7
Convention (IV) Respecting the Laws and Customs of War on Land and Its Annex: Regulation Concerning the Laws and Customs of War on Land (1907)	2(Art.23a,e)	I-7
Convention Respecting the Rights and Duties of Neutral Powers and Persons in Case of War on Land (Second Hague, V, [1907])	2 (Art.2,3)	I-8
Convention (VII) Relating to the Conversion of Merchant Ships into War Ships (1907)	NONE	I-9

INSTRUMENT	PEN. CHAR.	CHAPTER
Manual of the Laws of Naval War (1913)	1(Art.27-29)	I-37
Manual of the Laws of Naval War (1913)	1(Art. 54)	I-37
Manual of the Laws of Naval War (1913)	2(Art.16.1,2)	I-37
Manual of the Laws of Naval War (1913)	2(Art.19-24)	I-37
Convention Relating to the Non-Fortification and Neutralization of of the Aaland Islands (1921)	1 (Art. 3,4)	I-16
Treaty Relating to the Use of Submarines and Noxious Gases in Warfare (1922)	2(Art.1-5)	I-17
Treaty Relating to the Use of Submarines and Noxious Gases in Warfare (1922)	4 (Art.3)	I-17
Treaty Relating to the Use of Submarines and Noxious Gases in Warfare (1922)	5 (Art. 3)	I-17
Treaty Relating to the Use of Submarines and Noxious Gases in Warfare (1922)	8 (Art. 2)	I-17
Treaty Relating to the Use of Submarines and Noxious Gases in Warfare (1922)	10 (Art. 3)	I-17
Rules Concerning the Control of Wireless Telegraphy in Time of War and Air Warfare (1923)	1(Art.3,5,10)	I-18
Rules Concerning the Control of Wireless Telegraphy in Time of War and Air Warfare (1923)	2(Art.6,40)	I-18
Rules Concerning the Control of Wireless Telegraphy in Time of War and Air Warfare (1923)	2(Art.42,44)	I-18
Rules Concerning the Control of Wireless Telegraphy in Time of War and Air Warfare (1923)	2(Art.46,47)	I-18
Protocol for the Prohibition of the Use in War of Asphyxiating, Poisonous or Other Gases, and of Bacteriological Methods of Warfare (1925)	2 (Para.1)	II-1
Convention on Maritime Neutrality (1928)	2(Art.1,4-8)	I-19
Treaty for the Limitation and Reduction of Naval Armaments (London Treaty [1930])	2(Art.22)	I-20
Proces-verbal Relating to the Rules of Submarine Warfare Set Forth in Part IV of the Treaty of London (1936)	2(Art.22)	I-21
The Nyon Agreement (1937)	1(Sect.II,III)	I-22
Agreement Supplementary to the Nyon Agreement (1937)	1(Sect.II,III)	I-23
Draft Convention for the Protection of Civilian Populations Against New Engines of War (1938)	1(Art.2-6)	II-2
Draft Convention for the Protection of Civilian Populations Against New Engines of War (1938)	2(Art.7-9)	II-2

INSTRUMENT	PEN. CHAR.	CHAPTER
Convention on Maritime Neutrality (1928)	2(Art.1,4-8)	I-19
Treaty for the Limitation and Reduction of Naval Armaments (London Treaty [1930])	2(Art.22)	I-20
Proces-verbal Relating to the Rules of Submarine Warfare Set Forth in Part IV of the Treaty of London (1936)	2(Art.22)	I-21
The Nyon Agreement (1937)	1(Sect.II,III)	I-22
Agreement Supplementary to the Nyon Agreement (1937)	1(Sect.II,III)	I-23
Draft Convention for the Protection of Civilian Populations Against New Engines of War (1938)	1(Art.2-6)	II-2
Draft Convention for the Protection of Civilian Populations Against New Engines of War (1938)	2(Art.7-9)	II-2
Draft Convention for the Protection of Civilian Populations Against New Engines of War (1938)	7(Art.22,28,29)	II-2
Protocol No. III on the Control of Armaments (Treaty for Collaboration in Economic, Social and Cultural Matters of Collective Self-Defence Control of Armaments [1943])	NONE	I-24
The Antarctic Treaty (1959)	2 (Art. I,IV)	III-1
The Antarctic Treaty (1959)	8	III-1
Treaty Banning Nuclear Weapon Tests in the Atmosphere, in Outer Space and Under Water (1963)	2 (Art.I)	III-2
Treaty on Principles Governing the Activities of States in the Exploration of Outer Space, Including the Moon and Other Celestial Bodies (1967)	2 (Art.IV)	III-3
Treaty on Principles Governing the Activities of States in the Exploration of Outer Space, Including the Moon and Other Celestial Bodies (1967)	8 (Art.I,II)	III-3
Treaty for the Prohibition of Nuclear Weapons in Latin America (Treaty of Tlatelolco [1968])	2 (Art.1)	IV-1(a)
Additional Protocol I to the Treaty for the Prohibition of Nuclear Weapons in Latin America (1967)	NONE	IV-1(b)
Additional Protocol II to the Treaty for the Prohibition of Nuclear Weapons in Latin America (1967)	NONE	IV-1(c)
The Distinction Between Military Objectives and Non-Military Objectives in General and Particularly the Problems Associated with Weapons of Mass Destruction (1969)	NONE	II-4
Treaty on the Non-Proliferation of Nuclear Weapons (1968)	1(Art.6,7)	II-3

INSTRUMENT	PEN. CHAR.	CHAPTER
Treaty on the Prohibition of the Emplacement of Nuclear Weapons and Other Weapons of Mass Destruction on the Sea-Bed and the Ocean Floor and the Subsoil Thereof (1971)	2 (Art.I)	III-4
Convention on the Prohibition of the Development, Production and Stockpiling of Bacteriological (Biological) and Toxin Weapons and on Their Destruction (1972)	2 (Art.I,II,IV)	II-5
Convention on the Prohibition of Military or Any Other Hostile Use of Environmental Modification Techniques (1977)	2(Art.I)	I-28
Protocol Additional to the Geneva Convention of 12 August 1949, and Relating to the Protection of Victims of International Armed Conflicts (Protocol I [1977])	2(Art.35,36)	I-29
Protocol Additional to the Geneva Convention of 12 August 1949, and Relating to the Protection of Victims of International Armed Conflicts (Protocol I [1977])	2(Art.54-56)	I-29
Protocol Additional to the Geneva Convention of 12 August 1949, and Relating to the Protection of Victims of International Armed Conflicts (Protocol I [1977])	2(Art. 59)	I-29
Protocol Additional to the Geneva Convention of 12 August 1949, and Relating to the Protection of Victims of International Armed Conflicts (Protocol I [1977])	7(Art. 89)	I-29
Protocol Additional to the Geneva Convention of 12 August 1949, and Relating to the Protection of Victims of Non-International Armed Conflicts (Protocol II [1977])	2(Art.14,15)	I-30
Protocol Additional to the Geneva Convention of 12 August 1949, and Relating to the Protection of Victims of Non-International Armed Conflicts (Protocol II [1977])	4(Art. 6)	I-30
Resolution on Small-Calibre Weapons Systems by the United Nations Conference on Prohibitions or Restrictions on the Use of Certain Conventional Weapons (1979)	NONE	I-31
Agreement Governing the Activities of States on the Moon and Other Celestial Bodies (1979)	2(Art.2,3,4)	III-5
Convention on Prohibitions and Restrictions on the Use of Certain Conventional Weapons Which May Be Deemed to be Excessively Injurious or to Have Indiscriminate Effects (1980)	1(Prot.I;P.II	I-32

INSTRUMENT	PEN. CHAR.	CHAPTER
Convention on Prohibitions and Restrictions on the Use of Certain Conventional Weapons Which May Be Deemed to be Excessively Injurious or to Have Indiscriminate Effects (1980)	Art.3-6;P.III	I-32
Convention on Prohibitions and Restrictions on the Use of Certain Conventional Weapons Which May Be Deemed to be Excessively Injurious or to Have Indiscriminate Effects (1980)	Art.2)	I-32
Convention on Prohibitions and Restrictions on the Use of Certain Conventional Weapons Which May Be Deemed to be Excessively Injurious or to Have Indiscriminate Effects (1980)	2(Art.1,2,4)	I-32
Protocol on Non-Detectable Fragments to the Convention on Prohibitions or Restrictions on the Use of Certain Conventional Weapons (Protocol I [1980])	2(Art.1)	I-32(a)
Protocol on Prohibitions or Restrictions on the Use of Mines, Booby-Traps, and Other Devices to the Convention on Prohibitions or Restrictions on the Use of Certain Conventional Weapons (Protocol II [1980])	2(Art.3-6)	I-32(b)
Protocol on Prohibitions or Restrictions on the Use of Incendiary Weapons to the Convention on Prohibitions or Restrictions on the Use of Certain Conventional Weapons (Protocol III [1980])	2(Art.2)	I-32(c)
Protocol (IV) on Blinding Laser Weapons (1995)	2(Art.1,2,4)	I-32(d)
South Pacific Nuclear Free Zone Treaty (Treaty of Raratonga [1985])	2(Art.5-7)	IV-2
Convention on the Prohibition of the Development, Production, Stockpiling and Use of Chemical Weapons and on Their Destruction (1993)	2(Art.VII(1)(a,c)	II-6
Convention on the Prohibition of the Development, Production, Stockpiling and Use of Chemical Weapons and on Their Destruction (1993)	3(Art.VII(1)(c))	II-6
Convention on the Prohibition of the Development, Production, Stockpiling and Use of Chemical Weapons and on Their Destruction (1993)	4(Art.VII(1)(a)	II-6
Convention on the Prohibition of the Development, Production, Stockpiling and Use of Chemical Weapons and on Their Destruction (1993)	5(Art.VII(1)(a)	II-6
Convention on the Prohibition of the Development, Production, Stockpiling and Use of Chemical Weapons and on Their Destruction (1993)	7(Art.VII(2,3)	II-6

INSTRUMENT	PEN. CHAR.	CHAPTER
Convention on the Prohibition of the Development, Production, Stockpiling and Use of Chemical Weapons and on Their Destruction (1993)	8(Art.VII(1)(a)	II-6
San Remo Manual on International Law Applicable to Armed Conflicts at Sea (1994)	2(Art.16-18)	I-38
San Remo Manual on International Law Applicable to Armed Conflicts at Sea (1994)	2(Art.42,44)	I-38
San Remo Manual on International Law Applicable to Armed Conflicts at Sea (1994)	2(Art.78-91)	I-38
Treaty on South East Asia Nuclear Weapons Free Zone (1995)	2(Art.3)	IV-3
Africa Nuclear Weapon Free Zone Treaty (1996)	2(Art.4(1),5	IV-4(a)
Cairo Declaration (1996)	NONE	IV-4(b)
United Nations International Convention for the Suppression of Terrorist Bombings (1998)	1(Art.2)	I-34
United Nations International Convention for the Suppression of Terrorist Bombings (1998)	4(Art.4)	I-34
United Nations International Convention for the Suppression of Terrorist Bombings (1998)	5(Art.4)	I-34
United Nations International Convention for the Suppression of Terrorist Bombings (1998)	6(7-9)	I-34
United Nations International Convention for the Suppression of Terrorist Bombings (1998)	7(10,15)	I-34
United Nations International Convention for the Suppression of Terrorist Bombings (1998)	8(Art. 6)	I-34

CHART B
CONTEXTUAL APPLICABILITY

INSTRUMENT	WAR	PEACE	WAR & PEACE	CHAPTER
Instructions for the Government of Armies of the United States in the Field (Lieber Code [1863])	YES	NO	NO	I-31
Declaration Renouncing the Use, in Time of War, of Explosive Projectiles Under 400 Grammes Weight (St. Petersburg Declaration [1868])	YES	NO	NO	I-1
Project of an International Declaration Concerning the Laws and Customs of War (1874)	YES	NO	NO	I-2
The Laws of War on Land (Oxford Manual, [1880])	YES	NO	NO	I-36
Convention (II) Respecting the Laws and Customs of War on Land and Its Annex: Regulation Concerning the Laws and Customs of War on Land (1899)	YES	NO	NO	I-3
Declaration Concerning the Prohibition, for the Term of Five Years, the Launching of Projectiles and Explosives from Balloons, and Other Methods of a Similar Nature (First Hague, IV, 1 [1899])	YES	YES	YES	I-4
Declaration Concerning the Prohibition of the Use of Projectiles Diffusing Asphyxiating Gases (First Hague, IV, 2 [1899])	YES	NO	NO	I-5
Declaration Concerning the Prohibition of the Use of Expanding Bullets (First Hague, IV, 3 [1899])	YES	NO	NO	I-6
Convention (IV) Respecting the Laws and Customs of War on Land and Its Annex: Regulation Concerning the Laws and Customs of War on Land (1907)	YES	NO	NO	I-7
Convention Respecting the Rights and Duties of Neutral Powers and Persons in Case of War on Land (Second Hague, V, [1907])	YES	NO	NO	I-8
Convention (VII) Relating to the Conversion of Merchant Ships into War Ships (1907)	YES	NO	NO	I-9
Convention Relative to the Laying of Automatic Submarine Contact Mines (Second Hague, VIII [1907])	YES	YES	YES	I-10

INSTRUMENT	WAR	PEACE	WAR & PEACE	CHAPTER
Convention Concerning Bombardment By Naval Forces in Time of War (Second Hague, IX [1907])	YES	NO	NO	I-11
Convention (X) for the Adaptation to Maritime Warfare of the Principles of the Geneva Convention (1907)	YES	NO	NO	I-12
Convention Concerning the Rights and Duties of Neutral Powers in Naval War (Second Hague, XIII [1907])	YES	NO	NO	I-13
Declaration Relative to Prohibiting the Discharge of Projectiles and Explosives from Balloons (Second Hague, XIV [1907])	NO	YES	NO	I-14
Declaration Concerning the Laws of Naval War (1909)	YES	NO	NO	I-15
Manual of the Laws of Naval War (1913)	YES	NO	NO	I-37
Convention Relating to the Non-Fortification and Neutralization of of the Aaland Islands (1921)	YES	YES	YES	I-16
Treaty Relating to the Use of Submarines and Noxious Gases in Warfare (1922)	YES	NO	NO	I-17
Rules Concerning the Control of Wireless Telegraphy in Time of War and Air Warfare (1923)	YES	NO	NO	I-18
Protocol for the Prohibition of the Use in War of Asphyxiating, Poisonous or Other Gases, and of Bacteriological Methods of Warfare (1925)	YES	NO	NO	II-1
Convention on Maritime Neutrality (1928)	YES	NO	NO	I-19
Treaty for the Limitation and Reduction of Naval Armaments (London Treaty [1930])	YES	YES	YES	I-20
Proces-verbal Relating to the Rules of Submarine Warfare Set Forth in Part IV of the Treaty of London (1936)	YES	YES	YES	I-21
The Nyon Agreement (1937)	YES	YES	YES	I-22
Agreement Supplementary to the Nyon Agreement (1937)	YES	YES	YES	I-23
Draft Convention for the Protection of Civilian Populations Against New Engines of War (1938)	YES	NO	NO	II-2

International Humanitarian Law and Arms Control Agreements 75

INSTRUMENT	WAR	PEACE	WAR & PEACE	CHAPTER
Protocol No. III on the Control of Armaments (Treaty for Collaboration in Economic, Social and Cultural Matters of Collective Self-Defence Control of Armaments [1943])	YES	YES	YES	I-24
The Antarctic Treaty (1959)	NO	YES	NO	III-1
Treaty Banning Nuclear Weapon Tests in the Atmosphere, in Outer Space and Under Water (1963)	NO	YES	NO	III-2
Treaty on Principles Governing the Activities of States in the Exploration of Outer Space, Including the Moon and Other Celestial Bodies (1967)	YES	YES	YES	III-3
Treaty for the Prohibition of Nuclear Weapons in Latin America (Treaty of Tlatelolco [1968])	NO	YES	NO	IV-1(a)
Additional Protocol I to the Treaty for the Prohibition of Nuclear Weapons in Latin America (1967)	NO	YES	NO	IV-1(b)
Additional Protocol II to the Treaty for the Prohibition of Nuclear Weapons in Latin America (1967)	NO	YES	NO	IV-1(c)
The Distinction Between Military Objectives and Non-Military Objectives in General and Particularly the Problems Associated with Weapons of Mass Destruction (1969)	NO	YES	NO	II-4
Treaty on the Non-Proliferation of Nuclear Weapons (1968)	YES	YES	YES	II-3
Treaty on the Prohibition of the Emplacement of Nuclear Weapons and Other Weapons of Mass Destruction on the Sea-Bed and the Ocean Floor and the Subsoil Thereof (1971)	NO	YES	NO	III-4
Convention on the Prohibition of the Development, Production and Stockpiling of Bacteriological (Biological) and Toxin Weapons and on Their Destruction (1972)	YES	YES	YES	II-5
Convention on the Prohibition of Military or Any Other Hostile Use of Environmental Modification Techniques (1977)	YES	YES	YES	I-28

INSTRUMENT	WAR	PEACE	WAR & PEACE	CHAPTER
Protocol Additional to the Geneva Convention of 12 August 1949, and Relating to the Protection of Victims of International Armed Conflicts (Protocol I [1977])	YES	NO	NO	I-29
Protocol Additional to the Geneva Convention of 12 August 1949, and Relating to the Protection of Victims of Non-International Armed Conflicts (Protocol II [1977])	YES	YES	YES	I-30
Resolution on Small-Calibre Weapons Systems by the United Nations Conference on Prohibitions or Restrictions on the Use of Certain Conventional Weapons (1979)	NO	NO	NO	I-31
Agreement Governing the Activities of States on the Moon and Other Celestial Bodies (1979)	YES	YES	YES	III-5
Convention on Prohibitions and Restrictions on the Use of Certain Conventional Weapons Which May Be Deemed to be Excessively Injurious or to Have Indiscriminate Effects (1980)	YES	NO	NO	I-32
Protocol on Non-Detectable Fragments to the Convention on Prohibitions or Restrictions on the Use of Certain Conventional Weapons (Protocol I [1980])	YES	NO	NO	I-32(a)
Protocol on Prohibitions or Restrictions on the Use of Mines, Booby-Traps, and Other Devices to the Convention on Prohibitions or Restrictions on the Use of Certain Conventional Weapons (Protocol II [1980])	YES	NO	NO	I-32(b)
Protocol on Prohibitions or Restrictions on the Use of Incendiary Weapons to the Convention on Prohibitions or Restrictions on the Use of Certain Conventional Weapons (Protocol III [1980])	YES	NO	NO	I-32(c)
Protocol (IV) on Blinding Laser Weapons (1995)	YES	NO	NO	I-32(d)
South Pacific Nuclear Free Zone Treaty (Treaty of Raratonga [1985])	NO	YES	NO	IV-2

International Humanitarian Law and Arms Control Agreements

INSTRUMENT	WAR	PEACE	WAR & PEACE	CHAPTER
Convention on the Prohibition of the Development, Production, Stockpiling and Use of Chemical Weapons and on Their Destruction (1993)	YES	YES	YES	II-6
San Remo Manual on International Law Applicable to Armed Conflicts at Sea (1994)	YES	NO	NO	I-38
Treaty on South East Asia Nuclear Weapons Free Zone (1995)	YES	YES	YES	IV-3
Africa Nuclear Weapon Free Zone Treaty (1996)	NO	YES	NO	IV-4(a)
Cairo Declaration (1996)	NO	YES	NO	IV-4(b)
United Nations International Convention for the Suppression of Terrorist Bombings (1998)	NO	YES	NO	I-34

CHART C
TYPE OF CONTROL REGIME

INSTRUMENT	REGULATE	PROHIBIT	CHAPTER
Instructions for the Government of Armies of the United States in the Field (Lieber Code [1863])	YES	YES	I-35
Declaration Renouncing the Use, in Time of War, of Explosive Projectiles Under 400 Grammes Weight (St. Petersburg Declaration [1868])	NO	YES	I-1
Project of an International Declaration Concerning the Laws and Customs of War (1874)	YES	YES	I-2
The Laws of War on Land (Oxford Manual, [1880])	YES	YES	I-36
Convention (II) Respecting the Laws and Customs of War on Land and Its Annex: Regulation Concerning the Laws and Customs of War on Land (1899)	YES	YES	I-3
Declaration Concerning the Prohibition, for the Term of Five Years, the Launching of Projectiles and Explosives from Balloons, and Other Methods of a Similar Nature (First Hague, IV, 1 [1899])	YES	YES	I-4
Declaration Concerning the Prohibition of the Use of Projectiles Diffusing Asphyxiating Gases (First Hague, IV, 2 [1899])	NO	YES	I-5
Declaration Concerning the Prohibition of the Use of Expanding Bullets (First Hague, IV, 3 [1899])	NO	YES	I-6
Convention (IV) Respecting the Laws and Customs of War on Land and Its Annex: Regulation Concerning the Laws and Customs of War on Land (1907)	YES	YES	I-7
Convention Respecting the Rights and Duties of Neutral Powers and Persons in Case of War on Land (Second Hague, V, [1907])	YES	YES	I-8
Convention (VII) Relating to the Conversion of Merchant Ships into War Ships (1907)	YES	YES	I-9

INSTRUMENT	REGULATE	PROHIBIT	CHAPTER
Convention Relative to the Laying of Automatic Submarine Contact Mines (Second Hague, VIII [1907])	YES	YES	I-10
Convention Concerning Bombardment By Naval Forces in Time of War (Second Hague, IX [1907])	NO	YES	I-11
Convention (X) for the Adaptation to Maritime Warfare of the Principles of the Geneva Convention (1907)	YES	YES	I-12
Convention Concerning the Rights and Duties of Neutral Powers in Naval War (Second Hague, XIII [1907])	YES	YES	I-13
Declaration Relative to Prohibiting the Discharge of Projectiles and Explosives from Balloons (Second Hague, XIV [1907])	YES	YES	I-14
Declaration Concerning the Laws of Naval War (1909)	YES	NO	I-15
Manual of the Laws of Naval War (1913)	YES	YES	I-37
Convention Relating to the Non-Fortification and Neutralization of of the Aaland Islands (1921)	YES	YES	I-16
Treaty Relating to the Use of Submarines and Noxious Gases in Warfare (1922)	YES	YES	I-17
Rules Concerning the Control of Wireless Telegraphy in Time of War and Air Warfare (1923)	YES	YES	I-18
Protocol for the Prohibition of the Use in War of Asphyxiating, Poisonous or Other Gases, and of Bacteriological Methods of Warfare (1925)	NO	YES	II-1
Convention on Maritime Neutrality (1928)	YES	NO	I-19
Treaty for the Limitation and Reduction of Naval Armaments (London Treaty [1930])	YES	YES	I-20
Proces-verbal Relating to the Rules of Submarine Warfare Set Forth in Part IV of the Treaty of London (1936)	YES	YES	I-21
The Nyon Agreement (1937)	NO	YES	I-22
Agreement Supplementary to the Nyon Agreement (1937)	NO	YES	I-23
Draft Convention for the Protection of Civilian Populations Against New Engines of War (1938)	YES	YES	II-2

International Humanitarian Law and Arms Control Agreements 81

INSTRUMENT	REGULATE	PROHIBIT	CHAPTER
Protocol No. III on the Control of Armaments (Treaty for Collaboration in Economic, Social and Cultural Matters of Collective Self-Defence Control of Armaments [1943])	YES	YES	I-24
The Antarctic Treaty (1959)	YES	YES	III-1
Treaty Banning Nuclear Weapon Tests in the Atmosphere, in Outer Space and Under Water (1963)	YES	YES	III-2
Treaty on Principles Governing the Activities of States in the Exploration of Outer Space, Including the Moon and Other Celestial Bodies (1967)	YES	YES	III-3
Treaty for the Prohibition of Nuclear Weapons in Latin America (Treaty of Tlatelolco [1968])	YES	YES	IV-1(a)
Additional Protocol I to the Treaty for the Prohibition of Nuclear Weapons in Latin America (1967)	YES	YES	IV-1(b)
Additional Protocol II to the Treaty for the Prohibition of Nuclear Weapons in Latin America (1967)	YES	YES	IV-1(c)
The Distinction Between Military Objectives and Non Military Objectives in General and Particularly the Problems Associated with Weapons of Mass Destruction (1969)	YES	YES	II-4
Treaty on the Non-Proliferation of Nuclear Weapons (1968)	YES	YES	II-3
Treaty on the Prohibition of the Emplacement of Nuclear Weapons and Other Weapons of Mass Destruction on the Sea-Bed and the Ocean Floor and the Subsoil Thereof (1971)	YES	YES	III-4
Convention on the Prohibition of the Development, Production and Stockpiling of Bacteriological (Biological) and Toxin Weapons and on Their Destruction (1972)	YES	YES	II-5
Convention on the Prohibition of Military or Any Other Hostile Use of Environmental Modification Techniques (1977)	NO	YES	I-28
Protocol Additional to the Geneva Convention of 12 August 1949, and Relating to the Protection of Victims of International Armed Conflicts (Protocol I [1977])	YES	YES	I-29
Protocol Additional to the Geneva Convention of 12 August 1949, and Relating to the Protection of Victims of Non-International Armed Conflicts (Protocol II [1977])	YES	YES	I-30

INSTRUMENT	REGULATE	PROHIBIT	CHAPTER
Resolution on Small-Calibre Weapons Systems by the United Nations Conference on Prohibitions or Restrictions on the Use of Certain Conventional Weapons (1979)	NO	NO	I-31
Agreement Governing the Activities of States on the Moon and Other Celestial Bodies (1979)	YES	YES	III-5
Convention on Prohibitions and Restrictions on the Use of Certain Conventional Weapons Which May Be Deemed to be Excessively Injurious or to Have Indiscriminate Effects (1980)	YES	YES	I-32
Protocol on Non-Detectable Fragments to the Convention on Prohibitions or Restrictions on the Use of Certain Conventional Weapons (Protocol I [1980])	YES	YES	I-32(a)
Protocol on Prohibitions or Restrictions on the Use of Mines, Booby-Traps, and Other Devices to the Convention on Prohibitions or Restrictions on the Use of Certain Conventional Weapons (Protocol II [1980])	YES	YES	I-32(b)
Protocol on Prohibitions or Restrictions on the Use of Incendiary Weapons to the Convention on Prohibitions or Restrictions on the Use of Certain Conventional Weapons (Protocol III [1980])	YES	YES	I-32(c)
Protocol (IV) on Blinding Laser Weapons (1995)	YES	YES	I-32(d)
South Pacific Nuclear Free Zone Treaty (Treaty of Raratonga [1985])	NO	YES	IV-2
Convention on the Prohibition of the Development, Production, Stockpiling and Use of Chemical Weapons and on Their Destruction (1993)	YES	YES	II-6
San Remo Manual on International Law Applicable to Armed Conflicts at Sea (1994)	YES	YES	I-34
Treaty on South East Asia Nuclear Weapons Free Zone (1995)	NO	YES	IV-3
Africa Nuclear Weapon Free Zone Treaty (1996)	NO	YES	IV-4(a)
Cairo Declaration (1996)	NO	NO	IV-4(b)
United Nations International Convention for the Suppression of Terrorist Bombings (1998)	NO	YES	I-34

CHAPTER I

MULTILATERAL INSTRUMENTS ON THE REGULATION OF ARMED CONFLICTS AND WEAPONS CONTROL

INTRODUCTION

Chapter I is divided into two parts. The first part includes all relevant multilateral instruments on the regulation of armed conflicts and weapons control. The second part includes the principal manuals on the regulation of armed conflicts and weapons control evidencing customary international law. The first category of instruments included in this book is the most extensive. While this category includes the greatest number of conventions (thirty-eight instruments), it also covers the longest time period. Starting with the earliest instrument, the St. Petersburg Declaration of 1868, to the 1995 Protocol on Blinding Laser Weapons (Protocol IV to the Convention on Prohibitions or Restrictions on the Use of Certain Conventional Weapons). These two instruments illustrate the evolution of arms control regulation and prohibition, as well as the growing challenge of sophisticated weaponry that has developed since the ban on explosive projectiles of 400 grammes weight to the ban on blinding lasers.

Many of the instruments in Chapter I embody customary law, but the concept is broader than the specifics contained in these instruments. Some of the norms embodied in these instruments apply in time of war, while others also apply to peace times. More specifically, some conventions apply to use, while others apply to possession of certain weapons.

Unlawful use of weapons is defined as employment of weapons whose use is prohibited. This is to be distinguished from unauthorized use of permissible weapons, but whose use may be limited or controlled by general or specific norms. Because of the distinction between the contexts of war and peace, the use of certain weapons, paradoxically, may be deemed an international crime when used in time of war, but not when used in time of peace. However, the distinction is gradually eroding in contemporary legal doctrine.

Conventions on weapons of mass destruction such as chemical and biological weapons are not included in Chapter I, but are included in Chapter II because of their peculiar nature. So far there is no prohibition on the use of nuclear weapons, though an emerging rule of customary international law makes the "first use" of nuclear weapons a violation. Chapter I includes relevant provisions of the Geneva Conventions of 12 August 1949. These conventions do not contain a specific prohibition against weapons that cause unnecessary pain and suffering, nor does it have specific provisions that deal with weapons. However, insofar as the use of weapons can cause indiscriminate harm to protected persons such as civilians, POW's, the sick, wounded, and shipwrecked, they constitute violations of the 1949 Geneva Conventions. These violations are reflected in the grave breaches provisions. The 1982 Convention on the Law of the Sea is included because of its relevant provisions to the use of weapons. Lastly, Chapter I ends with the 1998 United Nations International Convention for the Suppression of Terrorist Bombings which is the only instrument in this chapter that also applies in time of peace and presumably also in time of war, unless it is a legitimate war-related action, which is doubtful.

The second part of Chapter I includes four principal manuals on the international law of war. While this is not an exhaustive list, it is a representative one. Two of the manuals concern the laws of war on land, and the remaining two focus on the laws of war at sea. The first manual included in this section is the Lieber Code of 1863, which were the instructions for the government of United States Army first developed during President Lincoln's term in office. The documents in this second category are not multilateral agreements, but they are included in this volume because of their importance to the development of customary international law. For example, the first document in this category, the Lieber Code, prohibits the use of poisons under Article 16. Subsequent conventions such as the Brussels Conference of 1874 and the Hague Conventions on Land Warfare in 1899 and 1907 followed this example.

Thus, these manuals evidence customary international law. But they have also set the course for future practice as now the armed forces of every country have their separate manuals or military codes that embody the provisions of the Geneva Conventions and customary international law.

International Humanitarian Law and Arms Control Agreements

I-1. **Declaration Renouncing the Use, in Time of War, of Explosive Projectiles Under 400 Grammes Weight [St. Petersburg Declaration]**, *signed at St. Petersburg*, **11 December 1868, 18 MARTENS (ser. 1) 474, entered into force 11 December 1868**.[1] Authentic Text: French

Relevant Penal Characteristics & Penal Provisions
2. Implicit recognition of the penal nature of the act by establishing a duty to prohibit, prevent, prosecute, punish, or the like: *See* text in italics

Applicability
War

Control
Prohibition

State Signatories
Austria-Hungary; Bavaria; Belgium; Denmark; France; Greece; Iran (Islamic Republic); Italy; the Netherlands; Norway; Portugal; Prussia & the North German Confederation; Russian Federation; Sweden; Switzerland; Turkey; United Kingdom; Wurtemberg

State Parties
Austria-Hungary; Baden; Bavaria; Belgium; Brazil; Denmark; Estonia; France; Great Britain; Greece; Italy; the Netherlands; Persia; Portugal; Prussia & the North German Confederation; Russia; Sweden-Norway; Switzerland; Turkey; Wurttemberg

Full Text[2]
On the proposition of the Imperial Cabinet of Russia, an International Military Commission having assembled at St. Petersburg in order to examine the expediency of forbidding the use of certain projectiles in time of war between civilized nations, and that Commission having by common agreement fixed the technical limits at which the necessities of war ought to yield to the requirements of humanity, the Undersigned are authorized by the orders of their Governments to declare as follows:

---

[1] *See also* 1 AM. J. INT'L L. 95 (1907), 138 Parry's 297.

[2] This Declaration has been relied upon in a number of subsequent arms control documents: Project of an International Declaration Concerning the Laws and Customs of War [Declaration of Brussels] (Brussles Conference on the Laws and Customs of War, No. 18), 27 August 1874; Convention with Respect to the Laws and Customs of War on Land [First Hague, II], 29 July 1899; Declaration Concerning the Prohibition, for the Term of Five Years, of the Launching of Projectiles and Explosives from Balloons or Other New Methods of a Similar Nature [First Hague, IV, 1], 29 July 1899; Declaration Concerning the Prohibition of the Use of Projectiles Diffusing Asphyxiating Gases, [First Hague, IV, 2], 29 July 1899; Declaration Concerning the Prohibition of the Use of Expanding Bullets [First Hague, IV, 3], 29 July 1899; Convention Respecting the Laws and Customs of War on Land [Second Hague, IV], 18 October 1907; Declaration Relative to Prohibiting the Discharge of Projectiles and Explosives from Balloons [Second Hague, XIV], 18 October 1907; Convention on Prohibitions or Restrictions on the Use of Certain Conventional Weapons Which May be Deemed to be Excessively Injurious or to Have Indiscriminate Effects, 10 October 1980.

Considering: That the progress of civilization should have the effect of alleviating as much as possible the calamities of war; That the only legitimate object which States should endeavour to accomplish during war is to weaken the military forces of the enemy;

That for this purpose it is sufficient to disable the greatest possible number of men;

That this object would be exceeded by the employment of arms which uselessly aggravate the sufferings of disabled men, or render their death inevitable;

That the employment of such arms would, therefore, be contrary to the laws of humanity;

The Contracting Parties engage mutually to renounce, in case of war among themselves, the employment by their military or naval troops of any projectile of a weight below 400 grammes, which is either explosive or charged with fulminating or inflammable substances.

They will invite all the States which have not taken part in the deliberations of the International Military Commission assembled at St. Petersburg by sending Delegates thereto, to accede to the present engagement.

This engagement is compulsory only upon the Contracting or Acceding Parties thereto in case of war between two or more of themselves; it is not applicable to non-Contracting Parties, or Parties who shall not have acceded to it.

It will also cease to be compulsory from the moment when, in a war between Contracting or Acceding Parties, a non-Contracting Party or a non-Acceding Party shall join one of the belligerents.

The Contracting or Acceding Parties reserve to themselves to come hereafter to an understanding whenever a precise proposition shall be drawn up in view of future improvements which science may effect in the armament of troops, in order to maintain the principles which they have established, and to conciliate the necessities of war with the laws of humanity.

Done at St. Petersburg, 29 November (11 December) 1868.

I-2. Project of an International Declaration Concerning the Laws and Customs of War *signed at Brussels,* **27 August 1874, 4 MARTENS (ser. 2) 219.** Authentic Text: French

Relevant Penal Characteristics & Penal Provisions

1. Explicit or implicit recognition of proscribed conduct as constituting an international crime, or a crime under international law, or a crime: Article 15 & Article 16
2. Implicit recognition of the penal nature of the act by establishing a duty to prohibit, prevent, prosecute, punish, or the like: Article 13 (a), (e)

Applicability
War

Control
Regulation & Prohibition

State Signatories
Austria-Hungary; Belgium; Denmark; France; Germany; Great Britain; Greece; Italy; Netherlands; Norway; Portugal; Russia; Spain; Sweden; Switzerland; Turkey

Full Text[3]

On military authority over hostile territory

Article 1. Territory is considered occupied when it is actually placed under the authority of the hostile army.

The occupation extends only to the territory where such authority has been established and can be exercised.

Art. 2. The authority of the legitimate Power being suspended and having in fact passed into the hands of the occupants, the latter shall take all the measures in his power to restore and ensure, as far as possible, public order and safety.

Art. 3. With this object he shall maintain the laws which were in force in the country in time of peace, and shall not modify, suspend or replace them unless necessary.

Art. 4. The functionaries and employees of every class who consent, on his invitation, to continue their functions, shall enjoy his protection. They shall not be dismissed or subjected to disciplinary punishment unless they fail in fulfilling the obligations undertaken by them, and they shall not be prosecuted unless they betray their trust.

Art. 5. The army of occupation shall only collect the taxes, dues, duties, and tolls imposed for the benefit of the State, or their equivalent, if it is impossible to collect them, and, as far as is possible, in accordance with the existing forms and practice. It shall devote them to defraying the expenses of the administration of the country to the same extent as the legitimate Government was so obligated.

Art. 6. An army of occupation can only take possession of cash, funds, and realizable securities which are strictly the property of the State, depots of arms, means of transport, stores and supplies, and generally, all movable property belonging to the State which may be used for the operations of the war.

---

[3] These rules were not adopted. *See also* LEON FRIEDMAN, 1 THE LAWS OF WAR, A DOCUMENTARY HISTORY 194 (1972).

Railway plant, land telegraphs, steamers and other ships, apart from cases governed by maritime law, as well as depots of arms and, generally, all kinds of war material, even if belonging to companies or to private persons, are likewise material which may serve for military operations and which cannot be left by the army of occupation at the disposal of the enemy. Railway plant, land telegraphs, as well as steamers and other ships above mentioned shall be restored and compensation fixed when peace is made.

Art. 7. The occupying State shall be regarded only as administrator and usufructuary of public buildings, real estate, forests, and agricultural estates belonging to the hostile State, and situated in the occupied country. It must safeguard the capital of these properties, and administer them in accordance with the rules of usufruct.

Art. 8. The property of municipalities, that of institutions dedicated to religion, charity and education, the arts and sciences even when State property, shall be treated as private property.

All seizure or destruction of, or wilful damage to, institutions of this character, historic monuments, works of art and science should be made the subject of legal proceedings by the competent authorities.

Who should be recognized as belligerents combatants and non-combatants

Art. 9. The laws, rights, and duties of war apply not only to armies, but also to militia and volunteer corps fulfilling the following conditions:

1. That they be commanded by a person responsible for his subordinates;
2. That they have a fixed distinctive emblem recognizable at a distance;
3. That they carry arms openly; and
4. That they conduct their operations in accordance with the laws and customs of war.

In countries where militia constitute the army, or form part of it, they are included under the denomination ' army '.

Art. 10. The population of a territory which has not been occupied, who, on the approach of the enemy, spontaneously take up arms to resist the invading troops without having had time to organize themselves in accordance with Article 9, shall be regarded as belligerents if they respect the laws and customs of war.

Art 11.The armed forces of the belligerent parties may consist of combatants and non-combatants. In case of capture by the enemy, both shall enjoy the rights of prisoners of war.

Means of injuring the enemy

Art. 12. The laws of war do not recognize in belligerents an unlimited power in the adoption of means of injuring the enemy.

Art. 13. According to this principle are especially ' forbidden ':

(a) Employment of poison or poisoned weapons;

(b) Murder by treachery of individuals belonging to the hostile nation or army;

(c) Murder of an enemy who, having laid down his arms or having no longer means of defense, has surrendered at discretion;

(d) The declaration that no quarter will be given;

(e) The employment of arms, projectiles or material calculated to cause unnecessary suffering, as well as the use of projectiles prohibited by the Declaration of St. Petersburg of 1868;

(f) Making improper use of a flag of truce, of the national flag or of the military insignia and uniform of the enemy, as well as the distinctive badges of the Geneva Convention;

(g) Any destruction or seizure of the enemy's property that is not imperatively demanded by the necessity of war.

Art. 14. Ruses of war and the employment of measures necessary for obtaining information about the enemy and the country (excepting the provisions of Article 36) are considered permissible.

Sieges and bombardments

Art. 15. Fortified places are alone liable to be besieged. Open towns, agglomerations of dwellings, or villages which are not defended can neither be attacked nor bombarded.

Art. 16. But if a town or fortress, agglomeration of dwellings, or village, is defended, the officer in command of an attacking force must, before commencing a bombardment, except in assault, do all in his power to warn the authorities.

Art. 17. In such cases all necessary steps must be taken to spare, as far as possible, buildings dedicated to art, science, or charitable purposes, hospitals, and places where the sick and wounded are collected provided they are not being used at the time for military purposes.

It is the duty of the besieged to indicate the presence of such buildings by distinctive and visible signs to be communicated to the enemy beforehand

Art. 18. A town taken by assault ought not to be given over to pillage by the victorious troops.

Spies

Art. 19. A person can only be considered a spy when acting clandestinely or on false pretenses he obtains or endeavours to obtain information in the districts occupied by the enemy, with the intention of communicating it to the hostile party.

Art. 20. A spy taken in the act shall be tried and treated according to the laws in force in the army which captures him.

Art. 21. A spy who rejoins the army to which he belongs and who is subsequently captured by the enemy is treated as a prisoner of war and incurs no responsibility for his previous acts.

Art. 22. Soldiers not wearing a disguise who have penetrated into the zone of operations of the hostile army, for the purpose of obtaining information, are not considered spies.

Similarly, the following should not be considered spies, if they are captured by the enemy: soldiers (and also civilians, carrying out their mission openly) entrusted with the delivery of dispatches intended either for their own army or for the enemy's army.

To this class belong likewise, if they are captured, persons sent in balloons for the purpose of carrying dispatches and, generally, of maintaining communications between the different parts of an army or a territory.

Prisoners of war

Art. 23. Prisoners of war are lawful and disarmed enemies.

They are in the power of the hostile Government, but not in that of the individuals or corps who captured them.

They must be humanely treated.

Any act of insubordination justifies the adoption of such measures of severity as may be necessary. All their personal belongings except arms shall remain their property.

Art. 24. Prisoners of war may be interned in a town, fortress, camp, or other place, under obligation not to go beyond certain fixed limits; but they can only be placed in confinement as an indispensable measure of safety.

Art. 25. Prisoners of war may be employed on certain public works which have no direct connection with the operations in the theatre of war and which are not excessive or humiliating to their military rank, if they belong to the army, or to their official or social position, if they do not belong to it.

They may also, subject to such regulations as may be drawn up by the military authorities, undertake private work.

Their wages shall go towards improving their position or shall be paid to them on their release. In this case the cost of maintenance may be deducted from said wages.

Art. 26. Prisoners of war cannot be compelled in any way to take any part whatever in carrying on the operations of the war.

Art. 27. The Government into whose hands prisoners of war have fallen charges itself with their maintenance.

The conditions of such maintenance may be settled by a reciprocal agreement between the belligerent parties.

In the absence of this agreement, and as a general principle, prisoners of war shall be treated as regards food and clothing, on the same footing as the troops of the Government which captured them.

Art. 28. Prisoners of war are subject to the laws and regulations in force in the army in whose power they are.

Arms may be used, after summoning, against a prisoner of war attempting to escape. If recaptured he is liable to disciplinary punishment or subject to a stricter surveillance.

If, after succeeding in escaping, he is again taken prisoner, he is not liable to punishment for his previous acts.

Art. 29. Every prisoner of war is bound to give, if questioned on the subject, his true name and rank, and if he infringes this rule, he is liable to a curtailment of the advantages accorded to the prisoners of war of his class.

Art. 30. The exchange of prisoners of war is regulated by a mutual understanding between the belligerent parties.

Art. 31. Prisoners of war may be set at liberty on parole if the laws of their country allow it, and, in such cases, they are bound, on their personal honour, scrupulously to fulfill, both towards their own Government and the Government by which they were made prisoners, the engagements they have contracted.

In such cases their own Government ought neither to require of nor accept from them any service incompatible with the parole given.

Art. 32. A prisoner of war cannot be compelled to accept his liberty on parole; similarly the hostile Government is not obliged to accede to the request of the prisoner to be set at liberty on parole.

Art. 33. Any prisoner of war liberated on parole and recaptured bearing arms against the Government to which he had pledged his honour may be deprived of the rights accorded to prisoners of war and brought before the courts.

Art. 34. Individuals in the vicinity of armies but not directly forming part of them, such as correspondents, newspaper reporters, sutlers, contractors, etc., can also be made prisoners. These prisoners should however be in possession of a permit issued by the competent authority and of a certificate of identity.

The sick and wounded

Art. 35. The obligations of belligerents with respect to the service of the sick and wounded are governed by the Geneva Convention of 22 August 1864, save such modifications as the latter may undergo.

On the military power with respect to private persons

Art. 36. The population of occupied territory cannot be forced to take part in military operations against its own country.

Art. 37. The population of occupied territory cannot be compelled to swear allegiance to the hostile Power.

Art. 38. Family honour and rights, and the lives and property of persons, as well as their religious convictions and their practice, must be respected.

Private property cannot be confiscated.

Art. 39. Pillage is formally forbidden.

On taxes and requisitions

Art. 40. As private property should be respected, the enemy will demand from communes or inhabitants only such payments and services as are connected with the generally recognized necessities of war, in proportion to the resources of the country, and not implying, with regard to the inhabitants, the obligation of taking part in operations of war against their country.

Art. 41. The enemy in levying contributions, whether as an equivalent for taxes (see Article 5) or for payments that should be made in kind, or as fines, shall proceed, so far as possible, only in accordance with the rules for incidence and assessment in force in the territory occupied.

The civil authorities of the legitimate Government shall lend it their assistance if they have remained at their posts.

Contributions shall be imposed only on the order and on the responsibility of the commander in chief or the superior civil authority established by the enemy in the occupied territory.

For every contribution, a receipt shall be given to the person furnishing it.

Art. 42. Requisitions shall be made only with the authorization of the commander in the territory occupied.

For every requisition indemnity shall be granted or a receipt delivered.

On parlementaires

Art. 43. A person is regarded as a parlementaire who has been authorized by one of the belligerents to enter into communication with the other, and who advances bearing a white flag, accompanied by a trumpeter (bugler or drummer) or also by a flag-bearer. He shall have a right to inviolability as well as the trumpeter (bugler or drummer) and the flag-bearer who accompany him.

Art. 44. The commander to whom a parlementaire is sent is not in all cases and under all conditions obliged to receive him.

It is lawful for him to take all the necessary steps to prevent the parlementaire taking advantage of his stay within the radius of the enemy's position to the prejudice of the latter, and if the parlementaire has rendered himself guilty of such an abuse of confidence, he has the right to detain him temporarily.

He may likewise declare beforehand that he will not receive parlementaires during a certain period. Parlementaires presenting themselves after such a notification, from the side to which it has been given, forfeit the right of inviolability.

Art. 45. The parlementaire loses his rights of inviolability if it is proved in a clear and incontestable manner that he has taken advantage of his privileged position to provoke or commit an act of treason.

Capitulations

Art. 46. The conditions of capitulations are discussed between the Contracting Parties. They must not be contrary to military honour. Once settled by a convention, they must be scrupulously observed by both parties.

Armistices

Art. 47. An armistice suspends military operations by mutual agreement, between the belligerent parties. If its duration is not defined, the belligerent parties may resume operations at any time, provided always that the enemy is warned within the time agreed upon, in accordance with the terms of the armistice.

Art. 48. The armistice may be general or local. The first suspends the military operations of the belligerent States everywhere; the second only between certain fractions of the belligerent armies and within a fixed radius.

Art. 49. An armistice must be officially and without delay notified to the competent authorities and to the troops. Hostilities are suspended immediately after the notification.

Art. 50. It rests with the Contracting Parties to settle, in the terms of the armistice, what communications may be held between the populations.

Art. 51. The violation of the armistice by one of the parties gives the other party the right of denouncing it.

Art. 52. A violation of the terms of the armistice by individuals acting on their own initiative only entitles the injured party to demand the punishment of the offenders or, if necessary, compensation for the losses sustained.

Interned belligerents and wounded cared for by neutrals

Art. 53. A neutral State which receives on its territory troops belonging to the belligerent armies shall intern them, as far as possible, at a distance from the theatre of war.

It may keep them in camps and even confine them in fortresses or in places set apart for this purpose.

It shall decide whether officers can be left at liberty on giving their parole not to leave the neutral territory without permission.

Art. 54. In the absence of a special convention, the neutral State shall supply the interned with the food, clothing and relief required by humanity.

At the conclusion of peace the expenses caused by the internment shall be made good.

Art. 55. A neutral State may authorize the passage through its territory of the wounded or sick belonging to the belligerent armies, on condition that the trains bringing them shall carry neither personnel nor material of war.

In such a case, the neutral State is bound to take whatever measures of safety and control are necessary for the purpose.

Art. 56. The Geneva Convention applies to sick and wounded interned in neutral territory.

I-3. Convention (II) with Respect to the Laws and Customs of War on Land and its annex: Regulation concerning the Laws and Customs of War on Land. *Signed at the Hague*, 29 July, 1899, 26 MARTENS (ser. 2) 949, 11 Malloy 2042, 1 AM. J. INT'L L. 129-153 (Supp. 1907) (English), I BEVANS 247-262 (English). Authentic Text: French

Relevant Penal Characteristics & Penal Provisions

1. Explicit or implicit recognition of proscribed conduct as constituting an international crime, or a crime under international law, or a crime: Article 25; Article 26

2. Implicit recognition of the penal nature of the act by establishing a duty to prohibit, prevent, prosecute, punish, or the like: Article 23(a),(e)

Applicability
War

Control
Regulation & Prohibition

State Parties
Argentina; Austria-Hungary; Belarus; Belgium; Bolivia; Brazil; Bulgaria; Chile; China; Colombia; Cuba; Denmark; Dominican Republic; Ecuador; El Salvador; Fiji; France; Germany; Greece; Guatemala; Haiti; Honduras; Iran (Islamic Republic); Italy; Japan; Korea; Luxembourg; Mexico; Montenegro; Netherlands; Nicaragua; Norway; Panama; Paraguay; Peru; Portugal; Romania; Russian Federation; South Africa; Spain; Sweden; Switzerland; Thailand; Turkey; United Kingdom; United States of America; Uruguay; Venezuela; Yugoslavia

Relevant Text

Considering that, while seeking means to preserve peace and prevent armed conflicts among nations, it is likewise necessary to have regard to cases where an appeal to arms may be caused by events which their solicitude could not avert;
Animated by the desire to serve, even in this extreme hypothesis, the interests of humanity and the ever increasing requirements of civilization; Thinking it important, with this object, to revise the laws and general customs of war, either with the view of defining them more precisely or of laying down certain limits for the purpose of modifying their severity as far as possible; Inspired by these views which are enjoined at the present day, as they were twenty-five years ago at the time of the Brussels Conference in 1874, by a wise and generous foresight; Have, in this spirit, adopted a great number of provisions, the object of which is to define and govern the usages of war on land. In view of the High Contracting Parties, these provisions, the wording of which has been inspired by the desire to diminish the evils of war so far as military necessities permit, are destined to serve as general rules of conduct for belligerents in their relations with each other and with populations. It has not, however, been possible to agree forthwith on provisions embracing all the circumstances which occur in practice. On the other hand, it could not be intended by the High Contracting Parties that the cases not provided for should, for want of a written provision, be left to the arbitrary judgment of the military commanders. Until a more complete code of the laws of war is issued, the High Contracting Parties think it right to declare that in cases not included in the Regulations adopted by them, populations and belligerents remain under the protection and empire of the principles of international law, as they result from the usages established between civilized nations, from the laws of humanity, and the

requirements of the public conscience;   They declare that it is in this sense especially that Articles 1 and 2 of the Regulations adopted must be understood;   The High Contracting Parties, desiring to conclude a Convention to this effect, have appointed as their Plenipotentiaries, to wit: (Here follow the names of Plenipotentiaries) Who, after communication of their full powers, found in good and due form, have agreed on the following:

Article. 1. The High Contracting Parties shall issue instructions to their armed land forces, which shall be in conformity with the "Regulations respecting the laws and customs of war on land" annexed to the present Convention.

Art. 2. The provisions contained in the Regulations mentioned in Article 1 are only binding on the Contracting Powers, in case of war between two or more of them. These provisions shall cease to be binding from the time when, in a war between Contracting Powers, a non-Contracting Power joins one of the belligerents.

Art. 3. The present Convention shall be ratified as speedily as possible. The ratifications shall be deposited at The Hague.   A ' procès-verbal ' shall be drawn up recording the receipt of each ratification, and a copy, duly certified, shall be sent through the diplomatic channel, to all the Contracting Powers.

Art. 4. Non-Signatory Powers are allowed to adhere to the present Convention. For this purpose they must make their adhesion known to the Contracting Powers by means of a written notification, addressed to the Netherlands Government, and by it communicated to all the other Contracting Powers.

Art. 5. In the event of one of the High Contracting Parties denouncing the present Convention, such denunciation would not take effect until a year after the written notification made to the Netherlands Government, and by it at once communicated to all the other Contracting Powers. This denunciation shall affect only the notifying Power. In faith of which the Plenipotentiaries have signed the present Convention and affixed their seals thereto. Done at The Hague 29 July 1899, in a single copy, which shall be kept in the archives of the Netherlands Government, and copies of which, duly certified, shall be delivered to the Contracting Powers through the diplomatic channel. (Here follow signatures)

ANNEX TO THE CONVENTION REGULATIONS RESPECTING THE LAWS AND CUSTOMS OF WAR ON LAND
SECTION I: ON BELLIGERENTS

CHAPTER I
On the qualifications of belligerents
Article 1. The laws, rights, and duties of war apply not only to armies, but also to militia and volunteer corps fulfilling the following conditions:
   1. To be commanded by a person responsible for his subordinates;
   2. To have a fixed distinctive emblem recognizable at a distance;
   3. To carry arms openly; and
   4. To conduct their operations in accordance with the laws and customs of war.   In countries where militia or volunteer corps constitute the army, or form part of it, they are included under the denomination "army."

Art. 2. The population of a territory which has not been occupied who, on the enemy's approach, spontaneously take up arms to resist the invading troops without having time to organize themselves in accordance with Article 1, shall be regarded as belligerent, if they respect the laws and customs of war.

Art. 3. The armed forces of the belligerent parties may consist of combatants and non-combatants. In case of capture by the enemy both have a right to be treated as prisoners of war.

***

SECTION II: ON HOSTILITIES
CHAPTER I
On means of injuring the enemy, sieges, and bombardments
Art. 22. The right of belligerents to adopt means of injuring the enemy is not unlimited.
Art. 23. Besides the prohibitions provided by special Conventions, it is especially prohibited
 (a) To employ poison or poisoned arms;
 (b) To kill or wound treacherously individuals belonging to the hostile nation or army;
 (c) To kill or wound an enemy who, having laid down arms, or having no longer means of defence, has surrendered at discretion;
 (d) To declare that no quarter will be given;
 (e) To employ arms, projectiles, or material of a nature to cause superfluous injury;
 (f) To make improper use of a flag of truce, the national flag or military ensigns and uniform of the enemy, as well as the distinctive badges of the Geneva Convention;
 (g) To destroy or seize the enemy's property, unless such destruction or seizure be imperatively demanded by the necessities of war.
Art. 24. Ruses of war and the employment of methods necessary to obtain information about the enemy and the country, are considered allowable.
Art. 25. The attack or bombardment of towns, villages, habitations or buildings which are not defended, is prohibited.
Art. 26. The commander of an attacking force, before commencing a bombardment, except in the case of an assault, should do all he can to warn the authorities.
Art. 27. In sieges and bombardments all necessary steps should be taken to spare as far as possible edifices devoted to religion, art, science, and charity, hospitals, and places where the sick and wounded are collected, provided they are not used at the same time for military purposes.   The besieged should indicate these buildings or places by some particular and visible signs, which should previously be notified to the assailants.
Art. 28. The pillage of a town or place, even when taken by assault is prohibited

***

I-4. Declaration Concerning the Prohibition, for the Term of Five Years, of the Launching of Projectiles and Explosives from Balloons or Other New Methods of a Similar Nature [First Hague, IV, 1], *signed at The Hague*, 29 July 1899, 32 Stat. 1839, 26 MARTENS (ser. 2) 994, entered into force 4 September 1900; entered into force with respect to the United States 4 September 1900.[1] Authentic Text: French

Relevant Penal Characteristics & Penal Provisions

1. Explicit or implicit recognition of proscribed conduct as constituting an international crime, or a crime under international law, or a crime: *See* text

Applicability
War & Peace

Control
Regulation & Prohibition

State Signatories
Austria-Hungary; Belgium; Bulgaria; China; Denmark; France; Germany; Greece; Italy; Japan; Luxembourg; Mexico; Montenegro; the Netherlands; Iran (Islamic Republic); Portugal; Romania; Russia; Serbia; Siam; Spain; Sweden-Norway; Switzerland; Turkey; United States of America

State Parties
Austria-Hungary; Belgium; Bulgaria; China;[2] Denmark; France; Germany; Greece; Iran (Islamic Republic); Italy; Japan; Luxembourg; Mexico; Montenegro; the Netherlands; Norway; Portugal; Romania; Russian Federation; Serbia; Siam; Spain; Sweden; Switzerland; Turkey; United States of America

Expired
4 September 1905

Full Text

The undersigned, Plenipotentiaries of the Powers represented at the International Peace Conference at The Hague, duly authorized to that effect by their Governments, inspired by the sentiments which found expression in the Declaration of St. Petersburg of 29 November (11 December) 1868, Declare that: The Contracting Powers agree to prohibit, for a term of five years, the launching of projectiles and explosives from balloons, or by other new methods of a similar nature. The present Declaration is only binding on the Contracting Powers in case of war between two or more of them. It shall cease to be binding from the time when, in a war between the Contracting Powers, one of the belligerents is joined by a non-Contracting Power. The present Declaration shall be ratified as soon as possible. The ratifications shall be deposited at The Hague. A ' procès-verbal ' shall be drawn up on the receipt of each ratification, of which a copy, duly certified, shall be sent through the diplomatic channel, to all the Contracting Powers. The non-Signatory Powers may adhere to the present Declaration. For this purpose they must make their adhesion known to the Contracting Powers by means of a written notification addressed to the Netherlands

---

[1] *See also* 1 AM. J. INT'L L. 153 (1907), 1 BEVANS 270, Malloy 2032, 187 Parry's 456.

[2] Pre-1949 convention, applicable only to Taiwan.

Government, and communicated by it to all the other Contracting Powers. In the event of one of the High Contracting Parties denouncing the present Declaration, such denunciation shall not take effect until a year after the notification made in writing to the Netherlands Government, and by it forthwith communicated to all the other Contracting Powers. This denunciation shall only affect the notifying Power. In faith of which the Plenipotentiaries have signed the present Declaration, and affixed their seais thereto. Done at The Hague, 29 July 1899, in single copy, which shall be kept in the archives of the Netherlands Government, and of which copies, duly certified, shall be sent through the diplomatic channel to the Contracting Powers.

I-5. **Declaration Concerning the Prohibition of the Use of Projectiles Diffusing Asphyxiating Gases [First Hague, IV, 2]**, *signed at The Hague*, 29 July 1899, 26 MARTENS (ser. 2) 998, entered into force 4 September 1900. Authentic Text: French

Relevant Penal Characteristics & Penal Provisions
2. Implicit recognition of the penal nature of the act by establishing a duty to prohibit, prevent, prosecute, punish, or the like: Paragraph 1

Applicability
War

Control
Prohibition

State Signatories
Austria-Hungary; Belgium; Bulgaria; China; Denmark; France; Germany; Greece; Italy; Japan; Luxembourg; Mexico; Montenegro; the Netherlands; Persia; Portugal; Romania; Russia; Serbia; Siam; Spain; Sweden-Norway; Switzerland; Turkey

State Parties
Austria-Hungary; Belgium; Bulgaria; Byelorussian Soviet Socialist Republic; China; Denmark; Ethiopia; Fiji; France; Germany; Great Britain & Ireland; Greece; Iran (Islamic Republic); Italy; Japan; Luxembourg; Mexico; Montenegro; the Netherlands; Nicaragua; Norway; Portugal; Romania; Siam; South Africa; Spain; Sweden; Switzerland; Turkey; Union of Soviet Socialist Republics; Yugoslavia

Full Text
The undersigned, Plenipotentiaries of the Powers represented at the International Peace Conference at The Hague, duly authorized to that effect by their Governments, inspired by the sentiments which found expression in the Declaration of St. Petersburg of 29 November (11 December) 1868, Declare as follows: The Contracting Powers agree to abstain from the use of projectiles the sole object of which is the diffusion of asphyxiating or deleterious gases. The present Declaration is only binding on the Contracting Powers in the case of a war between two or more of them. It shall cease to be binding from the time when, in a war between the Contracting Powers, one of the belligerents shall be joined by a non-Contracting Power. The present Declaration shall be ratified as soon as possible. The ratifications shall be deposited at The Hague. A ' procès-verbal ' shall be drawn up on the receipt of each ratification, a copy of which, duly certified, shall be sent through the diplomatic channel to all the Contracting Powers. The non-Signatory Powers can adhere to the present Declaration. For this purpose they must make their adhesion known to the Contracting Powers by means of a written notification addressed to the Netherlands Government, and by it communicated to all the other Contracting Powers. In the event of one of the High Contracting Parties denouncing the present Declaration, such denunciation shall not take effect until a year after the notification made in writing to the Government of the Netherlands, and forthwith communicated by it to all the other Contracting Powers. This denunciation shall only affect the notifying Power. In faith of which the Plenipotentiaries have signed the present Declaration, and affixed their seals thereto. Done at The Hague, 29 July 1899, in a single copy, which shall be kept in the archives of the Netherlands Government, and copies of which, duly certified, shall be sent by the diplomatic channel to the Contracting Powers.

I-6. Declaration Concerning the Prohibition of the Use of Expanding Bullets [First Hague, IV, 3], *signed at The Hague*, 29 July 1899, 26 MARTENS (ser. 2) 1002, entered into force 4 September 1900. Authentic Text: French

Relevant Penal Characteristics & Penal Provisions
2. Implicit recognition of the penal nature of the act by establishing a duty to prohibit, prevent, prosecute, punish, or the like: Paragraph 1

Applicability
War

Control
Prohibition

State Signatories
Austria-Hungary; Belgium; Bulgaria; China; Denmark; France; Germany; Greece; Italy; Japan; Luxembourg; Mexico; Montenegro; the Netherlands; Persia; Romania; Russia; Serbia; Siam; Spain; Sweden-Norway; Switzerland; Turkey

State Parties
Austria-Hungary; Belgium; Bulgaria; Byelorussian Soviet Socialist Republic; China; Denmark; Ethiopia; Fiji; France; German Democratic Republic; Great Britain & Ireland; Greece; Italy; Japan; Luxembourg; Mexico; Montenegro; the Netherlands; Nicaragua; Norway; Portugal; Romania; Siam; South Africa; Spain; Sweden; Switzerland; Turkey; Union of Soviet Socialist Republics; Yugoslavia

Full Text
The undersigned, Plenipotentiaries of the Powers represented at the International Peace Conference at The Hague, duly authorized to that effect by their Governments, inspired by the sentiments which found expression in the Declaration of St. Petersburg of 29 November (11 December) 1868, Declare as follows: The Contracting Parties agree to abstain from the use of bullets which expand or flatten easily in the human body, such as bullets with a hard envelope which does not entirely cover the core or is pierced with incisions. The present Declaration is only binding for the Contracting Powers in the case of a war between two or more of them. It shall cease to be binding from the time when, in a war between the Contracting Powers, one of the belligerents is joined by a non-Contracting Power. The present Declaration shall be ratified as soon as possible. The ratification shall be deposited at The Hague. A 'procès-verbal' shall be drawn up on the receipt of each ratification, a copy of which, duly certified, shall be sent through the diplomatic channel to all the Contracting Powers. The non-Signatory Powers may adhere to the present Declaration. For this purpose they must make their adhesion known to the Contracting Powers by means of a written notification addressed to the Netherlands Government, and by it communicated to all the other Contracting Powers. In the event of one of the High Contracting Parties denouncing the present Declaration, such denunciation shall not take effect until a year after the notification made in writing to the Netherlands Government, and forthwith communicated by it to all the other Contracting Powers. This denunciation shall only affect the notifying Power. In faith of which the Plenipotentiaries have signed the present Declaration, and have affixed their seals thereto. Done at The Hague, 29 July 1899, in a single copy, which shall be kept in the archives of the Netherlands Government, and copies of which, duly certified, shall be sent through the diplomatic channel to the Contracting Powers.

I-7. Convention (IV) respecting the Laws and Customs of War on Land and its annex: Regulation concerning the Laws and Customs of War on Land, *signed at the* Hague, 18 October 1907, 3 MARTENS (ser. 3) 461-503 (French, German), 2 AM. J. INT'L L. 90-117 (Supp. 1908) (English), 1 BEVANS 631-653 (English), 2 Malloy 2269-2290 (English). Authentic Text: French

Relevant Penal Characteristics & Penal Provisions

1. Explicit or implicit recognition of proscribed conduct as constituting an international crime, or a crime under international law, or a crime: Article 25; & Article 26

2. Implicit recognition of the penal nature of the act by establishing a duty to prohibit, prevent, prosecute, punish, or the like: Article 23 (a), (e)

Applicability
War

Control
Regulation & Prohibition

State Signatories
Argentina; Bulgaria; Chile; Colombia; Ecuador; Greece; Iran (Islamic Republic); Italy; Montenegro; Paraguay; Peru; Serbia; Turkey; Uruguay; Venezuela

State Parties
Austria-Hungary; Belarus; Belgium; Bolivia; Brazil; China; Cuba; Denmark; Dominican Republic; El Salvador; Ethiopia; Fiji; Finland; France; Germany; Guatemala; Haiti; Japan; Liberia; Luxembourg; Mexico; Netherlands; Nicaragua; Norway; Panama; Poland; Portugal; Romania; Russian Federation; South Africa; Sweden; Switzerland; Thailand; United Kingdom; United States of America

Relevant Text

Seeing that while seeking means to preserve peace and prevent armed conflicts between nations, it is likewise necessary to bear in mind the case where the appeal to arms has been brought about by events which their care was unable to avert; Animated by the desire to serve, even in this extreme case, the interests of humanity and the ever progressive needs of civilization; Thinking it important, with this object, to revise the general laws and customs of war, either with a view to defining them with greater precision or to confining them within such limits as would mitigate their severity as far as possible; Have deemed it necessary to complete and explain in certain particulars the work of the First Peace Conference, which, following on the Brussels Conference of 1874, and inspired by the ideas dictated by a wise and generous forethought, adopted provisions intended to define and govern the usages of war on land. According to the views of the High Contracting Parties, these provisions, the wording of which has been inspired by the desire to diminish the evils of war, as far as military requirements permit, are intended to serve as a general rule of conduct for the belligerents in their mutual relations and in their relations with the inhabitants. It has not, however, been found possible at present to concert regulations covering all the circumstances which arise in practice; On the other hand, the High Contracting Parties clearly do not intend that unforeseen cases should, in the absence of a written undertaking, be left to the arbitrary judgment of military commanders. Until a more complete code of the laws of war has been issued, the High Contracting Parties deem it expedient to declare that, in cases not included in the Regulations adopted by them, the inhabitants and the belligerents remain under the protection and the rule of the principles of the law of nations, as they result from the usages established among civilized peoples, from the laws of humanity, and the dictates of the public conscience. They declare that it is in this sense especially that Articles 1 and 2 of the Regulations adopted must be understood. The High Contracting Parties, wishing to conclude a fresh Convention to this effect, have appointed the following as their Plenipotentiaries:

(Here follow the names of Plenipotentiaries)

Who, after having deposited their full powers, found in good and due form, have agreed upon the following:

Article 1. The Contracting Powers shall issue instructions to their armed land forces which shall be in conformity with the Regulations respecting the laws and customs of war on land, annexed to the present Convention.

Art. 2. The provisions contained in the Regulations referred to in Article 1, as well as in the present Convention, do not apply except between Contracting powers, and then only if all the belligerents are parties to the Convention.

Art. 3. A belligerent party which violates the provisions of the said Regulations shall, if the case demands, be liable to pay compensation. It shall be responsible for all acts committed by persons forming part of its armed forces.

Art. 4. The present Convention, duly ratified, shall as between the Contracting Powers, be substituted for the Convention of 29 July 1899, respecting the laws land customs of war on land.

The Convention of 1899 remains in force as between the Powers which signed it, and which do not also ratify the present Convention.

Art. 5. The present Convention shall be ratified as soon as possible.

The ratifications shall be deposited at The Hague.

The first deposit of ratifications shall be recorded in a procès-verbal signed by the Representatives of the Powers which take part therein and by the Netherlands Minister for Foreign Affairs.

The subsequent deposits of ratifications shall be made by means of a written notification, addressed to the Netherlands Government and accompanied by the instrument of ratification.

A duly certified copy of the procès-verbal relative to the first deposit of ratifications, of the notifications mentioned in the preceding paragraph, as well as of the instruments of ratification, shall be immediately sent by the Netherlands Government, through the diplomatic channel, to the powers invited to the Second Peace Conference, as well as to the other Powers which have adhered to the Convention. In the cases contemplated in the preceding paragraph the said Government shall at the same time inform them of the date on which it received the notification.

Art. 6. Non-Signatory Powers may adhere to the present Convention.

The Power which desires to adhere notifies in writing its intention to the Netherlands Government, forwarding to it the act of adhesion, which shall be deposited in the archives of the said Government.

This Government shall at once transmit to all the other Powers a duly certified copy of the notification as well as of the act of adhesion, mentioning the date on which it received the notification.

Art. 7. The present Convention shall come into force, in the case of the Powers which were a party to the first deposit of ratifications, sixty days after the date of the procès-verbal of this deposit, and, in the case of the Powers which ratify subsequently or which adhere, sixty days after the notification of their ratification or of their adhesion has been received by the Netherlands Government.

Art. 8. In the event of one of the Contracting Powers wishing to denounce the present Convention, the denunciation shall be notified in writing to the Netherlands Government, which shall at once communicate a duly certified copy of the notification to all the other Powers, informing them of the date on which it was received.

The denunciation shall only have effect in regard to the notifying Power, land one year after the notification has reached the Netherlands Government.

Art. 9. A register kept by the Netherlands Ministry for Foreign Affairs shall give the date of the deposit of ratifications made in virtue of Article 5, paragraphs 3 land 4, as well as the date on which the notifications of adhesion (Article 6, paragraph 2), or of denunciation (Article 8, paragraph 1) were received.

Each Contracting Power is entitled to have access to this register and to be supplied with duly certified extracts.

In faith whereof the Plenipotentiaries have appended their signatures to the present Convention.

Done at The Hague 18 October 1907, in a single copy, which shall remain deposited in the archives of the Netherlands Government, and duly certified copies of which shall be sent, through the diplomatic channel to the Powers which have been invited to the Second Peace Conference.

ANNEX TO THE CONVENTION
REGULATIONS RESPECTING THE LAWS AND CUSTOMS OF WAR ON LAND
SECTION I
ON BELLIGERENTS
CHAPTER I
The qualifications of belligerents
Article 1. The laws, rights, and duties of war apply not only to armies, but also to militia and volunteer corps fulfilling the following conditions:

1. To be commanded by a person responsible for his subordinates;
2. To have a fixed distinctive emblem recognizable at a distance;
3. To carry arms openly; and
4. To conduct their operations in accordance with the laws and customs of war.

In countries where militia or volunteer corps constitute the army, or form part of it, they are included under the denomination "army."

Art. 2. The inhabitants of a territory which has not been occupied, who, on the approach of the enemy, spontaneously take up arms to resist the invading troops without having had time to organize themselves in accordance with Article 1, shall be regarded as belligerents if they carry arms openly and if they respect the laws and customs of war.

Art. 3. The armed forces of the belligerent parties may consist of combatants and non-combatants. In the case of capture by the enemy, both have a right to be treated as prisoners of war.

***

SECTION II
HOSTILITIES
CHAPTER I
Means of injuring the enemy, sieges, and bombardments

Art. 22. The right of belligerents to adopt means of injuring the enemy is not unlimited.

Art. 23. In addition to the prohibitions provided by special Conventions, it is especially forbidden

(a) To employ poison or poisoned weapons;

(b) To kill or wound treacherously individuals belonging to the hostile nation or army;

(c) To kill or wound an enemy who, having laid down his arms, or having no longer means of defence, has surrendered at discretion;

(d) To declare that no quarter will be given;

(e) To employ arms, projectiles, or material calculated to cause unnecessary suffering;

(f) To make improper use of a flag of truce, of the national flag or of the military insignia and uniform of the enemy, as well as the distinctive badges of the Geneva Convention;

(g) To destroy or seize the enemy's property, unless such destruction or seizure be imperatively demanded by the necessities of war;

(h) To declare abolished, suspended, or inadmissible in a court of law the rights and actions of

the nationals of the hostile party. A belligerent is likewise forbidden to compel the nationals of the

hostile party to take part in the operations of war directed against their own country, even if they were in the belligerent's service before the commencement of the war.

Art. 24. Ruses of war and the employment of measures necessary for obtaining information about the enemy and the country are considered permissible.

Art. 25. The attack or bombardment, by whatever means, of towns, villages, dwellings, or buildings which are undefended is prohibited.

Art. 26. The officer in command of an attacking force must, before commencing a bombardment, except in cases of assault, do all in his power to warn the authorities.

Art. 27. In sieges and bombardments all necessary steps must be taken to spare, as far as possible, buildings dedicated to religion, art, science, or charitable purposes, historic monuments, hospitals, and places where the sick and wounded are collected, provided they are not being used at the time for military purposes.

It is the duty of the besieged to indicate the presence of such buildings or places by distinctive

and visible signs, which shall be notified to the enemy beforehand.

Art. 28. The pillage of a town or place, even when taken by assault, is prohibited.

***

I-8. Convention Respecting the Rights and Duties of Neutral Powers and Powers in Case of War on Land [Second Hague, V], *signed at The Hague,* **18 October 1907, 36 Stat. 2310, 205 Consol. T.S. 299, 24 MARTENS (ser. 3) 504, entered into force 26 January 1910.**[1] Authentic Text: French

Relevant Penal Characteristics & Penal Provisions

2. Implicit recognition of the penal nature of the act by establishing a duty to prohibit, prevent, prosecute, punish, or the like: Article 2 and Article 3

5. Duty or right to punish the proscribed conduct: Article 5

Applicability
War

Control
Regulation & Prohibition

State Signatories
Argentina; Bulgaria; Chile; Colombia; Dominican Republic; Ecuador; Greece; Iran (Islamic Republic); Italy; Montenegro; Paraguay; Peru; Serbia; Turkey; United Kingdom; Uruguay; Venezuela

State Parties
Austria-Hungary; Belarus; Belgium; Bolivia; Brazil; China; Cuba; Denmark; El Salvador; Ethiopia; Finland; France; Germany; Guatemala; Haiti; Japan; Liberia; Luxembourg; Mexico; Netherlands; Nicaragua; Norway; Panama; Poland; Portugal; Romania; Russian Federation; Spain; Sweden; Switzerland; Thailand; United States of America

Reservations upon Signature, Accession or Ratification
Argentina

Full Text
With a view to laying down more clearly the rights and duties of neutral Powers in case of war on land and regulating the position of the belligerents who have taken refuge in neutral territory; Being likewise desirous of defining the meaning of the term "neutral," pending the possibility of settling, in its entirety, the position of neutral individuals in their relations with the belligerents; Have resolved to conclude a Convention to this effect, and have, in consequence, appointed the following as their plenipotentiaries: (Here follow the names of Plenipotentiaries.) Who, after having deposited their full powers, found in good and due form, have agreed upon the following provisions:

CHAPTER I
THE RIGHTS AND DUTIES OF NEUTRAL POWERS
Article 1. The territory of neutral Powers is inviolable.
Art. 2. Belligerents are forbidden to move troops or convoys of either munitions of war or supplies across the territory of a neutral Power.
Art. 3. Belligerents are likewise forbidden to:
(a) Erect on the territory of a neutral Power a wireless telegraphy station or other apparatus for the purpose of communicating with belligerent forces on land or sea;

---

[1] *See also* 205 CTS 299, 2 AM. J. INT'L L. Supp. 117, 1 BEVANS 723, 2 Malloy 2

(b) Use any installation of this kind established by them before the war on the territory of a neutral Power for purely military purposes, and which has not been opened for the service of public messages.   Art. 4. Corps of combatants cannot be formed nor recruiting agencies opened on the territory of a neutral Power to assist the belligerents.

Art. 5. A neutral Power must not allow any of the acts referred to in Articles 2 to 4 to occur on its territory.   It is not called upon to punish acts in violation of its neutrality unless the said acts have been committed on its own territory.

Art. 6. The responsibility of a neutral Power is not engaged by the fact of persons crossing the frontier separately to offer their services to one of the belligerents.

Art. 7. A neutral Power is not called upon to prevent the export or transport, on behalf of one or other of the belligerents, of arms, munitions of war, or, in general, of anything which can be of use to an army or a fleet.

Art. 8. A neutral Power is not called upon to forbid or restrict the use on behalf of the belligerents of telegraph or telephone cables or of wireless telegraphy apparatus belonging to it or to companies or private individuals.

Art. 9. Every measure of restriction or prohibition taken by a neutral Power in regard to the matters referred to in Articles 7 and 8 must be impartially applied by it to both belligerents. A neutral Power must see to the same obligation being observed by companies or private individuals owning telegraph or telephone cables or wireless telegraphy apparatus.

Art. 10. The fact of a neutral Power resisting, even by force, attempts to violate its neutrality cannot be regarded as a hostile act.

CHAPTER II
BELLIGERENTS INTERNED AND WOUNDED TENDED IN NEUTRAL TERRITORY

Art. 11. A neutral Power which receives on its territory troops belonging to the belligerent armies shall intern them, as far as possible, at a distance from the theatre of war.   It may keep them in camps and even confine them in fortresses or in places set apart for this purpose.   It shall decide whether officers can be left at liberty on giving their parole not to leave the neutral territory without permission.

Art. 12. In the absence of a special convention to the contrary, the neutral Power shall supply the interned with the food, clothing, and relief required by humanity.   At the conclusion of peace the expenses caused by the internment shall be made good.

Art. 13. A neutral Power which receives escaped prisoners of war shall leave them at liberty. If it allows them to remain in its territory it may assign them a place of residence. The same rule applies to prisoners of war brought by troops taking refuge in the territory of a neutral Power.

Art. 14. A neutral Power may authorize the passage over its territory of the sick and wounded belonging to the belligerent armies, on condition that the trains bringing them shall carry neither personnel nor war material. In such a case, the neutral Power is bound to take whatever measures of safety and control are necessary for the purpose.   The sick or wounded brought under the these conditions into neutral territory by one of the belligerents, and belonging to the hostile party, must be guarded by the neutral Power so as to ensure their not taking part again in the military operations. The same duty shall devolve on the neutral State with regard to wounded or sick of the other army who may be committed to its care.

Art. 15. The Geneva Convention applies to sick and wounded interned in neutral territory.

CHAPTER III
NEUTRAL PERSONS

Art. 16. The nationals of a State which is not taking part in the war are considered as neutrals.

Art. 17 A neutral cannot avail himself of his neutrality
(a) If he commits hostile acts against a belligerent;
(b) If he commits acts in favor of a belligerent, particularly if he voluntarily enlists in the ranks of the armed force of one of the parties. In such a case, the neutral shall not be more severly treated by the belligerent as against whom he has abandoned his neutrality than a national of the other belligerent State could be for the same act.

Art. 18. The following acts shall not be considered as committed in favour of one belligerent in the sense of Article 17, letter (b):
(a)Supplies furnished or loans made to one of the belligerents, provided that the person who furnishes the supplies or who makes the loans lives neither in the territory of the other party nor in the territory occupied by him, and that the supplies do not come from these territories;
(b) Services rendered in matters of police or civil administration.

CHAPTER IV
RAILWAY MATERIAL

Art. 19. Railway material coming from the territory of neutral Powers, whether it be the property of the said Powers or of companies or private persons, and recognizable as such, shall not be requisitioned or utilized by a belligerent except where and to the extent that it is absolutely necessary. It shall be sent back as soon possible to the country of origin. A neutral Power may likewise, in case of necessity, retain and utilize to an equal extent material coming from the territory of the belligerent Power. Compensation shall be paid by one Party or the other in proportion to the material used, and to the period of usage.

CHAPTER V
FINAL PROVISIONS

Art. 20. The provisions of the present Convention do not apply except between Contracting Powers and then only if all the belligerents are Parties to the Convention.

Art. 21. The present Convention shall be ratified as soon as possible. The ratifications shall be deposited at The Hague. The first deposit of ratifications shall be recorded in a ' procès-verbal ' signed by the representatives of the Powers which take part therein and by the Netherlands Minister for Foreign Affairs. The subsequent deposits of ratifications shall be made by means of a written notification, addressed to the Netherlands Government and accompanied by the instrument of ratification. A duly certified copy of the ' procès-verbal ' relative to the first deposit of ratifications, of the notifications mentioned in the preceding paragraph, and of the instruments of ratification shall be immediately sent by the Netherlands Government, through the diplomatic channel, to the Powers invited to the Second Peace Conference as well as to the other Powers which have adhered to the Convention. In the cases contemplated in the Preceding paragraph, the said Government shall at the same time inform them of the date on which it received the notification.

Art. 22. Non-Signatory Powers may adhere to the present Convention. The Power which desires to adhere notifies its intention in writing to the Netherlands Government, forwarding to it the act of adhesion, which shall be deposited in the archives of the said Government. This Government shall immediately forward to all the other Powers a duly certified copy of the notification as well as of the act of adhesion, mentioning the date on which it received the notification.

Art. 23. The present Convention shall come into force, in the case of the Powers, which were a Party to the first deposit of ratifications, sixty days after the date of the ' procès-verbal ' of this deposit, and, in the case of the Powers which ratify subsequently or which adhere, sixty days after the notification of their ratification or of their adhesion has been received by the Netherlands Government.

Art. 24. In the event of one of the Contracting Powers wishing to denounce the present Convention, the denunciation shall be notified in writing to the Netherlands Government, which shall immediately communicate a duly certified copy of the notification to all the other Powers, informing them at the same time of the date on which it was received. The denunciation shall only have effect in regard to the notifying Power, and one year after the notification has reached the Netherlands Government.

Art. 25. A register kept by the Netherlands Ministry of Foreign Affairs shall give the date of the deposit of ratifications made in virtue of Article 21, paragraphs 3 and 4, as well as the date on which the notifications of adhesion (Article 22, paragraph 2) or of denunciation (Article 24, paragraph I) have been received. Each Contracting Power is entitled to have access to this register and to be supplied with duly certified extracts from it. In faith whereof the Plenipotentiaries have appended their signatures to the present Convention. Done at The Hague, 18 October 1907, in a single copy, which shall remain deposited in the archives of the Netherlands Government and duly certified copies of which shall be sent, through the diplomatic channel, to the Powers which have been invited to the Second Peace Conference.

I-9. Convention (VII) Relating to the Conversion of Merchant Ships into War-Ships, signed at The Hague, 18 October 1907, 2 AM. J. INT'L L. 133 (Supp. 1908); 3 MARTENS (ser. 3) 557-579 (French, German); Authentic Text: French

Relevant Penal Characteristics & Penal Provisions
None

Applicability
War

Control
Regulation & Prohibition

State Signatories
Argentina; Austria-Hungary; Belgium; Bolivia; Brazil; Bulgaria; Chile; Colombia; Cuba; Denmark; Ecuador; El Salvador; France; Germany; Great Britain; Greece; Guatemala; Haiti; Iran (Islamic Republic); Italy; Montenegro; Paraguay; Peru; Portugal; Romania; Russia; Serbia; Siam; Spain; Sweden; Switzerland; Turkey; Venezuela

State Parties
Austria-Hungary; Belarus; Belgium; Brazil; China; Denmark; Ecuador; El Salvador; Ethiopia; Fiji; Finland; France; Germany; Guatemala; Haiti; Japan; Liberia; Luxembourg; Mexico; Netherlands; Nicaragua; Norway; Panama; Poland; Portugal; Romania; Russian Federation; South Africa; Spain; Sweden; Switzerland; Thailand; United Kingdom

Reservations upon Signature, Accession or Ratification
Turkey

Full Text

Whereas it is desirable, in view of the incorporation in time of war of merchant ships in the fighting fleet, to define the conditions subject to which this operation may be effected;

Whereas, however, the Contracting Powers have been unable to come to an agreement on the question whether the conversion of a merchant ship into a war-ship may take place upon the high seas, it is understood that the question of the place where such conversion is effected remains outside the scope of this agreement and is in no way affected by the following rules;

Being desirous of concluding a Convention to this effect, have appointed the following as their
Plenipotentiaries:

(Here follow the names of Plenipotentiaries)

Who, after having deposited their full powers, found in good and due form, have agreed upon the following
provisions:

Article 1. A merchant ship converted into a war-ship cannot have the rights and duties accruing to such vessels unless it is placed under the direct authority, immediate control, and responsibility of the Power whose flag it flies.

Art. 2. Merchant ships converted into war-ships must bear the external marks which distinguish the war-ships of their nationality.

Art. 3. The commander must be in the service of the State and duly commissioned by the competent authorities. His name must figure on the list of the officers of the fighting fleet.

Art. 4. The crew must be subject to military discipline.

Art. 5. Every merchant ship converted into a war-ship must observe in its operations the laws and customs of war.

Art. 6. A belligerent who converts a merchant ship into a war-ship must, as soon as possible, announce
such conversion in the list of war-ships.

Art. 7. The provisions of the present Convention do not apply except between Contracting Powers, and then only if all the belligerents are Parties to the Convention.

Art. 8. The present Convention shall be ratified as soon as possible.

The ratifications shall be deposited at The Hague.

The first deposit of ratifications shall be recorded in a ' procès-verbal ' signed by the representatives of the Powers who take part therein and by the Netherlands Minister for foreign Affairs.

The subsequent deposits of ratifications shall be made by means of a written notification, addressed to the Netherlands Government and accompanied by the instrument of ratification.

A duly certified copy of the ' procès-verbal ' relative to the first deposit of ratifications, of the notifications mentioned in the preceding paragraph, as well as of the instruments of ratification, shall be at once sent by the Netherlands Government, through the diplomatic channel, to the Powers invited to the Second Peace Conference, as well as to the other Powers which have adhered to the Convention. In the cases contemplated in the preceding paragraph the said Government shall at the same time inform them of the date on which it received the notification.

Art. 9. Non-Signatory Powers may adhere to the present Convention.

The Power which desires to adhere notifies its intention in writing to the Netherlands Government, forwarding to it the act of adhesion, which shall be deposited in the archives of the said Government.

That Government shall at once transmit to all the other Powers a duly certified copy of the notification as well as of the act of adhesion, stating the date on which it received the notification.

Art. 10. The present Convention shall come into force, in the case of the Powers which were a party to the first deposit of ratifications, sixty days after the date of the ' procès-verbal ' of this deposit, and, in the case of the Powers which ratify subsequently or which adhere, sixty days after the notification of their ratification or of their adhesion has been received by the Netherlands Government.

Art. 11. In the event of one of the Contracting Powers wishing to denounce the present Convention, the denunciation shall be notified in writing to the Netherlands Government, which shall at once communicate a duly certified copy of the notification to all the other Powers, informing them of the date on which it was received.

The denunciation shall only have effect in regard to the notifying Power, and one year after the notification has reached the Netherlands Government.

Art. 12. A register kept by the Netherlands Ministry for foreign Affairs shall give the date of the deposit of ratifications made in virtue of Article 8, paragraphs 3 and 4, as well as the date on which the notifications of adhesion (Article 9, paragraph 2) or of denunciation (Article 11, paragraph 1) have been received.

Each Contracting Power is entitled to have access to this register and to be supplied with duly certified extracts from it.

In faith whereof the Plenipotentiaries have appended their signatures to the present Convention.

Done at The Hague, 18 October 1907, in a single copy, which shall remain deposited in the archives of the Netherlands Government, and duly certified copies of which shall be sent, through the diplomatic channel, to the Powers which have been invited to the Second Peace Conference.

I-10. Convention Relative to the Laying of Automatic Submarine Contact Mines [Second Hague, VIII], *signed at The Hague,* **18 October 1907, 36 Stat. 2332, 3** MARTENS **(ser. 3) 580, entered into force 26 January 1910; entered into force with respect to the United States 26 January 1910.**[1] Authentic Text: French

Relevant Penal Characteristics & Penal Provisions

2. Implicit recognition of the penal nature of the act by establishing a duty to prohibit, prevent, prosecute, punish, or the like: Articles 1, 2, 5 (requires "notification of position of mines")

Applicability
War & Peace

Control
Regulation & Prohibition

State Signatories
Argentina; Austria-Hungary; Belgium; Bolivia; Brazil; Bulgaria; Chile; Colombia; Cuba; Denmark; Dominican Republic; Ecuador; El Salvador; France; Germany; Great Britain; Greece; Guatemala; Haiti; Iran (Islamic Republic); Italy; Japan; Luxembourg; Mexico; the Netherlands; Norway; Panama; Paraguay; Peru; Romania; Serbia; Siam; Switzerland; Turkey; United States of America; Uruguay; Venezuela

State Parties
Australia; Austria-Hungary; Belgium; Brazil; Canada; China;[2] Denmark; El Salvador; Ethiopia; Fiji; Finland; France; Germany; Guatemala; Haiti; India; Ireland; Japan; Laos; Liberia; Luxembourg; Mexico; the Netherlands; New Zealand; Nicaragua; Norway; Pakistan; Panama; the Philippines; Romania; South Africa; Sri Lanka; Switzerland; Thailand; United Kingdom; United States of America

Reservations upon Signature, Accession or Ratification
Australia; Canada; Dominican Republic; France; Germany; Great Britain; India; Ireland; Laos; New Zealand; Pakistan; Siam; South Africa; Sri Lanka; Thailand; Turkey; United Kingdom

Full Text
Inspired by the principle of the freedom of sea routes, the common highway of all nations;
Seeing that, although the existing position of affairs makes it impossible to forbid the employment of automatic submarine contact mines, it is nevertheless desirable to restrict and regulate their employment in order to mitigate the severity of war and to ensure, as far as possible, to peaceful navigation the security to which it is entitled, despite the existence of war;

---

[1] *See also* 2 AM. J. INT'L L. 138 (1908), 1 BEVANS 669, Malloy 2304, 205 Parry's 331.

[2] Pre-1949 convention, applicable only to Taiwan.

Until such time as it is found possible to formulate rules on the subject which shall ensure to the interests involved all the guarantees desirable; Have resolved to conclude a Convention for this purpose, and have appointed the following as their Plenipotentiaries: (Here follow the names of Plenipotentiaries) Who, after having deposited their full powers, found in good and due form, have agreed upon the following provisions:

Article 1. It is forbidden --

1. To lay unanchored automatic contact mines, except when they are so constructed as to become harmless one hour at most after the person who laid them ceases to control them;

2. To lay anchored automatic contact mines which do not become harmless as soon as they
have broken loose from their moorings;

3. To use torpedoes which do not become harmless when they have missed their mark.

Art. 2. It is forbidden to lay automatic contact mines off the coast and ports of the enemy, with the sole object of intercepting commercial shipping.

Art. 3. When anchored automatic contact mines are employed, every possible precaution must be taken for the security of peaceful shipping.

The belligerents undertake to do their utmost to render these mines harmless within a limited time, and, should they cease to be under surveillance, to notify the danger zones as soon as military exigencies permit, by a notice addressed to ship owners, which must also be communicated to the Governments through the diplomatic channel.

Art. 4. Neutral Powers which lay automatic contact mines off their coasts must observe the same rules and take the same precautions as are imposed on belligerents.

The neutral Power must inform ship owners, by a notice issued in advance, where automatic contact mines have been laid. This notice must be communicated at once to the Governments through the diplomatic channel.

Art. 5. At the close of the war, the Contracting Powers undertake to do their utmost to remove the mines which they have laid, each Power removing its own mines.

As regards anchored automatic contact mines laid by one of the belligerents off the coast of the other, their position must be notified to the other party by the Power which laid them, and each Power must proceed with the least possible delay to remove the mines in its own waters.

Art. 6. The Contracting Powers which do not at present own perfected mines of the pattern contemplated in the present Convention, and which, consequently, could not at present carry out the rules laid down in Articles 1 and 3, undertake to convert the ' matériel ' of their mines as soon as possible, so as to bring it into conformity with the foregoing requirements.

Art. 7. The provisions of the present Convention do not apply except between Contracting Powers, and then only if all the belligerents are parties to the Convention.

Art. 8. The present Convention shall be ratified as soon as possible.

The ratifications shall be deposited at The Hague.

The first deposit of ratifications shall be recorded in a ' procès-verbal ' signed by the representatives of the Powers which take part therein and by the Netherlands Minister for Foreign Affairs.

The subsequent deposits of ratifications shall be made by means of a written notification addressed to the Netherlands Government and accompanied by the instrument of ratification.

A duly certified copy of the ' procès-verbal ' relative to the first deposit of ratifications, of the notifications mentioned in the preceding paragraph, as well as of the instruments of ratification, shall be at once sent, by the Netherlands Government, through the diplomatic channel, to the Powers invited to the Second Peace Conference, as well as to the other Powers which have adhered to the Convention. In the cases contemplated in the preceding paragraph, the said Government shall inform them at the same time of the date on which it has received the notification.

Art. 9. Non-Signatory Powers may adhere to the present Convention.

The Power which desires to adhere notifies in writing its intention to the Netherlands Government, transmitting to it the act of adhesion, which shall be deposited in the archives of the said Government.

This Government shall at once transmit to all the other Powers a duly certified copy of the notification as well as of the act of adhesion, stating the date on which it received the notification.

Art. 10. The present Convention shall come into force, in the case of the Powers which were a party to the first deposit of ratifications, sixty days after the date of the ' procès-verbal ' of this deposit, and, in the case of the Powers which ratify subsequently or adhere, sixty days after the notification of their ratification or of their adhesion has been received by the Netherlands Government.

Art. 11. The present Convention shall remain in force for seven years, dating from the sixtieth day after the date of the first deposit of ratifications.

Unless denounced, it shall continue in force after the expiration of this period.

The denunciation shall be notified in writing to the Netherlands Government, which shall at once communicate a duly certified copy of the notification to all the Powers, informing them of the date on which it was received.

The denunciation shall only have effect in regard to the notifying Power, and six months after the notification has reached the Netherlands Government.

Art. 12. The Contracting Powers undertake to reopen the question of the employment of automatic contact mines six months before the expiration of the period contemplated in the first paragraph of the preceding article, in the event of the question not having been already reopened and settled by the Third Peace Conference.

If the Contracting Powers conclude a fresh Convention relative to the employment of mines, the present Convention shall cease to be applicable from the moment it comes into force.

Art. 13. A register kept by the Netherlands Ministry for foreign Affairs shall give the date of the deposit of ratifications made in virtue of Article 8, paragraphs 3 and 4, as well as the date on which the notifications of adhesion (Article 9, paragraph 2) or of denunciation (Article 11, paragraph 3) have been received.

Each Contracting Power is entitled to have access to this register and to be supplied with duly certified extracts from it.

In faith whereof the Plenipotentiaries have appended their signatures to the present Convention.

Done at The Hague, 18 October 1907, in a single copy, which shall remain deposited in the archives of the Netherlands Government, and duly certified copies of which shall be sent, through the diplomatic channel, to the Powers which have been invited to the Second Peace Conference.

I-11. Convention Concerning Bombardments by Naval Forces in Time of War, [Second Hague, IX], *signed at the Hague*, **18 October 1907, 36 Stat. 2351, U.S.T.S. 542, 3 Martens (ser. 3) 604, entered into force 26 January 1910.**[1] Authentic Text: French

Relevant Penal Characteristics and Penal Provisions
1. Explicit or implicit recognition of proscribed conduct as constituting an international crime, or a crime under international law, or a crime: Article 1

Applicability
War

Control
Prohibition

State Signatories
Argentina; Bulgaria; Chile; Colombia; Dominican Republic; Ecuador; Greece; Iran (Islamic Republic); Italy; Montenegro; Paraguay; Peru; Serbia; Turkey; Uruguay; Venezuela

State Parties
Austria-Hungary; Belarus; Belgium; Bolivia; Brazil; China; Cuba; Denmark; El Salvador; Ethiopia; Fiji; Finland; France; Germany; Guatemala; Haiti; Japan; Liberia; Luxembourg; Mexico; Netherlands; Nicaragua; Norway; Panama; Poland; Portugal; Romania; Russian Federation; South Africa; Spain; Sweden; Switzerland; Thailand; United Kingdom; United States of America

Full Text
Animated by the desire to realize the wish expressed by the first Peace Conference respecting the bombardment by naval forces of undefended ports, towns, and villages; Whereas it is expedient that bombardments by naval forces should be subject to rules of general application which would safeguard the rights of the inhabitants and assure the preservation of the more important buildings, by applying as far as Possible to this operation of war the principles of the Regulation of 1899 respecting the laws and customs of land war; Actuated, accordingly, by the desire to serve the interests of humanity and to diminish the severity and disasters of war; Have resolved to conclude a Convention to this effect, and have, for this purpose, appointed the following as their Plenipotentiaries: (Here follow the names of Plenipotentiaries) Who, after depositing their full powers, found in good and due form, have agreed upon the following provisions:

CHAPTER I
THE BOMBARDMENT OF UNDEFENDED PORTS, TOWNS, VILLAGES, DWELLINGS, OR BUILDINGS

Article 1. The bombardment by naval forces of undefended ports, towns, villages, dwellings, or buildings is forbidden. A place cannot be bombarded solely because automatic submarine contact mines are anchored off the harbour.

Article 2. Military works, military or naval establishments, depots of arms or war ' matériel, ' workshops or plant which could be utilized for the needs of the hostile fleet or army, and the ships of war in the harbour, are not, however, included in this prohibition. The commander of a naval force may destroy them with artillery, after a summons followed by a reasonable time of waiting, if all other means are impossible, and when the local authorities have not themselves destroyed them within the time fixed. He incurs no responsibility for any unavoidable damage which may be caused by a bombardment under such circumstances. If for military reasons immediate action is necessary, and no delay can be allowed the enemy, it is understood that the prohibition to bombard the undefended town holds good, as in the case given in paragraph l, and that the commander shall take all due measures in order that the town may suffer as little harm as possible.

Art. 3. After due notice has been given, the bombardment of undefended ports, towns, villages, dwellings, or buildings may be commenced, if the local authorities, after a formal summons has been made to them, decline to comply with requisitions for provisions or supplies necessary for the immediate use of the naval force before the place in question.

These requisitions shall be in proportion to the resources of the place. They shall only be demanded in the name of the commander of the said naval force, and they shall, as far as possible, be paid for in cash; if not, they shall be evidenced by receipts.

Art. 4. Undefended ports, towns, villages, dwellings, or buildings may not be bombarded on account of failure to pay money contributions.

CHAPTER II
GENERAL PROVISIONS

Art. 5. In bombardments by naval forces all the necessary measures must be taken by the commander to spare as far as possible sacred edifices, buildings used for artistic, scientific, or charitable purposes, historic monuments, hospitals, and places where the sick or wounded are collected, on the understanding that they are not used at the same time for military purposes.

It is the duty of the inhabitants to indicate such monuments, edifices, or places by visible signs, which shall consist of large, stiff rectangular panels divided diagonally into two coloured triangular portions, the upper portion black, the lower portion white.

Art. 6. If the military situation permits, the commander of the attacking naval force, before commencing the bombardment, must do his utmost to warn the authorities.

Art. 7. A town or place, even when taken by storm, may not be pillaged.

CHAPTER III
FINAL PROVISIONS

Art. 8. The provisions of the present Convention do not apply except between Contracting Powers, and then only if all the belligerents are parties to the Convention.

Art. 9. The present Convention shall be ratified as soon as possible. The ratifications shall be deposited at The Hague. The first deposit of ratifications shall be recorded in a ' procès-verbal ' signed by the representatives of the Powers which take part therein and by the Netherlands Minister of foreign Affairs. The subsequent deposits of ratifications shall be made by means of a written notification addressed to the Netherlands Government and accompanied by the instrument of ratification. A duly certified copy of the ' procès-verbal ' relative to the first deposit of ratifications, of the notifications mentioned in the preceding paragraph, as well as of the instruments of ratification, shall be at once sent by the Netherlands Government, through the diplomatic channel, to the Powers invited to the Second Peace Conference, as well as to the other Powers which have adhered to the Convention. In the cases contemplated in the preceding paragraph, the said Government shall inform them at the same time of the date on which it received the notification.

Art. 10. Non-Signatory Powers may adhere to the present Convention. The Power which desires to adhere shall notify its intention to the Netherlands Government, forwarding to it the act of adhesion, which shall be deposited in the archives of the said Government. This Government shall immediately forward to all the other Powers a duly certified copy of the notification, as well as of the act of adhesion, mentioning the date on which it received the notification.

Art. 11. The present Convention shall come into force, in the case of the Powers which were a party to the first deposit of ratifications, sixty days after the date of the ' procès-verbal ' of that deposit, and, in the case of the Powers which ratify subsequently or which adhere, sixty days after the notification of their ratification or of their adhesion has been received by the Netherlands Government.

Art. 12. In the event of one of the Contracting Powers wishing to denounce the present Convention, the denunciation shall be notified in writing to the Netherlands Government, which shall at once communicate a duly certified copy of the notification to all the other Powers informing them of the date on which it was received. The denunciation shall only have effect in regard to the notifying Power, and one year after the notification has reached the Netherlands Government.

Art. 13. A register kept by the Netherlands Minister for foreign Affairs shall give the date of the deposit of ratifications made in virtue of Article 9, paragraphs 3 and 4, as well as the date on which the notifications of adhesion (Article 10, paragraph 2) or of denunciation (Article 12, paragraph I) have been received.

Each Contracting Power is entitled to have access to this register and to be supplied with duly certified extracts from it.

In faith whereof the Plenipotentiaries have appended their signatures to the present Convention.

Done at The Hague, 18 October 1907, in a single copy, which shall remain deposited in the archives of the Netherlands Government, and duly certified copies of which shall be sent, through the diplomatic channel, to the Powers which have been invited to the Second Peace Conference.

I-12. **Convention (X) for the Adaptation to Maritime Warfare of the Principles of the Geneva Convention,** *signed at The Hague,* **18 October 1907,** 3 MARTENS (ser. 3) 630-662 (French, German), 2 Malloy 2326-2340 (English); 1 BEVANS 694-710 (English), 2 AM. J. INT'L L. 153-167 (Supp. 1908) (English, French). Authentic Text: French

Relevant Penal Characteristics & Penal Provisions
2. Implicit recognition of the penal nature of the act by establishing a duty to prohibit, prevent, prosecute, punish, or the like: Article 1; Article 4; Article 7

Applicability
War

Control
Regulation & Prohibition

State Signatories
Argentina; Austria-Hungary; Belgium; Bolivia; Brazil; Bulgaria; Chile; China; Colombia; Cuba; Denmark; Dominican Republic; Ecuador; El Salvador; France; Germany; Greece; Guatemala; Haiti; Italy; Japan; Luxembourg; Mexico; Iran (Islamic Republic); Montenegro; Netherlands; Norway; Panama; Paraguay; Peru; Portugal; Romania; Russia; Serbia; Siam; Spain; Sweden; Switzerland; Turkey; United States of America; United Kingdom; Uruguay; Venezuela

State Parties
Australia; Austria-Hungary; Belarus; Belgium; Bolivia; Brazil; Brazil; Canada; China; Cuba; Denmark; El Salvador; Ethiopia; Finland; France; Germany; Guatemala; Haiti; Hungary; India; Ireland; Japan; Laos; Liberia; Italy; Japan; Latvia; Luxembourg; Mexico; Netherlands; New Zealand; Nicaragua; Norway; Pakistan; Panama; Philippines; Poland; Portugal; Romania; South Africa; Russian Federation; Spain; Sri Lanka; Sweden; Switzerland; Thailand; United Kingdom; United States of America

Reservations upon Signature, Accession or Ratification
Australia; Canada; Chile; China; France; Germany; Great Britain; India; Ireland; Japan; Laos; New Zealand; Pakistan; South Africa; Sri Lanka; United Kingdom

Full Text
Animated alike by the desire to diminish, as far as depends on them, the inevitable evils of war; And wishing with this object to adapt to maritime warfare the principles of the Geneva Convention of 6 July 1906. Have resolved to conclude a Convention for the purpose of revising the Convention of 29 July 1899, relative to this question, and have appointed the following as their Plenipotentiaries: (Here follow the names of Plenipotentiaries) Who, after having deposited their full powers, found in good and due form, have agreed upon the following provisions:
Article 1. Military hospital ships, that is to say, ships constructed or assigned by States specially and solely with a view to assisting the wounded, sick and shipwrecked, the names of which have been communicated to the belligerent Powers at the commencement or during the course of hostilities, and in any case before they are employed, shall be respected, and cannot be captured while hostilities last. These ships, moreover, are not on the same footing as war-ships as regards their stay in a neutral port. Art. 2. Hospital ships, equipped wholly or in part at the expense of private individuals or officially recognized relief

societies, shall likewise be respected and exempt from capture, if the belligerent Power to whom they belong has given them an official commission and has notified their names to the hostile Power at the commencement of or during hostilities, and in any case before they are employed. These ships must be provided with a certificate from the competent authorities declaring that the vessels have been under their control while fitting out and on final departure.

Art. 3. Hospital ships, equipped wholly or in part at the expense of private individuals or officially recognized societies of neutral countries shall be respected and exempt from capture, on condition that they are placed under the control of one of the belligerents, with the previous consent of their own Government and with the authorization of the belligerent himself, and that the latter has notified their names to his adversary at the commencement of or during hostilities, and in any case, before they are employed.

Art. 4. The ships mentioned in Articles 1, 2, and 3 shall afford relief and assistance to the wounded, sick, and shipwrecked of the belligerents without distinction of nationality. The Governments undertake not to use these ships for any military purpose. These vessels must in no wise hamper the movements of the combatants. During and after an engagement they will act at their own risk and peril. The belligerents shall have the right to control and search them; they can refuse to help them, order them off, make them take a certain course, and put a commissioner on board; they can even detain them, if important circumstances require it. As far as possible, the belligerents shall enter in the log of the hospital ships the orders which they give them.

Art. 5. Military hospital ships shall be distinguished by being painted white outside with a horizontal band of green about a metre and a half in breadth. The ships mentioned in Articles 2 and 3 shall be distinguished by being painted white outside with a horizontal band of red about a metre and a half in breadth. The boats of the ships above mentioned, as also small craft which may be used for hospital work, shall be distinguished by similar painting. All hospital ships shall make themselves known by hoisting, with their national flag, the white flag with a red cross provided by the Geneva Convention, and further, if they belong to a neutral State, by flying at the mainmast the national flag of the belligerent under whose control they are placed. Hospital ships which, in the terms of Article 4, are detained by the enemy must haul down the national flag of the belligerent to whom they belong. The ships and boats above mentioned which wish to ensure by night the freedom from interference to which they are entitled, must, subject to the assent of the belligerent they are accompanying, take the necessary measures to render their special painting sufficiently plain.

Art. 6. The distinguishing signs referred to in Article 5 can only be used, whether in time of peace or war, for protecting or indicating the ships therein mentioned.

Art. 7. In the case of a fight on board a war-ship, the sick wards shall be respected and spared as far as possible. The said sick wards and the material belonging to them remain subject to the laws of war; they cannot, however, be used for any purpose other than that for which they were originally intended, so long is they are required for the sick and wounded. The commander, however, into whose power they have fallen may apply them to other purposes, if the military situation requires it, after seeing that the sick and wounded on board are properly provided for.

Art. 8. Hospital ships and sick wards of vessels are no longer entitled to protection if they are employed for the purpose of injuring the enemy. The fact of the staff of the said ships and sick wards bring armed for maintaining order and for defending the sick and wounded, and the presence of wireless telegraphy apparatus on board, is not a sufficient reason for withdrawing protection.

Art. 9. Belligerents may appeal to the charity of the commanders of neutral merchant ships, yachts, or boats to take on board and tend the sick and wounded.

Vessels responding to the appeal, and also vessels which have of their own accord rescued sick, wounded, or ship-wrecked men, shall enjoy special protection and certain immunities. In no case can they be captured for having such persons on board, but, apart from special undertakings that have been made to them, they remain liable to capture for any violations of neutrality they may have committed.

Art. 10. The religious, medical, and hospital staff of any captured ship is inviolable, and its members cannot be made prisoners of war. On leaving the ship they take away with them the objects and surgical instruments which are their own private property.

This staff shall continue to discharge its duties while necessary, and can afterwards leave, when the commander-in-chief considers it possible.

The belligerents must guarantee to the said staff, when it has fallen into their hands, the same allowances and pay which are given to the staff of corresponding rank in their own navy.

Art. 11. Sailors and soldiers on board, when sick or wounded, as well as other persons officially attached to fleets or armies, whatever their nationality, shall be respected and tended by the captors.

Art. 12. Any war-ship belonging to a belligerent may demand that sick, wounded, or shipwrecked men on board military hospital ships, hospital ships belonging to relief societies or to private individuals, merchant ships, yachts, or boats, whatever the nationality of these vessels, should be handed over.

Art. 13. If sick, wounded, or shipwrecked persons are taken on board a neutral warship, every possible precaution must be taken that they do not again take part in the operations of the war.

Art. 14. The shipwrecked, wounded, or sick of one of the belligerents who fall into the power of the other belligerent are prisoners of war. The captor must decide, according to circumstances, whether to keep them, send them to a port of his own country, to a neutral port, or even to an enemy port. In this last case, prisoners thus repatriated cannot serve again while the war lasts.

Art. 15. The shipwrecked, sick, or wounded, who are landed at a neutral port with the consent of the local authorities, must, unless an arrangement is made to the contrary between the neutral State and the belligerent States, be guarded by the neutral State, so as to prevent them again taking part in the operations of the war.

The expenses of tending them in hospital and interning them shall be borne by the State to which the shipwrecked, sick, or wounded persons belong.

Art. 16. After every engagement, the two belligerents, so far as military interests permit, shall take steps to look for the shipwrecked, sick, and wounded, and to protect them, as well as the dead, against pillage and ill-treatment.

They shall see that the burial, whether by land or sea, or cremation of the dead shall be preceded
by a careful examination of the corpse.

Art. 17. Each belligerent shall send, as early as possible, to the authorities of their country, navy, or army the military marks or documents of identity found on the dead and the description of the sick and wounded picked up by him.

The belligerents shall keep each other informed as to internments and transfers as well as to the admissions into hospital and deaths which have occurred among the sick and wounded in their hands. They shall collect all the objects of personal use, valuables, letters, etc., which are found in the captured ships, or which have been left by the sick or wounded who died in hospital, in order to have them forwarded to the persons concerned by the authorities of their own country.

Art. 18. The provisions of the present Convention do not apply except between Contracting Powers, and then only if all the belligerents are parties to the Convention.

Art. 19. The commanders-in-chief of the belligerent fleets must see that the above articles are properly carried out; they will have also to see to cases not covered thereby, in accordance with the instructions of their respective Governments and in conformity with the general principles of the present Convention.

Art. 20. The signatory Powers shall take the necessary measures for bringing the provisions of the present Convention to the knowledge of their naval forces, and especially of the members entitled thereunder to immunity, and for making them known to the public.

Art. 21. The Signatory Powers likewise undertake to enact or to propose to their legislatures, if their criminal laws are inadequate, the measures necessary for checking in time of war individual acts of pillage and ill-treatment in respect to the sick and wounded in the fleet, as well as for punishing, as an unjustifiable adoption of naval or military marks, the unauthorized use of the distinctive marks mentioned in Article 5 by vessels not protected by the present Convention.

They will communicate to each other, through the Netherlands Government, the enactments for preventing such acts at the latest within five years of the ratification of the present Convention.

Art. 22. In the case of operations of war between the land and sea forces of belligerents, the provisions of the present Convention do not apply except between the forces actually on board ship.

Art. 23. The present Convention shall be ratified as soon as possible.

The ratifications shall be deposited at The Hague.

The first deposit of ratifications shall be recorded in a ' procès-verbal ' signed by the representatives of the Powers taking part therein and by the Netherlands Minister for Foreign Affairs.

Subsequent deposits of ratifications shall be made by means of a written notification addressed to the Netherlands Government and accompanied by the instrument of ratification.

A certified copy of the ' procès-verbal ' relative to the first deposit of ratifications, of the notifications mentioned in the preceding paragraph, as well as of the instruments of ratification, shall be at once sent by the Netherlands Government through the diplomatic channel to the Powers invited to the Second Peace Conference, as well as to the other Powers which have adhered to the Convention. In the cases contemplated in the preceding paragraph the said Government shall inform them at the same time of the date on which it received the notification.

Art. 24. Non-signatory Powers which have accepted the Geneva Convention of 6 July 1906 may adhere to the present Convention.

The Power which desires to adhere notifies its intention to the Netherlands Government in writing, forwarding to it the act of adhesion, which shall be deposited in the archives of the said Government.

The said Government shall at once transmit to all the other Powers a duly certified copy of the notification as well as of the act of adhesion, mentioning the date on which it received the notification.

Art. 25. The present Convention, duly ratified, shall replace as between Contracting Powers, the Convention of 29 July 1899, for the adaptation to maritime warfare of the principles of the Geneva Convention.

The Convention of 1899 remains in force as between the Powers which signed it but which do not also ratify the present Convention.

Art. 26. The present Convention shall come into force, in the case of the Powers which were a party to the first deposit of ratifications, sixty days after the date of the ' procès-verbal ' of this deposit, and, in the case of the Powers which ratify subsequently or which adhere, sixty days after the notification of their ratification or of their adhesion has been received by the Netherlands Government.

Art. 27. In the event of one of the Contracting Powers wishing to denounce the present Convention, the denunciation shall be notified in writing to the Netherlands Government, which shall at once communicate a duly certified copy of the notification to all the other Powers, informing them at the same time of the date on which it was received.

The denunciation shall only have effect in regard to the notifying Power, and one year after the notification has reached the Netherlands Government.

Art. 28. A register kept by the Netherlands Ministry for Foreign Affairs shall give the date of the deposit of ratifications made in virtue of Article 23, paragraphs 3 and 4, as well as the date on which the notifications of adhesion (Article 24, paragraph 2) or of denunciation (Article 27, paragraph 1) have been received.

Each Contracting Power is entitled to have access to this register and to be supplied with duly certified extracts from it.

In faith whereof the Plenipotentiaries have appended their signatures to the Convention.

Done at The Hague, 18 October 1907, in a single copy, which shall remain deposited in the archives of the Netherlands Government, and duly certified copies of which shall be sent, through the diplomatic channel, to the Powers which have been invited to the Second Peace Conference.

International Humanitarian Law and Arms Control Agreements

I-13. **Convention Concerning the Rights and Duties of Neutral Powers in Naval War Second Hague, XIII],** *signed at The Hague,* **18 October 1907, 36 Stat. 2415, 205 Consol. T.S. 395, 3 Martens (ser. 3) 713 entered into force 26 January 1910.**[1] Authentic Text: French

Relevant Penal Characteristics & Penal Provisions

2. Implicit recognition of the penal nature of the act by establishing a duty to prohibit, prevent, prosecute, punish, or the like: Articles 2, 5, and 6

State Signatories

Argentina; Bolivia; Bulgaria; Chile; Colombia; Dominican Republic; Ecuador; Greece; Iran (Islamic Republic); Italy; Montenegro; Paraguay; Peru; Serbia; Turkey; United Kingdom; Uruguay; Venezuela

State Parties

Austria-Hungary; Belarus; Belgium; Brazil; China; Denmark; El Salvador; Ethiopia; Finland; France; Germany; Guatemala; Haiti; Hungary; Japan; Laos; Liberia; Luxembourg; Mexico; Netherlands; Nicaragua; Norway; Panama; the Philippines; Portugal; Romania; Russian Federation; Sweden; Switzerland; Thailand; United States of America

Reservations upon Signature, Accession or Ratification

China; Dominican Republic; Germany; Great Britain; Japan; Persia; the Philippines; Siam; Turkey; United States of America

Full Text

With a view to harmonizing the divergent views which, in the event of naval war, are still held on the relations between neutral Powers and belligerent Powers, and to anticipating the difficulties to which such divergence of views might give rise;

Seeing that, even if it is not possible at present to concert measures applicable to all circumstances which may in practice occur, it is nevertheless undeniably advantageous to frame, as far as possible, rules of general application to meet the case where war has unfortunately broken out;

Seeing that, in cases not covered by the present Convention, it is expedient to take into consideration the general principles of the law of nations;

Seeing that it is desirable that the Powers should issue detailed enactments to regulate the results of the attitude of neutrality when adopted by them;

Seeing that it is, for neutral Powers, an admitted duty to apply these rules impartially to several belligerents;

Seeing that, in this category of ideas, these rules should not, in principle, be altered in the course of the war, by a neutral Power, except in a case where experience has shown the necessity for such change for the protection of the rights of that Power;

Have agreed to observe the following common rules, which cannot however modify provisions laid down in existing general treaties, and have appointed as their Plenipotentiaries, namely:

(Here follow the names of Plenipotentiaries)

Who, after having deposited their full powers, found in good and due form, have agreed upon the following
provisions:

---

[1] *See also* 2 Am. J. Int'l L. 202 (1908), 1 Bevans 723, Malloy 2352, 205 Parry's 395.

Article 1. Belligerents are bound to respect the sovereign rights of neutral Powers and to abstain,
in neutral territory or neutral waters, from any act which would, if knowingly permitted by any
Power, constitute a violation of neutrality.

Art. 2. Any act of hostility, including capture and the exercise of the right of search, committed by belligerent war-ships in the territorial waters of a neutral Power, constitutes a violation of neutrality and is strictly forbidden.

Art. 3. When a ship has been captured in the territorial waters of a neutral Power, this Power
must employ, if the prize is still within its jurisdiction, the means at its disposal to release the prize
with its officers and crew, and to intern the prize crew.

If the prize is not in the jurisdiction of the neutral Power, the captor Government, on the demand of that Power, must liberate the prize with its officers and crew.

Art. 4. A prize court cannot be set up by a belligerent on neutral territory or on a vessel in neutral waters.

Art. 5. Belligerents are forbidden to use neutral ports and waters as a base of naval operations against their adversaries, and in particular to erect wireless telegraphy stations or any apparatus for the purpose of communicating with the belligerent forces on land or sea.

Art. 6. The supply, in any manner, directly or indirectly, by a neutral Power to a belligerent Power, of war-ships, ammunition, or war material of any kind whatever, is forbidden.

Art. 7. A neutral Power is not bound to prevent the export or transit, for the use of either belligerent, of arms, ammunition, or, in general, of anything which could be of use to an army or fleet.

Art. 8. A neutral Government is bound to employ the means at its disposal to prevent the fitting out or arming of any vessel within its jurisdiction which it has reason to believe is intended to cruise, or engage in hostile operations, against a Power with which that Government is at peace. It is also bound to display the same vigilance to prevent the departure from its jurisdiction of any vessel intended to cruise, or engage in hostile operations, which had been adapted entirely or partly within the said jurisdiction for use in war.

Art. 9. A neutral Power must apply impartially to the two belligerents the conditions, restrictions, or prohibitions made by it in regard to the admission into its ports, roadsteads, or territorial waters, of belligerent war-ships or of their prizes.

Nevertheless, a neutral Power may forbid a belligerent vessel which has failed to conform to the orders and regulations made by it, or which has violated neutrality, to enter its ports or roadsteads.

Art. 10. The neutrality of a Power is not affected by the mere passage through its territorial waters of war-ships or prizes belonging to belligerents.

Art. 11. A neutral Power may allow belligerent war-ships to employ its licensed pilots.

Art. 12. In the absence of special provisions to the contrary in the legislation of a neutral Power, belligerent war-ships are not permitted to remain in the ports, roadsteads, or territorial waters of the said Power for more than twenty-four hours, except in the cases covered by the present Convention.

Art. 13. If a Power which has been informed of the outbreak of hostilities learns that a belligerent war-ship is in one of its ports or roadsteads, or in its territorial waters, it must notify the said ship to depart within twenty-four hours or within the time prescribed by local regulations.

Art. 14. A belligerent war-ship may not prolong its stay in a neutral port beyond the permissible time except on account of damage or stress of weather. It must depart as soon as the cause of the delay is at an end.

The regulations as to the question of the length of time which these vessels may remain in neutral ports, roadsteads, or waters, do not apply to war-ships devoted exclusively to religious, scientific, or philanthropic purposes.

Art. 15. In the absence of special provisions to the contrary in the legislation of a neutral Power, the maximum number of warships belonging to a belligerent which may be in one of the ports or roadsteads of that Power simultaneously shall be three.

Art. 16. When war-ships belonging to both belligerents are present simultaneously in a neutral port or roadstead, a period of not less than twenty-four hours must elapse between the departure of the ship belonging to one belligerent and the departure of the ship belonging to the other.

The order of departure is determined by the order of arrival, unless the ship which arrived first is so circumstanced that an extension of its stay is permissible.

A belligerent war-ship may not leave a neutral port or roadstead until twenty-four hours after the departure of a merchant ship flying the flag of its adversary.

Art. 17. In neutral ports and roadsteads belligerent war-ships may only carry out such repairs as are absolutely necessary to render them seaworthy, and may not add in any manner whatsoever to their fighting force. The local authorities of the neutral Power shall decide what repairs are necessary, and these must be carried out with the least possible delay.

Art. 18. Belligerent war-ships may not make use of neutral ports, roadsteads, or territorial waters
for replenishing or increasing their supplies of war material or their armament, or for completing
their crews.

Art. 19. Belligerent war-ships may only revictual in neutral ports or roadsteads to bring up their supplies to the peace standard.

Similarly these vessels may only ship sufficient fuel to enable them to reach the nearest port in their own country. They may, on the other hand, fill up their bunkers built to carry fuel, when in neutral countries which have adopted this method of determining the amount of fuel to be supplied.

If, in accordance with the law of the neutral Power, the ships are not supplied with coal within twenty-four hours of their arrival, the permissible duration of their stay is extended by twenty-four hours.

Art. 20. Belligerent war-ships which have shipped fuel in a port belonging to a neutral Power may not within the succeeding three months replenish their supply in a port of the same Power.

Art. 21. A prize may only be brought into a neutral port on account of unseaworthiness, stress of weather, or want of fuel or provisions.

It must leave as soon as the circumstances which justified its entry are at an end. If it does not, the neutral Power must order it to leave at once; should it fail to obey, the neutral Power must employ the means at its disposal to release it with its officers and crew and to intern the prize crew.

Art. 22. A neutral Power must, similarly, release a prize brought into one of its ports under circumstances other than those referred to in Article 21.

Art. 23. A neutral Power may allow prizes to enter its ports and roadsteads, whether under convoy or not, when they are brought there to be sequestrated pending the decision of a Prize Court. It may have the prize taken to another of its ports.

If the prize is convoyed by a war-ship, the prize crew may go on board the convoying ship.

If the prize is not under convoy, the prize crew are left at liberty.

Art. 24. If, notwithstanding the notification of the neutral Power, a belligerent ship of war does not leave a port where it is not entitled to remain, the neutral Power is entitled to take such measures as it considers necessary to render the ship incapable of taking the sea during the war, and the commanding officer of the ship must facilitate the execution of such measures.

When a belligerent ship is detained by a neutral Power, the officers and crew are likewise detained.

The officers and crew thus detained may be left in the ship or kept either on another vessel or on land, and may be subjected to the measures of restriction which it may appear necessary to impose upon them. A sufficient number of men for looking after the vessel must, however, be always left on board.

The officers may be left at liberty on giving their word not to quit the neutral territory without permission.

Art. 25. A neutral Power is bound to exercise such surveillance as the means at its disposal allow to prevent any violation of the provisions of the above Articles occurring in its ports or roadsteads or in its waters.

Art. 26. The exercise by a neutral Power of the rights laid down in the present Convention can under no circumstances be considered as an unfriendly act by one or other belligerent who has accepted the articles relating thereto.

Art. 27. The Contracting Powers shall communicate to each other in due course all laws, proclamations, and other enactments regulating in their respective countries the status of belligerent war-ships in their ports and waters, by means of a communication addressed to the Government of the Netherlands, and forwarded immediately by that Government to the other Contracting Powers.

Art. 28. The provisions of the present Convention do not apply except between Contracting Powers, and then only if all the belligerents are parties to the Convention.

Art. 29. The present Convention shall be ratified as soon as possible.

The ratifications shall be deposited at The Hague.

The first deposit of ratifications shall be recorded in a ' procès-verbal ' signed by the representatives of the Powers which take part therein and by the Netherlands Minister for Foreign Affairs.

The subsequent deposits of ratifications shall be made by means of a written notification addressed to the Netherlands Government and accompanied by the instrument of ratification.

A duly certified copy of the ' procès-verbal ' relative to the first deposit of ratifications, of the ratifications mentioned in the preceding paragraph, as well as of the instruments of ratification, shall be at once sent by the Netherlands Government, through the diplomatic channel, to the Powers invited to the Second Peace Conference, as well as to the other Powers which have adhered to the Convention. In the cases contemplated in the preceding paragraph, the said Government shall inform them at the same time of the date on which it received the notification.

Art. 30. Non-Signatory Powers may adhere to the present Convention.

The Power which desires to adhere notifies in writing its intention to the Netherlands Government, forwarding to it the act of adhesion, which shall be deposited in the archives of the said Government.

That Government shall at once transmit to all the other Powers a duly certified copy of the notification as well as of the act of adhesion, mentioning the date on which it received the notification.

Art. 31. The present Convention shall come into force in the case of the Powers which were a party to the first deposit of the ratifications, sixty days after the date of the ' procès-verbal ' of that deposit, and, in the case of the Powers who ratify subsequently or who adhere, sixty days after the notification of their ratification or of their decision has been received by the Netherlands Government.

Art. 32. In the event of one of the Contracting Powers wishing to denounce the present Convention, the denunciation shall be notified in writing to the Netherlands Government, who shall at once communicate a duly certified copy of the notification to all the other Powers, informing them of the date on which it was received.

The denunciation shall only have effect in regard to the notifying Power, and one year after the notification has been made to the Netherlands Government.

Art. 33. A register kept by the Netherlands Ministry for Foreign Affairs shall give the date of the deposit of ratifications made by Article 29, paragraphs 3 and 4, as well as the date on which the notifications of adhesion (Article 30, paragraph 2) or of denunciation (Article 32, paragraph I) have been received.

Each Contracting Power is entitled to have access to this register and to be supplied with duly certified extracts.

In faith whereof the Plenipotentiaries have appended their signatures to the present Convention.

Done at The Hague, 18 October 1907, in a single copy, which shall remain deposited in the archives of the Netherlands Government, and duly certified copies of which shall be sent, through the diplomatic channel, to the Powers which have been invited to the Second Peace Conference.

I-14. **Declaration Relative to Prohibiting the Discharge of Projectiles and Explosives from Balloons, [Second Hague, XIV]**, *signed at The Hague, 18 October 1907, 36 Stat. 2439, 3 MARTENS (ser. 3) 745, entered into force 27 November 1909; entered into force with respect to the United States 27 November 1909.*[1] Authentic Text: French

Relevant Penal Characteristics & Penal Provisions

2. Implicit recognition of the penal nature of the act by establishing a duty to prohibit, prevent, prosecute, punish, or the like: Paragraph 1

Applicability
Peace

Control
Regulation & Prohibition

State Signatories
Argentina; Austria-Hungary; Belgium; Bolivia; Brazil;[1] Bulgaria; China; Colombia; Cuba; Dominican Republic; Ecuador; El Salvador; Great Britain; Greece; Haiti; Iran (Islamic Republic); Luxembourg; the Netherlands; Norway; Panama; Peru; Portugal; Siam; Switzerland; Turkey; United States of America; Uruguay

State Parties
Australia; Belgium; Bolivia; Brazil; Canada; China;[2] El Salvador; Ethiopia; Fiji; Finland; Haiti; India; Iceland; Liberia; Luxembourg; the Netherlands; New Zealand; Nicaragua; Norway; Pakistan; Panama; the Philippines; Portugal; South Africa; Sri Lanka; Switzerland; Thailand; United Kingdom; United States of America

Full Text
The undersigned, Plenipotentiaries of the Powers invited to the Second International Peace Conference at The Hague, duly authorized to that effect by their Governments, inspired by the sentiments which found expression in the Declaration of St. Petersburg of 29 November (11 December) 1868, and being desirous of renewing the declaration of The Hague of 29 July 1899, which has now expired, Declare: The Contracting Powers agree to prohibit, for a period extending to the close of the Third Peace Conference, the discharge of projectiles and explosives from balloons or by other new methods of a similar nature. The present Declaration is only binding on the Contracting Powers in case of war between two or more of them. It shall cease to be binding from the time when, in a war between the Contracting Powers, one of the belligerents is joined by a non-Contracting Power. The present Declaration shall be ratified as soon as possible. The ratifications shall be deposited at The Hague. A 'procès-verbal' shall be drawn up recording the receipt of the ratifications, of which a duly certified copy shall be sent, through the diplomatic channel, to all the Contracting Powers. Non-Signatory Powers may adhere to the present Declaration. To do so, they must make known their adhesion to the Contracting Powers by means of a written notification, addressed to the Netherlands Government, and communicated by it to all the other Contracting Powers.

---

[1] *See also* 2 AM. J. INT'L L. 216 (1908), 1 BEVANS 739; Malloy 2366; 205 Parry's 403.

[2] Pre-1949 convention, applicable only to Taiwan.

In the event of one of the High Contracting Parties denouncing the present Declaration, such denunciation shall not take effect until a year after the notification made in writing to the Netherlands Government, and forthwith communicated by it to all the other Contracting Powers.

This denunciation shall only have effect in regard to the notifying Power.

In faith whereof the Plenipotentiaries have appended their signatures to the present Declaration.

Done at The Hague, 18 October 1907 in a single copy, which shall remain deposited in the archives of the Netherlands Government, and duly certified copies of which shall be sent through the diplomatic channel, to the Contracting Powers.

I-15. **Declaration Concerning the Laws of Naval War**, *signed at The London Naval Conference, assembled at the Foreign Office,* **26 February, 1909,** ***British Blue Book,*** **Misc. No. 4 (1909), Cd. 4554; 3 Am. J. Int'l L. 179-220 (1909) (English, French).** Authentic Text: French

Relevant Penal Characteristics & Penal Provisions
None

State Signatories
Austria-Hungary; France; Germany; Italy; Japan; Netherlands; Russian Federation; Spain; United Kingdom; United States of America

Applicability
War

Control
Regulation

Full Text

Having regard to the terms in which the British Government invited various Powers to meet in conference in order to arrive at an agreement as to what are the generally recognized rules of international law within the meaning of Article 7 of the Convention of 18 October 1907, relative to the establishment of an International Prize Court; Recognizing all the advantages which an agreement as to the said rules would, in the unfortunate event of a naval war, present, both as regards peaceful commerce, and as regards the belligerents and their diplomatic relations with neutral Governments; Having regard to the divergence often found in the methods by which it is sought to apply in practice the general principles of international law; Animated by the desire to ensure henceforward a greater measure of uniformity in this respect; Hoping that a work so important to the common welfare will meet with general approval; Have appointed as their Plenipotentiaries, that is to say: (Here follow the names of Plenipotentiaries) Who, after having communicated their full powers, found to be in good and due form, have agreed to make the present Declaration: PRELIMINARY PROVISION The Signatory Powers are agreed that the rules contained in the following Chapters correspond in substance with the generally recognized principles of international law.

CHAPTER I BLOCKADE IN TIME OF WAR

Article 1. A blockade must not extend beyond the ports and coasts belonging to or occupied by the enemy.

Art. 2. In accordance with the Declaration of Paris of 1856, a blockade, in order to be binding, must be effective -- that is to say, it must be maintained by a force sufficient really to prevent access to the enemy coastline.

Art. 3. The question whether a blockade is effective is a question of fact.

Art. 4. A blockade is not regarded as raised if the blockading force is temporarily withdrawn on account of stress of weather.

Art. 5. A blockade must be applied impartially to the ships of all nations.

Art. 6. The commander of a blockading force may give permission to a warship to enter, and subsequently to leave, a blockaded port.

Art. 7. In circumstances of distress, acknowledged by an officer of the blockading force, a neutral vessel may enter a place under blockade and subsequently leave it, provided that she has neither discharged nor shipped any cargo there.

Art. 8. A blockade, in order to be binding, must be declared in accordance with Article 9, and notified in accordance with Articles 11 and 16.

Art. 9. A declaration of blockade is made either by the blockading Power or by the naval authorities acting in its name.

It specifies --

(1) The date when the blockade begins;

(2) the geographical limits of the coastline under blockade;

(3) the period within which neutral vessels may come out.

Art 10. If the operations of the blockading Power, or of the naval authorities acting in its name, do not tally with the particulars, which, in accordance with Article 9(1) and (2), must be inserted in the declaration of blockade, the declaration is void, and a new declaration is necessary in order to make the blockade operative.

Art. 11. A declaration of blockade is notified

(1) To neutral Powers, by the blockading Power, by means of a communication addressed to the Governments direct, or to their representatives accredited to it;

(2) To the local authorities, by the officer commanding the blockading force. The local authorities will, in turn, inform the foreign consular officers at the port or on the coastline under blockade as soon as possible.

Art. 12. The rules as to declaration and notification of blockade apply to cases where the limits of a blockade are extended, or where a blockade is re-established after having been raised.

Art. 13. The voluntary raising of a blockade, as also any restriction in the limits of a blockade, must be notified in the manner prescribed by Article 11.

Art. 14. The liability of a neutral vessel to capture for breach of blockade is contingent on her knowledge, actual or presumptive, of the blockade.

Art. 15. Failing proof to the contrary, knowledge of the blockade is presumed if the vessel left a neutral port subsequently to the notification of the blockade to the Power to which such port belongs, provided that such notification was made in sufficient time.

Art. 16. If a vessel approaching a blockaded port has no knowledge, actual or presumptive, of the blockade, the notification must be made to the vessel itself by an officer of one of the ships of the blockading force. This notification should be entered in the vessel's logbook, and must state the day and hour, and the geographical position of the vessel at the time.

If through the negligence of the officer commanding the blockading force no declaration of blockade has been notified to the local authorities, or, if in the declaration, as notified, no period has been mentioned within which neutral vessels may come out, a neutral vessel coming out of the blockaded port must be allowed to pass free.

Art. 17. Neutral vessels may not be captured for breach of blockade except within the area of operations of the warships detailed to render the blockade effective.

Art. 18. The blockading forces must not bar access to neutral ports or coasts.

Art. 19. Whatever may be the ulterior destination of a vessel or of her cargo, she cannot be captured for breach of blockade, if, at the moment, she is on her way to a non-blockaded port.

Art. 20. A vessel which has broken blockade outwards, or which has attempted to break blockade inwards, is liable to capture so long as she is pursued by a ship of the blockading force. If the pursuit is abandoned, or if the blockade is raised, her capture can no longer be effected.

Art. 21. A vessel found guilty of breach of blockade is liable to condemnation. The cargo is also condemned, unless it is proved that at the time of the shipment of the goods the shipper neither knew nor could have known of the intention to break the blockade.

CHAPTER II
CONTRABAND OF WAR

Art. 22. The following articles may, without notice (1), be treated as contraband of war, under the
name of absolute contraband:

(1) Arms of all kinds, including arms for sporting purposes, and their distinctive component parts.
(2) Projectiles, charges, and cartridges of all kinds, and their distinctive component parts.
(3) Powder and explosives specially prepared for use in war.
(4) Gun-mountings, limber boxes, limbers, military waggons, field forges, and their distinctive component parts.
(5) Clothing and equipment of a distinctively military character.
(6) All kinds of harness of a distinctively military character.
(7) Saddle, draught, and pack animals suitable for use in war.
(8) Articles of camp equipment, and their distinctive component parts.
(9) Armour plates.
(10) Warships, including boats, and their distinctive component parts of such a nature that they can only be used on a vessel of war.
(11) Implements and apparatus designed exclusively for the manufacture of munitions of war, for the manufacture or repair of arms, or war material for use on land or sea.

(1) In view of the difficulty of finding an exact equivalent in English for the expression "de plein droit", it has been decided to translate it by the words "without notice," which represent the meaning attached to it by the draftsman as appears from the General Report see p. 44 (note in the original).

Art. 23. Articles exclusively used for war may be added to the list of absolute contraband by a declaration, which must be notified.

Such notification must be addressed to the Governments of other Powers, or to their representatives accredited to the Power making the declaration. A notification made after the outbreak of hostilities is addressed only to neutral Powers.

Art. 24. The following articles, susceptible of use in war as well as for purposes of peace, may, without notice (1), be treated as contraband of war, under the name of conditional contraband:

(1) Foodstuffs.
(2) Forage and grain, suitable for feeding animals.
(3) Clothing, fabrics for clothing, and boots and shoes, suitable for use in war.
(4) Gold and silver in coin or bullion; paper money.
(5) Vehicles of all kinds available for use in war, and their component parts.
(6) Vessels, craft, and boats of all kinds; floating docks, parts of docks and their component parts.
(7) Railway material, both fixed and rolling-stock, and material for telegraphs, wireless telegraphs, and telephones.
(8) Balloons and flying machines and their distinctive component parts, together with accessories and articles recognizable as intended for use in connection with balloons and flying machines.
(9) Fuel; lubricants.
(10) Powder and explosives not specially prepared for use in war.
(11) Barbed wire and implements for fixing and cutting the same.
(12) Horseshoes and shoeing materials.
(13) Harness and saddlery.
(14) Field glasses, telescopes, chronometers, and all kinds of nautical instruments.

(1) See note relative to Article 22.

Art. 25. Articles susceptive of use in war as well as for purposes of peace, other than those enumerated in Articles 22 and 24, may be added to the list of conditional contraband by a declaration, which must be notified in the manner provided for in the second paragraph of Article 23.

Art. 26. If a Power waives, so far as it is concerned, the right to treat as contraband of war an article comprised in any of the classes enumerated in Articles 22 and 24, such intention shall be announced by a declaration, which must be notified in the manner provided for in the second paragraph of Article 23.

Art. 27. Articles which are not susceptible of use in war may not be declared contraband of war.

Art. 28. The following may not be declared contraband of war:

(1) Raw cotton, wool, silk, jute, flax, hemp, and other raw materials of the textile industries, and yarns of the same.

(2) Oil seeds and nuts; copra.

(3) Rubber, resins, gums, and lacs; hops.

(4) Raw hides and horns, bones, and ivory.

(5) Natural and artificial manures, including nitrates and phosphates for agricultural purposes.

(6) Metallic ores.

(7) Earths, clays, lime, chalk, stone, including marble, bricks, slates, and tiles.

(8) Chinaware and glass.

(9) Paper and paper-making materials.

(10) Soap, paint and colours, including articles exclusively used in their manufacture, and varnish.

(11) Bleaching powder, soda ash, caustic soda, salt cake, ammonia, sulphate of ammonia, and sulphate of copper.

(12) Agricultural, mining, textile, and printing machinery.

(13) Precious and semi-precious stones, pearls, mother-of-pearl, and coral.

(14) Clocks and watches, other than chronometers.

(15) Fashion and fancy goods.

(16) Feathers of all kinds, hairs, and bristles.

(17) Articles of household furniture and decoration; office furniture and requisites.

Art. 29. Likewise the following may not be treated as contraband of war:

(1) Articles serving exclusively to aid the sick and wounded. They can, however, in case of urgent military necessity and subject to the payment of compensation, be requisitioned, if their destination is that specified in Article 30.

(2) Articles intended for the use of the vessel in which they are found, as well as those intended for the use of her crew and passengers during the voyage.

Art. 30. Absolute contraband is liable to capture if it is shown to be destined to territory belonging to or occupied by the enemy, or to the armed forces of the enemy. It is immaterial whether the carriage of the goods is direct or entails transhipment or a subsequent transport by land.

Art. 31. Proof of the destination specified in Article 30 is complete in the following cases:

(1) When the goods are documented for discharge in an enemy port, or for delivery to the armed forces of the enemy.

(2) When the vessel is to call at enemy ports only, or when she is to touch at a enemy port or meet the armed forces of the enemy before reaching the neutral port for which the goods in question are documented.

Art. 32. Where a vessel is carrying absolute contraband, her papers are conclusive proof as to the voyage on which she is engaged, unless she is found clearly out of the course indicated by her papers, and unable to give adequate reasons to justify such deviation.

Art. 33. Conditional contraband is liable to capture if it is shown to be destined for the use of the armed forces or of a government department of the enemy State, unless in this latter case the circumstances show that the goods cannot in fact be used for the purposes of the war in progress. This latter exception does not apply to a consignment coming under Article 24 (4).

Art. 34. The destination referred to in Article 33 is presumed to exist if the goods are consigned to enemy authorities, or to a contractor established in the enemy country who, as a matter of common knowledge, supplies articles of this kind to the enemy. A similar presumption arises if the goods are consigned to a fortified place belonging to the enemy, or other place serving as a base for the armed forces of the enemy. No such presumption, however, arises in the case of a merchant vessel bound for one of these places if it is sought to prove that she herself is contraband.

In cases where the above presumptions do not arise, the destination is presumed to be innocent.

The presumptions set up by this Article may be rebutted.

Art. 35. Conditional contraband is not liable to capture, except when found on board a vessel bound for territory belonging to or occupied by the enemy, or for the armed forces of the enemy, and when it is not to be discharged in an intervening neutral port.

The ship's papers are conclusive proof both as to the voyage on which the vessel is engaged and as to the port of discharge of the goods, unless she is found clearly out of the course indicated by her papers, and unable to give adequate reasons to justify such deviation.

Art. 36. Notwithstanding the provisions of Article 35, conditional contraband, if shown to have the destination referred to in Article 33, is liable to capture in cases where the enemy country has no seaboard.

Art. 37. A vessel carrying goods liable to capture as absolute or conditional contraband may be captured on the high seas or in the territorial waters of the belligerents throughout the whole of her voyage, even if she is to touch at a port of call before reaching the hostile destination.

Art. 38. A vessel may not be captured on the ground that she has carried contraband on a previous occasion if such carriage is in point of fact at an end.

Art. 39. Contraband goods are liable to condemnation.

Art. 40. A vessel carrying contraband may be condemned if the contraband, reckoned either by value, weight, volume, or freight, forms more than half the cargo.

Art. 41. If a vessel carrying contraband is released, she may be condemned to pay the costs and expenses incurred by the captor in respect of the proceedings in the national prize court and the custody of the ship and cargo during the proceedings.

Art. 42. Goods which belong to the owner of the contraband and are on board the same vessel are liable to condemnation.

Art. 43. If a vessel is encountered at sea while unaware of the outbreak of hostilities or of the declaration of contraband which applies to her cargo, the contraband cannot be condemned except on payment of compensation; the vessel herself and the remainder of the cargo are not liable to condemnation or to the costs and expenses referred to in Article 41. The same rule applies if the master, after becoming aware of the outbreak of hostilities, or of the declaration of contraband, has had no opportunity of discharging the contraband.

A vessel is deemed to be aware of the existence of a state of war, or of a declaration of contraband, if she left a neutral port subsequently to the notification to the Power to which such port belongs of the outbreak of hostilities or of the declaration of contraband respectively, provided that such notification was made in sufficient time. A vessel is also deemed to be aware of the existence of a state of war if she left an enemy port after the outbreak of hostilities.

Art. 44. A vessel which has been stopped on the ground that she is carrying contraband, and which is not liable to condemnation on account of the proportion of contraband on board, may, when the circumstances permit, be allowed to continue her voyage if the master is willing to hand over the contraband to the belligerent warship.

The delivery of the contraband must be entered by the captor on the logbook of the vessel stopped, and the master must give the captor duly certified copies of all relevant papers.

The captor is at liberty to destroy the contraband that has been handed over to him under these conditions.

CHAPTER III
UNNEUTRAL SERVICE

Art. 45. A neutral vessel will be condemned and will, in a general way, receive the same treatment as a neutral vessel liable to condemnation for carriage of contraband:

(1) If she is on a voyage especially undertaken with a view to the transport of individual passengers who are embodied in the armed forces of the enemy, or with a view to the transmission of intelligence in the interest of the enemy.

(2) If, to the knowledge of either the owner, the charterer, or the master, she is transporting a military detachment of the enemy, or one or more persons who, in the course of the voyage, directly assist the operations of the enemy.

In the cases specified under the above heads, goods belonging to the owner of the vessel are likewise liable to condemnation. The provisions of the present Article do not apply if the vessel is encountered at sea while unaware of the outbreak of hostilities, or if the master, after becoming aware of the outbreak of hostilities, has had no opportunity of disembarking the passengers. The vessel is deemed to be aware of the existence of a state of war if she left an enemy port subsequently to the outbreak of hostilities, or a neutral port subsequently to the notification of the outbreak of hostilities to the Power to which such port belongs, provided that such notification was made in sufficient time.

Art. 46. A neutral vessel will be condemned and, in a general way, receive the same treatment as would be applicable to her if she were an enemy merchant vessel:

(1) if she takes a direct part in the hostilities;

(2) if she is under the orders or control of an agent placed on board by the enemy Government;

(3) if she is in the exclusive employment of the enemy Government;

(4) if she is exclusively engaged at the time either in the transport of enemy troops or in the transmission of intelligence in the interest of the enemy.

In the cases covered by the present Article, goods belonging to the owner of the vessel are likewise liable to condemnation.

Art. 47. Any individual embodied in the armed forces of the enemy who is found on board a neutral merchant vessel, may be made a prisoner of war, even though there be no ground for the capture of the vessel.

CHAPTER IV
DESTRUCTION OF NEUTRAL PRIZES

Art. 48. A neutral vessel which has been captured may not be destroyed by the captor; she must be taken into such port as is proper for the determination there of all questions concerning the validity of the capture.

Art. 49. As an exception, a neutral vessel which has been captured by a belligerent warship, and which would be liable to condemnation, may be destroyed if the observance of Article 48 would involve danger to the safety of the warship or to the success of the operations in which she is engaged at the time.

Art. 50. Before the vessel is destroyed all persons on board must be placed in safety, and all the ship's papers and other documents which the parties interested consider relevant for the purpose of deciding on the validity of the capture must be taken on board the warship.

Art. 51. A captor who has destroyed a neutral vessel must, prior to any decision respecting the validity of the prize, establish that he only acted in the face of an exceptional necessity of the nature contemplated in Article 49. If he fails to do this, he must compensate the parties interested and no examination shall be made of the question whether the capture was valid or not.

Art. 52. If the capture of a neutral vessel is subsequently held to be invalid, though the act of destruction has been held to have been justifiable, the captor must pay compensation to the parties interested, in place of the restitution to which they would have been entitled.

Art. 53. If neutral goods not liable to condemnation have been destroyed with the vessel, the owner of such goods is entitled to compensation.

Art. 54. The captor has the right to demand the handing over, or to proceed himself to the destruction of, any goods liable to condemnation found on board a vessel not herself liable to condemnation, provided that the circumstances are such as would, under Article 49, justify the destruction of a vessel herself liable to condemnation. The captor must enter the goods surrendered or destroyed in the logbook of the vessel stopped, and must obtain duly certified copies of all relevant papers. When the goods have been handed over or destroyed, and the formalities duly carried out, the master must be allowed to continue his voyage.

The provisions of Articles 51 and 52 respecting the obligations of a captor who has destroyed a neutral vessel are applicable.

CHAPTER V
TRANSFER TO A NEUTRAL FLAG

Art. 55. The transfer of an enemy vessel to a neutral flag, effected before the outbreak of hostilities, is valid, unless it is proved that such transfer was made in order to evade the consequences to which an enemy vessel, as such, is exposed. There is, however, a presumption, if the bill of sale is not on board a vessel which has lost her belligerent nationality less than sixty days before the outbreak of hostilities, that the transfer is void. This presumption may be rebutted.

Where the transfer was effected more than thirty days before the outbreak of hostilities, there is an absolute presumption that it is valid if it is unconditional, complete, and in conformity with the laws of the countries concerned, and if its effect is such that neither the control of, nor the profits arising from the employment of the vessel remain in the same hands as before the transfer. If, however, the vessel lost her belligerent nationality less than sixty days before the outbreak of hostilities and if the bill of sale is not on board, the capture of the vessel gives no right to damages.

Art. 56. The transfer of an enemy vessel to a neutral flag, effected after the outbreak of hostilities, is void unless it is proved that such transfer was not made in order to evade the consequences to which an enemy vessel, as such, is exposed.

There, however, is an absolute presumption that a transfer is void --

(1) If the transfer has been made during a voyage or in a blockaded port.
(2) If a right to repurchase or recover the vessel is reserved to the vendor.
(3) If the requirements of the municipal law governing the right to fly the flag under which the vessel is sailing, have not been fulfilled.

CHAPTER VI
ENEMY CHARACTER

Art. 57. Subject to the provisions respecting transfer to another flag, the neutral or enemy character of a vessel is determined by the flag which she is entitled to fly.

The case where a neutral vessel is engaged in a trade which is closed in time of peace, remains outside the scope of, and is in no wise affected by, this rule.

Art. 58. The neutral or enemy character of goods found on board an enemy vessel is determined by the neutral or enemy character of the owner.

Art. 59. In the absence of proof of the neutral character of goods found on board an enemy vessel, they are presumed to be enemy goods.

Art. 60. Enemy goods on board an enemy vessel retain their enemy character until they reach their destination, notwithstanding any transfer effected after the outbreak of hostilities while the goods are being forwarded.

If, however, prior to the capture, a former neutral owner exercises, on the bankruptcy of an existing enemy owner, a recognized legal right to recover the goods, they regain their neutral character.

CHAPTER VII
CONVOY

Art. 61. Neutral vessels under national convoy are exempt from search. The commander of a convoy gives, in writing, at the request of the commander of a belligerent warship, all information as to the character of the vessels and their cargoes, which could be obtained by search.

Art. 62. If the commander of the belligerent warship has reason to suspect that the confidence of the commander of the convoy has been abused, he communicates his suspicions to him. In such a case it is for the commander of the convoy alone to investigate the matter. He must record the result of such investigation in a report, of which a copy is handed to the officer of the warship. If, in the opinion of the commander of the convoy, the facts shown in the report justify the capture of one or more vessels, the protection of the convoy must be withdrawn from such vessels.

CHAPTER VIII
RESISTANCE TO SEARCH

Art. 63. Forcible resistance to the legitimate exercise of the right of stoppage, search, and capture, involves in all cases the condemnation of the vessel. The cargo is liable to the same treatment as the cargo of an enemy vessel. Goods belonging to the master or owner of the vessel are treated as enemy goods.

CHAPTER IX
COMPENSATION

Art. 64. If the capture of a vessel or of goods is not upheld by the prize court, or if the prize is released without any judgement being given, the parties interested have the right to compensation, unless there were good reasons for capturing the vessel or goods.

FINAL PROVISIONS

Art. 65. The provisions of the present Declaration must be treated as a whole, and cannot be separated.

Art. 66. The Signatory Powers undertake to insure the mutual observance of the rules contained in the present Declaration in any war in which all the belligerents are parties thereto. They will therefore issue the necessary instructions to their authorities and to their armed forces, and will take such measures as may be required in order to insure that it will be applied by their courts, and more particularly by their prize courts.

Art. 67. The present Declaration shall be ratified as soon as possible.

The ratifications shall be deposited in London.

The first deposit of ratifications shall be recorded in a Protocol signed by the representatives of the Powers taking part therein, and by His Britannic Majesty's Principal Secretary of State for Foreign Affairs.

The subsequent deposits of ratifications shall be made by means of a written notification addressed to the British Government, and accompanied by the instrument of ratification.

A duly certified copy of the Protocol relating to the first deposit of ratifications and of the notifications mentioned in the preceding paragraph as well as of the instruments of ratification which accompany them, shall be immediately sent by the British Government, through the diplomatic channel, to the Signatory Powers. The said Government shall, in the cases contemplated in the preceding paragraph, inform them at the same time of the date on which it received the notification.

Art. 68. The present Declaration shall take effect, in the case of the Powers which were parties to the first deposit of ratifications, sixty days after the date of the Protocol recording such deposit, and, in the case of the Powers which shall ratify subsequently, sixty days after the notification of their ratification shall have been received by the British Government.

Art 69. In the event of one of the Signatory Powers wishing to denounce the present Declaration, such denunciation can only be made to take effect at the end of a period of twelve years, beginning sixty days after the first deposit of ratifications, and, after that time, at the end of successive periods of six years, of which the first will begin at the end of the period of twelve years.

Such denunciation must be notified in writing, at least one year in advance, to the British Government, which shall inform all the other Powers.

It will only operate in respect of the denouncing Power.

Art. 70. The Powers represented at the London Naval Conference attach particular importance to the general recognition of the rules which they have adopted, and therefore express the hope that the Powers which were not represented there will accede to the present Declaration. They request the British Government to invite them to do so.

A Power which desires to accede shall notify its intention in writing to the British Government, and transmit simultaneously the act of accession, which will be deposited in the archives of the said Government.

The said Government shall forthwith transmit to all the other Powers a duly certified copy of the notification, together with the act of accession, and communicate the date on which such notification was received. The accession takes effect sixty days after such date.

In respect of all matters concerning this Declaration, Acceding Powers shall be on the same footing as the Signatory Powers.

Art. 71. The present Declaration, which bears the date of 26 February 1909, may be signed in London up till 30 June 1909, by the Plenipotentiaries of the Powers represented at the Naval Conference.

In faith whereof the Plenipotentiaries have signed the present Declaration, and have thereto affixed their seals.

Done at London, the twenty-sixth day of February, one thousand nine hundred and nine, in a single original, which shall remain deposited in the archives of the British Government, and of which duly certified copies shall be sent through the diplomatic channel to the Powers represented at the Naval Conference.

I-16. Convention Relating to the Non-Fortification and Neutralisation of the Aaland Islands, *signed at Geneva,* **20 October 1921, 9 L.N.T.S. 211, entered into force 6 April 1922.** Authentic Text: French

Relevant Penal Characteristics & Penal Provisions

1. Explicit or implicit recognition of proscribed conduct as constituting an international crime, or a crime under international law, or a crime: Articles 3, 4

Applicability
War & Peace

Control
Regulation & Prohibition

State Signatories
Denmark; Estonia; Finland; France; Germany; Italy; Latvia; Poland; Sweden; United Kingdom

State Parties
Denmark; Estonia; Finland; France; Germany; Italy; Latvia; Poland; Sweden; United Kingdom

Relevant Text

Article 3

No military or naval establishment or base of operations, no military aircraft establishment or base of operations, and no other installation used for war purposes shall be maintained or set up in the zone described in Article 2.

Article 4.

Except as provided in Article 7, no military, naval or air force of any Power shall enter or remain in the zone described in Article 2; the manufacture, import, transport and re-export of arms and implements of war in this zone are strictly forbidden.

The following provisions shall, however, be applied in time of peace:

(a) In addition to the regular police force necessary to maintain public order and security in the zone, in conformity with the general provisions in force in the Finnish Republic, Finland may, if exceptional circumstances demand, send into the zone and keep there temporarily such other armed forces as shall be strictly necessary for the maintenance of order.

(b) Finland also reserves the right for one or two of her light surface warships to visit the islands from time to time. These warships may then anchor temporarily in the waters of the islands. Apart from these ships, Finland may, if important special circumstances demand, send into the waters of the zone and keep there temporarily other surface ships, which must in no case exceed a total displacement of 6,000 tons.

The right the enter the archipelago and to anchor there temporarily cannot be granted by the Finnish Government to more than one warship of any other power at a time.

(c) Finland may fly her military or naval aircraft over the zone, but, except in cases of *force majeure,* landing there is prohibited.

I-17. Treaty in Relation to the Use of Submarines and Noxious Gases in Warfare, *signed at Washington*, **6 February 1922, 25 L.N.T.S. 202, 13 MARTENS (ser. 3) 643, never entered into force.**[1] Authentic Texts: English, French

Relevant Penal Characteristics & Penal Provisions

2. Implicit recognition of the penal nature of the act by establishing a duty to prohibit, prevent, prosecute, punish, or the like: Articles 1, 2, 3, 4, 5
4. Duty or right to prosecute: Article 3
5. Duty or right to punish the proscribed conduct: Article 3
8. Establishment of a criminal jurisdictional basis: Article 2
10. No defense of superior orders: Article 3

Applicability
War

Control
Regulation & Prohibition

State Signatories
Australia; Canada; France; India; Italy; Japan; New Zealand; South Africa; United Kingdom; United States of America

State Parties
Australia; Canada; Ethiopia; India; Italy; Japan; New Zealand; South Africa; United Kingdom; United States of America

Full Text

The United States of America, The British Empire, France, Italy and Japan, hereinafter referred to as the Signatory Powers, desiring to make more effective the rules adopted by civilized nations for the protection of the lives of neutrals and noncombatants at sea in time of war, and to prevent the use in war of noxious gases and chemicals, have determined to conclude a treaty to this
effect, and have appointed as their Plenipotentiaries:
 (Here follow the names of Plenipotentiaries)
 Who, having communicated their full powers, found in good and due form, have agreed as follows:
 Article 1. The Signatory Powers declare that among the rules adopted by civilized nations for the protection of the lives of neutrals and noncombatants at sea in time of war, the following are to be deemed an established part of international law:
 (1) A merchant vessel must be ordered to submit to visit and search to determine its character before it can be seized. A merchant vessel must not be attacked unless it refuses to submit to visit and search after warning, or to proceed as directed after seizure. A merchant vessel must not be destroyed unless the crew and passengers have been first placed in safety.

---

[1] This instrument never entered into force for failure to receive the necessary signatures, accessions or ratifications. Its historical relevance and significance warrants its inclusion herein. *See also* 16 AM. J. INT'L L. 57 (1922), 2 HUDSON 794, Malloy 3116.

(2) Belligerent submarines are not under any circumstances exempt from the universal rules above stated; and if a submarine cannot capture a merchant vessel in conformity with these rules the existing law of nations requires it to desist from attack and from seizure and to permit the merchant vessel to proceed unmolested.

Art. 2. The Signatory Powers invite all other civilized Powers to express their assent to the foregoing statement of established law so that there may be a clear public understanding throughout the world of the standards of conduct by which the public opinion of the world is to pass judgment upon future belligerents.

Art. 3. The Signatory Powers, desiring to ensure the enforcement of the humane rules of existing law declared by them with respect to attacks upon and the seizure and destruction of merchant ships, further declare that any person in the service of any Power who shall violate any of those rules, whether or not such person is under orders of a governmental superior, shall be deemed to have violated the laws of war and shall be liable to trial and punishment as if for an act of piracy and may be brought to trial before the civil or military authorities of any Power within the jurisdiction of which he may be found.

Art. 4. The Signatory Powers recognize the practical impossibility of using submarines as commerce destroyers without violating, as they were violated in the recent war of 1914-1918, the requirements universally accepted by civilized nations for the protection of the lives of neutrals and noncombatants, and to the end that the prohibition of the use of submarines as commerce destroyers shall be universally accepted as a part of the law of nations, they now accept that prohibition as henceforth binding as between themselves and they invite all other nations to adhere thereto.

Art. 5. The use in war of asphyxiating, poisonous or other gases, and all analogous liquids, materials or devices, having been justly condemned by the general opinion of the civilized world and a prohibition of such use having been declared in treaties to which a majority of the civilized Powers are parties.

The Signatory Powers, to the end that this prohibition shall be universally accepted as a part of international law binding alike the conscience and practice of nations, declare their assent to such prohibition, agree to be bound thereby as between themselves and invite all other civilized nations to adhere thereto.

Art. 6. The present Treaty shall be ratified as soon as possible in accordance with the constitutional methods of the Signatory Powers and shall take effect on the deposit of all the ratifications, which shall take place at Washington.

The Government of the United States will transmit to all the Signatory Powers a certified copy of the ' procès-verbal ' of the deposit of ratifications.

The present Treaty, of which the French and English texts are both authentic, shall remain deposited in the archives of the Government of the United States, and duly certified copies thereof will be transmitted by that Government to each of the Signatory Powers.

Art. 7. The Government of the United States will further transmit to each of the non-Signatory Powers a duly certified copy of the present Treaty and invite its adherence thereto.

Any non-Signatory Power may adhere to the present Treaty by communicating an instrument of adherence to the Government of the United States, which will thereupon transmit to each of the Signatory and Adhering Powers a certified copy of each instrument of adherence.

In faith whereof, the above named Plenipotentiaries have signed the present Treaty.

Done at the City of Washington, the sixth day of February, one thousand nine hundred and twenty-two.

I-18. **Rules concerning the Control of Wireless Telegraphy in Time of War and Air Warfare. Drafted by a Commission of Jurists at the Hague, December 1922 - February 1923, 17 AM. J. INT'L L. 245-260 (Supp. 1923) (English);** *La Guerre Aerienne, Revision des Lois de la Guerre,* **La Haye 1922-1923, Paris 1930 at 285-295 (French).** Authentic Text: English

Relevant Penal Characteristics & Penal Provisions

1. Explicit or implicit recognition of proscribed conduct as constituting an international crime, or a crime under international law, or a crime: Part I Article 3; Part I Article 5; Part I Article 10;

2. Implicit recognition of the penal nature of the act by establishing a duty to prohibit, prevent, prosecute, punish, or the like: Part I Article 6 (1), (2), (3); Part II Article 40; Part II Article 42; Part II Article 44; Part II Article 46 (1), (2), (3); & Part II Article 47

Applicability
War

Control
Regulation & Prohibition

Full Text[1]

FIRST PART
RULES FOR THE CONTROL OF WIRELESS TELEGRAPHY IN TIME OF WAR

Article 1. In time of war, the operation of wireless stations continues to be organized, so far as possible, in such manner as not to interfere with the service of other wireless stations. This rule does not apply to the wireless stations of the enemy.

Art. 2. The belligerent and neutral Powers may regulate or forbid the use of the wireless stations within their jurisdiction.

Art. 3. The installation or the operation of wireless stations, within a neutral jurisdiction, by a belligerent Power or by persons in its services, constitutes a violation of neutrality on the part of that belligerent as well as a breach of neutrality on the part of the neutral Power which permits the installation or the operation of such stations.

Art. 4. A neutral Power is not bound to restrict or to forbid the use of the wireless stations situated within its jurisdiction, save as far as this may be necessary to prevent the transmission of information, intended for a belligerent, concerning the military forces or military operations, and save the case provided for in Article 5.

Any restriction or prohibition enacted by a neutral Power shall apply to the belligerents uniformly.

Art. 5. Belligerent mobile wireless stations, when they are within a neutral jurisdiction, must abstain from any use of their wireless apparatus.

The neutral governments are bound to employ the means at their disposal in order to prevent such use.

Art. 6. 1. The wireless transmission, by an enemy or neutral vessel or aircraft while being on or above the high seas, of any military information intended for a belligerent's immediate use, shall be considered a hostile act exposing the vessel or aircraft to be fired at;

---

[1] This set of rules does not constitute an international treaty, but its historical significance to the customary law of aerial arms control warrants its inclusion herein.

2. A neutral vessel or a neutral aircraft which, while being on the high seas or above the high seas, transmits an information destined to a belligerent concerning the military forces or operations, is liable to capture. The prize court may pronounce the confiscation of the ship or the aircraft if it deems the confiscation justified by the circumstances;

3. The period within which a neutral vessel or aircraft may be captured on account of the acts referred to in paragraphs 1. and 2. shall not end with the current voyage or flight, but only after the expiration of one year, reckoning from the day on which the incriminated act was committed.

Art.7. If a belligerent commander is of the opinion that the presence of vessels or aircraft provided with wireless apparatus in the immediate vicinity of his armed force or the use of such installations will endanger the success of the operations in which he is engaged, he may order the neutral vessels or aircraft on the high seas or above the high seas:

1. To alter their course so far as necessary in order to prevent them from approaching the armed force operating under his command;

2. To abstain from making use of their wireless apparatus when they are in the immediate vicinity of that force.

A neutral ship or a neutral aircraft which does not comply with the directions that it has received, exposes itself to be fired at. It shall also liable to capture and can be confiscated if the prize court deems the confiscation justified by circumstances.

Art. 8. Neutral mobile wireless stations shall abstain from keeping a written copy of wireless messages received from belligerent military wireless stations, unless such messages are destined for the said neutral stations.

The violation of this rule entitles the belligerents to confiscate the texts in question.

Art. 9. Belligerents are bound to conform to the rules contained in the International Conventions regarding distress signals and distress messages, so far as their military operations permit them to do so.

The provisions contained in the present regulations cannot dispense the belligerents from such obligation, or forbid the transmission of distress signals, distress messages and messages which are indispensable for the safety of navigation.

Art. 10. Diverting wireless distress signals or distress messages, prescribed by the International Conventions, from their normal and legitimate use, constitutes a violation of the laws of war for which its author is personally responsible in accordance with international Law.

Art. 11. Acts which, in others respects, do not constitute acts of espionage, are not considered as such for the mere fact that they imply an infringement of the present rules.

Art. 12. Wireless operators incur no personal responsibility for merely carrying out the orders received in the exercise of their functions.

PART II
RULES OF AIR WARFARE
CHAPTER I.- DOMAIN OF APPLICATION: CLASSIFICATION AND MARKS

Article 1. The rules of air warfare apply to all aircraft, whether lighter or heavier than air, without discriminating whether or not they are capable of floating on water.

Art. 2. Are to be considered as public aircraft:

a) Military aircraft:

b) Non-military aircraft, assigned exclusively to a public service.

Any other aircraft is considered as private aircraft.

Art. 3. A military aircraft must carry an exterior mark indicating its nationality and its military character.

Art. 4. A non-military public aircraft assigned to customs or police service must carry papers attesting that it is exclusively used for a public service. Such aircraft must carry an exterior mark indicating its nationality and its non-military public character.

Art. 5. Non-military public aircraft other than those assigned to customs or police service must, in time of war, carry the same exterior marks and shall be treated, as regards the present rules, in the same manner as private aircraft.

Art. 6. Aircraft not contemplated in Articles 3 and 4 and considered as private aircraft shall carry such papers and exterior marks as are required by the rules in force in their own country. Such marks must indicate their nationality and their character.

Art. 7. The exterior marks required by the above articles shall be affixed in such manner as to make it impossible for them to be altered during flight. They shall be as large as possible and shall be visible from above, from below and from either side.

Art. 8. The exterior marks required by the regulations in force in each State shall be brought without delay to the knowledge of all the other Powers.

Modifications made in time of peace in the regulations requiring exterior marks shall be brought to the knowledge of all the other Powers before being put in force.

Modifications made in such regulations at the outbreak or in course of hostilities shall be brought by each Power to the knowledge of all the other Powers as soon as possible and at the latest when they are communicated to its fighting forces.

Art. 9. A belligerent non-military aircraft, whether public or private, may be transformed into a military aircraft provided that such transformation be made within the jurisdiction of the belligerent State to which the aircraft belongs, and not on the high seas.

Art. 10. No aircraft can possess more than one nationality.

CHAPTER II.- GENERAL PRINCIPLES

Art. 11. Outside the jurisdiction of any State, whether belligerent or neutral, all aircraft have full liberty to pass and to alight on water.

Art. 12. In time of war, every State, whether belligerent or neutral, may forbid or regulate the entry, the movements or the sojourn of aircrafts within its jurisdiction.

CHAPTER III.- BELLIGERENTS

Art. 13. Only military aircraft may exercise the rights of belligerents.

Art. 14. A military aircraft must be under the command of a person duly commissioned or matriculated military rolls of the State; the crew must be exclusively military.

Art. 15. The crews of military aircraft shall bear a fixed distinctive emblem of such a nature as to be recognizable at a distance in the event of crews finding themselves separated from the aircraft.

Art. 16. No aircraft other than a belligerent military aircraft may take part in hostilities in any form whatever.

The term "hostilities" includes the transmission, during a flight, of military information for the immediate use of a belligerent.

No private aircraft may be armed in time of war outside the jurisdiction of its own country.

Art. 17. The principles laid down by the Geneva Conference of 1906 and under the Convention for the adaptation of the said Convention to maritime warfare (Convention X of 1907) shall apply to air warfare and to ambulance planes as well as to the control of such ambulance planes by belligerent commanders.

In order to enjoy the protection and the privileges granted to mobile sanitary units by the Geneva Convention of 1906, the ambulance planes must carry, in addition to their normal distinctive marks, the distinctive emblem of the Red Cross.

CHAPTER IV.- HOSTILITIES

Art. 18. The use of tracer projectiles, whether incendiary or explosive, by or against an aircraft is not forbidden.

This rule applies as well to the States which are parties to the Declaration of St.Petersburg of 1866, as to those which are not.

Art. 19. The use of false exterior marks is forbidden.

Art. 20. In the event of an aircraft being disabled, the persons trying to escape by means of parachutes must not be attacked during their descent.

Art. 21. The use of aircraft for propaganda purposes shall not be considered as an illicit means of warfare.

The members of the crew of such aircraft are not to be deprived of their rights as prisoners of war on the ground that they have committed such an act.

Bombardment

Art. 22. Any air bombardment for the purpose of terrorizing the civil population or destroying or damaging private property without military character or injuring non-combatants, is forbidden.

Art. 23. Any air bombardment carried out for the purpose of enforcing requisitions in kind or payments of contributions in ready money, is forbidden.

Art. 24. 1. An air bombardment is legitimate only when is directed against a military objective, i.e. an objective whereof the total or partial destruction would constitute an obvious military advantage for the belligerent;

2. Such bombardment is legitimate only when directed exclusively against the following objectives: military forces, military works, military establishments or depots, manufacturing plants constituting important and well-known centres for the production of arms, ammunition or characterized military supplies, lines of communication or of transport which are used for military purposes.

3. Any bombardment of cities, towns, villages, habitations and building which are not situated in the immediate vicinity of the operations of the land forces, is forbidden. Should the objectives specified in paragraph 2 be so situated that they could not be bombed but that an undiscriminating bombardment of the civil population would result therefrom, the aircraft must abstain from bombing;

4. In the immediate vicinity of the operations of the land forces, the bombardment of cities, towns, villages, habitations and buildings is legitimate, provided there is a reasonable presumption that the military concentration is important enough to justify the bombardment, taking into account the danger to which the civil population will thus be exposed;

5. The belligerent State is bound to pay compensation for damage caused to persons or property, in violation of the provisions of this Article, by any one of his agents or any one of its military forces.

Art. 25. In bombardments by aircraft, all necessary steps should be taken by the commander to spare, as far as possible, buildings dedicated to public worship, art, science, and charitable purposes, historic monuments, hospital ships, hospitals and other places where the sick and wounded are gathered, provided that such buildings, objectives and places are not being used at the same time for military purposes. Such monuments, objects and places must be indicated, during the day, by signs visible from the aircraft. Using such signs to indicate buildings, objects or places other than those hereinbefore specified shall be considered a perfidious act. The signs of which the above mentioned use is to be made, shall be, in the case of buildings protected under the Geneva Convention, the red cross on a white ground and, in the case of the other protected buildings, a large rectangular panel divided diagonally into two triangles, the one white and the other black.

A belligerent who desired to ensure by night the protection of hospitals and other above mentioned privileged buildings, must take the necessary steps to make the aforesaid special signs sufficiently visible.

Art. 26. The following special rules have been adopted to permit the States to ensure a more efficient protection of monuments of great historic value situated on their territory provided they are disposed to abstain from using for military purposes not only such monuments and also the area surrounding them and to accept a special system for control to this end.

1. A State, if it deems it suitable, may establish a protected area around such monuments situated on its territory. In time of war, such areas shall be sheltered form bombardments;

2. Monuments around which such area is to be established, shall already be, in time of peace, the object of a notification addressed to the other Powers through the diplomatic channel; the notification shall also state the limits of such areas. This notification cannot be revoked in time of war;

3. The protected area may include, in addition to the space occupied by the monument or the group of monuments, a surrounding zone, the width of which may not exceed 500 metres from the periphery of the said space;

4. Marks well visible from the aircraft, both by day and by night, shall be employed to enable the belligerent aeronauts to identify the limits of the areas;

5. The marks placed on the monuments themselves shall be those mentioned in Article 25. The marks employed to indicate the areas surrounding the monuments shall be fixed by every State which accepts the provisions of this Article and shall be notified to the other Powers together with the list of the monuments and areas;

6. Every improper use of the marks referred to in paragraph 5 shall be considered an act of perfidy;

A State which accepts the provisions of this Article should abstain from making use of the historic monuments and the zone surrounding them for military purposes or for the benefit of its military organization in any manner whatsoever and should also abstain from committing, in the interior of such monument or within such zone, any act for military purposes;

8. A commission of control, composed of three neutral representatives accredited to the State which has accepted the provisions of the present Article, or of their delegates, shall be appointed for the purpose of ascertaining that no violation of the provisions of Paragraph 7 has been committed. One of the members of this commission of control shall be the representative, or his delegate, of the State which has been entrusted with the interests of the other belligerent.

Espionage

Art. 27. An individual, found on board a belligerent or neutral aircraft, can be considered as a spy only when, during a flight acting clandestinely or on false pretences, he obtains or endeavours to obtain information within the belligerent jurisdiction or in the zone of operations of a belligerent, with the intention of communicating it to the hostile party.

Art. 28. Acts of espionage committed, after leaving the aircraft, by members of the crew of an aircraft or by passengers transported by it, remain subject to the provisions of the Regulations concerning the laws and customs of war on land.

Art. 29. The repression of acts of espionage referred to in Articles 27 and 28 is subject to Articles 30 and 31 of the Regulations respecting the laws and customs of war on land.

CHAPTER V.- ON MILITARY AUTHORITY OVER ENEMY AND NEUTRAL AIRCRAFT AND PERSONS ON BOARD

Art. 30. When a belligerent commander deems the presence of aircraft to be able to endanger the success of the operations in which he is engaged, he may forbid the passage of neutral aircraft in the immediate vicinity of his own forces or impose on them an itinerary. A neutral aircraft which does not comply with such prescription of which it has cognizance through a publication of the belligerent commander, exposes itself to being fired at.

Art. 31. In accordance with the principles of Article 53 of the Regulations respecting the laws and customs of war on land, private neutral aircraft found by a belligerent occupying force when entering an enemy jurisdiction, may be requisitioned under payment of a full indemnity.

Art. 32. Enemy public aircraft other than those which are treated on the same footing as private aircraft are liable to confiscation without prize proceedings.

Art. 33. Belligerent non-military aircraft, whether public or private, flying within the jurisdiction of their State, are exposed to being fired at if they do not land at the nearest suitable point when an enemy military aircraft is approaching.

Art. 34. Belligerent non-military aircraft, whether public or private, are exposed to being fired at, when they are flying:
1. Within the jurisdiction of the enemy;
2. In the immediate vicinity of such jurisdiction and outside that of their own country;
3. In the immediate vicinity of the military land and sea operations of the enemy.

Art. 35. Neutral aircraft flying within the jurisdiction of a belligerent and warned of the approaching of military aircraft belonging to the other belligerent, must land at the nearest suitable point, failing which they expose themselves to being fired at.

Art. 36. When an enemy military aircraft falls into the hands of a belligerent, the members of the crew and the passengers, if any, may be made prisoners of war.

The same rule applies to members of the crew and to the passengers, if any, of an enemy non-military aircraft, except that in the case of public non-military aircraft exclusively employed for the transport of passengers, the latter are entitled to being released unless they be in the enemy's service or enemy subjects fit for military service.

If an enemy private aircraft falls into the hands of a belligerent, the members of the crew who are enemy subjects or neutral subjects in the enemy's service, may be made prisoners of war. The neutrals, members of the crew, who are not in the enemy's service, are entitled to being released, if they sign a written engagement to the effect that they will not serve on an enemy aircraft until the end of the hostilities. The passengers must be released unless they be in the enemy's service or enemy subjects fit for military service, in which cases they may be made prisoners of war.

The release may, in all cases, be postponed if the military interests of the belligerent require it.

The belligerent may keep as a prisoner of war every member of the crew or every passenger whose conduct during the flight at the end of which he has been arrested has been of a special and active assistance for the enemy.

The names of the persons released after signing the written engagement provided for in the third paragraph of the present article, shall be communicated to the other belligerent, who shall not employ them wittingly in violation of their engagement.

Art. 37. The members of the crew of a neutral aircraft who have been arrested by a belligerent shall be released unconditionally if they are neutral subjects and if they are not in the enemy's service. If they are enemy subjects or if they are in the enemy's service, they may be made prisoners of war.

The passengers must be released unless they are in the enemy's service or enemy subjects fit for military service, in which case they may be made prisoners of war.

The release may, in all cases, be postponed if the military interests of the belligerent require it.

The belligerent may retain as a prisoner of war every member of the crew or every passenger whose conduct during the flight at the end of which he has been arrested, was of a special active assistance to the enemy.

Art. 38. When the rules of Articles 37 and 37 provide that the members of the crew and the passengers may be made prisoners of war, it must be understood that, if they do not belong to the armed forces, they are entitled to a treatment which shall not be less favourable than that which is granted to prisoners of war.

CHAPTER VI.- DUTIES OF BELLIGERENTS TOWARDS NEUTRAL STATES AND DUTIES OF NEUTRALS TOWARDS BELLIGERENT STATES.

Art. 39. Belligerent aircraft are bound to respect the rights of neutral Powers and to abstain, within the jurisdiction of a neutral State, from all acts which it is the duty of such State to prevent.

Art. 40. Belligerent military aircraft are forbidden to penetrate into the jurisdiction of a neutral State.

Art. 41. Aircraft on board of warships, aircraft-carriers included, are considered as forming part of such ships.

Art. 42. A neutral Government is bound to use the means at its disposal to prevent belligerent military aircraft from entering its jurisdiction and to compel them to land or to alight on water if they have penetrated therein.

A neutral government is bound to employ the means at its disposal to intern every belligerent military aircraft which is found within its jurisdiction after landing or watering for whatever cause, as well as its crew and its passengers, if any.

Art. 43. The personnel of a disabled belligerent military aircraft who have been rescued outside the neutral territorial waters and brought into the jurisdiction of a neutral State by a neutral military aircraft and who have been landed there, shall be interned.

Art. 44. It is forbidden to a neutral government to supply a belligerent Power, whether directly or indirectly, with aircraft, component parts thereof or material or ammunition for aircraft.

Art. 45. Subject to the provisions of Article 46, a neutral Power is not bound to prevent the export or the transit of aircraft, component parts thereof or material or ammunition for aircraft, for the account of a belligerent.

Art. 46. A neutral government is bound to use the means at its disposal to:

1. Prevent the departure from its jurisdiction of an aircraft capable of perpetrating an attack against a belligerent Power, or carrying or accompanied by apparatus or material which could be assembled or utilized in such a way to enable it to perpetrate an attack, if there are reasons to believe that such aircraft is intended to be utilized against a belligerent Power;

2. Prevent the departure of an aircraft the crew of which includes any member of the fighting forces of a belligerent Power;

3. Prevent any work being carried out on an aircraft for the purpose of preparing its departure contrary to the objects of the present Article.

At the time of departure of any aircraft forwarded by airway to a belligerent Power by persons or corporations established within a neutral jurisdiction, the neutral government must prescribe for such aircraft a flying route avoiding the vicinity of the military operations of the other belligerent and must demand all the necessary guarantees to asceratin the itinerary followed by the aircraft to be the prescribed one.

Art. 47. A neutral State is bound to take the measures at its disposal to prevent aerial observations of the movements, operations and defense works of a belligerent from being made within its jurisdiction for the purpose of giving information to the other belligerent.

This rule also applies to a belligerent military aircraft on board a warship.

Art. 48. When a neutral Power, exercising its rights and performing its duties according to the present provisions, uses violence or any other means at its disposal, this cannot be considered as an act of hostility.

CHAPTER VII.- SEARCH, CAPTURE AND CONFISCATION

Art. 49. Private aircraft are liable to search and capture by belligerent military aircraft.

Art. 50. Belligerent military aircraft have the right to give order to public non-military aircraft to land or to alight on water, or to repair to a suitable and reasonably accessible place for the purpose of being searched. The refusal, after warning, to obey the order to land or to alight on water at such place for the purpose of being searched, exposes the aircraft to being fired at.

Art. 51. Neutral non-military public aircraft other than those which must be treated as private aircraft are only subject to the investigation of their papers.

Art. 52. An enemy private aircraft is liable to capture in all circumstances.

Art.53. A neutral private aircraft is liable to capture:

a) If it resists the legitimate exercise of the rights of the belligerents;

b) If it violates an interdiction whereof it has cognizance through a publication of a belligerent commander under the provision of Article 30:

c) If it is guilty of assistance to the enemy;

d) If it is armed, in time of war, outside the jurisdiction of its own country;

e) If it has no exterior marks or if it makes use of false marks;

f) If it has no papers or if its papers are insufficient or irregular;

g) If it is clearly out of the route between the point of departure and the point of destination indicated by its papers and if after such inquest as the belligerent may deem necessary, no reasons are given to justify such deviation. The aircraft as well as the members of the crew and the passengers, if any, may be retained by the belligerent during the inquest;

h) If it carries war contraband or must be considered as such itself;

i) If it tries to force a blockade duly established and effectively maintained;

k) If it has been transferred from the belligerent nationality to the neutral nationality at a date and under circumstances indicating the intention of escaping the risks to which an enemy aircraft is exposed as such.

Nevertheless, in each case, except that indicated under k), the reason of the capture must be an act committed during the flight in the course of which the aircraft has fallen into the hands of the belligerent, i.e. since it has left its point of departure and before it has reached its point of destination.

Art. 54. The papers of a private aircraft shall be considered insufficient or irregular if they do not establish the nationality of the aircraft and if they do not show the names and the nationality of each of the members of the crew and of the passengers, the point of departure and the destination of the flight, as well as precisions concerning the cargo and the condition on which it is conveyed. The books of the aircraft are included therein.

Art. 55. The capture of an aircraft or of goods on board an aircraft shall be submitted to a prize court in order that any neutral complaint may be duly examined and judged.

Art. 56. A private aircraft captured because it has no exterior marks or because it has made use of false marks or because it is armed, in time of war, outside the jurisdiction of its own country, is liable to confiscation.

A neutral private aircraft captured on account of having violated the order given by a belligerent commander in virtue of the provisions of Article 30, is liable to confiscation unless it justifies its presence in the forbidden zone.

In all other cases, the prize court adjudicating upon the validity of the capture of an aircraft, shall apply the same rules as it would to a merchant ship or to its cargo or to postal correspondence on board a merchant ship.

Art. 57. A private aircraft which after being searched turns out to be an enemy aircraft, may be destroyed if the belligerent commander deems it necessary, provided that all persons on board are previously placed in safety and all the papers of the aircraft are put in a safe place.

Art. 58. A private aircraft which after having been searched turns out to be neutral aircraft liable to confiscation on account of being guilty of hostile assistance or of being without exterior marks or of having carried false marks, may be destroyed if it is impossible to conduct it to the prize court or if such conduction might imperil the safety of the belligerent aircraft or the success of the operations in which it is engaged. In all cases other than those mentioned above, a neutral private aircraft may not be destroyed except in the event of a military necessity of extreme urgency which does not permit the commander to release it or to send it to the prize court for judgment.

Art. 59. Before a private aircraft is destroyed, all persons on board must be placed in safety and all the papers of the aircraft must be put in a safe place.

The captor who destroys a neutral private aircraft must submit the validity of the capture to the prize court and must, first of all, prove that he was entitled to destroy the aircraft under Article 58. If he fails to do so, the parties interested in the aircraft or in its cargo are entitled to compensation. If the capture of an aircraft the destruction of which has been held justified, is declared invalid, an indemnity must be paid to the parties interested in place of the restitution to which they would have been entitled.

Art. 60. If a neutral private aircraft has been captured for having carried contraband, the captor is at liberty to demand the handing over of the absolute contraband found on board or to proceed to the destruction of such absolute contraband, when the circumstances are such as to make it impossible to send the aircraft for judgment or if this would endanger the safety of the belligerent aircraft or the success of the operations in which it is engaged. The captor must enter the goods surrendered or destroyed in the logbook of the aircraft and, after having obtained the originals or the duplicates of the papers of the aircraft referring thereto, must allow the neutral aircraft to continue its flight.

The provisions of the second paragraph of Article 59 are applicable in the event of the absolute contraband on board of a neutral private aircraft having been surrendered or destroyed.

CHAPTER VIII.- DEFINITIONS

Art. 61. In the presents rules, the term "military" must be understood as referring to all elements of the armed forces, i.e. land, naval and air forces.

Art. 62. Except in so far as special provisions are laid down in the present regulations and save the provisions of Chapter VII of the present regulations or the international conventions indicating that maritime law and its proceedings are applicable, the aeronautical personnel taking part in the hostilities is subject to the laws of war and of neutrality applicable to the land troops in virtue of the custom and practice on International Law as well as of the various declarations and conventions to which interested States are parties.

I-19. Convention on Maritime Neutrality, *signed at Havana,* **20 February, 1928, 135 LNTS 187-217 (1932), 4 Malloy 4743-4750 (English), 2 Bevans 721-729 (English), 32 Am. J. Int'l L. 151-157 (Supp. 1928) (English).** Authentic Texts: English, French, Portuguese, & Spanish

Relevant Penal Characteristics & Penal Provisions
2. Implicit recognition of the penal nature of the act by establishing a duty to prohibit, prevent, prosecute, punish, or the like: Article 1 (1), (2); Article 4 (a), (b); Article 5; Article 6; Article 7; & Article 8

Applicability
War

Control
Regulation

State Signatories
Argentina; Brazil; Chile; Costa Rica; Cuba; El Salvador; Guatemala; Honduras; Mexico; Paraguay; Peru; Uruguay; Venezuela

State Parties
Bolivia; Colombia; Dominican Republic; Ecuador; Haiti; Nicaragua; Panama; United States of America

Full Text
The Governments of the Republics represented at the Sixth International Conference of America States, held in the City of Havana, Republic of Cuba, in the year 1928;

Desiring that, in case war breaks out between two or more states the other states may, in the service of peace, offer their good offices or mediation to bring the conflict to an end, without such an action being considered as an unfriendly act;

Convinced that in case this aim cannot be attained, neutral states have equal interest in having their rights respected by the belligerents;

Considering that neutrality is the juridical situation of states which do not take part in the hostilities, and that it creates rights and imposes obligations of impartiality, which should be regulated;

Recognizing that international solidarity requires that the liberty of commerce should be always respected, avoiding as far as Possible unnecessary burdens for the neutrals;

It being convenient, that as long as this object is not reached, to reduce those burdens as much as possible; and

In the hope that it will be possible to regulate the matter so that all interests concerned may have every desired guaranty;

Have resolved to formulate a convention to that effect and have appointed the following Plenipotentiaries:

(Here follow the names of Plenipotentiaries)

Who, after having presented their credentials, which were found in good and correct form, have agreed upon the following provisions:

SECTION I
FREEDOM OF COMMERCE IN TIME OF WAR
Article 1. The following rules shall govern commerce of war:

(1) Warships of the belligerents have the right to stop and visit on the high seas and in territorial waters that are not neutral any merchant ship with the object of ascertaining its character and nationality and of verifying whether it conveys cargo prohibited by international law or has committed any violation of blockade. If the merchant ship does not heed the signal to stop, it may be pursued by the warship and stopped by force; outside of such a case the ship cannot be attacked unless, after being hailed, it fails to observe the instructions given it.

The ship shall not be rendered incapable of navigation before the crew and passengers have been placed in safety.

(2) Belligerent submarines are subject to the foregoing rules. If the submarine cannot capture the ship while observing these rules, it shall not have the right to continue to attack or to destroy the ship.

Art. 2. Both the detention of the vessel and its crew for violation of neutrality shall be made in accordance with the procedure which best suits the state effecting it and at the expense of the transgressing ship. Said state, except in the case of grave fault on its Part, is not responsible for damages which the vessel may suffer.

SECTION II
DUTIES AND RIGHTS OF BELLIGERENTS

Art. 3. Belligerent states are obligated to refrain from performing acts of war in neutral waters or other acts which may constitute on the part of the state that tolerates them, a violation of neutrality.

Art. 4. Under the terms of the preceding article, a belligerent state is forbidden:

(a) To make use of neutral waters as a base of naval operations against the enemy, or to renew or augment military supplies or the armament of its ships, or to complete the equipment of the latter;

(b) To install in neutral waters radio-telegraph stations or any other apparatus which may serve as a means of communication with its military forces, or to make use of installations of this kind it may have established before the war and which may not have been opened to the public.

Art. 5. Belligerent warships are forbidden to remain in the ports or waters of a neutral state more than twenty-four hours. This provision will be communicated to the ship as soon as it arrives in port or in the territorial waters, and if already there at the time of the declaration of war, as soon as the neutral state becomes aware of this declaration.

Vessels used exclusively for scientific, religious, or philanthropic purposes are exempted from the foregoing provisions.

A ship may extend its stay in port more than twenty-four hours in case of damage or bad conditions at sea, but must depart as soon as the cause of the delay has ceased.

When, according to the domestic law of the neutral state, the ship may not receive fuel until twenty-four hours after its arrival in port the Period of its stay may be extended an equal length of time.

Art. 6. The ship which does not conform to the foregoing rules may be interned by order of the neutral government.

A ship shall be considered as interned from the moment it receives notice to that effect from the local neutral authority, even though a petition for reconsideration of the order has been interposed by the transgressing vessel, which shall remain under custody from the moment it receives the order.

Art. 7. In the absence of a special provision of the local legislation, the maximum number of ships of war of a belligerent which may be in a neutral port at the same time shall be three.

Art. 8. A ship of war may not depart from a neutral port within less than twenty-four hours after the departure of an enemy warship. The one entering first shall depart first, unless it is in such condition as to warrant extending its stay. In any case the ship which arrived later has the right to notify the other through the competent local authority that within twenty-four hours it will leave the port, the one first entering, however, having the right to depart within that time. If it leaves, the notifying ship must observe the interval which is above stipulated.

Art. 9. Damaged belligerent ships shall not be permitted to make repairs in neutral ports beyond those that are essential to the continuance of the voyage and which in no degree constitute an increase in its military strength.

Damages which are found to have been produced by the enemy's fire shall in no case be repaired.

The neutral state shall ascertain the nature of the repairs to be made and will see that they are made as rapidly as possible.

Art. 10. Belligerent warships may supply themselves with fuel and stores in neutral ports, under the conditions especially established by the local authority and in case there are no special provisions to that effect, they may supply themselves in the manner prescribed for provisioning in time of peace.

Art. 11. Warships which obtain fuel in a neutral port cannot renew their supply in the same state until a period of three months has elapsed.

Art. 12. Where the sojourn, supplying, and provisioning of belligerent ships in the ports and jurisdictional waters of neutrals are concerned, the provisions relative to ships of war shall apply equally:

(1) To ordinary auxiliary ships;

(2) To merchant ships transformed into warships, in accordance with Convention VII of The Hague of 1907. The neutral vessel shall be seized and in general subjected to the same treatment as enemy merchantmen:

(a) When taking a direct part in the hostilities.

(b) When at the orders or under direction of an agent placed on board by an enemy government;

(c) When entirely freight-loaded by an enemy government;

(d) When actually and exclusively destined for transporting enemy troops or for the transmission of information on behalf of the enemy. In the cases dealt with in this article, merchandise belonging to the owner of the vessel or ship shall also be liable to seizure.

(3) To armed merchantmen.

Art. 13. Auxiliary ships of belligerents, converted anew into merchantmen, shall be admitted as such in neutral ports subject to the following conditions:

(1) That the transformed vessel has not violated the neutrality of the country where it arrives;

(2) That the transformation has been made in the ports or jurisdictional waters of the country to which the vessel belongs, or in the ports of its allies;

(3) That the transformation be genuine, namely, that the vessel show neither in its crew nor in its equipment that it can serve the armed fleet of its country as an auxiliary, as it did before.

(4) That the government of the country to which the ship belongs communicate to the states the names of auxiliary craft which have lost such character in order to recover that of merchantmen; and

(5) That the same government obligate itself that said ships shall not again be used as auxiliaries to the war fleet.

Art. 14. The airships of belligerents shall not fly above the territorial waters of neutrals if it is not in conformity with the regulations of the latter.

SECTION III
RIGHTS AND DUTIES OF NEUTRALS

Art. 15. Of the acts of assistance coming from the neutral states, and the acts of commerce on the part of individuals, only the first are contrary to neutrality.

Art. 16. The neutral state is forbidden:

(a) To deliver to the belligerent, directly or indirectly, or for any reason whatever, ships of war, munitions or any other war material;

(b) To grant it loans, or to open credits for it during the duration of war.

Credits that a neutral state may give to facilitate the sale or exportation of its food products and raw materials are not included in this prohibition.

Art. 17. Prizes cannot be taken to a neutral port except in case of unseaworthiness, stress of weather, or want of fuel or provisions. When the cause has disappeared, the prizes must leave immediately; if none of the indicated conditions exist, the state shall suggest to them that they depart, and if not obeyed shall have recourse to the means at its disposal to disarm them with their officers and crew, or to intern the prize crew placed on board by the captor.

Art. 18. Outside of the cases provided for in Article 17, the neutral state must release the prizes which may have been brought into its territorial waters.

Art. 19. When a ship transporting merchandise is to be interned in a neutral state, cargo intended for said country shall be unloaded and that destined for others shall be transhipped.

Art. 20. The merchantman supplied with fuel or other stores in a neutral state which repeatedly delivers the whole or part of its supplies to a belligerent vessel, shall not again receive stores and fuel in the same state.

Art. 21. Should it be found that a merchantman flying a belligerent flag, by its preparations or other circumstances, can supply to warships of a state the stores which they need, the local authority may refuse it supplies or demand of the agent of the company a guaranty that the said ship will not aid or assist any belligerent vessel.

Art. 22. Neutral states are not obligated to prevent the export or transit at the expense of any one of the belligerents of arms, munitions and in general of anything which may be useful to their military forces.

Transit shall be permitted when, in the event of a war between two American nations, one of the belligerents is a Mediterranean country, having no other means of supplying itself, provided the vital interests of the country through which transit is requested do not suffer by the granting thereof.

Art. 23. Neutral states shall not oppose the voluntary departure of nationals of belligerent states even though they leave simultaneously in great numbers; but they may oppose the voluntary departure of their own nationals going to enlist in the armed forces.

Art. 24. The use by the belligerents of the means of communication of neutral states or which cross or touch their territory is subject to the measures dictated by the local authority.

Art. 25. If as the result of naval operations beyond the territorial waters of neutral states there should be dead or wounded on board belligerent vessels, said states may send hospital ships under the vigilance of the neutral government to the scene of the disaster. These ships shall enjoy complete immunity during the discharge of their mission.

Art. 26. Neutral states are bound to exert all the vigilance within their power in order to prevent in their ports or territorial waters any violation of the foregoing provisions.

SECTION IV
FULFILMENT AND OBSERVANCE OF THE LAWS OF NEUTRALITY

Art. 27. A belligerent shall indemnify the damage caused by its violation of the foregoing provisions. It shall likewise be responsible for the acts of persons who may belong to its armed forces.

Art. 28. The present Convention does not affect obligations previously undertaken by the Contracting Parties through international agreements.

Art. 29. After being signed, the present Convention shall be submitted to the ratification of the Signatory States. The Government of Cuba is charged with transmitting authentic certified copies to the governments for the aforementioned purpose of ratification. The instrument of ratification shall be deposited in the archives of the Pan American Union in Washington, the Union to notify the signatory governments of said deposit. Such notification shall be considered as an exchange of ratifications. This Convention shall remain open to the adherents of non-Signatory States.

In witness whereof, the aforenamed Plenipotentiaries sign the present Convention in Spanish, English, French and Portuguese, in the City of Havana, the twentieth day of February, 1928.

I-20. **Treaty for the Limitation and Reduction of Naval Armaments [London Treaty], (Part IV, Art. 22, relating to submarine warfare)** *signed at* **London, 22 April 1930,** *LNTS,* **Vol. 112, p. 88, 23 MARTENS (ser. 3) 645-680 (English, French), 4 Malloy 5268-5286 (English), 2 BEVANS 1055-1075 (English), 25 AM. J. INT'L L. 63-82 (Supp. 1931) (English).** Authentic Texts: English & French

Relevant Penal Characteristics & Penal Provisions
2. Implicit recognition of the penal nature of the act by establishing a duty to prohibit, prevent, prosecute, punish, or the like: Article 22

Applicability
War & Peace

Control
Regulation & Prohibition

State Signatories
Australia, Canada, France, India, Irish Free State, Italy, Japan, New Zealand, South Africa, United Kingdom (*including all parts of the British Empire not separate members of the League of Nations*), United States of America

State Parties
Australia; Canada; France; India; Ireland; Italy; Japan; New Zealand; South Africa; United Kingdom; United States of America

Full Text[1]
Art. 22. The following are accepted as established rules of international law:

(1) In their action with regard to merchant ships, submarines must conform to the rules of international law to which surface vessels are subject.

(2) In particular, except in the case of persistent refusal to stop on being duly summoned, or of active resistance to visit or search, a warship, whether surface vessel or submarine, may not sink or render incapable of navigation a merchant vessel without having first placed passengers, crew and ship's papers in a place of safety. For this purpose the ship's boats are not regarded as a place of safety unless the safety of the passengers and crew is assured, in the existing sea and weather conditions, by the proximity of land, or the presence of another vessel which is in a position to take them on board.

The High Contracting Parties invite all other Powers to express their assent to the above rules.

---

[1] The Treaty of London expired on 31 December, 1936. However, Article 23 provides for Article 22 to remain in force even after that date.

I-21. **Procès-verbal relating to the Rules of Submarine Warfare set forth in Part IV Of the Treaty of London of 22 April 1930,** *signed at London,* **6 November 1936, 173 LNTS 353-357 (1936) (English), 33 MARTENS (ser. 3) 3-5 (English, French), 3 BEVANS 298-299 (English), 31 AM. J. INT'L. L. 137-139 (1937) (English).** Authentic Texts: English & French

Relevant Penal Characteristics & Penal Provisions
2. Implicit recognition of the penal nature of the act by establishing a duty to prohibit, prevent, prosecute, punish, or the like: Rule 1 & Rule 2

Applicability
War & Peace

Control
Regulate & Prohibit

State Signatories
Australia; Canada; France; India; Ireland; Italy; Japan; New Zealand; South Africa; United Kingdom; United States of America

State Parties
Afghanistan; Albania; Austria; Belgium; Brazil; Bulgaria; Costa Rica; Czechoslovakia; Denmark; Egypt; El Salvador; Estonia; Fiji; Finland; Germany; Greece; Guatemala; Haiti; Holy See; Hungary; Iran (Islamic Republic); Iraq; Latvia; Lithuania; Mexico; Nepal; Netherlands; Norway; Panama; Peru; Poland; Russian Federation; Saudi Arabia; Sweden; Switzerland; Thailand; Tonga; Turkey; Yugoslavia

Full Text
Whereas the Treaty for the Limitation and Reduction of Naval Armaments signed in London on 22 April 1930, has not been ratified by all the Signatories;

And whereas the said Treaty will cease to be in force after 31 December 1936, with the exception of Part IV thereof, which sets forth rules as to the action of submarines with regard to merchant ships as being established rules of international law, and remains in force without limit of time;

And whereas the last paragraph of Article 22 in the said Part IV states that the High Contracting Parties invite all other Powers to express their assent to the said rules;

And whereas the Governments of the French Republic and the Kingdom of Italy have confirmed their acceptance of the said rules resulting from the signature of the said Treaty;

And whereas all the Signatories of the said Treaty desire that as great a number of Powers as possible should accept the rules contained in the said Part IV as established rules of international law;

The undersigned, representatives of their respective Governments, bearing in mind the said Article 22 of the Treaty, hereby request the Government of the United Kingdom of Great Britain and Northern Ireland forthwith to communicate the said rules, as annexed thereto, to the Governments of all Powers which are not Signatories of the said Treaty, with an Invitation to accede thereto definitely and without limit of time.

Rules

(1). In their action with regard to merchant ships, submarines must conform to the rules of international law to which surface vessels are subject.

(2). In particular, except in the case of persistent refusal to stop on being duly summoned, or of active resistance to visit or search, a warship, whether surface vessel or submarine, may not sink or render incapable of navigation a merchant vessel without having first placed passengers, crew and ship's papers in a place of safety. For this purpose the ship's boats are not regarded as a place of safety unless the safety of the passengers and crew is assured, in the existing sea and weather conditions, by the proximity of land, or the presence of another vessel which is in a position to take them on board.

Signed in London, the sixth day of November, nineteen hundred and thirty-six.

I-22. **The Nyon Agreement,** *signed at Nyon,* 14 September 1937; 181 L.N.T.S 137-152, No. 4284 (English, French), 34 MARTENS (ser. 3) 666-678 (English, French), 31 AM. J. INT'L L. 179-182 (Supp. 1937) (English). Authentic Texts: English & French

Relevant Penal Characteristics & Penal Provisions
1. Explicit or implicit recognition of proscribed conduct as constituting an international crime, or a crime under international law, or a crime: Section II & Section III

Applicability
War & Peace

Control
Prohibition

State Signatories
Bulgaria; Egypt; France; Greece; Romania; Russian Federation; Turkey; United Kingdom; Yugoslavia

Full Text
Whereas arising out of the Spanish conflict attacks have been repeatedly committed in the Mediterranean by submarines against merchant ships not belonging to either of the conflicting Spanish parties; and Whereas these attacks are violations of the rules of international law referred to in Part IV of the Treaty of London of 22 April 1930, with regard to the sinking of merchant ships and constitute acts contrary to the most elementary dictates of humanity, which should be justly treated as acts of piracy; and Whereas without in any way admitting the right of either party to the conflict in Spain to exercise belligerent rights or to interfere with merchant ships on the high seas even if the laws of warfare at sea are observed and without prejudice to the right of any participating Power to take such action as may be proper to protect its merchant shipping from any kind of interference on the high seas or to the possibility of further collective measures being agreed upon subsequently, it is necessary in the first place to agree upon certain special collective measures against piratical acts by submarines: In view thereof the undersigned, being authorized to this effect by their respective Governments, have met in conference at Nyon between the 9 and the 14 September 1937, and have agreed upon the following provisions which shall enter immediately into force:

I. The participating Powers will instruct their naval forces to take the action indicated in paragraphs II and III below with a view to the protection of all merchant ships not belonging to either of the conflicting Spanish parties.

II. Any submarine which attacks such a ship in a manner contrary to the rules of international law referred to in the International Treaty for the Limitation and Reduction of Naval Armaments signed in London on 22 April 1930, and confirmed in the Protocol signed in London on 6 November 1936, shall be counter-attacked and, if possible, destroyed.

III. The instruction mentioned in the preceding paragraph shall extend to any submarine encountered in the vicinity of a position where a ship not belonging to either of the conflicting Spanish parties has recently been attacked in violation of the rules referred to in the preceding paragraph in circumstances which give valid grounds for the belief that the submarine was guilty of the attack.

IV. In order to facilitate the putting into force of the above arrangements in a practical manner, the participating Powers have agreed upon the following arrangements:

1. In the western Mediterranean and in the Malta Channel, with the exception of the Tyrrhenean Sea, which may form the subject of special arrangements, the British and French fleets will operate both on the high seas and in the territorial waters of the participating Powers, in accordance with the division of the area agreed upon between the two Governments.
2. In the eastern Mediterranean,
(a) Each of the participating Powers will operate in its own territorial waters;
(b) On the high seas, with the exception of the Adriatic Sea, the British and French fleets will operate up to the entrance to the Dardanelles, in those areas where there is reason to apprehend danger to shipping in accordance with the division of the area agreed upon between the two Governments. The other participating Governments possessing a sea border on the Mediterranean undertake, within the limit of their resources, to furnish these fleets any assistance that may be asked for; in particular, they will permit them to take action in their territorial waters and to use such of their ports as they shall indicate.
3. It is further understood that the limits of the zones referred to in sub-paragraphs 1 and 2 above, and their allocation shall be subject at any time to revision by the participating Powers in order to take account of any charge in the situation.

V. The participating Powers agree that, in order to simplify the operation of the above-mentioned measures, they will for their part restrict the use of their submarines in the Mediterranean in the following manner:

(a) Except as stated in (b) and (c) below, no submarine will be sent to sea within the Mediterranean.

(b) Submarines may proceed on passage after notification to the other participating Powers, provided that they proceed on the surface and are accompanied by a surface ship.

(c) Each participating Power reserves for purposes of exercises certain areas defined in Annex I hereto in which its submarines are exempt from the restrictions mentioned in (a) or (b). The participating Powers further undertake not to allow the presence in their respective territorial waters of any foreign submarines except in case of urgent distress, or where the conditions prescribed in sub-paragraph (b) above are fulfilled.

VI. The participating Powers also agree that, in order to simplify the problem involved in carrying out the measures above described, they may severally advise their merchant shipping to follow certain main routes in the Mediterranean agreed upon between them and defined in Annex II hereto.

VII. Nothing in the present agreement restricts the right of any participating Power to send its surface vessels to any part of the Mediterranean.

VIII. Nothing in the present agreement in any way prejudices existing international engagements which have been registered with the Secretariat of the League of Nations.

IX. If any of the participating Powers notifies its intention of withdrawing from the present arrangement, the notification will take effect after the expiry of thirty days and any of the other participating Powers may withdraw on the same date if it communicates its intention to this effect before that date.

Done at Nyon, this fourteenth day of September nineteen hundred and thirty-seven, in a single copy, in the English and French languages, both texts being equally authentic, and which will be deposited in the archives of the Secretariat of the League of Nations.

I-23. **Agreement Supplementary to the Nyon Agreement, 1937; 181 L.N.T.S. 137-152, No. 4284 (English, French), 34 MARTENS (ser. 3) 666-678 (English, French), 31 AM. J. INT'L L. 179-182 (Supp. 1937) (English).** Authentic Texts: English & French

Relevant Penal Characteristics & Penal Provisions

1. Explicit or implicit recognition of proscribed conduct as constituting an international crime, or a crime under international law, or a crime: Section II & Section III

Applicability
War & Peace

Control
Prohibition

State Signatories
Bulgaria; Egypt; France; Greece; Romania; Russian Federation; Turkey; United Kingdom; Yugoslavia

Full Text

Whereas under the arrangement signed at Nyon on 14 September 1937, whereby collective measures were agreed upon relating to piratical acts by submarines in the Mediterranean, the participating Powers reserved the possibility of taking further collective measures; and

Whereas it is now considered expedient that such measures should be taken against similar acts by surface vessels and aircraft;

In view thereof, the undersigned, being authorized to this effect by their respective Governments, have met in conference at Geneva on the seventeenth day of September and have agreed upon the following provisions which shall enter immediately into force:

I. The present Agreement is supplementary to the Nyon Arrangement and shall be regarded as an integral part thereof.

II. The present Agreement applies to any attack by a surface vessel or an aircraft upon any merchant vessel in the Mediterranean not belonging to either of the conflicting Spanish parties, when such attack is accompanied by a violation of the humanitarian principles embodied in the rules of international law with regard to warfare at sea, which are referred to in Part IV of the Treaty of London of 22 April 1930, and confirmed in the Protocol signed in London on 6 November 1936.

III. Any surface war vessel, engaged in the protection of merchant shipping in conformity with the Nyon Arrangement, which witnesses an attack of the kind referred to in the preceding paragraph shall:

(a) If the attack is committed by an aircraft, open fire on the aircraft;

(b) If the attack is committed by a surface vessel, intervene to resist it within the limits of its powers, summoning assistance if such is available and necessary. In territorial waters each of the participating Powers concerned will give instructions as to the action to be taken by its own war vessels in the spirit of the present Agreement.

Done at Geneva, this seventeenth day of September 1937, in the English and French languages, both texts being equally authentic, in a single copy which will be deposited in the archives of the Secretariat of the League of Nations.

I-24. **Protocol No. III on the Control of Armaments [Treaty for Collaboration in Economic, Social and Cultural Matters and for Collective Self-Defence]**, *signed at Paris,* **23 October 1943, 211 U.N.T.S. 362, entered into force 6 May 1955.**
Authentic Texts: English, French

Relevant Penal Characteristics & Penal Provisions [1]
None

Applicability
War & Peace

Control
Regulation & Prohibition

State Signatories
Belgium; Federal Republic of Germany; France; Italy; Luxembourg; the Netherlands; United Kingdom

State Parties
Belgium; Federal Republic of Germany; France; Italy; Luxembourg; the Netherlands; United Kingdom

---

[1] This protocol provides for a variety of arms controls.

I-25 **Geneva Convention (I) for the Amelioration of the Condition of the Wounded and Sick in Armed Forces in the Field,** *signed in Geneva,* **12 August 1949, 75 U.N.T.S. 31, 6 U.S.T. 3114, T.I.A.S. No. 3362. Authentic Texts: English and French**

Relevant Penal Characteristics & Penal Provisions
1. Explicit or implicit recognition of proscribed conduct as constituting an international crime, or a crime under international law, or a crime.

Applicability
War

Control
Regulate and Prohibit

State Signatories

Afghanistan; Albania; Argentina; Australia; Austria; Belgium; Brazil; Bulgaria; Burma; Byelorussian Soviet Republic; Canada; Chile; China; Colombia; Costa Rica; Cuba; Czechoslovakia; Denmark; Ecuador; Egypt; Ethiopia; Finland; France; Greece; Guatemala; Holy See; Hungary; India; Iran; Ireland; Israel; Italy; Lebanon; Liechtenstein; Luxembourg; Mexico; Monaco; Netherlands; New Zealand; Nicaragua; Norway; Pakistan; Peru; Poland; Portugal; Romania; Spain; Sweden; Switzerland; Syria; Thailand; Turkey; Ukrainian Soviet Socialist Republic; Union of Soviet Socialist Republics; United Kingdom of Great Britain and Northern Ireland; United States of America; Uruguay; Venezuela; Yugoslavia

Relevant Text
Article 12

Members of the armed forces and other persons mentioned in the following Article, who are wounded or sick, shall be respected and protected in all circumstances.

They shall be treated humanely and cared for by the Party to the conflict in whose power they may be, without any adverse distinction founded on sex, race, nationality, religion, political opinions, or any other similar criteria. Any attempts upon their lives, or violence to their persons, shall be strictly prohibited; in particular, they shall not be murdered or exterminated, subjected to torture or to biological experiments; they shall not willfully be left without medical assistance and care, nor shall conditions exposing them to contagion or infection be created.

Only urgent medical reasons will authorize priority in the order of treatment to be administered.

Women shall be treated with all consideration due to their sex.

The Party to the conflict which is compelled to abandon wounded or sick to the enemy shall, as far as military considerations permit, leave with them a part of its medical personnel and material to assist in their care.

***

Article 20

Hospital ships entitled to the protection of the Geneva Convention for the Amelioration of the Condition of Wounded, Sick and Shipwrecked Members of Armed

Forces at Sea of August 12, 1949, shall not be attacked from the land.

***

Article 23
In time of peace, the High Contracting Parties and, after the outbreak of hostilities, the Parties to the conflict, may establish in their own territory and, if the need arises, in occupied areas, hospital zones and localities so organized as to protect the wounded and sick from the effects of war, as well as the personnel entrusted with the organization and administration of these zones and localities and with the care of the persons therein assembled.

Upon the outbreak and during the course of hostilities, the Parties concerned may conclude agreements on mutual recognition of hospital zones and localities they have created. They may for this purpose implement the provisions of the Draft Agreement annexed to the present Convention, with such amendments as they may consider necessary.

The Protecting Powers and the International Committee of the Red Cross are invited to lend their good offices in order to facilitate the institution and recognition of these hospital zones and localities.

***

Article 33
The material of mobile medical units of the armed forces which fall into the hands of the enemy, shall be reserved for the care of wounded and sick.

The buildings, material and stores of fixed medical establishments of the armed forces shall remain subject to the laws of war, but may not be diverted from that purpose as long as they are required for the care of wounded and sick. Nevertheless, the commanders of the forces in the field may make use of them, in case of urgent military necessity, provided that they make previous arrangements for the welfare of the wounded and sick who are nursed in them.

The material and stores defined in the present Article shall not be intentionally destroyed.

***

Article 35
Transports of wounded and sick or of medical equipment shall be resoected and protected in the same way as mobile medical units.

Should such transports or vehicles fall into the hands of the adverse Party, they shall be subject to the laws of war, on condition that the Party to the conflict who captures them shall in all cases ensure the care of the wounded and sick they contain.

The civilian personnel and all means of transport obtained by requisition shall be subject to the general rules of international law.

***

Article 50
Grave breaches to which the preceding Article relates shall be those involving any of the following acts, if committed against persons or property protected by the Convention: willful killing, torture or inhuman treatment, including biological experiments, willfully causing great suffering or serious injury to body or health, and extensive destruction and appropriation of property, not justified by military necessity and carried out unlawfully and wantonly.

***

I-26 Geneva Convention (II) for the Amelioration of the Wounded, Sick and Shipwrecked Members of Armed Forces at Sea, *Signed at Geneva*, 12 August 1949, 75 U.N.T.S. 85, 6 U.S.T. 3217, T.I.A.S. No. 3363. Authentic Texts: English and French

Relevant Penal Characteristics & Penal Provisions
1. Explicit or implicit recognition of proscribed conduct as constituting an international crime, or a crime under international law, or a crime.

Applicability
War

Control
Regulate and Prohibit

State Signatories

Afghanistan; Albania; Argentina; Australia; Austria; Belgium; Brazil; Bulgaria; Burma; Byelorussian Soviet Republic; Canada; Chile; China; Colombia; Costa Rica; Cuba; Czechoslovakia; Denmark; Ecuador; Egypt; Ethiopia; Finland; France; Greece; Guatemala; Holy See; Hungary; India; Iran; Ireland; Israel; Italy; Lebanon; Liechtenstein; Luxembourg; Mexico; Monaco; Netherlands; New Zealand; Nicaragua; Norway; Pakistan; Peru; Poland; Portugal; Romania; Spain; Sweden; Switzerland; Syria; Thailand; Turkey; Ukrainian Soviet Socialist Republic, Union of Soviet Socialist Republics; United Kingdom of Great Britain and Northern Ireland; United States of America; Uruguay; Venezuela; Yugoslavia

Relevant Text

Article 22
Military hospital ships, that is to say, ships built or equipped by the Powers specially and solely with a view to assisting the wounded, sick and shipwrecked, to treating them and to transporting them, may in no circumstances be attacked or captured, but shall at all times be respected and protected, on condition that their names and descriptions have been notified to the Parties to the conflict ten days before those ships are employed.
The characteristics which must appear in the notification shall include registered gross tonnage, the length from stem to stern and the number of masts and funnels.

Article 23
Establishments ashore entitled to the protection of the Geneva Convention for the Amelioration of the Condition of the Wounded and Sick in Armed Forces in the Field of August 12, 1949, shall be protected from bombardment or attack from the sea.

***

Article 27
Under the same conditions as those provided for in Articles 22 and 24, small craft employed by the State or by the officially recognized lifeboat institutions for coastal rescue operations, shall also be respected and protected, so far as operational requirements permit.

The same shall apply so far as possible to fixed coastal installations used exclusively by these craft for their humanitarian missions.

***

Article 51
Grave breaches to which the preceding Article relates shall be those involving any of the following acts, if committed against persons or property protected by the Convention: willful killing, torture or inhuman treatment, including biological experiments, willfully causing great suffering or serious injury to body or health, and extensive destruction and appropriation of property, not justified by military necessity and carried out unlawfully and wantonly.

I-27 Geneva Convention (IV) Relative to the Protection of Civilian Persons in Time of War, *Signed at Geneva*, 12 August 1949, 75 U.N.T.S. 287, 6 U.S.T. 3516, T.I.A.S. No. 3365. Authentic Texts: English and French

Relevant Penal Characteristics & Penal Provisions
1. Explicit or implicit recognition of proscribed conduct as constituting an international crime, or a crime under international law, or a crime.

Applicability
War

Control
Regulate and Prohibit

State Signatories

Afghanistan; Albania; Argentina; Australia; Austria; Belgium; Brazil; Bulgaria; Burma; Byelorussian Soviet Republic; Canada; Chile; China; Colombia; Costa Rica; Cuba; Czechoslovakia; Denmark; Ecuador; Egypt; Ethiopia; Finland; France; Greece; Guatemala; Holy See; Hungary; India; Iran; Ireland; Israel; Italy; Lebanon; Liechtenstein; Luxembourg; Mexico; Monaco; Netherlands; New Zealand; Nicaragua; Norway; Pakistan; Peru; Poland; Portugal; Romania; Spain; Sweden; Switzerland; Syria; Thailand; Turkey; Ukrainian Soviet Socialist Republic; Union of Soviet Socialist Republics; United Kingdom of Great Britain and Northern Ireland; United States of America; Uruguay; Venezuela; Yugoslavia

Relevant Text
Article 14

In time of peace, the High Contracting Parties and, after the outbreak of hostilities, the Parties thereto, may establish in their own territory and, if the need arises, in occupied areas, hospital and safety zones and localities so organized as to protect from the effects of war, wounded, sick and aged persons, children under fifteen, expectant mothers and mothers of children under seven.

Upon the outbreak and during the course of hostilities, the Parties concerned may conclude agreements on mutual recognition of the zones and localities they have created. They may for this purpose implement the provisions of the Draft Agreement annexed to the present Convention, with such amendments as they may consider necessary.

The Protecting Powers and the International Committee of the Red Cross are invited to lend their good offices in order to facilitate the institution and recognition of these hospital and safety zones and localities.

Article 15

Any Party to the conflict may, either direct or through a neutral State or some humanitarian organization, propose to the adverse Party to establish, in the regions where fighting is taking place, neutralized zones intended to shelter from the effects of war the following persons, without distinction: wounded and sick combatants or non-combatants; civilian persons who take no part in hostilities, and who, while they reside in the zones, perform no work of a military character. When the Parties concerned have agreed upon the geographical position, administration, food supply and supervision of the proposed neutralized zone, a written agreement shall be concluded and signed by the representatives of the Parties to the conflict. The agreement shall fix the beginning and the duration of the neutralization of the zone.

***

Article 53

Any destruction by the Occupying Power of real or personal property belonging individually or collectively to private persons, or to the State, or to other public authorities, or to social or cooperative organizations, is prohibited, except where such destruction is rendered absolutely necessary by military operations.*** Article 147 Grave breaches to which the preceding Article relates shall be those involving any of the following acts, if committed against persons or property protected by the Convention: willful killing, torture or inhuman treatment, including biological experiments, willfully causing great suffering or serious injury to body or health, unlawful deportation or transfer or unlawful confinement of a protected person, compelling a protected person to serve in the forces of a hostile Power, or willfully depriving a protected person of the rights of fair and regular trial prescribed in the present Convention, taking of hostages and extensive destruction and appropriation of property, not justified by military necessity and carried out unlawfully and wantonly.

I-28. **Convention on the Prohibition of Military or Any Other Hostile Use of Environmental Modification Techniques**, *opened for signature at Geneva*, **18 May 1977, U.N. G.A. Res. 31/721 (XXXI), 31 U.N. GAOR Supp. (No. 39), at 36, U.N. Doc. A/31/39 (1976), 31 U.S.T. 333, 1108 U.N.T.S. 151, 16 I.L.M. 88, entered into force 5 October 1978; entered into force with respect to the United States 17 January 1980.** Authentic Texts: Arabic, Chinese, English, French, Russian, Spanish

Relevant Penal Characteristics & Penal Provisions
2. Implicit recognition of the penal nature of the act by establishing a duty to prohibit, prevent, prosecute, punish, or the like: Article I

Applicability
War & Peace

Control
Prohibition

State Signatories
Australia; Belgium; Benin; Bolivia; Brazil; Bulgaria; Byelorussian Soviet Socialist Republic; Canada; Cuba; Cyprus; Czechoslovakia;[1] Denmark; Ethiopia; Finland; German Democratic Republic; Federal Republic of Germany; Ghana; the Holy See; Hungary; Iceland; India; Iran; Iraq; Ireland; Italy; Laos; Lebanon; Liberia; Luxembourg; Mongolia; Morocco; the Netherlands; Nicaragua; Norway; Poland; Portugal; Romania; Sierra Leone; Spain; Sri Lanka; Syria; Tunisia; Turkey;[2] Uganda; Ukrainian Soviet Socialist Republic; Union of Soviet Socialist Republics;[3] United Kingdom; United States of America; Yemen; Zaire

State Parties
Afghanistan; Algeria; Antigua & Barbuda; Argentina; Australia; Austria; Bangladesh; Belarus; Belgium; Benin; Brazil; Bulgaria; Canada; Cape Verde; Chile; Costa Rica; Cuba; Cyprus; Czech Republic; Democratic People's Republic of Korea; Denmark; Dominica; Egypt; Finland; Germany; Ghana; Greece; Guatemala; Hungary; India; Ireland; Italy; Japan; Kuwait;[4] Laos; Malawi; Mauritius; Mongolia; the Netherlands;[5] New Zealand; Niger; Norway; Pakistan; Papua New Guinea; Poland; Republic of Korea; Romania; Russian Federation; St. Christopher & Nevis; St. Lucia; St. Vincent & the Grenadines; Sao Tome & Principe; Slovakia; Solomon Islands; Spain; Sri Lanka; Sweden; Switzerland; Tunisia; Ukraine; United Kingdom;[6] United States of America; Uruguay; Uzbekistan; Vietnam; Yemen (Aden); Yemen (Sanaa)

---

[1] *See* Methodology, "State Succession."
[2] Interpretative statement upon signature.
[3] *See supra* note 1.
[4] With an understanding.
[5] With a declaration. For the Netherlands Kingdom in Europe and the Netherlands Antilles.
[6] Extended to St. Kitts-Nevis-Anguilla, Brunei, the Sovereign Base Areas of Akrotiri and Dhekelis in the Island of Cyprus, and territories under the territorial sovereignty of the United Kingdom.

Reservations upon Signature, Accession or Ratification
Austria; Germany; Guatemala; Kuwait; the Netherlands; New Zealand; Republic of Korea; Switzerland; Turkey

Full Text
The States Parties to this Convention,
Guided by the interest of consolidating peace, and wishing to contribute to the cause of halting the arms race, and of bringing about general and complete disarmament under strict and effective international control, and of saving mankind from the danger of using new means of warfare,

Determined to continue negotiations with a view to achieving effective progress toward further measures in the field of disarmament,

Recognizing that scientific and technical advances may open new possibilities with respect to modification of the environment,
Recalling the Declaration of the United Nations Conference on the Human Environment, adopted at Stockholm on 16 June 1972,
Realizing that the use of environmental modification techniques for peaceful purposes could improve the interrelationship of man and nature and contribute to the preservation and improvement of the environment for the benefit of present and future generations,
Recognizing, however, that military or any other hostile use of such techniques could have effects extremely harmful to human welfare,
Desiring to prohibit effectively military or any other hostile use of environmental modification techniques in order to eliminate the dangers to mankind from such use, and affirming their willingness to work towards the achievement of this objective,
Desiring also to contribute to the strengthening of trust among nations and to the further improvement of the international situation in accordance with the purposes and principles of the Charter of the United Nations, Have agreed as follows:

ARTICLE I
1. Each State Party to this Convention undertakes not to engage in military or any other hostile use of environmental modification techniques having widespread, longlasting or severe effects as the means of destruction, damage or injury to any other State Party.
2. Each State Party to this Convention undertakes not to assist, encourage or induce any State, group of States or international organization to engage in activities contrary to the provisions of paragraph 1 of this article.

ARTICLE II
As used in article I, the term "environmental modification techniques" refers to any technique for changing - through the deliberate manipulation of natural processes - the dynamics, composition or structure of the Earth, including its biota, lithosphere, hydrosphere and atmosphere, or of outer space.

ARTICLE III
1. The provisions of this Convention shall not hinder the use of environmental modification techniques for peaceful purposes and shall be without prejudice to the generally recognized principles and applicable rules of international law concerning such use.
2. The States Parties to this Convention undertake to facilitate, and have the right to participate in, the fullest possible exchange of scientific and technological information on the use of environmental modification techniques for peaceful purposes. States Parties in a position to do so shall contribute, alone or together with other States or international

organizations, to international economic and scientific co-operation in the preservation, improvement and peaceful utilization of the environment, with due consideration for the needs of the developing areas of the world.

ARTICLE IV
Each State Party to this Convention undertakes to take any measures it considers necessary in accordance with its constitutional processes to prohibit and prevent any activity in violation of the provisions of the Convention anywhere under its jurisdiction or control.

ARTICLE V
1. The States Parties to this Convention undertake to consult one another and to co-operate in solving any problems which may arise in relation to the objectives of, or in the application of the provisions of, the Convention. Consultation and co-operation pursuant to this article may also be undertaken through appropriate international procedures within the framework of the United Nations and in accordance with its Charter. These international procedures may include the services of appropriate international organizations, as well as of a Consultative Committee of Experts as provided for in paragraph 2 of this article.

2. For the purposes set forth in paragraph 1 of this article, the Depositary shall, within one month of the receipt of a request from any State Party to this Convention, convene a Consultative Committee of Experts. Any State Party may appoint an expert to the Committee whose functions and rules of procedure are set out in the annex, which constitutes an integral part of this Convention. The Committee shall transmit to the Depositary a summary of its findings of fact, incorporating all views and information presented to the Committee during its proceedings. The Depositary shall distribute the summary to all States Parties.

3. Any State Party to this Convention which has reason to believe that any other State Party is acting in breach of obligations deriving from the provisions of the Convention may lodge a complaint with the Security Council of the United Nations. Such a complaint should include all relevant information as well as all possible evidence supporting its validity.

4. Each State Party to this Convention undertakes to cooperate in carrying out any investigation which the Security Council may initiate, in accordance with the provisions of the Charter of the United Nations, on the basis of the complaint received by the Council. The Security Council shall inform the States Parties of the results of the investigation.

5. Each State Party to this Convention undertakes to provide or support assistance, in accordance with the provisions of the Charter of the United Nations, to any State Party which so requests, if the Security Council decides that such party has been harmed or is likely to be harmed as a result of violation of the Convention.

ARTICLE VI
1. Any State Party to this Convention may propose amendments to the Convention. The text of any proposed amendment shall be submitted to the Depositary, who shall promptly circulate it to all States Parties.

2. An amendment shall enter into force for all States Parties to this Convention which have accepted it, upon the deposit with the Depositary of instruments of acceptance by a majority of States Parties. Thereafter it shall enter into force for any remaining State Party on the date of deposit of its instrument of acceptance.

ARTICLE VII
This Convention shall be of unlimited duration.

ARTICLE VIII
1. Five years after the entry into force of this Convention, a conference of the States Parties to the Convention shall be convened by the Depositary at Geneva, Switzerland. The

conference shall review the operation of the Convention with a view to ensuring that its purposes and provisions are being realized, and shall in particular examine the effectiveness of the provisions of paragraph 1 of article I in eliminating the dangers of military or any other hostile use of environmental modification techniques.

2. At intervals of not less than five years thereafter, a majority of the States Parties to this Convention may obtain, by submitting a proposal to this effect to the Depositary, the convening of a conference with the same objectives.

3. If no conference has been convened pursuant to paragraph 2 of this article within ten years following the conclusion of a previous conference, the Depositary shall solicit the views of all States Parties to this Convention concerning the convening of such a conference. If one third or ten of the States Parties, whichever number is less, respond affirmatively, the Depositary shall take immediate steps to convene the conference.

ARTICLE IX

1. This Convention shall be open to all States for signature. Any State which does not sign the Convention before its entry into force in accordance with paragraph 3 of this article may accede to it at any time.

2. This Convention shall be subject to ratification by signatory States. Instruments of ratification or accession shall be deposited with the Secretary-General of the United Nations.

3. This Convention shall enter into force upon the deposit of instruments of ratification by twenty Governments of accordance with paragraph 2 of this article.

4. For those States whose instruments of ratification or accession are deposited after the entry into force of this Convention, it shall enter into force on the date of the deposit of their instruments of ratification or accession.

5. The Depositary shall promptly inform all signatory and acceding States of the date of each signature, the date of deposit of each instrument of ratification or accession and the date of the entry into force of this Convention and of any amendments thereto, as well as the receipt of other notices.

6. This Convention shall be registered by the Depositary in accordance with Aricle 102 of the Charter of the United Nations.

ARTICLE X

This Convention, of which the Arabic, Chinese, English, French, Russian and Spanish texts are equally authentic, shall be deposited with the Secretary-General of the United Nations, who shall send duly certified copies thereof to the Governments of the signatory and acceding States.

IN WITNESS WHEREOF, the undersigned, being duly authorized thereto, have signed this Convention.

Done at Geneva, on the 18 day of May 1977

Annex to the Convention
    Consultative Committee of Experts

1. The Consultative Committee of Experts shall undertake to make appropriate findings of fact and provide expert views relevant to any problem raised pursuant to paragraph 1 of article V of this Convention by the State Party requesting the convening of the Committee.

2. The work of the Consultative Committee of Experts shall be organized in such a way as to permit it to perform the functions set forth in paragraph 1 of this annex. The Committee shall decide procedural questions relative to the organization of its work, where possible by consensus, but otherwise by a majority of those present and voting. There shall be no voting on matters of substance.

3. The Depositary or his representative shall serve as the Chairman of the Committee.

4. Each expert may be assisted at meetings by one or more advisers.

5. Each expert shall have the right, through the Chairman, to request from States, and from international organizations, such information and assistance as the expert considers desirable for the accomplishment of the Committee's work.

Understandings regarding the Convention

It is the understanding of the Committee that, for the purposes of this Convention, the terms "widespread", "long-lasting" and "severe" shall be interpreted as follows:

    a) "widespread": encompassing an area on the scale of several hundred square kilometres;

    b) "long-lasting": lasting for a period of months, or approximately a season;

    c) "severe": involving serious or significant disruption or harm to human life, natural and economic resources or other assets. It is further understood that the interpretation set forth above is intended exclusively for this Convention and is not intended to prejudice the interpretation of the same or similar terms if used in connexion with any other international agreement.

Understanding relating to article II
It is the understanding of the Committee that the following examples are illustrative of phenomena that could be caused by the use of environmental modification techniques as defined in article II of the Convention: earthquakes; tsunamis; an upset in the ecological balance of a region; changes in weather patterns (clouds, precipitation, cyclones of various types and tornadic storms); changes in climate patterns; changes in ocean currents; changes in the state of the ozone layer; and changes in the state of the ionosphere.

It is further understood that all the phenomena listed above, when produced by a military or any other hostile use of environmental modification techiques, would result, or could reasonably be expected to result, in widespread, long-lasting or severe destruction, damage or injury. Thus, military or any other hostile use of environmental modification techniques as defined in article II, so as to cause those phenomena as a means of destruction, damage or injury to another State Party, would be prohibited.

It is recognized, moreover, that the list of examples set out above is not exhaustive. Other phenomena which could result from the use of environmental modification techniques as defined in article II could also be appropriately included. The absence of such phenomena from the list does not in any way imply that the undertaking contained in article I would not be applicable to those phenomena, provided the criteria set out in that article were met.

Understanding relating to article III
It is the understanding of the Committee that this Convention does not deal with the question whether or not a given use of environmental modification techniques for peaceful purposes is in accordance with generally recognized principles and applicable rules of international law.

Understanding relating to article VIII
It is the understanding of the Committee that a proposal to amend the Convention may also be considered at any conference of Parties held pursuant to article VIII. It is further understood that any proposed amendment that is intended for such consideration should, if possible, be submitted to the Depositary no less than 90 days before the commencement of the conference.

Note: These Understandings are not incorporated into the Convention but are part of the negotiating record and were included in the report transmitted by the Conference of the Committee on Disarmament to the United Nations General Assembly in September 1976 (Report of the Conference of the Committee on Disarmament, Volume I, General Assembly

Official records: Thirty-first session, Supplement No. 27 (A/31/27), New York, United Nations, 1976, pp. 91-92).

I-29. **Protocol Additional to the Geneva Conventions of 12 August 1949, and Relating to the Protection of Victims of International Armed Conflicts (Protocol I)**, *adopted at Geneva,* **8 June 1977**, *entered into force* **7 December, 1978, 3 U.N.T.S. 1125, 16 I.L.M. 1391-1449 (1977), 72 AM. J. INT'L L. 457-509 (1978) (English).** Authentic Texts: Arabic, Chinese, English, French, Russian, and Spanish

Relevant Penal Characteristics & Penal Provisions

2. Implicit recognition of the penal nature of the act by establishing a duty to prohibit, prevent, prosecute, punish, or the like: Article 35 (2), (3); Article 36; Article 54; Article 55; Article 56; & Article 59 (1), (2)(b)

7. Duty or right to cooperate in prosecution, punishment (including judicial assistance): Article 88; & Article 89

Applicability
War

Control
Regulation & Prohibition

State Signatories
Iran; Ireland; Morocco; Nicaragua; Pakistan; Phillippines; United Kingdom; United States of America

State Parties
Albania; Algeria; Angola; Antigua and Barbuda; Argentina; Armenia; Australia; Bahamas; Bahrain; Bangladesh; Barbados; Belarus; Belgium; Belize; Benin; Bolivia; Bosnia-Herzegovina; Botswana; Brazil; Brunei Darussalam; Bulgaria; Burkina Faso; Burundi; Cameroon; Canada; Cape Verde; Central African Republic; Chile; China; Colombia; Comoros; Congo; Costa Rica; Cote d'Ivoire; Croatia; Cuba; Cyprus; Czech Republic; Denmark; Djibouti; Dominica; Dominican Republic; Ecuador; Egypt; El Salvador; Equatorial Guinea; Estonia; Ethiopia; Finland; Gabon; Gambia; Georgia; Germany; Ghana; Greece; Guatemala; Guinea; Guinea-Bissau; Guyana; Holy See; Honduras; Hungary; Iceland; Italy; Jamaica; Jordan; Kazakhstan; Korea (Democratic Peoples Republic); Korea (Republic of); Kuwait; Kyrgyzstan; Lao People's Democratic Republic; Latvia; Lesotho; Liberia; Libyan Arab Jamahiriya; Liechtenstein; Luxembourg; Macedonia; Madagascar; Malawi; Maldives; Mali; Malta; Mauritania; Mauritius; Mexico; Micronesia; Moldova (Republic of); Mongolia; Mozambique; Namibia; Netherlands; New Zealand; Niger; Nigeria; Norway; Oman; Palau; Panama; Paraguay; Peru; Poland; Portugal; Qatar; Romania; Russian Federation; Rwanda; Saint Kitts and Nevis; Saint Lucia; Saint Vincent Grenadines; Samoa; San Marino; Sao Tome Principe; Saudi Arabia; Senegal; Seychelles; Sierra Leone; Slovakia; Solomon Islands; South Africa; Spain; Suriname; Swaziland; Sweden; Switzerland; Syrian Arab Republic; Tajikistan; Tanzania (United Republic of); Togo; Tunisia; Turkmenistan; Uganda; Ukraine; United Arab Emirates; Uruguay; Uzbekistan; Vanuatu; Viet Nam; Yemen; Yugoslavia; Zaire; Zambia; Zimbabwe

Relevant Text

***

Part III. Methods and Means of Warfare Combatant and Prisoners-Of-War

Section I. Methods and Means of Warfare

Art 35. Basic rules

1. In any armed conflict, the right of the Parties to the conflict to choose methods or means of warfare is not unlimited.

2. It is prohibited to employ weapons, projectiles and material and methods of warfare of a nature to cause superfluous injury or unnecessary suffering.

3. It is prohibited to employ methods or means of warfare which are intended, or may be expected, to cause widespread, long-term and severe damage to the natural environment.

Art 36. New weapons

In the study, development, acquisition or adoption of a new weapon, means or method of warfare, a High Contracting Party is under an obligation to determine whether its employment would, in some or all circumstances, be prohibited by this Protocol or by any other rule of international law applicable to the High Contracting Party.

Art 37. Prohibition of Perfidy

1. It is prohibited to kill, injure or capture an adversary by resort to perfidy. Acts inviting the confidence of an adversary to lead him to believe that he is entitled to, or is obliged to accord, protection under the rules of international law applicable in armed conflict, with intent to betray that confidence, shall constitute perfidy. The following acts are examples of perfidy:
(a) the feigning of an intent to negotiate under a flag of truce or of a surrender;
(b) the feigning of an incapacitation by wounds or sickness;
(c) the feigning of civilian, non-combatant status; and
(d) the feigning of protected status by the use of signs, emblems or uniforms of the United Nations or of neutral or other States not Parties to the conflict.

2. Ruses of war are not prohibited. Such ruses are acts which are intended to mislead an adversary or to induce him to act recklessly but which infringe no rule of international law applicable in armed conflict and which are not perfidious because they do not invite the confidence of an adversary with respect to protection under that law. The following are examples of such ruses: the use of camouflage, decoys, mock operations and misinformation.

Art 38. Recognized emblems

1. It is prohibited to make improper use of the distinctive emblem of the red cross, red crescent or red lion and sun or of other emblems, signs or signals provided for by the Conventions or by this Protocol. It is also prohibited to misuse deliberately in an armed conflict other internationally recognized protective emblems, signs or signals, including the flag of truce, and the protective emblem of cultural property.

2. It is prohibited to make use of the distinctive emblem of the United Nations, except as authorized by that Organization.

Art 39. Emblems of nationality

1. It is prohibited to make use in an armed conflict of the flags or military emblems, insignia or uniforms of neutral or other States not Parties to the conflict.

2. It is prohibited to make use of the flags or military emblems, insignia or uniforms of adverse Parties while engaging in attacks or in order to shield, favour, protect or impede military operations.

3. Nothing in this Article or in Article 37, paragraph 1 (d), shall affect the existing generally recognized rules of international law applicable to espionage or to the use of flags in the conduct of armed conflict at sea.

Art 40. Quarter
It is prohibited to order that there shall be no survivors, to threaten an adversary therewith or to conduct hostilities on this basis.

Art 41. Safeguard of an enemy hors de combat

1. A person who is recognized or who, in the circumstances should be recognized to be hors de combat shall not be made the object of attack.

2. A person is hors de combat if:
(a) he is in the power of an adverse Party;
(b) he clearly expresses an intention to surrender; or
(c) he has been rendered unconscious or is otherwise incapacitated by wounds or sickness, and therefore is incapable of defending himself; provided that in any of these cases he abstains from any hostile act and does not attempt to escape.

3. When persons entitled to protection as prisoners of war have fallen into the power or an adverse Party under unusual conditions of combat which prevent their evacuation as provided for in Part III, Section I, of the Third Convention, they shall be released and all feasible precautions shall be taken to ensure their safety.

Article 42 - Occupants of aircraft

1. No person parachuting from an aircraft in distress shall be made the object of attack during his descent.

2. Upon reaching the ground in territory controlled by an adverse Party, a person who has parachuted from an aircraft in distress shall be given an opportunity to surrender before being made the object of attack, unless it is apparent that he is engaging in a hostile act.

3. Airborne troops are not protected by this Article.

Section II. Combatants and Prisoners of War

Art 43. Armed forces

1. The armed forces of a Party to a conflict consist of all organized armed forces, groups and units which are under a command responsible to that Party for the conduct or its subordinates, even if that Party is represented by a government or an authority not recognized by an adverse Party. Such armed forces shall be subject to an internal disciplinary system which, inter alia, shall enforce compliance with the rules of international law applicable in armed conflict.

2. Members of the armed forces of a Party to a conflict (other than medical personnel and chaplains covered by Article 33 of the Third Convention) are combatants, that is to say, they have the right to participate directly in hostilities.

3. Whenever a Party to a conflict incorporates a paramilitary or armed law enforcement agency into its armed forces it shall so notify the other Parties to the conflict.

Art 44. Combatants and prisoners of war

1. Any combatant, as defined in Article 43, who falls into the power of an adverse Party shall be a prisoner of war.

2. While all combatants are obliged to comply with the rules of international law applicable in armed conflict, violations of these rules shall not deprive a combatant of his right to be a combatant or, if he falls into the power of an adverse Party, of his right to be a prisoner of war, except as provided in paragraphs 3 and 4.

3. In order to promote the protection of the civilian population from the effects of hostilities, combatants are obliged to distinguish themselves from the civilian population while they are engaged in an attack or in a military operation preparatory to an attack. Recognizing, however, that there are situations in armed conflicts where, owing to the nature of the hostilities an armed combatant cannot so distinguish himself, he shall retain his status as a combatant, provided that, in such situations, he
carries his arms openly:

(a) during each military engagement, and
(b) during such time as he is visible to the adversary while he is engaged in a military deployment preceding the launching of an attack in which he is to participate.

Acts which comply with the requirements of this paragraph shall not be considered as perfidious within the meaning of Article 37, paragraph 1 (c).

4. A combatant who falls into the power of an adverse Party while failing to meet the requirements set forth in the second sentence of paragraph 3 shall forfeit his right to be a prisoner of war, but he shall, nevertheless, be given protections equivalent in all respects to those accorded to prisoners of war by the Third Convention and by this Protocol. This protection includes protections equivalent to those accorded to prisoners of war by the Third Convention in the case where such a person is tried and punished for any offences he has committed.

5. Any combatant who falls into the power of an adverse Party while not engaged in an attack or in a military operation preparatory to an attack shall not forfeit his rights to be a combatant and a prisoner of war by virtue of his prior activities .

6. This Article is without prejudice to the right of any person to be a prisoner of war pursuant to Article 4 of the Third Convention.

7. This Article is not intended to change the generally accepted practice of States with respect to the wearing of the uniform by combatants assigned to the regular, uniformed armed units of a Party to the conflict.

8. In addition to the categories of persons mentioned in Article 13 of the First and Second Conventions, all members of the armed forces of a Party to the conflict, as defined in Article 43 of this Protocol, shall be entitled to protection under those Conventions if they are wounded or sick or, in the case of the Second Convention, shipwrecked at sea or in other waters.

Art 45. Protection of persons who have taken part in hostilities

1. A person who takes part in hostilities and falls into the power of an adverse Party shall be presumed to be a prisoner of war, and therefore shall be protected by the Third Convention, if he claims the status of prisoner of war, or if he appears to be entitled to such status, or if the Party on which he depends claims such status on his behalf by notification to the detaining Power or to the Protecting Power. Should any doubt arise as to whether any such person is entitled to the status of prisoner of war, he shall continue to have such status and, therefore, to be protected by the Third Convention and this Protocol until such time as his status has been determined by a competent tribunal.

2. If a person who has fallen into the power of an adverse Party is not held as a prisoner of war and is to be tried by that Party for an offence arising out of the hostilities, he shall have the right to assert his entitlement to prisoner-of-war status before a judicial tribunal and to have that question adjudicated. Whenever possible under the applicable procedure, this adjudication shall occur before the trial for the offence. The representatives of the Protecting Power shall be entitled to attend the proceedings in which that question is adjudicated, unless, exceptionally, the proceedings are held in camera in the interest of State security. In such a case the detaining Power shall advise the Protecting Power accordingly.

3. Any person who has taken part in hostilities, who is not entitled to prisoner-of-war status and who does not benefit from more favourable treatment in accordance with the Fourth Convention shall have the right at all times to the protection of Article 75 of this Protocol. In occupied territory, any such person, unless he is held as a spy, shall also be entitled, notwithstanding Article 5 of the Fourth Convention, to his rights of communication under that Convention.

Art 46. Spies

1. Notwithstanding any other provision of the Conventions or of this Protocol, any member of the armed forces of a Party to the conflict who falls into the power of an adverse Party while engaging in espionage shall not have the right to the status of prisoner of war and may be treated as a spy.

2. A member of the armed forces of a Party to the conflict who, on behalf of that Party and in territory controlled by an adverse Party, gathers or attempts to gather information shall not be considered as engaging in espionage if, while so acting, he is in the uniform of his armed forces.

3. A member of the armed forces of a Party to the conflict who is a resident of territory occupied by an adverse Party and who, on behalf of the Party on which he depends, gathers or attempts to gather information of military value within that territory shall not be considered as engaging in espionage unless he does so through an act of false pretences or deliberately in a clandestine manner. Moreover, such a resident shall not lose his right to the status of prisoner of war and may not be treated as a spy unless he is captured while engaging in espionage.

4. A member of the armed forces of a Party to the conflict who is not a resident of territory occupied by an adverse Party and who has engaged in espionage in that territory shall not lose his right to the status of prisoner of war and may not be treated as a spy unless he is captured before he has rejoined the armed forces to which he belongs.

Art 47. Mercenaries

1. A mercenary shall not have the right to be a combatant or a prisoner of war.

2. A mercenary is any person who:

(a) is specially recruited locally or abroad in order to fight in an armed conflict;
(b) does, in fact, take a direct part in the hostilities;
(c) is motivated to take part in the hostilities essentially by the desire for private gain and, in fact, is promised, by or on behalf of a Party to the conflict, material compensation substantially in excess of that promised or paid to combatants of similar ranks and functions in the armed forces of that Party;
(d) is neither a national of a Party to the conflict nor a resident of territory controlled by a Party to the conflict;
(e) is not a member of the armed forces of a Party to the conflict; and
(f) has not been sent by a State which is not a Party to the conflict on official duty as a member of its armed forces.

Part IV. Civilian Population

Section I. General Protection Against Effects of Hostilities

Chapter I. Basic rule and field of application

Art 48. Basic rule

In order to ensure respect for and protection of the civilian population and civilian objects, the Parties to the conflict shall at all times distinguish between the civilian population and combatants and between civilian objects and military objectives and accordingly shall direct their operations only against military objectives.

Art 49. Definition of attacks and scope of application

1. "Attacks" means acts of violence against the adversary, whether in offence or in defence.

2. The provisions of this Protocol with respect to attacks apply to all attacks in whatever territory conducted, including the national territory belonging to a Party to the conflict but under the control of an adverse Party.

3. The provisions of this section apply to any land, air or sea warfare which may affect the civilian population, individual civilians or civilian objects on land. They further apply to all attacks from the
sea or from the air against objectives on land but do not otherwise affect the rules of international law applicable in armed conflict at sea or in the air.
4. The provisions of this section are additional to the rules concerning humanitarian protection contained in the Fourth Convention, particularly in part II thereof, and in other international agreements binding upon the High Contracting Parties, as well as to other rules of international law relating to the protection of civilians and civilian objects on land, at sea or in the air against the effects of hostilities.

Chapter II. Civilians and civilian population

Art 50. Definition of civilians and civilian population

1. A civilian is any person who does not belong to one of the categories of persons referred to in Article 4 (A) (1), (2), (3) and (6) of the Third Convention and in Article 43 of this Protocol. In case of doubt whether a person is a civilian, that person shall be considered to be a civilian.

2. The civilian population comprises all persons who are civilians.

3. The presence within the civilian population of individuals who do not come within the definition of civilians does not deprive the population of its civilian character.

Art 51. - Protection of the civilian population

1. The civilian population and individual civilians shall enjoy general protection against dangers arising from military operations. To give effect to this protection, the following rules, which are additional to other applicable rules of international law, shall be observed in all circumstances.

2. The civilian population as such, as well as individual civilians, shall not be the object of attack. Acts or threats of violence the primary purpose of which is to spread terror among the civilian population are prohibited.

3. Civilians shall enjoy the protection afforded by this section, unless and for such time as they take a direct part in hostilities.

4. Indiscriminate attacks are prohibited. Indiscriminate attacks are:
(a) those which are not directed at a specific military objective;
(b) those which employ a method or means of combat which cannot be directed at a specific military objective; or
(c) those which employ a method or means of combat the effects of which cannot be limited as required by this Protocol; and consequently, in each such case, are of a nature to strike military objectives and civilians or civilian objects without distinction.

5. Among others, the following types of attacks are to be considered as indiscriminate:
(a) an attack by bombardment by any methods or means which treats as a single military objective a number of clearly separated and distinct military objectives located in a city, town, village or other area containing a similar concentration of civilians or civilian objects;
and
(b) an attack which may be expected to cause incidental loss of civilian life, injury to civilians, damage to civilian objects, or a combination thereof, which would be excessive in relation to the concrete and direct military advantage anticipated.

6. Attacks against the civilian population or civilians by way of reprisals are prohibited.

7. The presence or movements of the civilian population or individual civilians shall not be used to render certain points or areas immune from military operations, in particular in attempts to shield military objectives from attacks or to shield, favour or impede military operations. The Parties to the conflict shall not direct the movement of the civilian population or individual civilians in order to attempt to shield military objectives from attacks or to shield military operations.

8. Any violation of these prohibitions shall not release the Parties to the conflict from their legal obligations with respect to the civilian population and civilians, including the obligation to take the precautionary measures provided for in Article 57.

Chapter III. Civilian objects

Art 52. General Protection of civilian objects

1. Civilian objects shall not be the object of attack or of reprisals. Civilian objects are all objects which are not military objectives as defined in paragraph 2.

2. Attacks shall be limited strictly to military objectives. In so far as objects are concerned, military objectives are limited to those objects which by their nature, location, purpose or use make an effective contribution to military action and whose total or partial destruction, capture or neutralization, in the circumstances ruling at the time, offers a definite military advantage.

3. In case of doubt whether an object which is normally dedicated to civilian purposes, such as a place of worship, a house or other dwelling or a school, is being used to make an effective contribution to military action, it shall be presumed not to be so used.

Art 53. Protection of cultural objects and of places of worship

Without prejudice to the provisions of the Hague Convention for the Protection of Cultural Property in the Event of Armed Conflict of 14 May 1954, and of other relevant international instruments, it is prohibited:
(a) to commit any acts of hostility directed against the historic monuments, works of art or places of worship which constitute the cultural or spiritual heritage of peoples;

(b) to use such objects in support of the military effort;
(c) to make such objects the object of reprisals.

Art 54. Protection of objects indispensable to the survival of the civilian population

1. Starvation of civilians as a method of warfare is prohibited.
2. It is prohibited to attack, destroy, remove or render useless objects indispensable to the survival of the civilian population, such as food-stuffs, agricultural areas for the production of food-stuffs, crops, livestock, drinking water installations and supplies and irrigation works, for the specific purpose of denying them for their sustenance value to the civilian population or to the adverse Party, whatever the motive, whether in order to starve out civilians, to cause them to move away, or for any other motive.

3. The prohibitions in paragraph 2 shall not apply to such of the objects covered by it as are used by an adverse Party:
(a) as sustenance solely for the members of its armed forces; or
(b) if not as sustenance, then in direct support of military action, provided, however, that in no event shall actions against these objects be taken which may be expected to leave the civilian population with such inadequate food or water as to cause its starvation or force its movement.

4. These objects shall not be made the object of reprisals.

5. In recognition of the vital requirements of any Party to the conflict in the defence of its national territory against invasion, derogation from the prohibitions contained in paragraph 2 may be made by a Party to the conflict within such territory under its own control where required by imperative military necessity.

Art 55. Protection of the natural environment

1. Care shall be taken in warfare to protect the natural environment against widespread, long-term and severe damage. This protection includes a prohibition of the use of methods or means of warfare which are intended or may be expected to cause such damage to the natural environment and thereby to prejudice the health or survival of the population.

2. Attacks against the natural environment by way of reprisals are prohibited.

Art 56. Protection of works and installations containing dangerous forces

1. Works or installations containing dangerous forces, namely dams, dykes and nuclear electrical generating stations, shall not be made the object of attack, even where these objects are military objectives, if such attack may cause the release of dangerous forces and consequent severe losses among the civilian population. Other military objectives located at or in the vicinity of these works or installations shall not be made the object of attack if such attack may cause the release of dangerous forces from the works or installations and consequent severe losses among the civilian population.

2. The special protection against attack provided by paragraph 1 shall cease:
(a) for a dam or a dyke only if it is used for other than its normal function and in regular, significant and direct support of military operations and if such attack is the only feasible way to terminate such support;
(b) for a nuclear electrical generating station only if it provides electric power in regular, significant and direct support of military operations and if such attack is the only feasible way to terminate such support;
(c) for other military objectives located at or in the vicinity of these works or installations only if they are used in regular, significant and direct support of military operations and if such attack is the only feasible way to terminate such support.

3. In all cases, the civilian population and individual civilians shall remain entitled to all the protection accorded them by international law, including the protection of the precautionary measures provided for in Article 57. If the protection Ceases and any of the works, installations or military objectives mentioned in paragraph 1 is attacked, all practical precautions shall be taken to avoid the release of the dangerous forces.

4. It is prohibited to make any of the works, installations or military objectives mentioned in paragraph 1 the object of reprisals.

5. The Parties to the conflict shall endeavour to avoid locating any military objectives in the vicinity of the works or installations mentioned in paragraph 1. Nevertheless, installations erected for the sole purpose of defending the protected works or installations from attack are permissible and shall not themselves be made the object of attack, provided that they are not used in hostilities except for defensive actions necessary to respond to attacks against the protected works or installations and that their armament is limited to weapons capable only of repelling hostile action against the protected works or installations.

6. The High Contracting Parties and the Parties to the conflict are urged to conclude further agreements among themselves to provide additional protection for objects containing dangerous forces.

7. In order to facilitate the identification of the objects protected by this article, the Parties to the conflict may mark them with a special sign consisting of a group of three bright orange circles placed on the same axis, as specified in Article 16 of Annex I to this Protocol. The absence of such marking in no way relieves any Party to the conflict of its obligations under this Article.

Chapter IV. Precautionary measures

Art 57. Precautions in attack

1. In the conduct of military operations, constant care shall be taken to spare the civilian population, civilians and civilian objects.

2. With respect to attacks, the following precautions shall be taken:
(a) those who plan or decide upon an attack shall:
(i) do everything feasible to verify that the objectives to be attacked are neither civilians nor civilian objects and are not subject to special protection but are military objectives within the meaning of paragraph 2 of Article 52 and that it is not prohibited by the provisions of this Protocol to attack them;
(ii) take all feasible precautions in the choice of means and methods of attack with a view to avoiding, and in any event to minimizing, incidental loss or civilian life, injury to civilians and damage to civilian objects;
(iii) refrain from deciding to launch any attack which may be expected to cause incidental loss of civilian life, injury to civilians, damage to civilian objects, or a combination thereof, which would be excessive in relation to the concrete and direct military advantage anticipated;

(b) an attack shall be cancelled or suspended if it becomes apparent that the objective is not a military one or is subject to special protection or that the attack may be expected to cause incidental loss of civilian life, injury to civilians, damage to civilian objects, or a combination thereof, which would be excessive in relation to the concrete and direct military advantage anticipated;

(c) effective advance warning shall be given of attacks which may affect the civilian population, unless circumstances do not permit.

3. When a choice is possible between several military objectives for obtaining a similar military advantage, the objective to be selected shall be that the attack on which may be expected to cause the least danger to civilian lives and to civilian objects.

4. In the conduct of military operations at sea or in the air, each Party to the conflict shall, in conformity with its rights and duties under the rules of international law applicable in armed conflict, take all reasonable precautions to avoid losses of civilian lives and damage to civilian objects.

5. No provision of this article may be construed as authorizing any attacks against the civilian population, civilians or civilian objects.

Art 58. Precautions against the effects of attacks

The Parties to the conflict shall, to the maximum extent feasible:
(a) without prejudice to Article 49 of the Fourth Convention, endeavour to remove the civilian population, individual civilians and civilian objects under their control from the vicinity of military objectives;
(b) avoid locating military objectives within or near densely populated areas;

(c) take the other necessary precautions to protect the civilian population, individual civilians and civilian objects under their control against the dangers resulting from military operations.

Chapter V. Localities and zones under special protection
Art 59. Non-defended localities

1. It is prohibited for the Parties to the conflict to attack, by any means whatsoever, non-defended localities.
2. The appropriate authorities of a Party to the conflict may declare as a non-defended locality any inhabited place near or in a zone where armed forces are in contact which is open for occupation by an adverse Party.
Such a locality shall fulfil the following conditions:
(a) all combatants, as well as mobile weapons and mobile military equipment must have been evacuated;
(b) no hostile use shall be made of fixed military installations or establishments;
(c) no acts of hostility shall be committed by the authorities or by the population; and
(d) no activities in support of military operations shall be undertaken.

3. The presence, in this locality, of persons specially protected under the Conventions and this Protocol, and of police forces retained for the sole purpose of maintaining law and order, is not contrary to the conditions laid down in paragraph 2.

4. The declaration made under paragraph 2 shall be addressed to the adverse Party and shall define and describe, as precisely as possible, the limits of the non-defended locality. The Party to the conflict to which the declaration is addressed shall acknowledge its receipt and shall treat the locality as a non-defended locality unless the conditions laid down in paragraph 2 are not in fact fulfilled, in which event it shall immediately so inform the Party making the declaration. Even if the conditions laid down in paragraph 2 are not fulfilled, the locality shall continue to enjoy the protection provided by the other provisions of this Protocol and the other rules of international law applicable in armed conflict.

5. The Parties to the conflict may agree on the establishment of non-defended localities even if such localities do not fulfil the conditions laid down in paragraph 2. The agreement should define and describe, as precisely as possible, the limits of the non-defended locality; if necessary, it may lay down the methods of supervision.
6. The Party which is in control of a locality governed by such an agreement shall mark it, so far as possible, by such signs as may be agreed upon with the other Party, which shall be displayed where they are clearly visible, especially on its perimeter and limits and on highways.

7. A locality loses its status as a non-defended locality when its ceases to fulfil the conditions laid down in paragraph 2 or in the agreement referred to in paragraph 5. In such an eventuality, the locality shall continue to enjoy the protection provided by the other provisions of this Protocol and the other rules of international law applicable in armed conflict.

Art 60. Demilitarized zones
1. It is prohibited for the Parties to the conflict to extend their military operations to zones on which they have conferred by agreement the status of demilitarized zone, if such extension is contrary to the terms of this agreement.

2. The agreement shall be an express agreement, may be concluded verbally or in writing, either directly or through a Protecting Power or any impartial humanitarian organization, and may consist of reciprocal and concordant declarations. The agreement may be concluded in peacetime, as well as after the outbreak of hostilities, and should define and describe, as precisely as possible, the limits of the demilitarized zone and, if necessary, lay down the methods of supervision.

3. The subject of such an agreement shall normally be any zone which fulfils the following conditions:

(a) all combatants, as well as mobile weapons and mobile military equipment, must have been evacuated;
(b) no hostile use shall be made of fixed military installations or establishments;
(c) no acts of hostility shall be committed by the authorities or by the population; and
(d) any activity linked to the military effort must have ceased.

The Parties to the conflict shall agree upon the interpretation to be given to the condition laid down in subparagraph (d) and upon persons to be admitted to the demilitarized zone other than those mentioned in paragraph 4.

4. The presence, in this zone, of persons specially protected under the Conventions and this Protocol, and of police forces retained for the sole purpose of maintaining law and order, is not contrary to the conditions laid down in paragraph 3.

5. The Party which is in control of such a zone shall mark it, so far as possible, by such signs as may be agreed upon with the other Party, which shall be displayed where they are clearly visible, especially on its perimeter and limits and on highways.

6. If the fighting draws near to a demilitarized zone, and if the Parties to the conflict have so agreed, none of them may use the zone for purposes related to the conduct of military operations or unilaterally revoke its status.

7. If one of the Parties to the conflict commits a material breach of the provisions of paragraphs 3 or 6, the other Party shall be released from its obligations under the agreement conferring upon the zone the status of demilitarized zone. In such an eventuality, the zone loses its status but shall continue to enjoy the protection provided by the other provisions of this Protocol and the other rules of international law applicable in armed conflict.

***

Repression of Breaches of the Conventions and of this Protocol

Article 85 - Repression of breaches of this Protocol

1. The provisions of the Conventions relating to the repression of breaches and grave breaches, supplemented by this Section, shall apply to the repression of breaches and grave breaches of this Protocol.

2. Acts described as grave breaches in the Conventions are grave breaches of this Protocol if committed against persons in the power of an adverse Party protected by Articles 44, 45 and 73 of this Protocol, or against the wounded, sick and shipwrecked of the adverse Party who are protected by this Protocol, or against those medical or religious personnel, medical units or medical transports which are under the control of the adverse Party and are protected by this Protocol.

3. In addition to the grave breaches defined in Article 11, the following acts shall be regarded as grave breaches of this Protocol, when committed wilfully, in violation of the relevant provisions of this Protocol, and causing death or serious injury to body or health:
(a) making the civilian population or individual civilians the object of attack;
(b) launching an indiscriminate attack affecting the civilian population or civilian objects in the knowledge that such attack will cause excessive loss of life, injury to civilians or damage to civilian objects, as defined in Article 57, paragraph 2 (a)(iii);
(c) launching an attack against works or installations containing dangerous forces in the knowledge that such attack will cause excessive loss of life, injury to civilians or damage to civilian objects, as defined in Article 57, paragraph 2 (a)(iii);
(d) making non-defended localities and demilitarized zones the object of attack;
(e) making a person the object of attack in the knowledge that he is hors de combat;
(f) the perfidious use, in violation of Article 37, of the distinctive emblem of the red cross, red crescent or red lion and sun or of other protective signs recognized by the Conventions or this Protocol.

4. In addition to the grave breaches defined in the preceding paragraphs and in the Conventions, the following shall be regarded as grave breaches of this Protocol, when committed wilfully and in violation of the Conventions or the Protocol:
(a) the transfer by the occupying Power of parts of its own civilian population into the territory it occupies, or the deportation or transfer of all or parts of the population of the occupied territory within or outside this territory, in violation of Article 49 of the Fourth Convention;
(b) unjustifiable delay in the repatriation of prisoners of war or civilians;
(c) practices of apartheid and other inhuman and degrading practices involving outrages upon personal dignity, based on racial discrimination;

(d) making the clearly-recognized historic monuments, works of art or places of worship which constitute the cultural or spiritual heritage of peoples and to which special protection has been given by special arrangement, for example, within the framework of a competent international organization, the object of attack, causing as a result extensive destruction thereof, where there is no evidence of the violation by the adverse Party of Article 53, subparagraph (b), and when such historic monuments, works of art and places of worship are not located in the immediate proximity of military objectives;

(e) depriving a person protected by the Conventions or referred to in paragraph 2 or this Article of the rights of fair and regular trial.

5. Without prejudice to the application of the Conventions and of this Protocol, grave breaches of these instruments shall be regarded as war crimes.

Art 86. Failure to act

1. The High Contracting Parties and the Parties to the conflict shall repress grave breaches, and take measures necessary to suppress all other breaches, of the Conventions or of this Protocol which result from a failure to act when under a duty to do so.

2. The fact that a breach of the Conventions or of this Protocol was committed by a subordinate does not absolve his superiors from penal disciplinary responsibility, as the case may be, if they knew, or had information which should have enabled them to conclude in the circumstances at the time, that he was committing or was going to commit such a breach and if they did not take all feasible measures within their power to prevent or repress the breach.

Art 87. Duty of commanders

1. The High Contracting Parties and the Parties to the conflict shall require military commanders, with respect to members of the armed forces under their command and other persons under their control, to prevent and, where necessary, to suppress and to report to competent authorities breaches of the Conventions and of this Protocol.

2. In order to prevent and suppress breaches, High Contracting Parties and Parties to the conflict shall require that, commensurate with their level of responsibility, commanders ensure that members of the armed forces under their command are aware of their obligations under the Conventions and this Protocol.

3. The High Contracting Parties and Parties to the conflict shall require any commander who is aware that subordinates or other persons under his control are going to commit or have committed a breach of the Conventions or of this Protocol, to initiate such steps as are necessary to prevent such violations of the Conventions or this Protocol, and, where appropriate, to initiate disciplinary or penal action against violators thereof.

Art 88. Mutual assistance in criminal matters

1. The High Contracting Parties shall afford one another the greatest measure of assistance in connexion with criminal proceedings brought in respect of grave breaches of the Conventions or of this Protocol.

2. Subject to the rights and obligations established in the Conventions and in Article 85, paragraph 1 of this Protocol, and when circumstances permit, the High Contracting Parties shall co-operate in the matter of extradition. They shall give due consideration to the request of the State in whose territory the alleged offence has occurred.

3. The law of the High Contracting Party requested shall apply in all cases. The provisions of the preceding paragraphs shall not, however, affect the obligations arising from the provisions of any other treaty of a bilateral or multilateral nature which governs or will govern the whole or part of the subject of mutual assistance in criminal matters.

Art 89. Co-operation

In situations of serious violations or the Conventions or of this Protocol, the High Contracting Parties undertake to act jointly or individually, in co-operation with the United Nations and in conformity with the United Nations Charter.

Art 90. International Fact-Finding Commission

1. (a) An International Fact-Finding Commission (hereinafter referred to as "the Commission") consisting of 15 members of high moral standing and acknowledged impartiality shall be established;
(b) When not less than 20 High Contracting Parties have agreed to accept the competence of the Commission pursuant to paragraph 2, the depositary shall then, and at intervals of five years thereafter, convene a meeting of representatives of those High Contracting Parties for the purpose of electing the members of the Commission. At the meeting, the representatives shall elect the members of the Commission by secret ballot from a list of persons to which each of those High Contracting Parties may nominate one person;
(c) The members of the Commission shall serve in their personal capacity and shall hold office until the election of new members at the ensuing meeting;
(d) At the election, the High Contracting Parties shall ensure that the persons to be elected to the Commission individually possess the qualifications required and that, in the Commission as a whole, equitable geographical representation is assured;
(e) In the case of a casual vacancy, the Commission itself shall fill the vacancy, having due regard to the provisions of the preceding subparagraphs;
(f) The depositary shall make available to the Commission the necessary administrative facilities for the performance of its functions.

2. (a) The High Contracting Parties may at the time of signing, ratifying or acceding to the Protocol, or at any other subsequent time, declare that they recognize ipso facto and without special agreement, in relation to any other High Contracting Party accepting the same obligation, the competence of the Commission to inquire into allegations by such other Party, as authorized by this Article;
(b) The declarations referred to above shall be deposited with the depositary, which shall transmit copies thereof to the High Contracting Parties;
(c) The Commission shall be competent to:

(i) inquire into any facts alleged to be a grave breach as defined in the Conventions and this Protocol or other serious violation of the Conventions or of this Protocol;
(ii) facilitate, through its good offices, the restoration of an attitude of respect for the Conventions and this Protocol;
(d) In other situations, the Commission shall institute an inquiry at the request of a Party to the conflict only with the consent of the other Party or Parties concerned;

(e) Subject to the foregoing provisions or this paragraph, the provisions of Article 52 of the First Convention, Article 53 of the Second Convention, Article 132 or the Third Convention and Article 149 of the Fourth Convention shall continue to apply to any alleged violation of the Conventions and shall extend to any alleged violation of this Protocol.

3. (a) Unless otherwise agreed by the Parties concerned, all inquiries shall be undertaken by a Chamber consisting of seven members appointed as follows:
(i) five members of the Commission, not nationals of any Party to the conflict, appointed by the President of the Commission on the basis of equitable representation of the geographical areas, after consultation with the Parties to the conflict;
(ii) two ad hoc members, not nationals of any Party to the conflict, one to be appointed by each side;
(b) Upon receipt of the request for an inquiry, the President of the Commission shall specify an appropriate time-limit for setting up a Chamber. If any ad hoc member has not been appointed within the time-limit, the President shall immediately appoint such additional member or members of the Commission as may be necessary to complete the membership of the Chamber.

4. (a) The Chamber set up under paragraph 3 to undertake an inquiry shall invite the Parties to the conflict to assist it and to present evidence. The Chamber may also seek such other evidence as it deems appropriate and may carry out an investigation of the situation in loco;
(b) All evidence shall be fully disclosed to the Parties, which shall have the right to comment on it to the Commission;
(c) Each Party shall have the right to challenge such evidence.

5. (a) The Commission shall submit to the Parties a report on the findings of fact of the Chamber, with such recommendations as it may deem appropriate;
(b) If the Chamber is unable to secure sufficient evidence for factual and impartial findings, the Commission shall state the reasons for that inability;
(c) The Commission shall not report its findings publicly, unless all the Parties to the conflict have requested the Commission to do so.

6. The Commission shall establish its own rules, including rules for the presidency or the Commission and the presidency of the Chamber. Those rules shall ensure that the functions of the President of the Commission are exercised at all times and that, in the case of an inquiry, they are exercised by a person who is not a national of a Party to the conflict.

7. The administrative expenses of the Commission shall be met by contributions from the High Contracting Parties which made declarations under paragraph 2, and by voluntary contributions. The Party or Parties to the conflict requesting an inquiry shall advance the necessary funds for expenses incurred by a Chamber and shall be reimbursed by the Party or Parties against which the allegations are made to the extent of 50 per cent of the costs of the Chamber. Where there are counter allegations before the Chamber each side shall advance 50 per cent of the necessary funds.

Art 91. Responsibility

A Party to the conflict which violates the provisions of the Conventions or of this Protocol shall, if the case demands, be liable to pay compensation. It shall be responsible for all acts committed by persons forming part of its armed forces.

***

I-30. Protocol Additional to the Geneva Conventions of 12 August 1949, and Relating to the Protection of Victims of Non-International Armed Conflicts (Protocol II), 8 June 1977. [1]

Relevant Penal Characteristics & Penal Provisions
2. Implicit recognition of the penal nature of the act by establishing a duty to prohibit, prevent, prosecute, punish, or the like: Article 14 & Article 15

4. Duty or right to prosecute: Article 6

Applicability
War & Peace

Control
Regulation & Prohibition

Full Text
Preamble:The High Contracting Parties, Recalling that the humanitarian principles enshrined in Article 3 common to the Geneva Conventions of 12 August 1949, constitute the foundation of respect for the human person in cases of armed conflict not of an international character,
Recalling furthermore that international instruments relating to human rights offer a basic protection to the human person,
Emphasizing the need to ensure a better protection for the victims of those armed conflicts,
Recalling that, in cases not covered by the law in force, the human person remains under the protection of the principles of humanity and the dictates or the public conscience,
Have agreed on the following:

Part I. Scope of this Protocol
Art 1. Material field of application
1. This Protocol, which develops and supplements Article 3 common to the Geneva Conventions of 12 August 1949 without modifying its existing conditions or application, shall apply to all armed conflicts which are not covered by Article 1 of the Protocol Additional to the Geneva Conventions of 12 August 1949, and relating to the Protection of Victims of International Armed Conflicts (Protocol I) and which take place in the territory of a High Contracting Party between its armed forces and dissident armed forces or other organized armed groups which, under responsible command, exercise such control over a part of its territory as to enable them to carry out sustained and concerted military operations and to implement this Protocol.

---

[1] For Data, see Doc. I-29

2. This Protocol shall not apply to situations of internal disturbances and tensions, such as riots, isolated and sporadic acts of violence and other acts of a similar nature, as not being armed conflicts.

Art 2. Personal field of application

1. This Protocol shall be applied without any adverse distinction founded on race, colour, sex, language, religion or belief, political or other opinion, national or social origin, wealth, birth or other status, or on any other similar criteria (hereinafter referred to as "adverse distinction") to all persons affected by an armed conflict as defined in Article 1.
2. At the end of the armed conflict, all the persons who have been deprived of their liberty or whose liberty has been restricted for reasons related to such conflict, as well as those deprived of their liberty or whose liberty is restricted after the conflict for the same reasons, shall enjoy the protection of Articles 5 and 6 until the end of such deprivation or restriction of liberty.

Art 3. Non-intervention

1. Nothing in this Protocol shall be invoked for the purpose of affecting the sovereignty of a State or the responsibility of the government, by all legitimate means, to maintain or re-establish law and order in the State or to defend the national unity and territorial integrity of the State.
2. Nothing in this Protocol shall be invoked as a justification for intervening, directly or indirectly, for any reason whatever, in the armed conflict or in the internal or external affairs of the High Contracting Party in the territory of which that conflict occurs.

Part II. Humane Treatment

Art 4 Fundamental guarantees

1. All persons who do not take a direct part or who have ceased to take part in hostilities, whether or not their liberty has been restricted, are entitled to respect for their person, honour and convictions and religious practices. They shall in all circumstances be treated humanely, without any adverse distinction. It is prohibited to order that there shall be no survivors.

2. Without prejudice to the generality of the foregoing, the following acts against the persons referred to in paragraph I are and shall remain prohibited at any time and in any place whatsoever:(a) violence to the life, health and physical or mental well-being of persons, in particular murder as well as cruel treatment such as torture, mutilation or any form of corporal punishment;(b) collective punishments;(c) taking of hostages;(d) acts of terrorism;(e) outrages upon personal dignity, in particular humiliating and degrading treatment, rape, enforced prostitution and any form of indecent assault;

(f) slavery and the slave trade in all their forms;(g) pillage;(h) threats to commit any or the foregoing acts.

3. Children shall be provided with the care and aid they require, and in particular:

(a) they shall receive an education, including religious and moral education, in keeping with the wishes of their parents, or in the absence of parents, of those responsible for their care;

(b) all appropriate steps shall be taken to facilitate the reunion of families temporarily separated;

(c) children who have not attained the age of fifteen years shall neither be recruited in the armed forces or groups nor allowed to take part in hostilities;

(d) the special protection provided by this Article to children who have not attained the age of fifteen years shall remain applicable to them if they take a direct part in hostilities despite the provisions of subparagraph (c) and are captured;

(e) measures shall be taken, if necessary, and whenever possible with the consent of their parents or persons who by law or custom are primarily responsible for their care, to remove children temporarily from the area in which hostilities are taking place to a safer area within the country and ensure that they are accompanied by persons responsible for their safety and well-being.

Art 5. Persons whose liberty has been restricted

1. In addition to the provisions of Article 4 the following provisions shall be respected as a minimum with regard to persons deprived of their liberty for reasons related to the armed conflict, whether they are interned or detained;

(a) the wounded and the sick shall be treated in accordance with Article 7;

(b) the persons referred to in this paragraph shall, to the same extent as the local civilian population, be provided with food and drinking water and be afforded safeguards as regards health and hygiene and protection against the rigours of the climate and the dangers of the armed conflict;

(c) they shall be allowed to receive individual or collective relief;

(d) they shall be allowed to practise their religion and, if requested and appropriate, to receive spiritual assistance from persons, such as chaplains, performing religious functions;

(e) they shall, if made to work, have the benefit of working conditions and safeguards similar to those enjoyed by the local civilian population.

2. Those who are responsible for the internment or detention of the persons referred to in paragraph 1 shall also, within the limits of their capabilities, respect the following provisions relating to such persons:
(a) except when men and women of a family are accommodated together, women shall be held in quarters separated from those of men and shall be under the immediate supervision of women;
(b) they shall be allowed to send and receive letters and cards, the number of which may be limited by competent authority if it deems necessary;
(c) places of internment and detention shall not be located close to the combat zone. The persons referred to in paragraph 1 shall be evacuated when the places where they are interned or detained become particularly exposed to danger arising out of the armed conflict, if their evacuation can be carried out under adequate conditions of safety;
(d) they shall have the benefit of medical examinations;
(e) their physical or mental health and integrity shall not be endangered by any unjustified act or omission. Accordingly, it is prohibited to subject the persons described in this Article to any medical procedure which is not indicated by the state of health of the person concerned, and which is not consistent with the generally accepted medical standards applied to free persons under similar medical circumstances.
3. Persons who are not covered by paragraph 1 but whose liberty has been restricted in any way whatsoever for reasons related to the armed conflict shall be treated humanely in accordance with Article 4 and with paragraphs 1 (a), (c) and (d), and 2 (b) of this Article.
4. If it is decided to release persons deprived of their liberty, necessary measures to ensure their safety shall be taken by those so deciding.
Art 6. Penal prosecutions
1. This Article applies to the prosecution and punishment of criminal offences related to the armed conflict.
2. No sentence shall be passed and no penalty shall be executed on a person found guilty of an offence except pursuant to a conviction pronounced by a court offering the essential guarantees of independence and impartiality.
In particular:
(a) the procedure shall provide for an accused to be informed without delay of the particulars of the offence alleged against him and shall afford the accused before and during his trial all necessary rights and means of defence;
(b) no one shall be convicted of an offence except on the basis of individual penal responsibility;
(c) no one shall be held guilty of any criminal offence on account of any act or omission which did not constitute a criminal offence, under the law, at the time when it was committed; nor shall a heavier penalty be imposed than that which was applicable at the time when the criminal offence was committed; if, after the commission of the offence, provision is made by law for the imposition of a lighter penalty, the offender shall benefit thereby;
(d) anyone charged with an offence is presumed innocent until proved guilty according to law;

(e) anyone charged with an offence shall have the right to be tried in his presence;
(f) no one shall be compelled to testify against himself or to confess guilt.
3. A convicted person shall be advised on conviction of his judicial and other remedies and of the time-limits within which they may be exercised.
4. The death penalty shall not be pronounced on persons who were under the age of eighteen years at the time of the offence and shall not be carried out on pregnant women or mothers of young children.
5. At the end of hostilities, the authorities in power shall endeavour to grant the broadest possible amnesty to persons who have participated in the armed conflict, or those deprived of their liberty for reasons related to the armed conflict, whether they are interned or detained.

Part III. Wounded, Sick and Shipwrecked

Art 7. Protection and care
1. All the wounded, sick and shipwrecked, whether or not they have taken part in the armed conflict, shall be respected and protected.
2. In all circumstances they shall be treated humanely and shall receive to the fullest extent practicable and with the least possible delay, the medical care and attention required by their condition. There shall be no distinction among them founded on any grounds other than medical ones.

Art 8. Search
Whenever circumstances permit and particularly after an engagement, all possible measures shall be taken, without delay, to search for and collect the wounded, sick and shipwrecked, to protect them against pillage and ill-treatment, to ensure their adequate care, and to search for the dead, prevent their being despoiled, and decently dispose of them.

Art 9. Protection of medical and religious personnel
1. Medical and religious personnel shall be respected and protected and shall be granted all available help for the performance of their duties. They shall not be compelled to carry out tasks which are not compatible with their humanitarian mission.
2. In the performance of their duties medical personnel may not be required to give priority to any person except on medical grounds.

Art 10. General protection of medical duties
1. Under no circumstances shall any person be punished for having carried out medical activities compatible with medical ethics, regardless of the person benefiting therefrom.
2. Persons engaged in medical activities shall neither be compelled to perform acts or to carry out work contrary to, nor be compelled to refrain from acts required by, the rules of medical ethics or other rules designed for the benefit of the wounded and sick, or this Protocol.
3. The professional obligations of persons engaged in medical activities regarding information which they may acquire concerning the wounded and sick under their care shall, subject to national law, be respected.
4. Subject to national law, no person engaged in medical activities may be penalized in any way for refusing or failing to give information concerning the wounded and sick who are, or who have been, under his care.

Art 11. Protection of medical units and transports
1. Medical units and transports shall be respected and protected at all times and shall not be the object of attack.
2. The protection to which medical units and transports are entitled shall not cease unless they are used to commit hostile acts, outside their humanitarian function. Protection may, however, cease only after a warning has been given, setting, whenever appropriate, a reasonable time-limit, and after such warning has remained unheeded.
Art 12. The distinctive emblem
Under the direction of the competent authority concerned, the distinctive emblem of the red cross, red crescent or red lion and sun on a white ground shall be displayed by medical and religious personnel and medical units, and on medical transports. It shall be respected in all circumstances. It shall not be used improperly.
Part IV. Civilian Population
Art 13. Protection of the civilian population
1. The civilian population and individual civilians shall enjoy general protection against the dangers arising from military operations. To give effect to this protection, the following rules shall be observed in all circumstances.
2. The civilian population as such, as well as individual civilians, shall not be the object of attack. Acts or threats of violence the primary purpose of which is to spread terror among the civilian population are prohibited.
3. Civilians shall enjoy the protection afforded by this part, unless and for such time as they take a direct part in hostilities.
Art 14. Protection of objects indispensable to the survival of the civilian population
Starvation of civilians as a method of combat is prohibited. It is therefore prohibited to attack, destroy, remove or render useless for that purpose, objects indispensable to the survival of the civilian population such as food-stuffs, agricultural areas for the production of food-stuffs, crops, livestock, drinking water installations and supplies and irrigation works.
Art 15. Protection of works and installations containing dangerous forces
Works or installations containing dangerous forces, namely dams, dykes and nuclear electrical generating stations, shall not be made the object of attack, even where these objects are military objectives, if such attack may cause the release of dangerous forces and consequent severe losses among the civilian population.
Art 16. Protection of cultural objects and of places of worship
Without prejudice to the provisions of the Hague Convention for the Protection of Cultural Property in the Event of Armed Conflict of 14 May 1954, it is prohibited to commit any acts of hostility directed against historic monuments, works of art or places of worship which constitute the cultural or spiritual heritage of peoples, and to use them in support of the military effort.
Art 17. Prohibition of forced movement of civilians

1. The displacement of the civilian population shall not be ordered for reasons related to the conflict unless the security of the civilians involved or imperative military reasons so demand. Should such displacements have to be carried out, all possible measures shall be taken in order that the civilian population may be received under satisfactory conditions of shelter, hygiene, health, safety and nutrition.
2. Civilians shall not be compelled to leave their own territory for reasons connected with the conflict.

Art 18. Relief societies and relief actions
1. Relief societies located in the territory of the High Contracting Party, such as Red Cross (Red Crescent, Red Lion and Sun) organizations may offer their services for the performance of their traditional functions in relation to the victims of the armed conflict. The civilian population may, even on its own initiative, offer to collect and care for the wounded, sick and shipwrecked.
2. If the civilian population is suffering undue hardship owing to a lack of the supplies essential for its survival, such as food-stuffs and medical supplies, relief actions for the civilian population which are of an exclusively humanitarian and impartial nature and which are conducted without any adverse distinction shall be undertaken subject to the consent of the High Contracting Party concerned.

Part V. Final Provisions
Art 19. Dissemination
This Protocol shall be disseminated as widely as possible.
Art 20. Signature
This Protocol shall be open for signature by the Parties to the Conventions six months after the signing of the Final Act and will remain open for a period of twelve months.
Art 21. Ratification
This Protocol shall be ratified as soon as possible. The instruments of ratification shall be deposited with the Swiss Federal Council, depositary of the Conventions.
Art 22. Accession
This Protocol shall be open for accession by any Party to the Conventions which has not signed it. The instruments of accession shall be deposited with the depositary.
Art 23. Entry into force
1. This Protocol shall enter into force six months after two instruments of ratification or accession have been deposited.
2. For each Party to the Conventions thereafter ratifying or acceding to this Protocol, it shall enter into force six months after the deposit by such Party of its instrument of ratification or accession.
Art 24. Amendment

1. Any High Contracting Party may propose amendments to this Protocol. The text of any proposed amendment shall be communicated to the depositary which shall decide, after consultation with all the High Contracting Parties and the International Committee of the Red Cross, whether a conference should be convened to consider the proposed amendment.
2. The depositary shall invite to that conference all the High Contracting Parties as well as the Parties to the Conventions, whether or not they are signatories of this Protocol.

Art 25. Denunciation
1. In case a High Contracting Party should denounce this Protocol, the denunciation shall only take effect six months after receipt of the instrument of denunciation. If, however, on the expiry of six months, the denouncing Party is engaged in the situation referred to in Article 1, the denunciation shall not take effect before the end of the armed conflict. Persons who have been deprived of liberty, or whose liberty has been restricted, for reasons related to the conflict shall nevertheless continue to benefit from the provisions of this Protocol until their final release.
2. The denunciation shall be notified in writing to the depositary, which shall transmit it to all the High Contracting Parties.

Art 26. Notifications
The depositary shall inform the High Contracting Parties as well as the Parties to the Conventions, whether or not they are signatories of this Protocol, of:

(a) signatures affixed to this Protocol and the deposit of instruments of ratification and accession under Articles 21 and 22;
(b) the date of entry into force of this Protocol under Article 23; and
(c) communications and declarations received under Article 24.

Art 27. Registration
1. After its entry into force, this Protocol shall be transmitted by the depositary to the Secretariat of the United Nations for registration and publication, in accordance with Article 102 of the Charter of the United Nations.
2. The depositary shall also inform the Secretariat of the United Nations of all ratifications, accessions and denunciations received by it with respect to this Protocol.

Art 28. - Authentic texts
The original of this Protocol, of which the Arabic, Chinese, English, French, Russian and Spanish texts are equally authentic shall be deposited with the depositary, which shall transmit certified true copies thereof to all the Parties to the Conventions.

I-31. Resolution on Small-Calibre Weapon Systems, *adopted at Geneva,* by the United Nations Conference on Prohibitions or Restrictions on the Use of Certain Conventional Weapons, 28 September 1979, *Final Report of the Conference to the General Assembly,* A/CONF.95/15 Annex I, 27 October 1980. Authentic Texts: Arabic, Chinese, English, French, Russian, Spanish

Relevant Penal Characteristics & Penal Provisions
None

Applicability
Not Applicable

Control
Not Applicable

State Signatories
Afghanistan; Egypt; Iceland; Morocco; Nicaragua; Nigeria; Portugal; Sierra Leone; Sudan; Turkey; Viet Nam

State Parties
Argentina; Australia; Austria; Belarus; Belgium; Benin; Bosnia-Herzegovina; Brazil; Bulgaria; Canada; China; Croatia; Cuba; Cyprus; Czech Republic; Denmark; Djibouti; Ecuador; Finland; France; Georgia; Germany; Greece; Guatemala; Hungary; India; Ireland; Israel; Italy; Japan; Jordan; Lao People's Democratic Republic; Latvia; Liechtenstein; Luxembourg; Macedonia; Malta; Mauritius; Mexico; Mongolia; Netherlands; New Zealand; Niger; Norway; Pakistan; Philippines; Poland; Romania; Russian Federation; Slovakia; Slovenia; South Africa; Spain; Sweden; Switzerland; Togo; Tunisia; Uganda; Ukraine; United Kingdom; United States of America; Uruguay; Yugoslavia

Full Text
The United Nations Conference on Prohibitions or Restrictions of Use of Certain Conventional Weapons,

' Recalling ' United Nations General Assembly resolution 32/152 of 19 December 1977,
' Aware ' of the continuous development of small-calibre weapon systems (i.e., arms and projectiles),
' Anxious ' to prevent an unnecessary increase of the injurious effects of such weapon systems,
' Recalling ' the agreement embodied in The Hague Declaration of 29 July 1899, to abstain, in international armed conflict, from the use of bullets which expand or flatten easily in the human body,

'Convinced' that it is desirable to establish accurately the wounding effects of current and new generations of small calibre weapon systems including the various parameters that affect the energy transfer and the wounding mechanism of such systems,

1. 'Takes note' with appreciation of the intensive research carried out nationally and internationally in the area of wound ballistics, in particular relating to small-calibre weapon systems, as documented during the Conference;

2. 'Considers' that this research and the international discussion on the subject has led to an increased understanding of the wounding effects of small-calibre weapon systems and of the parameters involved;

3. 'Believes' that such research, including testing of small-calibre weapon systems, should be continued with a view to developing standardized assessment methodology relative to ballistic parameters and medical effects of such systems;

4. 'Invites' Governments to carry out further research, jointly or individually on the wounding effects of small-calibre weapon systems and to communicate, where possible, their findings and conclusions;

5. 'Welcomes' the announcement that an international scientific symposium on wound ballistics will be held in Gothenburg, Sweden, in late 1980 or in 1981, and hopes that the results of the symposium will be made available to the United Nations Disarmament Commission, the Committee on Disarmament and other interested fora;

6. 'Appeals' to all Governments to exercise the utmost care in the development of small-calibre weapon systems, so as to avoid an unnecessary escalation of the injurious effects of such systems.

I-32. **Convention on Prohibitions and Restrictions on the Use of Certain Conventional Weapons Which May be Deemed to be Excessively Injurious or to have Indiscriminate Effects**, *concluded at Geneva*, **10 October 1980, U.N. Doc. A/CONF.95/15, 1342 U.N.T.S. 7, 19 I.L.M. 1523, entered into force 2 December 1983**. Languages: Arabic, Chinese, English, French, Russian, Spanish

Relevant Penal Characteristics & Penal Provisions

1. Explicit recognition of proscribed conduct as constituting an international crime, or a crime under international law, or a crime: (Protocol I); (Protocol II) - Articles 3, 4, 5, 6; (Protocol III) - Article 2

2. Implicit recognition of the penal nature of the act by establishing a duty to prohibit, prevent, prosecute, punish, or the like: Articles 1, 2, 4

Applicability
War

Control
Regulation & Prohibition

State Signatories

Afghanistan; Argentina; Australia; Austria; Belarus; Belgium; Bulgaria; Byelorussian Soviet Socialist Republic; Canada; China;[1] Cuba; Czechoslovakia; Denmark; Ecuador; Egypt; Finland, France;[2] Germany; Greece; Hungary; Iceland; India; Ireland; Italy;[3] Japan; Liechtenstein; Luxembourg; Mexico; Mongolia; Morocco; the Netherlands; New Zealand; Nicaragua; Nigeria; Norway; Pakistan; the Philippines; Poland; Portugal; Romania; Russian Federation; Sierra Leone; Spain; Sudan; Sweden; Switzerland; Togo; Turkey; Ukraine; United Kingdom of Great Britain and Northern Ireland;[4] United States of America;[5] Vietnam; Yugoslavia

---

[1] With a statement.

[2] With an interpretive statement. With a declaration.

[3] With a declaration.

[4] With a statement.

[5] With a declaration.

States Parties

Argentina; Australia; Austria; Belarus; Belgium; Benin; Bosnia and Herzegovina; Brazil; Bulgaria; Cambodia; Canada; Cape Verde; China; Colombia; Costa Rica; Croatia; Cuba; Cyprus; Czech Republic; Denmark; Djibouti; Ecuador; El Salvador; Estonia; Finland; France; Germany; Georgia; Greece; Guatemala; Holy See; Hungary; India; Ireland; Israel; Italy; Japan; Jordan; Lao People's Republic; Latvia; Liechtenstein; Luxembourg; Malta; Mauritius; Mexico; Mongolia; the Netherlands; New Zealand; Niger; Norway; Pakistan; Panama; Peru; Philippines; Poland; Portugal; Romania; Russian Federation; Senegal; Slovakia; Slovenia; South Africa; Spain; Sweden; Switzerland; Tajikistan; the former Yugoslav Republic of Macedonia; Togo; Tunisia; Uganda; Ukraine; United Kingdom of Great Britain and Northern Ireland; United States of America; Uruguay; Uzbekistan; Yugoslavia

Reservations upon Signature, Accession or Ratification

Argentina; Canada; China; Cyprus; France; Israel; Holy See; Italy; the Netherlands, Romania; United Kingdom of Great Britain and Northern Ireland; United States of America

Full Text

The High Contracting Parties,

' Recalling ' that every State has the duty, in conformity with the Charter of the United Nations, to refrain in its international relations from the threat or use of force against the sovereignty, territorial integrity or political independence of any State, or in any other manner inconsistent with the purposes of the United Nations,

' Further recalling ' the general principle of the protection of the civilian population against the effects of hostilities,

' Basing themselves ' on the principle of international law that the right of the parties to an armed conflict to choose methods or means of warfare is not unlimited, and on the principle that prohibits the employment in armed conflicts of weapons, projectiles and material and methods of warfare of a nature to cause superfluous injury or unnecessary suffering,

' Also recalling ' that it is prohibited to employ methods or means of warfare which are intended, or may be expected, to cause widespread, long-term and severe damage to the natural environment,

' Confirming their determination ' that in cases not covered by this Convention and its annexed Protocols or by other international agreements, the civilian population and the combatants shall at all times remain under the protection and authority of the principles of international law derived from established custom, from the principles of humanity and from the dictates of public conscience,

' Desiring ' to contribute to international détente, the ending of the arms race and the building of confidence among States, and hence to the realization of the aspiration of all peoples to live in peace,

' Reaffirming ' the need to continue the codification and progressive development of the rules of international law applicable in armed conflict,

' Wishing ' to prohibit or restrict further the use of certain conventional weapons and believing that the positive results achieved in this area may facilitate the main talks on disarmament with a view to putting an end to the production, stockpiling and proliferation of such weapons,

' Emphasizing ' the desirability that all States become parties to this Convention and its annexed Protocols, especially the militarily significant States,

' Bearing in mind ' that the General Assembly of the United Nations and the United Nations Disarmament Commission may decide to examine the question of a possible broadening of the scope of the prohibitions and restrictions contained in this Convention and its annexed Protocols,

' Further bearing in mind ' that the Committee on Disarmament may decide to consider the question of adopting further measures to prohibit or restrict the use of certain conventional weapons,

Have agreed as follows:

Article 1
Scope of application

This Convention and its annexed Protocols shall apply in the situations referred to in Article 2 common to the Geneva Conventions of 12 August 1949 for the Protection of War Victims, including any situation described in paragraph 4 of Article 1 of Additional Protocol I to these Conventions.

Article 2
Relations with other international agreements

Nothing in this Convention or its annexed Protocols shall be interpreted as detracting from other obligations imposed upon the High Contracting Parties by international humanitarian law applicable in armed conflict.

Article 3
Signature

This Convention shall be open for signature by all States at United Nations Headquarters in New York for a period of twelve months from 10 April 1981.

Article 4
Ratification, acceptance, approval or accession

1. This Convention is subject to ratification, acceptance or approval by the Signatories. Any State which has not signed this Convention may accede to it.

2. The instruments of ratification, acceptance, approval or accession shall be deposited with the Depositary.

3. Expressions of consent to be bound by any of the Protocols annexed to this Convention shall be optional for each State, provided that at the time of the deposit of its instrument of ratification, acceptance or approval of this Convention or of accession thereto, that State shall notify the Depositary of its consent to be bound by any two or more of these Protocols.

4. At any time after the deposit of its instrument of ratification, acceptance or approval of this Convention or of accession thereto, a State may notify the Depositary of its consent to be bound by any annexed Protocol by which it is not already bound.

5. Any Protocol by which a High Contracting Party is bound shall for that Party form an integral part of this Convention.

Article 5
Entry into force

1. This Convention shall enter into force six months after the date of deposit of the twentieth instrument of ratification, acceptance, approval or accession.

2. For any State which deposits its instrument of ratification, acceptance, approval or accession after the date of the deposit of the twentieth instrument of ratification, acceptance, approval or accession, this Convention shall enter into force six months after the date on which that State has deposited its instrument of ratification, acceptance, approval or accession.

3. Each of the Protocols annexed to this Convention shall enter into force six months after the date by which twenty States have notified their consent to be bound by it in accordance with paragraph 3 or 4 of Article 4 of this Convention.

3. For any State which notifies its consent to be bound by a Protocol annexed to this Convention after the date by which twenty States have notified their consent to be bound by it, the Protocol shall enter into force six months after the date on which that State has notified its consent so to be bound.

Article 6
Dissemination

The High Contracting Parties undertake, in time of peace as in time of armed conflict, to disseminate this Convention and those of its annexed Protocols by which they are bound as widely as possible in their respective countries and, in particular, to include the study thereof in their programmes of military instruction, so that those instruments may become known to their armed forces.

Article 7
Treaty relations upon entry into force of this Convention

1. When one of the parties to a conflict is not bound by an annexed Protocol, the parties bound by this Convention and that annexed Protocol shall remain bound by them in their mutual relations.

2. Any High Contracting Party shall be bound by this Convention and any Protocol annexed thereto which is in force for it, in any situation contemplated by Article 1, in relation to any State which is not a party to this Convention or bound by the relevant annexed Protocol, if the latter accepts and applies this Convention or the relevant Protocol, and so notifies the Depositary.

3. The Depositary shall immediately inform the High Contracting Parties concerned of any notification received under paragraph 2 of this Article.

4. This Convention, and the annexed Protocols by which a High Contracting Party is bound, shall apply with respect to an armed conflict against that High Contracting Party of the type referred to in Article 1, paragraph 4, of Additional Protocol I to the Geneva Conventions of 12
August 1949 for the Protection of War Victims: (a) where the High Contracting Party is also a party to Additional Protocol I and an authority referred to in Article 96, paragraph 3, of that Protocol has undertaken to apply the Geneva Conventions and Additional Protocol I in accordance with Article 96, paragraph 3, of the said Protocol, and undertakes to apply this Convention and the relevant annexed Protocols in relation to that conflict; or (b) where the High Contracting Party is not a party to Additional Protocol I and an authority of the type referred to in subparagraph (a) above accepts and applies the obligations of the Geneva Conventions and of this Convention and the relevant annexed Protocols in relation to that conflict. Such an acceptance and application shall have in relation to that conflict the following effects:

(i) the Geneva Conventions and this Convention and its relevant annexed Protocols are brought into force for the parties to the conflict with immediate effect;

(ii) the said authority assumes the same rights and obligations as those which have been assumed by a High Contracting Party to the Geneva Conventions, this Convention and its relevant annexed Protocols; and

(iii) the Geneva Conventions, this Convention and its relevant annexed Protocols are equally binding upon all parties to the conflict.

The High Contracting Party and the authority may also agree to accept and apply the obligations of Additional Protocol I to the Geneva Conventions on a reciprocal basis.

Article 8
Review and amendments

1. (a) At any time after the entry into force of this Convention any High Contracting Party may propose amendments to this Convention or any annexed Protocol by which it is bound. Any proposal for an amendment shall be communicated to the Depositary, who shall notify it to all the High Contracting Parties and shall seek their views on whether a conference should be convened to consider the proposal. If a majority, that shall not be less than eighteen of the High

Contracting Parties so agree, he shall promptly convene a conference to which all High Contracting Parties shall be invited. States not parties to this Convention shall be invited to the conference as observers. (b) Such a conference may agree upon amendments which shall be adopted and shall enter into force in the same manner as this Convention and the annexed Protocols, provided that amendments to this Convention may be adopted only by the High Contracting Parties and that amendments to a specific annexed Protocol may be adopted only by the High Contracting Parties which are bound by that Protocol.

2. (a) At any time after the entry into force of this Convention any High Contracting Party may propose additional protocols relating to other categories of conventional weapons not covered by the existing annexed Protocols. Any such proposal for an additional protocol shall be communicated to the Depositary, who shall notify it to all the High Contracting Parties in accordance with subparagraph 1 (a) of this Article. If a majority, that shall not be less than eighteen of the High Contracting Parties so agree, the Depositary shall promptly convene a conference to which all States shall be invited. (b) Such a conference may agree, with the full participation of all States represented at the conference, upon additional protocols which shall be adopted in the same manner as this Convention, shall be annexed thereto and shall enter into force as provided in paragraphs 3 and 4 of Article 5 of this Convention.

3. (a) If, after a period of ten years following the entry into force of this Convention, no conference has been convened in accordance with subparagraph 1 (a) or 2 (a) of this Article, any High Contracting Party may request the Depositary to convene a conference to which all High Contracting Parties shall be invited to review the scope and operation of this Convention and the Protocols annexed thereto and to consider any proposal for amendments of this Convention or of the existing Protocols. States not parties to this Convention shall be invited as observers to the conference.

The conference may agree upon amendments which shall be adopted and enter into force in accordance with subparagraph 1 (b) above. (b) At such conference consideration may also be given to any proposal for additional protocols relating to other categories of conventional weapons not covered by the existing annexed Protocols. All States represented at the conference may participate fully in such consideration. Any additional protocols shall be adopted in the same manner as this Convention, shall be annexed thereto and shall enter into force as provided in paragraphs 3 and 4 of Article 5 of this Convention. (c) Such a conference may consider whether provision should be made for the convening of a further conference at the request of any High Contracting Party if, after a similar period to that referred to in subparagraph 3 (a) of this Article, no conference has been convened in accordance with subparagraph 1 (a) or 2 (a) of this Article.

Article 9
Denunciation

1. Any High Contracting Party may denounce this Convention or any of its annexed Protocols by so notifying the Depositary.

2. Any such denunciation shall only take effect one year after receipt by the Depositary of the notification of denunciation. If, however, on the expiry of that year the denouncing High Contracting Party is engaged in one of the situations referred to in Article 1, the Party shall continue to be bound by the obligations of this Convention and of the relevant annexed Protocols until the end of the armed conflict or occupation and, in any case, until the termination of operations connected with the final release, repatriation or re-establishment of the person protected by the rules of international law applicable in armed conflict, and in the case of any annexed Protocol containing provisions concerning situations in which peace-keeping, observation or similar functions are performed by United Nations forces or missions in the area concerned, until the termination of those functions.

3. Any denunciation of this Convention shall be considered as also applying to all annexed Protocols by which the denouncing High Contracting Party is bound.

4. Any denunciation shall have effect only in respect of the denouncing High Contracting Party.

5. Any denunciation shall not affect the obligations already incurred, by reason of an armed conflict, under this Convention and its annexed Protocols by such denouncing High Contracting Party in respect of any act committed before this denunciation becomes effective.

Article 10
Depositary

1. The Secretary-General of the United Nations shall be the Depositary of this Convention and of its annexed Protocols.

2. In addition to his usual functions, the Depositary shall inform all States of: (a) signatures affixed to this Convention under Article 3; (b) deposits of instruments of ratification, acceptance or approval or of accession to this Convention deposited under Article 4; (c) notifications of consent to be bound by annexed Protocols under Article 4; (d) the dates of entry into force of this Convention and of each of its annexed Protocols under Article 5; and (e) notifications of denunciation received under article 9, and their effective date.

Article 11
Authentic texts

The original of this Convention with the annexed Protocols, of which the Arabic, Chinese, English, French, Russian and Spanish texts are equally authentic, shall be deposited with the Depositary, who shall transmit certified true copies thereof to all States.

I-32(a). Protocol on Non-Detectable Fragments to the Convention on Prohibitions or Restrictions on the Use of Certain Conventional Weapons [Protocol I], *adopted at Geneva,* **10 October 1980, U.N. Doc. A/CONF.95/15 (1980), 19 I.L.M. 1529, entered into force 2 December 1983.**

Relevant Penal Characteristics & Penal Provisions

2. Implicit recognition of the penal nature of the act by establishing a duty to prohibit, prevent, prosecute, punish, or the like: Article 1

Applicability
War

Control
Regulation & Prohibition

State Signatories

Afghanistan; Argentina; Australia; Austria; Belgium; Bulgaria; Byelorussian Soviet Socialist Republic; Canada; China;[1] Cuba; Czechoslovakia; Denmark; Ecuador; Egypt; Finland, France;[2] German Democratic Republic; Federal Republic of Germany; Greece; Hungary; Iceland; India; Ireland; Italy;[3] Japan; Liechtenstein; Luxembourg; Mexico; Mongolia; Morocco; the Netherlands; New Zealand; Nicaragua; Nigeria; Norway; Pakistan; the Philippines; Poland; Portugal; Romania; Sierra Leone; Spain; Sudan; Sweden; Switzerland; Togo; Turkey; Ukrainian Soviet Socialist Republic; Union of Soviet Socialist Republics; United Kingdom;[4] United States of America;[5] Vietnam; Yugoslavia

State Parties

Argentina; Australia; Austria; Belarus; Belgium; Benin; Bosnia and Herzegovina; Brazil; Bulgaria; Canada; Cambodia; Cape Verde; China; Croatia; Cuba; Cyprus; Czech Republic; Denmark; Djibouti; Ecuador; Finland; former Yugoslav Republic of Macedonia; France; Germany; Georgia; Greece; Guatemala; Holy See; Hungary; India; Ireland; Israel; Italy; Japan; Jordan;

---

[1] With a statement.

[2] With an interpretive statement. With a declaration.

[3] With a declaration.

[4] With a statement.

[5] With a declaration.

Laos; Latvia; Liechtenstein; Luxembourg; Lithuania; Malta; Mauritius; Mexico; Mongolia; the Netherlands; New Zealand; Niger; Norway; Pakistan; Panama; Peru; Philippines; Poland; Portugal; Romania; Russian Federation; Slovak Rep.; Slovenia; South Africa; Spain; Sweden; Switzerland; Togo; Tunisia; Uganda; Ukraine; United Kingdom; United States of America; Uruguay; Yugoslavia

Reservations upon Signature, Accession or Ratification
Argentina; Canada; China; Cyprus; France; Israel; Italy; the Netherlands, Romania; Great Britain; United States of America

Full Text

Article 1. It is prohibited to use any weapon the primary effect of which is to injure by fragments which in the human body escape detection by X-rays.

I-32(b). Protocol on Prohibitions or Restrictions on the Use of Mines, Booby Traps and Other Devices to the Convention on Prohibitions or Restrictions on the Use of Certain Conventional Weapons, [Protocol II], *adopted at Geneva,* 10 October 1980, U.N. Doc. A/CONF.95/15 (1980), 19 I.L.M. 1529, entered into force 2 December 1983; entered into force with respect to the United States 24 September 1995.

Relevant Penal Characteristics & Penal Provisions
2.Implicit recognition of the penal nature of the act by establishing a duty to prohibit, prevent, prosecute, punish, or the like: Articles 3, 4, 5, 6

Applicability
War

Control
Regulation & Prohibition

State Signatories
Afghanistan; Argentina; Australia; Austria; Belgium; Bulgaria; Byelorussian Soviet Socialist Republic; Canada; China;[1] Cuba; Czechoslovakia; Denmark; Ecuador; Egypt, Finland, France,[2] German Democratic Republic; Federal Republic of Germany; Greece; Hungary; Iceland; India; Ireland; Italy;[3] Japan; Liechtenstein; Luxembourg; Mexico; Mongolia; Morocco; the Netherlands; New Zealand; Nicaragua; Nigeria; Norway; Pakistan; the Philippines; Poland; Portugal; Romania; Sierra Leone; Spain; Sudan; Sweden; Switzerland; Togo; Turkey; Ukrainian Soviet Socialist Republic; Union of Soviet Socialist Republics; United Kingdom;[4] United States of America;[5] Vietnam; Yugoslavia

State Parties
Argentina; Australia; Austria; Belarus; Belgium; Benin; Bosnia and Herzegovina; Brazil; Bulgaria; Cambodia; Canada; Cape Verde; China; Colombia; Costa Rica; Croatia; Cuba; Cyprus; Czech Republic; Denmark; El Salvador; Estonia; Ecuador; Finland; France; Germany; Georgia; Greece; Guatemala; Holy See; Hungary; India; Ireland; Israel; Italy; Japan; Jordan;

---

[1] With a statement.

[2] With an interpretive statement. With a declaration.

[3] With a declaration.

[4] With a statement.

[5] With a declaration.

Laos; Latvia; Liechtenstein; Luxembourg; Malta; Mauritius; Mexico; Monaco; Mongolia; the Netherlands; New Zealand; Niger; Norway; Pakistan; Panama; Peru; Poland; Philippines; Portugal; Romania; Russian Federation; Senegal; Slovakia; Slovenia; South Africa; Spain; Sweden; Switzerland; Tajikistan; Togo; Tunisia; Uganda; Ukraine; United Kingdom; United States of America; Uruguay; Yugoslavia

Reservations upon Signature, Accession or Ratification
Austria; Argentina; Belgium; Canada; China; Cyprus; Denmark; Finland; France; Germany; Greece; Hungary; Ireland; Israel; Italy; Liechtenstein; the Netherlands; Pakistan; Romania; South Africa; Ukraine; Great Britain; United States of America

Full Text

Article 1
Material scope of application

This Protocol relates to the use on land of the mines, booby-traps and other devices defined herein, including mines laid to interdict beaches, waterway crossings or river crossings, but does not apply to the use of anti-ship mines at sea or in inland waterways.

Article 2
Definitions

For the purpose of this Protocol:
1. "Mine" means any munition placed under, on or near the ground or other surface area and designed to be detonated or exploded by the presence, proximity or contact of a person or vehicle, and "remotely delivered mine" means any mine so defined delivered by artillery, rocket, mortar or similar means or dropped from an aircraft.
2. "Booby-trap" means any device or material which is designed, constructed or adapted to kill or injure and which functions unexpectedly when a person disturbs or approaches an apparently harmless object or performs an apparently safe act.
3. "Other devices" means manually-emplaced munitions and devices designed to kill, injure or damage and which are actuated by remote control or automatically after a lapse of time.
4. "Military objective" means, so far as objects are concerned, any object which by its nature, location, purpose or use makes an effective contribution to military action and whose total or partial destruction, capture or neutralization, in the circumstances ruling at the time, offers a definite military advantage.
5. "Civilian objects" are all objects which are not military objectives as defined in paragraph 4.

6. "Recording" means a physical, administrative and technical operation designed to obtain, for the purpose of registration in the official records, all available information facilitating the location of minefields, mines and booby-traps.

Article 3
General restrictions on the use of mines, booby-traps and other devices

1. This Article applies to: (a) mines (b) booby-traps; and (c) other devices.
2. It is prohibited in all circumstances to direct weapons to which this Article applies, either in offence, defence or by way of reprisals, against the civilian population as such or against individual civilians.
3. The indiscriminate use of weapons to which this Article applies is prohibited. Indiscriminate use is any placement of such weapons: (a) which is not on, or directed against, a military objective; or (b) which employs a method or means of delivery which cannot be directed at a specific military objective; or (c) which may be expected to cause incidental loss of civilian life, injury to civilians, damage to civilian objects, or a combination thereof, which would be excessive in relation to the concrete and direct military advantage anticipated.
4. All feasible precautions shall be taken to protect civilians from the effects of weapons to which this Article applies. Feasible precautions are those precautions which are practicable or practically possible taking into account all circumstances ruling at the time, including humanitarian and military considerations.

Article 4
Restrictions on the use of mines other than remotely delivered mines, booby-traps and other devices in populated areas

1. This Article applies to: (a) mines other than remotely delivered mines; (b) booby-traps; and (c) other devices.
2. It is prohibited to use weapons to which this Article applies in any city, town, village or other area containing a similar concentration of civilians in which combat between ground forces is not taking place or does not appear to be imminent, unless either: (a) they are placed on or in the close vicinity of a military objective belonging to or under the control of an adverse party; or (b) measures are taken to protect civilians from their effects, for example, the posting of warning signs, the posting of sentries, the issue of warnings or the provision of fences.

Article 5
Restrictions on the use of remotely delivered mines

1. The use of remotely delivered mines is prohibited unless such mines are only used within an area which is itself a military objective or which contains military

objectives, and unless: (a) their location can be accurately recorded in accordance with Article 7(1)(a); or (b) an effective neutralizing mechanism is used on each such mine, that is to say, a self-actuating mechanism which is designed to render a mine harmless or cause it to destroy itself when it is anticipated that the mine will no longer serve the military purpose for which it was placed in position, or a remotely-controlled mechanism which is designed to render harmless or destroy a mine when the mine no longer serves the military purpose for which it was placed in position.

2. Effective advance warning shall be given of any delivery or dropping of remotely delivered mines which may affect the civilian population, unless circumstances do not permit.

Article 6
Prohibition on the use of certain booby-traps

1. Without prejudice to the rules of international law applicable in armed conflict relating to treachery and perfidy, it is prohibited in all circumstances to use: (a) any booby-trap in the form of an apparently harmless portable object which is specifically designed and constructed to contain explosive material and to detonate when it is disturbed or approached, or (b) booby-traps which are in any way attached to or associated with:

(i) internationally recognized protective emblems, signs or signals;

(ii) sick, wounded or dead persons;

(iii) burial or cremation sites or graves;

(iv) medical facilities, medical equipment, medical supplies or medical transportation;

(v) children's toys or other portable objects or products specially designed for the feeding, health, hygiene, clothing or education of children;

(vi) food or drink;

(vii) kitchen utensils or appliances except in military establishments, military locations or military supply depots;

(viii) objects clearly of a religious nature;

(ix) historic monuments, works of art or places or worship which constitute the cultural or spiritual heritage of peoples;

(x) animals or their carcasses.

3. It is prohibited in all circumstances to use any booby-trap which is designed to cause superfluous injury or unnecessary suffering.

Article 7
Recording and publication of the location of minefields, mines and booby-traps

1. The parties to a conflict shall record the location
of: (a) all pre-planned minefields laid by them; and (b) all areas in which they have made large-scale and pre-planned use of booby-traps.

2. The parties shall endeavour to ensure the recording of the location of all other minefields, mines and booby-traps which they have laid or placed in position.

3. All such records shall be retained by the parties who shall:
(a) immediately after the cessation of active hostilities:

(i) take all necessary and appropriate measures, including the use of such records, to protect civilians from the effects of minefields, mines and booby-traps; and either

(ii) in cases where the forces of neither party are in the territory of the adverse party, make available to each other and to the Secretary-General of the United Nations all information in their possession concerning the location of minefields, mines and booby-traps in the territory of the adverse party; or

(iii) once complete withdrawal of the forces of the parties from the territory of the adverse party has taken place, make available to the adverse party and to the Secretary-General of the United Nations all information in their possession concerning the location of minefields, mines and booby traps in the territory of the adverse party; (b) when a United Nations force or mission performs functions in any area, make available to the authority mentioned in Article 8 such information as is required by that Article; (c) whenever possible, by mutual agreement, provide for the release of information concerning the location of minefields, mines and booby traps, particularly in agreements governing the cessation of hostilities.

Article 8
Protection of United Nations forces and missions from the effects of minefields, mines and booby-traps

1. When a United Nations force or mission performs functions of peacekeeping, observation or similar functions in any area, each party to the conflict shall, if requested by the head of the United Nations force or mission in that area, as far as it is able: (a) remove or render harmless all mines or booby traps in that area; (b) take such measures as may be necessary to protect the force or mission from the effects of minefields, mines and booby traps while carrying out its duties; and (c) make available to the head of the United Nations force or mission in that area, all information in the party's possession concerning the location of minefields, mines and booby traps in that area.

3. When a United Nations fact-finding mission performs functions in any area, any party to the conflict concerned shall provide protection to that mission except where, because of the size of such mission, it cannot adequately provide such protection. In that case it shall make available to the head of the mission the information in its possession concerning the location of minefields, mines and booby-traps in that area.

Article 9
International co-operation in the removal of minefields, mines and booby-traps

After the cessation of active hostilities, the parties shall endeavour to reach agreement, both among themselves and, where appropriate, with other States and with international organizations, on the provision of information and technical and material assistance -- including, in appropriate circumstances, joint operations -- necessary to remove or otherwise render ineffective minefields, mines and booby-traps placed in position during the conflict.

TECHNICAL ANNEX TO THE PROTOCOL ON PROHIBITIONS OR RESTRICTIONS ON THE USE OF MINES, BOOBY-TRAPS AND OTHER DEVICES (Protocol II)

Guidelines on recording

Whenever an obligation for the recording of the location of minefields, mines and booby traps arises under the Protocol, the following guidelines shall be taken into account.

1. With regard to pre-planned minefields and large-scale and pre-planned use of booby traps: (a) maps, diagrams or other records should be made in such a way as to indicate the extent of the minefield or booby-trapped area; and (b) the location of the minefield or booby-trapped area should be specified by relation to the co-ordinates of a single reference point and by the estimated dimensions of the area containing mines and booby traps in relation to that single reference point.

2. With regard to other minefields, mines and booby traps laid or placed in position: In so far as possible, the relevant information specified in paragraph I above should be recorded so as to enable the areas containing minefields, mines and booby traps to be identified.

Protocol on Prohibitions or Restrictions on the Use of Mines, Booby-Traps and Other Devices as amended on 3 May 1996 (Protocol II as amended on 3 May 1996)

Full Text

Article 1 - Scope of application
1.   This Protocol relates to the use on land of the mines, booby-traps and other devices, defined herein, including mines laid to interdict beaches, waterway crossings or river crossings, but does not apply to the use of anti-ship mines at sea or in inland waterways.
2.   This Protocol shall apply, in addition to situations referred to in Article I of this Convention, to situations referred to in Article 3 common to the Geneva Conventions of 12 August 1949. This Protocol shall not apply to situations of internal disturbances and tensions, such as riots, isolated and sporadic acts of violence and other acts of a similar nature, as not being armed conflicts.

3. In case of armed conflicts not of an international character occurring in the territory of one of the High Contracting Parties, each party to the conflict shall be bound to apply the prohibitions and restrictions of this Protocol.
4. Nothing in this Protocol shall be invoked for the purpose of affecting the sovereignty of a State or the responsibility of the Government, by all legitimate means, to maintain or re-establish law and order in the State or to defend the national unity and territorial integrity of the State.
5. Nothing in this Protocol shall be invoked as a justification for intervening, directly or indirectly, for any reason whatever, in the armed conflict or in the internal or external affairs of the High Contracting Party in the territory of which that conflict occurs.
6. The application of the provisions of this Protocol to parties to a conflict, which are not High Contracting Parties that have accepted this Protocol, shall not change their legal status or the legal status of a disputed territory, either explicitly or implicitly.

Article 2 -Definitions
For the purpose of this Protocol:
1. "Mine" means a munition placed under, on or near the ground or other surface area and designed to be exploded by the presence, proximity or contact of a person or vehicle.
2. "Remotely-delivered mine" means a mine not directly emplaced but delivered by artillery, missile, rocket, mortar, or similar means, or dropped from an aircraft. Mines delivered from a land-based system from less than 500 metres are not considered to be "remotely delivered", provided that they are used in accordance with Article 5 and other relevant Articles of this Protocol.
3. "Anti-personnel mine" means a mine primarily designed to be exploded by the presence, proximity or contact of a person and that will incapacitate, injure or kill one or more persons.
4. "Booby-trap" means any device or material which is designed, constructed or adapted to kill or injure, and which functions unexpectedly when a person disturbs or approaches an apparently harmless object or performs an apparently safe act.
5. "Other devices" means manually-emplaced munitions and devices including improvised explosive devices designed to kill, injure or damage and which are actuated manually, by remote control or automatically after a lapse of time.
6. "Military objective" means, so far as objects are concerned, any object which by its nature, location, purpose or use makes an effective contribution to military action and whose total or partial destruction, capture or neutralization, in the circumstances ruling at the time, offers a definite military advantage.
7. "Civilian objects" are all objects which are not military objectives as defined in paragraph 6 of this Article.

8. "Minefield" is a defined area in which mines have been emplaced and "mined area" is an area which is dangerous due to the presence of mines. "Phoney minefield" means an area free of mines that simulates a minefield. The term "minefield" includes phoney minefields.

9. "Recording" means a physical, administrative and technical operation designed to obtain, for the purpose of registration in official records, all available information facilitating the location of minefields, mined areas, mines, booby-traps and other devices.

10. "Self-destruction mechanism" means an incorporated or externally attached automatically-functioning mechanism which secures the destruction of the munition into which it is incorporated or to which it is attached.

11. "Self-neutralization mechanism" means an incorporated automatically-functioning mechanism which renders inoperable the munition into which it is incorporated.

12. "Self-deactivating" means automatically rendering a munition inoperable by means of the irreversible exhaustion of a component, for example, a battery, that is essential to the operation of the munition.

13. "Remote control" means control by commands from a distance.

14. "Anti-handling device" means a device intended to protect a mine and which is part of, linked to, attached to or placed under the mine and which activates when an attempt is made to tamper with the mine.

15. "Transfer" involves, in addition to the physical movement of mines into or from national territory, the transfer of title to and control over the mines, but does not involve the transfer of territory containing emplaced mines.

Article 3 - General restrictions on the use, of mines, booby-traps and other devices

1. This Article applies to:
(a) mines;
(b) booby-traps; and
(c) other devices.

2. Each High Contracting Party or party to a conflict is, in accordance with the provisions of this Protocol, responsible for all mines, booby-traps, and other devices employed by it and undertakes to clear, remove, destroy or maintain them as specified in Article 10 of this Protocol.

3. It is prohibited in all circumstances to use any mine, booby-trap or other device which is designed or of a nature to cause superfluous injury or unnecessary suffering.

4. Weapons to which this Article applies shall strictly comply with the standards and limitations specified in the Technical Annex with respect to each particular category.

5. It is prohibited to use mines, booby-traps or other devices which employ a mechanism or device specifically designed to detonate the munition by the presence of commonly available mine detectors as a result of their magnetic or other non-contact influence during normal use in detection operations.

6. It is prohibited to use a self-deactivating mine equipped with an anti-handling device that is designed in such a manner that the anti-handling device is capable of functioning after the mine has ceased to be capable of functioning.

7. It is prohibited in all circumstances to direct weapons to which this Article applies, either in offence, defence or by way of reprisals, against the civilian population as such or against individual civilians or civilian objects.

8. The indiscriminate use of weapons to which this Article applies is prohibited. Indiscriminate use is any placement of such weapons:

(a) which is not on, or directed against, a military objective. In case of doubt as to whether an object which is normally dedicated to civilian purposes, such as a place of worship, a house or other dwelling or a school, is being used to make an effective contribution to military action, it shall be presumed not to be so used; or

(b) which employs a method or means of delivery which cannot be directed at a specific military objective; or

(c) which may be expected to cause incidental loss of civilian life, injury to civilians, damage to civilian objects, or a combination thereof, which would be excessive in relation to the concrete and direct military advantage anticipated.

9. Several clearly separated and distinct military objectives located in a city, town, village or other area containing a similar concentration of civilians or civilian objects are not to be treated as a single military objective.

10. All feasible precautions shall be taken to protect civilians from the effects of weapons to which this Article applies. Feasible precautions are those precautions which are practicable or practically possible taking into account all circumstances ruling at the time, including humanitarian and military considerations. These circumstances include, but are not limited to:

(a) the short- and long-term effect of mines upon the local civilian population for the duration of the minefield;

(b) possible measures to protect civilians (for example, fencing, signs, warning and monitoring);

(c) the availability and feasibility of using alternatives; and

(d) the short- and long-term military requirements for a minefield.

11. Effective advance warning shall be given of any emplacement of mines, booby-traps and other devices which may affect the civilian population, unless circumstances do not permit.

Article 4 - Restrictions on the use of anti-personnel mines
It is prohibited to use anti-personnel mines which are not detectable, as specified in paragraph 2 of the Technical Annex.

Article 5 - Restrictions on the use of anti-personnel mines other than remotely-delivered mines

1. This Article applies to anti-personnel mines other than remotely-delivered mines.

2. It is prohibited to use weapons to which this Article applies which are not in compliance with the provisions on self-destruction and self-deactivation in the Technical Annex, unless:
(a) such weapons are placed within a perimeter-marked area which is monitored by military personnel and protected by fencing or other means, to ensure the effective exclusion of civilians from the area. The marking must be of a distinct and durable character and must at least be visible to a person who is about to enter the perimeter-marked area; and
(b) such weapons are cleared before the area is abandoned, unless the area is turned over to the forces of another State which accept responsibility for the maintenance of the protections required by this Article and the subsequent clearance of those weapons.
3. A party to a conflict is relieved from further compliance with the provisions of sub-paragraphs 2 (a) and 2 (b) of this Article only if such compliance is not feasible due to forcible loss of control of the area as a result of enemy military action, including situations where direct enemy military action makes it impossible to comply. If that party regains control of the area, it shall resume compliance with the provisions of sub-paragraphs 2 (a) and 2 (b) of this Article.
4. If the forces of a party to a conflict gain control of an area in which weapons to which this Article applies have been laid, such forces shall, to the maximum extent feasible, maintain and, if necessary, establish the protections required by this Article until such weapons have been cleared.
5. All feasible measures shall be taken to prevent the unauthorized removal, defacement, destruction or concealment of any device, system or material used to establish the perimeter of a perimeter-marked area.
6. Weapons to which this Article applies which propel fragments in a horizontal arc of less than 90 degrees and which are placed on or above the ground may be used without the measures provided for in sub-paragraph 2 (a) of this Article for a maximum period of 72 hours, if:
(a) they are located in immediate proximity to the military unit that emplaced them; and
(b) the area is monitored by military personnel to ensure the effective exclusion of civilians.

Article 6 - Restrictions on the use of remotely-delivered mines
1. It is prohibited to use remotely-delivered mines unless they are recorded in accordance with sub-paragraph I (b) of the Technical Annex.
2. It is prohibited to use remotely-delivered anti-personnel mines which are not in compliance with the provisions on self-destruction and self-deactivation in the Technical Annex.
3. It is prohibited to use remotely-delivered mines other than anti-personnel mines, unless, to the extent feasible, they are equipped with an effective self-destruction or self-neutralization mechanism and have a back-up self-deactivation feature, which is designed so that the mine will no longer function as a mine when the mine no longer serves the military purpose for which it was placed in position.

4. Effective advance warning shall be given of any delivery or dropping of remotely-delivered mines which may affect the civilian population, unless circumstances do not permit.

Article 7 - Prohibitions on the use of booby-traps and other devices

1. Without prejudice to the rules of international law applicable in armed conflict relating to treachery and perfidy, it is prohibited in all circumstances to use booby-traps and other devices which are in any way attached to or associated with:

    (a) internationally recognized protective emblems, signs or signals;

    (b) sick, wounded or dead persons;

    (c) burial or cremation sites or graves;

    (d) medical facilities, medical equipment, medical supplies or medical transportation;

    (e) children's toys or other portable objects or products specially designed for the feeding, health, hygiene, clothing or education of children;

    (f) food or drink;

    (g) kitchen utensils or appliances except in military establishments, military locations or military supply depots;

    (h) objects clearly of a religious nature;

    (i) historic monuments, works of art or places of worship which constitute the cultural or spiritual heritage of peoples; or

    (j) animals or their carcasses.

2. It is prohibited to use booby-traps or other devices in the form of apparently harmless portable objects which are specifically designed and constructed to contain explosive material.

3. Without prejudice to the provisions of Article 3, it is prohibited to use weapons to which this Article applies in any city, town, village or other area containing a similar concentration of civilians in which combat between ground forces is not taking place or does not appear to be imminent, unless either:

    (a) they are placed on or in the close vicinity of a military objective; or

    (b) measures are taken to protect civilians from their effects, for example, the posting of warning sentries, the issuing of warnings or the provision of fences

Article 8 - Transfers

1. In order to promote the purposes of this Protocol, each High Contracting Party:

    (a) undertakes not to transfer any mine the use of which is prohibited by this Protocol;

    (b) undertakes not to transfer any mine to any recipient other than a State or a State agency authorized to receive such transfers;

(c) undertakes to exercise restraint in the transfer of any mine the use of which is restricted by this Protocol. In particular, each High Contracting Party undertakes not to transfer any anti-personnel mines to States which are not bound by this Protocol, unless the recipient State agrees to apply this Protocol; and

(d) undertakes to ensure that any transfer in accordance with this Article takes place in full compliance, by both the transferring and the recipient State, with the relevant provisions of this Protocol and the applicable norms of international humanitarian law.

2. In the event that a High Contracting Party declares that it will defer compliance with specific provisions on the use of certain mines, as provided for in the Technical Annex, sub-paragraph I (a) of this Article shall however apply to such mines.

3. All High Contracting Parties, pending the entry into force of this Protocol, will refrain from any actions which would be inconsistent with sub-paragraph I (a) of this Article.

Article 9 -Recording and use of information on minefields, mined areas, mines, booby-traps and other devices

1. All information concerning minefields, mined areas, mines, booby-traps and other devices shall be recorded in accordance with the provisions of the Technical Annex.

2. All such records shall be retained by the parties to a conflict, who shall, without delay after the cessation of active hostilities, take all necessary and appropriate measures, including the use of such information, to protect civilians from the effects of minefields, mined areas, mines, booby-traps and other devices in areas under their control. At the same time, they shall also make available to the other party or parties to the conflict and to the Secretary-General of the United Nations all such information in their possession concerning minefields, mined areas, mines, booby-traps and other devices laid by them in areas no longer under their control; provided, however, subject to reciprocity, where the forces of a party to a conflict are in the territory of an adverse party, either party may withhold such information from the Secretary-General and the other party, to the extent that security interests require such withholding, until neither party is in the territory of the other. In the latter case, the information withheld shall be disclosed as soon as those security interests permit. Wherever possible, the parties to the conflict shall seek, by mutual agreement, to provide for the release of such information at the earliest possible time in a manner consistent with the security interests of each party.

3. This Article is without prejudice to the provisions of Articles 10 and 12 of this Protocol.

Article 10 - Removal of minefields, mined areas, mines, booby-traps and other devices and international cooperation
1. Without delay after the cessation of active hostilities, all minefields, mined areas, mines, booby-traps and other devices shall be cleared, removed, destroyed or maintained in accordance with Article 3 and paragraph 2 of Article 5 of this Protocol.
2. High Contracting Parties and parties to a conflict bear such responsibility with respect to minefields, mined areas, mines, booby-traps and other devices in areas under their control.

3. With respect to minefields, mined areas, mines, booby-traps and other devices laid by a party in areas over which it no longer exercises control, such party shall provide to the party in control of the area pursuant to paragraph 2 of this Article, to the extent permitted by such party, technical and material assistance necessary to fulfil such responsibility.
4. At all times necessary, the parties shall endeavour to reach agreement, both among themselves and, where appropriate, with other States and with international organizations, on the provision of technical and material assistance, including, in appropriate circumstances, the undertaking of joint operations necessary to fulfil such responsibilities.

Article 11 - Technological cooperation and assistance
1. Each High Contracting Party undertakes to facilitate and shall have the right to participate in the fullest possible exchange of equipment, material and scientific and technological information concerning the implementation of this Protocol and means of mine clearance. In particular, High Contracting Parties shall not impose undue restrictions on the provision of mine clearance equipment and related technological information for humanitarian purposes.
2. Each High Contracting Party undertakes to provide information to the database on mine clearance established within the United Nations System, especially information concerning various means and technologies of mine clearance, and lists of experts, expert agencies or national points of contact on mine clearance.
3. Each high Contracting Party in a position to do so shall provide assistance for mine clearance through the United Nations System, other international bodies or on a bilateral basis, or contribute to the United Nations Voluntary Trust Fund for Assistance in Mine Clearance.
4. Requests by High Contracting Parties for assistance, substantiated by relevant information, may be submitted to the United Nations, to other appropriate bodies or to other States. These requests may be submitted to the Secretary-General of the United Nations, who shall transmit them to all High Contracting Parties and to relevant international organizations.

5. In the case of requests to the United Nations, the Secretary-General of the United Nations, within the resources available to the Secretary-General of the United Nations, may take appropriate steps to assess the situation and, in cooperation with the requesting High Contracting Party, determine the appropriate provision of assistance in mine clearance or implementation of the Protocol. The Secretary-General may also report to High Contracting Parties on any such assessment as well as on the type and scope of assistance required.

6. Without prejudice to their constitutional and other legal provisions, the High Contracting Parties undertake to cooperate and transfer technology to facilitate the implementation of the relevant prohibitions and restrictions set out in this Protocol.

7. Each High Contracting Party has the right to seek and receive technical assistance, where appropriate, from another High Contracting Party on specific relevant technology, other than weapons technology, as necessary and feasible, with a view to reducing any period of deferral for which provision is made in the Technical Annex.

Article 12 - Protection from the effects of minefields, mined areas, mines, booby-traps and other devices

1. Application

(a) With the exception of the forces and missions referred to in sub-paragraph 2(a) (i) of this Article, this Article applies only to missions which are performing functions in an area with the consent of the High Contracting Party on whose territory the functions are performed.

(b) The application of the provisions of this Article to parties to a conflict which are not High Contracting Parties shall not change their legal status or the legal status of a disputed territory, either explicitly or implicitly.

(c) The provisions of this Article are without prejudice to existing international humanitarian law, or other international instruments as applicable, or decisions by the Security Council of the United Nations, which provide for a higher level of protection to personnel functioning in accordance with this Article.

2. Peace-keeping and certain other forces and missions

(a) This paragraph applies to: (i) any United Nations force or mission performing peace-keeping, observation or similar functions in any area in accordance with the Charter of the United Nations; (ii) any mission established pursuant to Chapter VIII of the Charter of the United Nations and performing its functions in the area of a conflict.

(b) Each High Contracting Party or party to a conflict, if so requested by the head of a force or mission to which this paragraph applies, shall: (i) so far as it is able, take such measures as are necessary to protect the force or mission from the effects of mines, booby-traps and other devices in any area under its control; (ii) if necessary in order effectively to protect such personnel, remove or render harmless, so far as it is able, all mines, booby-traps and other devices in that area; and (iii) inform the head of the force or mission of the location of all known minefields, mined areas, mines, booby-traps and other devices in the area in which the force or mission is performing its functions and, so far as is feasible, make available to the head of the force or mission all information in its possession concerning such minefields, mined areas, mines, booby-traps and other devices.

3. Humanitarian and fact-finding missions of the United Nations System

(a) This paragraph applies to any humanitarian or fact-finding mission of the United Nations System.

(b) Each High Contracting Party or party to a conflict, if so requested by the head of a mission to which this paragraph applies, shall: (i) provide the personnel of the mission with the protections set out in sub-paragraph 2(b) (i) of this Article; and (ii) if access to or through any place under its control is necessary for the performance of the mission's functions and in order to provide the personnel of the mission with safe passage to or through that place:

(aa) unless on-going hostilities prevent, inform the head of the mission of a safe route to that place if such information is available; or

(bb) if information identifying a safe route is not provided in accordance with sub-paragraph (aa), so far as is necessary and feasible, clear a lane through minefields.

4. Missions of the International Committee of the Red Cross

(a) This paragraph applies to any mission of the International Committee of the Red Cross performing functions with the consent of the host State or States as provided for by the Geneva Conventions of 12 August 1949 and, where applicable, their Additional Protocols.

(b) Each High Contracting Party or party to a conflict, if so requested by the head of a mission to which this paragraph applies, shall: (i) provide the personnel of the mission with the protections set out in sub-paragraph 2(b) (i) of this Article; and (ii) take the measures set out in sub-paragraph 3(b) (ii) of this Article.

5. Other humanitarian missions and missions of enquiry

(a) Insofar as paragraphs 2, 3 and 4 above do not apply to them, this paragraph applies to the following missions when they are performing functions in the area of a conflict or to assist the victims of a conflict: (i) any humanitarian mission of a national Red Cross or Red Crescent Society or of their International Federation; (ii) any mission of an impartial humanitarian organization, including any impartial humanitarian demining mission; and (iii) any mission of enquiry established pursuant to the provisions of the Geneva Conventions of 12 August 1949 and, where applicable, their Additional Protocols.

(b) Each High Contracting Party or party to a conflict, if so requested by the head of a mission to which this paragraph applies, shall, so far as is feasible:

(i) provide the personnel of the mission with the protections set out in sub-paragraph 2(b) (i) of this Article, and (ii) take the measures set out in sub-paragraph 3(b) (ii) of this Article.

6. Confidentiality - All information provided in confidence pursuant to this Article shall be treated by the recipient in strict confidence and shall not be released outside the force or mission concerned without the express authorization of the provider of the information.

7. Respect for laws and regulations - Without prejudice to such privileges and immunities as they may enjoy or to the requirements of their duties, personnel participating in the forces and missions referred to in this Article shall:
    (a) respect the laws and regulations of the host State; and
    (b) refrain from any action or activity incompatible with the impartial and international nature of their duties.

Article 13 - Consultations of High Contracting Parties

1. The High Contracting Parties undertake to consult and cooperate with each other on all issues related to the operation of this Protocol. For this purpose, a conference of High Contracting Parties shall be held annually.

2. Participation in the annual conferences shall be determined by their agreed Rules of Procedure.

3. The work of the conference shall include:
    (a) review of the operation and status of this Protocol;
    (b) consideration of matters arising from reports by High Contracting Parties according to paragraph 4 of this Article;
    (c) preparation for review conferences; and
    (d) consideration of the development of technologies to protect civilians against indiscriminate effects of mines.

4. The High Contracting Parties shall provide annual reports to the Depositary, who shall circulate them to all High Contracting Parties in advance of the Conference, on any of the following matters:
    (a) dissemination of information on this Protocol to their armed forces and to the civilian population;
    (b) mine clearance and rehabilitation programmes;
    (c) steps taken to meet technical requirements of this Protocol and any other relevant information pertaining thereto;
    (d) legislation related to this Protocol;
    (e) measures taken on international technical information exchange, on international cooperation on mine clearance, and on technical cooperation and assistance; and
    (f) other relevant matters.

5. The cost of the Conference of High Contracting Parties shall be borne by the High Contracting Parties and States not parties participating in the work of the Conference, in accordance with the United Nations scale of assessment adjusted appropriately.

Article 14 - Compliance

1. Each High Contracting Party shall take all appropriate steps, including legislative and other measures, to prevent and suppress violations of this Protocol by persons or on territory under its jurisdiction or control.

2. The measures envisaged in paragraph 1 of this Article include appropriate measures to ensure the imposition of penal sanctions against persons who, in relation to an armed conflict and contrary to the provisions of this Protocol, wilfully kill or cause serious injury to civilians and to bring such persons to justice.

3. Each High Contracting Party shall also require that its armed forces issue relevant military instructions and operating procedures and that armed forces personnel receive training commensurate with their duties and responsibilities to comply with the provisions of this Protocol.

4. The High Contracting Parties undertake to consult each other and to cooperate with each other bilaterally, through the Secretary-General of the United Nations or through other appropriate international procedures, to resolve any problems that may arise with regard to the interpretation and application of the provisions of this Protocol.

Technical Annex
1. Recording

(a) Recording of the location of mines other than remotely-delivered mines, minefields, mined areas, booby-traps and other devices shall be carried out in accordance with the following provisions:

(i) the location of the minefields, mined areas and areas of booby-traps and other devices shall be specified accurately by relation to the coordinates of at least two reference points and the estimated dimensions of the area containing these weapons in relation to those reference points;

(ii) maps, diagrams or other records shall be made in such a way as to indicate the location of minefields, mined areas, booby-traps and other devices in relation to reference points, and these records shall also indicate their perimeters and extent;

(iii) for purposes of detection and clearance of mines, booby-traps and other devices, maps, diagrams or other records shall contain complete information on the type, number, emplacing method, type of fuse and life time, date and time of laying, anti-handling devices (if any) and other relevant information on all these weapons laid. Whenever feasible the minefield record shall show the exact location of every mine, except in row minefields where the row location is sufficient. The precise location and operating mechanism of each booby-trap laid shall be individually recorded.

(b) The estimated location and area of remotely-delivered mines shall be specified by coordinates of reference points (normally corner points) and shall be ascertained and when feasible marked on the ground at the earliest opportunity. The total number and types of mines laid, the date and time of laying and the self-destruction time periods shall also be recorded.

(c) Copies of records shall be held at a level of command sufficient to guarantee their safety as far as possible.

(d) The use of mines produced after the entry into force of this Protocol is prohibited unless they are marked in English or in the respective national language or languages with the following information: (i) name of the country of origin; (ii) month and year of production; and (iii) serial number or lot number.

The marking should be visible, legible, durable and resistant to environmental effects, as far as possible.

2. Specifications on detectability

(a) With respect to anti-personnel mines produced after 1 January 1997, such mines shall incorporate in their construction a material or device that enables the mine to be detected by commonly-available technical mine detection equipment and provides a response signal equivalent to a signal from 8 grammes or more of iron in a single coherent mass.

(b) With respect to anti-personnel mines produced before 1 January 1997, such mines shall either incorporate in their construction, or have attached prior to their emplacement, in a manner not easily removable, a material or device that enables the mine to be detected by commonly-available technical mine detection equipment and provides a response signal equivalent to a signal from 8 grammes or more of iron in a single coherent mass.

(c) In the event that a High Contracting Party determines that it cannot immediately comply with sub-paragraph (b), it may declare at the time of its notification of consent to be bound by this Protocol that it will defer compliance with sub-paragraph (b) for a period not to exceed 9 years from the entry into force of this Protocol. In the meantime it shall, to the extent feasible, minimize the use of anti-personnel mines that do not so comply.

3. Specifications on self-destruction and self-deactivation

(a) All remotely-delivered anti-personnel mines shall be designed and constructed so that no more than 10% of activated mines will fail to self-destruct within 30 days after emplacement, and each mine shall have a back-up self-deactivation feature designed and constructed so that, in combination with the self-destruction mechanism, no more than one in one thousand activated mines will function as a mine 120 days after emplacement.

(b) All non-remotely delivered anti-personnel mines, used outside marked areas, as defined in Article 5 of this Protocol, shall comply with the requirements for self-destruction and self-deactivation stated in sub-paragraph (a).

(c) In the event that a High Contracting Party determines that it cannot immediately comply with sub-paragraphs (a) and/or (b), it may declare at the time of its notification of consent to be bound by this Protocol, that it will, with respect to mines produced prior to the entry into force of this Protocol defer compliance with sub-paragraphs (a) and/or (b) for a period not to exceed 9 years from the entry into force of this Protocol.

During this period of deferral, the High Contracting Party shall:
(i) undertake to minimize, to the extent feasible, the use of anti-personnel mines that do not so comply, and (ii) with respect to remotely-delivered anti-personnel mines, comply with either the requirements for self-destruction or the requirements for self-deactivation and, with respect to other anti-personnel mines comply with at least the requirements for self-deactivation.

4. International signs for minefields and mined areas

Signs similar to the example attached [1] and as specified below shall be utilized in the marking of minefields and mined areas to ensure their visibility and recognition by the civilian population:

(a) size and shape: a triangle or square no smaller than 28 centimetres (11 inches) by 20 centimetres (7.9 inches) for a triangle, and 15 centimetres (6 inches) per ide for a square;
(b) colour: red or orange with a yellow reflecting border.

I-32(c). Protocol on Prohibitions or Restrictions on the Use of Incendiary Weapons to the Convention on Prohibitions or Restrictions on the Use of Certain Conventional Weapons [Protocol III], *adopted at Geneva, 10 October 1980, U.N. Doc. A/CONF.95/15 (1980), 19 I.L.M. 1534, entered into force 2 December 1983 with provisions.*

Relevant Penal Characteristics & Penal Provisions
2. Implicit recognition of the penal nature of the act by establishing a duty to prohibit, prevent, prosecute, punish, or the like: Article 2

Applicability
War

Control
Regulation & Prohibition

State Signatories
Afghanistan; Argentina; Australia; Austria; Belgium; Bulgaria; Byelorussian Soviet Socialist Republic; Canada; China;[1] Cuba; Czechoslovakia; Denmark; Ecuador; Egypt; Finland, France;[2] German Democratic Republic; Federal Republic of Germany; Greece; Hungary; Iceland; India; Ireland; Italy;[3] Japan; Liechtenstein; Luxembourg; Mexico; Mongolia; Morocco; the Netherlands; New Zealand; Nicaragua; Nigeria; Norway; Pakistan; the Philippines; Poland; Portugal; Romania; Sierra Leone; Spain; Sudan; Sweden; Switzerland; Togo; Turkey; Ukrainian Soviet Socialist Republic; Union of Soviet Socialist Republics; United Kingdom;[4] United States of America;[5] Vietnam; Yugoslavia

State Parties
Argentina; Australia; Austria; Belarus; Belgium; Benin; Bosnia and Herzegovina; Brazil; Bulgaria; Canada; China; Croatia; Cuba; Cyprus; Czech Republic; Denmark; Ecuador; Finland; France; Germany; Georgia; Greece; Guatemala; Hungary; India; Ireland; Israel; Italy; Japan; Jordan; Laos;

---

[1] With a statement.

[2] With an interpretive statement. With a declaration.

[3] With a declaration.

[4] With a statement.

[5] With a declaration.

Latvia; Liechtenstein; Luxembourg; Malta; Mauritius; Mexico; Mongolia; the Netherlands; New Zealand; Niger; Norway; Pakistan; Poland; Romania; Russian Federation; Slovakia; Slovenia; South Africa; Spain; Sweden; Switzerland; Togo; Tunisia; Uganda; Ukraine; United Kingdom; United States of America; Uruguay; Yugoslavia

Reservations upon Signature, Accession or Ratification
Argentina; Canada; China; Cyprus; France; Israel; Italy; the Netherlands, Romania; Great Britain; United States of America

Full Text

Article 1
Definitions

For the purpose of this Protocol:
1. "Incendiary weapon" means any weapon or munition which is primarily designed to set fire to objects or to cause burn injury to persons through the action of flame, heat, or combination thereof, produced by a chemical reaction of a substance delivered on the target.
(a) Incendiary weapons can take the form of, for example, flame throwers, fougasses, shells, rockets, grenades, mines, bombs and other containers of incendiary substances.
(b) Incendiary weapons do not include:
   (i) Munitions which may have incidental incendiary effects, such as illuminants, tracers, smoke or signalling systems;
   (ii) Munitions designed to combine penetration, blast or fragmentation effects with an additional incendiary effect, such as armour-piercing projectiles, fragmentation shells, explosive bombs and similar combined-effects munitions in which the incendiary effect is not specifically designed to cause burn injury to persons, but to be used against military objectives, such as armoured vehicles, aircraft and installations or facilities.
2. "Concentration of civilians" means any concentration of civilians, be it permanent or temporary, such as in inhabited parts of cities, or inhabited towns or villages, or as in camps or columns of refugees or evacuees, or groups of nomads.
3. "Military objective" means, so far as objects are concerned, any object which by its nature, location, purpose or use makes an effective contribution to military action and whose total or partial destruction, capture or neutralization, in the circumstances ruling at the time, offers a definite military advantage.
4. "Civilian objects" are all objects which are not military objectives as defined in paragraph 3.
5. "Feasible precautions" are those precautions which are practicable or practically possible taking into account all circumstances ruling at the time, including humanitarian and military considerations.

Article 2
Protection of civilians and civilian objects

1. It is prohibited in all circumstances to make the civilian population as such, individual civilians or civilian objects the object of attack by incendiary weapons.
2. It is prohibited in all circumstances to make any military objective located within a concentration of civilians the object of attack by air-delivered incendiary weapons.
3. It is further prohibited to make any military objective located within a concentration of civilians the object of attack by means of incendiary weapons other than air-delivered incendiary weapons, except when such military objective is clearly separated from the concentration of civilians and all feasible precautions are taken with a view to limiting the incendiary effects to the military objective and to avoiding, and in any event to minimizing, incidental loss of civilian life, injury to civilians and damage to civilian objects.
4. It is prohibited to make forests or other kinds of plant cover the object of attack by incendiary weapons except when such natural elements are used to cover, conceal or camouflage combatants or other military objectives, or are themselves military objectives.

I-32(d). **Additional Protocol to the Convention on Prohibitions or Restrictions on the Use of Certain Conventional Weapons Which May be Deemed to be Excessively Injurious or to have Indiscriminate Effects (Protocol IV) on Blinding Laser Weapons,** *adopted,* 12 October 1995, *see* 90 AM. J. INT'L L. 484 (1996), not yet in force.

Relevant Penal Characteristics & Penal Provisions
1. Explicit recognition of proscribed conduct as constituting an international crime, or a crime under international law, or a crime: Article 1

State Parties
Argentina; Australia; Austria; Belgium; Brazil; Bulgaria; Cambodia; Canada; Cape Verde; China; Colombia; Costa Rica; Czech Republic; Denmark; El Salvador; Estonia; Finland; France; Germany; Greece; Holy See; Hungary; India; Ireland; Italy; Japan; Latvia; Liechtenstein; Lithuania; Luxembourg; Mexico; Mongolia; Netherlands; New Zealand; Norway; Panama; Peru; Philippines; Russian Federation; Slovakia; South Africa; Spain; Sweden; Switzerland; Tajikistan; United Kingdom of Great Britain and Northern Ireland; Uruguay; Uzbekistan

Declarations and Reservations
Australia; Austria; Belgium; Canada; Germany; Greece; Ireland; Italy; Liechtenstein; Netherlands; South Africa; Sweden; Switzerland; United Kingdom of Great Britain and Northern Ireland

Applicability
War

Control
Regulation & Prohibition

Full Text

Article 1
It is prohibited to employ laser weapons specifically designed, as their sole combat function or as one of their combat functions, to cause permanent blindness to unenhanced vision, that is to the naked eye or to the eye with corrective eyesight devices. The High Contracting Parties shall not transfer such weapons to any State or non-State entity.

Article 2
In the employment of laser systems, the High Contracting Parties shall take all feasible precautions to avoid the incidence of permanent blindness to unenhanced vision. Such precautions shall include training of their armed forces and other practical measures.

Article 3
Blinding as an incidental or collateral effect of the legitimate military employment of laser systems, including laser systems used against optical equipment, is not covered by the prohibition of this Protocol.

Article 4
For the purpose of this protocol "permanent blindness" means irreversible and uncorrectable loss of vision which is seriously disabling with no prospect of recovery. Serious disability is equivalent to visual acuity of less than 20/200 Snellen measured using both eyes.

I-33. United Nations Convention on the Law of the Sea (1982); Montego Bay, 10 December, 1982, A/CONF. 62/122, 7 October 1982. Authentic Languages: Arabic, Chinese, English, French, Russian and Spanish

Relevant Penal Characteristics and Penal Provisions

1. Explicit or implicit recognition of proscribed conduct as constituting an international crime, or a crime under international law, or a crime;
2. Implicit recognition of the penal nature of the act by establishing a duty to prohibit, prevent, prosecute, punish, or the like;
8. Establishment of a criminal jurisdictional basis;

Applicability
Peace

Control
Regulate

State Signatories

Afghanistan; Albania; Algeria; Angola; Antigua and Barbuda; Argentina; Australia; Austria; Bahamas; Bahrain; Bangladesh; Barbados; Belgium; Belize; Benin; Bhutan; Bolivia; Botswana; Brazil; Brunei; Bulgaria; Burkina Faso; Burma; Burundi; Byelorussia; Cameroon; Canada; Cape Verde; Central African Republic; Chad; Chile; China; Colombia; Comoros; Congo; Costa Rica; Cyprus; Czechoslovakia; Democratic Kampuchea; Democratic People's Republic of Korea; Democratic Yemen; Denmark; Djibouti; Dominica; Dominican Republic; Ecuador; Egypt; El Salvador; Equatorial Guinea; Ethiopia; Fiji; Finland; France; Gabon; Gambia; German Democratic Republic; German Federal Republic; Ghana; Greece; Grenada; Guatemala; Guinea-Bissau; Guinea; Guyana;

Haiti; Holy See; Honduras; Hungary; Iceland; India; Indonesia; Iran; Iraq; Ireland; Israel; Italy; Ivory Coast; Jamaica; Japan; Jordan; Kenya; Kiribati; Kuwait; Lao People's Democratic Republic; Lebanon; Lesotho; Liberia; Libya; Liechtenstein; Luxembourg; Madagascar; Malawi; Malaysia; Maldives; Mali; Malta; Mauritania; Mauritius; Mexico; Monaco; Mongolia; Morocco; Mozambique; Nauru; Nepal; Netherlands; New Zealand; Nicaragua; Niger; Nigeria; Norway; Niue; Oman; Pakistan; Panama; Papua New Guinea; Paraguay; Peru; Philippines; Poland; Portugal; Qatar; Republic of Korea; Romania; Rwanda; St. Christopher & Nevis; St. Lucia; St. Vincent and the Grenadines; Samoa; San Marino; Sao Tome and Principe; Saudi Arabia; Senegal; Seyechelles; Sierra Leone; Singapore; Solomon Islands; Somalia; South Africa; Spain; Sri Lanka; Sudan; Suriname; Swaziland; Sweden; Switzerland; Syria; Thailand; Togo; Tonga; Trinidad and Tobago; Tunisia; Turkey; Tuvalu; Uganda; Ukraine; USSR; United Arab Emirates; United

Kingdom; United Republic of Tanzania; United States of America; Uruguay; Vanuatu; Venezuela; Viet Nam; Yugoslavia; Zaire; Zambia; Zimbabwe.

State Parties

Fiji; Zambia; Mexico; Jamaica; Namibia; Ghana; Bahamas; Belize; Egypt; Ivory Coast; Philippines; Gambia; Cuba; Senegal; Sudan; Saint Lucia; Togo; Tunisia; Bahrain; Iceland; Mali; Iraq; Guinea; United Republic of Tanzania; Cameroon; Indonesia; Trinidad and Tobago; Kuwait; Yugoslavia; Nigeria; Guinea-Bissau; Paraguay; Yemen; Cape Verde; Sao Tome and Principe; Cyprus; Brazil; Antigua and Barbuda; Zaire; Kenya; Somalia; Oman; Botswana; Uganda; Angola; Grenada; Micronesia; Marshall Islands; Seychelles; Djibouti; Dominica; Costa Rica; Uruguay; St. Kitts and Nevis; Zimbabwe; Malta; St. Vincent and the Grenadines; Honduras; Barbados; Guyana; Bosnia Herzegovina; Comoros; Sri Lanka; Viet Nam; The former Yugoslav Republic of Macedonia; Australia; Germany; Mauritius; Singapore;

Relevant Text

Article 19
Meaning of innocent passage

1. Passage is innocent so long as it is not prejudicial to the peace, good order or security of the coastal State. Such passage shall take place in conformity with this Convention and with other rules of international law.

2. Passage of a foreign ship shall be considered to be prejudicial to the peace, good order or security of the coastal State if in the territorial sea it engages in any of the following activities:

(a) any threat or use of force against the sovereignty, territorial integrity or political independence of the coastal State, or in any other manner in violation of the principles of international law embodied in the Charter of the United Nations;
(b) any exercise or practice with weapons of any kind;
(c) any act aimed at collecting information to the prejudice of the defence or security of the coastal State;
(d) any act of propaganda aimed at affecting the defence or security of the coastal State;
(e) the launching, landing or taking on board of any aircraft;
(f) the launching, landing or taking on board of any military device;
(g) the loading or unloading of any commodity, currency or person contrary to the customs, fiscal, immigration or sanitary laws and regulations of the coastal State;
(h) any act of wilful and serious pollution contrary to this Convention;

(i) any fishing activities;
(j) the carrying out of research or survey activities;
(k) any act aimed at interfering with any systems of communication or any other facilities or installations of the coastal State;
(l) any other activity not having a direct bearing on passage.

Article 20
Submarines and other underwater vehicles

In the territorial sea, submarines and other underwater vehicles are required to navigate on the surface and to show their flag.

***

Article 23
Foreign nuclear-powered ships and ships carrying nuclear or other inherently dangerous or noxious substances

Foreign nuclear-powered ships and ships carrying nuclear or other inherently dangerous or noxious substances shall, when exercising the right of innocent passage through the territorial sea, carry documents and observe special precautionary measures established for such ships by international agreements.

***

SUBSECTION C. RULES APPLICABLE TO WARSHIPS AND OTHER GOVERNMENT SHIPS OPERATED FOR NON-COMMERCIAL PURPOSES

Article 29
Definition of warships

For the purposes of this Convention, "warship" means a ship belonging to the armed forces of a State bearing the external marks distinguishing such ships of its nationality, under the command of an officer duly commissioned by the government of the State and whose name appears in the appropriate service list or its equivalent, and manned by a crew which is under regular armed forces discipline.

Article 30
Non-compliance by warships with the laws and regulations of the coastal State

If any warship does not comply with the laws and regulations of the coastal State concerning passage through the territorial sea and disregards any request for compliance therewith which is made to it, the coastal State may require it to leave the territorial sea immediately.

Article 31
Responsibility of the flag State for damage caused by a warship or other government ship operated for non-commercial purposes

The flag State shall bear international responsibility for any loss or damage to the coastal State resulting from the non-compliance by a warship or other government ship operated for non-commercial purposes with the laws and regulations of the coastal State concerning passage through the territorial sea or with the provisions of this Convention or other rules of international law.

Article 32
Immunities of warships and other government ships operated for non-commercial purposes

With such exceptions as are contained in subsection A and in articles 30 and 31, nothing in this Convention affects the immunities of warships and other government ships operated for non-commercial purposes.

***

Article 95
Immunity of warships on the high seas

Warships on the high seas have complete immunity from the jurisdiction of any State other than the flag State.

***

Article 298
Optional exceptions to applicability of section 2

1. When signing, ratifying or acceding to this Convention or at any time thereafter, a State may, without prejudice to the obligations arising under section 1, declare in writing that it does not accept any one or more of the procedures provided for in section 2 with respect to one or more of the following categories of disputes:

(b) disputes concerning military activities, including military activities by government vessels and aircraft engaged in non-commercial service, and disputes concerning law enforcement activities in regard to the exercise of sovereign rights or jurisdiction excluded from the jurisdiction of a court or tribunal under article 297, paragraph 2 or 3;

***

Article 301
Peaceful uses of the seas

In exercising their rights and performing their duties under this Convention, States Parties shall refrain from any threat or use of force against the territorial integrity or political independence of any State, or in any other manner inconsistent with the principles of international law embodied in the Charter of the United Nations.

International Humanitarian Law and Arms Control Agreements

I-34. **United Nations International Convention for the Suppression of Terrorist Bombings, January 12, 1998., U.N. Doc A/Res/52/164; <http://www.sipri.se/cbw/docs/terrorism-conv-text.html>. Authentic Texts: Arabic, Chinese, English, French, Russian and Spanish.**

Relevant Penal Characteristics & Penal Provisions

1. Explicit or implicit recognition of proscribed conduct as constituting an international crime, or a crime under international law, or a crime: Article 2

2. Implicit recognition of the penal nature of the act by establishing a duty to prohibit, prevent, prosecute, punish, or the like: Article 15

3. Criminalization of the proscribed conduct: Articles 4, 5

4. Duty or right to prosecute: Article 7 (implicit) (Duty or right to prosecute if no extradition: Articles 8)

5. Duty or right to punish the proscribed conduct: Articles 4

6. Duty or right to extradite: Articles 9

7. Duty or right to cooperate in prosecution, punishment (including judicial assistance): Article 10

8. Establishment of a criminal jurisdictional basis: Articles 3, 6

Applicability

War and Peace

Control

Prohibition

State Signatories

Algeria; Argentina; Austria; Belarus; Belgium; Brazil; Burundi; Canada; Comoros; Costa Rica; Côte d'Ivoire; Cyprus Czech Republic; Denmark; Egypt; Estonia; Finland; France; Germany; Greece; Hungary; Iceland; India; Ireland; Israel; Italy; Japan; Lithuania; Luxembourg; Madagascar; Monaco; Nepal; Netherlands; Norway; Panama; Philippines; Poland; Portugal; Republic of Korea; Romania; Russian Federation, Slovakia, Slovenia; South Africa; Spain; Sri Lanka; Sudan; Sweden; the former Yugoslav Republic of Macedonia; Togo; Turkmenistan; Uganda; United Kingdom of Great Britain and Northern Ireland; United States of America; Uruguay; Uzbekistan; Venezuela.

State Parties

Norway; Panama; Spain; Sri Lanka; Turkmenistan; Uzbekistan.

Full Text

The States Parties to this Convention,

Having in mind the purposes and principles of the Charter of the United Nations concerning the maintenance of international peace and security and the promotion of good-neighbourliness and friendly relations and cooperation among States,

Deeply concerned about the worldwide escalation of acts of terrorism in all its forms and manifestations,

Recalling the Declaration on the Occasion of the Fiftieth Anniversary of the United Nations of 24 October 1995, *

Recalling also the Declaration on Measures to Eliminate International Terrorism, annexed to General Assembly resolution 49/60 of 9 December 1994, in which, inter alia, "the States Members of the United Nations solemnly reaffirm their unequivocal condemnation of all acts,
methods and practices of terrorism as criminal and unjustifiable, wherever and by whomever committed, including those which jeopardize the friendly relations among States and peoples and threaten the territorial integrity and security of States",

Noting that the Declaration also encouraged States "to review urgently the scope of the existing international legal provisions on the prevention, repression and elimination of terrorism in all its forms and manifestations, with the aim of ensuring that there is a comprehensive legal framework covering all aspects of the matter",

Recalling General Assembly resolution 51/210 of 17 December 1996 and the Declaration to Supplement the 1994 Declaration on Measures to Eliminate International Terrorism annexed thereto,

Noting that terrorist attacks by means of explosives or other lethal devices have become increasingly widespread,

Noting also that existing multilateral legal provisions do not adequately address these attacks,

Being convinced of the urgent need to enhance international cooperation between States in devising and adopting effective and practical measures for the prevention of such acts of terrorism and for the prosecution and punishment of their perpetrators,

Considering that the occurrence of such acts is a matter of grave concern to the international community as a whole,

Noting that the activities of military forces of States are governed by rules of international law outside the framework of this Convention and that the exclusion of certain actions from the coverage of this Convention does not condone or make lawful otherwise unlawful acts, or preclude prosecution under other laws,

Have agreed as follows:

Article 1

For the purposes of this Convention:

1. "State or government facility" includes any permanent or temporary facility or conveyance that is used or occupied by representatives of a State, members of Government, the legislature or the judiciary or by officials or employees of a State or any other public authority or entity or by employees or officials of an intergovernmental organization in connection with their official duties.

2. "Infrastructure facility" means any publicly or privately owned facility providing or distributing services for the benefit of the public, such as water, sewage, energy, fuel or communications.

3. "Explosive or other lethal device" means:

(a) An explosive or incendiary weapon or device that is designed, or has the capability, to cause death, serious bodily injury or substantial material damage; or

(b) A weapon or device that is designed, or has the capability, to cause death, serious bodily injury or substantial material damage through the release, dissemination or impact of toxic chemicals, biological agents or toxins or similar substances or radiation or radioactive material.

4. "Military forces of a State" means the armed forces of a State which are organized, trained and equipped under its internal law for the primary purpose of national defence or security and persons acting in support of those armed forces who are under their formal command, control and responsibility.

5. "Place of public use" means those parts of any building, land, street, waterway or other location that are accessible or open to members of the public, whether continuously, periodically or occasionally, and encompasses any commercial,

business, cultural, historical, educational, religious, governmental, entertainment, recreational or similar place that is so accessible or open to the public.

6. "Public transportation system" means all facilities, conveyances and instrumentalities, whether publicly or privately owned, that are used in or for publicly available services for the transportation of persons or cargo.

Article 2

1. Any person commits an offence within the meaning of this Convention if that person unlawfully and intentionally delivers, places, discharges or detonates an explosive or other lethal device in, into or against a place of public use, a State or government facility, a public transportation system or an infrastructure facility:

(a) With the intent to cause death or serious bodily injury; or

(b) With the intent to cause extensive destruction of such a place, facility or system, where such destruction results in or is likely to result in major economic loss.

2. Any person also commits an offence if that person attempts to commit an offence as set forth in paragraph 1 of the present article.

3. Any person also commits an offence if that person:

(a) Participates as an accomplice in an offence as set forth in paragraph 1 or 2 of the present article; or

(b) Organizes or directs others to commit an offence as set forth in paragraph 1 or 2 of the present article; or

(c) In any other way contributes to the commission of one or more offences as set forth in paragraph 1 or 2 of the present article by a group of persons acting with a common purpose; such contribution shall be intentional and either be made with the aim of furthering the general criminal activity or purpose of the group or be made in the knowledge of the intention of the group to commit the offence or offences concerned.

Article 3

This Convention shall not apply where the offence is committed within a single State, the alleged offender and the victims are nationals of that State, the alleged offender is found in the territory of that State and no other State has a basis under article 6, paragraph 1 or paragraph 2, of this Convention to exercise jurisdiction, except that the provisions of articles 10 to 15 shall, as appropriate, apply in those cases.

Article 4

Each State Party shall adopt such measures as may be necessary:

(a) To establish as criminal offences under its domestic law the offences set forth in article 2 of this Convention;

(b) To make those offences punishable by appropriate penalties which take into account the grave nature of those offences.

Article 5

Each State Party shall adopt such measures as may be necessary, including, where appropriate, domestic legislation, to ensure that criminal acts within the scope of this Convention, in particular where they are intended or calculated to provoke a state of terror in the general public or in a group of persons or particular persons, are under no circumstances justifiable by considerations of a political, philosophical, ideological, racial, ethnic, religious or other similar nature and are punished by penalties consistent with their grave nature.

Article 6

1. Each State Party shall take such measures as may be necessary to establish its jurisdiction over the offences set forth in article 2 when:

(a) The offence is committed in the territory of that State; or

(b) The offence is committed on board a vessel flying the flag of that State or an aircraft which is registered under the laws of that State at the time the offence is committed; or

(c) The offence is committed by a national of that State.

2. A State Party may also establish its jurisdiction over any such offence when:

(a) The offence is committed against a national of that State; or

(b) The offence is committed against a State or government facility of that State abroad, including an embassy or other diplomatic or consular premises of that State; or

(c) The offence is committed by a stateless person who has his or her habitual residence in the territory of that State; or

(d) The offence is committed in an attempt to compel that State to do or abstain from doing any act; or

(e) The offence is committed on board an aircraft which is operated by the Government of that State.

3. Upon ratifying, accepting, approving or acceding to this Convention, each State Party shall notify the Secretary-General of the United Nations of the jurisdiction it has established under its domestic law in accordance with paragraph 2 of the present article. Should any change take place, the State Party concerned shall immediately notify the Secretary-General.

4. Each State Party shall likewise take such measures as may be necessary to establish its jurisdiction over the offences set forth in article 2 in cases where the alleged offender is present in its territory and it does not extradite that person to any of the States Parties which have established their jurisdiction in accordance with paragraph 1 or 2 of the present article.

5. This Convention does not exclude the exercise of any criminal jurisdiction established by a State Party in accordance with its domestic law.

Article 7

1. Upon receiving information that a person who has committed or who is alleged to have committed an offence as set forth in article 2 may be present in its territory, the State Party concerned shall take such measures as may be necessary under its domestic law to investigate the facts contained in the information.

2. Upon being satisfied that the circumstances so warrant, the State Party in whose territory the offender or alleged offender is present shall take the appropriate measures under its domestic law so as to ensure that person's presence for the purpose of prosecution or extradition.

3. Any person regarding whom the measures referred to in paragraph 2 of the present article are being taken shall be entitled to:

(a) Communicate without delay with the nearest appropriate representative of the

State of which that person is a national or which is otherwise entitled to protect that person's rights or, if that person is a stateless person, the State in the territory of which that person habitually resides;

(b) Be visited by a representative of that State;

(c) Be informed of that person's rights under subparagraphs (a) and (b).

4. The rights referred to in paragraph 3 of the present article shall be exercised in conformity with the laws and regulations of the State in the territory of which the offender or alleged offender is present, subject to the provision that the said laws and regulations must enable full effect to be given to the purposes for which the rights accorded under paragraph 3 are intended.

5. The provisions of paragraphs 3 and 4 of the present article shall be without prejudice to the right of any State Party having a claim to jurisdiction in accordance with article 6, subparagraph 1 (c) or 2 (c), to invite the International Committee of the Red Cross to communicate with and visit the alleged offender.

6. When a State Party, pursuant to the present article, has taken a person into custody, it shall immediately notify, directly or through the Secretary-General of the United Nations, the States Parties which have established jurisdiction in accordance with article 6, paragraphs 1 and 2, and, if it considers it advisable, any other interested States Parties, of the fact that that person is in custody and of the circumstances which warrant that person's detention. The State which makes the investigation contemplated in paragraph 1 of the present article shall promptly inform the said States Parties of its findings and shall indicate whether it intends to exercise jurisdiction.

Article 8

1. The State Party in the territory of which the alleged offender is present shall, in cases to which article 6 applies, if it does not extradite that person, be obliged, without exception whatsoever and whether or not the offence was committed in its territory, to submit the case without undue delay to its competent authorities for the purpose of prosecution, through proceedings in accordance with the laws of that State. Those authorities shall take their decision in the same manner as in the case of any other offence of a grave nature under the law of that State.

2. Whenever a State Party is permitted under its domestic law to extradite or otherwise surrender one of its nationals only upon the condition that the person will be returned to that State to serve the sentence imposed as a result of the trial or proceeding for which the extradition or surrender of the person was sought, and this State and the State seeking the extradition of the person agree with this option and other terms they may deem appropriate, such a conditional extradition or

surrender shall be sufficient to discharge the obligation set forth in paragraph 1 of the present article.

Article 9

1. The offences set forth in article 2 shall be deemed to be included as extraditable offences in any extradition treaty existing between any of the States Parties before the entry into force of this Convention. States Parties undertake to include such offences as extraditable offences in every extradition treaty to be subsequently concluded between them.

2. When a State Party which makes extradition conditional on the existence of a treaty receives a request for extradition from another State Party with which it has no extradition treaty, the requested State Party may, at its option, consider this Convention as a legal basis for extradition in respect of the offences set forth in article 2. Extradition shall be subject to the other conditions provided by the law of the requested State.

3. States Parties which do not make extradition conditional on the existence of a treaty shall recognize the offences set forth in article 2 as extraditable offences between themselves, subject to the conditions provided by the law of the requested State.

4. If necessary, the offences set forth in article 2 shall be treated, for the purposes of extradition between States Parties, as if they had been committed not only in the place in which they occurred but also in the territory of the States that have established jurisdiction in accordance with article 6, paragraphs 1 and 2.

5. The provisions of all extradition treaties and arrangements between States Parties with regard to offences set forth in article 2 shall be deemed to be modified as between State Parties to the extent that they are incompatible with this Convention.

Article 10

1. States Parties shall afford one another the greatest measure of assistance in connection with investigations or criminal or extradition proceedings brought in respect of the offences set forth in article 2, including assistance in obtaining evidence at their disposal necessary for the proceedings.

2. States Parties shall carry out their obligations under paragraph 1 of the present article in conformity with any treaties or other arrangements on mutual legal assistance that may exist between them. In the absence of such treaties or arrangements, States Parties shall afford one another assistance in accordance with their domestic law.

Article 11

None of the offences set forth in article 2 shall be regarded, for the purposes of extradition or mutual legal assistance, as a political offence or as an offence connected with a political offence or as an offence inspired by political motives. Accordingly, a request for extradition or for mutual legal assistance based on such an offence may not be refused on the sole ground that it concerns a political offence or an offence connected with a political offence or an offence inspired by political motives.

Article 12

Nothing in this Convention shall be interpreted as imposing an obligation to extradite or to afford mutual legal assistance, if the requested State Party has substantial grounds for believing that the request for extradition for offences set forth in article 2 or for mutual legal assistance with respect to such offences has been made for the purpose of prosecuting or punishing a person on account of that person's race, religion, nationality, ethnic origin or political opinion or that compliance with the request would cause prejudice to that person's position for any of these reasons.

Article 13

1. A person who is being detained or is serving a sentence in the territory of one State Party whose presence in another State Party is requested for purposes of testimony, identification or otherwise providing assistance in obtaining evidence for the investigation or prosecution of offences under this Convention may be transferred if the following conditions are met:

(a) The person freely gives his or her informed consent; and

(b) The competent authorities of both States agree, subject to such conditions as those States may deem appropriate.

2. For the purposes of the present article:

(a) The State to which the person is transferred shall have the authority and obligation to keep the person transferred in custody, unless otherwise requested or authorized by the State from which the person was transferred;

(b) The State to which the person is transferred shall without delay implement its obligation to return the person to the custody of the State from which the person was transferred as agreed beforehand, or as otherwise agreed, by the competent authorities of both States;

(c) The State to which the person is transferred shall not require the State from which the person was transferred to initiate extradition proceedings for the return of the person;

(d) The person transferred shall receive credit for service of the sentence being served in the State from which he was transferred for time spent in the custody of the State to which he was transferred.

3. Unless the State Party from which a person is to be transferred in accordance with the present article so agrees, that person, whatever his or her nationality, shall not be prosecuted or detained or subjected to any other restriction of his or her personal liberty in the territory of the State to which that person is transferred in respect of acts or convictions anterior to his or her departure from the territory of the State from which such person was transferred.

Article 14

Any person who is taken into custody or regarding whom any other measures are taken or proceedings are carried out pursuant to this Convention shall be guaranteed fair treatment, including enjoyment of all rights and guarantees in conformity with the law of the State in the territory of which that person is present and applicable provisions of international law, including international law of human rights.

Article 15

States Parties shall cooperate in the prevention of the offences set forth in article 2, particularly:

(a) By taking all practicable measures, including, if necessary, adapting their domestic legislation, to prevent and counter preparations in their respective territories for the commission of those offences within or outside their territories, including measures to prohibit in their territories illegal activities of persons, groups and organizations that encourage, instigate, organize, knowingly finance or engage in the perpetration of offences as set forth in article 2;

(b) By exchanging accurate and verified information in accordance with their national law, and coordinating administrative and other measures taken as appropriate to prevent the commission of offences as set forth in article 2;

(c) Where appropriate, through research and development regarding methods of detection of explosives and other harmful substances that can cause death or bodily injury, consultations on the development of standards for marking explosives in order to identify their origin in post-blast investigations, exchange of information on preventive measures, cooperation and transfer of technology, equipment and related materials.

Article 16

The State Party where the alleged offender is prosecuted shall, in accordance with its domestic law or applicable procedures, communicate the final outcome of the proceedings to the Secretary-General of the United Nations, who shall transmit the information to the other States Parties.

Article 17

The States Parties shall carry out their obligations under this Convention in a manner consistent with the principles of sovereign equality and territorial integrity of States and that of non-intervention in the domestic affairs of other States.

Article 18

Nothing in this Convention entitles a State Party to undertake in the territory of another State Party the exercise of jurisdiction and performance of functions which are exclusively reserved for the authorities of that other State Party by its domestic law.

Article 19

1. Nothing in this Convention shall affect other rights, obligations and responsibilities of States and individuals under international law, in particular the purposes and principles of the Charter of the United Nations and international humanitarian law.

2. The activities of armed forces during an armed conflict, as those terms are understood under international humanitarian law, which are governed by that law, are not governed by this Convention, and the activities undertaken by military forces of a State in the exercise of their official duties, inasmuch as they are governed by other rules of international law, are not governed by this Convention.

Article 20

1. Any dispute between two or more States Parties concerning the interpretation or application of this Convention which cannot be settled through negotiation within a reasonable time shall, at the request of one of them, be submitted to arbitration. If, within six months from the date of the request for arbitration, the parties are unable to agree on the organization of the arbitration, any one of those parties may refer the dispute to the International Court of Justice, by application, in conformity with the Statute of the Court.

2. Each State may at the time of signature, ratification, acceptance or approval of this Convention or accession thereto declare that it does not consider itself bound by paragraph 1 of the present article. The other States Parties shall not be bound by paragraph 1 with respect to any State Party which has made such a reservation.

3. Any State which has made a reservation in accordance with paragraph 2 of the present article may at any time withdraw that reservation by notification to the Secretary-General of the United Nations.

Article 21

1. This Convention shall be open for signature by all States from 12 January 1998 until 31 December 1999 at United Nations Headquarters in New York.

2. This Convention is subject to ratification, acceptance or approval. The instruments of ratification, acceptance or approval shall be deposited with the Secretary-General of the United Nations.

3. This Convention shall be open to accession by any State. The instruments of accession shall be deposited with the Secretary-General of the United Nations.

Article 22

1. This Convention shall enter into force on the thirtieth day following the date of

the deposit of the twenty-second instrument of ratification, acceptance, approval or accession with the Secretary-General of the United Nations.

2. For each State ratifying, accepting, approving or acceding to the Convention after the deposit of the twenty-second instrument of ratification, acceptance, approval or accession, the Convention shall enter into force on the thirtieth day after deposit by such State of its instrument of ratification, acceptance, approval or accession.

Article 23

1. Any State Party may denounce this Convention by written notification to the Secretary-General of the United Nations.

2. Denunciation shall take effect one year following the date on which notification is received by the Secretary-General of the United Nations.

Article 24

The original of this Convention, of which the Arabic, Chinese, English, French, Russian and Spanish texts are equally authentic, shall be deposited with the Secretary-General of the United Nations, who shall send certified copies thereof to all States.

IN WITNESS WHEREOF, the undersigned, being duly authorized thereto by their respective Governments, have signed this Convention, opened for signature at United Nations Headquarters in New York on 12 January 1998.

* See resolution 50/6.

PRINCIPAL MANUALS ON THE REGULATION OF ARMED CONFLICTS AND WEAPONS CONTROL EVIDENCING CUSTOMARY INTERNATIONAL LAW

I-35. Instructions for the Government of Armies of the United States in the Field (Lieber Code). Prepared by Francis Lieber, promulgated as General Orders No. 100, Adjutant General's Office, 1863, Washington, 1898: Government Printing Office, 24 April 1863.[1]
Authentic Text: English

Relevant Penal Characteristics & Penal Provisions
2. Implicit recognition of the penal nature of the act by establishing a duty to prohibit, prevent, prosecute, punish, or the like: Article 16 and Article 30

Applicability
War
Control
Regulation & Prohibition

Full Text
Section I : Martial law -- Military jurisdiction -- Military necessity -- Retaliation
　　Article 1. A place, district, or country occupied by an enemy stands, in consequence of the occupation, under the Martial Law of the invading or occupying army, whether any proclamation declaring Martial Law, or any public warning to the inhabitants, has been issued or not. Martial Law is the immediate and direct effect and consequence of occupation or conquest.The presence of a hostile army proclaims its Martial Law.
　　Art. 2. Martial Law does not cease during the hostile occupation, except by special proclamation, ordered by the commander in chief; or by special mention in the treaty of peace concluding the war, when the occupation of a place or territory continues beyond the conclusion of peace as one of the conditions of the same.
　　Art. 3. Martial Law in a hostile country consists in the suspension, by the occupying military authority, of the criminal and civil law, and of the domestic administration and government in the occupied place or territory, and in the substitution of military rule and force for the same, as well as in the dictation of general laws, as far as military necessity requires this suspension, substitution, or dictation. The commander of the forces may proclaim that the administration of all civil and penal law shall continue either wholly or in part, as in times of peace, unless

---

[1] Although the *Lieber Code* is not a multilateral convention, it is included here because it is the first example of weapons regulation (prohibition of the use of poisons under Article 16). In addition, the *Lieber Code* provisions influenced subsequent codification of the laws of war on the international level, as can be seen in the Brussels Conference of 1874 and the Hague Conventions on Land Warfare in 1899 and 1907. *See also* SCHINDLER/TOMAN, THE LAWS OF ARMED CONFLICTS 3-98 (1988).

otherwise ordered by the military authority.

Art. 4. Martial Law is simply military authority exercised in accordance with the laws and usages of war. Military oppression is not Martial Law: It is the abuse of the power which that law confers. As Martial Law is executed by military force, it is incumbent upon those who administer it to be strictly guided by the principles of justice, honor, and humanity -- virtues adorning a soldier even more than other men, for the very reason that he possesses the power of his arms against the unarmed.

Art. 5. Martial Law should be less stringent in places and countries fully occupied and fairly conquered. Much greater severity may be exercised in places or regions where actual hostilities exist, or are expected and must be prepared for. Its most complete sway is allowed -- even in the commander's own country -- when face to face with the enemy, because of the absolute necessities of the case, and of the paramount duty to defend the country against invasion.

To save the country is paramount to all other considerations.

Art. 6. All civil and penal law shall continue to take its usual course in the enemy's places and territories under Martial Law, unless interrupted or stopped by order of the occupying military power; but all the functions of the hostile government -- legislative executive, or administrative -- whether of a general, provincial, or local character, cease under Martial Law, or continue only with the sanction, or, if deemed necessary, the participation of the occupier or invader.

Art. 7. Martial Law extends to property, and to persons, whether they are subjects of the enemy or aliens to that government.

Art. 8. Consuls, among American and European nations, are not diplomatic agents.
Nevertheless, their offices and persons will be subjected to Martial Law in cases of urgent necessity only: their property and business are not exempted. Any delinquency they commit against the established military rule may be punished as in the case of any other inhabitant, and such punishment furnishes no reasonable ground for international complaint.

Art. 9. The functions of Ambassadors, Ministers, or other diplomatic agents accredited by neutral powers to the hostile government, cease, so far as regards the displaced government; but the conquering or occupying power usually recognizes them as temporarily accredited to itself.

Art. 10. Martial Law affects chiefly the police and collection of public revenue and taxes, whether imposed by the expelled government or by the invader, and refers mainly to the support and efficiency of the army, its safety, and the safety of its operations.

Art. 11. The law of war does not only disclaim all cruelty and bad faith concerning engagements concluded with the enemy during the war, but also the breaking of stipulations solemnly contracted by the belligerents in time of peace, and avowedly intended to remain in force in case of war between the contracting powers. It disclaims all extortions and other transactions for individual gain; all acts of private revenge, or connivance at such acts. Offenses to the contrary shall be severely punished, and especially so if committed by officers.

Art. 12. Whenever feasible, Martial Law is carried out in cases of individual offenders by Military Courts; but sentences of death shall be executed only with the approval of the chief executive, provided the urgency of the case does not require a speedier execution, and then only with the approval of the chief commander.

Art. 13. Military jurisdiction is of two kinds: First, that which is conferred and defined by statute; second, that which is derived from the common law of war. Military offenses under the statute law must be tried in the manner therein directed; but military offenses which do not come within the statute must be tried and punished under the common law of war. The character of the courts which exercise these jurisdictions depends upon the local laws of each particular country.

In the armies of the United States the first is exercised by courts-martial, while cases which do not come within the "Rules and Articles of War," or the jurisdiction conferred by statute on courts-martial, are tried by military commissions.

Art. 14. Military necessity, as understood by modern civilized nations, consists in the necessity of those measures which are indispensable for securing the ends of the war, and which are lawful according to the modern law and usages of war.

Art. 15. Military necessity admits of all direct destruction of life or limb of ' armed ' enemies, and of other persons whose destruction is incidentally ' unavoidable ' in the armed contests of the war; it allows of the capturing of every armed enemy, and every enemy of importance to the hostile government, or of peculiar danger to the captor; it allows of all destruction of property, and obstruction of the ways and channels of traffic, travel, or communication, and of all withholding of sustenance or means of life from the enemy; of the appropriation of whatever an enemy's country affords necessary for the subsistence and safety of the army, and of such deception as does not involve the breaking of good faith either positively pledged, regarding agreements entered into during the war, or supposed by the modern law of war to exist. Men who take up arms against one another in public war do not cease on this account to be moral beings, responsible to one another and to God.

Art. 16. Military necessity does not admit of cruelty -- that is, the infliction of suffering for the sake of suffering or for revenge, nor of maiming or wounding except in fight, nor of torture to extort confessions. It does not admit of the use of poison in any way, nor of the wanton devastation of a district. It admits of deception, but disclaims acts of perfidy; and, in general, military necessity does not include any act of hostility which makes the return to peace unnecessarily difficult.

Art. 17. War is not carried on by arms alone. It is lawful to starve the hostile belligerent, armed or unarmed, so that it leads to the speedier subjection of the enemy.

Art. 18. When a commander of a besieged place expels the noncombatants, in order to lessen the number of those who consume his stock of provisions, it is lawful, though an extreme measure, to drive them back, so as to hasten on the surrender.

Art. 19. Commanders, whenever admissible, inform the enemy of their intention to bombard a place, so that the noncombatants, and especially the women and children, may be removed before the bombardment commences. But it is no infraction of the common law of war to omit thus to inform the enemy. Surprise may be a necessity.

Art. 20. Public war is a state of armed hostility between sovereign nations or governments. It is a law and requisite of civilized existence that men live in political, continuous societies, forming organized units, called states or nations, whose constituents bear, enjoy, suffer, advance and retrograde together, in peace and in war.

Art. 21. The citizen or native of a hostile country is thus an enemy, as one of the constituents of the hostile state or nation, and as such is subjected to the hardships of the war.

Art. 22. Nevertheless, as civilization has advanced during the last centuries, so has likewise steadily advanced, especially in war on land, the distinction between the private individual belonging to a hostile country and the hostile country itself, with its men in arms. The principle has been more and more acknowledged that the unarmed citizen is to be spared in person, property, and honor as much as the exigencies of war will admit.

Art. 23. Private citizens are no longer murdered, enslaved, or carried off to distant parts, and the inoffensive individual is as little disturbed in his private relations as the commander of the hostile troops can afford to grant in the overruling demands of a vigorous war.

Art. 24. The almost universal rule in remote times was, and continues to be with barbarous armies, that the private individual of the hostile country is destined to suffer every privation of liberty and protection, and every disruption of family ties. Protection was, and still is with uncivilized people, the exception.

Art. 25. In modern regular wars of the Europeans, and their descendants in other portions of the globe, protection of the inoffensive citizen of the hostile country is the rule; privation and disturbance of private relations are the exceptions.

Art. 26. Commanding generals may cause the magistrates and civil officers of the hostile country to take the oath of temporary allegiance or an oath of fidelity to their own victorious government or rulers, and they may expel everyone who declines to do so. But whether they do so or not, the people and their civil officers owe strict obedience to them as long as they hold sway over the district or country, at the peril of their lives.

Art. 27. The law of war can no more wholly dispense with retaliation than can the law of nations, of which it is a branch. Yet civilized nations acknowledge retaliation as the sternest feature of war. A reckless enemy often leaves to his opponent no other means of securing himself against the repetition of barbarous outrage.

Art. 28. Retaliation will, therefore, never be resorted to as a measure of mere revenge, but only as a means of protective retribution, and moreover, cautiously and unavoidably; that is to say, retaliation shall only be resorted to after careful inquiry into the real occurrence, and the character of the misdeeds that may demand retribution.

Unjust or inconsiderate retaliation removes the belligerents farther and farther from the mitigating rules of regular war, and by rapid steps leads them nearer to the internecine wars of savages.

Art. 29. Modern times are distinguished from earlier ages by the existence, at one and the same time, of many nations and great governments related to one another in close intercourse.

Peace is their normal condition; war is the exception. The ultimate object of all modern war is a renewed state of peace.

International Humanitarian Law and Arms Control Agreements 277

The more vigorously wars are pursued, the better it is for humanity. Sharp wars are brief.

Art. 30. Ever since the formation and coexistence of modern nations, and ever since wars have become great national wars, war has come to be acknowledged not to be its own end, but the means to obtain great ends of state, or to consist in defense against wrong; and no conventional restriction of the modes adopted to injure the enemy is any longer admitted; but the law of war imposes many limitations and restrictions on principles of justice, faith, and honor.

Section II : Public and private property of the enemy -- Protection of persons, and especially of women, of religion, the arts and sciences -- Punishment of crimes against the inhabitants of hostile countries

Art. 31. A victorious army appropriates all public money, seizes all public movable property until further direction by its government, and sequesters for its own benefit or of that of its government all the revenues of real property belonging to the hostile government or nation. The title to such real property remains in abeyance during military occupation, and until the conquest is made complete.

Art. 32. A victorious army, by the martial power inherent in the same, may suspend, change, or abolish, as far as the martial power extends, the relations which arise from the services due, according to the existing laws of the invaded country, from one citizen, subject, or native of the same to another.
The commander of the army must leave it to the ultimate treaty of peace to settle the permanency of this change.

Art. 33. It is no longer considered lawful -- on the contrary, it is held to be a serious breach of the law of war -- to force the subjects of the enemy into the service of the victorious government, except the latter should proclaim, after a fair and complete conquest of the hostile country or district, that it is resolved to keep the country, district, or place permanently as its own and make it a portion of its own country.

Art. 34. As a general rule, the property belonging to churches, to hospitals, or other establishments of an exclusively charitable character, to establishments of education, or foundations for the promotion of knowledge, whether public schools, universities, academies of learning or observatories, museums of the fine arts, or of a scientific character -- such property is not to be considered public property in the sense of paragraph 31; but it may be taxed or used when the public service may require it.

Art. 35. Classical works of art, libraries, scientific collections, or precious instruments, such as astronomical telescopes, as well as hospitals, must be secured against all avoidable injury, even when they are contained in fortified places whilst besieged or bombarded.

Art. 36. If such works of art, libraries, collections, or instruments belonging to a hostile nation or government, cam be removed without injury, the ruler of the conquering state or nation may order them to be seized and removed for the benefit of the said nation. The ultimate ownership is to be settled by the ensuing treaty of peace.

In no case shall they be sold or given away, if captured by the armies of the United

States, nor shall they ever be privately appropriated, or wantonly destroyed or injured.

Art. 37. The United States acknowledge and protect, in hostile countries occupied by them, religion and morality; strictly private property; the persons of the inhabitants, especially those of women: and the sacredness of domestic relations. Offenses to the contrary shall be rigorously punished.

This rule does not interfere with the right of the victorious invader to tax the people or their property, to levy forced loans, to billet soldiers, or to appropriate property, especially houses, lands, boats or ships, and churches, for temporary and military uses.

Art. 38. Private property, unless forfeited by crimes or by offenses of the owner, can be seized only by way of military necessity, for the support or other benefit of the army or of the United States.

If the owner has not fled, the commanding officer will cause receipts to be given, which may serve the spoliated owner to obtain indemnity.

Art. 39. The salaries of civil officers of the hostile government who remain in the invaded territory, and continue the work of their office, and can continue it according to the circumstances arising out of the war -- such as judges, administrative or police officers, officers of city or communal governments -- are paid from the public revenue of the invaded territory, until the military government has reason wholly or partially to discontinue it. Salaries or incomes connected with purely honorary titles are always stopped.

Art. 40. There exists no law or body of authoritative rules of action between hostile armies, except that branch of the law of nature and nations which is called the law and usages of war on land.

Art. 41. All municipal law of the ground on which the armies stand, or of the countries to which they belong, is silent and of no effect between armies in the field.

Art. 42. Slavery, complicating and confounding the ideas of property, (that is of a ' thing ',) and of personality, (that is of ' humanity ',) exists according to municipal or local law only. The law of nature and nations has never acknowledged it. The digest of the Roman law enacts the early dictum of the pagan jurist, that "so far as the law of nature is concerned, all men are equal." Fugitives escaping from a country in which they were slaves, villains, or serfs, into another country, have, for centuries past, been held free and acknowledged free by judicial decisions of European countries, even though the municipal law of the country in which the slave had taken refuge acknowledged slavery within its own dominions.

Art. 43. Therefore, in a war between the United States and a belligerent which admits of slavery, if a person held in bondage by that belligerent be captured by or come as a fugitive under the protection of the military forces of the United States, such person is immediately entitled to the rights and privileges of a freeman. To return such person into slavery would amount to enslaving a free person, and neither the United States nor any officer under their authority can enslave any human being. Moreover, a person so made free by the law of war is under the shield of the law of nations, and the former owner or State can have, by the law of postliminy, no belligerent lien or claim of service.

Art. 44. All wanton violence committed against persons in the invaded country, all destruction of property not commanded by the authorized officer, all robbery, all pillage or sacking, even after taking a place by main force, all rape, wounding, maiming, or killing of such inhabitants, are prohibited under the penalty of death, or such other severe punishment as may seem adequate for the gravity of the offense.

A soldier, officer or private, in the act of committing such violence, and disobeying a superior ordering him to abstain from it, may be lawfully killed on the spot by such superior.

Art. 45. All captures and booty belong, according to the modern law of war, primarily to the government of the captor.

Prize money, whether on sea or land, can now only be claimed under local law.

Art. 46. Neither officers nor soldiers are allowed to make use of their position or power in the hostile country for private gain, not even for commercial transactions otherwise legitimate. Offenses to the contrary committed by commissioned officers will be punished with cashiering or such other punishment as the nature of the offense may require; if by soldiers, they shall be punished according to the nature of the offense.

Art. 47. Crimes punishable by all penal codes, such as arson, murder, maiming, assaults, highway robbery, theft, burglary, fraud, forgery, and rape, if committed by an American soldier in a hostile country against its inhabitants, are not only punishable as at home, but in all cases in which death is not inflicted, the severer punishment shall be preferred.

Section III : Deserters -- Prisoners of war -- Hostages -- Booty on the battle-field

Art. 48. Deserters from the American Army, having entered the service of the enemy, suffer death if they fall again into the hands of the United States, whether by capture, or being delivered up to the American Army; and if a deserter from the enemy, having taken service in the Army of the United States, is captured by the enemy, and punished by them with death or otherwise, it is not a breach against the law and usages of war, requiring redress or retaliation.

Art. 49. A prisoner of war is a public enemy armed or attached to the hostile army for active aid, who has fallen into the hands of the captor, either fighting or wounded, on the field or in the hospital, by individual surrender or by capitulation.

All soldiers, of whatever species of arms; all men who belong to the rising en masse of the hostile country; all those who are attached to the army for its efficiency and promote directly the object of the war, except such as are hereinafter provided for; all disabled men or officers on the field or elsewhere, if captured; all enemies who have thrown away their arms and ask for quarter, are prisoners of war, and as such exposed to the inconveniences as well as entitled to the privileges of a prisoner of war.

Art. 50. Moreover, citizens who accompany an army for whatever purpose, such as sutlers, editors, or reporters of journals, or contractors, if captured, may be made prisoners of war, and be detained as such.

The monarch and members of the hostile reigning family, male or female, the chief, and chief officers of the hostile government, its diplomatic agents, and all persons who are of particular and singular use and benefit to the hostile army or its government, are, if captured on belligerent ground, and if unprovided with a safe conduct granted by the captor's government, prisoners of war.

Art. 51. If the people of that portion of an invaded country which is not yet occupied by the enemy, or of the whole country, at the approach of a hostile army, rise, under a duly authorized levy ' en masse ' to resist the invader, they are now treated as public enemies, and, if captured, are prisoners of war.

Art. 52. No belligerent has the right to declare that he will treat every captured man in arms of a levy ' en masse ' as a brigand or bandit.

If, however, the people of a country, or any portion of the same, already occupied by an army, rise against it, they are violators of the laws of war, and are not entitled to their protection.

Art. 53. The enemy's chaplains, officers of the medical staff, apothecaries, hospital nurses and servants, if they fall into the hands of the American Army, are not prisoners of war, unless the commander has reasons to retain them. In this latter case, or if, at their own desire, they are allowed to remain with their captured companions, they are treated as prisoners of war, and may be exchanged if the commander sees fit.

Art. 54. A hostage is a person accepted as a pledge for the fulfillment of an agreement concluded between belligerents during the war, or in consequence of a war. Hostages are rare in the present age.

Art. 55. If a hostage is accepted, he is treated like a prisoner of war, according to rank and condition, as circumstances may admit.

Art. 56. A prisoner of war is subject to no punishment for being a public enemy, nor is any revenge wreaked upon him by the intentional infliction of any suffering, or disgrace, by cruel imprisonment, want of food, by mutilation, death, or any other barbarity.

Art. 57. So soon as a man is armed by a sovereign government and takes the soldier's oath of fidelity, he is a belligerent; his killing, wounding, or other warlike acts are not individual crimes or offenses. No belligerent has a right to declare that enemies of a certain class, color, or condition, when properly organized as soldiers, will not be treated by him as public enemies.

Art. 58. The law of nations knows of no distinction of color, and if an enemy of the United States should enslave and sell any captured persons of their army, it would be a case for the severest retaliation, if not redressed upon complaint.

The United States cannot retaliate by enslavement; therefore death must be the retaliation for this crime against the law of nations.

Art. 59. A prisoner of war remains answerable for his crimes committed against the captor's army or people, committed before he was captured, and for which he has not been punished by his own authorities.

All prisoners of war are liable to the infliction of retaliatory measures.

Art. 60. It is against the usage of modern war to resolve, in hatred and revenge, to give no quarter. No body of troops has the right to declare that it will not give, and therefore will not expect, quarter; but a commander is permitted to direct his troops to give no quarter, in great straits, when his own salvation makes it impossible to cumber himself with prisoners.

Art. 61. Troops that give no quarter have no right to kill enemies already disabled on the ground, or prisoners captured by other troops.

Art. 62. All troops of the enemy known or discovered to give no quarter in general, or to any portion of the army, receive none.

Art. 63. Troops who fight in the uniform of their enemies, without any plain, striking, and uniform mark of distinction of their own, can expect no quarter.

Art. 64. If American troops capture a train containing uniforms of the enemy, and the commander considers it advisable to distribute them for use among his men, some striking mark or sign must be adopted to distinguish the American soldier from the enemy.

Art. 65. The use of the enemy's national standard, flag, or other emblem of nationality, for the purpose of deceiving the enemy in battle, is an act of perfidy by which they lose all claim to the protection of the laws of war.

Art. 66. Quarter having been given to an enemy by American troops, under a misapprehension of his true character, he may, nevertheless, be ordered to suffer death if, within three days after the battle, it be discovered that he belongs to a corps which gives no quarter.

Art. 67. The law of nations allows every sovereign government to make war upon another sovereign state, and, therefore, admits of no rules or laws different from those of regular warfare, regarding the treatment of prisoners of war, although they may belong to the army of a government which the captor may consider as a wanton and unjust assailant.

Art. 68. Modern wars are not internecine wars, in which the killing of the enemy is the object. The destruction of the enemy in modern war, and, indeed, modern war itself, are means to obtain that object of the belligerent which lies beyond the war.

Unnecessary or revengeful destruction of life is not lawful.

Art. 69. Outposts, sentinels, or pickets are not to be fired upon, except to drive them in, or when a positive order, special or general, has been issued to that effect.

Art. 70. The use of poison in any manner, be it to poison wells, or food, or arms, is wholly excluded from modern warfare. He that uses it puts himself out of the pale of the law and usages of war.

Art. 71. Whoever intentionally inflicts additional wounds on an enemy already wholly disabled, or kills such an enemy, or who orders or encourages soldiers to do so, shall suffer death, if duly convicted, whether he belongs to the Army of the United States, or is an enemy captured after having committed his misdeed.

Art. 72. Money and other valuables on the person of a prisoner, such as watches or jewelry, as well as extra clothing, are regarded by the American Army as the private property of the prisoner, and the appropriation of such valuables or money is considered dishonorable, and is prohibited.

Nevertheless, if ' large ' sums are found upon the persons of prisoners, or in their possession, they shall be taken from them, and the surplus, after providing for their own support, appropriated for the use of the army, under the direction of the commander, unless otherwise ordered by the government. Nor can prisoners claim, as private property, large sums found and captured in their train, although they have been placed in the private luggage of the prisoners.

Art. 73. All officers, when captured, must surrender their side arms to the captor. They may be restored to the prisoner in marked cases, by the commander, to signalize admiration of his distinguished bravery or approbation of his humane treatment of prisoners before his capture. The captured officer to whom they may be restored can not wear them during captivity.

Art. 74. A prisoner of war, being a public enemy, is the prisoner of the government, and not of the captor. No ransom cam be paid by a prisoner of war to his individual captor or to any officer in command. The government alone releases captives, according to rules prescribed by itself.

Art. 75. Prisoners of war are subject to confinement or imprisonment such as may be deemed necessary on account of safety, but they are to be subjected to no other intentional suffering or indignity. The confinement and mode of treating a prisoner may be varied during his captivity according to the demands of safety.

Art. 76. Prisoners of war shall be fed upon plain and wholesome food, whenever practicable, and treated with humanity.

They may be required to work for the benefit of the captor's government, according to their rank and condition.

Art. 77. A prisoner of war who escapes may be shot or otherwise killed in his flight; but neither death nor any other punishment shall be inflicted upon him simply for his attempt to escape, which the law of war does not consider a crime. Stricter means of security shall be used after an unsuccessful attempt at escape.

If, however, a conspiracy is discovered, the purpose of which is a united or general escape, the conspirators may be rigorously punished, even with death; and capital punishment may also be inflicted upon prisoners of war discovered to have plotted rebellion against the authorities of the captors, whether in union with fellow prisoners or other persons.

Art. 78. If prisoners of war having given no pledge nor made any promise on their honor, forcibly or otherwise escape, and are captured again in battle after having rejoined their own army, they shall not be punished for their escape, but shall be treated as simple prisoners of war, although they will be subjected to stricter confinement.

Art. 79. Every captured wounded enemy shall be medically treated, according to the ability of the medical staff.

Art. 80. Honorable men, when captured, will abstain from giving to the enemy information concerning their own army, and the modern law of war permits no longer the use of any violence against prisoners in order to extort the desired information or to punish them for having given false information.

Section IV : Partisans -- Armed enemies not belonging to the hostile army -- Scouts -- Armed prowlers -- War-rebels

Art. 81. Partisans are soldiers armed and wearing the uniform of their army, but belonging to a corps which acts detached from the main body for the purpose of making in roads into the territory occupied by the enemy. If captured, they are entitled to all the privileges of the prisoner of war.

Art. 82. Men, or squads of men, who commit hostilities, whether by fighting, or inroads for destruction or plunder, or by raids of any kind, without commission, without being part and portion of the organized hostile army, and without sharing continuously in the war, but who do so with intermitting returns to their homes and avocations, or with the occasional assumption of the semblance of peaceful pursuits, divesting themselves of the character or appearance of soldiers -- such men, or squads of men, are not public enemies, and, therefore, if captured, are not entitled to the privileges of prisoners of war, but shall be treated summarily as highway in the uniform of the army hostile to their own, employed in obtaining information, if found within or lurking about the lines of the captor, are treated as spies, and suffer death.

Art. 84. Armed prowlers, by whatever names they may be called, or persons of the enemy's territory, who steal within the lines of the hostile army for the purpose of robbing, killing, or of destroying bridges, roads or canals, or of robbing or destroying the mail, or of cutting the telegraph wires, are not entitled to the privileges of the prisoner of war.

Art. 85. War-rebels are persons within an occupied territory who rise in arms against the occupying or conquering army, or against the authorities established by the same. If captured, they may suffer death, whether they rise singly, in small or large bands, and whether called upon to do so by their own, but expelled, government or not. They are not prisoners of war; nor are they if discovered and secured before their conspiracy has matured to an actual rising or armed violence.

Section V : Safe-conduct -- Spies -- War-traitors -- Captured messengers -- Abuse of the flag of truce

Art. 86. All intercourse between the territories occupied by belligerent armies, whether by traffic, by letter, by travel, or in any other way, ceases. This is the general rule, to be observed without special proclamation.

Exceptions to this rule, whether by safe-conduct, or permission to trade on a small or large scale, or by exchanging mails, or by travel from one territory into the other, can take place only according to agreement approved by the government, or by the highest military authority.

Contraventions of this rule are highly punishable.

Art. 87. Ambassadors, and all other diplomatic agents of neutral powers, accredited to the enemy, may receive safe-conducts through the territories occupied by the belligerents, unless there are military reasons to the contrary, and unless they may reach the place of their destination conveniently by another route. It implies no international affront if the safe-conduct is declined. Such passes are usually given by the supreme authority of the State, and not by subordinate officers.

Art. 88. A spy is a person who secretly, in disguise or under false pretense, seeks information with the intention of communicating it to the enemy.

The spy is punishable with death by hanging by the neck, whether or not he succeed in obtaining the information or in conveying it to the enemy.

Art. 89. If a citizen of the United States obtains information in a legitimate manner, and betrays it to the enemy, be he a military or civil officer, or a private citizen, he shall suffer death.

Art. 90. A traitor under the law of war, or a war-traitor, is a person in a place or district under Martial Law who, unauthorized by the military commander, gives information of any kind to the enemy, or holds intercourse with him.

Art. 91. The war-traitor is always severely punished. If his offense consists in betraying to the enemy anything concerning the condition, safety, operations, or plans of the troops holding or occupying the place or district, his punishment is death.

Art. 92. If the citizen or subject of a country or place invaded or conquered gives information to his own government, from which he is separated by the hostile army, or to the army of his government, he is a war-traitor, and death is the penalty of his offense.

Art. 93. All armies in the field stand in need of guides, and impress them if they cannot obtain them otherwise.

Art. 94. No person having been forced by the enemy to serve as guide is punishable for having done so.

Art. 95. If a citizen of a hostile and invaded district voluntarily serves as a guide to the enemy, or offers to do so, he is deemed a war-traitor, and shall suffer death.

Art. 96. A citizen serving voluntarily as a guide against his own country commits treason, and will be dealt with according to the law of his country.

Art. 97. Guides, when it is clearly proved that they have misled intentionally, may be put to death.

Art. 98. All unauthorized or secret communication with the enemy is considered treasonable by the law of war.

Foreign residents in an invaded or occupied territory, or foreign visitors in the same, can claim no immunity from this law. They may communicate with foreign parts, or with the inhabitants of the hostile country, so far as the military authority permits, but no further. Instant expulsion from the occupied territory would be the very least punishment for the infraction of this rule.

Art. 99. A messenger carrying written dispatches or verbal messages from one portion of the army, or from a besieged place, to another portion of the same army, or its government, if armed, and in the uniform of his army, and if captured, while doing so, in the territory occupied by the enemy, is treated by the captor as a prisoner of war. If not in uniform, nor a soldier, the circumstances connected with his capture must determine the disposition that shall be made of him.

Art. 100. A messenger or agent who attempts to steal through the territory occupied by the enemy, to further, in any manner, the interests of the enemy, if captured, is not entitled to the privileges of the prisoner of war, and may be dealt with according to the circumstances of the case.

Art. 101. While deception in war is admitted as a just and necessary means of hostility, and is consistent with honorable warfare, the common law of war allows even capital punishment for clandestine or treacherous attempts to injure an enemy, because they are so dangerous, and it is difficult to guard against them.

Art. 102. The law of war, like the criminal law regarding other offenses, makes no difference on account of the difference of sexes, concerning the spy, the war-traitor, or the war-rebel.

Art. 103. Spies, war-traitors, and war-rebels are not exchanged according to the common law of war. The exchange of such persons would require a special cartel, authorized by the government, or, at a great distance from it, by the chief commander of the army in the field.

Art. 104. A successful spy or war-traitor, safely returned to his own army, and afterwards captured as an enemy, is not subject to punishment for his acts as a spy or war-traitor, but he may be held in closer custody as a person individually dangerous.

Section VI : Exchange of prisoners -- Flags of truce -- Flags of protection

Art. 105. Exchanges of prisoners take place -- number for number -- rank for rank -- wounded for wounded -- with added condition for added condition -- such, for instance, as not to serve for a certain period.

Art. 106. In exchanging prisoners of war, such numbers of persons of inferior rank may be substituted as an equivalent for one of superior rank as may be agreed upon by cartel, which requires the sanction of the government, or of the commander of the army in the field.

Art. 107. A prisoner of war is in honor bound truly to state to the captor his rank; and he is not to assume a lower rank than belongs to him, in order to cause a more advantageous exchange, nor a higher rank, for the purpose of obtaining better treatment. Offenses to the contrary have been justly punished by the commanders of released prisoners, and may be good cause for refusing to release such prisoners.

Art. 108. The surplus number of prisoners of war remaining after an exchange has taken place is sometimes released either for the payment of a stipulated sum of money, or, in urgent cases, of provision, clothing, or other necessaries.

Such arrangement, however, requires the sanction of the highest authority.

Art. 109. The exchange of prisoners of war is an act of convenience to both belligerents. If no general cartel has been concluded, it cannot be demanded by either of them. No belligerent is obliged to exchange prisoners of war. A cartel is voidable as soon as either party has violated it.

Art. 110. No exchange of prisoners shall be made except after complete capture, and after an accurate account of them, and a list of the captured officers, has been taken.

Art. 111. The bearer of a flag of truce cannot insist upon being admitted. He must always be admitted with great caution. Unnecessary frequency is carefully to be avoided.

Art. 112. If the bearer of a flag of truce offer himself during an engagement, he can be admitted as a very rare exception only. It is no breach of good faith to retain such flag of truce, if admitted during the engagement. Firing is not required to cease on the appearance of a flag of truce in battle.

Art. 113. If the bearer of a flag of truce, presenting himself during an engagement, is killed or wounded, it furnishes no ground of complaint whatever.

Art. 114. If it be discovered, and fairly proved, that a flag of truce has been abused for surreptitiously obtaining military knowledge, the bearer of the flag thus abusing his sacred character is deemed a spy.

So sacred is the character of a flag of truce, and so necessary is its sacredness, that while its abuse is an especially heinous offense, great caution is requisite, on the other hand, in convicting the bearer of a flag of truce as a spy.

Art. 115. It is customary to designate by certain flags (usually yellow) the hospitals in places which are shelled, so that the besieging enemy may avoid firing on them. The same has been done in battles, when hospitals are situated within the field of the engagement.

Art. 116. Honorable belligerents often request that the hospitals within the territory of the enemy may be designated, so that they may be spared. An honorable belligerent allows himself to be guided by flags or signals of protection as much as the contingencies and the necessities of the fight will permit.

Art. 117. It is justly considered an act of bad faith, of infamy or fiendishness, to deceive the enemy by flags of protection. Such act of bad faith may be good cause for refusing to respect such flags.

Art. 118. The besieging belligerent has sometimes requested the besieged to designate the buildings containing collections of works of art, scientific museums, astronomical observatories, or precious libraries, so that their destruction may be avoided as much as possible.

Section VII : Parole

Art. 119. Prisoners of war may be released from captivity by exchange, and, under certain circumstances, also by parole.

Art. 120. The term Parole designates the pledge of individual good faith and honor to do, or to omit doing, certain acts after he who gives his parole shall have been dismissed, wholly or partially, from the power of the captor.

Art. 121. The pledge of the parole is always an individual, but not a private act.

Art. 122. The parole applies chiefly to prisoners of war whom the captor allows to return to their country, or to live in greater freedom within the captor's country or territory, on conditions stated in the parole.

Art. 123. Release of prisoners of war by exchange is the general rule; release by parole is the exception.

Art. 124. Breaking the parole is punished with death when the person breaking the parole is captured again. Accurate lists, therefore, of the paroled persons must be kept by the belligerents.

Art. 125. When paroles are given and received there must be an exchange of two written documents, in which the name and rank of the paroled individuals are accurately and truthfully stated.

Art. 126. Commissioned officers only are allowed to give their parole, and they can give it only with the permission of their superior, as long as a superior in rank is within reach.

Art. 127. No noncommissioned officer or private can give his parole except through an officer. Individual paroles not given through an officer are not only void, but subject the individuals giving them to the punishment of death as deserters. The only admissible exception is where individuals, properly separated from their commands, have suffered long confinement without the possibility of being paroled through an officer.

Art. 128. No paroling on the battlefield; no paroling of entire bodies of troops after a battle; and no dismissal of large numbers of prisoners, with a general declaration that they are paroled, is permitted, or of any value.

Art. 129. In capitulations for the surrender of strong places or fortified camps the commanding officer, in cases of urgent necessity, may agree that the troops under his command shall not fight again during the war, unless exchanged

Art. 130. The usual pledge given in the parole is not to serve during the existing war, unless exchanged.

This pledge refers only to the active service in the field, against the paroling belligerent or his allies actively engaged in the same war. These cases of breaking the parole are patent acts, and can be visited with the punishment of death; but the pledge does not refer to internal service, such as recruiting or drilling the recruits, fortifying places not besieged, quelling civil commotions, fighting against belligerents unconnected with the paroling belligerents, or to civil or diplomatic service for which the paroled officer may be employed.

Art. 131. If the government does not approve of the parole, the paroled officer must return into captivity, and should the enemy refuse to receive him, he is free of his parole.

Art. 132. A belligerent government may declare, by a general order, whether it will allow paroling, and on what conditions it will allow it. Such order is communicated to the enemy.

Art. 133. No prisoner of war can be forced by the hostile government to parole himself, and no government is obliged to parole prisoners of war, or to parole all captured officers, if it paroles any. As the pledging of the parole is an individual act, so is paroling, on the other hand, an act of choice on the part of the belligerent.

Art. 134. The commander of an occupying army may require of the civil officers of the enemy, and of its citizens, any pledge he may consider necessary for the safety or security of his army, and upon their failure to give it he may arrest, confine, or detain them.

Section VIII : Armistice -- Capitulation

Art. 135. An armistice is the cessation of active hostilities for a period agreed between belligerents. It must be agreed upon in writing, and duly ratified by the highest authorities of the contending parties.

Art. 136. If an armistice be declared, without conditions, it extends no further than to require a total cessation of hostilities along the front of both belligerents. If conditions be agreed upon, they should be clearly expressed, and must be rigidly adhered to by both parties. If either party violates any express condition, the armistice may be declared null and void by the other.

Art. 137. An armistice may be general, and valid for all points and lines of the belligerents; or special, that is, referring to certain troops or certain localities only. An armistice may be concluded for a definite time; or for an indefinite time, during which either belligerent may resume hostilities on giving the notice agreed upon to the other.

Art. 138. The motives which induce the one or the other belligerent to conclude an armistice, whether it be expected to be preliminary to a treaty of peace, or to prepare during the armistice for a more vigorous prosecution of the war, does in no way affect the character of the armistice itself.

Art. 139. An armistice is binding upon the belligerents from the day of the agreed commencement, but the officers of the armies are responsible from the day only when they receive official information of its existence.

Art. 140. Commanding officers have the right to conclude armistices binding on the district over which their command extends, but such armistice is subject to the ratification of the superior authority, and ceases so soon as it is made known to the enemy that the armistice is not ratified, even if a certain time for the elapsing between giving notice of cessation and the resumption of hostilities should have been stipulated for.

Art. 141. It is incumbent upon the contracting parties of an armistice to stipulate what intercourse of persons or traffic between the inhabitants of the territories occupied by the hostile armies shall be allowed, if any.

If nothing is stipulated the intercourse remains suspended, as during actual hostilities.

Art. 142. An armistice is not a partial or a temporary peace; it is only the suspension of military operations to the extent agreed upon by the parties.

Art. 143. When an armistice is concluded between a fortified place and the army besieging it, it is agreed by all the authorities on this subject that the besieger must cease all extension, perfection, or advance of his attacking works as much so as from attacks by main force.

But as there is a difference of opinion among martial jurists, whether the besieged have the right to repair breaches or to erect new works of defense within the place during an armistice, this point should be determined by express agreement between the parties.

Art. 144. So soon as a capitulation is signed, the capitulator has no right to demolish, destroy, or injure the works, arms, stores, or ammunition, in his possession, during the time which elapses between the signing and the execution of the capitulation, unless otherwise stipulated in the same.

Art. 145. When an armistice is clearly broken by one of the parties, the other party is released from all obligation to observe it.

Art. 146. Prisoners taken in the act of breaking an armistice must be treated as prisoners of war, the officer alone being responsible who gives the order for such a violation of an armistice. The highest authority of the belligerent aggrieved may demand redress for the infraction of an armistice.

Art. 147. Belligerents sometimes conclude an armistice while their plenipotentiaries are met to discuss the conditions of a treaty of peace; but plenipotentiaries may meet without a preliminary armistice; in the latter case, the war is carried on without any abatement.

Section IX : Assassination

Art. 148. The law of war does not allow proclaiming either an individual belonging to the hostile army, or a citizen, or a subject of the hostile government, an outlaw, who may be slain without trial by any captor, any more than the modern law of peace allows such intentional outlawry; on the contrary, it abhors such outrage. The sternest retaliation should follow the murder committed in consequence of such proclamation, made by whatever authority. Civilized nations look with horror upon offers of rewards for the assassination of enemies as relapses into barbarism.

Section X : Insurrection -- Civil war -- Rebellion

Art. 149. Insurrection is the rising of people in arms against their government, or a portion of it, or against one or more of its laws, or against an officer or officers of the government. It may be confined to mere armed resistance, or it may have greater ends in view.

Art. 150. Civil war is war between two or more portions of a country or state, each contending for the mastery of the whole, and each claiming to be the legitimate government. The term is also sometimes applied to war of rebellion, when the rebellious provinces or portions of the state are contiguous to those containing the seat of government.

Art. 151. The term rebellion is applied to an insurrection of large extent, and is usually a war between the legitimate government of a country and portions of provinces of the same who seek to throw off their allegiance to it and set up a government of their own.

Art. 152. When humanity induces the adoption of the rules of regular war to ward rebels, whether the adoption is partial or entire, it does in no way whatever imply a partial or complete acknowledgement of their government, if they have set up one, or of them, as an independent and sovereign power. Neutrals have no right to make the adoption of the rules of war by the assailed government toward rebels the ground of their own acknowledgment of the revolted people as an independent power.

Art. 153. Treating captured rebels as prisoners of war, exchanging them, concluding of cartels, capitulations, or other warlike agreements with them; addressing officers of a rebel army by the rank they may have in the same; accepting flags of truce; or, on the other hand, proclaiming Martial Law in their territory, or levying wartaxes or forced loans, or doing any other act sanctioned or demanded by the law and usages of public war between sovereign belligerents, neither proves nor establishes an acknowledgment of the rebellious people, or of the government which they may have erected, as a public or sovereign power. Nor does the adoption of the rules of war toward rebels imply an engagement with them extending beyond the limits of these rules. It is victory in the field that ends the strife and settles the future relations between the contending parties.

Art. 154. Treating, in the field, the rebellious enemy according to the law and usages of war has never prevented the legitimate government from trying the leaders of the rebellion or chief rebels for high treason, and from treating them accordingly, unless they are included in a general amnesty.

Art. 155. All enemies in regular war are divided into two general classes -- that is to say, into combatants and noncombatants, or unarmed citizens of the hostile government.

The military commander of the legitimate government, in a war of rebellion, distinguishes between the loyal citizen in the revolted portion of the country and the disloyal citizen. The disloyal citizens may further be classified into those citizens known to sympathize with the rebellion without positively aiding it, and those who, without taking up arms, give positive aid and comfort to the rebellious enemy without being bodily forced thereto.

Art. 156. Common justice and plain expediency require that the military commander protect the manifestly loyal citizens, in revolted territories, against the hardships of the war as much as the common misfortune of all war admits.

The commander will throw the burden of the war, as much as lies within his power, on the disloyal citizens, of the revolted portion or province, subjecting them to a stricter police than the noncombatant enemies have to suffer in regular war; and if he deems it appropriate, or if his government demands of him that every citizen shall, by an oath of allegiance, or by some other manifest act, declare his fidelity to the legitimate government, he may expel, transfer, imprison, or fine the revolted citizens who refuse to pledge themselves anew as citizens obedient to the law and loyal to the government.

Whether it is expedient to do so, and whether reliance can be placed upon such oaths, the commander or his government have the right to decide.

Art. 157. Armed or unarmed resistance by citizens of the United States against the lawful movements of their troops is levying war against the United States, and is therefore treason.

I-36. The Laws of War on Land (Oxford Manual), *signed at Oxford*, Manual adopted and published by the Institute of International Law, 9 September 1880, 5 Annuaire de l'Institute de Droit International 156-174.[1] (1881-1882). Authentic Text: French

Relevant Penal Characteristics & Penal Provisions

2. Implicit recognition of the penal nature of the act by establishing a duty to prohibit, prevent, prosecute, punish, or the like: Article 8(a); Article 9(a)

5. Duty or right to punish the proscribed conduct: Article 32(c); & Article 84

Applicability
War

Control
Regulation & Prohibition

Full Text

PREFACE

War holds a great place in history, and it is not to be supposed that men will soon give it up -- in spite of the protests which it arouses and the horror which it inspires -- because it appears to be the only possible issue of disputes which threaten the existence of States, their liberty, their vital interests. But the gradual improvement in customs should be reflected in the method of conducting war. It is worthy of civilized nations to seek, as has been well said (Baron Jomini), "to restrain the destructive force of war, while recognizing its inexorable necessities".

This problem is not easy of solution; however, some points have already been solved, and very recently the draft of Declaration of Brussels has been a solemn pronouncement of the good intentions of governments in this connection. It may be said that independently of the international laws existing on this subject, there are to-day certain principles of justice which guide the public conscience, which are manifested even by general customs, but which it would be well to fix and make obligatory. That is what the Conference of Brussels attempted, at the suggestion of His Majesty the Emperor of Russia, and it is what the Institute of International Law, in its turn, is trying to-day to contribute. The Institute attempts this although the governments have not ratified the draft issued by the Conference at Brussels, because since 1874 ideas, aided by reflection and experience, have had time to mature, and because it seems less difficult than it did then to trace rules which would be acceptable to all peoples.

The Institute, too, does not propose an international treaty, which might perhaps be premature or at least very difficult to obtain; but, being bound by its by-laws to work, among other things, for the observation of the laws of war, it believes it is fulfilling a

---

[1] This document is not a multilateral agreement, but is nonetheless an authoritative manual. It is included here because of its early importance as a statement of general principles that states could use in drafting and codifying agreements regulating warfare.

duty in offering to the governments a ' Manual ' suitable as the basis for national legislation in each State, and in accord with both the progress of juridical science and the needs of civilized armies.

Rash and extreme rules will not, furthermore, be found therein. The Institute has not sought innovations in drawing up the ' Manual '; it has contented itself with stating clearly and codifying the accepted ideas of our age so far as this has appeared allowable and practicable.

By so doing, it believes it is rendering a service to military men themselves. In fact so long as the demands of opinion remain indeterminate, belligerents are exposed to painful uncertainty and to endless accusations. A positive set of rules, on the contrary, if they are judicious, serves the interests of belligerents and is far from hindering them, since by preventing the unchaining of passion and savage instincts -- which battle always awakens, as much as it awakens courage and manly virtues, -- it strengthens the discipline which is the strength of armies; it also ennobles their patriotic mission in the eyes of the soldiers by keeping them within the limits of respect due to the rights of humanity.

But in order to attain this end it is not sufficient for sovereigns to promulgate new laws. It is essential, too, that they make these laws known among all people, so that when a war is declared, the men called upon to take up arms to defend the causes of the belligerent States, may be thoroughly impregnated with the special rights and duties attached to the execution of such a command.

The Institute, with a view to assisting the authorities in accomplishing this part of their task, has given its work a popular form, attaching thereto statements of the reasons therefor, from which the text of a law may be easily secured when desired.

PART I : GENERAL PRINCIPLES

Article 1. The state of war does not admit of acts of violence, save between the armed forces of belligerent States.

Persons not forming part of a belligerent armed force should abstain from such acts.

' This rule implies a distinction between the individuals who compose the "armed force" of a State and its other ' ressortissants '. A definition of the term "armed force" is, therefore, necessary. '

Art. 2. The armed force of a State includes:

1. The army properly so called, including the militia;

2. The national guards, landsturm, free corps, and other bodies which fulfil the three following conditions:

(a) That they are under the direction of a responsible chief;

(b) That they must have a uniform, or a fixed distinctive emblem recognizable at a distance, and worn by individuals composing such corps;

(c) That they carry arms openly;

3. The crews of men-of-war and other military boats;

4. The inhabitants of non-occupied territory, who, on the approach of the enemy, take up arms spontaneously and openly to resist the invading troops, even if they have not had time to organize themselves.

Art. 3. Every belligerent armed force is bound to conform to the laws of war.

' The only legitimate end that States may have in war being to weaken the military strength of the enemy ' (Declaration of St. Petersburg, 1868), '

Art. 4. The laws of war do not recognize in belligerents an unlimited liberty as to the means of injuring the enemy.

They are to abstain especially from all needless severity, as well as from all perfidious, unjust, or tyrannical acts.

Art. 5. Military conventions made between belligerents during the continuance of war, such as armistices and capitulations, must be scrupulously observed and respected.

Art. 6. No invaded territory is regarded as conquered until the end of the war; until that time the occupant exercises, in such territory, only a ' de facto ' power, essentially provisional in character.

PART II : APPLICATION OF GENERAL PRINCIPLES
I. HOSTILITIES
A. Rules of conduct with regard to individuals
(a) Inoffensive populations
    ' The contest being carried on by "armed forces" only (Article 1), '

Art. 7. It is forbidden to maltreat inoffensive populations.
(b) Means of injuring the enemy
    ' As the struggle must be honourable (Article 4), '

Art. 8. It is forbidden:

(a) To make use of poison, in any form whatever;

(b) To make treacherous attempts upon the life of an enemy; as, for example, by keeping assassins in pay or by feigning to surrender;

(c) To attack an enemy while concealing the distinctive signs of an armed force;

(d) To make improper use of the national flag, military insignia or uniform of the enemy, of the flag of truce and of the protective signs prescribed by the ' Geneva Convention ' (Articles 17 and 40).

    ' As needless severity should be avoided (Article 4), '

Art. 9. It is forbidden:

(a) To employ arms, projectiles, or materials of any kind calculated to cause superfluous suffering, or to aggravate wounds - notably projectiles of less weight than four hundred grams which are explosive or are charged with fulminating or inflammable substances ' (Declaration of St. Petersburg); '

(b) To injure or kill an enemy who has surrendered at discretion or is disabled, and to declare in advance that quarter will not be given, even by those who do not ask it for themselves.

(c) The sick and wounded, and the sanitary service
    ' The following provisions (Articles 10 to 18), drawn from the ' Geneva Convention, ' exempt the sick and wounded, and the personnel of the sanitary service, from many of the needless hardships to which they were formerly exposed: '

Art. 10. Wounded or sick soldiers should be brought in and cared for, to whatever nation they belong.

Art. 11. Commanders in chief have power to deliver immediately to the enemy outposts hostile soldiers who have been wounded in an engagement, when circumstances permit and with the consent of both parties.

Art. 12. Evacuations, together with the persons under whose direction they take place, shall be protected by neutrality.

Art. 13. Persons employed in hospitals and ambulances -- including the staff for superintendence, medical service, administration and transport of wounded, as well as the chaplains, and the members and agents of relief associations which are duly authorized to assist the regular sanitary staff -- are considered as neutral while so employed, and so long as there remain any wounded to bring in or to succour.

Art. 14. The personnel designated in the preceding article should continue, after occupation by the enemy, to tend, according to their needs, the sick and wounded in the ambulance or hospital which it serves.

Art. 15. When such personnel requests to withdraw, the commander of the occupying troops sets the time of departure, which however he can only delay for a short time in case of military necessity.

Art. 16. Measures should be taken to assure, if possible, to neutralized persons who have fallen into the hands of the enemy, the enjoyment of fitting maintenance.

Art. 17. The neutralized sanitary staff should wear a white arm-badge with a red cross, but the delivery thereof belongs exclusively to the military authority.

Art. 18. The generals of the belligerent Powers should appeal to the humanity of the inhabitants, and should endeavour to induce them to assist the wounded by pointing out to them the advantages that will result to themselves from so doing (Articles 36 and 59). They should regard as inviolable those who respond to this appeal.

(d) The dead

Art. 19. It is forbidden to rob or mutilate the dead lying on the field of battle.

Art. 20. The dead should never be buried until all articles on them which may serve to fix their identity, such as pocket-books, numbers, etc., shall have been collected.

The articles thus collected from the dead of the enemy are transmitted to its army or government.

(e) Who may be made prisoners of war

Art. 21. Individuals who form a part of the belligerent armed force, if they fall into the hands of the enemy, are to be treated as prisoners of war, in conformity with Articles 61 et seq.

The same rule applies to messengers openly carrying official dispatches, and to civil aeronauts charged with observing the enemy, or with the maintenance of communications between the various parts of the army or territory.

Art. 22. Individuals who accompany an army, but who are not a part of the regular armed force of the State, such as correspondents, traders, sutlers, etc., and who fall into the hands of the enemy, may be detained for such length of time only as is warranted by strict military necessity.

(f) Spies

Art. 23. Individuals captured as spies cannot demand to be treated as prisoners of war.

'But'

Art. 24. Individuals may not be regarded as spies, who, belonging to the armed force of either belligerent, have penetrated, without disguise, into the zone of operations of the enemy, -- nor bearers of official dispatches, carrying out their mission openly, nor aeronauts (Article 21).

' In order to avoid the abuses to which accusations of espionage too often give rise in war it is important to assert emphatically that '

Art. 25. No person charged with espionage shall be punished until the judicial authority shall have pronounced judgment.

' Moreover, it is admitted that '

Art. 26. A spy who succeeds in quitting the territory occupied by the enemy incurs no responsibility for his previous acts, should he afterwards fall into the hands of that enemy. (g) Parlementaires.

Art. 27. A person is regarded as a parlementaire and has a right to inviolability who has been authorized by one of the belligerents to enter into communication with the other, and who advances bearing a white flag.

Art. 28. He may be accompanied by a bugler or a drummer, by a colour-bearer, and, if need be, by a guide and interpreter, who also are entitled to inviolability.

' The necessity of this prerogative is evident. It is moreover, frequently exercised in the interest of humanity. But it must not be injurious to the adverse party. This is why '

Art. 29. The commander to whom a parlementaire is sent is not in all cases obliged to receive him.

' Besides, '

Art. 30. The commander who receives a parlementaire has a right to take all the necessary steps to prevent the presence of the enemy within his lines from being prejudicial to him.

' The parlementaire and those who accompany him should behave fairly towards the enemy receiving them (Article 4). '

Art. 31. If a parlementaire abuse the trust reposed in him he may be temporarily detained, and, if it be proved that he has taken advantage of his privileged position to abet a treasonable act, he forfeits his right to inviolability.

B. Rules of conduct with regard to things

(a) Means of injuring -- Bombardment

' Certain precautions are made necessary by the rule that a belligerent must abstain from useless severity (Article 4). In accordance with this principle '

Art. 32. It is forbidden:

(a) To pillage, even towns taken by assault;

(b) To destroy public or private property, if this destruction is not demanded by an imperative necessity of war;

(c) To attack and to bombard undefended places.

' If it is incontestable that belligerents have the right to resort to bombardment against fortresses and other places in which the enemy is intrenched, considerations of humanity require that this means of coercion be surrounded with certain modifying influences which will restrict as far as possible the effects to the hostile armed force and its means of defense.

Art. 33. The commander of an attacking force, save in cases of open assault, shall, before undertaking a bombardment, make every due effort to give notice thereof to the local authorities.

Art. 34. In case of bombardment all necessary steps must be taken to spare, if it can be done, buildings dedicated to religion, art, science and charitable purposes, hospitals and places where the sick and wounded are gathered on the condition that they are not being utilized at the time, directly or indirectly, for defense.

It is the duty of the besieged to indicate the presence of such buildings by visible signs notified to the assailant beforehand.

(b) Sanitary material

' The arrangements for the relief of the wounded, which are made the subject of Articles 10 let seq., would be inadequate were not sanitary establishments also granted special protection. Hence, in accordance with the ' Geneva Convention, '

Art. 35. Ambulances and hospitals for the use of armies are recognized as neutral and should, as such, be protected and respected by belligerents, so long as any sick or wounded are therein.

Art. 36. The same rule applies to private buildings, or parts of buildings, in which sick or wounded are gathered and cared for.

' Nevertheless, '

Art. 37. The neutrality of hospitals and ambulances ceases if they are guarded by a military force; this does not preclude the presence of police guard.

Art. 38. As the equipment of military hospitals remains subject to the laws of war, persons attached to such hospitals cannot, in withdrawing, carry away any articles but such as are their private property. Ambulances, on the contrary, retain all their equipment.

Art. 39. In the circumstances referred to in the above paragraph, the term "ambulance" is applied to field hospitals and other temporary establishments which follow the troops on the field of battle to receive the sick and wounded.

Art. 40. A distinctive and uniform flag is adopted for ambulances, hospitals, and evacuations. It bears a red cross on a white ground It must always be accompanied by the national flag.

II. OCCUPIED TERRITORY

A. Definition

Art. 41. Territory is regarded as occupied when, as the consequence of invasion by hostile forces, the State to which it belongs has ceased, in fact, to exercise its ordinary authority therein, and the invading State is alone in a position to maintain order there. The limits within which this state of affairs exists determine the extent and duration of the occupation.

B. Rules of conduct with respect to persons

' In consideration of the new relations which arise from the provisional change of government (Article 6), '

Art. 42. It is the duty of the occupying military authority to inform the inhabitants at the earliest practicable moment, of the powers that it exercises, as well as of the local extent of the occupation.

Art. 43. The occupant should take all due and needful measures to restore and ensure public order and public safety.

' To that end '

Art. 44. The occupant should maintain the laws which were in force in the country in time of peace, and should not modify, suspend, or replace them, unless necessary.

Art. 45. The civil functionaries and employees of every class who consent to continue to perform their duties are under the protection of the occupant.

They may always be dismissed, and they always have the right to resign their places.

They should not be summarily punished unless they fail to fulfil obligations accepted by them, and should be handed over to justice only if they violate these obligations.

Art. 46. In case of urgency, the occupant may demand the cooperation of the inhabitants, in order to provide for the necessities of local administration.

' As occupation does not entail upon the inhabitants a change of nationality, '

Art. 47. The population of the invaded district cannot be compelled to swear allegiance to the hostile Power; but inhabitants who commit acts of hostility against the occupant are punishable (Article 1).

Art. 48. The inhabitants of an occupied territory who do not submit to the orders of the occupant may be compelled to do so.

The occupant, however, cannot compel the inhabitants to assist him in his works of attack or defense, or to take part in military operations against their own country (Article 4).

' Besides, '

Art. 49. Family honour and rights, the lives of individuals, as well as their religious convictions and practice, must be respected (Article 4).

C. Rules of conduct with regard to property

(a) Public property

' Although the occupant replaces the enemy State in the government of the invaded territory, his power is not absolute. So long as the fate of this territory remains in suspense -- that is, until peace -- the occupant is not free to dispose of what still belongs to the enemy and is not of use in military operation. Hence the following rules'

Art. 50. The occupant can only take possession of cash, funds and realizable or negotiable securities which are strictly the property of the State, depots of arms, supplies, and, in general, movable property of the State of such character as to be useful in military operations.

Art. 51. Means of transportation (railways, boats, & c.), as well as land telegraphs and landing-cables, can only be appropriated to the use of the occupant. Their destruction is forbidden, unless it be demanded by military necessity. They are restored when peace is made in the condition in which they then are.

Art. 52. The occupant can only act in the capacity of provisional administrator in respect to real property, such as buildings, forests, agricultural establishments, belonging to the enemy State (Article 6).

It must safeguard the capital of these properties and see to their maintenance.

Art. 53. The property of municipalities, and that of institutions devoted to religion, charity, education, art and science, cannot be seized.

All destruction or wilful damage to institutions of this character, historic monuments, archives, works of art, or science, is formally forbidden, save when urgently demanded by military necessity.

(b) Private property

' If the powers of the occupant are limited with respect to the property of the enemy State, with greater reason are they limited with respect to the property of individuals. '

Art. 54. Private property, whether belonging to individuals or corporations, must be respected, and can be confiscated only under the limitations contained in the following articles.

Art. 55. Means of transportation (railways, boats, & c.), telegraphs, depots of arms and munitions of war, although belonging to companies or to individuals, may be seized by the occupant, but must be restored, if possible, and compensation fixed when peace is made.

Art. 56. Impositions in kind (requisitions) demanded from communes or inhabitants should be in proportion to the necessities of war as generally recognized, and in proportion to the resources of the country.

Requisitions can only be made on the authority of the commander in the locality occupied.

Art. 57. The occupant may collect, in the way of dues and taxes, only those already established for the benefit of the State. He employs them to defray the expenses of administration of the country, to the extent in which the legitimate government was bound.

Art. 58. The occupant cannot collect extraordinary contributions of money, save as an equivalent for fines, or imposts not paid, or for payments not made in kind.

Contributions in money can be imposed only on the order and responsibility of the general in chief, or of the superior civil authority established in the occupied territory, as far as possible, in accordance with the rules of assessment and incidence of the taxes in force.

Art. 59. In the apportionment of burdens relating to the quartering of troops and war contributions, account is taken of the charitable zeal displayed by the inhabitants in behalf of the wounded.

Art. 60. Requisitioned articles, when they are not paid for in cash, and war contributions are evidenced by receipts. Measures should be taken to assure the ' bona fide ' character and regularity of these receipts.

III. Prisoners of war

A. Rules for captivity

' The confinement of prisoners of war is not in the nature of a penalty for crime (Article 21): neither is it an act of vengeance. It is a temporary detention only, entirely without penal character.

In the following provisions, therefore, regard has been had to the consideration due them as prisoners, and to the necessity of their secure detention. '

Art. 61. Prisoners of war are in the power of the hostile government, but not in that of the individuals or corps who captured them.

Art. 62. They are subject to the laws and regulations in force in the army of the enemy.

Art. 63. They must be humanely treated.

Art. 64. All their personal belongings, except arms, remain their property.

Art. 65. Every prisoner is bound to give, if questioned on the subject, his true name and rank. Should he fail to do so, he may be deprived of all, or a part, of the advantages accorded to prisoners of his class.

Art. 66. Prisoners may be interned in a town, a fortress, a camp, or other place, under obligation not to go beyond certain fixed limits; but they may only be placed in confinement as an indispensable measure of safety.

Art. 67. Any act of insubordination justifies the adoption towards them of such measure of severity as may be necessary.

Art. 68. Arms may be used, after summoning, against a prisoner attempting to escape.

If he is recaptured before being able to rejoin his own army or to quit the territory of his captor, he is only liable to disciplinary punishment, or subject to a stricter surveillance.

But if, after succeeding in escaping, he is again captured, he is not liable to punishment for his previous flight.

If, however, the fugitive so recaptured or retaken has given his parole not to escape, he may be deprived of the rights of a prisoner of war.

Art. 69. The government into whose hands prisoners have fallen is charged with their maintenance.

In the absence of an agreement on this point between the belligerent parties, prisoners are treated, as regards food and clothing, on the same peace footing as the troops of the government which captured them.

Art. 70. Prisoners cannot be compelled in any manner to take any part whatever in the operations of war, nor compelled to give information about their country or their army.

Art. 71. They may be employed on public works which have no direct connection with the operations in the theatre of war, which are not excessive and are not humiliating either to their military rank, if they belong to the army, or to their official or social position, if they do not form part thereof.

Art. 72. In case of their being authorized to engage in private industries, their pay for such services may be collected by the authority in charge of them. The sums so received may be employed in bettering their condition, or may be paid to them on their release, subject to deduction, if that course be deemed expedient, of the expense of their maintenance.

B. Termination of captivity

' The reasons justifying detention of the captured enemy exist only during the continuance of the war. '

Art. 73. The captivity of prisoners of war ceases, as a matter of right, at the conclusion of peace; but their liberation is then regulated by agreement between the belligerents.

' Before that time, and by virtue of the ' Geneva Convention, ' '

Art. 74. It also ceases as of right for wounded or sick prisoners who, after being cured, are found to be unfit for further military service. The captor should then send them back to their country.

' During the war '

Art. 75. Prisoners of war may be released in accordance with a cartel of exchange, agreed upon by the belligerent parties.

' Even without exchange '

Art. 76. Prisoners may be set at liberty on parole, if the laws of their country do not forbid it.

In this case they are bound, on their personal honour, scrupulously to fulfil the engagements which they have freely contracted, and which should be clearly specified. On its part, their own government should not demand or accept from them any service incompatible with the parole given.

Art. 77. A prisoner cannot be compelled to accept his liberty on parole. Similarly, the hostile government is not obliged to accede to the request of a prisoner to be set at liberty on parole.

Art. 78. Any prisoner liberated on parole and recaptured bearing arms against the government to which he had given such parole may be deprived of his rights as a prisoner of war, unless since his liberation he has been included in an unconditional exchange of prisoners.

IV. PERSONS INTERNED IN NEUTRAL TERRITORY

' It is universally admitted that a neutral State cannot, without compromising its neutrality, lend aid to either belligerent, or permit them to make use of its territory. On the other hand, considerations of humanity dictate that asylum should not be refused to individuals who take refuge in neutral territory to escape death or captivity. Hence the following provisions, calculated to reconcile the opposing interests involved. '

Art. 79. A neutral State on whose territory troops or individuals belonging to the armed forces of the belligerents take refuge should intern them, as far as possible, at a distance from the theatre of war.

It should do the same towards those who make use of its territory for military operations or services.

Art. 80. The interned may be kept in camps or even confined in fortresses or other places.

The neutral State decides whether officers can be left at liberty on parole by taking an engagement not to leave the neutral territory without permission.

Art. 81. In the absence of a special convention concerning the maintenance of the interned, the neutral State supplies them with the food, clothing, and relief required by humanity.

It also takes care of the ' matériel ' brought in by the interned.

When peace has been concluded, or sooner if possible, the expenses caused by the internment are repaid to the neutral State by the belligerent State to which the interned belong.

Art. 82. The provisions of the ' Geneva Convention ' of 22 August 1864 (Articles 10-18, 35-40, 59 and 74 above given), are applicable to the sanitary staff, as well as to the sick and wounded, who take refuge in, or are conveyed to, neutral territory.

' In particular, '

Art. 83. Evacuations of wounded and sick not prisoners may pass through neutral territory, provided the personnel and material accompanying them are exclusively sanitary. The neutral State through whose territory these evacuations are made is bound to take whatever measures of safety and control are necessary to secure the strict observance of the above conditions.

PART III : PENAL SANCTION

' If any of the foregoing rules be violated, the offending parties should be punished, after a judicial hearing, by the belligerent in whose hands they are. Therefore '

Art. 84. Offenders against the laws of war are liable to the punishments specified in the penal law.

' This mode of repression, however, is only applicable when the person of the offender can be secured. In the contrary case, the criminal law is powerless, and, if the injured party deem the misdeed so serious in character as to make it necessary to recall the enemy to a respect for law, no other recourse than a resort to reprisals remains.

Reprisals are an exception to the general rule of equity, that an innocent person ought not to suffer for the guilty. They are also at variance with the rule that each belligerent should conform to the rules of war, without reciprocity on the part of the enemy. This necessary rigour, however, is modified to some extent by the following restrictions: '

Art. 85. Reprisals are formally prohibited in case the injury complained of has been repaired.

Art. 86. In grave cases in which reprisals appear to be absolutely necessary, their nature and scope shall never exceed the measure of the infraction of the laws of war committed by the enemy.

They can only be resorted to with the authorization of the commander in chief.

They must conform in all cases to the laws of humanity and morality.

I-37. Manual of the Laws of Naval War, *signed at Oxford,* 9 August 1913, 26 Annuaire de l'Institut de Droit international 610-640 (1913).
Authentic Text: French

Relevant Penal Characteristics & Penal Provisions

1. Explicit or implicit recognition of proscribed conduct as constituting an international crime, or a crime under international law, or a crime: Article 25; Article 27; Article 28; Article 29; & Article 54

2. Implicit recognition of the penal nature of the act by establishing a duty to prohibit, prevent, prosecute, punish, or the like: Article 16 (1), (2); Article 19; Article 20; Article 21 (1), (2); Article 22; Article 23; Article 24

Applicability
War

Control
Regulation & Prohibition

Full Text

The Institute of International Law, at its Christiania session, declared itself in favour of firmly upholding its former Resolutions on the abolition of capture and of confiscation of enemy private property in naval warfare. But at the same time being aware that this principle is not yet accepted, and deeming that, for so long as it shall not be, regulation of the right of capture is indispensable, it entrusted a commission with the task of drawing up stipulations providing for either contingency. In pursuance of this latter action, the Institute, at its Oxford session on 9 August 1913, adopted the following Manual, based on the right of capture (1).

(1) ' Definitions.- Capture ' is the act by which the commander of a war-ship substitutes his authority for that of the captain of the enemy ship, subject to the subsequent judgment of the prize court as to the ultimate fate of the ship and its cargo.

' Seizure, ' when applied to a ship, is the act by which a war-ship takes possession of the vessel detained, with or without the consent of the captain of the latter. Seizure differs from capture in that the ultimate fate of the vessel may not be involved as a result of its condemnation.

Applied to goods alone, seizure is the act by which the war-ship, with or without the consent of the captain of the vessel detained, takes possession of the goods and holds them or disposes of them subject to the subsequent judgment of the prize court.

' Confiscation ' is the act by which the prize court renders valid the capture of a vessel or the seizure of its goods.

The word ' prize ' is a general expression applying to a captured ship or to seized goods.

By ' public ships ' are meant all ships other than war-ships which, belonging to the State or to individuals, are set apart for public service and are under the orders of an officer duly commissioned by the State. (Note in the original).

SECTION I
ON LOCALITIES WHERE HOSTILITIES MAY TAKE PLACE

Article 1. Rules peculiar to naval warfare are applicable only on the high seas and in the territorial waters of the belligerents, exclusive of those waters which, from the standpoint of navigation, ought not to be considered as maritime.

SECTION II
ON THE ARMED FORCE OF BELLIGERENT STATES

Art. 2. War-ships. Constituting part of the armed force of a belligerent State and, therefore, subject as
such to the laws of naval warfare are:

(1) All ships belonging to the State which, under the direction of a military commander and manned by a military crew, carry legally the ensign and the pendant of the national navy.

(2) Ships converted by the State into war-ships in conformity with Articles 36.

Art. 3. Conversion of public and private vessels into war-ships. A vessel converted into a war-ship cannot have the rights and duties accruing to such vessels, unless it is placed under the direct authority, immediate control, and responsibility of the Power whose flag it flies.

Art. 4. Vessels converted into war-ships must bear the exterior marks which distinguish the war-
ships of their nationality.

Art. 5. The commander must be in the service of the State and duly commissioned by the competent authorities; his name must appear on the list of officers of the fighting fleet.

Art. 6. The crew must be subject to the rules of military discipline.

Art. 7. Every vessel converted into a war-ship must observe in its operations the laws and customs of war.

Art. 8. The belligerent who converts a vessel into a war-ship must, as soon as possible, announce such conversion in the list of war-ships.

Art. 9. The conversion of a vessel into a war-ship may be accomplished by a belligerent only in its own waters, in those of an allied State also a belligerent, in those of the adversary, or, lastly, in those of a territory occupied by the troops of one of these States.

Art. 10. Conversion of war-ships into public or private vessels. A war-ship may not, while hostilities last, be converted into a public or a private vessel.

Art. 11. Belligerent personnel. Constituting part of the armed force of a belligerent State and, therefore, in so far as they carry on operations at sea, subject as such to the laws of naval warfare, are:

(1) The personnel of the ships mentioned in Article 2;

(2) The troops of the naval forces, active or reserve;

(3) The militarized personnel on the seacoasts;

(4) The regular forces, other than naval forces, or those regularly organized in conformity with Article 1 of the Hague Regulations of 18 October 1907, concerning the laws and customs of war on land.

Art. 12. Privateering, private vessels, public vessels not war-ships. Privateering is forbidden.

Apart from the conditions laid down in Articles 3 and following, neither public nor private vessels, nor their personnel, may commit acts of hostility against the enemy.

Both may, however, use force to defend themselves against the attack of an enemy vessel.

Art. 13. Population of unoccupied territory. The inhabitants of a territory which has not been occupied who, upon the approach of the enemy, spontaneously arm vessels to fight him, without having had time to convert them into war-ships in conformity with Articles 3 and following, shall be considered as belligerents, if they act openly and if they respect the laws and usages of war.

SECTION III
ON MEANS OF INJURING THE ENEMY

Art. 14. Principle. The right of belligerents to adopt means of injuring the enemy is not unlimited.

Art. 15. Treacherous and barbarous methods. Ruses of war are considered permissible. Methods, however, which involve treachery are forbidden.

Thus it is forbidden:

(1) To kill or wound treacherously individuals belonging to the opposite side;

(2) To make improper use of a flag of truce, to make use of false flags, uniforms, or insignia, of whatever kind, especially those of the enemy, as well as of the distinctive badges of the medical corps indicated in Articles 41 and 42.

Art. 16. In addition to the prohibitions which shall be established by special conventions, it is forbidden:

(1) To employ poison or poisoned weapons, or projectiles the sole object of which is the diffusion of asphyxiating or deleterious gases;

(2) To employ arms, projectiles, or materials calculated to cause unnecessary suffering. Entering especially into this category are explosive projectiles or those charged with fulminating or inflammable materials, less than 400 grammes in weight, and bullets which expand or flatten easily in the human body, such as bullets with a hard envelope which does not cover the core entirely or is pierced with incisions.

Art. 17. It is also forbidden:

(1) To kill or to wound an enemy who, having laid down his arms or having no longer means of defense, has surrendered at discretion;

(2) To sink a ship which has surrendered, before having taken off the crew;

(3) To declare that no quarter will be given.

Art. 18. Pillage and devastation are forbidden.

It is forbidden to destroy enemy property, except in the cases where such destruction is imperatively required by the necessities of war or authorized by provisions of the present regulations.

Art. 19. Torpedoes. It is forbidden to employ torpedoes which do not become harmless when they have missed their mark.

Art. 20. Submarine mines. It is forbidden to lay automatic contact mines, anchored or not, in the open sea.

Art. 21. Belligerents may lay mines in their territorial waters and in those of the enemy.

But it is forbidden, even in territorial waters:

(1) To lay unanchored automatic contact mines unless they are so constructed as to become harmless one hour at most after the person who laid them ceases to control them;

(2) To lay anchored automatic contact mines which do not become harmless as soon as they have broken loose from their moorings.

Art. 22. A belligerent may not lay mines along the coast and harbours of his adversary except for naval and military ends. He is forbidden to lay them there in order to establish or to maintain a commercial blockade.

Art. 23. When automatic contact mines, anchored or unanchored, are employed, every precaution must be taken for the security of peaceful shipping. The belligerents must do their utmost to render these mines harmless within a limited time. Should the mines cease to be under surveillance, the belligerents shall notify the danger zones. as soon as military exigencies permit, by a notice addressed to ship-owners, which must also be communicated to the governments through the diplomatic channel.

Art. 24. At the close of the war, the belligerent States shall do their utmost to remove the mines that they have laid, each one its own.

As regards the anchored automatic contact mines laid by one of the belligerents off the coast of the other, their position must be notified to the other party by the State that has laid them, and each State must proceed, with the least possible delay, to remove the mines in its own waters.

Belligerent States upon whom rests the obligation of removing these mines after the war is over shall, with as little delay as possible, make known the fact that, so far as is possible, the mines have been removed.

Art. 25. Bombardment. The bombardment of undefended ports, towns, villages, dwellings, or buildings is forbidden.

A place cannot be bombarded solely because submarine automatic contact mines are anchored off its coast.

Art. 26. Military works, military or naval establishments, depots of arms or war ' matériel, ' workshops or plants which could be utilized for the needs of the hostile fleet or army, and the war-ships in the harbour, are not, however, included in this prohibition. The commander of a naval force may destroy them with artillery, after a summons followed by a reasonable time of waiting, if all other means are impossible, and when the local authorities have not themselves destroyed them within the time fixed.

He incurs no responsibility for any unavoidable damage which may be caused by a bombardment under such circumstances.

If for military reasons immediate action is necessary, and no delay can be allowed the enemy, it is understood that the prohibition to bombard the undefended town holds good, as in the case given in paragraph 1, and that the commander shall take all due measures in order that the town may suffer as little harm as possible.

Art. 27. The bombardment of undefended ports, towns, villages, dwellings, or buildings because of the non-payment of contributions of money, or the refusal to comply with requisitions for provisions or supplies is forbidden.

Art. 28. In bombardments all useless destruction is forbidden, and especially should all necessary measures be taken by the commander of the attacking force to spare, as far as possible, sacred edifices, buildings used for artistic, scientific, or charitable purposes, historic monuments, hospitals, and places where the sick or wounded are collected. on condition that they are not used at the same time for military purposes.

It is the duty of the inhabitants to indicate such monuments, edifices, or places by visible signs, which shall consist of large stiff rectangular panels divided diagonally into two coloured triangular portions, the upper portion black, the lower portion white.

Art. 29. If the military situation permits, the commander of the attacking naval force, before commencing the bombardment, must do his utmost to warn the authorities.

Art. 30. Blockade. Ports and coasts belonging to the enemy or occupied by him may be subjected to blockade according to the rules of international law.

SECTION IV
ON THE RIGHTS AND DUTIES OF THE BELLIGERENT WITH REGARD TO ENEMY PROPERTY

Art. 31. A. Ships and cargoes -- War-ships. The armed forces of a State may attack the enemy's war-ships, to take possession of them or to destroy them, together with their equipment and supplies, whether these ships, at the beginning of the struggle, are in a harbour of the State, or are encountered at sea, in ignorance of hostilities; or by ' force majeure ' are either compelled to enter a port, or are cast on the shores of said State.

Art. 32. Public and private vessels -- Stopping, visit, and search. All vessels other than those of the navy, whether they belong to the State or to individuals, may be summoned by a belligerent war-ship to stop, that a visit and search may be conducted on board them.

The belligerent war-ship, in ordering a vessel to stop, shall fire a charge of powder as a summons and, if that warning is not sufficient, shall fire a projectile across the bow of the vessel. Previously or at the same time, the war-ship shall hoist its flag, above which, at night, a signal light shall be placed. The vessel answers the signal by hoisting its own flag and by stopping at once; whereupon, the war-ship shall send to the stopped vessel a launch manned by an officer and a sufficient number of men, of whom only two or three shall accompany the officer on board the stopped vessel.

Visit consists in the first place in an examination of the ship's papers.

If the ship's papers are insufficient or not of a nature to allay suspicion, the officer conducting the visit has the right to proceed to a search of the vessel, for which purpose he must ask the cooperation of the captain.

Visit of post packets must, as Article 53 says, be conducted with all the consideration and all the expedition possible.

Vessels convoyed by a neutral war-ship are not subject to visit except in so far as permitted by the rules relating to convoys.

Art. 33. Principle of capture. Public and private vessels of enemy nationality are subject to capture, and enemy goods on board, public or private, are liable to seizure.

Art. 34. Capture and seizure are permitted even when the vessels or the goods have fallen into the power of the belligerent because of ' force majeure,' through shipwreck or by being compelled to put into port.

Art. 35. Vessels which possess no ship's papers, which have intentionally destroyed or hidden those that they had, or which offer false ones, are liable to seizure.

Art. 36. Extenuation of the principle of capture. When a public or private vessel belonging to one of the belligerent Powers is, at the commencement of hostilities, in an enemy port, it is allowed to depart freely, immediately or after a reasonable number of days of grace, and to proceed, after having been furnished with a passport, to its port of destination, or to any other port indicated.

The same rule should apply in the case of a ship which has left its last port of departure before the commencement of the war and entered an enemy port while still ignorant of hostilities.

Art. 37. The public or private vessel unable, owing to circumstances of ' force majeure, ' to leave the enemy port within the period contemplated in the preceding article, cannot be captured.

The belligerent may only detain it without payment of compensation but subject to the obligation of restoring it after the war, or requisition it on payment of compensation.

Art. 38. Enemy vessels, public or private, which left their last port of departure before the commencement of the war and which are encountered on the high seas while still ignorant of the outbreak of hostilities, cannot be captured. They are only liable to detention on the understanding that they shall be restored after the war without compensation, or requisitioned, or even destroyed, on payment of compensation, but in such case provision must be made for the safety of the passengers on board as well as for the security of the ship's papers.

But, where these vessels shall be encountered at sea before the expiration of a sufficient period to be granted by the belligerent, seizure is not permissible. Vessels thus encountered are free to proceed to their port of destination or to any other port indicated.

After touching at a port in their own country or at a neutral port, these vessels are subject to capture.

Art. 39. Enemy cargo found on board the ships detained under Articles 37 and 38 may likewise be held. It must be restored after the termination of the war without payment of indemnity, unless requisitioned on payment of compensation.

The same rule is applicable to goods which are contraband of war found on board the vessels mentioned in Articles 36, 37 and 38, even when these vessels are not subject to capture.

Art. 40. In all cases considered in Articles 36, 37 and 38, public or private ships whose build shows that they are intended for conversion into war-ships, may be seized or requisitioned upon payment of compensation. These vessels shall be restored after the war.

Goods found on board these ships shall be dealt with according to the rules in Article 39.

Art. 41. Exceptions to the principles in Articles 31 and 32 -- Hospital ships. Military hospital ships, that is to say, ships constructed or assigned by States specially and solely with a view to assisting the wounded, sick and shipwrecked, the names of which have been communicated to the belligerent Powers at the commencement or during the course of hostilities, and in any case before they are employed, shall be respected, and cannot be captured while hostilities last.

Military hospital ships shall be distinguished by being painted white outside with a horizontal band of green about a metre and a half (five feet) in breadth.

The boats of the ships above mentioned, as also small craft which may be used for hospital work, shall be distinguished by similar painting.

All hospital ships shall make themselves known by hoisting, with their national flag the white flag with the red cross provided by the Geneva Convention.

The ships and boats above mentioned which wish to ensure by night the freedom from interference to which they are entitled, must, subject to the belligerent they are accompanying, take the measures necessary to render their special painting sufficiently plain.

The distinguishing signs referred to in this article can be used only outside with a horizontal band of green about a metre and a half (five feet) in breadth.

These ships cannot be used for any military purpose.

They must in no wise hamper the movements of the combatants.

During and after an engagement, they will act at their own risk and peril.

The belligerents shall have the right to control and search them; they can refuse to help them, order them off, make them take a certain course, and put a commissioner on board; they can even detain them, if important circumstances require it.

As far as possible, the belligerents shall enter in the log of the hospital ships the orders which they give them.

Hospital ships which, under the terms of this Article, are detained by the enemy, must haul down the national flag of the belligerent to whom they belong.

Art. 42. Hospital ships, equipped wholly or in part at the expense of private individuals or officially recognized relief societies, shall likewise be respected and exempt from capture, if the belligerent Power to whom they belong has given them an official commission and has notified their names to the hostile Power at the commencement of or during hostilities, and in any case before they are employed.

These ships must be provided with a certificate from competent authorities declaring that the vessels have been under their control while fitting out and on final departure.

The ships in question shall be distinguished by being painted white outside with a horizontal band of red about a metre and a half (five feet) in breadth.

They are subject to the regulations laid down for military hospital ships by Article 41.

Art. 43. In case of a fight on board a war-ship, the sick-wards and the ' matériel ' belonging to them shall be respected and spared as far as possible. Although remaining subject to the laws of war, they cannot be used for any purpose other than that for which they were originally intended, so long as they are required for the sick and wounded. The commander into whose power they have fallen may, however, apply them to other purposes, if the military situation requires it, after seeing that the sick and wounded on board are properly provided for.

Art. 44. Hospital ships and sick-wards of vessels are no longer entitled to protection if they are employed for the purpose of injuring the enemy. The fact that the staff of the said ships and sick-wards is armed for maintaining order and for defending the sick and wounded, and the presence of wireless telegraphy apparatus on board, are not sufficient reasons for withdrawing protection.

Art. 45. Cartel ships. Ships called cartel ships, which act as bearers of a flag of truce, may not be seized while fulfilling their mission, even if they belong to the navy.

A ship authorized by one of the belligerents to enter into a parley with the other and carrying a white flag is considered a cartel ship.

The commanding officer to whom a cartel ship is sent is not obliged to receive it under all circumstances. He can take all measures necessary to prevent the cartel ship from profiting by its mission to obtain information. In case it abuses its privileges, he has the right to hold the cartel ship temporarily.

A cartel ship loses its rights of inviolability if it is proved, positively and unexceptionably, that the commander has profited by the privileged position of his vessel to provoke or to commit a treacherous act.

Art. 46. Vessels charged with missions. Vessels charged with religious, scientific, or philanthropic missions are exempt from seizure.

Art. 47. Vessels used exclusively for fishing along the coast and for local trade. Vessels used exclusively for fishing along the coast, or for local trade, under which term are included those used exclusively for piloting or for light-house service, as well as the boats meant principally for the navigation of rivers, canals, and lakes, are exempt from seizure, together with their appliances, rigging, tackle and cargo.

It is forbidden to take advantage of the harmless character of said boats in order to use them for military purposes while preserving their peaceful appearance.

Art. 48. Vessels furnished with a safe-conduct or a licence. Enemy vessels provided with a safe-conduct or a licence are exempt from seizure.

Art. 49. Suspension of immunities. The exceptions considered in Articles 41, 42, 45, 46, 47 and 48 cease to be applicable if the vessels to which they refer participate in the hostilities in any manner whatsoever or commit other acts which are forbidden to neutrals as unneutral service.

The same suspension occurs if, summoned to stop to submit to search, they seek to escape by force or by flight.

Art. 50. Rights of the belligerent in the zone of operations. When a belligerent has not the right of seizing or of capturing enemy vessels, he may, even on the high seas, forbid them to enter the zone corresponding to the actual sphere of his operations.

He may also forbid them within this zone to perform certain acts calculated to interfere with his activities, especially certain acts of communication, such, for example, as the use of wireless telegraphy.

The simple infraction of these prohibitions will entail driving the vessel back, even by force, from the forbidden zone and the sequestration of the apparatus. The vessel, if it be proved that it has communicated with the enemy to furnish him with information concerning the conduct of hostilities, can be considered as having placed itself at the service of the enemy and, consequently, with its apparatus, shall be liable to capture.

Art. 51. Enemy character. The enemy or neutral character of a vessel is determined by the flag which it is entitled to fly.

The enemy or neutral character of goods found on board an enemy vessel is determined by the enemy or the neutral character of the owner.

Each State must declare, not later than the outbreak of hostilities, whether the enemy or neutral character of the owner of the goods is determined by his place of residence or his nationality.

Enemy goods found on board an enemy ship retain their enemy character until they reach their destination, notwithstanding any transfer effected after the outbreak of hostilities while the goods are being forwarded.

If, however, prior to the capture, a former neutral owner exercises, on the bankruptcy of an existing enemy owner, a recognized legal right to recover the goods, they regain their neutral character.

Art. 52. Transfer to a neutral flag. The transfer of an enemy vessel to a neutral flag, effected before the outbreak of hostilities, is valid, unless it is proved that such transfer was made in order to evade the consequences to which an enemy vessel as such is exposed. There is, however, a presumption, if the bill of sale is not on board a vessel which has lost its belligerent nationality less than sixty days before the outbreak of hostilities, that the transfer is void; this presumption may be rebutted.

Where the transfer was effected more than thirty days before the outbreak of hostilities, there is an absolute presumption that it is valid if it is unconditional, complete, and in conformity with the laws of the countries concerned, and if its effect is such that neither the control of, nor the profits arising from the employment of, the vessel remain in the same hands as before the transfer. If, however, the vessel lost her belligerent nationality less than sixty days before the outbreak of hostilities and if the bill of sale is not on board, the capture of the vessel gives no right to damages.

The transfer of an enemy vessel to a neutral flag effected after the outbreak of hostilities, is void unless it is proved that such transfer was not made in order to evade the consequences to which an enemy vessel, as such, is exposed.

There is, however, an absolute presumption that a transfer is void:

(1) if the transfer has been made during a voyage or in a blockaded port;

(2) if a right to repurchase or recover the vessel is reserved to the vendor;

(3) if the requirements of the municipal law governing the right to fly the flag under which the vessel is sailing, have not been fulfilled.

Art. 53. B. Postal correspondence. Postal correspondence, whatever its official or private character may be, found on the high seas on board an enemy ship, is inviolable, unless it is destined for or proceeding from a blockaded port.

The inviolability of postal correspondence does not exempt mail-boats from the laws and customs of maritime war as to ships in general. The ship, however, may not be searched except when absolutely necessary, and then only with as much consideration and expedition as possible.

If the ship on which the mail is sent be seized, the correspondence is forwarded by the captor with the least possible delay.

Art. 54. C. Submarine cables. In the conditions stated below, belligerent States are authorized to destroy or to seize only the submarine cables connecting their territories or two points in these territories, and the cables connecting the territory of one of the nations engaged in the war with a neutral territory.

The cable connecting the territories of the two belligerents or two points in the territory of one of the belligerents, may be seized or destroyed throughout its length, except in the waters of a neutral State.

A cable connecting a neutral territory with the territory of one of the belligerents may not, under any circumstances, be seized or destroyed in the waters under the power of a neutral territory. On the high seas, this cable may not be seized or destroyed unless there exists an effective blockade and within the limits of that blockade, on consideration of the restoration of the cable in the shortest time possible. This cable may be seized or destroyed on the territory of and in the waters belonging to the territory of the enemy for a distance of three marine miles from low tide. Seizure or destruction may never take place except in case of absolute necessity.

In applying the preceding rules no distinction is to be made between cables, according to whether they belong to the State or to individuals; nor is any regard to be paid to the nationality of their owners.

Submarine cables connecting belligerent territory with neutral territory, which have been seized or destroyed, shall be restored and compensation fixed when peace is made.

SECTION V
ON THE RIGHTS AND DUTIES OF THE BELLIGERENT WITH REGARD TO INDIVIDUALS

Art. 55. A. Personnel of vessels -- War-ships. When a war-ship is captured by the enemy, combatants and non-combatants forming part of the armed forces of the belligerents, arc to be treated as prisoners of war.

Art. 56. Public or private vessels. When an enemy ship, public or private, is seized by a belligerent, such of its crew as are nationals of a neutral State, are not made prisoners of war. The same rule applies in the case of the captain and officers likewise nationals of a neutral State, if they promise in writing not to take, during hostilities, any service connected with the operations of the war. The captain, officers and members of the crew, when nationals of the enemy State, are not made prisoners of war, on condition that they make a formal promise in writing not to undertake, while hostilities last, any service connected with the operations of the war.

Art. 57. The names of the persons retaining their liberty on condition of the promise provided for by the preceding article, are notified by the belligerent captor to the other belligerent. The latter is forbidden knowingly to employ the said persons.

Art. 58. All persons constituting part of the crew of a public or a private enemy ship are, in the absence of proof to the contrary, presumed to be of enemy nationality.

Art. 59. Members of the personnel of an enemy ship which, because of its special character, is itself exempt from seizure, cannot be held as enemies.

Art. 60. When a public or a private ship has directly or indirectly taken part in the hostilities, the enemy may retain as prisoners of war the whole personnel of the ship, without prejudice to the penalties he might otherwise incur.

Art. 61. Members of the personnel of a public or of a private vessel, who are personally guilty of an act of hostility towards the enemy, may be held by him as prisoners of war, without prejudice to the penalties he might otherwise incur.

Art. 62. B. Passengers. When individuals who follow a naval force without belonging to it, such as contractors, newspaper correspondents, etc., fall into the enemy's hands, and when the latter thinks it expedient to detain them, they may be detained only so long as military exigencies require. They are entitled to be treated as prisoners of war.

Art. 63. Passengers who, without forming part of the crew, are on board an enemy ship, may not be detained as prisoners of war, unless they have been guilty of a hostile act.

All passengers included in the armed force of the enemy may be made prisoners of war, even if the vessel is not subject to seizure.

Art. 64. C. Religious, medical, and hospital personnel. The religious, medical, and hospital staff of every vessel taken or seized is inviolable, and its members may not be made prisoners of war. On leaving the ship they take away with them the objects and surgical instruments which are their own private property.

This staff shall continue to discharge its duties while necessary, and can afterwards leave, when the commander in chief considers it possible.

The belligerents must guarantee to the said staff, when it has fallen into their hands, the same allowances and pay which are given to the staff of corresponding rank in their own navy.

The commissioner put by the belligerent on board the hospital ship of his adversary, in conformity with paragraph 10 of Article 41, enjoys the same protection as the medical staff.

The religious, medical, and hospital staffs lose their rights of inviolability, if they take part in hostilities, if, for example, they use their arms otherwise than for defense.

Art. 65. D. Parlementaires. The personnel of cartel ships is inviolable.

It loses its rights of inviolability if it is proved in a clear and incontestable manner that it has taken advantage of its privileged position to provoke or commit an act of treason.

Art. 66. E. Spies. A spy, even when taken in the act, may not be punished without first being tried.

Art. 67. A person can be considered a spy only when, acting clandestinely or on false pretenses, thus concealing his operations, he obtains or endeavours to obtain information in the zone of operations of a belligerent, with the intention of communicating it to the hostile party.

Hence, soldiers not wearing a disguise who have penetrated into the zone of operations of the hostile fleet for the purpose of obtaining information, may not be considered as spies but are to be treated as prisoners of war. Similarly, soldiers or civilians, carrying out their mission openly, entrusted with the delivery of dispatches, or engaged in transmitting and receiving dispatches by wireless telegraphy, are not to be considered as spies. To this class belong likewise persons sent in air-ships or in hydro-aeroplanes to act as scouts in the zone of operations of the enemy fleet or to maintain communications.

Art. 68. The spy who succeeds in escaping from the zone corresponding to the enemy's actual sphere of operations, or who has rejoined the armed force to which he belongs, if he later falls into the power of the enemy, incurs no responsibility for his previous acts.

Art. 69. F. Requisition of nationals of the enemy State -- Guides, pilots, and hostages. A belligerent has no right to force persons who fall into his power, or nationals of the adverse party in general, to take part in the operations of the war directed against their own country, even when they were in his service before the beginning of the war, or to compel them to furnish information concerning their own

State, its forces, its military position, or its means of defense.

He cannot force them to act as guides or as pilots.

He may, however, punish those who knowingly and voluntarily offer themselves in order to mislead him.

Compelling nationals of a belligerent to swear allegiance to the enemy Power is not permitted.

The taking of hostages is forbidden.

Art. 70. G. Prisoners of war. Prisoners of war are in the power of the hostile government, but not of the individuals or corps who capture them.

They must be humanely treated.

All their personal belongings, except arms, horses, military papers, and all objects in general which are specially adapted to a military end, remain their property.

Art. 71. Prisoners of war may be interned on a ship only in case of necessity and temporarily.

Art. 72. The government into whose hands prisoners of war have fallen is charged with their maintenance.

Art. 73. All prisoners of war, so long as they are on board a ship, shall be subject to the laws, regulations, and orders in force in the navy of the State in whose power they are.

Art. 74. Escaped prisoners who are retaken before succeeding in escaping from the enemy's actual sphere of action, or before being able to rejoin the armed force to which they belong, are liable to disciplinary punishment.

Prisoners who, after succeeding in escaping, are again taken prisoners, are not liable to any punishment on account of the previous flight.

Art. 75. Every prisoner of war is bound to give, if he is questioned on the subject, his true name and rank, and if he infringes this rule, he is liable to have the advantages given to prisoners of his class curtailed.

Art. 76. Prisoners of war may be set at liberty on parole if the laws of their country allow, and, in such cases, they are bound, on their personal honour, scrupulously to fulfil, both towards their own government and the government by whom they were made prisoners, the engagements they have contracted.

In such cases their own government is bound neither to require nor to accept from them any service incompatible with the parole given.

Art. 77. A prisoner of war cannot be compelled to accept his liberty on parole; similarly the hostile government is not obliged to accede to the request of the prisoner to be set at liberty on parole.

Art. 78. Prisoners of war liberated on parole and recaptured bearing arms against the government to whom they had pledged their honour, or against the allies of that government, forfeit their right to be treated as prisoners of war, and can be brought before the courts, unless, subsequent to their liberation, they have been included in an unconditional cartel of exchange.

Art. 79. Prisoners in naval warfare disembarked on land are subject to the rules laid down for prisoners in land warfare.

The same regulations should be applied, as far as possible, to prisoners of war interned on a vessel.

The preceding rules must, as far as it is possible to apply them, be followed toward prisoners of war from the moment they are captured, when they are on the ship which takes them to the place of their internment.

Art. 80. After the conclusion of peace, the repatriation of prisoners of war shall be carried out as quickly as possible.

Art. 81. H. Wounded, sick, shipwrecked and dead. Vessels used for hospital service shall afford relief and assistance to the wounded, sick and shipwrecked of the belligerents without distinction of nationality.

Art. 82. In case of the capture or seizure of an enemy vessel or a hospital ship that has failed in its duty, the sailors and soldiers on board, when sick or wounded, as well as other persons officially attached to fleets or armies, whatever their nationality, shall be respected and tended by their captors.

Art. 83. Any war-ship belonging to a belligerent may demand that sick, wounded or shipwrecked men on board military hospital ships, hospital ships belonging to relief societies or to private individuals, merchant ships, yachts, or boats, whatever the nationality of these vessels, should be handed over.

Art. 84. The shipwrecked, wounded, or sick of one of the belligerents who fall into the power of the other belligerent are prisoners of war. The captor must decide, according to circumstances, whether to keep them, send them to a port of his own country, to a neutral port, or even to an enemy port. In this last case, prisoners thus repatriated cannot serve again while the war lasts.

Art. 85. After every engagement, the two belligerents, so far as military interests permit, shall take steps to look for the shipwrecked and wounded, and to protect them, as well as the dead, from pillage and ill-treatment.

They shall see that the burial, whether by land or sea, or the cremation of the dead shall be preceded by a careful examination of the corpse.

Art. 86. Each belligerent shall send, as early as possible, to the authorities of their country, their navy, or their army the military marks or documents of identity found on the dead and the description of the sick and wounded picked up by him.

The belligerents shall keep each other informed as to internments and transfers as well as to admissions into hospitals and the deaths which have occurred among the sick and wounded in their hands. They shall collect, in order to have them forwarded to the persons concerned by the authorities of their own country, all the objects of personal use, valuables, letters, etc., which are found in the captured or seized ships, or which have been left by the sick or wounded who died in hospital.

Art. 87. In the case of operations of war between the land and sea forces of belligerents, the provisions of the present regulations on hospital assistance do not apply except between the forces actually on board ship.

SECTION VI
ON THE RIGHTS AND DUTIES OF THE BELLIGERENT IN OCCUPIED TERRITORY

Art. 88. Occupation: extent and effects. Occupation of maritime territory, that is of gulfs, bays, roadsteads, ports, and territorial waters, exists only when there is at the same time an occupation of continental territory, by either a naval or a military force. The occupation, in that case, is subject to the laws and usages of war on land.

SECTION VII
ON CONVENTIONS BETWEEN BELLIGERENTS

Art. 89. General rules. The commander of any belligerent naval force may conclude agreements of a purely military character concerning the forces under his command.

He may not, without authority from his government, conclude any agreement of a political character, such as a general armistice.

Art. 90. All agreements between belligerents must take into account the rules of military honour, and, once settled, must be scrupulously observed by the two parties.

Art. 91. Capitulation. After having concluded a capitulation the commander may neither damage nor destroy the ships, objects, or supplies in his possession, but must surrender them unless the right of so doing has been expressly reserved to him in the terms of the capitulation.

Art. 92. Armistice. An armistice suspends military operations.

Blockades established at the time of the armistice are not raised, unless by a special stipulation of the agreement.

The exercise of the right of visit continues to be permitted. The right of capture ceases except in cases where it exists with regard to neutral vessels.

Art. 93. An armistice may be general or partial. The first suspends the military operations of the belligerent States everywhere; the second, only between certain portions of the belligerent forces and within a fixed radius.

Art. 94. The agreement which proclaims an armistice must indicate precisely the moment it is to begin and the moment it is to end.

An armistice must be notified officially and in good time to the competent authorities as well as to the forces engaged.

Art. 95. Hostilities are suspended at the date fixed by the agreement, or, if no date has been set, immediately after the notification.

If the duration of the armistice has not been defined, the belligerent parties may resume operations at any time, provided always that the enemy is warned in good time.

Art. 96. The terms of a naval armistice shall settle, in cases where they permit the approach of enemy war-ships to certain points of the enemy's coast, the conditions of this approach and the communications of these ships either with the local authorities, or with the inhabitants.

Art. 97. Any serious violation of the armistice by one of the parties gives the other party the right of denouncing it, and even, in cases of urgency, of recommencing hostilities immediately.

Art. 98. A violation of the terms of the armistice by isolated individuals, acting on their own initiative, entitles the injured party only to demand the punishment of the offenders or, if necessary, compensation for the losses sustained.

Art. 99. Suspension of arms. A suspension of arms must, like an armistice, determine precisely the moment when hostilities are to be suspended and the moment when it ceases to be effective.

If no time is set for resuming hostilities, the belligerent who intends to continue the struggle must warn the enemy of his intention in good time.

The rupture of a suspension of arms by one of the belligerents or by isolated individuals entails the consequences stated in Articles 97 and 98.

SECTION VIII
ON THE FORMALITIES OF SEIZURE AND ON PRIZE PROCEDURE

Art. 100. Formalities of seizure. When, after the search has been conducted, the vessel is considered subject to capture, the officer who seizes the ship must:

(1) Seal all the ship's papers after having inventoried them;

(2) Draw up a report of the seizure, as well as a short inventory of the vessel stating its condition;

(3) State the condition of the cargo which he has inventoried, then close the hatchways of the hold, the chests and the store-room and, as far as circumstances will permit, seal them;

(4) Draw up a list of the persons found on board;

(5) Put on board the seized vessel a crew sufficient to retain possession of it, maintain order upon it, and conduct it to such port as he may see fit.

If he thinks fit, the captain may, instead of sending a crew aboard a vessel, confine himself to escorting it.

Art. 101. Except for persons who may be considered prisoners of war or who are liable to Punishment, a belligerent may not detain on a seized ship for more than a reasonable time, those necessary as witnesses in ascertaining the facts; but for insurmountable obstacles he must set them at liberty after the 'procès-verbal' of their depositions has been drawn up.

If special circumstances require it, the captain, the officers, and a part of the crew of the captured ship may be taken on board the captor.

The captor shall attend to the maintenance of the persons detained, and shall always give them, as well as the crew, when they are set at liberty, means temporarily necessary for their further maintenance.

Art. 102. The seized ship must be taken to the nearest possible port belonging either to the captor State or to an allied belligerent Power, which offers safe refuge, and has means of easy communication with the prize court charged with deciding upon the capture.

During the voyage, the prize shall sail under the flag and the pendant carried by the war-ships of the State.

Art. 103. The seized ship and its cargo shall, as far as possible, be kept intact during the voyage to port.

If the cargo includes articles liable to deteriorate easily, the captor, so far as possible with the consent of the captain of the seized ship and in his presence, shall take the best measures toward the preservation of these articles.

Art. 104. Destruction of vessels and goods liable to confiscation. Belligerents are not permitted to destroy seized enemy ships, except in so far as they are subject to confiscation and because of exceptional necessity, that is, when the safety of the captor ship or the success of the war operations in which it is at that time engaged, demands it. Before the vessel is destroyed all persons on board must be placed in safety, and all the ship's papers and other documents which the parties interested consider relevant for the purpose of deciding on the validity of the capture must be taken on board the war-ship. The same rule shall hold, as far as possible, for the goods.

A 'procès-verbal' of the destruction of the captured ship and of the reasons which led to it must be drawn up.

Art. 105. The captor has the right to demand the handing over, or to proceed himself to the destruction of, any goods liable to condemnation found on board a vessel not herself liable to condemnation, provided that the circumstances are such as would, under the preceding article, justify the destruction of a vessel herself liable to condemnation. The captor must enter the goods surrendered or destroyed in the log-book of the vessel stopped, and must obtain duly certified copies of all relevant papers. When the goods have been handed over or destroyed, and the formalities duly carried out, the master must be allowed to continue his voyage.

Art. 106. Use of captured ships. If the captured ship or its cargo is necessary to the captor for immediate public use, he may use them thus. In this case, impartial persons shall make a careful estimate and inventory of the ship and its cargo, and this estimate shall be sent, together with the account of the capture, to the prize court.

Art. 107. Loss of prizes through the perils of the sea. If a prize is lost by the perils of the sea, the fact must be carefully ascertained. In that case no indemnity is due, either for the ship or for the cargo, provided that if the prize be subsequently annulled the captor is able to prove that the loss would have occurred even without capture.

Art. 108. Recapture. When a ship has been taken and retaken and is then captured from the recaptor, the last captor only has the right to it.

Art. 109. Prize procedure. The captured vessel and its cargo, once in the port of the captor or of an allied State, shall be turned over, with all necessary documents, to the competent authority.

Art. 110. The legality and the regularity of the capture of enemy vessels and of the seizure of goods must be established before a prize court.

Art. 111. All recaptures must likewise be judged by a prize court.

Art. 112. A belligerent State shall not obtain possession of the ship or goods that it has seized during the war until such time as, by final decree, the prize court shall have adjudged the confiscation of the said ship or said goods in its favour.

Art. 113. If the seizure of the ship or of the goods is not upheld by the prize court, or if the prize is released without any judgment being given, the parties interested have the right to compensation, unless there were good reasons for capturing the vessel or the goods.

Art. 114. In case of the destruction of a vessel, the captor shall be required to compensate the parties interested, unless he is able to justify the exceptional necessity of the destruction, or unless, the destruction having been justified, the capture is subsequently declared void.

The same rule is applicable to the case provided for in Article 105.

If goods not liable to confiscation have been destroyed, the owner of the goods has a right to an indemnity.

In the case of a captor's using the ship or the cargo after the seizure, he must, if his act is held to have been illegal, pay the interested parties an equitable indemnity, according to the documents drawn up at the time the vessel or goods were used.

Art. 115. Unlike non-military public ships and enemy private ships, belligerent warships taken by the adversary, as well as their ' matériel, ' become the property of the latter as soon as they fall into his possession, without the decision of a prize court being necessary.

SECTION IX
ON THE END OF HOSTILITIES

Art. 116. Peace. Acts of hostility must cease upon the signing of the treaty of peace.

Notice of the end of the war shall be communicated by each government to the commander of its naval forces with as little delay as possible.

When hostile acts have been committed after the signing of the treaty of peace, the former status must, as far as possible, be restored.

When they have been committed after the official notification of the treaty of peace, they entail the payment of an indemnity and the punishment of the guilty.

ADDITIONAL ARTICLE

In conformity with Article 3 of the Hague Convention of 18 October 1907, concerning the laws and customs of war on land, the belligerent party which violates the provisions of the present regulations shall, if the case demands, be obliged to pay compensation; it shall be responsible for all acts committed by persons forming part of its armed naval forces.

I-38. San Remo Manual on International Law Applicable to Armed Conflicts at Sea, 12 June 1994, *San Remo Manual on International Law Applicable to Armed Conflicts at Sea,* Cambridge, Cambridge University Press, 1-44 (1995). Authentic text: English

Relevant Penal Characteristics & Penal Provisions

2. Implicit recognition of the penal nature of the act by establishing a duty to prohibit, prevent, prosecute, punish, or the like: Article 16 (c); Article 17; Article 18; Article 42 (a),(b); Article 44; Article 45; Article 78; Article 79; Article 80; Article 81; Article 83; Article 84; Article 85; Article 86; Article 87; Article 88; Article 89; Article 90; Article 91

Applicability
War

Control
Regulation & Prohibition

Full Text
PART I : GENERAL PROVISIONS
SECTION I : SCOPE OF APPLICATION OF THE LAW

1. The parties to an armed conflict at sea are bound by the principles and rules of international humanitarian law from the moment armed force is used.

2. In cases not covered by this document or by international agreements, civilians and combatants remain under the protection and authority of the principles of international law derived from established custom, from the principles of humanity and from the dictates of the public conscience.

SECTION II : ARMED CONFLICTS AND THE LAW OF SELF-DEFENCE

3. The exercise of the right of individual or collective self-defence recognized in Article 51 of the Charter of the United Nations is subject to the conditions and limitations laid down in the Charter, and arising from general international law, including in particular the principles of necessity and proportionality.

4. The principles of necessity and proportionality apply equally to armed conflict at sea and require that the conduct of hostilities by a State should not exceed the degree and kind of force, not otherwise prohibited by the law of armed conflict, required to repel an armed attack against it and to restore its security.

5. How far a State is justified in its military actions against the enemy will depend upon the intensity and scale of the armed attack for which the

enemy is responsible and the gravity of the threat posed.

6. The rules set out in this document and any other rules of international humanitarian law shall apply equally to all parties to the conflict. The equal application of these rules to all parties to the conflict shall not be affected by the international responsibility that may have been incurred by any of them for the outbreak of the conflict.

SECTION III : ARMED CONFLICTS IN WHICH THE SECURITY COUNCIL HAS TAKEN ACTION

7. Notwithstanding any rule in this document or elsewhere on the law of neutrality, where the Security Council, acting in accordance with its powers under Chapter VII of the Charter of the United Nations, has identified one or more of the parties to an armed conflict as responsible for resorting to force in violation of international law, neutral States:

(a) are bound not to lend assistance other than humanitarian assistance to that State; and

(b) may lend assistance to any State which has been the victim of a breach of the peace or an act of aggression by that State.

8. Where, in the course of an international armed conflict, the Security Council has taken preventive or enforcement action involving the application of economic measures under Chapter VII of the Charter, Member States of the United Nations may not rely upon the law of neutrality to justify conduct which would be incompatible with their obligations under the Charter or under decisions of the Security Council.

9. Subject to paragraph 7, where the Security Council has taken a decision to use force, or to authorize the use of force by a particular State or States, the rules set out in this document and any other rules of international humanitarian law applicable to armed conflicts at sea shall apply to all parties to any such conflict which may ensue.

SECTION IV : AREAS OF NAVAL WARFARE

10. Subject to other applicable rules of the law of armed conflict at sea contained in this document or elsewhere, hostile actions by naval forces may be conducted in, on or over:

(a) the territorial sea and internal waters, the land territories, the exclusive economic zone and continental shelf and, where applicable, the archipelagic waters, of belligerent States;
(b) the high seas; and

(c) subject to paragraphs 34 and 35, the exclusive economic zone and the continental shelf of neutral States.

11. The parties to the conflict are encouraged to agree that no hostile actions will be conducted in marine areas containing:
(a) rare or fragile ecosystems; or
(b) the habitat of depleted, threatened or endangered species or other forms of marine life.

12. In carrying out operations in areas where neutral States enjoy sovereign rights, jurisdiction, or other rights under general international law, belligerents shall have due regard for the legitimate rights and duties of those neutral States.

SECTION V : DEFINITIONS

13. For the purposes of this document:

(a) international humanitarian law means international rules, established by treaties or custom, which limit the right of parties to a conflict to use the methods or means of warfare of their choice, or which protect States not party to the conflict or persons and objects that are, or may be, affected by the conflict;
(b) attack means an act of violence, whether in offence or in defence;
(c) collateral casualties or collateral damage means the loss of life of, or injury to, civilians or other protected persons, and damage to or the destruction of the natural environment or objects that are not in themselves military objectives;
(d) neutral means any State not party to the conflict;
(e) hospital ships, coastal rescue craft and other medical transports means vessels that are protected under the Second Geneva Convention of 1949 and Additional Protocol I of 1977;
(f) medical aircraft means an aircraft that is protected under the Geneva Conventions of 1949 and Additional Protocol I of 1977;
(g) warship means a ship belonging to the armed forces of a State bearing the external marks distinguishing the character and nationality of such a ship, under the command of an officer duly commissioned by the government of that State and whose name appears in the appropriate service list or its equivalent, and manned by a crew which is under regular armed forces discipline;
(h) auxiliary vessel means a vessel, other than a warship, that is owned by or under the exclusive control of the armed forces of a State and used for the time being on government non-commercial service;
(i) merchant vessel means a vessel, other than a warship, an auxiliary vessel, or a State vessel such as a customs or police vessel, that is engaged in commercial or private service;

(j) military aircraft means an aircraft operated by commissioned units of the armed forces of a State having the military marks of that State, commanded by a member of the armed forces and manned by a crew subject to regular armed forces discipline;

(k) auxiliary aircraft means an aircraft, other than a military aircraft, that is owned by or under the exclusive control of the armed forces of a State and used for the time being on government non-commercial service;

(l) civil aircraft means an aircraft other than a military, auxiliary, or State aircraft such as a customs or police aircraft, that is engaged in commercial or private service;

(m) civil airliner means a civil aircraft that is clearly marked and engaged in carrying civilian passengers in scheduled or non-scheduled services along Air Traffic Service routes.

PART II : REGIONS OF OPERATIONS
SECTION I: INTERNAL WATERS, TERRITORIAL SEA AND ACHIPELAGIC WATERS

14. Neutral waters consist of the internal waters, territorial sea, and, where applicable, the archipelagic waters, of neutral States. Neutral airspace consists of the airspace over neutral waters and the land territory of neutral States.

15. Within and over neutral waters, including neutral waters comprising an international strait and waters in which the right of archipelagic sea lanes passage may be exercised, hostile actions by belligerent forces are forbidden. A neutral State must take such measures as are consistent with Section II of this Part, including the exercise of surveillance, as the means at its disposal allow, to prevent the violation of its neutrality by belligerent forces.

16. Hostile actions within the meaning of paragraph 15 include, inter alia:

(a) attack on or capture of persons or objects located in, on or over neutral waters or territory;
(b) use as a base of operations, including attack on or capture of persons or objects located outside neutral waters, if the attack or seizure is conducted by belligerent forces located in, on or over neutral waters;
(c) laying of mines; or
(d) visit, search, diversion or capture.

17. Belligerent forces may not use neutral waters as a sanctuary.

18. Belligerent military and auxiliary aircraft may not enter neutral airspace. Should they do so, the neutral State shall use the means at its

disposal to require the aircraft to land within its territory and shall intern the aircraft and its crew for the duration of the armed conflict. Should the aircraft fail to follow the instructions to land, it may be attacked, subject to the special rules relating to medical aircraft as specified in paragraphs 181-183.

19. Subject to paragraphs 29 and 33, a neutral State may, on a non-discriminatory basis, condition, restrict or prohibit the entrance to or passage through its neutral waters by belligerent warships and auxiliary vessels.

20. Subject to the duty of impartiality, and to paragraphs 21 and 23-33, and under such regulations as it may establish, a neutral State may, without jeopardizing its neutrality, permit the following acts within its neutral waters:

(a) passage through its territorial sea, and where applicable its archipelagic waters, by warships, auxiliary vessels and prizes of belligerent States; warships, auxiliary vessels and prizes may employ pilots of the neutral State during passage;
(b) replenishment by a belligerent warship or auxiliary vessel of its food, water and fuel sufficient to reach a port in its own territory; and
(c) repairs of belligerent warships or auxiliary vessels found necessary by the neutral State to make them seaworthy; such repairs may not restore or increase their fighting strength.

21. A belligerent warship or auxiliary vessel may not extend the duration of its passage through neutral waters, or its presence in those waters for replenishment or repair, for longer than 24 hours unless unavoidable on account of damage or the stress of weather. The foregoing rule does not apply in international straits and waters in which the right of archipelagic sea lanes passage is exercised.

22. Should a belligerent State be in violation of the regime of neutral waters, as set out in this document, the neutral State is under an obligation to take the measures necessary to terminate the violation. If the neutral State fails to terminate the violation of its neutral waters by a belligerent, the opposing belligerent must so notify the neutral State and give that neutral State a reasonable time to terminate the violation by the belligerent. If the violation of the neutrality of the State by the belligerent constitutes a serious and immediate threat to the security of the opposing belligerent and the violation is not terminated, then that belligerent
may, in the absence of any feasible and timely alternative, use such force as is strictly necessary to respond to the threat posed by the violation.

SECTION II : INTERNATIONAL STRAITS AND ARCHIPELAGIC SEA LANES

General rules

23. Belligerent warships and auxiliary vessels and military and auxiliary aircraft may exercise the rights of passage through, under or over neutral international straits and of archipelagic sea lanes passage provided by general international law.

24. The neutrality of a State bordering an international strait is not jeopardized by the transit passage of belligerent warships, auxiliary vessels, or military or auxiliary aircraft, nor by the innocent passage of belligerent warships or auxiliary vessels through that strait.

25. The neutrality of an archipelagic State is not jeopardized by the exercise of archipelagic sea lanes passage by belligerent warships, auxiliary vessels, or military or auxiliary aircraft.

26. Neutral warships, auxiliary vessels, and military and auxiliary aircraft may exercise the rights of passage provided by general international law through, under and over belligerent international straits and archipelagic waters. The neutral State should, as a precautionary measure, give timely notice of its exercise of the rights of passage to the belligerent State.

Transit passage and archipelagic sea lanes passage

27. The rights of transit passage and archipelagic sea lanes passage applicable to international straits and archipelagic waters in peacetime continue to apply in times of armed conflict. The laws and regulations of States bordering straits and archipelagic States relating to transit passage and archipelagic sea lanes passage adopted in accordance with general international law remain applicable.

28. Belligerent and neutral surface ships, submarines and aircraft have the rights of transit passage and archipelagic sea lanes passage through, under, and over all straits and archipelagic waters to which these rights generally apply.

29. Neutral States may not suspend, hamper, or otherwise impede the right of transit passage nor the right of archipelagic sea lanes passage.

30. A belligerent in transit passage through, under and over a neutral international strait, or in archipelagic sea lanes passage through, under and over neutral archipelagic waters, is required to proceed without delay, to refrain from the threat or use of force against the territorial integrity or political independence of the neutral littoral or archipelagic State, or in any

other manner inconsistent with the purposes of the Charter of the United Nations, and otherwise to refrain from any hostile actions or other activities not incident to their transit.

Belligerents passing through, under and over neutral straits or waters in which the right of archipelagic sea lanes passage applies are permitted to take defensive measures consistent with their security, including launching and recovery of aircraft, screen formation steaming, and acoustic and electronic surveillance. Belligerents in transit or archipelagic sea lanes passage may not, however, conduct offensive operations against enemy forces, nor use such neutral waters as a place of sanctuary nor as a base of operations.

Innocent passage

31. In addition to the exercise of the rights of transit and archipelagic sea lanes passage, belligerent warships and auxiliary vessels may, subject to paragraphs 19 and 21, exercise the right of innocent passage through neutral international straits and archipelagic waters in accordance with general international law.

32. Neutral vessels may likewise exercise the right of innocent passage through belligerent international straits and archipelagic waters.

33. The right of non-suspendable innocent passage ascribed to certain international straits by international law may not be suspended in time of armed conflict.

SECTION III : EXCLUSIVE ECONOMIC ZONE AND CONTINENTAL SHELF

34. If hostile actions are conducted within the exclusive economic zone or on the continental shelf of a neutral State, belligerent States shall, in addition to observing the other applicable rules of the law of armed conflict at sea, have due regard for the rights and duties of the coastal State, inter alia, for the exploration and exploitation of the economic resources of the exclusive economic zone and the continental shelf and the protection and preservation of the marine environment. They shall, in particular, have due regard for artificial islands, installations, structures and safety zones established by neutral States in the exclusive economic zone and on the continental shelf.

35. If a belligerent considers it necessary to lay mines in the exclusive economic zone or the continental shelf of a neutral State, the belligerent shall notify that State, and shall ensure, inter alia, that the size of the minefield and the type of mines used do not endanger artificial islands, installations and structures, nor interfere with access thereto, and shall avoid so far as practicable interference with the exploration or exploitation of the zone by the

neutral State. Due regard shall also be given to the protection and preservation of the marine environment.

SECTION IV : HIGH SEAS AND SEA-BED BEYOND NATIONAL JURISDICTION

36. Hostile actions on the high seas shall be conducted with due regard for the exercise by neutral States of rights of exploration and exploitation of the natural resources of the sea-bed, and ocean floor, and the subsoil thereof, beyond national jurisdiction.

37. Belligerents shall take care to avoid damage to cables and pipelines laid on the sea-bed which do not exclusively serve the belligerents.

PART III : BASIC RULES AND TARGET DISCRIMINATION

SECTION I : BASIC RULES

38. In any armed conflict the right of the parties to the conflict to choose methods or means of warfare is not unlimited.

39. Parties to the conflict shall at all times distinguish between civilians or other protected persons and combatants and between civilian or exempt objects and military objectives.

40. In so far as objects are concerned, military objectives are limited to those objects which by their nature, location, purpose or use make an effective contribution to military action and whose total or partial destruction, capture or neutralization, in the circumstances ruling at the time, offers a definite military advantage.

41. Attacks shall be limited strictly to military objectives. Merchant vessels and civil aircraft are civilian objects unless they are military objectives in accordance with the principles and rules set forth in this document.

42. In addition to any specific prohibitions binding upon the parties to a conflict, it is forbidden to employ methods or means of warfare which:

(a) are of a nature to cause superfluous injury or unnecessary suffering; or
(b) are indiscriminate, in that:
(i) they are not, or cannot be, directed against a specific military objective; or
(ii) their effects cannot be limited as required by international law as reflected in this document.

43. It is prohibited to order that there shall be no survivors, to threaten an adversary therewith or to conduct hostilities on this basis.

44. Methods and means of warfare should be employed with due regard for the natural environment taking into account the relevant rules of international law. Damage to or destruction of the natural environment not justified by military necessity and carried out wantonly is prohibited.

45. Surface ships, submarines and aircraft are bound by the same principles and rules.

SECTION II : PRECAUTIONS IN ATTACK

46. With respect to attacks, the following precautions shall be taken:

(a) those who plan, decide upon or execute an attack must take all feasible measures to gather information which will assist in determining whether or not objects which are not military objectives are present in an area of attack;
(b) in the light of the information available to them, those who plan, decide upon or execute an attack shall do everything feasible to ensure that attacks are limited to military objectives;
(c) they shall furthermore take all feasible precautions in the choice of methods and means in order to avoid or minimize collateral casualties or damage; and
(d) an attack shall not be launched if it may be expected to cause collateral casualties or damage which world be excessive in relation to the concrete and direct military advantage anticipated from the attack as a whole; an attack shall be cancelled or suspended as soon as it becomes apparent that the collateral casualties or damage would be excessive.

Section VI of this Part provides additional precautions regarding civil aircraft.

SECTION III : ENEMY VESSELS AND AIRCRAFT EXEMPT FROM ATTACK

Classes of vessels exempt from attack

47. The following classes of enemy vessels are exempt from attack:

(a) hospital ships;
(b) small craft used for coastal rescue operations and other medical transports;
(c) vessels granted safe conduct by agreement between the belligerent parties including:
(i) cartel vessels, e.g., vessels designated for and engaged in the transport of prisoners of war;
(ii) vessels engaged in humanitarian missions, including vessels carrying supplies indispensable to the survival of the civilian population, and vessels engaged in relief actions and rescue operations;

(d) vessels engaged in transporting cultural property under special protection;
(e) passenger vessels when engaged only in carrying civilian passengers;
(f) vessels charged with religious, non-military scientifc or philanthropic missions, vessels collecting scientific data of likely military applications are not protected;
(g) small coastal fishing vessels and small boats engaged in local coastal trade, but they are subject to the regulations of a belligerent naval commander operating in the area and to inspection;
(h) vessels designated or adapted exclusively for responding to pollution incidents in the marine environment;
(i) vessels which have surrendered;
(j) life rafts and life boats.

Conditions of exemption

48. Vessels listed in paragraph 47 are exempt from attack only if they:

(a) are innocently employed in their normal role;
(b) submit to identification and inspection when required; and

(c) do not intentionally hamper the movement of combatants and obey orders to stop or move out of the way when required.

Loss of exemption

Hospital ships
49. The exemption from attack of a hospital ship may cease only by reason of a breach of a condition of exemption in paragraph 48 and, in such a case, only after due warning has been given naming in all appropriate cases a reasonable time limit to discharge itself of the cause endangering its exemption, and after such warning has remained unheeded.

50. If after due warning a hospital ship persists in breaking a condition of its exemption, it renders itself liable to capture or other necessary measures to enforce compliance.

51. A hospital ship may only be attacked as a last resort if:

(a) diversion or capture is not feasible;
(b) no other method is available for exercising military control;
(c) the circumstances of non-compliance are sufficiently grave that the hospital ship has become, or may be reasonably assumed to be, a military objective; and
(d) the collateral casualties or damage will not be disproportionate to the military advantage gained or expected.

International Humanitarian Law and Arms Control Agreements 331

All other categories of vessels exempt from attack

52. If any other class of vessel exempt from attack breaches any of the conditions of its exemption in paragraph 48, it may be attacked only if:

(a) diversion or capture is not feasible;
(b) no other method is available for exercising military control;
(c) the circumstances of non-compliance are sufficiently grave that the vessel has become, or may be reasonably assumed to be, a military objective; and
(d) the collateral casualties or damage will not be disproportionate to the military advantage gained or expected.

Classes of aircraft exempt from attack

53. The following classes of enemy aircraft are exempt from attack:

(a) medical aircraft;
(b) aircraft granted safe conduct by agreement between the parties to the conflicts; and
(c) civil airliners.

Conditions of exemption for medical aircraft

54. Medical aircraft are exempt from attack only if they:

(a) have been recognized as such;
(b) are acting in compliance with an agreement as specified in paragraph 177;
(c) fly in areas under the control of own or friendly forces; or
(d) fly outside the area of armed conflict.

In other instances, medical aircraft operate at their own risk.

Conditions of exemption for aircraft granted safe conduct

55. Aircraft granted safe conduct are exempt from attack only if they:

(a) are innocently employed in their agreed role;
(b) do not intentionally hamper the movements of combatants; and
(c) comply with the details of the agreement, including availability for inspection.

Conditions of exemption for civil airliners

56. Civil airliners are exempt from attack only if they:

(a) are innocently employed in their normal role; and

(b) do not intentionally hamper the movements of combatants.

Loss of exemption

57. If aircraft exempt from attack breach any of the applicable conditions of their exemption as set forth in paragraphs 54-56, they may be attacked only if:

(a) diversion for landing, visit and search, and possible capture, is not feasible;
(b) no other method is available for exercising military control;

(c) the circumstances of non-compliance are sufficiently grave that the aircraft has become, or may be reasonably assumed to be, a military objective; and
(d) the collateral casualties or damage will not be disproportionate to the military advantage gained or anticipated.

58. In case of doubt whether a vessel or aircraft exempt from attack is being used to make an effective contribution to military action, it shall be presumed not to be so used.

SECTION IV : OTHER ENEMY VESSELS AND AIRCRAFT

Enemy merchant vessels

59. Enemy merchant vessels may only be attacked if they meet the definition of a military objective in paragraph 40.

60. The following activities may render enemy merchant vessels military objectives:

(a) engaging in belligerent acts on behalf of the enemy, e.g., laying mines, minesweeping, cutting undersea cables and pipelines, engaging in visit and search of neutral merchant vessels or attacking other merchant vessels;
(b) acting as an auxiliary to an enemy's armed forces, e.g., carrying troops or replenishing warships;
(c) being incorporated into or assisting the enemy s intelligence gathering system, e.g., engaging in reconnaissance, early warning, surveillance, or command, control and communications missions;
(d) sailing under convoy of enemy warships or military aircraft;
(e) refusing an order to stop or actively resisting visit, search or capture;
(f) being armed to an extent that they could inflict damage to a warship; this excludes light individual weapons for the defence of personnel, e.g., against pirates, and purely deflective systems such as chaff ; or
(g) otherwise making an effective contribution to military action, e.g., carrying military materials.

61.   Any attacks on these vessels is subject to the basic rules set out in paragraphs 38-46.

Enemy civil aircraft

62.   Enemy civil aircraft may only be attacked if they meet the definition of a military objective in paragraph 40.

63.   The following activities may render enemy civil aircraft military objectives:
(a) engaging in acts of war on behalf of the enemy, e.g., laying mines, minesweeping, laying or monitoring acoustic sensors, engaging in electronic warfare, intercepting or attacking other civil aircraft, or providing targeting information to enemy forces;
(b) acting as an auxiliary aircraft to an enemy's armed forces, e.g., transporting troops or military cargo, or refuelling military aircraft;
(c) being incorporated into or assisting the enemy's intelligence-gathering system, e.g., engaging in reconnaissance, early warning, surveillance, or command, control and communications missions;
(d) flying under the protection of accompanying enemy warships or military aircraft;
(e) refusing an order to identify itself, divert from its track, or proceed for visit and search to a belligerent airfield that is safe for the type of aircraft involved and reasonably accessible, or operating fire control equipment that could reasonably be construed to be part of an aircraft weapon system, or on being intercepted clearly manoeuvring to attack the intercepting belligerent military aircraft;
(f) being armed with air-to-air or air-to-surface weapons; or
(g) otherwise making an effective contribution to military action.

64.   Any attack on these aircraft is subject to the basic rules set out in paragraphs 38-46.

Enemy warships and military aircraft

65.   Unless they are exempt from attack under paragraphs 47 or 53, enemy warships and military aircraft and enemy auxiliary vessels and aircraft are military objectives within the meaning of paragraph 40.

66.   They may be attacked, subject to the basic rules in paragraphs 38-46.

SECTION V : NEUTRAL MERCHANT VESSELS AND CIVIL AIRCRAFT

Neutral merchant vessels

67. Merchant vessels flying the flag of neutral States may not be attacked unless they:

(a) are believed on reasonable grounds to be carrying contraband or breaching a blockade, and after prior warning they intentionally and clearly refuse to stop, or intentionally and clearly resist visit, search or capture;
(b) engage in belligerent acts on behalf of the enemy;
(c) act as auxiliaries to the enemy's armed forces;
(d) are incorporated into or assist the enemy s intelligence system;
(e) sail under convoy of enemy warships or military aircraft; or
(f) otherwise make an effective contribution to the enemy s military action, e.g., by carrying military materials, and it is not feasible for the attacking forces to first place passengers and crew in a place of safety. Unless circumstances do not permit, they are to be given a warning, so that they can re-route, off-load, or take other precautions.

68. Any attack on these vessels is subject to the basic rules in paragraphs 38-46.

69. The mere fact that a neutral merchant vessel is armed provides no grounds for attacking it.

Neutral civil aircraft

70. Civil aircraft bearing the marks of neutral States may not be attacked unless they:

(a) are believed on reasonable grounds to be carrying contraband, and, after prior warning or interception, they intentionally and clearly refuse to divert from their destination, or intentionally and clearly refuse to proceed for visit and search to a belligerent airfield that is safe for the type of aircraft involved and reasonably accessible;
(b) engage in belligerent acts on behalf of the enemy;
(c) act as auxiliaries to the enemy's armed forces;
(d) are incorporated into or assist the enemy's intelligence system; or
(e) otherwise make an effective contribution to the enemy's military action, e.g., by carrying military materials, and, after prior warning or interception, they intentionally and clearly refuse to divert from their destination, or intentionally and clearly refuse to proceed for visit and search to a belligerent airfield that is safe for the type of aircraft involved and reasonably accessible.

71. Any attack on these aircraft is subject to the basic rules in paragraphs 38-46.

SECTION VI : PRECAUTIONS REGARDING CIVIL AIRCRAFT

72. Civil aircraft should avoid areas of potentially hazardous military

International Humanitarian Law and Arms Control Agreements 335

activity.

73. In the immediate vicinity of naval operations, civil aircraft shall comply with instructions from the belligerents regarding their heading and altitude.

74. Belligerent and neutral States concerned, and authorities providing air traffic services, should establish procedures whereby commanders of warships and military aircraft are aware on a continuous basis of designated routes assigned to or flight plans filed by civil aircraft in the area of military operations, including information on communication channels, identification modes and codes, destination, passengers and cargo.

75. Belligerent and neutral States should ensure that a Notice to Airmen (NOTAM) is issued providing information on military activities in areas potentially hazardous to civil aircraft, including activation of danger areas or temporary airspace restrictions. This NOTAM should include information on:

(a) frequencies upon which the aircraft should maintain a continuous listening watch;
(b) continuous operation of civil weather-avoidance radar and identification modes and codes;
(c) altitude, course and speed restrictions;
(d) procedures to respond to radio contact by the military forces and to establish two-way communications; and
(e) possible action by the military forces if the NOTAM is not complied with and the civil aircraft is perceived by those military forces to be a threat.

76. Civil aircraft should file the required flight plan with the cognizant Air Traffic Service, complete with information as to registration, destination, passengers, cargo, emergency communication channels, identification modes and codes, updates en route and carry certificates as to registration, airworthiness, passengers and cargo. They should not deviate from a designated Air Traffic Service route or flight plan without Air Traffic Control clearance unless unforeseen conditions arise, e.g., safety or distress, in which case appropriate notification should be made immediately.

77. If a civil aircraft enters an area of potentially hazardous military activity, it should comply with relevant NOTAMs. Military forces should use all available means to identify and warn the civil aircraft, by using, inter alia, secondary surveillance radar modes and codes, communications, correlation with flight plan information, interception by military aircraft, and, when possible, contacting the appropriate Air Traffic Control facility.

PART IV : METHODS AND MEANS OF WARFARE AT SEA

SECTION I : MEANS OF WARFARE

Missiles and other projectiles

78. Missiles and projectiles, including those with over-the-horizon capabilities, shall be used in conformity with the principles of target discrimination as set out in paragraphs 38-46.

Torpedoes

79. It is prohibited to use torpedoes which do not sink or otherwise become harmless when they have completed their run.

Mines

80. Mines may only be used for legitimate military purposes including the denial of sea areas to the enemy.

81. Without prejudice to the rules set out in paragraph 82, the parties to the conflict shall not lay mines unless effective neutralization occurs when they have become detached or control over them is otherwise lost.

82. It is forbidden to use free-floating mines unless:

(a) they are directed against a military objective; and
(b) they become harmless within an hour after loss of control over them.

83. The laying of armed mines or the arming of pre-laid mines must be notified unless the mines can only detonate against vessels which are military objectives.

84. Belligerents shall record the locations where they have laid mines.

85. Mining operations in the internal waters, territorial sea or archipelagic waters of a belligerent State should provide, when the mining is first executed, for free exit of shipping of neutral States.

86. Mining of neutral waters by a belligerent is prohibited.

87. Mining shall not have the practical effect of preventing passage between neutral waters and international waters.

88. The minelaying States shall pay due regard to the legitimate uses of the high seas by, inter alia, providing safe alternative routes for shipping of

neutral States.

89. Transit passage through international straits and passage through waters subject to the right of archipelagic sea lanes passage shall not be impeded unless safe and convenient alternative routes are provided.

90. After the cessation of active hostilities, parties to the conflict shall do their utmost to remove or render harmless the mines they have laid, each party removing its own mines. With regard to mines laid in the territorial seas of the enemy, each party shall notify their position and shall proceed with the least possible delay to remove the mines in its territorial sea or otherwise render the territorial sea safe for navigation.

91. In addition to their obligations under paragraph 90, parties to the conflict shall endeavour to reach agreement, both among themselves and, where appropriate, with other States and with international organizations, on the provision of information and technical and material assistance, including in appropriate circumstances joint operations, necessary to remove minefields or otherwise render them harmless.

92. Neutral States do not commit an act inconsistent with the laws of neutrality by clearing mines laid in violation of international law.

SECTION II : METHODS OF WARFARE

Blockade

93. A blockade shall be declared and notified to all belligerents and neutral States.

94. The declaration shall specify the commencement, duration, location, and extent of the blockade and the period within which vessels of neutral States may leave the blockaded coastline.

95. A blockade must be effective. The question whether a blockade is effective is a question of fact.

96. The force maintaining the blockade may be stationed at a distance determined by military requirements.

97. A blockade may be enforced and maintained by a combination of legitimate methods and means of warfare provided this combination does not result in acts inconsistent with the rules set out in this document.

98. Merchant vessels believed on reasonable grounds to be breaching a blockade may be captured. Merchant vessels which, after prior warning, clearly resist capture may be attacked.

99. A blockade must not bar access to the ports and coasts of neutral States.

100. A blockade must be applied impartially to the vessels of all States.

101. The cessation, temporary lifting, re-establishment, extension or other alteration of a blockade must be declared and notified as in paragraphs 93 and 94.

102. The declaration or establishment of a blockade is prohibited if:

(a) it has the sole purpose of starving the civilian population or denying it other objects essential for its survival; or
(b) the damage to the civilian population is, or may be expected to be, excessive in relation to the concrete and direct military advantage anticipated from the blockade.

103. If the civilian population of the blockaded territory is inadequately provided with food and other objects essential for its survival, the blockading party must provide for free passage of such foodstuffs and other essential supplies, subject to:

(a) the right to prescribe the technical arrangements, including search, under which such passage is permitted; and

(b) the condition that the distribution of such supplies shall be made under the local supervision of a Protecting Power or a humanitarian organization which offers guarantees of impartiality, such as the International Committee of the Red Cross.

104. The blockading belligerent shall allow the passage of medical supplies for the civilian population or for the wounded and sick members of armed forces, subject to the right to prescribe technical arrangements, including search, under which such passage is permitted.

Zones

105. A belligerent cannot be absolved of its duties under international humanitarian law by establishing zones which might adversely affect the legitimate uses of defined areas of the sea.

106. Should a belligerent, as an exceptional measure, establish such a zone:

(a) the same body of law applies both inside and outside the zone;
(b) the extent, location and duration of the zone and the measures imposed

shall not exceed what is strictly required by military necessity and the principles of proportionality;

(c) due regard shall be given to the rights of neutral States to legitimate uses of the seas;

(d) necessary safe passage through the zone for neutral vessels and aircraft shall be provided:

(i) where the geographical extent of the zone significantly impedes free and safe access to the ports and coasts of a neutral State;

(ii) in other cases where normal navigation routes are affected, except where military requirements do not permit; and

(e) the commencement, duration, location and extent of the zone, as well as the restrictions imposed, shall be publicly declared and appropriately notified.

107. Compliance with the measures taken by one belligerent in the zone shall not be construed as an act harmful to the opposing belligerent.

108. Nothing in this Section should be deemed to derogate from the customary belligerent right to control neutral vessels and aircraft in the immediate vicinity of naval operations.

SECTION III : DECEPTION, RUSES OF WAR AND PERFIDY

109. Military and auxiliary aircraft are prohibited at all times from feigning exempt, civilian or neutral status.

110. Ruses of war are permitted. Warships and auxiliary vessels, however, are prohibited from launching an attack whilst flying a false flag, and at all times from actively simulating the status of:

(a) hospital ships, small coastal rescue craft or medical transports;
(b) vessels on humanitarian missions;
(c) passenger vessels carrying civilian passengers;
(d) vessels protected by the United Nations flag;
(e) vessels guaranteed safe conduct by prior agreement between the parties, including cartel vessels;
(f) vessels entitled to be identified by the emblem of the red cross or red crescent; or
(g) vessels engaged in transporting cultural property under special protection.

111. Perfidy is prohibited. Acts inviting the confidence of an adversary to lead it to believe that it is entitled to, or is obliged to accord, protection under the rules of international law applicable in armed conflict, with intent to betray that confidence, constitute perfidy. Perfidious acts include the launching of an attack while feigning:

(a) exempt, civilian, neutral or protected United Nations status;

(b) surrender or distress by, e.g., sending a distress signal or by the crew taking to life rafts.

PART V : MEASURES SHORT OF ATTACK: INTERCEPTION, VISIT, SEARCH, DIVERSION AND CAPTURE

SECTION I : DETERMINATION OF ENEMY CHARACTER OF VESSELS AND AIRCRAFT

112. The fact that a merchant vessel is flying the flag of an enemy State or that a civil aircraft bears the marks of an enemy State is conclusive evidence of its enemy character.

113. The fact that a merchant vessel is flying the flag of a neutral State or a civil aircraft bears the marks of a neutral State is prima facie evidence of its neutral character.

114. If the commander of a warship suspects that a merchant vessel flying a neutral flag in fact has enemy character, the commander is entitled to exercise the right of visit and search, including the right of diversion for search under paragraph 121.

115. If the commander of a military aircraft suspects that a civil aircraft with neutral marks in fact has enemy character, the commander is entitled to exercise the right of interception and, if circumstances require, the right to divert for the purpose of visit and search.

116. If, after visit and search, there is reasonable ground for suspicion that the merchant vessel flying a neutral flag or a civil aircraft with neutral marks has enemy character, the vessel or aircraft may be captured as prize subject to adjudication.

117. Enemy character can be determined by registration, ownership, charter or other criteria.

SECTION II : VISIT AND SEARCH OF MERCHANT VESSELS

Basic rules

118. In exercising their legal rights in an international armed conflict at sea, belligerent warships and military aircraft have a right to visit and search merchant vessels outside neutral waters where there are reasonable grounds for suspecting that they are subject to capture.

119. As an alternative to visit and search, a neutral merchant vessel may, with its consent, be diverted from its declared destination.

Merchant vessels under convoy of accompanying neutral warships

120. A neutral merchant vessel is exempt from the exercise of the right of visit and search if it meets the following conditions:

(a) it is bound for a neutral port;
(b) it is under the convoy of an accompanying neutral warship of the same nationality or a neutral warship of a State with which the flag State of the merchant vessel has concluded an agreement providing for such convoy;
(c) the flag State of the neutral warship warrants that the neutral merchant vessel is not carrying contraband or otherwise engaged in activities inconsistent with its neutral status; and
(d) the commander of the neutral warship provides, if requested by the commander of an intercepting belligerent warship or military aircraft, all information as to the character of the merchant vessel and its cargo as could otherwise be obtained by visit and search.

Diversion for the purpose of visit and search

121. If visit and search at sea is impossible or unsafe, a belligerent warship or military aircraft may divert a merchant vessel to an appropriate area or port in order to exercise the right of visit and search.

Measures of supervision

122. In order to avoid the necessity of visit and search, belligerent States may establish reasonable measures for the inspection of cargo of neutral merchant vessels and certification that a vessel is not carrying contraband.

123. The fact that a neutral merchant vessel has submitted to such measures of supervision as the inspection of its cargo and grant of certificates of non contraband cargo by one belligerent is not an act of unneutral service with regard to an opposing belligerent.

124. In order to obviate the necessity for visit and search, neutral States are encouraged to enforce reasonable control measures and certification procedures to ensure that their merchant vessels are not carrying contraband.

SECTION III : INTERCEPTION, VISIT AND SEARCH OF CIVIL AIRCRAFT

Basic rules

125. In exercising their legal rights in an international armed conflict at sea, belligerent military aircraft have a right to intercept civil aircraft outside

neutral airspace where there are reasonable grounds for suspecting they are subject to capture. If, after interception, reasonable grounds for suspecting that a civil aircraft is subject to capture still exist, belligerent military aircraft have the right to order the civil aircraft to proceed for visit and search to a belligerent airfield that is safe for the type of aircraft involved and reasonably accessible.

If there is no belligerent airfield that is safe and reasonably accessible for visit and search, a civil aircraft may be diverted from its declared destination.

126.   As an alternative to visit and search:

(a) an enemy civil aircraft may be diverted from its declared destination;
(b) a neutral civil aircraft may be diverted from its declared destination with its consent.

Civil aircraft under the operational control of an accompanying neutral military aircraft or warship

127.   A neutral civil aircraft is exempt from the exercise of the right of visit and search if it meets the following conditions:

(a) it is bound for a neutral airfield;
(b) it is under the operational control of an accompanying:
   (i) neutral military aircraft or warship of the same nationality; or
   (ii) neutral military aircraft or warship of a State with which the flag State of the civil aircraft has concluded an agreement providing for such control;
(c) the flag State of the neutral military aircraft or warship warrants that the neutral civil aircraft is not carrying contraband or otherwise engaged in activities inconsistent with its neutral status; and
(d) the commander of the neutral military aircraft or warship provides, if requested by the commander of an intercepting belligerent military aircraft, all information as to the character of the civil aircraft and its cargo as could otherwise be obtained by visit and search.

Measures of interception and supervision

128.   Belligerent States should promulgate and adhere to safe procedures for intercepting civil aircraft as issued by the competent international organization.

129.   Civil aircraft should file the required flight plan with the cognizant Air Traffic Service, complete with information as to registration, destination, passengers, cargo, emergency communication channels, identification modes and codes, updates en route and carry certificates as to registration, airworthiness, passengers and cargo. They should not deviate from a

International Humanitarian Law and Arms Control Agreements 343

designated Air Traffic Service route or flight plan without Air Traffic Control clearance unless unforeseen conditions arise, e.g., safety or distress, in which case appropriate notification should be made immediately.

130.   Belligerents and neutrals concerned, and authorities providing air traffic services, should establish procedures whereby commanders of warships and military aircraft are continuously aware of designated routes assigned to and flight plans filed by civil aircraft in the area of military operations, including information on communication channels, identification modes and codes, destination, passengers and cargo.

131.   In the immediate vicinity of naval operations, civil aircraft shall comply with instructions from the combatants regarding their heading and altitude.

132.   In order to avoid the necessity of visit and search, belligerent States may establish reasonable measures for the inspection of the cargo of neutral civil aircraft and certification that an aircraft is not carrying contraband.

133.   The fact that a neutral civil aircraft has submitted to such measures of supervision as the inspection of its cargo and grant of certificates of non-contraband cargo by one belligerent is not an act of unneutral service with regard to an opposing belligerent.

134.   In order to obviate the necessity for visit and search, neutral States are encouraged to enforce reasonable control measures and certification procedures to ensure that their civil aircraft are not carrying contraband.

SECTION IV : CAPTURE OF ENEMY VESSELS AND GOODS

135.   Subject to the provisions of paragraph 136, enemy vessels, whether merchant or otherwise, and goods on board such vessels may be captured outside neutral waters. Prior exercise of visit and search is not required.

136.   The following vessels are exempt from capture:

(a) hospital ships and small craft used for coastal rescue operations;
(b) other medical transports, so long as they are needed for the wounded, sick and shipwrecked on board;
(c) vessels granted safe conduct by agreement between the belligerent parties including: (i) cartel vessels, e.g., vessels designated for and engaged in the transport of prisoners of war; and (ii) vessels engaged in humanitarian missions, including vessels carrying supplies indispensable to the survival of the civilian population, and vessels engaged in relief actions and rescue operations;

(d) vessels engaged in transporting cultural property under special protection;
(e) vessels charged with religious, non-military scientific or philanthropic missions; vessels collecting scientific data of likely military applications are not protected;
(f) small coastal fishing vessels and small boats engaged in local coastal trade, but they are subject to the regulations of a belligerent naval commander operating in the area and to inspectiorr, and
(g) vessels designed or adapted exclusively for responding to pollution incidents in the marine environment when actually engaged in such activities.

137. Vessels listed in paragraph 136 are exempt from capture only if they:

(a) are innocently employed in their normal role;
(b) do not commit acts harmful to the enemy;
(c) immediately submit to identification and inspection when required; and
(d) do not intentionally hamper the movement of combatants and obey orders to stop or move out of the way when required.

138. Capture of a merchant vessel is exercised by taking such vessel as prize for adjudication. If military circumstances preclude taking such a vessel as prize at sea, it may be diverted to an appropriate area or port in order to complete capture. As an alternative to capture, an enemy merchant vessel may be diverted from its declared destination.

139. Subject to paragraph 140, a captured enemy merchant vessel may, as an exceptional measure, be destroyed when military circumstances preclude taking or sending such a vessel for adjudication as an enemy prize, only if the following criteria are met beforehand:

(a) the safety of passengers and crew is provided for; for this purpose, the ship's boats are not regarded as a place of safety unless the safety of the passengers and crew is assured in the prevailing sea and weather conditions by the proximity of land or the presence of another vessel which is in a position to take them on board;
(b) documents and papers relating to the prize are safeguarded; and
(c) if feasible, personal effects of the passengers and crew are saved.

140. The destruction of enemy passenger vessels carrying only civilian passengers is prohibited at sea. For the safety of the passengers, such vessels shall be diverted to an appropriate area or port in order to complete capture.

SECTION V : CAPTURE OF ENEMY CIVIL AIRCRAFT AND GOODS

141. Subject to the provisions of paragraph 142, enemy civil aircraft and goods on board such aircraft may be captured outside neutral airspace. Prior exercise of visit and search is not required.

142. The following aircraft are exempt from capture:

(a) medical aircraft; and
(b) aircraft granted safe conduct by agreement between the parties to the conflict.

143. Aircraft listed in paragraph 142 are exempt from capture only if they:

(a) are innocently employed in their normal role;
(b) do not commit acts harmful to the enemy;
(c) immediately submit to interception and identification when required;
(d) do not intentionally hamper the movement of combatants and obey orders to divert from their track when required; and
(e) are not in breach of a prior agreement.

144. Capture is exercised by intercepting the enemy civil aircraft, ordering it to proceed to a belligerent airfield that is safe for the type of aircraft involved and reasonably accessible and, on landing, taking the aircraft as a prize for adjudication. As an alternative to capture, an enemy civil aircraft may be diverted from its declared destination.

145. If capture is exercised, the safety of passengers and crew and their personal effects must be provided for. The documents and papers relating to the prize must be safeguarded.

SECTION VI : CAPTURE OF NEUTRAL MERCHANT VESSELS AND GOODS

146. Neutral merchant vessels are subject to capture outside neutral waters if they are engaged in any of the activities referred to in paragraph 67 or if it is determined as a result of visit and search or by other means, that they:

(a) are carrying contraband;
(b) are on a voyage especially undertaken with a view to the transport of individual passengers who are embodied in the armed forces of the enemy;
(c) are operating directly under enemy control, orders, charter, employment or direction;
(d) present irregular or fraudulent documents, lack necessary documents, or destroy, deface or conceal documents;
(e) are violating regulations established by a belligerent within the immediate area of naval operations; or
(f) are breaching or attempting to breach a blockade.

Capture of a neutral merchant vessel is exercised by taking such vessel as prize for adjudication.

147. Goods on board neutral merchant vessels are subject to capture only if they are contraband.

148. Contraband is defined as goods which are ultimately destined for territory under the control of the enemy and which may be susceptible for use in armed conflict.

149. In order to exercise the right of capture referred to in paragraphs 146(a) and 147, the belligerent must have published contraband lists. The precise nature of a belligerent's contraband list may vary according to the particular circumstances of the armed conflict. Contraband lists shall be reasonably specific.

150. Goods not on the belligerent's contraband list are 'free goods', that is, not subject to capture. As a minimum, 'free goods' shall include the following:

(a) religious objects;
(b) articles intended exclusively for the treatment of the wounded and sick and for the prevention of disease;
(c) clothing, bedding, essential foodstuffs, and means of shelter for the civilian population in general, and women and children in particular, provided there is not serious reason to believe that such goods will be diverted to other purpose, or that a definite military advantage would accrue to the enemy by their substitution for enemy goods that would thereby become available for military purposes;
(d) items destined for prisoners of war, including individual parcels and collective relief shipments containing food, clothing, educational, cultural, and recreational articles;
(e) goods otherwise specifically exempted from capture by international treaty or by special arrangement between belligerents; and
(f) other goods not susceptible for use in armed conflict,

151. Subject to paragraph 152, a neutral vessel captured in accordance with paragraph 146 may, as an exceptional measure, be destroyed when military circumstances preclude taking or sending such a vessel for adjudication as an enemy prize, only if the following criteria are met beforehand:

(a) the safety of passengers and crew is provided for; for this purpose the ship's boats are not regarded as a place of safety unless the safety of the passengers and crew is assured in the prevailing sea and weather conditions, by the proximity of land, or the presence of another vessel which is in a position to take them on board;

(b) documents and papers relating to the captured vessel are safeguarded; and

(c) if feasible, personal effects of the passengers and crew are saved.

Every effort should be made to avoid destruction of a captured neutral vessel. Therefore, such destruction shall not be ordered without there being entire satisfaction that the captured vessel can neither be sent into a belligerent port, nor diverted, nor properly released. A vessel may not be destroyed under this paragraph for carrying contraband unless the contraband, reckoned either by value, weight, volume or freight, forms more than half the cargo. Destruction shall be subject to adjudication.

152. The destruction of captured neutral passenger vessels carrying civilian passengers is prohibited at sea. For the safety of the passengers, such vessels shall be diverted to an appropriate port in order to complete capture provided for in paragraph 146.

SECTION VII : CAPTURE OF NEUTRAL CIVIL AIRCRAFT AND GOODS

153. Neutral civil aircraft are subject to capture outside neutral airspace if they are engaged in any of the activities in paragraph 70 or if it is determined as a result of visit and search or by any other means, that they:

(a) are carrying contraband;
(b) are on a flight especially undertaken with a view to the transport of individual passengers who are embodied in the armed forces of the enemy;
(c) are operating directly under enemy control, orders, charter, employment or direction;
(d) present irregular or fraudulent documents, lack necessary documents, or destroy, deface or conceal documents;
(e) are violating regulations established by a belligerent within the immediate area of naval operations; or
(f) are engaged in a breach of blockade.

154. Goods on board neutral civil aircraft are subject to capture only if they are contraband.

155. The rules regarding contraband as prescribed in paragraphs 148-150 shall also apply to goods on board neutral civil aircraft.

156. Capture is exercised by intercepting the neutral civil aircraft, ordering it to proceed to a belligerent airfield that is safe for the type of aircraft involved and reasonably accessible and, on landing and after visit and search, taking it as prize for adjudication. If there is no belligerent airfield that is safe and reasonably accessible, a neutral civil aircraft may be diverted

from its declared destination.

157. As an alternative to capture, a neutral civil aircraft may, with its consent, be diverted from its declared destination.

158. If capture is exercised, the safety of passengers and crew and their personal effects must be provided for. The documents and papers relating to the prize must be safeguarded.

PART VI : PROTECTED PERSONS, MEDICAL TRANSPORTS AND MEDICAL AIRCRAFT

GENERAL RULES

159. Except as provided for in paragraph 171, the provisions of this Part are not to be construed as in any way departing from the provisions of the Second Geneva Convention of 1949 and Additional Protocol I of 1977 which contain detailed rules for the treatment of the wounded, sick and shipwrecked and for medical transports.

160. The parties to the conflict may agree, for humanitarian purposes, to create a zone in a defined area of the sea in which only activities consistent with those humanitarian purposes are permitted.

SECTION I : PROTECTED PERSONS

161. Persons on board vessels and aircraft having fallen into the power of a belligerent or neutral shall be re spected and protected. While at sea and thereafter until determination of their status, they shall be subject to the jurisdiction of the State exercising power over them.

162. Members of the crews of hospital ships may not be captured during the time they are in the service of these vessels. Members of the crews of rescue craft may not be captured while engaging in rescue operations.

163. Persons on board other vessels or aircraft exempt from capture listed in paragraphs 136 and 142 may not be captured.

164. Religious and medical personnel assigned to the spiritual and medical care of the wounded, sick and shipwrecked shall not be considered prisoners of war. They may, however, be retained as long as their services for the medical or spiritual needs of prisoners of war are needed.

165. Nationals of an enemy State, other than those specified in paragraphs 162-164, are entitled to prisoner-of-war status and may be made prisoners of war if they are:

(a) members of the enemy's armed forces;
(b) persons accompanying the enemy's armed forces;
(c) crew members of auxiliary vessels or auxiliary aircraft;
   (d) crew members of enemy merchant vessels or civil aircraft not exempt from capture, unless they benefit from more favourable treatment under other provisions of international law; or
   (e) crew members of neutral merchant vessels or civil aircraft that have taken a direct part in the hostilities on the side of the enemy, or served as an auxiliary for the enemy.

166.   Nationals of a neutral State:

   (a) who are passengers on board enemy or neutral vessels or aircraft are to be released and may not be made prisoners of war unless they are members of the enemy's armed forces or have personally committed acts of hostility against the captor;
   (b) who are members of the crew of enemy warships or auxiliary vessels or military aircraft or auxiliary aircraft are entitled to prisoner-of-war status and may be made prisoners of war;
   (c) who are members of the crew of enemy or neutral merchant vessels or civil aircraft are to be released and may not be made prisoners of war unless the vessel or aircraft has committed an act covered by paragraphs 60, 63, 67 or 70, or the member of the crew has personally committed an act of hostility against the captor.

167.   Civilian persons other than those specified in paragraphs 162-166 are to be treated in accordance with the Fourth Geneva Convention of 1949.

168.   Persons having fallen into the power of a neutral State are to be treated in accordance with Hague Conventions V and XIII of 1907 and the Second Geneva Convention of 1949.

SECTION II : MEDICAL TRANSPORTS

169.   In order to provide maximum protection for hospital ships from the moment of the outbreak of hostilities, States may beforehand make general notification of the characteristics of their hospital ships as specified in Article 22 of the Second Geneva Convention of 1949. Such notification should include all available information on the means whereby the ship may be identified.

170.   Hospital ships may be equipped with purely deflective means of defence, such as chaff and flares. The presence of such equipment should be notified.

171.   In order to fulfil most effectively their humanitarian mission,

hospital ships should be permitted to use cryptographic equipment. The equipment shall not be used in any circumstances to transmit intelligence data nor in any other way to acquire any military advantage.

172. Hospital ships, small craft used for coastal rescue operations and other medical transports are encouraged to implement the means of identification set out in Annex I of Additional Protocol I of 1977.

173. These means of identification are intended only to facilitate identification and do not, of themselves, confer protected status.

SECTION III : MEDICAL AIRCRAFT

174. Medical aircraft shall be protected and respected as specified in the provisions of this document.

175. Medical aircraft shall be clearly marked with the emblem of the red cross or red crescent, together with their national colours, on their lower, upper and lateral surfaces. Medical aircraft are encouraged to implement the other means of identification set out in Annex I of Additional Protocol I of 1977 at all times. Aircraft chartered by the International Committee of the Red Cross may use the same means of identification as medical aircraft. Temporary medical aircraft which cannot, either for lack of time or because of their characteristics, be marked with the distinctive emblem should use the most effective means of identification available.

176. Means of identification are intended only to facilitate identification and do not, of themselves, confer protected status.

177. Parties to the conflict are encouraged to notify medical flights and conclude agreements at all times, especially in areas where control by any party to the conflict is not clearly established. When such an agreement is concluded, it shall specify the altitudes, times and routes for safe operation and should include means of identification and communications.

178. Medical aircraft shall not be used to commit acts harmful to the enemy. They shall not carry any equipment intended for the collection or transmission of intelligence data. They shall not be armed, except for small arms for self-defence, and shall only carry medical personnel and equipment.

179. Other aircraft, military or civilian, belligerent or neutral, that are employed in the search for, rescue or transport of the wounded, sick and shipwrecked, operate at their own risk, unless pursuant to prior agreement between the parties to the conflict.

180. Medical aircraft flying over areas which are physically controlled by the opposing belligerent, or over areas the physical control of which is not

International Humanitarian Law and Arms Control Agreements 351

clearly established, may be ordered to land to permit inspection. Medical aircraft shall obey any such order.

181. Belligerent medical aircraft shall not enter neutral airspace except by prior agreement. When within neutral airspace pursuant to agreement, medical aircraft shall comply with the terms of the agreement. The terms of the agreement may require the aircraft to land for inspection at a designated airport within the neutral State. Should the agreement so require, the inspection and follow-on action shall be conducted in accordance with paragraphs 182-183.

182. Should a medical aircraft, in the absence of an agreement or in deviation from the terms of an agreement, enter neutral airspace, either through navigational error or because of an emergency affecting the safety of the flight, it shall make every effort to give notice and to identify itself. Once the aircraft is recognized as a medical aircraft by the neutral State, it shall not be attacked but may be required to land for inspection. Once it has been inspected, and if it is determined in fact to be a medical aircraft, it shall be allowed to resume its flight.

183. If the inspection reveals that the aircraft is not a medical aircraft, it may be captured, and the occupants shall, unless agreed otherwise between the neutral State and the parties to the conflict, be detained in the neutral State where so required by the rules of international law applicable in armed conflict, in such a manner that they cannot again take part in the hostilities.

CHAPTER II

MULTILATERAL INSTRUMENTS ON THE REGULATION, CONTROL, AND PROHIBITION OF WEAPONS OF MASS DESTRUCTION

INTRODUCTION

Chapter II contains eight multilateral instruments on the regulation, control, and prohibition of weapons of mass destruction. They start with the 1925 Protocol for the Prohibition of the Use in War of Asphyxiating, Poisonous or Other Gases, and of Bacteriological Methods of Warfare, to the 1998 Draft Convention on Nuclear Terrorism, which was still being negotiated at the U.N. in July 2000. The capabilities of these weapons justifies the growing concern of the international community with preventing the use of these devices by state and non-State actors.

Chapter II also includes the 1996 International Court of Justice Advisory Opinion on the Legality of Threat of Use of Nuclear Weapons, which proscribes the first use of nuclear weapons. These instruments which deal with weapons of mass destruction also fall in the category of customary international law. The overall concept derives from the Preamble of the 1907 Hague Convention which codifies customary international law as it existed then. It states:

> *It has not been found possible at present to concert regulations covering all the circumstances which arise in practice. On the other hand, the High Contracting Parties clearly do not intend that unforeseen cases should, in the absence of a written undertaking, be left to the arbitrary judgment of military commanders. Until a more complete code of the laws of war has been issued, the High Contracting Parties deem it expedient to declare that, in cases not included in the Regulations adopted by them, the inhabitants and the belligerents remain under the protection and the rule of the principles of the law of nations, as they result from the usages established among civilized peoples, from the laws of humanity, and the dictates of the public conscience.*[1]
> (emphasis added).

This language embodies the well-known Martens clause[2] which permits the resort to "general principles" as a means of interpreting provisions in international instruments and to fill gaps in conventional textual language.[3]

---

[1] BASSIOUNI, CRIMES AGAINST HUMANITY, 75; 1907 Hague Convention Respecting the Laws and Customs of War on Land, Oct. 18, 1907, 36 Stat. 2277, T.S. No. 539, 3 MARTENS (ser. 3) 461, reprinted in 2 AM. J. INT'L L. 90 (Supp 1908) at ¶¶ 6-8 of the Pmbl.

[2] The Martens Clause is named after Fyodor Martens, the Russian diplomat and jurist who drafted it. A similar formula appears in each of the 1949 Geneva Conventions and in the 1977

The extension of the "general principle" contained in Preamble of the 1899 and 1907 Conventions is reflected in Article 22 of the Hague Regulations in the 1899 and 1907 Conventions which provides for another general norm that *"the right of belligerents to adopt means of injuring the enemy is not unlimited."* (emphasis added).[4]

Moreover, the 1907 Hague Convention IV with Respect to the Laws and Customs of War on Land expressly prohibited the use of "arms, projectiles, or material calculated to cause unnecessary pain and suffering." The 1907 Hague Convention applies only to states and to armed conflicts between states. The 1949 Geneva Convention extended the protection against unnecessary pain and suffering in Article 35 of Part III, Section I of Protocol I, which applies to international conflicts:

1. In any armed conflict, the right of the Parties to the conflict to choose methods or means of warfare is not unlimited.

Protocols. *See* First Geneva Convention for the Amelioration of the Condition of the Wounded and Sick in Armed Forces in the Field, 75 U.N.T.S. 31, 6 U.S.T. 3114, T.I.A.S. No. 3362 at art. 63(4); Second Geneva Convention of 1949 for the Amelioration of the Condition of Wounded, Sick, and Shipwrecked Members of the Armed Forces at Sea, 75 U.N.T.S. 85, 6 U.S.T. 3217, T.I.A.S. No. 3363 at art. 62(4); Third Geneva Convention of 1949 relative to the Treatment of Prisoners of War, 75 U.N.T.S. 135, 6 U.S.T. 3316, T.I.A.S. No. 3364 at art. 142(4); Fourth Geneva Convention of 1949 relative to the Protection of Civilian Persons in Time of War, U.N.T.S. 287, 6 U.S.T. 3516, T.I.A.S. No. 3365 at art. 158(4); Protocol Additional to Geneva Conventions of August 12, 1949, and Relating to the Protection of Victims of International Armed Conflicts, *open for signature* Dec. 12, 1977, U.N. Doc. A/32/144 Annex I, *reprinted in* 16 I.L.M. 1391 (1977), 72 AM. J. INT'L L. 457 (1977) at art. 1(2) [hereinafter Protocol I]; Protocol Additional to Geneva Convention of Aug. 12, 1949, and Relating to the Protection of Vistims of Non-International Armed Conflicts, *opened for signature*, Dec. 12, 1977, U.N. Doc. A/32/144 Annex II, *reprinted in* 16 I.L.M. 1391 at pmbl [hereinafter Protocol II].; PAOLO BENVENUTI, *La Clausola MARTENS e la Tradizione Classica del Diritto Naturale nella Codificazione del Conflicts Armati, in* SCRITTI DEGLI ALLIEVI IN MEMORIA DI GUISEPPE BARILE 173 (1995).

[3] *See* M. Cherif Bassiouni, *A Functional Approach to A General Principles of International Law*, 11 MICH J. INT'L L. 768 (1990). The same formulation of the Hague Conventions has been used in the latest international instrument on the humanitarian law of armed conflicts, Protocol I states in Article 1:

> *In cases not covered by this Protocol or by other international agreements, civilians and combatants remain under the protection and authority of the principles of international law derived from established custom, from the principles of humanity and from the dictates of public conscience.* (emphasis added).

Protocol I at art. 1. *See also* Waldemar A. Solf, *Protection of Civilians Against the Effects of Hostilities Under Customary International Law and Under Protocol I*, 1 AM. U. J. INT'L & POL'Y 117 (1986).

[4] Protocol I, *supra* note 2, at art. 35 (1) which parallels the Hague Conventions' general norm on the implicit limitation on the "methods" of war. That article states *"in any armed conflict, the right of the parties to the conflict to choose methods or means of warfare is not unlimited."* (emphasis added).

2. It is prohibited to employ weapons, projectiles and material and methods of warfare of a nature to cause superfluous injury or unnecessary suffering.[5]

The normative provisions contained in some of these conventions are thus reinforced by the general limitations contained in customary international law.

---

[5] *Id.*

II-1. Protocol for the Prohibition of the Use in War of Asphyxiating, Poisonous or Other Gases, and of Bacteriological Methods of Warfare, *signed at Geneva,* 17 June 1925, 26 U.S.T. 571, 94 L.N.T.S. 65, 14 I.L.M. 49, entered into force with respect to each party to the Protocol upon the date of deposit of its ratification or act of accession; entered into force with respect to the United States 10 April 1975. Authentic Texts: English, French

Relevant Penal Characteristics & Penal Provisions

2. Implicit recognition of the penal nature of the act by establishing a duty to prohibit, prevent, prosecute, punish, or the like: Paragraph 1 (operative)

Applicability
War
Control
Prohibition

State Signatories

Austria; Belgium; Brazil; Bulgaria; Canada; Chile; Czechoslovakia; Denmark; Egypt; El Salvador; Estonia; Ethiopia; Finland; France; Germany; Greece; India; Italy; Japan; Latvia; Lithuania; Luxembourg; the Netherlands; Nicaragua; Norway; Poland; Portugal; Romania; Kingdom of the Serbs, Croats & Slovenes; Siam; Spain; Sweden; Switzerland; Turkey; United Kingdom; United States of America; Uruguay; Venezuela

State Parties

Afghanistan; Angola; Antigua & Barbuda; Argentina; Australia; Austria; the Bahamas; Bahrain; Bangladesh; Barbados; Belgium; Belize; Benin; Bhutan, Bolivia, Botswana; Brazil; Bulgaria; Burkina Faso; Burma; Cambodia; Cameroon; Canada; Cape Verde; Central African Republic; Chile; China; Cote d'Ivoire; Cuba; Cyprus; Czech Republic; Denmark; Dominica; Dominican Republic; Ecuador; Equatorial Guinea; Egypt; Estonia; Ethiopia; Fiji; Finland; France; the Gambia; German Democratic Republic; Federal Republic of Germany; Ghana; Greece; Grenada; Guatemala; Guinea-Bissau; Guyana; the Holy See; Hungary; Iceland, India; Indonesia; Iran; Iraq; Ireland; Israel; Italy; Jamaica; Japan; Jordan; Kenya; Kiribati; Korea, Dem. People's Rep.; Korea, Rep.; Kuwait; Latvia; Laos; Lebanon; Lesotho; Liberia; Libya; Lithuania; Luxembourg; Liechtenstein; Madagascar; Malawi; Malaysia; the Maldives; Mali; Malta; Mauritius; Mexico; Monaco; Mongolia; Morocco; Nepal; the Netherlands; New Zealand; Nicaragua; Niger; Nigeria; Norway; Pakistan; Panama; Papua New Guinea; Paraguay; Peru; The Philippines; Poland; Portugal; Qatar; Romania; Russian Federation; Rwanda; St. Kitts & Nevis; St. Lucia; St. Vincent & the Grenadines; Saudi Arabia; the Seychelles; Sierra Leone; Singapore; Slovak Republic; Solomon Islands; South Africa; Spain; Sri Lanka; Sudan; Suriname, Swaziland; Sweden; Switzerland; Syria; Tanzania; Thailand; Togo; Tonga; Trinidad

& Tobago; Tunisia; Turkey; Tuvalu; Uganda; United Kingdom; United States of America; Uruguay; Venezuela; Socialist Republic of Vietnam; Yemen (Sanaa); Yemen (Aden); Yugoslavia; Zambia; Zimbabwe

Reservations upon Signature, Accession or Ratification

Angola; Antigua & Barbuda; Austria; Australia; the Bahamas; Bahrain; Belgium; Belize; Botswana; Bulgaria; Burma; Canada; Chile; China; Czechoslovakia; Dominica; Estonia; Fiji; France; Grenada; Guyana; India; Iraq; Israel; Jordan; Kiribati; Kuwait; Libya; Malaysia; Mongolia; New Zealand; Nigeria; Papua New Guinea; Portugal; Romania; St. Christopher & Nevis; St. Lucia; St. Vincent & the Grenadines; the Seychelles; Singapore; Solomon Islands; South Africa; Spain; Suriname; Swaziland; Syria; Tuvalu; Union of Soviet Socialist Republics; United Kingdom; United States of America; Socialist Republic of Vietnam; Yugoslavia; Zambia; Zimbabwe

Full Text

The undersigned Plenipotentiaries, in the name of their respective Governments:
(Here follow the names of Plenipotentiaries)

Whereas the use in war of asphyxiating, poisonous or other gases, and of all analogous liquids materials or devices, has been justly condemned by the general opinion of the civilized world; and

Whereas the prohibition of such use has been declared in Treaties to which the majority of Powers of the world are Parties; and

To the end that this prohibition shall be universally accepted as a part of International Law, binding alike the conscience and the practice of nations;

Declare:

That the High Contracting Parties, so far as they are not already Parties to Treaties prohibiting such use, accept this prohibition, agree to extend this prohibition to the use of bacteriological methods of warfare and agree to be bound as between themselves according to the terms of this declaration.

The High Contracting Parties will exert every effort to induce other States to accede to the present Protocol. Such accession will be notified to the Government of the French Republic, and by the latter to all Signatory and Acceding Powers, and will take effect on the date of the notification by the Government of the French Republic.

The present Protocol of which the French and English texts are both authentic, shall be ratified as soon as possible. It shall bear today's date.

The ratifications of the present Protocol shall be addressed to the Government of the French Republic, which will at once notify the deposit of such ratification to each of the Signatory and Acceding Powers.

The instruments of ratification and accession to the present Protocol will remain deposited in the archives of the Government of the French Republic.

The present Protocol will come into force for each Signatory Power as from the date of deposit of its ratification, and, from that moment, each Power will be bound as regards other Powers which have already deposited their ratifications.

In witness whereof the Plenipotentiaries have signed the present Protocol.

Done at Geneva in a single copy, the seventeenth day of June, One Thousand Nine Hundred and Twenty-Five.

II-2. **Draft Convention for the Protection of Civilian Populations Against New Engines of War**, *signed at Amsterdam, by the International Law Association,* **2 September 1938, The International Law Association, Report to the Fortieth Conference held at Amsterdam 29 August to September 1938 at 41-54;** Authentic Texts: English & French

Relevant Penal Characteristics & Penal Provisions

1. Explicit or implicit recognition of proscribed conduct as constituting an international crime, or a crime under international law, or a crime: Article 2; Article 3; Article 4; Article 5 (1), (2); & Article 6

2. Implicit recognition of the penal nature of the act by establishing a duty to prohibit, prevent, prosecute, punish, or the like: Article 7; Article 8; & Article 9

7. Duty or right to cooperate in prosecution, punishment (including judicial assistance): Article 22; Article 28; & Article 29

Full Text

All the High Contracting Parties,

Affirming their fidelity to their obligations under the Pact of Paris of 27 August 1928,

Declaring that in any war which they may wage they would necessarily be the victims of aggression, or such war would on their part be a war of legitimate assistance to a victim of aggression,

Undertaking to observe the following rules, which they acknowledge to embody principles of humanity demanded by the conscience of civilization,

Have decided to conclude a Treaty and for that purpose have appointed as their respective Plenipotentiaries

Who, having communicated to one another their full powers, found in good and due form, have agreed upon the following articles:

Article 1. The civilian population of a State shall not form the object of an act of war. The phrase "civilian population" within the meaning of this Convention shall include all those not enlisted in any branch of the combatant services nor for the time being employed or occupied in any belligerent establishment as defined in Article 2.

ATTACK OR BOMBARDMENT OF UNDEFENDED TOWNS

Art. 2. The bombardment by whatever means of towns, ports, villages or buildings which are undefended is prohibited in all circumstances. A town, port, village or isolated building shall be considered undefended provided that not only (a) no combatant troops, but also (b) no military, naval or air establishment, or barracks, arsenal, munition stores or factories, aerodromes or aeroplane workshops or ships of war, naval dockyards, forts, or fortifications for defensive or offensive purposes, or entrenchments (in this Convention referred to as "belligerent establishments") exist within its boundaries or within a radius of "x" kilometres from such boundaries.

BOMBARDMENT OF DEFENDED TOWNS

Art. 3. The bombardment by whatever means of towns, ports, villages or buildings which are defended is prohibited at any time (whether at night or day) when objects of military character cannot be clearly recognized.

Art. 4. Aerial bombardment for the purpose of terrorising the civilian population is expressly prohibited.

Art. 5. 1. Aerial bombardment is prohibited unless directed at combatant forces or belligerent establishments or lines of communication or transportation used for military purposes.

2. In cases where the objectives above specified are so situated that they cannot be bombarded
without the indiscriminate bombardment of the civilian population, the aircraft must abstain from bombardment.

CHEMICAL, INCENDIARY OR BACTERIAL WEAPONS

Art. 6. The use of chemical, incendiary or bacterial weapons as against any State, whether or not a party to the present Convention, and in any war, whatever its character, is prohibited.

The application of this rule shall be regulated by the following three articles.

Art. 7. (a) The prohibition of the use of chemical weapons shall apply to the use, by any method whatsoever, for the purpose of injuring an adversary, of any natural or synthetic substance (whether solid, liquid or gaseous) which is harmful to the human or animal organism by reason of its being a toxic, asphyxiating, irritant or vesicant substance.

(b) The said prohibition shall not apply:

I. to explosives that are not in the last-mentioned category;

II. to the noxious substances arising from the combustion or detonation of such explosives, provided that such explosives have not been designed or used with the object of producing such noxious substances;

III. to smoke or fog used to screen objectives or for other military purpose, provided that such smoke or fog is not liable to produce harmful effects under normal conditions of use;

IV. to gas that is merely lachrymatory.

Art. 8. The prohibition of the use of incendiary weapons shall apply to projectiles specifically intended to cause fires except when used for defence against aircraft. The prohibition shall not apply:

I. to projectiles specially constructed to give light or to be luminous;

II. to pyrotechnics not normally likely to cause fires;

III. to projectiles of all kinds which, though capable of producing incendiary effects accidentally, are not normally likely to produce such effects;

IV. to incendiary projectiles designed specifically for defence against aircraft when used exclusively for that purpose;

V. to appliances, such as flame-projectors, used to attack individual combatants by fire.

Art. 9. The prohibition of the use of bacterial weapons shall apply to the use for the purpose of injuring an adversary of all methods for the dissemination of pathogenic microbes or of filter-passing viruses, or of infected substances, whether for the purpose of bringing them into immediate contact with human beings, animals or plants, or for the purpose of affecting any of the latter in any manner whatsoever, as, for example, by polluting the atmosphere, water, foodstuffs or any other objects of human use or consumption.

SAFETY ZONES

Art. 10. For the purpose of better enabling a State to obtain protection for the non-belligerent part of its civil population, a State may, if it thinks fit, declare a specified part or parts of its territory to be a "safety zone" or "safety zones" and, subject to the conditions following, such safety zones shall enjoy immunity from attack or bombardment by whatsoever means, and shall not form the legitimate object of any act of war.

Art. 11. A safety zone shall consist of either:

(a) a camp specially erected for that purpose and so situated as to ensure that there is no defended town, port, village or building within "x" kilometres of any part of such camp, or

(b) an undefended town, port, village or building as defined in Article 2.

Art. 12. The inhabitants of a safety zone shall consist of persons who form part of the non-combatant civil population of the State concerned, and shall comprise only the following classes of persons:

(a) persons over the age of 60 years,

(b) persons under the age of 15 years,

(c) persons between 15 and 60 years of age who, by reason of physical or mental infirmity, or by reason of their being expectant mothers or mothers who are suckling infants, are unfit or unable to take part in any work that would enable the State concerned to carry on the war. The question whether any person is or is not within this category is one for the decision of the Controlling Authority hereafter referred to, and

(d) such other persons (not exceeding in the aggregate five percent of the number of such non-combatants) as shall be necessary for the purpose of tending such non-combatants and maintaining law and order within the safety zone, as well as the Controlling Authority hereafter referred to.

Art. 13. The situation of any such safety zone and the road, permanent way, river or canal whereby supplies will be brought to such safety zone shall be notified to other Powers in time of peace through diplomatic channels by means of a map and written description, and such notification shall indicate the precise site and limits of the zone. In time of war such notification shall be given through the agency of one of the States signatory to this Convention and not participating in the war. It shall be the duty of such State forthwith to inform directly the Governments of all States actively concerned in any such war of the contents of such notification, and as soon as may be to acquaint therewith the representatives of all States accredited to its Government and not actively participating in such war. A safety zone notified in time of war shall not be deemed to be such until the expiration of 48 hours after such State as aforesaid has informed the Governments of all States actively concerned in any such war as aforesaid.

Art. 14. Such safety zones must be circular in shape and clearly indicated by marks visible by day to aircraft, and the nature of such marks shall be set out in the notification to other Powers as provided in the last-mentioned Article. The marks used for its safety zones by a State must all be of the same size, colour and pattern. The distinctive flag of the Geneva Convention shall not be used as a mark for such safety zones, nor shall the national flag of any State be so used.

Art. 15. It shall be unlawful during time of war to export any article whatsoever from any such safety zone.

Art. 16. No person other than those specified in Article 12 shall during time of war be permitted to enter any such safety zone. It shall be lawful for the purposes of providing food, clothing and other necessaries of life to those within the zones for transport services (whether by land, sea or air) to proceed as far as the limits of the safety zone as indicated in the notification to other Powers, but not to enter within or fly over such limits, and to remain there for such period only as shall enable the articles transported to be unloaded. For such period as it is engaged upon or returning from such service, and provided it bears the same distinctive marks as those by which such safety zone is indicated, any railway, motor, steam or electric vehicle, ship or aircraft shall whilst within "x" kilometres of any part of the safety zone enjoy the same immunity as such safety zone, and such immunity shall extend to the road, permanent way, river or canal (so far as the same is within the said "x" kilometres of any part of the safety zone) along which such railway, vehicle or ship must necessarily travel in bringing supplies to or returning from the safety zone. No road, permanent way, river or canal which shall have been used for military purposes at any time whilst the safety zone existed as such shall be entitled to the immunity aforesaid.

Art. 17. Every safety zone shall in time of war be subject to the supervision of a Controlling Authority composed of one or more nationals of a non-belligerent State, and it shall be the duty of such Controlling Authority to satisfy itself that the rules herein contained relating to the establishment of safety zones are in all respects complied with. The Controlling Authority shall be accorded every facility for the carrying out of its duties by the Government of the State concerned, and shall enjoy diplomatic privileges.

Art. 18. The Controlling Authority shall be chosen by and be responsible to a Commission of Control appointed to any State which desires to avail itself of the protection hereby afforded to safety zones by the President of the Permanent Court of International Justice, and may be so appointed in time of peace as well as in time of war. Such Commission of Control shall consist of not less than three nationals of non-belligerent States, and shall be accorded every facility for the carrying out of its duties by the Government of the State to which it is appointed, and shall enjoy diplomatic privileges, but shall not interfere with the territorial sovereignty of such State.

Art. 19. The Controlling Authority of a safety zone shall also satisfy itself that the provisions of Article 16 are complied with by any transport service proceeding to or from such safety zone, and that the permanent way, road, river or canal used by such transport service had not been used for military purposes whilst such safety zone existed as such.

Art. 20. It shall be the duty of a Controlling Authority which becomes aware of any breach of any of the provisions of this Convention by any belligerent forthwith to notify the Commission of Control to which it is responsible, and the Commission of Control, if satisfied that such breach has occurred shall forthwith notify the President of the Permanent Court of International Justice, specifying the breach and naming the State by which such breach is committed, and shall also forthwith notify the Governments of all belligerents.

Art. 21. If any State seeking to avail itself of the protection hereby afforded to safety zones commits a breach of any of the provisions relating to safety zones contained in this Convention in respect of one or more of its own safety zones, and such breach is notified as provided in the preceding article, and the safety zone or safety zones affected by such breach are specified in such notice, it shall be lawful for any other belligerent to give notice to such State that the safety zone or safety zones concerned will after the receipt of such notice no longer be recognized as such, but it shall not be lawful to cause any injury to civilian populations by way of reprisals for such breach.

SANCTIONS

Art. 22. Any party claiming that a breach of any of the provisions of this Convention (other than a breach of the provisions relating to the establishment of safety zones committed by a State seeking to obtain the protection hereby afforded to such safety zones, for which breach the provisions of the last preceeding Article shall be the sole remedy) has occurred shall notify the President of the Permanent Court of International Justice with a view to the immediate constitution of a Commission of Investigation.

Art. 23. The Commission of Investigation shall proceed with all possible speed to make such inquiries as are necessary to determine whether any such breach has occurred.

It shall report to the Permanent Court of International Justice.

Art. 24. The Permanent Court of International Justice shall invite the party (1) against which the complaint has been made to furnish explanations.

It may send commissioners to the territory under the control of that party or of the party making such complaint for the purpose of proceeding to an inquiry, to determine whether any such breach has occurred.

(1) Signatory States not already adhering to the Statute of the Permanent Court would have to undertake to do so. ' (Note in the original). '

Art. 25. The Permanent Court of International Justice may also carry out any other inquiry with the same object, and may determine any question which may arise requiring determination by a judicial tribunal, such decision to be given with all possible speed.

Art. 26. The parties involved in the above-mentioned operations, and, in general, all the parties to the present Convention, shall take the necessary measures to facilitate these operations, particularly as regards the rapid transport of persons and correspondence.

Art. 27. According to the result of the above-mentioned operations, the Permanent Court of International Justice, acting with all possible speed, shall establish whether any such breach has occurred.

Art. 28. In the event of any such breach being established to its satisfaction the Permanent Court of International Justice shall publish its findings, specifying the State or States which has or have committed such breach, and thereupon it shall be lawful for any Signatory State not being a party to such breach without thereby committing any breach of its treaty obligations or of International Law to do all or any of the following things:

(a) assist with armed forces the State against which such breach shall have been committed,

(b) supply such last-mentioned State with financial or material assistance, including munitions of war,

(c) refuse to admit the exercise by the State or States committing such breach of belligerent rights,

(d) decline to observe towards the State or States committing such breach the duties prescribed by International Law for a neutral in relation to a belligerent.

Art. 29. Any State committing a breach of this Convention is liable to pay compensation for all damage caused by such breach to a State injured thereby or any of its nationals.

Art. 30. Each of the High Contracting Parties agrees that it will without delay enact such domestic legislation as may be required to carry into effect the obligations entered into by it hereunder.

Art. 31. This Convention is in addition to, and not in substitution for, the humanitarian obligation imposed upon any Signatory State by any general treaty such as the Hague Conventions of 1899 and 1907 and the International Convention relating to the Treatment of Prisoners of War, 1929.

Art. 32. Non-Signatory Powers may adhere to this Convention. To do so they must make known their adhesion to the High Contracting Parties by means of a written notification addressed to all the High Contracting Parties.

II-3. Treaty on the Non-Proliferation of Nuclear Weapons, *signed at Washington, London and Moscow,* 1 July 1968, 21 U.S.T. 483, 729 U.N.T.S. 161, 7 I.L.M. 809, entered into force 5 March 1970; entered into force with respect to the United States 5 March 1970.[1] Authentic Texts: Chinese, English, French, Russian, Spanish

Relevant Penal Characteristics & Penal Provisions
None

Applicability
War & Peace

Control
Regulation & Prohibition

State Signatories
Afghanistan; Australia; Austria; Barbados; Belgium; Bolivia; Botswana; Bulgaria; Cameroon; Canada; Ceylon; China; Colombia; the Congo; Costa Rica; Cyprus; Czechoslovakia; Dahomey; Denmark; Dominican Republic; Ecuador; El Salvador; Ethiopia; Finland; the Gambia; Federal Republic of Germany; Ghana; Greece; Guatemala; Haiti; Honduras; Hungary; Iceland; Indonesia; Iran; Ireland; Italy; Ivory Coast; Jamaica; Japan; Jordan; Kenya; Korea; Kuwait; Laos; Lebanon; Lesotho; Liberia; Libya; Luxembourg; Malagasy Republic; Malaysia; the Maldives; Mali; Malta; Mauritius; Mexico; Morocco; Nepal; the Netherlands; New Zealand; Nicaragua; Nigeria; Norway; Panama; Paraguay; Peru; the Philippines; Poland; Romania; San Marino; Senegal; Singapore; Somalia; Sweden; Switzerland; Togo; Trinidad & Tobago; Tunisia; Turkey; Union of Soviet Socialist Republics; United Kingdom; United States of America; Upper Volta; Uruguay; Venezuela; Vietnam; Yugoslavia

State Parties
Afghanistan; Albania; Algeria; Andorra; Angola; Antigua & Barbuda; Australia; Argentina; Armenia; Australia; Austria; Azerbaijan; the Bahamas; Bahrain; Bangladesh; Barbados; Belgium; Belize; Benin; Bhutan; Bolivia; Bosnia and

---

1 *See* International Court of Justice Advisory Opinion on the Legality of Threat or Use of Nuclear Weapons *infra* Chapter II-8.

Herzegovina; Botswana; Brazil; Brunei Darussalam; Burkina Faso; Bulgaria; Burundi; Cambodia; Cameroon; Canada; Cape Verde; Central African Republic; Chad; Chile; China (Taiwan); Colombia; Comoros; the Congo; Costa Rica; Cote d' Ivoire; Croatia; Cyprus; Czech Republic; Democratic People's Republic of Korea; Democratic Republic of the Congo; Denmark; Djibouti; Dominica; Dominican Republic; Ecuador; Egypt; El Salvador; Equatorial Guinea; Eritrea; Estonia; Ethiopia; Fiji; Finland; France; Gabon; the Gambia; Georgia; Germany; Ghana; Greece; Grenada; Guatemala; Guinea; Guinea-Bissau; Guyana; Haiti; the Holy See; Honduras; Hungary; Iceland; Indonesia; Iran; Iraq; Ireland; Italy; Ivory Coast; Jamaica; Japan; Jordan; Kampuchea; Kazakhstan; Kenya; Kiribati; Republic of Korea; Kuwait; Kyrgyzstan; Lao People's Democratic Republic; Laos; Latvia; Lebanon; Lesotho; Liberia; Libya; Liechtenstein; Luxembourg; Madagascar; Malawi; Malaysia; the Maldives; Mali; Malta; Marshall Islands; Mauritania; Mauritius; Mexico; Micronesia; Monaco; Mongolia; Morocco; Mozambique; Myanmar; Namibia; Nauru; Nepal; the Netherlands; New Zealand; Nicaragua; Niger; Nigeria; Norway; Oman; Palau; Panama; Papua New Guinea; Paraguay; Peru; the Philippines; Poland; Portugal; Qatar; Republic of Korea; Republic of Moldovia; Romania; Russian Federation; Rwanda; St. Kitts & Nevis; St. Lucia; St. Vincent and the Grenadines; Samoa; San Marino; Sao Tome & Principe; Saudi Arabia; Senegal; Seychelles; Sierra Leone; Singapore; Solomon Islands; Somalia; South Africa; Spain; Sri Lanka; Sudan; Suriname; Swaziland; Sweden; Switzerland; Syria; Tajikistan; Thailand; the former Yugoslav Republic of Macedonia; Togo; Tonga; Tunisia; Turkey; Turkmenistan; Tuvalu; Uganda; Ukraine; United Arab Emirates; United Kingdom of Great Britain and Northern Ireland; United Republic of Tanzania; United States of America; Upper Volta; Uruguay; Venezuela; Socialist Republic of Vietnam; Western Samoa; Yemen (Aden); Yugoslavia; Zambia; Zaire; Zimbabwe

Full Text

The States concluding this Treaty, hereinafter referred to as the "Parties to the Treaty",

Considering the devastation that would be visited upon all mankind by a nuclear war and the consequent need to make every effort to avert the danger of such a war and to take measures to safeguard the security of peoples,

Believing that the proliferation of nuclear weapons would seriously enhance the danger of nuclear war,

In conformity with resolutions of the United Nations General Assembly calling for the conclusion of an agreement on the prevention of wider dissemination of nuclear weapons,

Undertaking to co-operate in facilitating the application of International Atomic Energy Agency safeguards on peaceful nuclear activities,

Expressing their support for research, development and other efforts to further the application, within the framework of the International Atomic Energy Agency safeguards system, of the principle of safeguarding effectively the flow of source and special fissionable materials by use of instruments and other techniques at certain strategic points,

Affirming the principle that the benefits of peaceful applications of nuclear technology, including any technological by-products which may be derived by nuclear-weapon States from the development of nuclear explosive devices, should be available for peaceful purposes to all Parties to the Treaty, whether nuclear-weapon or non-nuclear-weapon States,

Convinced that, in furtherance of this principle, all Parties to the Treaty are entitled to participate in the fullest possible exchange of scientific information for, and to contribute alone or in co-operation with other States to, the further development of the applications of atomic energy for peaceful purposes,

Declaring their intention to achieve at the earliest possible date the cessation of the nuclear arms race and to undertake effective measures in the direction of nuclear disarmament,

Urging the co-operation of all States in the attainment of this objective,

Recalling the determination expressed by the Parties to the 1963 Treaty banning nuclear weapon tests in the atmosphere, in outer space and under water in its Preamble to seek to achieve the discontinuance of all test explosions of nuclear weapons for all time and to continue negotiations to this end,

Desiring to further the easing of international tension and the strengthening of trust between States in order to facilitate the cessation of the manufacture of nuclear weapons, the liquidation of all their existing stockpiles, and the elimination from national arsenals of nuclear weapons and the means of their delivery pursuant to a Treaty on general and complete disarmament under strict and effective international control,

Recalling that, in accordance with the Charter of the United Nations, States must refrain in their international relations from the threat or use of force against the territorial integrity or political independence of any State, or in any other manner inconsistent with the Purposes of the United Nations, and that the establishment and maintenance of international peace and security are to be promoted with the least diversion for armaments of the world's human and economic resources,

Have agreed as follows:

Article I

Each nuclear-weapon State Party to the Treaty undertakes not to transfer to any recipient whatsoever nuclear weapons or other nuclear explosive devices or control over such weapons or explosive devices directly, or indirectly; and not in any way to assist, encourage, or induce any non-nuclear-weapon State to manufacture or otherwise acquire nuclear weapons or other nuclear explosive devices, or control over such weapons or explosive devices.

Article II

Each non-nuclear-weapon State Party to the Treaty undertakes not to receive the transfer from any transferor whatsoever of nuclear weapons or other nuclear explosive devices or of control over such weapons or explosive devices directly, or indirectly; not to manufacture or otherwise acquire nuclear weapons or other nuclear explosive devices; and not to seek or receive any assistance in the manufacture of nuclear weapons or other nuclear explosive devices.

Article III

1. Each non-nuclear-weapon State Party to the Treaty undertakes to accept safeguards, as set forth in an agreement to be negotiated and concluded with the International Atomic Energy Agency in accordance with the Statute of the International Atomic Energy Agency and the Agency's safeguards system, for the exclusive purpose of verification of the fulfilment of its obligations assumed under this Treaty with a view to preventing diversion of nuclear energy from peaceful uses to nuclear weapons or other nuclear explosive devices. Procedures for the safeguards required by this Article shall be followed with respect to source or special fissionable material whether it is being produced, processed or used in any principal nuclear facility or is outside any such facility. The safeguards required by this Article shall be applied on all source or special fissionable material in all peaceful nuclear activities within the territory of such State, under its jurisdiction, or carried out under its control anywhere.

2. Each State Party to the Treaty undertakes not to provide: (a) source or special fissionable material, or (b) equipment or material especially designed or prepared for the processing, use or production of special fissionable material, to any non-nuclear-weapon State for peaceful purposes, unless the source or special fissionable material shall be subject to the safeguards required by this Article.

3. The safeguards required by this Article shall be implemented in a manner designed to comply with Article IV of this Treaty, and to avoid hampering the economic or technological development of the Parties or international co-operation in the field of peaceful nuclear activities, including the international exchange of nuclear material and equipment for the processing, use or production of nuclear material for peaceful purposes in accordance with the provisions of this Article and the principle of safeguarding set forth in the Preamble of the Treaty.

4. Non-nuclear-weapon States Party to the Treaty shall conclude agreements with the International Atomic Energy Agency to meet the requirements of this Article either individually or together with other States in accordance with the Statute of the International Atomic Energy Agency. Negotiation of such agreements shall commence within 180 days from the original entry into force of this Treaty. For States

depositing their instruments of ratification or accession after the 180-day period, negotiation of such agreements shall commence not later than the date of such deposit. Such agreements shall enter into force not later than eighteen months after the date of initiation of negotiations.

Article IV

1. Nothing in this Treaty shall be interpreted as affecting the inalienable right of all the Parties to the Treaty to develop research, production and use of nuclear energy for peaceful purposes without discrimination and in conformity with Articles I and II of this Treaty.

2. All the Parties to the Treaty undertake to facilitate, and have the right to participate in, the fullest possible exchange of equipment, materials and scientific and technological information for the peaceful uses of nuclear energy. Parties to the Treaty in a position to do so shall also co-operate in contributing alone or together with other States or international organizations to the further development of the applications of nuclear energy for peaceful purposes, especially in the territories of non-nuclear-weapon States Party to the Treaty, with due consideration for the needs of the developing areas of the world.

Article V

Each Party to the Treaty undertakes to take appropriate measures to ensure that, in accordance with this Treaty, under appropriate international observation and through appropriate international procedures, potential benefits from any peaceful applications of nuclear explosions will be made available to non-nuclear-weapon States Party to the Treaty on a non-discriminatory basis and that the charge to such Parties for the explosive devices used will be as low as possible and exclude any charge for research and development. Non-nuclear-weapon States Party to the Treaty shall be able to obtain such benefits, pursuant to a special international agreement or agreements, through an appropriate international body with adequate representation of non-nuclear-weapon States. Negotiations on this subject shall commence as soon as possible after the Treaty enters into force. Non-nuclear-weapon States Party to the Treaty so desiring may also obtain such benefits pursuant to bilateral agreements.

Article VI

Each of the Parties to the Treaty undertakes to pursue negotiations in good faith on effective measures relating to cessation of the nuclear arms race at an early date and to nuclear disarmament, and on a treaty on general and complete disarmament under strict and effective international control.

Article VII

Nothing in this Treaty affects the right of any group of States to conclude regional treaties in order to assure the total absence of nuclear weapons in their respective territories.

Article VIII

1. Any Party to the Treaty may propose amendments to this Treaty. The text of any proposed amendment shall be submitted to the Depositary Governments which shall circulate it to all Parties to the Treaty. Thereupon, if requested to do so by one-third or more of the Parties to the Treaty, the Depositary Governments shall convene a conference, to which they shall invite all the Parties to the Treaty, to consider such an amendment.

2. Any amendment to this Treaty must be approved by a majority of the votes of all the Parties to the Treaty, including the votes of all nuclear-weapon States Party to the Treaty and all other Parties which, on the date the amendment is circulated, are members of the Board of Governors of the International Atomic Energy Agency. The amendment shall enter into force for each Party that deposits its instrument of ratification of the amendment upon the deposit of such instruments of ratification by a majority of all the Parties, including the instruments of ratification of all nuclear-weapon States Party to the Treaty and all other Parties which, on the date the amendment is circulated, are members of the Board of Governors of the International Atomic Energy Agency. Thereafter, it shall enter into force for any other Party upon the deposit of its instrument of ratification of the amendment.

3. Five years after the entry into force of this Treaty, a conference of Parties to the Treaty shall be held in Geneva, Switzerland, in order to review the operation of this Treaty with a view to assuring that the purposes of the Preamble and the provisions of the Treaty are being realised. At intervals of five years thereafter, a majority of the Parties to the Treaty may obtain, by submitting a proposal to this effect to the Depositary Governments, the convening of further conferences with the same objective of reviewing the operation of the Treaty.

Article IX

1. This Treaty shall be open to all States for signature. Any State which does not sign the Treaty before its entry into force in accordance with paragraph 3 of this Article may accede to it at any time.

2. This Treaty shall be subject to ratification by signatory States. Instruments of ratification and instruments of accession shall be deposited with the Governments of the United Kingdom of Great Britain and Northern Ireland, the Union of Soviet Socialist Republics and the United States of America, which are hereby designated the Depositary Governments.

3. This Treaty shall enter into force after its ratification by the States, the Governments of which are designated Depositaries of the Treaty, and forty other States signatory to this Treaty and the deposit of their instruments of ratification. For the purposes of this Treaty, a nuclear-weapon State is one which has manufactured

and exploded a nuclear weapon or other nuclear explosive device prior to 1 January, 1967.

4. For States whose instruments of ratification or accession are deposited subsequent to the entry into force of this Treaty, it shall enter into force on the date of the deposit of their instruments of ratification or accession.

5. The Depositary Governments shall promptly inform all signatory and acceding States of the date of each signature, the date of deposit of each instrument of ratification or of accession, the date of the entry into force of this Treaty, and the date of receipt of any requests for convening a conference or other notices.

6. This Treaty shall be registered by the Depositary Governments pursuant to Article 102 of the Charter of the United Nations.

Article X

1. Each Party shall in exercising its national sovereignty have the right to withdraw from the Treaty if it decides that extraordinary events, related to the subject matter of this Treaty, have jeopardized the supreme interests of its country. It shall give notice of such withdrawal to all other Parties to the Treaty and to the United Nations Security Council three months in advance. Such notice shall include a statement of the extraordinary events it regards as having jeopardized its supreme interests.

2. Twenty-five years after the entry into force of the Treaty, a conference shall be convened to decide whether the Treaty shall continue in force indefinitely, or shall be extended for an additional fixed period or periods. This decision shall be taken by a majority of the Parties to the Treaty.

Article XI

This Treaty, the English, Russian, French, Spanish and Chinese texts of which are equally authentic, shall be deposited in the archives of the Depositary Governments. Duly certified copies of this Treaty shall be transmitted by the Depositary Governments to the Governments of the signatory and acceding States.

IN WITNESS WHEREOF the undersigned, duly authorised, have signed this Treaty. DONE in triplicate, at the cities of London, Moscow and Washington, the first day of July, one thousand nine hundred and sixty-eight.

II-4. **The Distinction between Military Objectives and Non-Military Objectives in General and Particularly the Problems Associated with Weapons of Mass Destruction,** *resolution adopted at Edinburgh*, 9 September 1969, by the Institute of International Law, 53 Annuaire de l'Institut de Droit International, Session d'Edinbourg 358 (French), 375 (English) (1969), 66 AM. J. INT'L L. 470-471 (English) Authentic Text: French

Relevant Penal Characteristics & Penal Provisions
1. Explicit or implicit recognition of proscribed conduct as constituting an international crime, or a crime under international law, or a crime: Article 6 & Article 7

Applicability
Peace

Control
Regulate & Prohibit

Full Text
The Institute of International Law,

' Reaffirming ' the existing rules of international law whereby the recourse to force is prohibited in international relations,

' Considering ' that, if an armed conflict occurs in spite of these rules, the protection of civilian populations is one of the essential obligations of the parties,

' Having in mind ' the general principles of international law, the customary rules and the conventions and agreements which clearly restrict the extent to which the parties engaged in a conflict may harm the adversary,

' Having also in mind ' that these rules, which are enforced by international and national courts, have been formally confirmed on several occasions by a large number of international organizations and especially by the United Nations Organization,

' Being of the opinion ' that these rules have kept their full validity notwithstanding the infringements suffered,

' Having in mind ' that the consequences which the indiscriminate conduct of hostilities and particularly the use of nuclear, chemical and bacteriological weapons, may involve for civilian populations and for mankind as a whole,

' Notes ' that the following rules form part of the principles to be observed in armed conflicts by any ' de jure ' or ' de facto ' government, or by any other authority responsible for the conduct of hostilities:

1. The obligation to respect the distinction between military objectives and non-military objects as well as between persons participating in the hostilities and members of the civilian population remains a fundamental principle of the international law in force.

2. There can be considered as military objectives only those which, by their very nature or purpose or use, make an effective contribution to military action, or exhibit a generally recognized military significance, such that their total or partial destruction in the actual circumstances gives a substantial, specific and immediate military advantage to those who are in a position to destroy them.

3. Neither the civilian population nor any of the objects expressly protected by conventions or agreements can be considered as military objectives, nor yet

(a) under whatsoever circumstances the means indispensable for the survival of the civilian population,

(b) those objects which, by their nature or use, serve primarily humanitarian or peaceful purposes such as religious or cultural needs.

4. Existing international law prohibits all armed attacks on the civilian populations as such, as well as on non-military objects, notably dwellings or other buildings sheltering the civilian population, so long as these are not used for military purposes to such an extent as to justify action against them under the rules regarding military objectives as set forth in the second paragraph hereof.

5. The provisions of the preceding paragraphs do not affect the application of the existing rules of international law which prohibit the exposure of civilian populations and of non-military objects to the destructive effects of military means.

6. Existing international law prohibits, irrespective of the type of weapon used, any action whatsoever designed to terrorize the civilian population.

7. Existing international law prohibits the use of all weapons which, by their nature, affect indiscriminately both military objectives and non-military objects, or both armed forces and civilian populations. In particular, it prohibits the use of weapons the destructive effect of which is so great that it cannot be limited to specific military objectives or is otherwise uncontrollable (self-generating weapons), as well as of "blind" weapons.

8. Existing international law prohibits all attacks for whatsoever motive or by whatsoever means for the annihilation of any group, region or urban centre with no possible distinction between armed forces and civilian populations or between military objectives and non-military objects.

II-5. Convention on the Prohibition of the Development, Production and Stockpiling of Bacteriological (Biological) and Toxin Weapons and on Their Destruction, *signed at Washington, London and Moscow,* **10 April 1972, 26 U.S.T. 583, 1015 U.N.T.S. 163, 11 I.L.M. 309, entered into force 26 March 1975; entered into force with respect to the United States 26 March 1975.** Languages: Chinese, English, French, Russian, Spanish

Relevant Penal Characteristics & Penal Provisions
2. Implicit recognition of the penal nature of the act by establishing a duty to prohibit, prevent, prosecute, punish, or the like: Article I; Article II; Article IV; & Article VIII

Applicability
War & Peace

Control
Regulation & Prohibition

State Signatories
Afghanistan; Argentina; Australia; Austria; Barbados; Belgium; Bolivia; Botswana; Brazil; Bulgaria; Burma; Burundi; Canada; Central African Republic; Ceylon; Chile; China (Taiwan); Colombia; Costa Rica; Cyprus; Czechoslovakia; Dahomey; Denmark; Dominican Republic; Ecuador; El Salvador; Ethiopia; Finland; the Gambia; Federal Republic of Germany; Ghana; Greece; Guatemala; Guyana; Haiti; Honduras; Hungary; Iceland; India; Indonesia; Iran; Ireland; Italy; Ivory Coast; Japan; Jordan; Khmer Republic; Korea; Kuwait; Laos; Lebanon; Lesotho; Liberia; Luxembourg; Malawi; Malaysia; Mali; Mauritius; Mexico; Mongolia; Morocco; Nepal; the Netherlands; New Zealand; Nicaragua; Niger; Nigeria; Norway; Pakistan; Panama; Peru; the Philippines; Poland; Portugal; Romania; Rwanda; San Marino; Saudi Arabia; Senegal; Sierra Leone; Singapore; South Africa; Spain; Sweden; Switzerland; Thailand; Togo; Tunisia; Turkey; Union of Soviet Socialist Republics; United Kingdom; United States of America; Venezuela; Vietnam; Yemen; Yugoslavia; Zaire

State Parties
Afghanistan; Albania; Argentina; Australia; Austria; Bahamas; Bahrain; Bangladesh; Barbados; Belarus; Belgium; Belize; Benin; Bhutan; Bolivia; Bosnia and Herzegovina; Brazil; Brunei; Bulgaria; Burkina Faso; Cambodia; Canada; Cape Verde; Chile; China (Taiwan); Colombia; the Congo; Congo, Dem. Rep.; Costa Rica;

Croatia; Cuba; Cyprus; Czech Republic; Denmark; Dominica; Dominican Republic; Ecuador; El Salvador; Equatorial Guinea; Estonia; Ethiopia; Fiji; Finland; former Yugoslav Republic of Macedonia; France; Gambia; Georgia; German Democratic Republic; Federal Republic of Germany; Ghana; Greece; Grenada; Guatemala; Guinea-Bissau; Honduras; Hungary; Iceland; India; Iran; Iraq; Ireland; Italy; Jamaica; Japan; Jordan; Kenya; Korea, Dem. People's Rep.; Korea, Rep.; Kuwait Laos; Lebanon; Lesotho; Libya; Lithuania; Liechtenstein; Luxembourg; Malaysia; Malta; Maldives; Mauritius; Mexico; Mongolia; the Netherlands; New Zealand; Nicaragua; Niger; Nigeria; Norway; Oman; Pakistan; Panama; Papua New Guinea; Paraguay; the Philippines; Poland; Portugal; Qatar; Romania; Russian Federation; Rwanda; San Marino; Sao Tome & Principe; St. Lucia; St. Kitts and Nevis; Saudi Arabia; Senegal; the Seychelles; Sierra Leone; Singapore; Solomon Islands; Slovak Rep.; Slovenia; South Africa; Spain; Sri Lanka; Suriname; Sweden; Swaziland; Switzerland; Thailand; Togo; Tonga; Tunisia; Turkey; Turkmenistan; Uganda; Ukraine; Union of Soviet Socialist Republics; United Kingdom; United States of America; Uruguay; Vanuatu; Venezuela; Socialist Republic of Vietnam; Yemen (Aden); Yugoslavia; Zimbabwe

Reservations Upon Signature, Accession, or Ratification
Austria; Bahrain; Malaysia

Full Text
The States Parties to this Convention, Determined to act with a view to achieving effective progress towards general and complete disarmament, including the prohibition and elimination of all types of weapons of mass destruction, and convinced that the prohibition of the development, production and stockpiling of chemical and bacteriological (biological) weapons and their elimination, through effective measures, will facilitate the achievement of general and complete disarmament under strict and effective international control, Recognising the important significance of the Protocol for the Prohibition of the Use in War of Asphyxiating, Poisonous or Other Gases and of Bacteriological Methods of Warfare, signed at Geneva on 17 June 1925, and conscious also of the contribution which the said Protocol has already made, and continues to make, to mitigating the horrors of war,
Reaffirming their adherence to the principles and objectives of that Protocol and calling upon all States to comply strictly with them,

Recalling that the General Assembly of the United Nations has repeatedly condemned all actions contrary to the principles and objectives of the Geneva Protocol of 17 June 1925,

Desiring to contribute to the strengthening of confidence between peoples and the general improvement of the international atmosphere,

Desiring also to contribute to the realisation of the purposes and principles of the Charter of the United Nations,

Convinced of the importance and urgency of eliminating from the arsenals of States, through effective measures, such dangerous weapons of mass destruction as those using chemical or bacteriological (biological) agents,

Recognising that an agreement on the prohibition of bacteriological (biological) and toxin weapons represents a first possible step towards the achievement of agreement on effective measures also for the prohibition of the development, production and stockpiling of chemical weapons, and determined to continue negotiations to that end,

Determined, for the sake of all mankind, to exclude completely the possibility of bacteriological (biological) agents and toxins being used as weapons,

Convinced that such use would be repugnant to the conscience of mankind and that no effort should be spared to minimise this risk,

Have agreed as follows

ARTICLE I

Each State Party to this Convention undertakes never in any circumstances to develop, produce, stockpile or otherwise acquire or retain:

1. microbial or other biological agents, or toxins whatever their origin or method of production, of types and in quantities that have no justification for prophylactic, protective or other peaceful purposes;

2. weapons, equipment or means of delivery designed to use such agents or toxins for hostile purposes or in armed conflict.

ARTICLE II

Each State Party to this Convention undertakes to destroy, or to divert to peaceful purposes, as soon as possible but not later than nine months after the entry into force of the Convention, all agents, toxins, weapons, equipment and means of delivery specified in Article I of the Convention, which are in its possession or under its jurisdiction or control. In implementing the provisions of this Article all necessary safety precautions shall be observed to protect populations and the environment.

ARTICLE III

Each State Party to this Convention undertakes not to transfer to any recipient whatsover, directly or indirectly, and not in any way to assist, encourage, or induce any State, group of States or international organisations to manufacture or otherwise acquire any of the agents, toxins, weapons, equipment or means of delivery specified in Article I of the Convention.

ARTICLE IV
Each State Party to this Convention shall, in accordance with its constitutional processes, take any necessary measures to prohibit and prevent the development, production, stockpiling, acquisition or retention of the agents, toxins, weapons, equipment and means of delivery specified in Article I of the Convention, within the territory of such State, under its jurisdiction or under its control anywhere.

ARTICLE V
The States Parties to this Convention undertake to consult one another and to cooperate in solving any problems which may arise in relation to the objective of, or in the application of the provisions of, the Convention. Consultation and cooperation pursuant to this Article may also be undertaken through appropriate international procedures within the framework of the United Nations and in accordance with its Charter.

ARTICLE VI
1. Any State Party to this Convention which finds that any other State Party is acting in breach of obligations deriving from the provisions of the Convention may lodge a complaint with the Security Council of the United Nations. Such a complaint should include all possible evidence confirming its validity, as well as a request for its consideration by the Security Council.
2. Each State Party to this Convention undertakes to co-operate in carrying out any investigation which the Security Council may initiate, in accordance with the provisions of the Charter of the United Nations, on the basis of the complaint received by the Council. The Security Council shall inform the States Parties to the Convention of the results of the investigation.

ARTICLE VII
Each State Party to this Convention undertakes to provide or support assistance, in accordance with the United Nations Charter, to any Party to the Convention which so requests, if the Security Council decides that such Party has been exposed to danger a result of violation of the Convention.

ARTICLE VIII
Nothing in this Convention shall be interpreted as in any way limiting or detracting from the obligations assumed by any State under the Protocol for the Prohibition of the Use in War of Asphyxiating, Poisonous or Other Gases, and of Bacteriological Methods of Warfare, signed at Geneva on 17 June 1925.

ARTICLE IX

Each State Party to this Convention affirms the recognised objective of effective prohibition of chemical weapons and, to this end, undertakes to continue negotiations in good faith with a view to reaching early agreement on effective measures for the prohibition of their development, production and stockpiling and for their destruction, and on appropriate measures concerning equipment and means of delivery specifically designed for the production or use of chemical agents for weapons purposes.

ARTICLE X

1. The State Parties to this Convention undertake to facilitate, and have the right to participate in, the fullest possible exchange of equipment, materials and scientific and technological information for the use of bacteriological (biological) agents and toxins for peaceful purposes. Parties to the Convention in a position to do so shall also co-operate in contributing individually or together with other States or international organisations to the further development and application of scientific discoveries in the field of bacteriology (biology) for the prevention of disease, or for other peaceful purposes.

2. This Convention shall be implemented in a manner designed to avoid hampering the economic or technological development of States Parties to the Convention or international co-operation in the field of peaceful bacteriological (biological) activities, including the international exchange of bacteriological (biological) agents and toxins and equipment for the processing, use or production of bacteriological (biological) agents and toxins for peaceful purposes in accordance with the provisions of the Convention.

ARTICLE XI

Any State Party may propose amendments to this Convention. Amendments shall enter into force for each State Party accepting the amendments upon their acceptance by a majority of the States Parties to the Convention and thereafter for each remaining State Party on the date of acceptance by it.

ARTICLE XII

Five years after the entry into force of this Convention, or earlier if it is requested by a majority of Parties to the Convention by submitting a proposal to this effect to the Depositary Governments, a conference of States Parties to the Convention shall be held at Geneva, Switzerland, to review the operation of the Convention, with a view to assuring that the purposes of the preamble and the provisions of the Convention, including the provisions concerning negotiations on chemical weapons, are being realised. Such review shall take into account any new scientific and technological developments relevant to the Convention.

ARTICLE XIII

1. This Convention shall be of unlimited duration.
2. Each State Party to this Convention shall in exercising its national sovereignty have the right to withdraw from the Convention if it decides that extraordinary events, related to the subject matter of the Convention, have jeopardised the supreme interests of its country. It shall give notice of such withdrawal to all other States Parties to the Convention and to the United Nations Security Council three months in advance. Such notice shall include a statement of the extraordinary events it regards as having jeopardised its supreme interests.

ARTICLE XIV

1. This Convention shall be open to all States for signature. Any State which does not sign the Convention before its entry into force in accordance with paragraph 3 of this Article may accede to it at any time.
2. This Convention shall be subject to ratification by signatory States. Instruments of ratification and instruments of accession shall be deposited with the Governments of the United Kingdom of Great Britain and Northern Ireland, the Union of Soviet Socialist Republics and the United States of America, which are hereby designated the Depositary Governments.
3. This Convention shall enter into force after the deposit of instruments of ratification by twenty-two Governments, including the Governments designated as Depositaries of the Convention.
4. For States whose instruments of ratification or accession are deposited subsequent to the entry into force of this Convention, it shall enter into force on the date of the deposit of their instruments of ratification or accession.
5. The Depositary Governments shall promptly inform all signatory and acceding States of the date of each signature, the date of deposit of each instrument of ratification or of accession and the date of the entry into force of this Convention, and of the receipt of other notices.
6. This Convention shall be registered by the Depositary Governments pursuant to Article 102 of the Charter of the United Nations.

ARTICLE XV

This Convention, the English, Russian, French, Spanish and Chinese texts of which are equally authentic, shall be deposited in the archives of the Depositary Governments. Duly certified copies of the Convention shall be transmitted by the Depositary Governments to the Governments of the signatory and acceding States.

II-6. **Convention on the Prohibition of the Development, Production, Stockpiling and Use of Chemical Weapons and on their Destruction,** *signed at Paris,* **13 January 1993, S. TREATY DOC. NO. 103-21, 32 I.L.M. 800, entered into force 29 April 1997.** Languages: Arabic, Chinese, English, French, Russian and Spanish

Relevant Penal Characteristics & Penal Provisions

2. Implicit recognition of the penal nature of the act by establishing a duty to prohibit, prevent, prosecute, punish, or the like: Article VII (1)(a) and VII (1)(c)

3. Criminalization of the proscribed conduct: Article VII (1)(c)

4. Duty or right to prosecute: Article VII (1)(a)

5. Duty or right to punish the proscribed conduct: Article VII (1)(a) (implicit)

7. Duty or right to cooperate in prosecution, punishment (including judicial assistance): Article VII (2), (3)

8. Establishment of a criminal jurisdictional basis: Article VII (1)(a)

Applicability
War & Peace

Control
Regulation & Prohibition

State Signatories

Afghanistan; Albania; Algeria; Argentina; Armenia; Australia; Austria; Azerbaijan; Bahamas; Bahrain; Bangladesh; Belarus; Belgium; Benin; Bhutan; Bolivia; Bosnia and Herzegovina; Brazil; Brunei Darussalam; Bulgaria; Burkina Faso; Burundi; Cambodia; Cameroon; Canada; Cape Verde; Central African Republic; Chad; Chile; China; Colombia; Comoros; Congo; Cook Islands; Costa Rica; Cote d'Ivoire; Croatia; Cuba; Cyprus; Czech Republic; Democratic Republic of the Congo; Denmark; Djibouti; Dominica; Dominican Republic; Ecuador; El Salvador; Equatorial Guinea; Estonia; Ethiopia; Fiji; Finland; France; Gabon; the Gambia; Georgia; Germany; Ghana; Granada; Greece; Grenada; Guatemala; Guinea; Guinea-Bissau; Guyana; Haiti; the Holy See; Honduras; Hungary; Iceland;

India; Indonesia; Iran; Ireland; Israel; Italy; Jamaica; Japan; Kazakhstan; Kenya; Kuwait; Kyrgyzstan; Lao People's Democratic Republic; Latvia; Lesotho; Liberia; Liechtenstein; Lithuania; Luxembourg; Madagascar; Malawi; Malaysia; Maldives; Mali; Malta; Marshall Islands; Mauritania; Mauritius; Mexico; Micronesia; Monaco; Mongolia; Morocco; Myanmar; Namibia; Nauru; Nepal; Netherlands; New Zealand; Nicaragua; Niger; Nigeria; Norway; Oman; Pakistan; Panama; Papua New Guinea; Paraguay; Peru; the Philippines; Poland; Portugal; Qatar; Republic of Korea; Republic of Moldova; Romania; Russian Federation; Rwanda; Samoa; St. Kitts & Nevis; St. Lucia; St. Vincent & the Grenadines; San Marino; Saudi Arabia; Senegal; Seychelles; Sierra Leone; Singapore; Slovakia; Slovenia; South Africa; Spain; Sri Lanka; Suriname; Swaziland; Sweden; Switzerland; Tajikistan; Thailand; the former Yugoslav Republic of Macedonia; Togo; Tunisia; Turkey; Turkmenistan; Ukraine; Uganda; United Arab Emirates; United Kingdom of Great Britain and Northern Ireland; United Republic of Tanzania; United States of America; Uruguay; Uzbekistan; Venezuela; Vietnam; Yemen; Yugoslavia; Zaire; Zambia; Zimbabwe

State Parties

Albania; Algeria; Argentina; Armenia; Australia; Austria; Azerbaijan; Bahrain; Bangladesh; Belarus; Belgium; Benin; Bolivia; Bosnia & Herzegovina; Botswana; Brazil; Brunei Darussalam; Bulgaria; Burkina Faso; Burundi; Cameroon; Canada; Chile; China; Colombia; Cook Islands; Costa Rica; Cote d'Ivoire; Croatia; Cuba; Cyprus; Czech Republic; Denmark; Ecuador; El Salvador; Equatorial Guinea; Eritrea; Estonia; Ethiopia; Fiji; Finland; France; Gambia; Georgia; Germany; Ghana; Greece; Guinea; Guyana; Holy See; Hungary; Iceland; India; Indonesia; Ireland; Islamic Republic of Iran; Italy; Japan; Jordan; Kazakhstan; Kenya; Kuwait; Lao People's Democratic Republic; Latvia; Lesotho; Liechtenstein; Lithuania; Luxembourg; Malawi; Malaysia; Maldives; Mali; Malta; Mauritania; Mauritius; Mexico; Micronesia; Monaco; Mongolia; Morocco; Namibia; Nepal; the Netherlands; New Zealand; Nicaragua; Niger; Nigeria; Norway; Oman; Pakistan; Panama; Papua New Guinea; Paraguay; Peru; the Philippines; Poland; Portugal; Qatar; Republic of Korea; Republic of Moldovia; Romania; Russian Federation; Saint Lucia; San Marino; Saudi Arabia; Senegal; Seychelles; Singapore; Slovakia; Slovenia; South Africa; Spain; Sri Lanka; Sudan; Suriname; Swaziland; Sweden; Switzerland; Tajikistan; Turkmenistan; the former Yugoslav Republic pf Macedonia; Togo; Trinidad and Tobago; Tunisia; Turkey; Ukraine; United Kingdom of Great Britain & Northern Ireland; United Republic of Tanzania; United States of America; Uruguay; Uzbekistan; Venezuela; Viet Nam; Yugoslavia; Zimbabwe

Reservations upon Signature, Accession or Ratification

Austria; Belgium; China; Cuba; Denmark; France; Germany; Greece; Holy See; Ireland; Islamic Republic of Iran; Italy; Luxembourg; Netherlands; Pakistan; Portugal; Spain; Sudan; United Kingdom of Great Britain and Northern Ireland; United States of America

Full Text

PREAMBLE

The State Parties to this Convention,

Determined to act with a view to achieving effective progress towards general and complete disarmament under strict and effective international control, including the prohibition and elimination of all types of weapons of mass destruction,

Desiring to contribute to the realization of the purposes and principles of the Charter of the United Nations,

Recalling that the General Assembly of the United Nations has repeatedly condemned all actions contrary to the principles and objectives of the Protocol for the Prohibition of the Use in War of Asphyxiating, Poisonous or Other Gases, and of Bacteriological Methods of Warfare, signed at Geneva on 17 June 1925 (the Geneva Protocol of 1925),

Recognizing that this Convention reaffirms principles and objectives of and obligations assumed under the Geneva Protocol of 1925, and the Convention on the Prohibition of the Development, Production and Stockpiling of Bacteriological (Biological) and Toxin Weapons and on their Destruction signed at London, Moscow and Washington, on 10 April 1972,

Bearing in mind the objective contained in Article IX of the Convention on the Prohibition of the Development, Production and Stockpiling of Bacteriological (Biological) and Toxin Weapons and on their Destruction,

Determined for the sake of all mankind, to exclude completely the possibility of the use of chemical weapons, through the implementation of the provisions of this Convention, thereby complementing the obligations assumed under the Geneva Protocol of 1925,

Recognizing the prohibition, embodied in the pertinent agreements and relevant principles of international law, of the use of herbicides as a method of warfare,

Considering that achievements in the field of chemistry should be used exclusively for the benefit of mankind,

Desiring to promote free trade in chemicals as well as international cooperation and exchange of scientific and technical information in the field of chemical activities for purposes not prohibited under this Convention in order to enhance the economic and technological development of all States Parties,

Convinced that the complete and effective prohibition of the development, production, acquisition, stockpiling, retention, transfer and use of chemical weapons, and their destruction, represent a necessary step towards the achievement of these common objectives,
Have agreed as follows:

ARTICLE I
GENERAL OBLIGATIONS

1. Each State Party to this Convention undertakes never under any circumstances:
   (a) To develop, produce, otherwise acquire, stockpile or retain chemical weapons, or transfer, directly or indirectly, chemical weapons to anyone;
   (b) To use chemical weapons;
   (c) To engage in any military preparations to use chemical weapons;
   (d) To assist, encourage or induce, in any way, anyone to engage in any activity prohibited to a State Party under this Convention.

2. Each State Party undertakes to destroy chemical weapons it owns or possesses, or that are located in any place under its jurisdiction or control, in accordance with the provisions of this Convention.

3. Each State Party undertakes to destroy all chemical weapons it abandoned on the territory of another State Party, in accordance with the provisions of this Convention.

4. Each State Party undertakes to destroy any chemical weapons production facilities it owns or possesses, or that are located in any place under its jurisdiction or control, in accordance with the provisions of this Convention.

5. Each State Party undertakes not to use riot control agents as a method of warfare.

ARTICLE II
DEFINITIONS AND CRITERIA

For the purposes of this Convention:

1. "Chemical Weapons" means the following, together or separately:

   (a) Toxic chemicals and their precursors, except where intended for purposes not prohibited under this Convention, as long as the types and quantities are consistent with such purposes;

   (b) Munitions and devices, specifically designed to cause death or other harm through the toxic properties of those toxic chemicals specified in subparagraph (a), which would be released as a result of the employment of such munitions and devices;

   (c) Any equipment specifically designed for use directly in connection with the employment of munitions and devices specified in subparagraph (b).

2. "Toxic Chemical" means:

Any chemical which through its chemical action on life processes can cause death, temporary incapacitation or permanent harm to humans or animals. This includes all such chemicals, regardless of their origin or of their method of production, and regardless of whether they are produced in facilities, in munitions or elsewhere. (For the purpose of implementing this Convention, toxic chemicals which have been identified for the application of verification measures are listed in Schedules contained in the Annex on Chemicals.)

3. "Precursor" means:

Any chemical reactant which takes part at any stage in the production by whatever method of a toxic chemical. This includes any key component of a binary or multicomponent chemical system.

(For the purpose of implementing this Convention, precursors which have been identified for the application of verification measures are listed in Schedules contained in the Annex on Chemicals.)

4. "Key Component of Binary or Multicomponent Chemical Systems" (hereinafter referred to as "key component") means:

The precursor which plays the most important role in determining the toxic properties of the final product and reacts rapidly with other chemicals in the binary or multicomponent system.

5. "Old Chemical Weapons" means:

  (a) Chemical weapons which were produced before 1925; or

  (b) Chemical weapons produced in the period between 1925 and 1946 that have deteriorated to such extent that they can no longer be used as chemical weapons.

6. "Abandoned Chemical Weapons" means:

Chemical weapons, including old chemical weapons, abandoned by a State after 1 January 1925 on the territory of another State without the consent of the latter.

7. "Riot Control Agent" means:

Any chemical not listed in a Schedule, which can produce rapidly in humans sensory irritation or disabling physical effects which disappear within a short time following termination of exposure.

8. "Chemical Weapons Production Facility":

  (a) Means any equipment, as well as any building housing such equipment, that was designed, constructed or used at any time since 1 January 1946:

  (i) As part of the stage in the production of chemicals ("final technological stage") where the material flows would contain, when the equipment is in operation:

(1) Any chemical listed in Schedule 1 in the Annex on Chemicals;

or

(2) Any other chemical that has no use, above 1 tonne per year on the territory of a State Party or in any other place under the jurisdiction or control of a State Party, for purposes not prohibited under this Convention, but can be used for chemical weapons purposes;

or

(ii) For filling chemical weapons, including, inter alia, the filling of chemicals listed in Schedule 1 into munitions, devices or bulk storage containers; the filling of chemicals into containers that form part of assembled binary munitions and devices or into chemical submunitions that form part of assembled unitar munitions and devices, and the loading of the containers and chemical submunitions into the respective munitions and devices;

(b) Does not mean:

(i) Any facility having a production capacity for synthesis of chemicals specified in subparagraph (a) (i) that is less than 1 tonne;

(ii) Any facility in which a chemical specified in subparagraph (a) (i) is or was produced as an unavoidable by-product of activities for purposes not prohibited under this Convention, provided that the chemical does not exceed 3 per cent of the total product and that the facility is subject to declaration and inspection under the Annex on Implementation and Verification (hereinafter referred to as "Verification Annex"); or

(iii) The single small-scale facility for production of chemicals listed in Schedule 1 for purposes not prohibited under this Convention as referred to in Part VI of the Verification Annex.

9. "Purposes Not Prohibited Under this Convention" means:

(a) Industrial, agricultural, research, medical, pharmaceutical or other peaceful purposes;

(b) Protective purposes, namely those purposes directly related to protection against toxic chemicals and to protection against chemical weapons;

(c) Military purposes not connected with the use of chemical weapons and not dependent on the use of the toxic properties of chemicals as a method of warfare;

(d) Law enforcement including domestic riot control purposes.

10. "Production Capacity" means:

The annual quantitative potential for manufacturing a specific chemical based on the technological process actually used or, if the process is not yet operational, planned to be used at the relevant facility. It shall be deemed to be equal to the nameplate capacity or, if the nameplate capacity is not available, to the design capacity. The nameplate capacity is the product output under conditions optimized for maximum quantity for the production facility, as demonstrated by one or more test-runs. The design capacity is the corresponding theoretically calculated product output.

11. "Organization" means the Organization for the Prohibition of Chemical Weapons established pursuant to Article VIII of this Convention.

12. For the purposes of Article VI:

(a) "Production" of a chemical means its formation through chemical reaction;

(b) "Processing" of a chemical means a physical process, such as formulation, extraction and purification, in which a chemical is not converted into another chemical;

(c) "Consumption" of a chemical means its conversion into another chemical via a chemical reaction.

ARTICLE III
DECLARATIONS

1. Each State Party shall submit to the Organization, not later than 30 days after this Convention enters into force for it, he following declarations, in which it shall:

 (a) With respect to chemical weapons:

　　(i) Declare whether it owns or possesses any chemical weapons, or whether there are any chemical weapons located in any place under its jurisdiction or control;

　　(ii) Specify the precise location, aggregate quantity and detailed inventory of chemical weapons it owns or possesses, or that are located in any place under its jurisdiction or control, in accordance with Part IV (A), paragraphs 1 to 3, of the Verification Annex, except for those chemical weapons referred to in sub-subparagraph (iii);

　　(iii) Report any chemical weapons on its territory that are owned and possessed by another State and located in any place under the jurisdiction or control of another State, in accordance with Part IV (A), paragraph 4, of the Verification Annex;

　　(iv) Declare whether it has transferred or received, directly or indirectly, any chemical weapons since 1 January 1946 and specify the transfer or receipt of such weapons, in accordance with Part IV (A), paragraph 5, of the Verification Annex;

　　(v) Provide its general plan for destruction of chemical weapons that it owns or possesses, or that are located in any place under its jurisdiction or control, in accordance with Part IV (A), paragraph 6, of the Verification Annex;

 (b) With respect to old chemical weapons and abandoned chemical weapons:

　　(i) Declare whether it has on its territory old chemical weapons and provide all available information in accordance with Part IV (B), paragraph 3, of the Verification Annex;

(ii)Declare whether there are abandoned chemical weapons on its territory and provide all available information in accordance with Part IV (B), paragraph 8, of the Verification Annex;

(iii)Declare whether it has abandoned chemical weapons on the territory of other States and provide all available information in accordance with Part IV (B), paragraph 10, of the Verification Annex;

(c) With respect to chemical weapons production facilities:

(i) Declare whether it has or has had any chemical weapons production facility under its ownership or possession, or that is or has been located in any place under its jurisdiction or control at any time since 1 January 1946;

(ii)Specify any chemical weapons production facility it has or has had under its ownership or possession or that is or has been located in any place under its jurisdiction or control at any time since 1 January 1946, in accordance with Part V, paragraph 1, of the Verification Annex, except for those facilities referred to in sub-subparagraph (iii);

(iii)Report any chemical weapons production facility on its territory that another State has or has had under its ownership and possession and that is or has been located in any place under the jurisdiction or control of another State at any time since 1 January 1946, in accordance with Part V, paragraph 2, of the Verification Annex;

(iv)Declare whether it has transferred or received, directly or indirectly, any equipment for the production of chemical weapons since 1 January 1946 and specify the transfer or receipt of such equipment, in accordance with Part V, paragraphs 3 to 5, of the Verification Annex;

(v)Provide its general plan for destruction of any chemical weapons production facility it owns or possesses, or that is located in any place under its jurisdiction or control, in accordance with Part V, paragraph 6, of the Verification Annex;

(vi)Specify actions to be taken for closure of any chemical weapons production facility it owns or possesses, or that is located in any place under its jurisdiction or control, in accordance with Part V, paragraph 1 (i), of the Verification Annex;

(vii) Provide its general plan for any temporary conversion of any chemical weapons production facility it owns or possesses, or that is located in any place under its jurisdiction or control, into chemical weapons destruction facility, in accordance with Part V, paragraph 7, of the Verification Annex;

(d) With respect to other facilities: Specify the precise location, nature and general scope of activities of any facility or establishment under its ownership or possession, or located in any place under its jurisdiction or control, and that has been designed, constructed or used since 1 January 1946 primarily for development of chemical weapons. Such declaration shall include, inter alia, laboratories and test and evaluation sites;

(e) With respect to riot control agents: Specify the chemical name, structural formula and Chemical Abstracts Service (CAS) registry number, if assigned, of each chemical it holds for riot control purposes. This declaration shall be updated not later than 30 days after any change becomes effective.

2. The provisions of this Article and the relevant provisions of Part IV of the Verification Annex shall not, at the discretion of a State Party, apply to chemical weapons buried on its territory before 1 January 1977 and which remain buried, or which had been dumped at sea before 1 January 1985.

ARTICLE IV
CHEMICAL WEAPONS

1. The provisions of this Article and the detailed procedures for its implementation shall apply to all chemical weapons owned or possessed by a State Party, or that are located in any place under its jurisdiction or control, except old chemical weapons and abandoned chemical weapons to which Part IV (B) of the Verification Annex applies.

2. Detailed procedures for the implementation of this Article are set forth in the Verification Annex.

3. All locations at which chemical weapons specified in paragraph 1 are stored or destroyed shall be subject to systematic verification through on-site inspection

and monitoring with on-site instruments, in accordance with Part IV(A) of the Verification Annex.

4. Each State Party shall, immediately after the declaration under Article III, paragraph 1 (a), has been submitted, provide access to chemical weapons specified in paragraph 1 for the purpose of systematic verification of the declaration through on-site inspection. Thereafter, each State Party shall not remove any of these chemical weapons, except to a chemical weapons destruction facility. It shall provide access to such chemical weapons, for the purpose of systematic on-site verification.

5. Each State Party shall provide access to any chemical weapons destruction facilities and their storage areas, that it owns or possesses, or that are located in any place under its jurisdiction or control, for the purpose of systematic verification through on-site inspection and monitoring with on-site instruments.

6. Each State Party shall destroy all chemical weapons specified in paragraph 1 pursuant to the Verification Annex and in accordance with the agreed rate and sequence of destruction (hereinafter referred to as "order of destruction"). Such destruction shall begin not later than two years after this Convention enters into force for it and shall finish not later than 10 years after entry into force of this Convention. A State Party is not precluded from destroying such chemical weapons at a faster rate.

7. Each State Party shall:

(a) Submit detailed plans for the destruction of chemical weapons specified in paragraph 1 not later than 60 days before each annual destruction period begins, in accordance with Part IV (A), paragraph 29, of the Verification Annex; the detailed plans shall encompass all stocks to be destroyed during the next annual destruction period;

(b) Submit declarations annually regarding the implementation of its plans for destruction of chemical weapons specified in paragraph 1, not later than 60 days after the end of each annual destruction period; and

(c) Certify, not later than 30 days after the destruction process has been completed, that all chemical weapons specified in paragraph 1 have been destroyed.

8. If a State ratifies or accedes to this Convention after the 10-year period for destruction set forth in paragraph 6, it shall destroy chemical weapons specified in paragraph 1 as soon as possible. The order of destruction and procedures for stringent verification for such a State Party shall be determined by the Executive Council.

9. Any chemical weapons discovered by a State Party after the initial declaration of chemical weapons shall be reported, secured and destroyed in accordance with Part IV (A) of the Verification Annex.

10. Each State Party, during transportation, sampling, storage and destruction of chemical weapons, shall assign the highest priority to ensuring the safety of people and to protecting the environment.

Each State Party shall transport, sample, store and destroy chemical weapons in accordance with its national standards for safety and emissions.

11. Any State Party which has on its territory chemical weapons that are owned or possessed by another State, or that are located in any place under the jurisdiction or control of another State, shall make the fullest efforts to ensure that these chemical weapons are removed from its territory not later than one year after this Convention enters into force for it. If they are not removed within one year, the State Party may request the Organization and other States Parties to provide assistance in the destruction of these chemical weapons.

12. Each State Party undertakes to cooperate with other States Parties that request information or assistance on a bilateral basis or through the Technical Secretariat regarding methods and technologies for the safe and efficient destruction of chemical weapons.

13. In carrying out verification activities pursuant to this Article and Part IV (A) of the Verification Annex, the Organization shall consider measures to avoid unnecessary duplication of bilateral or multilateral agreements on verification of chemical weapons storage and their destruction among States Parties.

To this end, the Executive Council shall decide to limit verification to measures complementary to those undertaken pursuant to such a bilateral or multilateral agreement, if it considers that:

(a) Verification provisions of such an agreement are consistent with the verification provisions of this Article and Part IV (A) of the Verification Annex;

(b) Implementation of such an agreement provides for sufficient assurance of compliance with the relevant provisions of this Convention; and

(c) Parties to the bilateral or multilateral agreement keep the Organization fully informed about their verification activities.

14. If the Executive Council takes a decision pursuant to paragraph 13, the Organization shall have the right to monitor the implementation of the bilateral or multilateral agreement.

15. Nothing in paragraphs 13 and 14 shall affect the obligation of a State Party to provide declarations pursuant to Article III, this Article and Part IV (A) of the Verification Annex.

16. Each State Party shall meet the costs of destruction of chemical weapons it is obliged to destroy. It shall also meet the costs of verification of storage and destruction of these chemical weapons unless the Executive Council decides otherwise. If the Executive Council decides to limit verification measures of the Organization pursuant to paragraph 13, the costs of complementary verification and monitoring by the Organization shall be paid in accordance with the United Nations scale of assessment, as specified in Article VIII, paragraph 7.

17. The provisions of this Article and the relevant provisions of Part IV of the Verification Annex shall not, at the discretion of a State Party, apply to chemical weapons buried on its territory before 1 January 1977 and which remain buried, or which had been dumped at sea before 1 January 1985.

ARTICLE V
CHEMICAL WEAPONS PRODUCTION FACILITIES

1. The provisions of this Article and the detailed procedures for its implementation shall apply to any and all chemical weapons production facilities owned or possessed by a State Party, or that are located in any place under its

jurisdiction or control.

2. Detailed procedures for the implementation of this Article are set forth in the Verification Annex.

3. All chemical weapons production facilities specified in paragraph 1 shall be subject to systematic verification through on-site inspection and monitoring with on-site instruments in accordance with Part V of the Verification Annex.

4. Each State Party shall cease immediately all activity at chemical weapons production facilities specified in paragraph 1, except activity required for closure.

5. No State Party shall construct any new chemical weapons production facilities or modify any existing facilities for the purpose of chemical weapons production or for any other activity prohibited under this Convention.

6. Each State Party shall, immediately after the declaration under Article III, paragraph 1 (c), has been submitted, provide access to chemical weapons production facilities specified in paragraph 1, for the purpose of systematic verification of the declaration through on-site inspection

7. Each State Party shall:

(a) Close, not later than 90 days after this Convention enters into force for it, all chemical weapons production facilities specified in paragraph 1, in accordance with Part V of the Verification Annex, and give notice thereof; and

(b) Provide access to chemical weapons production facilities specified in paragraph 1, subsequent to closure, for the purpose of systematic verification through on-site inspection and monitoring with on-site instruments in order to ensure that the facility remains closed and is subsequently destroyed.

8. Each State Party shall destroy all chemical weapons production facilities specified in paragraph 1 and related facilities and equipment, pursuant to the Verification Annex and in accordance with an agreed rate and sequence of destruction (hereinafter referred to as "order of destruction"). Such destruction shall begin not later than one year after this Convention enters into force for it, and shall finish not later than 10 years after entry into force of this Convention. A

State Party is not precluded from destroying such facilities at a faster rate.

9. Each State Party shall:

(a) Submit detailed plans for destruction of chemical weapons production facilities specified in paragraph 1, not later than 180 days before the destruction of each facility begins;

(b) Submit declarations annually regarding the implementation of its plans for the destruction of all chemical weapons production facilities specified in paragraph 1, not later than 90 days after the end of each annual destruction period; and

(c) Certify, not later than 30 days after the destruction process has been completed, that all chemical weapons production facilities specified in paragraph 1 have been destroyed.

10. If a State ratifies or accedes to this Convention after the 10-year period bfor destruction set forth in paragraph 8, it shall destroy chemical weapons production facilities specified in paragraph 1 as soon as possible. The order of destruction and procedures for stringent verification for such a State Party shall be determined by the Executive Council.

11. Each State Party, during the destruction of chemical weapons production facilities, shall assign the highest priority to ensuring the safety of people and to protecting the environment. Each State Party shall destroy chemical weapons production facilities in accordance with its national standards for safety and emissions.

12. Chemical weapons production facilities specified in paragraph 1 may be temporarily converted for destruction of chemical weapons in accordance with Part V, paragraphs 18 to 25, of the Verification Annex. Such a converted facility must be destroyed as soon as it is no longer in use for destruction of chemical weapons but, in any case, not later than 10 years after entry into force of this Convention.

13. A State Party may request, in exceptional cases of compelling need, permission to use a chemical weapons production facility specified in paragraph 1 for purposes not prohibited under this Convention. Upon the recommendation of

the Executive Council, the Conference of the States Parties shall decide whether or not to approve the request and shall establish the conditions upon which approval is contingent in accordance with Part V, Section D, of the Verification Annex.

14. The chemical weapons production facility shall be converted in such a manner that the converted facility is not more capable of being reconverted into a chemical weapons production facility than any other facility used for industrial, agricultural, research, medical, pharmaceutical or other peaceful purposes not involving chemicals listed in Schedule 1.

15. All converted facilities shall be subject to systematic verification through on-site inspection and monitoring with on-site instruments in accordance with Part V, Section D, of the Verification Annex.

16. In carrying out verification activities pursuant to this Article and Part V of the Verification Annex, the Organization shall consider measures to avoid unnecessary duplication of bilateral or multilateral agreements on verification of chemical weapons production facilities and their destruction among States Parties.

To this end, the Executive Council shall decide to limit the verification to measures complementary to those undertaken pursuant to such a bilateral or multilateral agreement, if it considers that:

(a) Verification provisions of such an agreement are consistent with the verification provisions of this Article and Part V of the Verification Annex;

(b) Implementation of the agreement provides for sufficient assurance of compliance with the relevant provisions of this Convention; and

(c) Parties to the bilateral or multilateral agreement keep the Organization fully informed about their verification activities.

17. If the Executive Council takes a decision pursuant to paragraph 16, the Organization shall have the right to monitor the implementation of the bilateral or multilateral agreement.

18. Nothing in paragraphs 16 and 17 shall affect the obligation of a State Party to

make declarations pursuant to Article III, this Article and Part V of the Verification Annex.

19. Each State Party shall meet the costs of destruction of chemical weapons production facilities it is obliged to destroy. It shall also meet the costs of verification under this Article unless the Executive Council decides otherwise. If the Executive Council decides to limit verification measures of the Organization pursuant to paragraph 16, the costs of complementary verification and monitoring by the Organization shall be paid in accordance with the United Nations scale of assessment, as specified in Article VIII, paragraph 7.

ARTICLE VI
ACTIVITIES NOT PROHIBITED UNDER THIS CONVENTION

1. Each State Party has the right, subject to the provisions of this Convention, to develop, produce, otherwise acquire, retain, transfer and use toxic chemicals and their precursors for purposes not prohibited under this Convention.

2. Each State Party shall adopt the necessary measures to ensure that toxic chemicals and their precursors are only developed, produced, otherwise acquired, retained, transferred, or used within its territory or in any other place under its jurisdiction or control for purposes not prohibited under this Convention. To this end, and in order to verify that activities are in accordance with obligations under this Convention, each State Party shall subject toxic chemicals and their precursors listed in Schedules 1, 2 and 3 of the Annex on Chemicals, facilities related to such chemicals, and other facilities as specified in the Verification Annex, that are located on its territory or in any other place under its jurisdiction or control, to verification measures as provided in the Verification Annex.

3. Each State Party shall subject chemicals listed in Schedule 1 (hereinafter referred to as "Schedule 1 chemicals") to the prohibitions on production, acquisition, retention, transfer and use as specified in Part VI of the Verification Annex. It shall subject Schedule 1 chemicals and facilities specified in Part VI of the Verification Annex to systematic verification through on-site inspection and monitoring with on-site instruments in accordance with that Part of the Verification Annex.

4. Each State Party shall subject chemicals listed in Schedule 2 (hereinafter referred to as "Schedule 2 chemicals") and facilities specified in Part VII of the

Verification Annex to data monitoring and on-site verification in accordance with that Part of the Verification Annex.

5. Each State Party shall subject chemicals listed in Schedule 3 (hereinafter referred to as "Schedule 3 chemicals") and facilities specified in Part VIII of the Verification Annex to data monitoring and on-site verification in accordance with that Part of the Verification Annex.

6. Each State Party shall subject facilities specified in Part IX of the Verification Annex to data monitoring and eventual on-site verification in accordance with that Part of the Verification Annex unless decided otherwise by the Conference of the States Parties pursuant to Part IX, paragraph 22, of the Verification Annex.

7. Not later than 30 days after this Convention enters into force for it, each State Party shall make an initial declaration on relevant chemicals and facilities in accordance with the Verification Annex.

8. Each State Party shall make annual declarations regarding the relevant chemicals and facilities in accordance with the Verification Annex.

9. For the purpose of on-site verification, each State Party shall grant to the inspectors access to facilities as required in the Verification Annex.

10. In conducting verification activities, the Technical Secretariat shall avoid undue intrusion into the State Party's chemical activities for purposes not prohibited under this Convention and, in particular, abide by the provisions set forth in the Annex on the Protection of Confidential Information (hereinafter referred to as "Confidentiality Annex").

11. The provisions of this Article shall be implemented in a manner which avoids hampering the economic or technological development of States Parties, and international cooperation in the field of chemical activities for purposes not prohibited under this Convention including the international exchange of scientific and technical information and chemicals and equipment for the production, processing or use of chemicals for purposes not prohibited under this Convention.

ARTICLE VII
NATIONAL IMPLEMENTATION MEASURES

General undertakings

1. Each State Party shall, in accordance with its constitutional processes, adopt the necessary measures to implement its obligations under this Convention. In particular, it shall:

   (a) Prohibit natural and legal persons anywhere on its territory or in any other place under its jurisdiction as recognized by international law from undertaking any activity prohibited to a State Party under this Convention, including enacting penal legislation with respect to such activity;

   (b) Not permit in any place under its control any activity prohibited to a State Party under this Convention; and

   (c) Extend its penal legislation enacted under subparagraph (a) to any activity prohibited to a State Party under this Convention undertaken anywhere by natural persons, possessing its nationality, in conformity with international law.

2. Each State Party shall cooperate with other States Parties and afford the appropriate form of legal assistance to facilitate the implementation of the obligations under paragraph 1.

3. Each State Party, during the implementation of its obligations under this Convention, shall assign the highest priority to ensuring the safety of people and to protecting the environment, and shall cooperate as appropriate with other State Parties in this regard.

Relations between the State Party and the Organization

4. In order to fulfil its obligations under this Convention, each State Party shall designate or establish a National Authority to serve as the national focal point for effective liaison with the Organization and other States Parties. Each State Party shall notify the Organization of its National Authority at the time that this Convention enters into force for it.

5. Each State Party shall inform the Organization of the legislative and administrative measures taken to implement this Convention.

6. Each State Party shall treat as confidential and afford special handling to information and data that it receives in confidence from the Organization in connection with the implementation of this Convention. It shall treat such information and data exclusively in connection with its rights and obligations under this Convention and in accordance with the provisions set forth in the Confidentiality Annex.

7. Each State Party undertakes to cooperate with the Organization in the exercise of all its functions and in particular to provide assistance to the Technical Secretariat.

ARTICLE VIII
THE ORGANIZATION

A. GENERAL PROVISIONS

1. The States Parties to this Convention hereby establish the Organization for the Prohibition of Chemical Weapons to achieve the object and purpose of this Convention, to ensure the implementation of its provisions, including those for international verification of compliance with it, and to provide a forum for consultation and cooperation among States Parties.

2. All States Parties to this Convention shall be members of the Organization. A State Party shall not be deprived of its membership in the Organization.

3. The seat of the Headquarters of the Organization shall be The Hague, Kingdom of the Netherlands.

4. There are hereby established as the organs of the Organization: the Conference of the States Parties, the Executive Council, and the Technical Secretariat.

5. The Organization shall conduct its verification activities provided for under this Convention in the least intrusive manner possible consistent with the timely and efficient accomplishment of their objectives. It shall request only the information

and data necessary to fulfil its responsibilities under this Convention. It shall take every precaution to protect the confidentiality of information on civil and military activities and facilities coming to its knowledge in the implementation of this Convention and, in particular, shall abide by the provisions set forth in the Confidentiality Annex.

6. In undertaking its verification activities the Organization shall consider measures to make use of advances in science and technology.

7. The costs of the Organization's activities shall be paid by States Parties in accordance with the United Nations scale of assessment adjusted to take into account differences in membership between the United Nations and this Organization, and subject to the provisions of Articles IV and V. Financial contributions of States Parties to the Preparatory Commission shall be deducted in an appropriate way from their contributions to the regular budget. The budget of the Organization shall comprise two separate chapters, one relating to administrative and other costs, and one relating to verification costs.

8. A member of the Organization which is in arrears in the payment of its financial contribution to the Organization shall have no vote in the Organization if the amount of its arrears equals or exceeds the amount of the contribution due from it for the preceding two full years. The Conference of the States Parties may, nevertheless, permit such a member to vote if it is satisfied that the failure to pay is due to conditions beyond the control of the member.

B. THE CONFERENCE OF THE STATES PARTIES

Composition, procedures and decision-making

9. The Conference of the States Parties (hereinafter referred to as "the Conference") shall be composed of all members of this Organization. Each member shall have one representative in the Conference, who may be accompanied by alternates and advisers.

10. The first session of the Conference shall be convened by the depositary not later than 30 days after the entry into force of this Convention.

11. The Conference shall meet in regular sessions which shall be held annually unless it decides otherwise.

12. Special sessions of the Conference shall be convened:

(a) When decided by the Conference;

(b) When requested by the Executive Council;

(c) When requested by any member and supported by one third of the members; or

(d) In accordance with paragraph 22 to undertake reviews of the operation of this Convention.

Except in the case of subparagraph (d), the special session shall be convened not later than 30 days after receipt of the request by the Director-General of the Technical Secretariat, unless specified otherwise in the request.

13. The Conference shall also be convened in the form of an Amendment Conference in accordance with Article XV, paragraph 2.

14. Sessions of the Conference shall take place at the seat of the Organization unless the Conference decides otherwise.

15. The Conference shall adopt its rules of procedure. At the beginning of each regular session, it shall elect its Chairman and such other officers as may be required. They shall hold office until a new Chairman and other officers are elected at the next regular session.

16. A majority of the members of the Organization shall constitute a quorum for the Conference.

17. Each member of the Organization shall have one vote in the Conference.

18. The Conference shall take decisions on questions of procedure by a simple majority of the members present and voting. Decisions on matters of substance should be taken as far as possible by consensus. If consensus is not attainable when an issue comes up for decision, the Chairman shall defer any vote for 24 hours and during this period of deferment shall make every effort to facilitate achievement of consensus, and shall report to the Conference before the end of

this period. If consensus is not possible at the end of 24 hours, the Conference shall take the decision by a two-thirds majority of members present and voting unless specified otherwise in this Convention. When the issue arises as to whether the question is one of substance or not, that question shall be treated as a matter of substance unless otherwise decided by the Conference by the majority required for decisions on matters of substance.

Powers and functions

19. The Conference shall be the principal organ of the Organization. It shall consider any questions, matters or issues within the scope of this Convention, including those relating to the powers and functions of the Executive Council and the Technical Secretariat. It may make recommendations and take decisions on any questions, matters or issues related to this Convention raised by a State Party or brought to its attention by the Executive Council.

20. The Conference shall oversee the implementation of this Convention, and act in order to promote its object and purpose. The Conference shall review compliance with this Convention. It shall also oversee the activities of the Executive Council and the Technical Secretariat and may issue guidelines in accordance with this Convention to either of them in the exercise of their functions.

21. The Conference shall:

(a) Consider and adopt at its regular sessions the report, programme and budget of the Organization, submitted by the Executive Council, as well as consider other reports;

(b) Decide on the scale of financial contributions to be paid by States Parties in accordance with paragraph 7;

(c) Elect the members of the Executive Council;

(d) Appoint the Director-General of the Technical Secretariat (hereinafter referred to as "the Director-General");

(e) Approve the rules of procedure of the Executive Council submitted by the latter;

(f) Establish such subsidiary organs as it finds necessary for the exercise of its functions in accordance with this Convention;

(g) Foster international cooperation for peaceful purposes in the field of chemical activities;

(h) Review scientific and technological developments that could affect the operation of this Convention and, in this context, direct the Director-General to establish a Scientific Advisory Board to enable him, in the performance of his functions, to render specialized advice in areas of science and technology relevant to this Convention, to the Conference, the Executive Council or States Parties. The Scientific Advisory Board shall be composed of independent experts appointed in accordance with terms of reference adopted by the Conference;

(i) Consider and approve at its first session any draft agreements, provisions and guidelines developed by the Preparatory Commission;

(j) Establish at its first session the voluntary fund for assistance in accordance with Article X;

(k) Take the necessary measures to ensure compliance with this Convention and to redress and remedy any situation which contravenes the provisions of this Convention, in accordance with Article XII.

22. The Conference shall not later than one year after the expiry of the fifth and the tenth year after the entry into force of this Convention, and at such other times within that time period as may be decided upon, convene in special sessions to undertake reviews of the operation of this Convention. Such reviews shall take into account any relevant scientific and technological developments. At intervals of five years thereafter, unless otherwise decided upon, further sessions of the Conference shall be convened with the same objective.

C. THE EXECUTIVE COUNCIL

Composition, procedure and decision-making

23. The Executive Council shall consist of 41 members. Each State Party shall have the right, in accordance with the principle of rotation, to serve on the Executive Council. The members of the Executive Council shall be elected by the

Conference for a term of two years. In order to ensure the effective functioning of this Convention, due regard being specially paid to equitable geographical distribution, to the importance of chemical industry, as well as to political and security interests, the Executive Council shall be composed as follows:

(a) Nine States Parties from Africa to be designated by States Parties located in this region. As a basis for this designation it is understood that, out of these nine States Parties, three members shall, as a rule, be the States Parties with the most significant national chemical industry in the region as determined by internationally reported and published data; in addition, the regional group shall agree also to take into account other regional factors in designating these three members;

(b) Nine States Parties from Asia to be designated by States Parties located in this region. As a basis for this designation it is understood that, out of these nine States Parties, four members shall, as a rule, be the States Parties with the most significant national chemical industry in the region as determined by internationally reported and published data; in addition, the regional group shall agree also to take into account other regional factors in designating these four members;

(c) Five States Parties from Eastern Europe to be designated by States Parties located in this region. As a basis for this designation it is understood that, out of these five States Parties, one member shall, as a rule, be the State Party with the most significant national chemical industry in the region as determined by internationally reported and published data; in addition, the regional group shall agree also to take into account other regional factors in designating this one member;

(d) Seven States Parties from Latin America and the Caribbean to be designated by States Parties located in this region. As a basis for this designation it is understood that, out of these seven States Parties, three members shall, as a rule, be the States Parties with the most significant national chemical industry in the region as determined by internationally reported and published data; in addition, the regional group shall agree also to take into account other regional factors in designating these three members;

(e) Ten States Parties from among Western European and other States to be designated by States Parties located in this region. As a basis for this designation it is understood that, out of these 10 States Parties, 5 members shall, as a rule, be the States Parties with the most significant national chemical industry in the region as determined by internationally reported and published data; in addition, the regional group shall agree also to take into account other regional factors in designating these five members;

(f) One further State Party to be designated consecutively by States Parties located in the regions of Asia and Latin America and the Caribbean. As a basis for this designation it is understood that this State Party shall be a rotating member from these regions.

24. For the first election of the Executive Council 20 members shall be elected for a term of one year, due regard being paid to the established numerical proportions as described in paragraph 23.

25. After the full implementation of Articles IV and V the Conference may, upon the request of a majority of the members of the Executive Council, review the composition of the Executive Council taking into account developments related to the principles specified in paragraph 23 that are governing its composition.

26. The Executive Council shall elaborate its rules of procedure and submit them to the Conference for approval.

27. The Executive Council shall elect its Chairman from among its members.

28. The Executive Council shall meet for regular sessions. Between regular sessions it shall meet as often as may be required for the fulfilment of its powers and functions.

29. Each member of the Executive Council shall have one vote. Unless otherwise specified in this Convention, the Executive Council shall take decisions on matters of substance by a two-thirds majority of all its members. The Executive Council shall take decisions on questions of procedure by a simple majority of all its members. When the issue arises as to whether the question is one of substance or not, that question shall be treated as a matter of substance unless otherwise decided by the Executive Council by the majority required for decisions on matters of substance.

Powers and functions

30. The Executive Council shall be the executive organ of the Organization. It shall be responsible to the Conference. The Executive Council shall carry out the powers and functions entrusted to it under this Convention, as well as those functions delegated to it by the Conference. In so doing, it shall act in conformity with the recommendations, decisions and guidelines of the Conference and assure their proper and continuous implementation.

31. The Executive Council shall promote the effective implementation of, and compliance with, this Convention. It shall supervise the activities of the Technical Secretariat, cooperate with the National Authority of each State Party and facilitate consultations and cooperation among States Parties at their request.

32. The Executive Council shall:

(a) Consider and submit to the Conference the draft programme and budget of the Organization;

(b) Consider and submit to the Conference the draft report of the Organization on the implementation of this Convention, the report on the performance of its own activities and such special reports as it deems necessary or which the Conference may request;

(c) Make arrangements for the sessions of the Conference including the preparation of the draft agenda.

33. The Executive Council may request the convening of a special session of the Conference.

34. The Executive Council shall:

(a) Conclude agreements or arrangements with States and international organizations on behalf of the Organization, subject to prior approval by the Conference;

(b) Conclude agreements with States Parties on behalf of the Organization in connection with Article X and supervise the voluntary fund referred to in Article X;

(c) Approve agreements or arrangements relating to the implementation of verification activities, negotiated by the Technical Secretariat with States Parties.

35. The Executive Council shall consider any issue or matter within its competence affecting this Convention and its implementation, including concerns regarding compliance, and cases of non-compliance, and, as appropriate, inform States Parties and bring the issue or matter to the attention of the Conference.

36. In its consideration of doubts or concerns regarding compliance and cases of non-compliance, including, inter alia, abuse of the rights provided for under this Convention, the Executive Council shall consult with the States Parties involved and, as appropriate, request the State Party to take measures to redress the situation within a specified time. To the extent that the Executive Council considers further action to be necessary, it shall take, inter alia, one or more of the following measures.

(a) Inform all States Parties of the issue or matter;

(b) Bring the issue or matter to the attention of the Conference;

(c) Make recommendations to the Conference regarding measures to redress the situation and to ensure compliance.

The Executive Council shall, in cases of particular gravity and urgency, bring the issue or matter, including relevant information and conclusions, directly to the attention of the United Nations General Assembly and the United Nations Security Council. It shall at the same time inform all States Parties of this step.

D. THE TECHNICAL SECRETARIAT

37. The Technical Secretariat shall assist the Conference and the Executive Council in the performance of their functions. The Technical Secretariat shall carry out the verification measures provided for in this Convention. It shall carry out the other functions entrusted to it under this Convention as well as those functions delegated to it by the Conference and the Executive Council.

38. The Technical Secretariat shall:

(a) Prepare and submit to the Executive Council the draft programme and budget of the Organization;

(b) Prepare and submit to the Executive Council the draft report of the Organization on the implementation of this Convention and such other reports as the Conference or the Executive Council may request;

(c) Provide administrative and technical support to the Conference, the Executive Council and subsidiary organs;

(d) Address and receive communications on behalf of the Organization to and from States Parties on matters pertaining to the implementation of this Convention;

(e) Provide technical assistance and technical evaluation to States Parties in the implementation of the provisions of this Convention, including evaluation of scheduled and unscheduled chemicals.

39. The Technical Secretariat shall:

(a) Negotiate agreements or arrangements relating to the implementation of verification activities with States Parties, subject to approval by the Executive Council;

(b) Not later than 180 days after entry into force of this Convention, coordinate the establishment and maintenance of permanent stockpiles of emergency and humanitarian assistance by States Parties in accordance with Article X, paragraphs 7 (b) and (c). The Technical Secretariat may inspect the items maintained for serviceability. Lists of items to be stockpiled shall be considered and approved by the Conference pursuant to paragraph 21(i) above;

(c) Administer the voluntary fund referred to in Article X, compile declarations made by the States Parties and register, when requested, bilateral agreements concluded between States Parties or between a State Party and the Organization for the purposes of Article X.

40. The Technical Secretariat shall inform the Executive Council of any problem that has arisen with regard to the discharge of its functions, including doubts, ambiguities or uncertainties about compliance with this Convention that have come to its notice in the performance of its verification activities and that it has been unable to resolve or clarify through its consultations with the State Party

concerned.

41. The Technical Secretariat shall comprise a Director-General, who shall be its head and chief administrative officer, inspectors and such scientific, technical and other personnel as may be required.

42. The Inspectorate shall be a unit of the Technical Secretariat and shall act under the supervision of the Director-General.

43. The Director-General shall be appointed by the Conference upon the recommendation of the Executive Council for a term of four years, renewable for one further term, but not thereafter.

44. The Director-General shall be responsible to the Conference and the Executive Council for the appointment of the staff and the organization and functioning of the Technical Secretariat. The paramount consideration in the employment of the staff and in the determination of the conditions of service shall be the necessity of securing the highest standards of efficiency, competence and integrity. Only citizens of States Parties shall serve as the Director-General, as inspectors or as other members of the professional and clerical staff. Due regard shall be paid to the importance of recruiting the staff on as wide a geographical basis as possible. Recruitment shall be guided by the principle that the staff shall be kept to a minimum necessary for the proper discharge of the responsibilities of the Technical Secretariat.

45. The Director-General shall be responsible for the organization and functioning of the Scientific Advisory Board referred to in paragraph 21 (h). The Director-General shall, in consultation with States Parties, appoint members of the Scientific Advisory Board, who shall serve in their individual capacity. The members of the Board shall be appointed on the basis of their expertise in the particular scientific fields relevant to the implementation of this Convention. The Director-General may also, as appropriate, in consultation with members of the Board, establish temporary working groups of scientific experts to provide recommendations on specific issues. In regard to the above, States Parties may submit lists of experts to the Director-General.

46. In the performance of their duties, the Director-General, the inspectors and the other members of the staff shall not seek or receive instructions from any Government or from any other source external to the Organization. They shall

refrain from any action that might reflect on their positions as international officers responsible only to the Conference and the Executive Council.

47. Each State Party shall respect the exclusively international character of the responsibilities of the Director-General, the inspectors and the other members of the staff and not seek to influence them in the discharge of their responsibilities.

E. PRIVILEGES AND IMMUNITIES

48. The Organization shall enjoy on the territory and in any other place under the jurisdiction or control of a State Party such legal capacity and such privileges and immunities as are necessary for the exercise of its functions.

49. Delegates of States Parties, together with their alternates and advisers, representatives appointed to the Executive Council together with their alternates and advisers, the Director-General and the staff of the Organization shall enjoy such privileges and immunities as are necessary in the independent exercise of their functions in connection with the Organization.

50. The legal capacity, privileges, and immunities referred to in this Article shall be defined in agreements between the Organization and the States Parties as well as in an agreement between the Organization and the State in which the headquarters of the Organization is seated. These agreements shall be considered and approved by the Conference pursuant to paragraph 21 (i).

51. Notwithstanding paragraphs 48 and 49, the privileges and immunities enjoyed by the Director-General and the staff of the Technical Secretariat during the conduct of verification activities shall be those set forth in Part II, Section B, of the Verification Annex.

ARTICLE IX
CONSULTATIONS, COOPERATION AND FACT-FINDING

1. States Parties shall consult and cooperate, directly among themselves, or through the Organization or other appropriate international procedures, including procedures within the framework of the United Nations and in accordance with its Charter, on any matter which may be raised relating to the object and purpose, or the implementation of the provisions, of this Convention.

2. Without prejudice to the right of any State Party to request a challenge inspection, States Parties should, whenever possible, first make every effort to clarify and resolve, through exchange of information and consultations among themselves, any matter which may cause doubt about compliance with this Convention, or which gives rise to concerns about a related matter which may be considered ambiguous. A State Party which receives a request from another State Party for clarification of any matter which the requesting State Party believes causes such a doubt or concern shall provide the requesting State Party as soon as possible, but in any case not later than 10 days after the request, with information sufficient to answer the doubt or concern raised along with an explanation of how the information provided resolves the matter. Nothing in this Convention shall affect the right of any two or more States Parties to arrange by mutual consent for inspections or any other procedures among themselves to clarify and resolve any matter which may cause doubt about compliance or gives rise to a concern about a related matter which may be considered ambiguous. Such arrangements shall not affect the rights and obligations of any State Party under other provisions of this Convention.

Procedure for requesting clarification

3. A State Party shall have the right to request the Executive Council to assist in clarifying any situation which may be considered ambiguous or which gives rise to a concern about the possible non-compliance of another State Party with this Convention. The Executive Council shall provide appropriate information in its possession relevant to such a concern.

4. A State Party shall have the right to request the Executive Council to obtain clarification from another State Party on any situation which may be considered ambiguous or which gives rise to a concern about its possible non-compliance with this Convention. In such a case, the following shall apply:

(a) The Executive Council shall forward the request for clarification to the State Party concerned through the Director-General not later than 24 hours after its receipt;

(b) The requested State Party shall provide the clarification to the Executive Council as soon as possible, but in any case not later than 10 days after the receipt of the request;

(c) The Executive Council shall take note of the clarification and forward it to the requesting State Party not later than 24 hours after its receipt;

(d) If the requesting State Party deems the clarification to be inadequate, it shall have the right to request the Executive Council to obtain from the requested State Party further clarification;

(e) For the purpose of obtaining further clarification requested under subparagraph (d), the Executive Council may call on the Director-General to establish a group of experts from the Technical Secretariat, or if appropriate staff are not available in the Technical Secretariat, from elsewhere, to examine all available information and data relevant to the situation causing the concern. The group of experts shall submit a factual report to the Executive Council on its findings;

(f) If the requesting State Party considers the clarification obtained under subparagraphs (d) and (e) to be unsatisfactory, it shall have the right to request a special session of the Executive Council in which States Parties involved that are not members of the Executive Council shall be entitled to take part. In such a special session, the Executive Council shall consider the matter and may recommend any measure it deems appropriate to resolve the situation.

5. A State Party shall also have the right to request the Executive Council to clarify any situation which has been considered ambiguous or has given rise to a concern about its possible non-compliance with this Convention. The Executive Council shall respond by providing such assistance as appropriate.

6. The Executive Council shall inform the States Parties about any request for clarification provided in this Article.

7. If the doubt or concern of a State Party about a possible non-compliance has not been resolved within 60 days after the submission of the request for clarification to the Executive Council, or it believes its doubts warrant urgent consideration, notwithstanding its right to request a challenge inspection, it may request a special session of the Conference in accordance with Article VIII, paragraph 12 (c). At such a special session, the Conference shall consider the matter and may recommend any measure it deems appropriate to resolve the situation.

Procedures for challenge inspections

8. Each State Party has the right to request an on-site challenge inspection of any facility or location in the territory or in any other place under the jurisdiction or control of any other State Party for the sole purpose of clarifying and resolving any questions concerning possible non-compliance with the provisions of this Convention, and to have this inspection conducted anywhere without delay by an inspection team designated by the Director-General and in accordance with the Verification Annex.

9. Each State Party is under the obligation to keep the inspection request within the scope of this Convention and to provide in the inspection request all appropriate information on the basis of which a concern has arisen regarding possible non-compliance with this Convention as specified in the Verification Annex. Each State Party shall refrain from unfounded inspection requests, care being taken to avoid abuse. The challenge inspection shall be carried out for the sole purpose of determining facts relating to the possible non-compliance.

10. For the purpose of verifying compliance with the provisions of this Convention, each State Party shall permit the Technical Secretariat to conduct the on-site challenge inspection pursuant to paragraph 8.

11. Pursuant to a request for a challenge inspection of a facility or location, and in accordance with the procedures provided for in the Verification Annex, the inspected State Party shall have.

    (a) The right and the obligation to make every reasonable effort to demonstrate its compliance with this Convention and, to this end, to enable the inspection team to fulfil its mandate;

    (b) The obligation to provide access within the requested site for the sole purpose of establishing facts relevant to the concern regarding possible non-compliance; and

    (c) The right to take measures to protect sensitive installations, and to prevent disclosure of confidential information and data, not related to this Convention.

12. With regard to an observer, the following shall apply:

(a) The requesting State Party may, subject to the agreement of the inspected State Party, send a representative who may be a national either of the requesting State Party or of a third State Party, to observe the conduct of the challenge inspection.

(b) The inspected State Party shall then grant access to the observer in accordance with the Verification Annex.

(c) The inspected State Party shall, as a rule, accept the proposed observer, but if the inspected State Party exercises a refusal, that fact shall be recorded in the final report.

13. The requesting State Party shall present an inspection request for an on-site challenge inspection to the Executive Council and at the same time to the Director-General for immediate processing.

14. The Director-General shall immediately ascertain that the inspection request meets the requirements specified in Part X, paragraph 4, of the Verification Annex, and, if necessary, assist the requesting State Party in filing the inspection request accordingly. When the inspection request fulfils the requirements, preparations for the challenge inspection shall begin.

15. The Director-General shall transmit the inspection request to the inspected State Party not less than 12 hours before the planned arrival of the inspection team at the point of entry.

16. After having received the inspection request, the Executive Council shall take cognizance of the Director-General's actions on the request and shall keep the case under its consideration throughout the inspection procedure. However, its deliberations shall not delay the inspection process.

17. The Executive Council may, not later than 12 hours after having received the inspection request, decide by a three-quarter majority of all its members against carrying out the challenge inspection, if it considers the inspection request to be frivolous, abusive or clearly beyond the scope of this Convention as described in paragraph 8. Neither the requesting nor the inspected State Party shall participate in such a decision. If the Executive Council decides against the challenge inspection, preparations shall be stopped, no further action on the inspection request shall be taken, and the States Parties concerned shall be informed accordingly.

18. The Director-General shall issue an inspection mandate for the conduct of the challenge inspection. The inspection mandate shall be the inspection request referred to in paragraphs 8 and 9 put into operational terms, and shall conform with the inspection request.

19. The challenge inspection shall be conducted in accordance with Part X or, in the case of alleged use, in accordance with Part XI of the Verification Annex. The inspection team shall be guided by the principle of conducting the challenge inspection in the least intrusive manner possible, consistent with the effective and timely accomplishment of its mission.

20. The inspected State Party shall assist the inspection team throughout the challenge inspection and facilitate its task. If the inspected State Party proposes, pursuant to Part X, Section C, of the Verification Annex, arrangements to demonstrate compliance with this Convention, alternative to full and comprehensive access, it shall make every reasonable effort, through consultations with the inspection team, to reach agreement on the modalities for establishing the facts with the aim of demonstrating its compliance.

21. The final report shall contain the factual findings as well as an assessment by the inspection team of the degree and nature of access and cooperation granted for the satisfactory implementation of the challenge inspection. The Director-General shall promptly transmit the final report of the inspection team to the requesting State Party, to the inspected State Party, to the Executive Council and to all other States Parties. The Director-General shall further transmit promptly to the Executive Council the assessments of the requesting and of the inspected States Parties, as well as the views of other States Parties which may be conveyed to the Director-General for that purpose, and then provide them to all States Parties.

22. The Executive Council shall, in accordance with its powers and functions, review the final report of the inspection team as soon as it is presented, and address any concerns as to:

(a) Whether any non-compliance has occurred;

(b) Whether the request had been within the scope of this Convention; and

(c) Whether the right to request a challenge inspection had been abused.

23. If the Executive Council reaches the conclusion, in keeping with its powers and functions, that further action may be necessary with regard to paragraph 22, it shall take the appropriate measures to redress the situation and to ensure compliance with this Convention, including specific recommendations to the Conference. In the case of abuse, the Executive Council shall examine whether the requesting State Party should bear any of the financial implications of the challenge inspection.

24. The requesting State Party and the inspected State Party shall have the right to participate in the review process. The Executive Council shall inform the States Parties and the next session of the Conference of the outcome of the process.

25. If the Executive Council has made specific recommendations to the Conference, the Conference shall consider action in accordance with Article XII.

ARTICLE X
ASSISTANCE AND PROTECTION AGAINST CHEMICAL WEAPONS

1. For the purposes of this Article, "Assistance" means the coordination and delivery to States Parties of protection against chemical weapons, including, inter alia, the following: detection equipment and alarm systems; protective equipment; decontamination equipment and decontaminants; medical antidotes and treatments; and advice on any of these protective measures.

2. Nothing in this Convention shall be interpreted as impeding the right of any State Party to conduct research into, develop, produce, acquire, transfer or use means of protection against chemical weapons, for purposes not prohibited under this Convention.

3. Each State Party undertakes to facilitate, and shall have the right to participate in, the fullest possible exchange of equipment, material and scientific and technological information concerning means of protection against chemical weapons.

4. For the purposes of increasing the transparency of national programmes related to protective purposes, each State Party shall provide annually to the Technical Secretariat information on its programme, in accordance with procedures to be

considered and approved by the Conference pursuant to Article VIII, paragraph 21 (i).

5. The Technical Secretariat shall establish, not later than 180 days after entry into force of this Convention and maintain, for the use of any requesting State Party, a data bank containing freely available information concerning various means of protection against chemical weapons as well as such information as may be provided by States Parties.

The Technical Secretariat shall also, within the resources available to it, and at the request of a State Party, provide expert advice and assist the State Party in identifying how its programmes for the development and improvement of a protective capacity against chemical weapons could be implemented.

6. Nothing in this Convention shall be interpreted as impeding the right of States Parties to request and provide assistance bilaterally and to conclude individual agreements with other States Parties concerning the emergency procurement of assistance.

7. Each State Party undertakes to provide assistance through the Organization and to this end to elect to take one or more of the following measures:

(a) To contribute to the voluntary fund for assistance to be established by the Conference at its first session;

(b) To conclude, if possible not later than 180 days after this Convention enters into force for it, agreements with the Organization concerning the procurement, upon demand, of assistance;

(c) To declare, not later than 180 days after this Convention enters into force for it, the kind of assistance it might provide in response to an appeal by the Organization. If, however, a State Party subsequently is unable to provide the assistance envisaged in its declaration, it is still under the obligation to provide assistance in accordance with this paragraph.

8. Each State Party has the right to request and, subject to the procedures set forth in paragraphs 9, 10 and 11, to receive assistance and protection against the use or threat of use of chemical weapons if it considers that:

(a) Chemical weapons have been used against it;

(b) Riot control agents have been used against it as a method of warfare; or

(c) It is threatened by actions or activities of any State that are prohibited for States Parties by Article I.

9. The request, substantiated by relevant information, shall be submitted to the Director-General, who shall transmit it immediately to the Executive Council and to all States Parties. The Director-General shall immediately forward the request to States Parties which have volunteered, in accordance with paragraphs 7 (b) and (c), to dispatch emergency assistance in case of use of chemical weapons or use of riot control agents as a method of warfare, or humanitarian assistance in case of serious threat of use of chemical weapons or serious threat of use of riot control agents as a method of warfare to the State Party concerned not later than 12 hours after receipt of the request. The Director-General shall initiate, not later than 24 hours after receipt of the request, an investigation in order to provide foundation for further action. He shall complete the investigation within 72 hours and forward a report to the Executive Council. If additional time is required for completion of the investigation, an interim report shall be submitted within the same time-frame. The additional time required for investigation shall not exceed 72 hours. It may, however, be further extended by similar periods. Reports at the end of each additional period shall be submitted to the Executive Council. The investigation shall, as appropriate and in conformity with the request and the information accompanying the request, establish relevant facts related to the request as well as the type and scope of supplementary assistance and protection needed.

10. The Executive Council shall meet not later than 24 hours after receiving an investigation report to consider the situation and shall take a decision by simple majority within the following 24 hours on whether to instruct the Technical Secretariat to provide supplementary assistance. The Technical Secretariat shall immediately transmit to all States Parties and relevant international organizations the investigation report and the decision taken by the Executive Council. When so decided by the Executive Council, the Director-General shall provide assistance immediately. For this purpose, the Director-General may cooperate with the requesting State Party, other States Parties and relevant international organizations. The States Parties shall make the fullest possible efforts to provide assistance.

11. If the information available from the ongoing investigation or other reliable sources would give sufficient proof that there are victims of use of chemical weapons and immediate action is indispensable, the Director-General shall notify all States Parties and shall take emergency measures

of assistance, using the resources the Conference has placed at his disposal for such contingencies. The Director-General shall keep the Executive Council informed of actions undertaken pursuant to this paragraph.

ARTICLE XI
ECONOMIC AND TECHNOLOGICAL DEVELOPMENT

1. The provisions of this Convention shall be implemented in a manner which avoids hampering the economic or technological development of States Parties, and international cooperation in the field of chemical activities for purposes not prohibited under this Convention including the international exchange of scientific and technical information and chemicals and equipment for the production, processing or use of chemicals for purposes not prohibited under this Convention.

2. Subject to the provisions of this Convention and without prejudice to the principles and applicable rules of international law, the States Parties shall:

  (a) Have the right, individually or collectively, to conduct research with, to develop, produce, acquire, retain, transfer, and use chemicals;

  (b) Undertake to facilitate, and have the right to participate in, the fullest possible exchange of chemicals, equipment and scientific and technical information relating to the development and application of chemistry for purposes not prohibited under this Convention;

  (c) Not maintain among themselves any restrictions, including those in any international agreements, incompatible with the obligations undertaken under this Convention, which would restrict or impede trade and the development and promotion of scientific and technological knowledge in the field of chemistry for industrial, agricultural, research, medical, pharmaceutical or other peaceful purposes;

(d) Not use this Convention as grounds for applying any measures other than those provided for, or permitted, under this Convention nor use any other international agreement for pursuing an objective inconsistent with this Convention;

(e) Undertake to review their existing national regulations in the field of trade in chemicals in order to render them consistent with the object and purpose of this Convention.

ARTICLE XII
MEASURES TO REDRESS A SITUATION AND TO ENSURE COMPLIANCE, INCLUDING SANCTIONS

1. The Conference shall take the necessary measures, as set forth in paragraphs 2, 3 and 4, to ensure compliance with this Convention and to redress and remedy any situation which contravenes the provisions of this Convention. In considering action pursuant to this paragraph, the Conference shall take into account all information and recommendations on the issues submitted by the Executive Council.

2. In cases where a State Party has been requested by the Executive Council to take measures to redress a situation raising problems with regard to its compliance, and where the State Party fails to fulfil the request within the specified time, the Conference may, inter alia, upon the recommendation of the Executive Council, restrict or suspend the State Party's rights and privileges under this Convention until it undertakes the necessary action to conform with its obligations under this Convention.

3. In cases where serious damage to the object and purpose of this Convention may result from activities prohibited under this Convention, in particular by Article I, the Conference may recommend collective measures to States Parties in conformity with international law.

4. The Conference shall, in cases of particular gravity, bring the issue, including relevant information and conclusions, to the attention of the United Nations General Assembly and the United Nations Security Council.

ARTICLE XIII
RELATION TO OTHER INTERNATIONAL AGREEMENTS

Nothing in this Convention shall be interpreted as in any way limiting or detracting from the obligations assumed by any State under the Protocol for the Prohibition of the Use in War of Asphyxiating, Poisonous or Other Gases, and of Bacteriological Methods of Warfare, signed at Geneva on 17 June 1925, and under the Convention on the Prohibition of the Development, Production and Stockpiling of Bacteriological (Biological) and Toxin Weapons and on Their Destruction, signed at London, Moscow and Washington on 10 April 1972.

ARTICLE XIV
SETTLEMENT OF DISPUTES

1. Disputes that may arise concerning the application or the interpretation of this Convention shall be settled in accordance with the relevant provisions of this Convention and in conformity with the provisions of the Charter of the United Nations.

2. When a dispute arises between two or more States Parties, or between one or more States Parties and the Organization, relating to the interpretation or application of this Convention, the parties concerned shall consult together with a view to the expeditious settlement of the dispute by negotiation or by other peaceful means of the parties' choice, including recourse to appropriate organs of this Convention and, by mutual consent, referral to the International Court of Justice in conformity with the Statute of the Court. The States Parties involved shall keep the Executive Council informed of actions being taken.

3. The Executive Council may contribute to the settlement of a dispute by whatever means it deems appropriate, including offering its good offices, calling upon the States Parties to a dispute to start the settlement process of their choice and recommending a time-limit for any agreed procedure.

4. The Conference shall consider questions related to disputes raised by States Parties or brought to its attention by the Executive Council. The Conference shall,

as it finds necessary, establish or entrust organs with tasks related to the settlement of these disputes in conformity with Article VIII, paragraph 21 (f).

5. The Conference and the Executive Council are separately empowered, subject to authorization from the General Assembly of the United Nations, to request the International Court of Justice to give an advisory opinion on any legal question arising within the scope of the activities of the Organization. An agreement between the Organization and the United Nations shall be concluded for this purpose in accordance with Article VIII, paragraph 34 (a).

6. This Article is without prejudice to Article IX or to the provisions on measures to redress a situation and to ensure compliance, including sanctions.

ARTICLE XV
AMENDMENTS

1. Any State Party may propose amendments to this Convention. Any State Party may also propose changes, as specified in paragraph 4, to the Annexes of this Convention. Proposals for amendments shall be subject to the procedures in paragraphs 2 and 3. Proposals for changes, as specified in paragraph 4, shall be subject to the procedures in paragraph 5.

2. The text of a proposed amendment shall be submitted to the Director-General for circulation to all States Parties and to the Depositary. The proposed amendment shall be considered only by an Amendment Conference. Such an Amendment Conference shall be convened if one third or more of the States Parties notify the Director-General not later than 30 days after its circulation that they support further consideration of the proposal. The Amendment Conference shall be held immediately following a regular session of the Conference unless the requesting States Parties ask for an earlier meeting. In no case shall an Amendment Conference be held less than 60 days after the circulation of the proposed amendment.

3. Amendments shall enter into force for all States Parties 30 days after deposit of the instruments of ratification or acceptance by all the States Parties referred to under subparagraph (b) below:

 (a) When adopted by the Amendment Conference by a positive vote of a majority of all States Parties with no State Party casting a negative vote; and

(b) Ratified or accepted by all those States Parties casting a positive vote at the Amendment Conference.

4. In order to ensure the viability and the effectiveness of this Convention, provisions in the Annexes shall be subject to changes in accordance with paragraph 5, if proposed changes are related only to matters of an administrative or technical nature. All changes to the Annex on Chemicals shall be made in accordance with paragraph 5. Sections A and C of the Confidentiality Annex, Part X of the Verification Annex, and those definitions in Part I of the Verification Annex which relate exclusively to challenge inspections, shall not be subject to changes in accordance with paragraph 5.

5. Proposed changes referred to in paragraph 4 shall be made in accordance with the following procedures:

(a) The text of the proposed changes shall be transmitted together with the necessary information to the Director-General. Additional information for the evaluation of the proposal may be provided by any State Party and the Director-General. The Director-General shall promptly communicate any such proposals and information to all States Parties, the Executive Council and the Depositary;

(b) Not later than 60 days after its receipt, the Director-General shall evaluate the proposal to determine all its possible consequences for the provisions of this Convention and its implementation and shall communicate any such information to all States Parties and the Executive Council;

(c) The Executive Council shall examine the proposal in the light of all information available to it, including whether the proposal fulfils the requirements of paragraph 4. Not later than 90 days after its receipt, the Executive Council shall notify its recommendation, with appropriate explanations, to all States Parties for consideration. States Parties shall acknowledge receipt within 10 days;

(d) If the Executive Council recommends to all States Parties that the proposal be adopted, it shall be considered approved if no State Party objects to it within 90 days after receipt of the recommendation. If the Executive Council recommends that the proposal be rejected, it shall be considered rejected if no

State Party objects to the rejection within 90 days after receipt of the recommendation;

(e) If a recommendation of the Executive Council does not meet with the acceptance required under subparagraph (d), a decision on the proposal, including whether it fulfils the requirements of paragraph 4, shall be taken as a matter of substance by the Conference at its next session;

(f) The Director-General shall notify all States Parties and the Depositary of any decision under this paragraph;

(g) Changes approved under this procedure shall enter into force for all States Parties 180 days after the date of notification by the Director-General of their approval unless another time period is recommended by the Executive Council or decided by the Conference.

ARTICLE XVI
DURATION AND WITHDRAWAL

1. This Convention shall be of unlimited duration.

2. Each State Party shall, in exercising its national sovereignty, have the right to withdraw from this Convention if it decides that extraordinary events, related to the subject-matter of this Convention, have jeopardized the supreme interests of its country. It shall give notice of such withdrawal 90 days in advance to all other States Parties, the Executive Council, the Depositary and the United Nations Security Council. Such notice shall include a statement of the extraordinary events it regards as having jeopardized its supreme interests.

3. The withdrawal of a State Party from this Convention shall not in any way affect the duty of States to continue fulfilling the obligations assumed under any relevant rules of international law, particularly the Geneva Protocol of 1925.

ARTICLE XVII
STATUS OF THE ANNEXES

The Annexes form an integral part of this Convention. Any reference to this Convention includes the Annexes.

ARTICLE XVIII
SIGNATURE

This Convention shall be open for signature for all States before its entry into force.

ARTICLE XIX
RATIFICATION

This Convention shall be subject to ratification by States Signatories according to their respective constitutional processes.

ARTICLE XX
ACCESSION

Any State which does not sign this Convention before its entry into force may accede to it at any time thereafter.

ARTICLE XXI
ENTRY INTO FORCE

1. This Convention shall enter into force 180 days after the date of the deposit of the 65th instrument of ratification, but in no case earlier than two years after its opening for signature.
2. For States whose instruments of ratification or accession are deposited subsequent to the entry into force of this Convention, it shall enter into force on the 30th day following the date of deposit of their instrument of ratification or accession.

ARTICLE XXII
RESERVATIONS

The Articles of this Convention shall not be subject to reservations. The Annexes of this Convention shall not be subject to reservations incompatible with its object and purpose.

ARTICLE XXIII
DEPOSITARY

The Secretary-General of the United Nations is hereby designated as the Depositary of this Convention and shall, inter alia:

(a) Promptly inform all signatory and acceding States of the date of each signature, the date of deposit of each instrument of ratification or accession and the date of the entry into force of this Convention, and of the receipt of other notices;

(b) Transmit duly certified copies of this Convention to the Governments of all signatory and acceding States; and

(c) Register this Convention pursuant to Article 102 of the Charter of the United Nations.

ARTICLE XXIV
AUTHENTIC TEXTS

This Convention, of which the Arabic, Chinese, English, French, Russian and Spanish texts are equally authentic, shall be deposited with the Secretary-General of the United Nations.

IN WITNESS WHEREOF the undersigned, being duly authorized to that effect, have signed this Convention.

Done at Paris on the thirteenth day of January, one thousand nine hundred and ninety-three.

II-7. Draft International Convention for the Suppression of Acts of Nuclear Terrorism; Revised Text Proposed by the Friends of the Chairman (October 1998) United Nations General Assembly, Fifty-third Session, Sixth Committee, A/C.6/53/L.4. Original Language: English.

Full Text

The States Parties to this Convention,
Having in mind the purposes and principles of the Charter of the United Nations concerning the maintenance of international peace and security and the promotion of good-neighbourliness and friendly relations and cooperation among States,
Recalling the Declaration on the Occasion of the Fiftieth Anniversary of the United Nations of 24 October 1995, 1
Recognizing the right of all States to develop and apply nuclear energy for peaceful purposes and their legitimate interests in the potential benefits to be derived from the peaceful application of nuclear energy,
Bearing in mind the Convention on the Physical Protection of Nuclear Material of 1980,
Deeply concerned about the worldwide escalation of acts of terrorism in all its forms and manifestations,
Recalling also the Declaration on Measures to Eliminate International Terrorism, annexed to General Assembly resolution 49/60 of 9 December 1994, in which, *inter alia*, the States Members of the United Nations solemnly reaffirm their unequivocal condemnation of all acts, methods and practices of terrorism as criminal and unjustifiable, wherever and by whomever committed, including those which jeopardize the friendly relations among States and peoples and threaten the territorial integrity and security of States,
Noting that the Declaration also encouraged States to review urgently the scope of the existing international legal provisions on the prevention, repression and elimination of terrorism in all its forms and manifestations, with the aim of ensuring that there is a comprehensive legal framework covering all aspects of the matter,
Recalling General Assembly resolution 51/210 of 17 December 1996 and the Declaration to Supplement the 1994 Declaration on Measures to Eliminate International Terrorism annexed thereto,
Recalling also that, pursuant to General Assembly resolution 51/210, an ad hoc committee was established to elaborate, *inter alia*, an international convention for the suppression of acts of nuclear terrorism to supplement related existing international instruments,
Noting that acts of nuclear terrorism may result in the gravest consequences and may pose a threat to international peace and security,
Noting also that existing multilateral legal provisions do not adequately address those attacks,
Being convinced of the urgent need to enhance international cooperation between States in devising and adopting effective and practical measures for the prevention of such acts of terrorism and for the prosecution and punishment of their perpetrators,
Noting that the activities of military forces of States are governed by rules of international law outside of the framework of this Convention and that the exclusion of certain actions from the coverage of this Convention does not condone or make lawful otherwise unlawful acts, or preclude prosecution under other laws,
Have agreed as follows:

Article 1
For the purposes of this Convention:
1. Radioactive material means nuclear material and other radioactive substances which contain nuclides which undergo spontaneous disintegration (a process accompanied by emission of one or more types of ionizing radiation, such as alpha-, beta-, neutron particles and gamma rays) and which may, owing to their radiological or fissile properties, cause death, serious bodily injury or substantial damage to property or to the environment.
2. Nuclear material means plutonium, except that with isotopic concentration exceeding 80 per cent in plutonium-238; uranium-233; uranium enriched in the isotopes 235 or 233; uranium containing the mixture of isotopes as occurring in nature other than in the form of ore or ore residue; or any material containing one or more of the foregoing;
Whereby Auranium enriched in the isotope 235 or 233 means uranium containing the isotope 235 or 233 or both in an amount such that the abundance ratio of the sum of these isotopes to the isotope 238 is greater than the ratio of the isotope 235 to the isotope 238 occurring in nature.
3. Nuclear facility means:
(a) Any nuclear reactor, including reactors installed on vessels, vehicles, aircraft or space objects for use as an energy source in order to propel such vessels, vehicles, aircraft or space objects or for any other purpose;
(b) Any plant or conveyance being used for the production, storage, processing or transport of radioactive material.
4. Device means:
(a) Any nuclear explosive device; or
(b) Any radioactive material dispersal or radiation-emitting device which may, owing to its radiological properties, cause death, serious bodily injury or substantial damage to property or the environment.
5. State or government facility includes any permanent or temporary facility or conveyance that is used or occupied by representatives of a State, members of Government, the legislature or the judiciary or by officials or employees of a State or any other public authority or entity or by employees or officials of an intergovernmental organization in connection with their official duties.
6. Military forces of a State means the armed forces of a State which are organized, trained and equipped under its internal law for the primary purpose of national defence or security and persons acting in support of those armed forces who are under their formal command, control and responsibility.

Article 2
1. Any person commits an offence within the meaning of this Convention if that person unlawfully and intentionally:
(a) Possesses radioactive material or makes or possesses a device:
(i) With the intent to cause death or serious bodily injury; or
(ii) With the intent to cause substantial damage to property or the environment;
(b) Uses in any way radioactive material or a device, or uses or damages a nuclear facility in a manner which releases or risks the release of radioactive material:
(i) With the intent to cause death or serious bodily injury; or
(ii) With the intent to cause substantial damage to property or the environment; or
(iii) With the intent to compel a natural or legal person, an international organization or a State to do or refrain from doing an act.
2. Any person also commits an offence if that person:

(a) Threatens, under circumstances which indicate the credibility of the threat, to commit an offence as set forth in subparagraph 1 (b) of the present article; or
(b) Demands unlawfully and intentionally radioactive material, a device or a nuclear facility by threat, under circumstances which indicate the credibility of the threat, or by use of force.
3. Any person also commits an offence if that person attempts to commit an offence as set forth in paragraph 1 of the present article.
4. Any person also commits an offence if that person:
(a) Participates as an accomplice in an offence as set forth in paragraph 1, 2 or 3 of the present article; or
(b) Organizes or directs others to commit an offence as set forth in paragraph 1, 2 or 3 of the present article; or
(c) In any other way contributes to the commission of one or more offences as set forth in paragraph 1, 2 or 3 of the present article by a group of persons acting with a common purpose; such contribution shall be intentional and either be made with the aim of furthering the general criminal activity or purpose of the group or be made in the knowledge of the intention of the group to commit the offence or offences concerned.

Article 3
This Convention shall not apply where the offence is committed within a single State, the alleged offender and the victims are nationals of that State, the alleged offender is found in the territory of that State and no other State has a basis under article 9, paragraph 1 or paragraph 2, to exercise jurisdiction, except that the provisions of articles 7, 12, 14, 15, 16 and 17 shall, as appropriate, apply in those cases.

Article 4
1. Nothing in this Convention shall affect other rights, obligations and responsibilities of States and individuals under international law, in particular the purposes and principles of the Charter of the United Nations and international humanitarian law.
2. The activities of armed forces during an armed conflict, as those terms are understood under international humanitarian law, which are governed by that law are not governed by this Convention, and the activities undertaken by military forces of a State in the exercise of their official duties, inasmuch as they are governed by other rules of international law, are not governed by this Convention.
3. The provisions of paragraph 2 of the present article shall not be interpreted as condoning or making lawful otherwise unlawful acts, or precluding prosecution under other laws.

Article 5
Each State Party shall adopt such measures as may be necessary:
(a) To establish as criminal offences under its national law the offences set forth in article 2;
(b) To make those offences punishable by appropriate penalties which take into account the grave nature of these offences.

Article 6
Each State Party shall adopt such measures as may be necessary, including, where appropriate, domestic legislation, to ensure that criminal acts within the scope of this Convention, in particular where they are intended or calculated to provoke a state of terror in the general public or in a group of persons or particular persons, are under no

circumstances justifiable by considerations of a political, philosophical, ideological, racial, ethnic, religious or other similar nature and are punished by penalties consistent with their grave nature.

Article 7
1. States Parties shall cooperate by:
(a) Taking all practicable measures, including, if necessary, adapting their national law, to prevent and counter preparations in their respective territories for the commission within or outside their territories of the offences set forth in article 2, including measures to prohibit in their territories illegal activities of persons, groups and organizations that encourage, instigate, organize, knowingly finance or knowingly provide technical assistance or information or engage in the perpetration of those offences;
(b) Exchanging accurate and verified information in accordance with their national law and in the manner of and subject to the conditions specified herein, and coordinating administrative and other measures taken as appropriate to detect, prevent, suppress and investigate the offences set forth in article 2 and also in order to institute criminal proceedings against persons alleged to have committed those crimes. In particular, a State Party shall take appropriate measures in order to inform without delay the other States referred to in article 9 in respect of the commission of the offences set forth in article 2 as well as preparations to commit such offences about which it has learned, and also to inform, where appropriate, international organizations.
2. States Parties shall take appropriate measures consistent with their national law to protect the confidentiality of any information which they receive in confidence by virtue of the provisions of this Convention from another State Party or through participation in an activity carried out for the implementation of this Convention. If States Parties provide information to international organizations in confidence, steps shall be taken to ensure that the confidentiality of such information is protected.
3. States Parties shall not be required by this Convention to provide any information which they are not permitted to communicate pursuant to national law or which would jeopardize the security of the State concerned or the physical protection of nuclear material.
4. States Parties shall inform the Secretary-General of the United Nations of their competent authorities and liaison points responsible for sending and receiving the information referred to in the present article. The Secretary-General of the United Nations shall communicate such information regarding competent authorities and liaison points to all States Parties and the International Atomic Energy Agency. Such authorities and liaison points must be accessible on a continuous basis.

Article 8
For purposes of preventing offences under this Convention, States Parties shall make every effort to adopt appropriate measures to ensure the protection of radioactive material, taking into account relevant recommendations and functions of the International Atomic Energy Agency.

Article 9
1. Each State Party shall take such measures as may be necessary to establish its jurisdiction over the offences set forth in article 2 when:
(a) The offence is committed in the territory of that State; or
(b) The offence is committed on board a vessel flying the flag of that State or an

aircraft which is registered under the laws of that State at the time the offence is committed; or
(c) The offence is committed by a national of that State.
2. A State Party may also establish its jurisdiction over any such offence when:
(a) The offence is committed against a national of that State; or
(b) The offence is committed against a State or government facility of that State abroad, including an embassy or other diplomatic or consular premises of that State; or
(c) The offence is committed by a stateless person who has his or her habitual residence in the territory of that State; or
(d) The offence is committed in an attempt to compel that State to do or abstain from doing any act; or
(e) The offence is committed on board an aircraft which is operated by the Government of that State.
3. Upon ratifying, accepting, approving or acceding to this Convention, each State Party shall notify the Secretary-General of the United Nations of the jurisdiction it has established under its national law in accordance with paragraph 2 of the present article. Should any change take place, the State Party concerned shall immediately notify the Secretary-General.
4. Each State Party shall likewise take such measures as may be necessary to establish its jurisdiction over the offences set forth in article 2 in cases where the alleged offender is present in its territory and it does not extradite that person to any of the States Parties which have established their jurisdiction in accordance with paragraph 1 or 2 of the present article.
5. This Convention does not exclude the exercise of any criminal jurisdiction established by a State Party in accordance with its national law.

Article 10
1. Upon receiving information that an offence set forth in article 2 has been committed or is being committed in the territory of a State Party or that a person who has committed or who is alleged to have committed such an offence may be present in its territory, the State Party concerned shall take such measures as may be necessary under its national law to investigate the facts contained in the information.
2. Upon being satisfied that the circumstances so warrant, the State Party in whose territory the offender or alleged offender is present shall take the appropriate measures under its national law so as to ensure that person's presence for the purpose of prosecution or extradition.
3. Any person regarding whom the measures referred to in paragraph 2 of the present article are being taken shall be entitled to:
(a) Communicate without delay with the nearest appropriate representative of the State of which that person is a national or which is otherwise entitled to protect that person's rights or, if that person is a stateless person, the State in the territory of which that person habitually resides;
(b) Be visited by a representative of that State;
(c) Be informed of that person's rights under subparagraphs (a) and (b).
4. The rights referred to in paragraph 3 of the present article shall be exercised in conformity with the laws and regulations of the State in the territory of which the offender or alleged offender is present, subject to the provision that the said laws and regulations must enable full effect to be given to the purposes for which the rights accorded under paragraph 3 are intended.
5. The provisions of paragraphs 3 and 4 of the present article shall be without prejudice to the right of any State Party having a claim to jurisdiction in accordance with article 9,

subparagraph 1 (c) or 2 (c), to invite the International Committee of the Red Cross to communicate with and visit the alleged offender.

6. When a State Party, pursuant to the present article, has taken a person into custody, it shall immediately notify, directly or through the Secretary-General of the United Nations, the States Parties which have established jurisdiction in accordance with article 9, paragraphs 1 and 2 and, if it considers it advisable, any other interested States Parties, of the fact that that person is in custody and of the circumstances which warrant that person's detention. The State which makes the investigation contemplated in paragraph 1 of the present article shall promptly inform the said States Parties of its findings and shall indicate whether it intends to exercise jurisdiction.

Article 11

1. The State Party in the territory of which the alleged offender is present shall, in cases to which article 9 applies, if it does not extradite that person, be obliged, without exception whatsoever and whether or not the offence was committed in its territory, to submit the case without undue delay to its competent authorities for the purpose of prosecution, through proceedings in accordance with the laws of that State. Those authorities shall take their decision in the same manner as in the case of any other offence of a grave nature under the law of that State.

2. Whenever a State Party is permitted under its national law to extradite or otherwise surrender one of its nationals only upon the condition that the person will be returned to that State to serve the sentence imposed as a result of the trial or proceeding for which the extradition or surrender of the person was sought, and this State and the State seeking the extradition of the person agree with this option and other terms they may deem appropriate, such a conditional extradition or surrender shall be sufficient to discharge the obligation set forth in paragraph 1 of the present article.

Article 12

Any person who is taken into custody or regarding whom any other measures are taken or proceedings are carried out pursuant to this Convention shall be guaranteed fair treatment, including enjoyment of all rights and guarantees in conformity with the law of the State in the territory of which that person is present and applicable provisions of international law, including international law of human rights.

Article 13

1. The offences set forth in article 2 shall be deemed to be included as extraditable offences in any extradition treaty existing between any of the States Parties before the entry into force of this Convention. States Parties undertake to include such offences as extraditable offences in every extradition treaty to be subsequently concluded between them.

2. When a State Party which makes extradition conditional on the existence of a treaty receives a request for extradition from another State Party with which it has no extradition treaty, the requested State Party may, at its option, consider this Convention as a legal basis for extradition in respect of the offences set forth in article 2. Extradition shall be subject to the other conditions provided by the law of the requested State.

3. States Parties which do not make extradition conditional on the existence of a treaty shall recognize the offences set forth in article 2 as extraditable offences between themselves, subject to the conditions provided by the law of the requested State.

4. If necessary, the offences set forth in article 2 shall be treated, for the purposes of extradition between States Parties, as if they had been committed not only in the place in

which they occurred but also in the territory of the States that have established jurisdiction in accordance with article 9, paragraphs 1 and 2.

5. The provisions of all extradition treaties and arrangements between States Parties with regard to offences set forth in article 2 shall be deemed to be modified as between States Parties to the extent that they are incompatible with this Convention.

Article 14

1. States Parties shall afford one another the greatest measure of assistance in connection with investigations or criminal or extradition proceedings brought in respect of the offences set forth in article 2, including assistance in obtaining evidence at their disposal necessary for the proceedings.
2. States Parties shall carry out their obligations under paragraph 1 of the present article in conformity with any treaties or other arrangements on mutual legal assistance that may exist between them. In the absence of such treaties or arrangements, States Parties shall afford one another assistance in accordance with their national law.

Article 15

None of the offences set forth in article 2 shall be regarded, for the purposes of extradition or mutual legal assistance, as a political offence or as an offence connected with a political offence or as an offence inspired by political motives. Accordingly, a request for extradition or for mutual legal assistance based on such an offence may not be refused on the sole ground that it concerns a political offence or an offence connected with a political offence or an offence inspired by political motives.

Article 16

Nothing in this Convention shall be interpreted as imposing an obligation to extradite or to afford mutual legal assistance if the requested State Party has substantial grounds for believing that the request for extradition for offences set forth in article 2 or for mutual legal assistance with respect to such offences has been made for the purpose of prosecuting or punishing a person on account of that person's race, religion, nationality, ethnic origin or political opinion or that compliance with the request would cause prejudice to that person's position for any of these reasons.

Article 17

1. A person who is being detained or is serving a sentence in the territory of one State Party whose presence in another State Party is requested for purposes of testimony, identification or otherwise providing assistance in obtaining evidence for the investigation or prosecution of offences under this Convention may be transferred if the following conditions are met:
(a) The person freely gives his or her informed consent; and
(b) The competent authorities of both States agree, subject to such conditions as those States may deem appropriate.
2. For the purposes of the present article:
(a) The State to which the person is transferred shall have the authority and obligation to keep the person transferred in custody, unless otherwise requested or authorized by the State from which the person was transferred;
(b) The State to which the person is transferred shall without delay implement its obligation to return the person to the custody of the State from which the person was transferred as agreed beforehand, or as otherwise agreed, by the competent authorities of both States;

(c) The State to which the person is transferred shall not require the State from which the person was transferred to initiate extradition proceedings for the return of the person;
(d) The person transferred shall receive credit for service of the sentence being served in the State from which he was transferred for time spent in the custody of the State to which he was transferred.
3. Unless the State Party from which a person is to be transferred in accordance with the present article so agrees, that person, whatever his or her nationality, shall not be prosecuted or detained or subjected to any other restriction of his or her personal liberty in the territory of the State to which that person is transferred in respect of acts or convictions anterior to his or her departure from the territory of the State from which such person was transferred.

Article 18
1. Upon seizing or otherwise taking control of radioactive material, devices or nuclear facilities, following the commission of an offence set forth in article 2, the State Party in possession of it shall:
(a) Take steps to render harmless the radioactive material, device or nuclear facility;
(b) Ensure that any nuclear material is held in accordance with applicable International Atomic Energy Agency safeguards; and
(c) Have regard to physical protection recommendations and health and safety standards published by the International Atomic Energy Agency.
2. Upon the completion of any proceedings connected with an offence set forth in article 2, or sooner if required by international law, any radioactive material, device or nuclear facility shall be returned, after consultations (in particular, regarding modalities of return and storage) with the States Parties concerned to the State Party to which it belongs, to the State Party of which the natural or legal person owning such radioactive material, device or facility is a national or resident, or to the State Party from whose territory it was stolen or otherwise unlawfully obtained.
3(1) Where a State Party is prohibited by national or international law from returning or accepting such radioactive material, device or nuclear facility or where the States Parties concerned so agree, subject to paragraph 3(2) of the present article, the State Party in possession of the radioactive material, devices or nuclear facilities shall continue to take the steps described in paragraph 1 of the present article; such radioactive material, devices or nuclear facilities shall be used only for peaceful purposes.
3(2) Where it is not lawful for the State Party in possession of the radioactive material, devices or nuclear facilities to possess them, that State shall ensure that they are as soon as possible where appropriate, has provided assurances consistent with the requirements of paragraph 1 of the present article in consultation with that State, for the purpose of rendering it harmless; such radioactive material, devices or nuclear facilities shall be used only for peaceful purposes.
4. If the radioactive material, devices or nuclear facilities referred to in paragraphs 1 and 2 of the present article do not belong to any of the States Parties or to a national or resident of a State Party or was not stolen or otherwise unlawfully obtained from the territory of a State Party, or if no State is willing to receive such item pursuant to paragraph 3 of the present article, a separate decision concerning its disposition shall, subject to paragraph 3(2) of the present article, be taken after consultations between the States concerned and any relevant international organizations.
5. For the purposes of paragraphs 1, 2, 3 and 4 of the present article, the State Party in possession of the radioactive material, device or nuclear facility may request the assistance and cooperation of other States Parties, in particular the States Parties concerned, and any

relevant international organizations, in particular the International Atomic Energy Agency. States Parties and the relevant international organizations are encouraged to provide assistance pursuant to this paragraph to the maximum extent possible.

6. The States Parties involved in the disposition or retention of the radioactive material, device or nuclear facility pursuant to the present article shall inform the Director General of the International Atomic Energy Agency of the manner in which such an item was disposed of or retained. The Director General of the International Atomic Energy Agency shall transmit the information to the other States Parties.

7. In the event of any dissemination in connection with an offence set forth in article 2, nothing in the present article shall affect in any way the rules of international law governing liability for nuclear damage, or other rules of international law.

Article 19
The State Party where the alleged offender is prosecuted shall, in accordance with its national law or applicable procedures, communicate the final outcome of the proceedings to the Secretary-General of the United Nations, who shall transmit the information to the other States Parties.

Article 20
States Parties shall conduct consultations with one another directly or through the Secretary-General of the United Nations, with the assistance of international organizations as necessary, to ensure effective implementation of this Convention.

Article 21
The States Parties shall carry out their obligations under this Convention in a manner consistent with the principles of sovereign equality and territorial integrity of States and that of non-intervention in the domestic affairs of other States.

Article 22
Nothing in this Convention entitles a State Party to undertake in the territory of another State Party the exercise of jurisdiction and performance of functions which are exclusively reserved for the authorities of that other State Party by its national law.

Article 23
1. Any dispute between two or more States Parties concerning the interpretation or application of this Convention which cannot be settled through negotiation within a reasonable time shall, at the request of one of them, be submitted to arbitration. If, within six months from the date of the request for arbitration, the parties are unable to agree on the organization of the arbitration, any one of those parties may refer the dispute to the International Court of Justice, by application, in conformity with the Statute of the Court.

2. Each State may, at the time of signature, ratification, acceptance or approval of this Convention or accession thereto, declare that it does not consider itself bound by paragraph 1 of the present article. The other States Parties shall not be bound by paragraph 1 with respect to any State Party which has made such a reservation.

3. Any State which has made a reservation in accordance with paragraph 2 of the present article may at any time withdraw that reservation by notification to the Secretary-General of the United Nations.

Article 24

1. This Convention shall be open for signature by all States from _____ until _____ at United Nations Headquarters in New York.
2. This Convention is subject to ratification, acceptance or approval. The instruments of ratification, acceptance or approval shall be deposited with the Secretary-General of the United Nations.
3. This Convention shall be open to accession by any State. The instruments of accession shall be deposited with the Secretary-General of the United Nations.

Article 25

1. This Convention shall enter into force on the thirtieth day following the date of the deposit of the twenty-second instrument of ratification, acceptance, approval or accession with the Secretary-General of the United Nations.
2. For each State ratifying, accepting, approving or acceding to the Convention after the deposit of the twenty-second instrument of ratification, acceptance, approval or accession, the Convention shall enter into force on the thirtieth day after deposit by such State of its instrument of ratification, acceptance, approval or accession.

Article 26

1. A State Party may propose an amendment to this Convention. The proposed amendment shall be submitted to the Depositary, who circulates it immediately to all States Parties.
2. If the majority of the States Parties request the Depositary to convene a Conference to consider the proposed amendments, the Depositary shall invite all States Parties to attend such a Conference to begin not sooner than three months after the invitations are issued.
3. The Conference shall make every effort to ensure amendments are adopted by consensus. Should this not be possible, amendments shall be adopted by a two-thirds majority of all States Parties. Any amendment adopted at the Conference shall be promptly circulated by the Depositary to all States Parties.
4. The amendment adopted pursuant to paragraph 3 of the present article shall enter into force for each State Party that deposits its instrument of ratification, acceptance, accession or approval of the amendment on the thirtieth day after the date on which two thirds of the States Parties have deposited their relevant instrument. Thereafter, the amendment shall enter into force for any State Party on the thirtieth day after the date on which that State deposits its relevant instrument.

Article 27

1. Any State Party may denounce this Convention by written notification to the Secretary-General of the United Nations.
2. Denunciation shall take effect one year following the date on which notification is received by the Secretary-General of the United Nations.

Article 28

The original of this Convention, of which the Arabic, Chinese, English, French, Russian and Spanish texts are equally authentic, shall be deposited with the Secretary-General of the United Nations, who shall send certified copies thereof to all States.

In witness whereof, the undersigned, being duly authorized thereto by their respective Governments, have signed this Convention, opened for signature at United Nations Headquarters in New York on _____.

II-8. International Court of Justice Advisory Opinion on the Legality of Threat or Use of Nuclear Weapons, American Society of International Law, Washington, D.C., 35 I.L.M. 809 (1996).

Full Text

ADVISORY OPINION
Present: President BEDJAOUI; Vice-President SCHWEBEL; Judges ODA, GUILLAUME, SHAHABUDDEEN, WEERAMANTRY, RANJEVA, HERCZEGH, SHI, FLEISCHHAUER, KOROMA, VERESHCHETIN, FERRARI BRAVO, HIGGINS; Registrar VALENCIA-OSPINA.

On the legality of the threat or use of nuclear weapons,

THE COURT,

composed as above,

gives the following Advisory Opinion:

1. The question upon which the advisory opinion of the Court has been requested is set forth in resolution 49/75 K adopted by the General Assembly of the United Nations (hereinafter called the "General Assembly") on 15 December 1994. By a letter dated 19 December 1994, received in the Registry by facsimile on 20 December 1994 and filed in the original on 6 January 1995, the [*815] Secretary-General of the United Nations officially communicated to the Registrar the decision taken by the General Assembly to submit the question to the Court for an advisory opinion. Resolution 49/75 K, the English text of which was enclosed with the letter, reads as follows:

"The General Assembly,

Conscious that the continuing existence and development of nuclear weapons pose serious risks to humanity,

Mindful that States have an obligation under the Charter of the United Nations to refrain from the threat or use of force against the territorial integrity or political independence of any State.

Recalling its resolutions 1653 (XVI) of 24 November 1961, 33/71 B of 14 December 1978, 34/83 G of 11 December 1979, 35/152 D of 12 December 1980, 36/92 I of 9 December 1981, 45/59 B of 4 December 1990 and 46/37 D of 6 December 1991, in which it declared that the use of nuclear weapons would be a violation of the Charter and a crime against humanity,

Welcoming the progress made on the prohibition and elimination of weapons of mass destruction, including the Convention on the Prohibition of the Development, Production and Stockpiling of Bacteriological (Biological) and Toxin Weapons and on Their Destruction and the Convention on the Prohibition of the Development, Production, Stockpiling and Use of Chemical Weapons and on Their Destruction,

Convinced that the complete elimination of nuclear weapons is the only guarantee against the threat of nuclear war,

Noting the concerns expressed in the Fourth Review Conference of the Parties to the Treaty on the Non-Proliferation of Nuclear Weapons that insufficient progress had been made towards the complete elimination of nuclear weapons at the earliest possible time,

Recalling that, convinced of the need to strengthen the rule of law in international relations, it has declared the period 1990-1999 the United Nations Decade of International Law,

Noting that Article 96, paragraph 1, of the Charter empowers the General Assembly to request the International Court of Justice to give an advisory opinion on any legal question,

Recalling the recommendation of the Secretary-General, made in his report entitled 'An Agenda for Peace', that United Nations organs that are authorized to take advantage of the advisory competence of the International Court of Justice turn to the Court more frequently for such opinions,

Welcoming resolution 46/40 of 14 May 1993 of the Assembly of the World Health Organization, in which the organization requested the International Court of Justice to give an advisory opinion on whether the use of nuclear weapons by a State in war or other armed conflict would be a breach of its obligations under international law, including the Constitution of the World Health Organization,

Decides, pursuant to Article 96, paragraph 1, of the Charter of the United Nations, to request the International Court of Justice urgently to render its advisory opinion on the following question: 'Is the threat or use of nuclear weapons in any circumstance permitted under international law?'"

2. Pursuant to Article 65, paragraph 2, of the Statute, the Secretary-General of the United Nations communicated to the Court a dossier of documents likely to throw light upon the question.

3. By letters dated 21 December 1994, the Registrar, pursuant to Article 66, paragraph 1, of the Statute, gave notice of the request for an advisory opinion to all States entitled to appear before the Court.

4. By an Order dated 1 February 1995 the Court decided that the States entitled to appear before it and the United Nations were likely to be able to furnish information on the question, in accordance with Article 66, paragraph 2, of the Statute. By the same Order, the Court fixed, respectively, 20 June 1995 as the time-limit within which written statements might be submitted to it on the question, and 20 September 1995 as the time-limit within which States and

organizations having presented written statements might submit written comments on the other written statements in accordance with Article 66, paragraph 4, of the Statute. In the aforesaid Order, it was stated in particular that the General Assembly had requested that the advisory opinion of the Court be rendered "urgently"; reference was also made to the procedural time-limits already fixed for the request for an advisory opinion previously submitted to the Court by the World Health Organization on the question of the Legality of the use by a State of nuclear weapons in armed conflict.

On 8 February 1995, the Registrar addressed to the States entitled to appear before the Court and to the United Nations the special and direct communication provided for in Article 66, paragraph 2, of the Statute.

5. Written statements were filed by the following States: Bosnia and Herzegovina, Burundi, Democratic People's Republic of Korea, Ecuador, Egypt, Finland, France, Germany, India, Ireland, Islamic Republic of Iran, Italy, Japan, Lesotho, Malaysia, Marshall Islands, Mexico, Nauru, Netherlands, New Zealand, Qatar, Russian Federation, Samoa, San Marino, Solomon Islands, Sweden, United Kingdom of Great Britain and Northern Ireland, and United States of America. In addition, written comments on those written statements were submitted by the following States: Egypt, Nauru and Solomon Islands. Upon receipt of those statements and comments, the Registrar communicated the text to all States having taken part in the written proceedings.

6. The Court decided to hold public sittings, opening on 30 October 1995, at which oral statements might be submitted to the Court by any State or organization which had been considered likely to be able to furnish information on the question before the Court. By letters dated [*816] 23 June 1995, the Registrar requested the States entitled to appear before the Court and the United Nations to inform him whether they intended to take part in the oral proceedings; it was indicated, in those letters, that the Court had decided to hear, during the same public sittings, oral statements relating to the request for an advisory opinion from the General Assembly as well as oral statements concerning the above-mentioned request for an advisory opinion laid before the Court by the World Health Organization, on the understanding that the United Nations would be entitled to speak only in regard to the request submitted by the General Assembly, and it was further specified therein that the participants in the oral proceedings which had not taken part in the written proceedings would receive the text of the statements and comments produced in the course of the latter.

7. By a letter dated 20 October 1995, the Republic of Nauru requested the Court's permission to withdraw the written comments submitted on its behalf in a document entitled "Response to submissions of other States". The Court granted the request and, by letters dated 30 October 1995, the Deputy-Registrar notified the States to which the document had been communicated, specifying that the document consequently did not form part of the record before the Court.

8. Pursuant to Article 106 of the Rules of Court, the Court decided to make the written statements and comments submitted to the Court accessible to the public, with effect from the opening of the oral proceedings.

9. In the course of public sittings held from 30 October 1995 to 15 November 1995, the Court heard oral statements in the following order by:

For the Commonwealth of Australia:	Mr. Gavan Griffith, Q.C., Solicitor-General of Australia, Counsel; The Honourable Gareth Evans, Q.C., Senator, Minister for Foreign Affairs, Counsel;
For the Arab Republic of Egypt	Mr. George Abi-Saab, Professor of International Law, Graduate Institute of International Studies, Geneva, Member of the Institute of International Law;
For the French Republic:	Mr. Marc Perrin de Brichambaut, Director of Le Affairs, Ministry of Foreign Affairs; Mr. Alain Pellet, Professor of International Law University of Paris X and Institute of Political Studies, Paris;
For the Federal Republic of Germany:	Mr. Hartmut Hillgenberg, Director-General of L Affairs, Ministry of Foreign Affairs;
For Indonesia:	H.E. Mr. Johannes Berchmans Soedarmanto Kardarisman, Ambassador of Indonesia to the Netherlands;
For Mexico:	H.E. Mr. Sergio Gonzalez Galvez, Ambassador Under-Secretary of Foreign Relations;
For the Islamic Republic of Iran:	H.E. Mr. Mohammad J. Zarif, Deputy Minister, Legal and International Affairs, Ministry of Foreign Affairs;
For Italy:	Mr. Umberto Leanza, Professor of International Law at the Faculty of Law at the University of Rome "Tor Vergata", Head of the Diplomatic Legal Service at the Ministry of Foreign Affairs;
For Japan:	H.E. Mr. Takekazu Kawamura, Ambassador,

International Humanitarian Law and Arms Control Agreements 447

	Director General for Arms Control and Scientific Affairs, Ministry of Foreign Affairs; Mr. Takashi Hiraoka, Mayor of Hiroshima; Mr. Iccho Itoh, Mayor of Nagasaki;
For Malaysia:	H.E. Mr. Tan Sri Razali Ismail, Ambassador, Permanent Representative of Malaysia to the United Nations; Dato Mohtar Abdullah, Attorney-General;
For New Zealand:	The Honourable Paul East, Q.C., Attorney-General of New Zealand; Mr. Allan Bracegirdle, Deputy Director of Legal Division of the New Zealand Ministry for Foreign Affairs and Trade;
For the Philippines:	H.E. Mr. Rodolfo S. Sanchez, Ambassador of the Philippines to the Netherlands; Professor Merlin N. Magallona, Dean, College of Law, University of the Philippines;
For Qatar:	H.E. Mr. Najeeb ibn Mohammed Al-Nauimi, Minister of Justice;
For the Russian Federation:	Mr. A. G. Khodakov, Director, Legal Department, Ministry of Foreign Affairs;
For San Marino:	Mrs. Federica Bigi, Embassy Counsellor, Official in Charge of Political Directorate, Department of Foreign Affairs;
For Samoa:	H.E. Mr. Neroni Slade, Ambassador and Permanent Representative of Samoa to the United Nations; Mrs. Laurence Boisson de Chazournes, Assistant Professor, Graduate Institute of International Studies, Geneva; Mr. Roger S. Clark, Distinguished Professor of Law, Rutgers University School of Law, Camden, New Jersey;
For the Marshall	The Honourable Theodore G. Kronmiller, Legal

Islands:	Counsel, Embassy of the Marshall Islands to the United States of America; Mrs. Lijon Eknilang, Council Member, Rongelap Atoll Local Government;
For the Solomon Islands:	The Honourable Victor Ngele, Minister of Police and National Security; Mr. Jean Salmon, Professor of Law, Universite libre de Bruxelles; Mr. Eric David, Professor of Law, Universite libre de Bruxelles; Mr. Philippe Sands, Lecturer in Law, School of Oriental and African Studies, London University, and Legal Director, Foundation for International Environmental Law and Development; Mr. James Crawford, Whewell Professor International Law, University of Cambridge;
For Costa Rica:	Mr. Carlos Vargas-Pizarro, Legal Counsel and Special Envoy of the Government of Costa Rica;
For the United Kingdom of Great Britain and Northern Ireland:	The Rt. Honourable Sir Nicholas Lyell, Q.C., M Her Majesty's Attorney-General;
For the United States of America:	Mr. Conrad K. Harper, Legal Adviser, US Department of State; Mr. Michael J. Matheson, Principal Deputy Legal Adviser, US Department of State; Mr. John H. McNeill, Senior Deputy General Counsel, US Department of Defense;
For Zimbabwe:	Mr. Jonathan Wutawunashe, Charge d'affaires a Embassy of the Republic of Zimbabwe in the Netherlands;

[*817] Questions were put by Members of the Court to particular participants in the oral proceedings, who replied in writing, as requested, within the prescribed time-limits; the Court having decided that the other participants could also reply to those questions on the same terms, several of them did so. Other questions put by Members of the Court were addressed, more generally, to any participant in the

oral proceedings; several of them replied in writing, as requested, within the prescribed time-limits.

10. The Court must first consider whether it has the jurisdiction to give a reply to the request of the General Assembly for an Advisory Opinion and whether, should the answer be in the affirmative, there is any reason it should decline to exercise any such jurisdiction.

The Court draws its competence in respect of advisory opinions from Article 65, paragraph 1, of its Statute. Under this Article, the Court "may give an advisory opinion on any legal question at the request of whatever body may be authorized by or in accordance with the Charter of the United Nations to make such a request".

11. For the Court to be competent to give an advisory opinion, it is thus necessary at the outset for the body requesting the opinion to be "authorized by or in accordance with the Charter of the United Nations to make such a request". The Charter provides in Article 96, paragraph 1, that:

"The General Assembly or the Security Council may request the International Court of Justice to give an advisory opinion on any legal question."

Some States which oppose the giving of an opinion by the Court argued that the General Assembly and Security Council are not entitled to ask for opinions on matters totally unrelated to their work. They suggested that, as in the case of organs and agencies acting under Article 96, paragraph 2, of the Charter, and notwithstanding the difference in wording between that provision and paragraph 1 of the same Article, the General Assembly and Security Council may ask for an advisory opinion on a legal question only within the scope of their activities.

In the view of the Court, it matters little whether this interpretation of Article 96, paragraph 1, is or is not correct; in the present case, the General Assembly has competence in any event to seise the Court. Indeed, Article 10 of the Charter has conferred upon the General Assembly a competence relating to "any questions or any matters" within the scope of the Charter. Article 11 has specifically provided it with a competence to "consider the general principles . . . in the maintenance of international peace and security, including the principles governing disarmament and the regulation of armaments". Lastly, according to Article 13, the General Assembly "shall initiate studies and make recommendations for the purpose of . . . encouraging the progressive development of international law and its codification".

12. The question put to the Court has a relevance to many aspects of the activities and concerns of the General Assembly including those relating to the threat or use of force in international relations, the disarmament process, and the progressive development of international law. The General Assembly has a long-standing interest in these matters and in their relation to nuclear weapons. This interest has been manifested in the annual First Committee debates, and the

Assembly resolutions on nuclear weapons; in the holding of three special sessions on disarmament (1978, 1982 and 1988) by the General Assembly, and the annual meetings of the Disarmament Commission since 1978; and also in the commissioning of studies on the effects of the use of nuclear weapons. In this context, it does not matter that important recent and current activities relating to nuclear disarmament are being pursued in other fora.

Finally, Article 96, paragraph 1, of the Charter cannot be read as limiting the ability of the Assembly to request an opinion only in those circumstances in which it can take binding decisions. The fact that the Assembly's activities in the above-mentioned field have led it only to the making of recommendations thus has no bearing on the issue of whether it had the competence to put to the Court the question of which it is seised.

13. The Court must furthermore satisfy itself that the advisory opinion requested does indeed relate to a "legal question" within the meaning of its Statute and the United Nations Charter.

The Court has already had occasion to indicate that questions "framed in terms of law and raising problems of international law . . . are by their very nature susceptible of a reply based on law . . . [and] appear . . . to be questions of a legal character" (Western Sahara, Advisory Opinion, I.C.J. Reports 1975, p. 18, para. 15).

[*818] The question put to the Court by the General Assembly is indeed a legal one, since the Court is asked to rule on the compatibility of the threat or use of nuclear weapons with the relevant principles and rules of international law. To do this, the Court must identify the existing principles and rules, interpret them and apply them to the threat or use of nuclear weapons, thus offering a reply to the question posed based on law.

The fact that this question also has political aspects, as, in the nature of things, is the case with so many questions which arise in international life, does not suffice to deprive it of its character as a "legal question" and to "deprive the Court of a competence expressly conferred on it by its Statute" (Application for Review of Judgement No. 158 of the United Nations Administrative Tribunal, Advisory Opinion, I.C.J. Reports 1973, p. 172, para. 14). Whatever its political aspects, the Court cannot refuse to admit the legal character of a question which invites it to discharge an essentially judicial task, namely, an assessment of the legality of the possible conduct of States with regard to the obligations imposed upon them by international law (cf. Conditions of Admission of a State to Membership in the United Nations (Article 4 of the Charter), Advisory Opinion, I.C.J. Reports 1947-1948, pp. 61-62; Competence of the General Assembly for the Admission of a State to the United Nations, Advisory Opinion, I.C.J. Reports 1950, pp. 6-7; Certain Expenses of the United Nations (Article 17, paragraph 2, of the Charter), Advisory Opinion, I.C.J. Reports 1962, p. 155).

Furthermore, as the Court said in the Opinion it gave in 1980 concerning the Interpretation of the Agreement of 25 March 1951 between the WHO and Egypt:

"Indeed, in situations in which political considerations are prominent it may be particularly necessary for an international organization to obtain an advisory opinion from the Court as to the legal principles applicable with respect to the matter under debate . . ." (Interpretation of the Agreement of 25 March 1951 between the WHO and Egypt, Advisory Opinion, I.C.J. Reports 1980, p. 87, para. 33.)

The Court moreover considers that the political nature of the motives which may be said to have inspired the request and the political implications that the opinion given might have are of no relevance in the establishment of its jurisdiction to give such an opinion.

14. Article 65, paragraph 1, of the Statute provides: "The Court may give an advisory opinion . . ." (Emphasis added.) This is more than an enabling provision. As the Court has repeatedly emphasized, the Statute leaves a discretion as to whether or not it will give an advisory opinion that has been requested of it, once it has established its competence to do so. In this context, the Court has previously noted as follows:

"The Court's Opinion is given not to the States, but to the organ which is entitled to request it; the reply of the Court, itself an 'organ of the United Nations', represents its participation in the activities of the Organization, and, in principle, should not be refused." (Interpretation of Peace Treaties with Bulgaria, Hungary and Romania, First Phase, Advisory Opinion, I.C.J. Reports 1950, p. 71; see also Reservations to the Convention on the Prevention and Punishment of the Crime of Genocide, Advisory Opinion, I.C.J. Reports 1951, p. 19; Judgments of the Administrative Tribunal of the ILO upon Complaints Made against Unesco, Advisory Opinion, I.C.J. Reports 1956, p. 86; Certain Expenses of the United Nations (Article 17, paragraph 2, of the Charter), Advisory Opinion, I.C.J. Reports 1962, p. 155; and Applicability of Article VI, Section 22, of the Convention on the Privileges and Immunities of the United Nations, Advisory Opinion, I.C.J. Reports 1989, p. 189.)

The Court has constantly been mindful of its responsibilities as "the principal judicial organ of the United Nations" (Charter, Art. 92). When considering each request, it is mindful that it should not, in principle, refuse to give an advisory opinion. In accordance with the consistent jurisprudence of the Court, only "compelling reasons" could lead it to such a refusal (Judgments of the Administrative Tribunal of the ILO upon Complaints Made against Unesco, Advisory Opinion, I.C.J. Reports 1956, p. 86; Certain Expenses of the United Nations (Article 17, paragraph 2, of the Charter), Advisory Opinion, I.C.J. Reports 1962, p. 155; Legal Consequences for States of the Continued Presence of South

Africa in Namibia (South West Africa) notwithstanding Security Council Resolution 276 (1970), Advisory Opinion, I.C.J. Reports 1971, p. 27; Application for Review of Judgement No. 158 of the United Nations Administrative Tribunal, Advisory Opinion, I.C.J. Reports 1973, p. 183; Western Sahara, Advisory Opinion, I.C.J. Reports 1975, p. 21; and Applicability of Article VI, Section 22, of the Convention on the Privileges and Immunities of the United Nations, Advisory Opinion, I.C.J. Reports 1989, p. 191). There has been no refusal, based on the discretionary power of the Court, to act upon a request for advisory opinion in the history of the present Court; in the case concerning the Legality of the Use by a State of Nuclear Weapons in Armed Conflict, the refusal to give the World Health Organization the advisory opinion requested by it was justified by the Court's lack of jurisdiction in that case. The Permanent Court of International Justice took the view on only one occasion that it could not reply to a question put to it, having regard to the very particular circumstances of the case, among which were that the question directly concerned an already existing dispute, one of the States parties to which was neither a party to the Statute of the Permanent Court nor a Member of the League of Nations, objected to the proceedings, and refused to take part in any way (Status of Eastern Carelia, P.C.I.J., Series B, No. 5).

15. Most of the reasons adduced in these proceedings in order to persuade the Court that in the exercise of its discretionary power it should decline to render the opinion requested by General Assembly resolution 49/75K were summarized in the following statement made by one State in the written proceedings:

"The question presented is vague and abstract, addressing complex issues which are the subject of consideration among interested States and within other bodies of the United Nations which have an express mandate to address these matters. An opinion by the Court in regard to the question presented would provide no practical assistance to the General Assembly in carrying out its functions under the Charter. Such an opinion has the potential of undermining progress already made or being made on this sensitive subject and, therefore, is contrary to the interest of the United Nations Organization." (United States of America, Written Statement, pp. 1-2; cf. pp. 3-7, II. See also United Kingdom, Written Statement, pp. 9-20, paras. 2.23-2.45; France, Written Statement, pp. 13-20, paras. 5-9; Finland, Written Statement, pp. 1-2; Netherlands, Written Statement, pp. 3-4, paras. 6-13; Germany, Written Statement, pp. 3-6, para. 2(b).))

In contending that the question put to the Court is vague and abstract, some States appeared to mean by this that there exists no specific dispute on the subject-matter of the question. In order to respond to this argument, it is necessary to distinguish between requirements governing contentious procedure and those applicable to advisory opinions. The purpose of the advisory function is not to settle -- at least directly -- disputes between States, but to offer legal advice to [*819] the organs and institutions requesting the opinion (cf. Interpretation of Peace Treaties I.C.J. Reports 1950, p. 71). The fact that the question put to the

Court does not relate to a specific dispute should consequently not lead the Court to decline to give the opinion requested.

Moreover, it is the clear position of the Court that to contend that it should not deal with a question couched in abstract terms is "a mere affirmation devoid of any justification", and that "the Court may give an advisory opinion on any legal question, abstract or otherwise" (Conditions of Admission of a State to Membership in the United Nations (Article 4 of the Charter), Advisory Opinion, 1948, I.C.J. Reports 1947-1948, p. 61; see also Effect of Awards of Compensation Made by the United Nations Administrative Tribunal, Advisory Opinion, I.C.J. Reports 1954, p. 51; and Legal Consequences for States of the Continued Presence of South Africa in Namibia (South West Africa) notwithstanding Security Council Resolution 276 (1970), Advisory Opinion, I.C.J. Reports 1971, p. 27, para. 40).

Certain States have however expressed the fear that the abstract nature of the question might lead the Court to make hypothetical or speculative declarations outside the scope of its judicial function. The Court does not consider that, in giving an advisory opinion in the present case, it would necessarily have to write "scenarios", to study various types of nuclear weapons and to evaluate highly complex and controversial technological, strategic and scientific information. The Court will simply address the issues arising in all their aspects by applying the legal rules relevant to the situation.

16. Certain States have observed that the General Assembly has not explained to the Court for what precise purposes it seeks the advisory opinion. Nevertheless, it is not for the Court itself to purport to decide whether or not an advisory opinion is needed by the Assembly for the performance of its functions. The General Assembly has the right to decide for itself on the usefulness of an opinion in the light of its own needs.

Equally, once the Assembly has asked, by adopting a resolution, for an advisory opinion on a legal question, the Court, in determining whether there are any compelling reasons for it to refuse to give such an opinion, will not have regard to the origins or to the political history of the request, or to the distribution of votes in respect of the adopted resolution.

17. It has also been submitted that a reply from the Court in this case might adversely affect disarmament negotiations and would, therefore, be contrary to the interest of the United Nations. The Court is aware that, no matter what might be its conclusions in any opinion it might give, they would have relevance for the continuing debate on the matter in the General Assembly and would present an additional element in the negotiations on the matter. Beyond that, the effect of the opinion is a matter of appreciation. The Court has heard contrary positions advanced and there are no evident criteria by which it can prefer one assessment to another. That being so, the Court cannot regard this factor as a compelling reason to decline to exercise its jurisdiction.

18. Finally, it has been contended by some States that in answering the question posed, the Court would be going beyond its judicial role and would be taking upon itself a law-making capacity. It is clear that the Court cannot legislate, and, in the circumstances of the present case, it is not called upon to do so. Rather its task is to engage in its normal judicial function of ascertaining the existence or otherwise of legal principles and rules applicable to the threat or use of nuclear weapons. The contention that the giving of an answer to the question posed would require the Court to legislate is based on a supposition that the present corpus juris is devoid of relevant rules in this matter. The Court could not accede to this argument; it states the existing law and does not legislate. This is so even if, in stating and applying the law, the Court necessarily has to specify its scope and sometimes note its general trend.

19. In view of what is stated above, the Court concludes that it has the authority to deliver an opinion on the question posed by the General Assembly, and that there exist no "compelling reasons" which would lead the Court to exercise its discretion not to do so.

An entirely different question is whether the Court, under the constraints placed upon it as a judicial organ, will be able to give a complete answer to the question asked of it. However, that is a different matter from a refusal to answer at all.

20. The Court must next address certain matters arising in relation to the formulation of the question put to it by the General Assembly. The English text asks: "Is the threat or use of nuclear weapons in any circumstance permitted under international law?" The French text of the question reads as follows: "Est-il permis en droit international de recourir a la menace ou a l'emploi d'armes nucleaires en toute circonstance?" It was suggested that the Court was being asked by the General Assembly whether it was permitted to have recourse to nuclear weapons in every circumstance, and it was contended that such a question would inevitably invite a simple negative answer.

The Court finds it unnecessary to pronounce on the possible divergences between the English and French texts of the question posed. Its real objective is clear: to determine the legality or illegality of the threat or use of nuclear weapons.

21. The use of the word "permitted" in the question put by the General Assembly was criticized before the Court by certain States on the ground that this implied that the threat or the use of nuclear weapons would only be permissible if authorization could be found in a treaty provision or in customary international law. Such a starting point, those States submitted, was incompatible with the very basis of international law, which rests upon the principles of sovereignty and consent; accordingly, and contrary to what was implied by use of the word "permitted", States are free to threaten or use nuclear weapons unless it can be shown that they are bound not to do so by reference to a prohibition in either treaty law or customary international law. Support for this contention was found in dicta

of the Permanent Court of International Justice in the "Lotus" case that "restrictions upon the independence of States cannot . . . be presumed" and that international law leaves to States "a wide measure of discretion which is only limited in certain cases by prohibitive rules" (P.C.I.J., Series A, No. 10, pp. 18 and 19). Reliance was also placed on the dictum of the present Court in the case concerning Military and Paramilitary Activities in and against Nicaragua (Nicaragua v United States of America) that:
"in international law there are no rules, other than such rules as may be accepted by the State concerned, by treaty or otherwise, whereby the level of armaments of a sovereign State can be limited" (I.C.J. Reports 1986, p. 135, para. 269).

[*820] For other States, the invocation of these dicta in the "Lotus" case was inapposite; their status in contemporary international law and applicability in the very different circumstances of the present case were challenged. It was also contended that the above-mentioned dictum of the present Court was directed to the possession of armaments and was irrelevant to the threat or use of nuclear weapons.

Finally, it was suggested that, were the Court to answer the question put by the Assembly, the word "permitted" should be replaced by "prohibited".

22. The Court notes that the nuclear-weapon States appearing before it either accepted, or did not dispute, that their independence to act was indeed restricted by the principles and rules of international law, more particularly humanitarian law (see below, paragraph 86), as did the other States which took part in the proceedings.

Hence, the argument concerning the legal conclusions to be drawn from the use of the word "permitted", and the questions of burden of proof to which it was said to give rise, are without particular significance for the disposition of the issues before the Court.

23. In seeking to answer the question put to it by the General Assembly, the Court must decide, after consideration of the great corpus of international law norms available to it, what might be the relevant applicable law.

24. Some of the proponents of the illegality of the use of nuclear weapons have argued that such use would violate the right to life as guaranteed in Article 6 of the International Covenant on Civil and Political Rights, as well as in certain regional instruments for the protection of human rights. Article 6, paragraph 1, of the International Covenant provides as follows:

"Every human being has the inherent right to life. This right shall be protected by law. No one shall be arbitrarily deprived of his life."

In reply, others contended that the International Covenant on Civil and

Political Rights made no mention of war or weapons, and it had never been envisaged that the legality of nuclear weapons was regulated by that instrument. It was suggested that the Covenant was directed to the protection of human rights in peacetime, but that questions relating to unlawful loss of life in hostilities were governed by the law applicable in armed conflict.

25. The Court observes that the protection of the International Covenant of Civil and Political Rights does not cease in times of war, except by operation of Article 4 of the Covenant whereby certain provisions may be derogated from in a time of national emergency. Respect for the right to life is not, however, such a provision. In principle, the right not arbitrarily to be deprived of one's life applies also in hostilities. The test of what is an arbitrary deprivation of life, however, then falls to be determined by the applicable lex specialis, namely, the law applicable in armed conflict which is designed to regulate the conduct of hostilities. Thus whether a particular loss of life, through the use of a certain weapon in warfare, is to be considered an arbitrary deprivation of life contrary to Article 6 of the Covenant, can only be decided by reference to the law applicable in armed conflict and not deduced from the terms of the Covenant itself.

26. Some States also contended that the prohibition against genocide, contained in the Convention of 9 December 1948 on the Prevention and Punishment of the Crime of Genocide, is a relevant rule of customary international law which the Court must apply. The Court recalls that, in Article II of the Convention genocide is defined as
"any of the following acts committed with intent to destroy, in whole or in part, a national, ethnical, racial or religious group, as such:
(a) Killing members of the group;
(b) Causing serious bodily or mental harm to members of the group;
(c) Deliberately inflicting on the group conditions of life calculated to being about its physical destruction in whole or in part;
(d) Imposing measures intended to prevent births within the group;
(e) Forcibly transferring children of the group to another group."

It was maintained before the Court that the number of deaths occasioned by the use of nuclear weapons would be enormous; that the victims could, in certain cases, include persons of a particular national, ethnic, racial or religious group; and that the intention to destroy such groups could be inferred from the fact that the user of the nuclear weapon would have omitted to take account of the well-known effects of the use of such weapons.

The Court would point out in that regard that the prohibition of genocide would be pertinent in this case if the recourse to nuclear weapons did indeed entail the element of intent, towards a group as such, required by the provision quoted above. In the view of the Court, it would only be possible to arrive at such a conclusion after having taken due account of the circumstances specific to each case.

27. In both their written and oral statements, some States furthermore argued that any use of nuclear weapons would be unlawful by reference to existing norms relating to the safeguarding and protection of the environment, in view of their essential importance.

Specific references were made to various existing international treaties and instruments. These included Additional Protocol I of 1977 to the Geneva Conventions of 1949, Article 35, paragraph 3, of which prohibits the employment of "methods or means of warfare which are intended, or may be expected, to cause widespread, long-term and severe damage to the natural environment"; and the Convention of 18 May 1977 on the Prohibition of Military or Any Other Hostile Use of Environmental Modification Techniques, which prohibits the use of weapons which [*821] have "widespread, long-lasting or severe effects" on the environment (Art. 1). Also cited were Principle 21 of the Stockholm Declaration of 1972 and Principle 2 of the Rio Declaration of 1992 which express the common conviction of the States concerned that they have a duty "to ensure that activities within their jurisdiction or control do not cause damage to the environment of other States or of areas beyond the limits of national jurisdiction". These instruments and other provisions relating to the protection and safeguarding of the environment were said to apply at all times, in war as well as in peace, and it was contended that they would be violated by the use of nuclear weapons whose consequences would be widespread and would have transboundary effects.

28. Other States questioned the binding legal quality of these precepts of environmental law; or, in the context of the Convention on the Prohibition of Military or Any Other Hostile Use of Environmental Modification Techniques, denied that it was concerned at all with the use of nuclear weapons in hostilities; or, in the case of Additional Protocol I, denied that they were generally bound by its terms, or recalled that they had reserved their position in respect of Article 35, paragraph 3, thereof.

It was also argued by some States that the principal purpose of environmental treaties and norms was the protection of the environment in time of peace. It was said that those treaties made no mention of nuclear weapons. It was also pointed out that warfare in general, and nuclear warfare in particular, were not mentioned in their texts and that it would be destabilizing to the rule of law and to confidence in international negotiations if those treaties were now interpreted in such a way as to prohibit the use of nuclear weapons.

29. The Court recognizes that the environment is under daily threat and that the use of nuclear weapons could constitute a catastrophe for the environment. The Court also recognizes that the environment is not an abstraction but represents the living space, the quality of life and the very health of human beings, including generations unborn. The existence of the general obligation of States to ensure that activities within their jurisdiction and control respect the environment of other States or of areas beyond national control is now part of the corpus of international

law relating to the environment.

30. However, the Court is of the view that the issue is not whether the treaties relating to the protection of the environment are or not applicable during an armed conflict, but rather whether the obligations stemming from these treaties were intended to be obligations of total restraint during military conflict.

The Court does not consider that the treaties in question could have intended to deprive a State of the exercise of its right of self-defence under international law because of its obligations to protect the environment. Nonetheless, States must take environmental considerations into account when assessing what is necessary and proportionate in the pursuit of legitimate military objectives. Respect for the environment is one of the elements that go to assessing whether an action is in conformity with the principles of necessity and proportionality.

This approach is supported, indeed, by the terms of Principle 24 of the Rio Declaration, which provides that:

"Warfare is inherently destructive of sustainable development. States shall therefore respect international law providing protection for the environment in times of armed conflict and cooperate in its further development, as necessary."

31. The Court notes furthermore that Articles 35, paragraph 3, and 55 of Additional Protocol 1 provide additional protection for the environment. Taken together, these provisions embody a general obligation to protect the natural environment against widespread, long-term and severe environmental damage; the prohibition of methods and means of warfare which are intended, or may be expected, to cause such damage; and the prohibition of attacks against the natural environment by way of reprisals.

These are powerful constraints for all the States having subscribed to these provisions.

32. General Assembly resolution 47/37 of 25 November 1992 on the Protection of the Environment in Times of Armed Conflict, is also of interest in this context. It affirms the general view according to which environmental considerations constitute one of the elements to be taken into account in the implementation of the principles of the law applicable in armed conflict: it states that "destruction of the environment, not justified by military necessity and carried out wantonly, is clearly contrary to existing international law". Addressing the reality that certain instruments are not yet binding on all States, the General Assembly in this resolution "appeals to all States that have not yet done so to consider becoming parties to the relevant international conventions."

In its recent Order in the Request for an Examination of the Situation in Accordance with Paragraph 63 of the Court's Judgment of 20 December 1974 in the Nuclear Tests (New Zealand v. France) Case, the Court stated that its conclusion was "without prejudice to the obligations of States to respect and protect the natural environment" (Order of 22 September 1995, I.C.J. Reports 1995, p. 306, para. 64). Although that statement was made in the context of nuclear testing, it naturally also applies to the actual use of nuclear weapons in armed conflict.

33. The Court thus finds that while the existing international law relating to the protection and safeguarding of the environment does not specifically prohibit the use of nuclear weapons, it indicates important environmental factors that are properly to be taken into account in the context of the implementation of the principles and rules of the law applicable in armed conflict.

34. In the light of the foregoing the Court concludes that the most directly relevant applicable law governing the question of which it was seised, is that relating to the use of force enshrined in the United Nations Charter and the law applicable in armed conflict which regulates the conduct of hostilities, together with any specific treaties on nuclear weapons that the Court might determine to be relevant.

35. In applying this law to the present case, the Court cannot however fail to take into account certain unique characteristics of nuclear weapons.

[*822] The Court has noted the definitions of nuclear weapons contained in various treaties and accords. It also notes that nuclear weapons are explosive devices whose energy results from the fusion or fission of the atom. By its very nature, that process, in nuclear weapons as they exist today, releases not only immense quantities of heat and energy, but also powerful and prolonged radiation. According to the material before the Court, the first two causes of damage are vastly more powerful than the damage caused by other weapons, while the phenomenon of radiation is said to be peculiar to nuclear weapons. These characteristics render the nuclear weapon potentially catastrophic. The destructive power of nuclear weapons cannot be contained in either space or time. They have the potential to destroy all civilization and the entire ecosystem of the planet.

The radiation released by a nuclear explosion would affect health, agriculture, natural resources and demography over a very wide area. Further, the use of nuclear weapons would be a serious danger to future generations. Ionizing radiation has the potential to damage the future environment, food and marine ecosystem, and to cause genetic defects and illness in future generations.

36. In consequence, in order correctly to apply to the present case the Charter law on the use of force and the law applicable in armed conflict, in particular humanitarian law, it is imperative for the Court to take account of the unique characteristics of nuclear weapons, and in particular their destructive capacity, their capacity to cause untold human suffering, and their ability to cause damage to generations to come.

37. The Court will now address the question of the legality or illegality of recourse to nuclear weapons in the light of the provisions of the Charter relating to the threat or use of force.

38. The Charter contains several provisions relating to the threat and use of force. In Article 2, paragraph 4, the threat or use of force against the territorial integrity or political independence of another State or in any other manner inconsistent with the purposes of the United Nations is prohibited. That paragraph provides:

"All Members shall refrain in their international relations from the threat or use of force against the territorial integrity or political independence of any State, or in any other manner inconsistent with the Purposes of the United Nations."

This prohibition of the use of force is to be considered in the light of other relevant provisions of the Charter. In Article 51, the Charter recognizes the inherent right of individual or collective self-defence if an armed attack occurs. A further lawful use of force is envisaged in Article 42, whereby the Security Council may take military enforcement measures in conformity with Chapter VII of the Charter.

39. These provisions do not refer to specific weapons. They apply to any use of force, regardless of the weapons employed. The Charter neither expressly prohibits, nor permits, the use of any specific weapon, including nuclear weapons. A weapon that is already unlawful per se, whether by treaty or custom, does not become lawful by reason of its being used for a legitimate purpose under the Charter.

40. The entitlement to resort to self-defence under Article 51 is subject to certain constraints. Some of these constraints are inherent in the very concept of self defence. Other requirements are specified in Article 51.

41. The submission of the exercise of the right of self-defence to the conditions of necessity and proportionality is a rule of customary international law. As the Court stated in the case concerning Military and Paramilitary Activities in and against Nicaragua (Nicaragua v United States of America) (I.C.J. Reports 1986, p. 94, para. 176): "there is a specific rule whereby self-defence would warrant only measures which are proportional to the armed attack and necessary to respond to it, a rule well established in customary international law". This dual condition applies equally to Article 51 of the Charter, whatever the means of force employed.

42. The proportionality principle may thus not in itself exclude the use of nuclear weapons in self-defence in all circumstances. But at the same time, a use of force that is proportionate under the law of self-defence, must, in order to be lawful, also meet the requirements of the law applicable in armed conflict which comprise in particular the principles and rules of humanitarian law.

43. Certain States have in their written and oral pleadings suggested that in the

case of nuclear weapons, the condition of proportionality must be evaluated in the light of still further factors. They contend that the very nature of nuclear weapons, and the high probability of an escalation of nuclear exchanges, mean that there is an extremely strong risk of devastation. The risk factor is said to negate the possibility of the condition of proportionality being complied with. The Court does not find it necessary to embark upon the quantification of such risks; nor does it need to enquire into the question whether tactical nuclear weapons exist which are sufficiently precise to limit those risks: it suffices for the Court to note that the very nature of all nuclear weapons and the profound risks associated therewith are further considerations to be borne in mind by States believing they can exercise a nuclear response in self-defence in accordance with the requirements of proportionality.

44. Beyond the conditions of necessity and proportionality, Article 51 specifically requires that measures taken by States in the exercise of the right of self-defence shall be immediately reported to the Security Council; this article further provides that these measures shall not in any way affect the authority and responsibility of the Security Council under the Charter to take at any time such action as it deems necessary in order to maintain or restore international peace and security. These requirements of Article 51 apply whatever the means of force used in self-defence.

45. The Court notes that the Security Council adopted on 11 April 1995, in the context of the extension of the Treaty on the Non-Proliferation of Nuclear Weapons, resolution 984 (1995) by the terms of which, on the one hand, it [*823] "takes note with appreciation of the statements made by each of the nuclear-weapon States (S/1995/261, S/1995/262, S/1995/263, S/1995/264, S/1995/265), in which they give security assurances against the use of nuclear weapons to non-nuclear-weapon States that are Parties to the Treaty on the Non-Proliferation of Nuclear Weapons,"

and, on the other hand, it "welcomes the intention expressed by certain States that they will provide or support immediate assistance, in accordance with the Charter, to any non-nuclear-weapon State Party to the Treaty on the Non-Proliferation of Nuclear Weapons that is a victim of an act of, or an object of a threat of, aggression in which nuclear weapons are used".

46. Certain States asserted that the use of nuclear weapons in the conduct of reprisals would be lawful. The Court does not have to examine, in this context, the question of armed reprisals in time of peace, which are considered to be unlawful. Nor does it have to pronounce on the question of belligerent reprisals save to observe that in any case any right of recourse to such reprisals would, like self-defence, be governed inter alia by the principle of proportionality.

47. In order to lessen or eliminate the risk of unlawful attack, States

sometimes signal that they possess certain weapons to use in self-defence against any State violating their territorial integrity or political independence. Whether a signalled intention to use force if certain events occur is or is not a "threat" within Article 2, paragraph 4, of the Charter depends upon various factors. If the envisaged use of force is itself unlawful, the stated readiness to use it would be a threat prohibited under Article 2, paragraph 4. Thus it would be illegal for a State to threaten force to secure territory from another State, or to cause it to follow or not follow certain political or economic paths. The notions of "threat" and "use" of force under Article 2, paragraph 4, of the Charter stand together in the sense that if the use of force itself in a given case is illegal -- for whatever reason -- the threat to use such force will likewise be illegal. In short, if it is to be lawful, the declared readiness of a State to use force must be a use of force that is in conformity with the Charter. For the rest, no State -- whether or not it defended the policy of deterrence -- suggested to the Court that it would be lawful to threaten to use force if the use of force contemplated would be illegal.

48. Some States put forward the argument that possession of nuclear weapons is itself an unlawful threat to use force. Possession of nuclear weapons may indeed justify an inference of preparedness to use them. In order to be effective, the policy of deterrence, by which those States possessing or under the umbrella of nuclear weapons seek to discourage military aggression by demonstrating that it will serve no purpose, necessitates that the intention to use nuclear weapons be credible. Whether this is a "threat" contrary to Article 2, paragraph 4, depends upon whether the particular use of force envisaged would be directed against the territorial integrity or political independence of a State, or against the Purposes of the United Nations or whether, in the event that it were intended as a means of defence, it would necessarily violate the principles of necessity and proportionality. In any of these circumstances the use of force, and the threat to use it, would be unlawful under the law of the Charter.

49. Moreover, the Security Council may take enforcement measures under Chapter VII of the Charter. From the statements presented to it the Court does not consider it necessary to address questions which might, in a given case, arise from the application of Chapter VII.

50. The terms of the question put to the Court by the General Assembly in resolution 49/75K could in principle also cover a threat or use of nuclear weapons by a State within its own boundaries. However, this particular aspect has not been dealt with by any of the States which addressed the Court orally or in writing in these proceedings. The Court finds that it is not called upon to deal with an internal use of nuclear weapons.

51. Having dealt with the Charter provisions relating to the threat or use of force, the Court will now turn to the law applicable in situations of armed conflict. It will first address the question whether there are specific rules in international law regulating the legality or illegality of recourse to nuclear weapons per se; it will then examine the question put to it in the light of the law applicable in armed

conflict proper, i.e. the principles and rules of humanitarian law applicable in armed conflict, and the law of neutrality.

52. The Court notes by way of introduction that international customary and treaty law does not contain any specific prescription authorizing the threat or use of nuclear weapons or any other weapon in general or in certain circumstances, in particular those of the exercise of legitimate self-defence. Nor, however, is there any principle or rule of international law which would make the legality of the threat or use of nuclear weapons or of any other weapons dependent on a specific authorization. State practice shows that the illegality of the use of certain weapons as such does not result from an absence of authorization but, on the contrary, is formulated in terms of prohibition.

53. The Court must therefore now examine whether there is any prohibition of recourse to nuclear weapons as such; it will first ascertain whether there is a conventional prescription to this effect.

54. In this regard, the argument has been advanced that nuclear weapons should be treated in the same way as poisoned weapons. In that case, they would be prohibited under:
(a) the Second Hague Declaration of 29 July 1899, which prohibits "the use of projectiles the object of which is the diffusion of asphyxiating or deleterious gases";
[*824] (b) Article 23 (a) of the Regulations respecting the laws and customs of war on land annexed to the Hague Convention IV of 18 October 1907, whereby "it is especially forbidden: ...to employ poison or poisoned weapons"; and
(c) the Geneva Protocol of 17 June 1925 which prohibits "the use in war of asphyxiating, poisonous or other gases, and of all analogous liquids, materials or devices".

55. The Court will observe that the Regulations annexed to the Hague Convention IV do not define what is to be understood by "poison or poisoned weapons" and that different interpretations exist on the issue. Nor does the 1925 Protocol specify the meaning to be given to the term "analogous materials or devices". The terms have been understood, in the practice of States, in their ordinary sense as covering weapons whose prime, or even exclusive, effect is to poison or asphyxiate. This practice is clear, and the parties to those instruments have not treated them as referring to nuclear weapons.

56. In view of this, it does not seem to the Court that the use of nuclear weapons can be regarded as specifically prohibited on the basis of the above-mentioned provisions of the Second Hague Declaration of 1899, the Regulations annexed to the Hague Convention IV of 1907 or the 1925 Protocol (see paragraph 54 above).

57. The pattern until now has been for weapons of mass destruction to be declared illegal by specific instruments. The most recent such instruments are the

Convention of 10 April 1972 on the Prohibition of the Development, Production and Stockpiling of Bacteriological (Biological) and Toxin Weapons and on their destruction -- which prohibits the possession of bacteriological and toxic weapons and reinforces the prohibition of their use -- and the Convention of 13 January 1993 on the Prohibition of the Development, Production, Stockpiling and Use of Chemical Weapons and on Their Destruction -- which prohibits all use of chemical weapons and requires the destruction of existing stocks. Each of these instruments has been negotiated and adopted in its own context and for its own reasons. The Court does not find any specific prohibition of recourse to nuclear weapons in treaties expressly prohibiting the use of certain weapons of mass destruction.

58. In the last two decades, a great many negotiations have been conducted regarding nuclear weapons; they have not resulted in a treaty of general prohibition of the same kind as for bacteriological and chemical weapons. However, a number of specific treaties have been concluded in order to limit:
(a) the acquisition, manufacture and possession of nuclear weapons (Peace Treaties of 10 February 1947; State Treaty for the Re-establishment of an Independent and Democratic Austria of 15 May 1955; Treaty of Tlatelolco of 14 February 1967 for the Prohibition of Nuclear Weapons in Latin America, and its Additional Protocols; Treaty of 1 July 1968 on the Non-Proliferation of Nuclear Weapons; Treaty of Rarotonga of 6 August 1985 on the Nuclear-Weapon-Free Zone of the South Pacific, and its Protocols; Treaty of 12 September 1990 on the Final Settlement with respect to Germany);
(b) the deployment of nuclear weapons (Antarctic Treaty of 1 December 1959; Treaty of 27 January 1967 on Principles Governing the Activities of States in the Exploration and Use of Outer Space, including the Moon and Other Celestial Bodies; Treaty of Tlatelolco of 14 February 1967 for the Prohibition of Nuclear Weapons in Latin America, and its Additional Protocols; Treaty of 11 February 1971 on the Prohibition of the Emplacement of Nuclear Weapons and Other Weapons of Mass Destruction on the Sea-Bed and the Ocean Floor and in the Subsoil Thereof; Treaty of Rarotonga of 6 August 1985 on the Nuclear-Weapon-Free Zone of the South Pacific, and its Protocols); and
(c) the testing of nuclear weapons (Antarctic Treaty of 1 December 1959; Treaty of 5 August 1963 Banning Nuclear Weapon Tests in the Atmosphere, in Outer Space and under Water; Treaty of 27 January 1967 on Principles Governing the Activities of States in the Exploration and Use of Outer Space, including the Moon and Other Celestial Bodies; Treaty of Tlatelolco of 14 February 1967 for the Prohibition of Nuclear Weapons in Latin America, and its Additional Protocols; Treaty of Rarotonga of 6 August 1985 on the Nuclear-Weapon-Free Zone of the South Pacific, and its Protocols).

59. Recourse to nuclear weapons is directly addressed by two of these Conventions and also in connection with the indefinite extension of the Treaty on the Non-Proliferation of Nuclear Weapons of 1968:
(a) the Treaty of Tlatelolco of 14 February 1967 for the Prohibition of Nuclear Weapons in Latin America prohibits, in Article 1, the use of nuclear weapons by

the Contracting Parties. It further includes an Additional Protocol II open to nuclear-weapon States outside the region, Article 3 of which provides:

"The Governments represented by the undersigned Plenipotentiaries also undertake not to use or threaten to use nuclear weapons against the Contracting Parties of the Treaty for the Prohibition of Nuclear Weapons in Latin America." The Protocol was signed and ratified by the five nuclear-weapon States. Its ratification was accompanied by a variety of declarations. The United Kingdom Government, for example, stated that "in the event of any act of aggression by a Contracting Party to the Treaty in which that Party was supported by a nuclear-weapon State", the United Kingdom Government would "be free to reconsider the extent to which they could be regarded as committed by the provisions of Additional Protocol II". The United States made a similar statement. The French Government, for its part, stated that it "interprets the undertaking made in article 3 of the Protocol as being without prejudice to the full exercise of the right of self-defence confirmed by Article 51 of the Charter". China reaffirmed its commitment not to be the first to make use of nuclear weapons. The Soviet Union reserved "the right to review" the obligations imposed upon it by Additional Protocol II, particularly in the event of an attack by a State party either "in support of a nuclear-weapon State or jointly with that State". None of these statements drew comment or objection from the parties to the Treaty of Tlatelolco.

(b) the Treaty of Rarotonga of 6 August 1985 establishes a South Pacific Nuclear Free Zone in which the Parties undertake not to manufacture, acquire or possess any nuclear explosive device (Art. 3). Unlike the Treaty of Tlatelolco, the Treaty of Rarotonga does not expressly prohibit the use of such weapons. But such a prohibition is for the States parties the necessary consequence of the prohibitions stipulated by the Treaty. The Treaty has a number of protocols. Protocol 2, open to the five nuclear-weapon States, specifies in its Article 1 that:

"Each Party undertakes not to use or threaten to use any nuclear explosive device against:

[*825] (a) Parties to the Treaty; or

(b) any territory within the South Pacific Nuclear Free Zone for which a State that has become a Party to Protocol 1 is internationally responsible."

China and Russia are parties to that Protocol. In signing it, China and the Soviet Union each made a declaration by which they reserved the " right to reconsider" their obligations under the said Protocol; the Soviet Union also referred to certain circumstances in which it would consider itself released from those obligations. France, the United Kingdom and the United States, for their part, signed Protocol 2 on 25 March 1996, but have not yet ratified it. On that occasion, France declared, on the one hand, that no provision in that Protocol "shall impair the full exercise of the inherent right of self-defence provided for in Article 51 of the ... Charter" and, on the other hand, that "the commitment set out in Article 1 of [that] Protocol amounts to the negative security assurances given by France to non-nuclear-weapon States which are parties to the Treaty on . . . Non-Proliferation", and that "these assurances shall not apply to States which are not parties" to that Treaty. For its part, the United Kingdom made a declaration setting out the precise circumstances in which it "will not be bound by [its] undertaking under Article 1" of the Protocol.

(c) as to the Treaty on the Non-Proliferation of Nuclear Weapons, at the time of its signing in 1968 the United States, the United Kingdom and the USSR gave various security assurances to the non-nuclear-weapon States that were parties to the Treaty. In resolution 255 (1968) the Security Council took note with satisfaction of the intention expressed by those three States to "provide or support immediate assistance, in accordance with the Charter, to any non-nuclear-weapon State Party to the Treaty on the Non-Proliferation . . . that is a victim of an act of, or an object of a threat of, aggression in which nuclear weapons are used".

On the occasion of the extension of the Treaty in 1995, the five nuclear-weapon States gave their non-nuclear-weapon partners, by means of separate unilateral statements on 5 and 6 April 1995, positive and negative security assurances against the use of such weapons. All the five nuclear-weapon States first undertook not to use nuclear weapons against non-nuclear-weapon States that were parties to the Treaty on the Non-Proliferation of Nuclear Weapons. However, these States, apart from China, made an exception in the case of an invasion or any other attack against them, their territories, armed forces or allies, or on a State towards which they had a security commitment, carried out or sustained by a non-nuclear-weapon State party to the Non-Proliferation Treaty in association or alliance with a nuclear-weapon State. Each of the nuclear-weapon States further undertook, as a permanent Member of the Security Council, in the event of an attack with the use of nuclear weapons, or threat of such attack, against a non-nuclear-weapon State, to refer the matter to the Security Council without delay and to act within it in order that it might take immediate measures with a view to supplying, pursuant to the Charter, the necessary assistance to the victim State (the commitments assumed comprising minor variations in wording). The Security Council, in unanimously adopting resolution 984 (1995) of 11 April 1995, cited above, took note of those statements with appreciation. It also recognized "that the nuclear-weapon State permanent members of the Security Council will bring the matter immediately to the attention of the Council and seek Council action to provide, in accordance with the Charter, the necessary assistance to the State victim"; and welcomed the fact that "the intention expressed by certain States that they will provide or support immediate assistance, in accordance with the Charter, to any non-nuclear- weapon State Party to the Treaty on the Non-Proliferation of Nuclear Weapons that is a victim of an act of, or an object of a threat of, aggression in which nuclear weapons are used."

60. Those States that believe that recourse to nuclear weapons is illegal stress that the conventions that include various rules providing for the limitation or elimination of nuclear weapons in certain areas (such as the Antarctic Treaty of 1959 which prohibits the deployment of nuclear weapons in the Antarctic, or the Treaty of Tlatelolco of 1967 which creates a nuclear-weapon-free zone in Latin America), or the conventions that apply certain measures of control and limitation to the existence of nuclear weapons (such as the 1963 Partial Test-Ban Treaty or the Treaty on the Non-Proliferation of Nuclear Weapons) all set limits to the use of nuclear weapons. In their view, these treaties bear witness, in their own way, to the emergence of a rule of complete legal prohibition of all uses of nuclear weapons.

61. Those States who defend the position that recourse to nuclear weapons is legal in certain circumstances see a logical contradiction in reaching such a conclusion. According to them, those Treaties, such as the Treaty on the Non-Proliferation of Nuclear Weapons, as well as Security Council resolutions 255 (1968) and 984 (1995) which take note of the security assurances given by the nuclear-weapon States to the non-nuclear-weapon States in relation to any nuclear aggression against the latter, cannot be understood as prohibiting the use of nuclear weapons, and such a claim is contrary to the very text of those instruments. For those who support the legality in certain circumstances of recourse to nuclear weapons, there is no absolute prohibition against the use of such weapons. The very logic and construction of the Treaty on the Non-Proliferation of Nuclear Weapons, they assert, confirm this. This Treaty, whereby, they contend, the possession of nuclear weapons by the five nuclear-weapon States has been accepted, cannot be seen as a treaty banning their use by those States; to accept the fact that those States possess nuclear weapons is tantamount to recognizing that such weapons may be used in certain circumstances. Nor, they contend, could the security assurances given by the nuclear-weapon States in 1968, and more recently in connection with the Review and Extension Conference of the Parties to the Treaty on the Non-Proliferation of Nuclear Weapons in 1995, have been conceived without its being supposed that there were circumstances in which nuclear weapons could be used in a lawful manner. For those who defend the legality of the use, in certain circumstances, of nuclear weapons, the acceptance of those instruments by the different non-nuclear-weapon States confirms and reinforces the evident logic upon which those instruments are based.

62. The Court notes that the treaties dealing exclusively with acquisition, manufacture, possession, deployment and testing of nuclear weapons, without specifically addressing their threat or use, certainly point to an increasing concern in the international community with these weapons; the Court concludes from this that these treaties could therefore be seen as foreshadowing a future general prohibition of the use of such weapons, but they do not constitute such a prohibition by themselves. As to the treaties of Tlatelolco and Rarotonga and their Protocols, and also the declarations made in connection with the indefinite extension of the Treaty on the Non-Proliferation of Nuclear Weapons, it emerges

from these instruments that:

[*826] (a) a number of States have undertaken not to use nuclear weapons in specific zones (Latin America; the South Pacific) or against certain other States (non-nuclear-weapon States which are parties to the Treaty on the Non-Proliferation of Nuclear Weapons);

(b) nevertheless, even within this framework, the nuclear-weapon States have reserved the right to use nuclear weapons in certain circumstances; and

(c) these reservations met with no objection from the parties to the Tlatelolco or Rarotonga Treaties or from the Security Council.

63. These two treaties, the security assurances given in 1995 by the nuclear-weapon States and the fact that the Security Council took note of them with satisfaction, testify to a growing awareness of the need to liberate the community of States and the international public from the dangers resulting from the existence of nuclear weapons. The Court moreover notes the signing, even more recently, on 15 December 1995, at Bangkok, of a Treaty on the Southeast Asia Nuclear-Weapon-Free Zone, and on 11 April 1996, at Cairo, of a treaty on the creation of a nuclear-weapons-free zone in Africa. It does not, however, view these elements as amounting to a comprehensive and universal conventional prohibition on the use, or the threat of use, of those weapons as such.

64. The Court will now turn to an examination of customary international law to determine whether a prohibition of the threat or use of nuclear weapons as such flows from that source of law. As the Court has stated, the substance of that law must be "looked for primarily in the actual practice and opinio juris of States" (Continental Shelf (Libyan Arab Jamahiriya/Malta), Judgment, I.C.J. Reports 1985, p. 29, para. 27).

65. States which hold the view that the use of nuclear weapons is illegal have endeavoured to demonstrate the existence of a customary rule prohibiting this use. They refer to a consistent practice of non-utilization of nuclear weapons by States since 1945 and they would see in that practice the expression of an opinio juris on the part of those who possess such weapons.

66. Some other States, which assert the legality of the threat and use of nuclear weapons in certain circumstances, invoked the doctrine and practice of deterrence in support of their argument. They recall that they have always, in concert with certain other States, reserved the right to use those weapons in the exercise of the right to self-defence against an armed attack threatening their vital security interests. In their view, if nuclear weapons have not been used since 1945, it is not on account of an existing or nascent custom but merely because circumstances that might justify their use have fortunately not arisen.

67. The Court does not intend to pronounce here upon the practice known as the "policy of deterrence." It notes that it is a fact that a number of States adhered to that practice during the greater part of the Cold War and continue to adhere to it. Furthermore, the Members of the international community are profoundly divided

on the matter of whether non-recourse to nuclear weapons over the past fifty years constitutes the expression of an opinio juris. Under these circumstances the Court does not consider itself able to find that there is such an opinio juris.

68. According to certain States, the important series of General Assembly resolutions, beginning with resolution 1653 (XVI) of 24 November 1961, that deal with nuclear weapons and that affirm, with consistent regularity, the illegality of nuclear weapons, signify the existence of a rule of international customary law which prohibits recourse to those weapons. According to other States, however, the resolutions in question have no binding character on their own account and are not declaratory of any customary rule of prohibition of nuclear weapons; some of these States have also pointed out that this series of resolutions not only did not meet with the approval of all of the nuclear-weapon States but of many other States as well.

69. States which consider that the use of nuclear weapons is illegal indicated that those resolutions did not claim to create any new rules, but were confined to a confirmation of customary law relating to the prohibition of means or methods of warfare which, by their use, overstepped the bounds of what is permissible in the conduct of hostilities. In their view, the resolutions in question did no more than apply to nuclear weapons the existing rules of international law applicable in armed conflict; they were no more than the "envelope" or instrumentum containing certain pre-existing customary rules of international law. For those States it is accordingly of little importance that the instrumentum should have occasioned negative votes, which cannot have the effect of obliterating those customary rules which have been confirmed by treaty law.

70. The Court notes that General Assembly resolutions, even if they are not binding, may sometimes have normative value. They can, in certain circumstances, provide evidence important for establishing the existence of a rule or the emergence of an opinio juris. To establish whether this is true of a given General Assembly resolution, it is necessary to look at its content and the conditions of its adoption; it is also necessary to see whether an opinio juris exists as to its normative character. Or a series of resolutions may show the gradual evolution of the opinio juris required for the establishment of a new rule.

71. Examined in their totality, the General Assembly resolutions put before the Court declare that the use of nuclear weapons would be "a direct violation of the Charter of the United Nations"; and in certain formulations that such use "should be prohibited". The focus of these resolutions has sometimes shifted to diverse related matters; however, several of the resolutions under consideration in the present case have been adopted with substantial numbers of negative votes and abstentions; thus, although those resolutions are a clear sign of deep concern regarding the problem of nuclear weapons, they still fall short of establishing the existence of an opinio juris on the illegality of the use of such weapons.

72. The Court further notes that the first of the resolutions of the General

Assembly expressly proclaiming the illegality of the use of nuclear weapons, resolution 1653 (XVI) of 24 November 1961 (mentioned in subsequent resolutions), after referring to certain international declarations and binding agreements, from the Declaration of St. Petersburg of 1868 to the Geneva Protocol of 1925, proceeded to qualify the legal nature of nuclear weapons, determine their effects, and apply general rules of customary international law to nuclear weapons in particular. That application by the General Assembly of general rules of customary law to the particular case of nuclear weapons indicates that, in its view, there was no specific rule of customary law which prohibited the use of nuclear weapons; if such a rule had existed, the General Assembly could simply have referred to it and would not have needed to undertake such an exercise of legal qualification.

[*827] 73. Having said this, the Court points out that the adoption each year by the General Assembly, by a large majority, of resolutions recalling the content of resolution 1653 (XVI), and requesting the member States to conclude a convention prohibiting the use of nuclear weapons in any circumstance, reveals the desire of a very large section of the international community to take, by a specific and express prohibition of the use of nuclear weapons, a significant step forward along the road to complete nuclear disarmament. The emergence, as lex lata, of a customary rule specifically prohibiting the use of nuclear weapons as such is hampered by the continuing tensions between the nascent opinio juris on the one hand, and the still strong adherence to the practice of deterrence on the other.

74. The Court not having found a conventional rule of general scope, nor a customary rule specifically proscribing the threat or use of nuclear weapons per se, it will now deal with the question whether recourse to nuclear weapons must be considered as illegal in the light of the principles and rules of international humanitarian law applicable in armed conflict and of the law of neutrality.

75. A large number of customary rules have been developed by the practice of States and are an integral part of the international law relevant to the question posed. The "laws and customs of war" -- as they were traditionally called -- were the subject of efforts at codification undertaken in The Hague (including the Conventions of 1899 and 1907), and were based partly upon the St. Petersburg Declaration of 1868 as well as the results of the Brussels Conference of 1874. This "Hague Law" and, more particularly, the Regulations Respecting the Laws and Customs of War on Land, fixed the rights and duties of belligerents in their conduct of operations and limited the choice of methods and means of injuring the enemy in an international armed conflict. One should add to this the "Geneva Law" (the Conventions of 1864, 1906, 1929 and 1949), which protects the victims of war and aims to provide safeguards for disabled armed forces personnel and persons not taking part in the hostilities. These two branches of the law applicable in armed conflict have become so closely interrelated that they are considered to have gradually formed one single complex system, known today as international humanitarian law. The provisions of the Additional Protocols of 1977 give

expression and attest to the unity and complexity of that law.

76. Since the turn of the century, the appearance of new means of combat has -- without calling into question the longstanding principles and rules of international law -- rendered necessary some specific prohibitions of the use of certain weapons, such as explosive projectiles under 400 grammes, dum-dum bullets and asphyxiating gases. Chemical and bacteriological weapons were then prohibited by the 1925 Geneva Protocol. More recently, the use of weapons producing "non-detectable fragments", of other types of "mines, booby traps and other devices", and of "incendiary weapons", was either prohibited or limited, depending on the case, by the Convention of 10 October 1980 on Prohibitions or Restrictions on the Use of Certain Conventional Weapons Which May Be Deemed to Be Excessively Injurious or to Have Indiscriminate Effects. The provisions of the Convention on "mines, booby traps and other devices" have just been amended, on 3 May 1996, and now regulate in greater detail, for example, the use of anti-personnel land mines.

77. All this shows that the conduct of military operations is governed by a body of legal prescriptions. This is so because "the right of belligerents to adopt means of injuring the enemy is not unlimited" as stated in Article 22 of the 1907 Hague Regulations relating to the laws and customs of war on land. The St. Petersburg Declaration had already condemned the use of weapons "which uselessly aggravate the suffering of disabled men or make their death inevitable". The aforementioned Regulations relating to the laws and customs of war on land, annexed to the Hague Convention IV of 1907, prohibit the use of "arms, projectiles, or material calculated to cause unnecessary suffering" (Art. 23).

78. The cardinal principles contained in the texts constituting the fabric of humanitarian law are the following. The first is aimed at the protection of the civilian population and civilian objects and establishes the distinction between combatants and non-combatants; States must never make civilians the object of attack and must consequently never use weapons that are incapable of distinguishing between civilian and military targets. According to the second principle, it is prohibited to cause unnecessary suffering to combatants: it is accordingly prohibited to use weapons causing them such harm or uselessly aggravating their suffering. In application of that second principle, States do not have unlimited freedom of choice of means in the weapons they use.

The Court would likewise refer, in relation to these principles, to the MARTENS Clause, which was first included in the Hague Convention II with Respect to the Laws and Customs of War on Land of 1899 and which has proved to be an effective means of addressing the rapid evolution of military technology. A modern version of that clause is to be found in Article 1, paragraph 2, of Additional Protocol I of 1977, which reads as follows:

"In cases not covered by this Protocol or by other international agreements, civilians and combatants remain under the protection and authority of the principles of international law derived from established custom, from the principles of humanity and from the dictates of public conscience."

In conformity with the aforementioned principles, humanitarian law, at a very early stage, prohibited certain types of weapons either because of their indiscriminate effect on combatants and civilians or because of the unnecessary suffering caused to combatants, that is to say, a harm greater than that unavoidable to achieve legitimate military objectives. If an envisaged use of weapons would not meet the requirements of humanitarian law, a threat to engage in such use would also be contrary to that law.

79. It is undoubtedly because a great many rules of humanitarian law applicable in armed conflict are so fundamental to the respect of the human person and "elementary considerations of humanity" as the Court put it in its Judgment of 9 April 1949 in the Corfu Channel case (I.C.J. Reports 1949, p. 22), that the Hague and Geneva Conventions have enjoyed a broad accession. Further these fundamental rules are to be observed by all States whether or not they have ratified the conventions that contain them, because they constitute intransgressible principles of international customary law.

80. The Nuremberg International Military Tribunal had already found in 1945 that the humanitarian rules included in the Regulations annexed to the Hague Convention IV of 1907 "were recognized by all civilized nations and were regarded as being declaratory of the laws and customs of war" (International Military Tribunal, Trial of the Major War Criminals, 14 November 1945 -- 1 October 1946, Nuremberg, 1947, Vol. 1, p. 254).

[*828] 81. The Report of the Secretary-General pursuant to paragraph 2 of Security Council resolution 808 (1993), with which he introduced the Statute of the International Tribunal for the Prosecution of Persons Responsible for Serious Violations of International Humanitarian Law Committed in the Territory of the Former Yugoslavia since 1991, and which was unanimously approved by the Security Council (resolution 827 (1993)), stated:

"In the view of the Secretary-General, the application of the principle nullum crimen sine lege requires that the international tribunal should apply rules of international humanitarian law which are beyond any doubt part of customary law .

The part of conventional international humanitarian law which has beyond doubt become part of international customary law is the law applicable in armed conflict as embodied in: the Geneva Conventions of 12 August 1949 for the Protection of War Victims; the Hague Convention (IV) Respecting the Laws and Customs of War on Land and the Regulations annexed thereto of 18 October 1907; the Convention on the Prevention and Punishment of the Crime of Genocide of 9 December 1948; and the Charter of the International Military Tribunal of 8 August 1945."

82. The extensive codification of humanitarian law and the extent of the accession to the resultant treaties, as well as the fact that the denunciation clauses that existed in the codification instruments have never been used, have provided the international community with a corpus of treaty rules the great majority of which had already become customary and which reflected the most universally recognized humanitarian principles. These rules indicate the normal conduct and behaviour expected of States.

83. It has been maintained in these proceedings that these principles and rules of humanitarian law are part of jus cogens as defined in Article 53 of the Vienna Convention on the Law of Treaties of 23 May 1969. The question whether a norm is part of the jus cogens relates to the legal character of the norm. The request addressed to the Court by the General Assembly raises the question of the applicability of the principles and rules of humanitarian law in cases of recourse to nuclear weapons and the consequences of that applicability for the legality of recourse to these weapons. But it does not raise the question of the character of the humanitarian law which would apply to the use of nuclear weapons. There is, therefore, no need for the Court to pronounce on this matter.

84. Nor is there any need for the Court elaborate on the question of the applicability of Additional Protocol I of 1977 to nuclear weapons. It need only observe that while, at the Diplomatic Conference of 1974-1977, there was no substantive debate on the nuclear issue and no specific solution concerning this question was put forward, Additional Protocol I in no way replaced the general customary rules applicable to all means and methods of combat including nuclear weapons. In particular, the Court recalls that all States are bound by those rules in Additional Protocol I which, when adopted, were merely the expression of the pre-existing customary law, such as the MARTENS Clause, reaffirmed in the first article of Additional Protocol I. The fact that certain types of weapons were not specifically dealt with by the 1974-1977 Conference does not permit the drawing of any legal conclusions relating to the substantive issues which the use of such weapons would raise.

85. Turning now to the applicability of the principles and rules of humanitarian law to a possible threat or use of nuclear weapons, the Court notes that doubts in this respect have sometimes been voiced on the ground that these principles and rules had evolved prior to the invention of nuclear weapons and that the Conferences of Geneva of 1949 and 1974-1977 which respectively adopted the four Geneva Conventions of 1949 and the two Additional Protocols thereto did not deal with nuclear weapons specifically. Such views, however, are only held by a small minority. In the view of the vast majority of States as well as writers there can be no doubt as to the applicability of humanitarian law to nuclear weapons.

86. The Court shares that view. Indeed, nuclear weapons were invented after most of the principles and rules of humanitarian law applicable in armed conflict

had already come into existence; the Conferences of 1949 and 1974-1977 left these weapons aside, and there is a qualitative as well as quantitative difference between nuclear weapons and all conventional arms. However, it cannot be concluded from this that the established principles and rules of humanitarian law applicable in armed conflict did not apply to nuclear weapons. Such a conclusion would be incompatible with the intrinsically humanitarian character of the legal principles in question which permeates the entire law of armed conflict and applies to all forms of warfare and to all kinds of weapons, those of the past, those of the present and those of the future. In this respect it seems significant that the thesis that the rules of humanitarian law do not apply to the new weaponry, because of the newness of the latter, has not been advocated in the present proceedings. On the contrary, the newness of nuclear weapons has been expressly rejected as an argument against the application to them of international humanitarian law:

"In general, international humanitarian law bears on the threat or use of nuclear weapons as it does of other weapons.

International humanitarian law has evolved to meet contemporary circumstances, and is not limited in its application to weaponry of an earlier time. The fundamental principles of this law endure: to mitigate and circumscribe the cruelty of war for humanitarian reasons." (New Zealand, Written Statement, p. 15, paras. 63-64.)

None of the statements made before the Court in any way advocated a freedom to use nuclear weapons without regard to humanitarian constraints. Quite the reverse; it has been explicitly stated,

"Restrictions set by the rules applicable to armed conflicts in respect of means and methods of warfare definitely also extend to nuclear weapons" (Russian Federation, CR 95/29, p. 52);

"So far as the customary law of war is concerned, the United Kingdom has always accepted that the use of nuclear weapons is subject to the general principles of the jus in bello" (United Kingdom, CR 95/34, p. 45); and

"The United States has long shared the view that the law of armed conflict governs the use of nuclear weapons -- just as it governs the use of conventional weapons" (United States of America, CR 95/34, p. 85.)

87. Finally, the Court points to the MARTENS Clause, whose continuing existence and applicability is not to be doubted, as an affirmation that the principles and rules of humanitarian law apply to nuclear weapons.

*

[*829] 88. The Court will now turn to the principle of neutrality which was raised by several States. In the context of the advisory proceedings brought before

the Court by the WHO concerning the Legality of the Use by a State of Nuclear Weapons in Armed Conflict, the position was put as follows by one State:

"The principle of neutrality, in its classic sense, was aimed at preventing the incursion of belligerent forces into neutral territory, or attacks on the persons or ships of neutrals. Thus: 'the territory of neutral powers is inviolable' (Article 1 of the Hague Convention (V) Respecting the Rights and Duties of Neutral Powers and Persons in Case of War on Land, concluded on 18 October 1907); 'belligerents are bound to respect the sovereign rights of neutral powers . . .' (Article 1 to the Hague Convention (XIII) Respecting the Rights and Duties of Neutral Powers in Naval War, concluded on 18 October 1907), 'neutral states have equal interest in having their rights respected by belligerents . . .' (Preamble to Convention on Maritime Neutrality, concluded on 20 February 1928). It is clear, however, that the principle of neutrality applies with equal force to transborder incursions of armed forces and to the transborder damage caused to a neutral State by the use of a weapon in a belligerent State." (Legality of the Use by a State of Nuclear Weapons in Armed Conflict, Nauru, Written Statement (I), p. 35, IV E.)

The principle so circumscribed is presented as an established part of the customary international law.

89. The Court finds that as in the case of the principles of humanitarian law applicable in armed conflict, international law leaves no doubt that the principle of neutrality, whatever its content, which is of a fundamental character similar to that of the humanitarian principles and rules, is applicable (subject to the relevant provisions of the United Nations Charter), to all international armed conflict, whatever type of weapons might be used.

90. Although the applicability of the principles and rules of humanitarian law and of the principle of neutrality to nuclear weapons is hardly disputed, the conclusions to be drawn from this applicability are, on the other hand, controversial.

91. According to one point of view, the fact that recourse to nuclear weapons is subject to and regulated by the law of armed conflict does not necessarily mean that such recourse is as such prohibited. As one State put it to the Court:

"Assuming that a State's use of nuclear weapons meets the requirements of self-defence, it must then be considered whether it conforms to the fundamental principles of the law of armed conflict regulating the conduct of hostilities" (United Kingdom, Written Statement, p. 40, para. 3.44);
"the legality of the use of nuclear weapons must therefore be assessed in the light of the applicable principles of international law regarding the use of force and the conduct of hostilities, as is the case with other methods and means of warfare" (United Kingdom, Written Statement, p. 75, para. 4.2(3)); and

"The reality . . . is that nuclear weapons might be used in a wide variety of circumstances with very different results in terms of likely civilian casualties. In some cases, such as the use of a low yield nuclear weapon against warships on the High Seas or troops in sparsely populated areas, it is possible to envisage a nuclear attack which caused comparatively few civilian casualties. It is by no means the case that every use of nuclear weapons against a military objective would inevitably cause very great collateral civilian casualties." (United Kingdom, Written Statement, p. 53, para. 3.70; see also United States of America, Oral Statement, CR 95/34, pp. 89-90.)

92. Another view holds that recourse to nuclear weapons could never be compatible with the principles and rules of humanitarian law and is therefore prohibited. In the event of their use, nuclear weapons would in all circumstances be unable to draw any distinction between the civilian population and combatants, or between civilian objects and military objectives, and their effects, largely uncontrollable, could not be restricted, either in time or in space, to lawful military targets. Such weapons would kill and destroy in a necessarily indiscriminate manner, on account of the blast, heat and radiation occasioned by the nuclear explosion and the effects induced; and the number of casualties which would ensue would be enormous. The use of nuclear weapons would therefore be prohibited in any circumstance, notwithstanding the absence of any explicit conventional prohibition. That view lay at the basis of the assertions by certain States before the Court that nuclear weapons are by their nature illegal under customary international law, by virtue of the fundamental principle of humanity.

93. A similar view has been expressed with respect to the effects of the principle of neutrality. Like the principles and rules of humanitarian law, that principle has therefore been considered by some to rule out the use of a weapon the effects of which simply cannot be contained within the territories of the contending States.

94. The Court would observe that none of the States advocating the legality of the use of nuclear weapons under certain circumstances, including the "clean" use of smaller, low yield, tactical nuclear weapons, has indicated what, supposing such limited use were feasible, would be the precise circumstances justifying such use; nor whether such limited use would not tend to escalate into the all-out use of high yield nuclear weapons. This being so, the Court does not consider that it has a sufficient basis for a determination on the validity of this view.

95. Nor can the Court make a determination on the validity of the view that the recourse to nuclear weapons would be illegal in any circumstance owing to their inherent and total incompatibility with the law applicable in armed conflict. Certainly, as the Court has already indicated, the principles and rules of law applicable in armed conflict -- at the heart of which is the overriding consideration of humanity -- make the conduct of armed hostilities subject to a number of strict requirements. Thus, methods and means of warfare, which would preclude any distinction between civilian and military targets, or which would result in

unnecessary suffering to combatants, are prohibited. In view of the unique characteristics of nuclear weapons, to which the Court has referred above, the use of such weapons in fact seems scarcely reconcilable with respect for such requirements. Nevertheless, the Court considers that it does not have sufficient elements to enable it to conclude with certainty that the use of nuclear weapons would necessarily be at variance with the principles and rules of law applicable in armed conflict in any circumstance.

[*830] 96. Furthermore, the Court cannot lose sight of the fundamental right of every State to survival, and thus its right to resort to self-defence, in accordance with Article 51 of the Charter, when its survival is at stake.

Nor can it ignore the practice referred to as "policy of deterrence", to which an appreciable section of the international community adhered for many years. The Court also notes the reservations which certain nuclear-weapon States have appended to the undertakings they have given, notably under the Protocols to the Treaties of Tlatelolco and Rarotonga, and also under the declarations made by them in connection with the extension of the Treaty on the Non-Proliferation of Nuclear Weapons, not to resort to such weapons.

97. Accordingly, in view of the present state of international law viewed as a whole, as examined above by the Court, and of the elements of fact at its disposal, the Court is led to observe that it cannot reach a definitive conclusion as to the legality or illegality of the use of nuclear weapons by a State in an extreme circumstance of self-defence, in which its very survival would be at stake.

98. Given the eminently difficult issues that arise in applying the law on the use of force and above all the law applicable in armed conflict to nuclear weapons, the Court considers that it now needs to examine one further aspect of the question before it, seen in a broader context.

In the long run, international law, and with it the stability of the international order which it is intended to govern, are bound to suffer from the continuing difference of views with regard to the legal status of weapons as deadly as nuclear weapons. It is consequently important to put an end to this state of affairs: the long-promised complete nuclear disarmament appears to be the most appropriate means of achieving that result.

99. In these circumstances, the Court appreciates the full importance of the recognition by Article VI of the Treaty on the Non-Proliferation of Nuclear Weapons of an obligation to negotiate in good faith a nuclear disarmament. This provision is worded as follows:

"Each of the Parties to the Treaty undertakes to pursue negotiations in good faith on effective measures relating to cessation of the nuclear arms race at an early date and to nuclear disarmament, and on a treaty on general and complete disarmament under strict and effective international control."

The legal import of that obligation goes beyond that of a mere obligation of conduct; the obligation involved here is an obligation to achieve a precise result -- nuclear disarmament in all its aspects -- by adopting a particular course of conduct, namely, the pursuit of negotiations on the matter in good faith.

100. This twofold obligation to pursue and to conclude negotiations formally concerns the 182 States parties to the Treaty on the Non-Proliferation of Nuclear Weapons, or, in other words, the vast majority of the international community.

Virtually the whole of this community appears moreover to have been involved when resolutions of the United Nations General Assembly concerning nuclear disarmament have repeatedly been unanimously adopted. Indeed, any realistic search for general and complete disarmament, especially nuclear disarmament, necessitates the co-operation of all States.

101. Even the very first General Assembly resolution, unanimously adopted on 24 January 1946 at the London session, set up a commission whose terms of reference included making specific proposals for, among other things, "the elimination from national armaments of atomic weapons and of all other major weapons adaptable to mass destruction". In a large number of subsequent resolutions, the General Assembly has reaffirmed the need for nuclear disarmament. Thus, in resolution 808 A (IX) of 4 November 1954, which was likewise unanimously adopted, it concluded
"that a further effort should be made to reach agreement on comprehensive and co-ordinated proposals to be embodied in a draft international disarmament convention providing for: . . . (b) The total prohibition of the use and manufacture of nuclear weapons and weapons of mass destruction of every type, together with the conversion of existing stocks of nuclear weapons for peaceful purposes."

The same conviction has been expressed outside the United Nations context in various instruments.

102. The obligation expressed in Article VI of the Treaty on the Non-Proliferation of Nuclear Weapons includes its fulfilment in accordance with the basic principle of good faith. This basic principle is set forth in Article 2, paragraph 2, of the Charter. It was reflected in the Declaration on Friendly Relations between States (resolution 2625 (XXV) of 24 October 1970) and in the Final Act of the Helsinki Conference of 1 August 1975. It is also embodied in Article 26 of the Vienna Convention on the Law of Treaties of 23 May 1969, according to which "every treaty in force is binding upon the parties to it and must be performed by them in good faith".

Nor has the Court omitted to draw attention to it, as follows:

"One of the basic principles governing the creation and performance of legal obligations, whatever their source, is the principle of good faith. Trust and confidence are inherent in international co-operation, in particular in an age when this co-operation in many fields is becoming increasingly essential." (Nuclear Tests (Australia v. France), Judgment of 20 December 1974, I.C.J. Reports 1974, p. 268, para. 46.)

103. In its resolution 984 (1995) dated 11 April 1995, the Security Council took care to reaffirm "the need for all States Parties to the Treaty on the Non-Proliferation of Nuclear Weapons to comply fully with all their obligations" and urged
"all States, as provided for in Article VI of the Treaty on the Non-Proliferation of Nuclear Weapons, to pursue negotiations in good faith on effective measures relating to nuclear disarmament and on a treaty on general and complete disarmament under strict and effective international control which remains a universal goal".

[*831] The importance of fulfilling the obligation expressed in Article VI of the Treaty on the Non-Proliferation of Nuclear Weapons was also reaffirmed in the final document of the Review and Extension Conference of the parties to the Treaty on the Non-Proliferation of Nuclear Weapons, held from 17 April to 12 May 1995.

In the view of the Court, it remains without any doubt an objective of vital importance to the whole of the international community today.

104. At the end of the present Opinion, the Court emphasizes that its reply to the question put to it by the General Assembly rests on the totality of the legal grounds set forth by the Court above (paragraphs 20 to 103), each of which is to be read in the light of the others. Some of these grounds are not such as to form the object of formal conclusions in the final paragraph of the Opinion; they nevertheless retain, in the view of the Court, all their importance.

105. For these reasons,

THE COURT,

(1) By thirteen votes to one,

Decides to comply with the request for an advisory opinion;
IN FAVOUR: President Bedjaoui; Vice-President Schwebel; Judges Guillaume, Shahabuddeen, Weeramantry, Ranjeva, Herczegh, Shi, Fleischhauer, Koroma, Vereshchetin, Ferrari Bravo, Higgins;
AGAINST: Judge Oda.

(2) Replies in the following manner to the question put by the General Assembly:

A. Unanimously,

There is in neither customary nor conventional international law any specific authorization of the threat or use of nuclear weapons;

    B. By eleven votes to three,
There is in neither customary nor conventional international law any comprehensive and universal prohibition of the threat or use of nuclear weapons as such;

IN FAVOUR: President Bedjaoui; Vice-President Schwebel; Judges Oda, Guillaume, Ranjeva, Herczegh, Shi, Fleischhauer, Vereshchetin, Ferrari Bravo, Higgins;
AGAINST: Judges Shahabuddeen, Weeramantry, Koroma.

    C. Unanimously,
A threat or use of force by means of nuclear weapons that is contrary to Article 2, paragraph 4, of the United Nations Charter and that fails to meet all the requirements of Article 51, is unlawful;

    D. Unanimously,
A threat or use of nuclear weapons should also be compatible with the requirements of the international law applicable in armed conflict, particularly those of the principles and rules of international humanitarian law, as well as with specific obligations under treaties and other undertakings which expressly deal with nuclear weapons;

    E. By seven votes to seven, by the President's casting vote,
It follows from the above-mentioned requirements that the threat or use of nuclear weapons would generally be contrary to the rules of international law applicable in armed conflict, and in particular the principles and rules of humanitarian law;
However, in view of the current state of international law, and of the elements of fact at its disposal, the Court cannot conclude definitively whether the threat or use of nuclear weapons would be lawful or unlawful in an extreme circumstance of self-defence, in which the very survival of a State would be at stake;

IN FAVOUR: President Bedjaoui; Judges Ranjeva, Herczegh, Shi, Fleischhauer, Vereschetin, Ferrari Bravo;
AGAINST: Vice-President Schwebel; Judges Oda, Guillaume, Shahabuddeen, Weeramantry, Koroma, Higgins.

    F. Unanimously,
There exists an obligation to pursue in good faith and bring to a conclusion negotiations leading to nuclear disarmament in all its aspects under strict and effective international control.

[*832] Done in English and in French, the English text being authoritative, at the Peace Palace, The Hague, this eighth day of July, one thousand nine hundred and ninety-six, in two copies, one of which will be placed in the archives of the Court and the other transmitted to the Secretary-General of the United Nations.

(Signed) Mohammed BEDJAOUI, President.

(Signed) Eduardo VALENCIA-OSPINA, Registrar.

President BEDJAOUI, Judges HERCZEGH, SHI, VERESHCHETIN and FERRARI BRAVO append declarations to the Advisory Opinion of the Court.

Judges GUILLAUME, RANJEVA and FLEISCHHAUER append separate opinions to the Advisory Opinion of the Court.

Vice-President SCHWEBEL, Judges ODA, SHAHABUDDEEN, WEERAMANTRY, KOROMA and HIGGINS append dissenting opinions to the Advisory Opinion of the Court.

(Initialled) M. B.

(Initialled) E. V. O.

CHAPTER III

MULTILATERAL INSTRUMENTS ON THE PROHIBITION OF EMPLACEMENT OF WEAPONS OF MASS DESTRUCTION IN CERTAIN MEDIA

INTRODUCTION

Chapter III includes five major multilateral treaties on the prohibition of emplacement of weapons of mass destruction in certain media. This category includes specialized arms control agreements that prohibit the emplacement of nuclear, chemical, and biological weapons in media such as outer space, the moon, and the ocean floor. Significantly, the instruments in this section span the high period of Cold War activity, starting with the 1959 Antarctic Treaty banning nuclear weapon tests in Antarctica and culminating with the 1979 Agreement Governing the Activities of States on the Moon and Other Celestial Bodies. Illustrative of the Cold War influence on this period is the fact that three treaties were signed at Moscow, and four were signed in the United States.

A very positive development in these treaties is that in addition to proscribing military activities involving weapons of mass destruction in areas traditionally deemed to be global commons, the treaties also encourage international cooperation for peaceful scientific research in the commons. Chapter III also includes treaties with provisions that proscribe nuclear weapons tests in outer space, under water, or in the atmosphere, as well as emplacement of nuclear weapons on the sea-bed, ocean floor, or sub-soil.

The five instruments included in this section are illustrative of the trend starting in the Cold War of prohibiting the emplacement of certain weapons in particular areas. The rationale for these prohibitions is to enhance the peace and security of humankind, and the instruments are thus related to the preservation of peace and the prohibition of aggression. They are, however, also intended explicitly or implicitly to protect the environment. However, their primary subject matter is weapons and consequently these documents are included here.

A violation of the obligations contained in these instruments constitutes a violation of international law, and may be deemed an emerging customary law violation includable in war crimes. These conventions do not however contain penal elements, and they are therefore at this time only the foundation for future criminalization.

III-1. The Antarctic Treaty, *signed at Washington*, 1 December 1959, 12 U.S.T. 794, 402 U.N.T.S. 71, 54 AM. J. INT'L L. 477 (1960), entered into force 23 June 1961; entered into force with respect to the United States 23 June 1961.[1] Authentic Texts: English, French, Russian, Spanish

Relevant Penal Characteristics & Penal Provisions

2. Implicit recognition of the penal nature of the act by establishing a duty to prohibit, prevent, prosecute, punish, or the like: Article I & Article V

8. Establishment of a criminal jurisdictional basis: (excludes the exercise of national sovereignty)

Applicability
Peace

Control
Regulation & Prohibition

State Signatories
Argentina; Australia; Belgium; Chile; France; Japan; New Zealand; Norway; South Africa; Union of Soviet Socialist Republics;[2] United Kingdom; United States of America.

State Parties
Argentina;[3] Australia;[4] Austria; Belgium;[5] Brazil; Bulgaria; Chile;[6] China; Colombia; Cuba; Czechoslovakia;[7] Denmark; Ecuador; Finland; France;[8] German Democratic Republic;[9] Federal Republic of Germany;[10] Greece; Guatemala;

---

[1] *See also* 54 AM. J. INT'L L. 477 (1960).

[2] *See* Methodology, State Succession.

[3] Consulting members under art. IX of the Treaty.

[4] *Id.*

[5] *Id.*

[6] *Id.*

[7] *See* Methodology, State Succession.

[8] Consulting members under art. IX of the Treaty.

[9] With a statement.

Hungary; India; Italy; Japan;[11] Korea; the Netherlands;[12] New Zealand;[13] Norway;[14] Papua New Guinea; Peru; Poland;[15] Romania;[16] South Africa;[17] Slovak Rep.; Spain; Sweden; Switzerland; Turkey; Ukraine; Union of Soviet Socialist Republics;[18] United Kingdom;[19] United States of America;[20] Uruguay[21]

Full Text

The Governments of Argentina, Australia, Belgium, Chile, the French Republic, Japan, New Zealand, Norway, the Union of South Africa, the Union of Soviet Socialist Republics, the United Kingdom of Great Britain and Northern Ireland and the United States of America, Recognizing that it is in the interest of all mankind that Antarctica shall continue forever to be used exclusively for peaceful purposes and shall not become the scene or object of international discord; Acknowledging the substantial contributions to scientific knowledge resulting from international co-operation in scientific investigation in Antarctica; Convinced that the establishment of a firm foundation for the continuation and development of such co-operation on the basis of freedom of scientific investigation in Antarctica as applied during the International Geophysical Year accords with the interests of science and the progress of all mankind; Convinced also that a treaty ensuring the use of Antarctica for peaceful purposes only and the continuance of international harmony in Antarctica will further the purposes and principles embodied in the Charter of the United Nations; Have agreed as follows:

---

[10] Consulting members under art. IX of the Treaty. Applicable to Land Berlin.

[11] Consulting members under art. IX of the Treaty.

[12] Extended to the Netherlands Antilles.

[13] Consulting members under art. IX of the Treaty.

[14] *Id.*

[15] *Id.*

[16] With a statement.

[17] Consulting members under art. IX of the Treaty..

[18] *Id.* and *see* Methodology, State Succession.

[19] Consulting members under art. IX of the Treaty.

[20] *Id.*

[21] With a statement.

Article I

1. Antarctica shall be used for peaceful purposes only. There shall be prohibited, inter alia, any measures of a military nature, such as the establishment of military bases and fortifications, the carrying out of military maneuvers, as well as the testing of any types of weapons.
2. The present Treaty shall not prevent the use of military personnel or equipment for scientific research or for any other peaceful purpose.

Article II

Freedom of scientific investigation in Antarctica and co-operation toward that end, as applied during the International Geophysical Year, shall continue, subject to the provisions of the present Treaty.

Article III

1. In order to promote international co-operation in scientific investigation in Antarctica, as provided for in Article II of the present Treaty, the Contracting Parties agree that, to the greatest extent feasible and practicable:
a) information regarding plans for scientific programs in Antarctica shall be exchanged to permit maximum economy and efficiency of operations;
b) scientific personnel shall be exchanged in Antarctica between expeditions and stations;
c) scientific observations and results from Antarctica shall be exchanged and made freely available.
2. In implementing this Article, every encouragement shall be given to the establishment of co-operative working relations with those Specialized Agencies of the United Nations and other international organizations having a scientific or technical interest in Antarctica.

Article IV

1. Nothing contained in the present Treaty shall be interpreted as:
a) a renunciation by any Contracting Party of previously asserted rights of or claims to territorial sovereignty in Antarctica;
b) a renunciation or diminution by any Contracting Party of any basis of claim to territorial sovereignty in Antarctica which it may have whether as a result of its activities or those of its nationals in Antarctica, or otherwise;
c) prejudicing the position of any Contracting Party as regards its recognition or non-recognition of any other State's right of or claim or basis of claim to territorial sovereignty in Antarctica.
2. No acts or activities taking place while the present Treaty is in force shall constitute a basis for asserting, supporting or denying a claim to territorial sovereignty in Antarctica or create any rights of sovereignty in Antarctica. No new claim, or enlargement of an existing claim, to territorial sovereignty in Antarctica shall be asserted while the present Treaty is in force.

Article V

1. Any nuclear explosions in Antarctica and the disposal there of radioactive waste material shall be prohibited.

2. In the event of the conclusion of international agreements concerning the use of nuclear energy, including nuclear explosions and the disposal of radioactive waste material, to which all of the Contracting Parties whose representatives are entitled to participate in the meetings provided for under Article IX are parties the rules established under such agreements shall apply in Antarctica.

Article VI

The provisions of the present Treaty shall apply to the area south of 60 deg South Latitude, including all ice shelves, but nothing in the present Treaty shall prejudice or in any way affect the rights, or the exercise of the rights, of any State under international law with regard to the high seas within that area.

Article VII

1. In order to promote the objectives and ensure the observance of the provisions of the present Treaty, each Contracting Party whose representatives are entitled to participate in the meetings referred to in Article IX of the Treaty shall have the right to designate observers to carry out any inspection provided for by the present Article. Observers shall be nationals of the Contracting Parties which designate them. The names of observers shall be communicated to every other Contracting Party having the right to designate observers, and like notice shall be given of the termination of their appointment.

2. Each observer designated in accordance with the provisions of paragraph 1 of this Article shall have complete freedom of access at any time to any or all areas of Antarctica.

3. All areas of Antarctica, including all stations, installations and equipment within those areas, and all ships and aircraft at points of discharging or embarking cargoes or personnel in Antarctica, shall be open at all times to inspection by any observers designated in accordance with paragraph 1 of this article.

4. Aerial observation may be carried out at any time over any or all areas of Antarctica by any of the Contracting Parties having the right to designate observers.

5. Each Contracting Party shall, at the time when the present Treaty enters into force for it, inform the other Contracting Parties, and thereafter shall give them notice in advance, of

a) all expeditions to and within Antarctica, on the part of its ships or nationals, and all expeditions to Antarctica organized in or proceeding from its territory;

b) all stations in Antarctica occupied by its nationals; and

c) any military personnel or equipment intended to be introduced by it into Antarctica subject to the conditions prescribed in paragraph 2 of Article I of the present Treaty.

Article VIII

1. In order to facilitate the exercise of their functions under the present Treaty, and without prejudice to the respective positions of the Contracting Parties relating to jurisdiction over all other persons in Antarctica, observers designated under paragraph 1 of Article VII and scientific personnel exchanged under subparagraph 1 (b) of Article III of the Treaty, and members of the staffs accompanying any such persons, shall be subject only to the jurisdiction of the Contracting Party of which they are nationals in respect of all acts or omissions occurring while they are in

Antarctica for the purpose of exercising their functions.
2. Without prejudice to the provisions of paragraph 1 of this Article, and pending the adoption of measures In pursuance of subparagraph 1 (e) of Article IX, the Contracting Parties concerned in any case of dispute with regard to the exercise of jurisdiction in Antarctica shall immediately consult together with a view to reaching a mutually acceptable solution.
Article IX
1. Representatives of the Contracting Parties named in the preamble to the present Treaty shall meet at the City of Canberra within two months after the date of entry into force of the Treaty, and thereafter at suitable intervals and places, for the purpose of exchanging information, consulting together on matters of common interest pertaining to Antarctica, and formulating and considering, and recommending to their Governments, measures in furtherance of the principles and objectives of the Treaty, including measures regarding:
    a) use of Antarctica for peaceful purposes only;
    b) facilitation of scientific research in Antarctica;
    c) facilitation of international scientific cooperation in Antarctica;
    d) facilitation of the exercise of the rights of inspection provided for in Article VII of the Treaty;
    e) questions relating to the exercise of jurisdiction in Antarctica;
    f) preservation and conservation of living resources in Antarctica.
2. Each Contracting Party which has become a party to the present Treaty by accession under Article XIII shall be entitled to appoint representatives to participate in the meetings referred to in paragraph 1 of the present Article, during such time as that Contracting Party demonstrates its interest in Antarctica by conducting substantial scientific research activity there, such as the establishment of a scientific station or the dispatch of a scientific expedition.
3. Reports from the observers referred to in Article VII of the present Treaty shall be transmitted to the representatives of the Contracting Parties participating in the meetings referred to in paragraph 1 of the present Article.
4. The measures referred to in paragraph 1 of this Article shall become effective when approved by all the Contracting Parties whose representatives were entitled to participate in the meetings held to consider those measures.
5. Any or all of the rights established in the present Treaty may be exercised as from the date of entry into force of the Treaty whether or not any measures facilitating the exercise of such rights have been proposed, considered or approved as provided in this Article.
Article X
Each of the Contracting Parties undertakes to exert appropriate efforts consistent with the Charter of the United Nations, to the end that no one engages in any activity in Antarctica contrary to the principles or purposes of the present Treaty.
Article XI
1. If any dispute arises between two or more of the Contracting Parties concerning the interpretation or application of the present Treaty, those Contracting Parties shall consult among themselves with a view to having the dispute resolved by

negotiation, inquiry, mediation, conciliation, arbitration, judicial settlement or other peaceful means of their own choice.

2. Any dispute of this character not so resolved shall, with the consent, in each case, of all parties to the dispute, be referred to the International Court of Justice for settlement; but failure to reach agreement or reference to the International Court shall not absolve parties to the dispute from the responsibility of continuing to seek to resolve it by any of the various peaceful means referred to in paragraph 1 of this Article.

Article XII

1.a) The present Treaty may be modified or amended at any time by unanimous agreement of the Contracting Parties whose representatives are entitled to participate in the meeting provided for under Article IX. Any such modification or amendment shall enter into force when the depositary Government has received notice from all such contracting Parties that they have ratified it.

b) Such modification or amendment shall thereafter enter into force as to any other Contracting Party when notice of ratification by it has been received by the depositary Government.

c) Any such Contracting Party from which no notice of ratification is received within a period of two years from the date of entry into force of the modification or amendment in accordance with the provisions of subparagraph 1 (a) of this Article shall be deemed to have withdrawn from the present Treaty on the date of the expiration of such period.

2. a) If after the expiration of thirty years from the date of entry into force of the present Treaty, any of the Contracting Parties whose representatives are entitled to participate in the meetings provided for under Article IX so requests by a communication addressed to the depositary Government, a Conference of all the Contracting Parties shall be held as soon as practicable to review the operation of the Treaty.

b) Any modification or amendment to the present Treaty which is approved at such a Conference by a majority of the Contracting Parties there represented, including a majority of those whose representatives are entitled to participate in the meetings provided for under Article IX, shall be communicated by the depositary Government to all the Contracting Parties immediately after the termination of the Conference and shall enter into force in accordance with the provisions of paragraph 1 of the present Article.

c) If any such modification or amendment has not entered into force in accordance with the provisions of subparagraph 1 (a) of this Article within a period of two years after the date of its communication to all the Contracting Parties, any Contracting Party may at any time after the expiration of that period give notice to the depositary Government of its withdrawal from the present Treaty, and such withdrawal shall take effect two years after the receipt of the notice by the depositary Government.

Article XIII
1. The present Treaty shall be subject to ratification by the signatory States. It shall be open for accession by any State which is a Member of the United Nations, or by any other State which may be invited to accede to the Treaty with the consent of all the Contracting Parties whose representatives are entitled to participate in the meetings provided for under Article IX of the Treaty.
2. Ratification of or accession to the present Treaty shall be effected by each State in accordance with its constitutional processes.
3. Instruments of ratification and instruments of accession shall be deposited with the Government of the United States of America, hereby designated as the depositary Government.
4. The depositary Government shall inform all signatory and acceding States of the date of each deposit of an instrument of ratification or accession, and the date of entry into force of the Treaty and of any modification or amendment thereto.
5. Upon the deposit of instruments of ratification by all the signatory States, the present Treaty shall enter into force for these States and for States which have deposited instruments of accession. Thereafter the Treaty shall enter into force for any acceding State upon the deposit of its instruments of accession.
6. The present Treaty shall be registered by the depositary Government pursuant to Article 102 of the Charter of the United Nations.
Article XIV
The present Treaty, done in the English, French, Russian and Spanish languages, each version being equally authentic, shall be deposited in the archives of the Government of the United States of America, which shall transmit duly certified copies thereof to the Governments of the signatory and acceding States.
In Witness Whereof, the undersigned Plenipotentiaries, duly authorized, have signed the present Treaty.
Done at Washington this first day of December, one thousand nine hundred and fifty-nine.

III-2. Treaty Banning Nuclear Weapon Tests in the Atmosphere, in Outer Space and Under Water, *signed at Moscow,* **5 August 1963, 14 U.S.T. 1313, 480 U.N.T.S. 43, 2 I.L.M. 883, entered into force 10 October 1963; entered into force with respect to the United States 10 October 1963.**[1] Authentic Texts: English, Russian

Relevant Penal Characteristics & Penal Provisions
2. Implicit recognition of the penal nature of the act by establishing a duty to prohibit, prevent, prosecute, punish, or the like: Article I

Applicability
Peace

Control
Regulation & Prohibition

State Signatories
Afghanistan; Algeria; Argentina; Australia; Austria; Belgium; Benin; Bolivia; Brazil; Bulgaria; Burma; Burundi; Byelorussian Soviet Socialist Republic; Cameroon; Canada; Ceylon; Chad; Chile; China (Taiwan); Colombia; the Congo (Leopoldville); Costa Rica; Cyprus; Czechoslovakia;[2] Dahomey; Denmark; Dominican Republic; Ecuador; Egypt; El Salvador; Ethiopia; Finland; Gabon; Federal Republic of Germany; German Democratic Republic; Ghana; Greece; Guatemala; Haiti; Honduras; Hungary; Iceland; India; Indonesia; Iran; Iraq; Ireland; Israel; Italy; Ivory Coast; Jamaica; Japan; Jordan; Republic of Korea; Kuwait; Laos; Lebanon; Liberia; Libya; Luxembourg; Malagasy Republic; Malaya; Mali; Mauritania; Mexico; Mongolia; Morocco; Nepal; the Netherlands; New Zealand; Nicaragua; Niger; Nigeria; Norway; Pakistan; Panama; Paraguay; Peru; the Philippines; Poland; Portugal; Romania; Rwanda; San Marino; Senegal; Sierra Leone; Somalia; Spain; Sudan; Sweden; Switzerland; Syria; Tanganyika; Thailand; Togo; Trinidad & Tobago; Tunisia; Turkey; Uganda; Ukrainian Soviet Socialist Republic; Union of Soviet Socialist Republics;[3] United Arab Republic; United Kingdom; United States of America; Upper Volta; Uruguay; Venezuela; Republic of Vietnam; Vietnam; Western Samoa; Yemen (Sanaa); Yugoslavia[4]

---

[1] *See* 57 AM. J. INT'L L. 1026 (1963).

[2] *See* Methodology, State Succession.

[3] *Id.*

[4] *Id.*

State Parties

Afghanistan; Antigua and Barbuda; Argentina; Armenia; Australia; Austria; the Bahamas; Bangladesh; Belarus; Belgium; Benin; Bhutan; Bolivia; Botswana; Bosnia-Herzegovina; Botswana; Brazil; Bulgaria; Burma; Canada; Cape Verde; Central African Republic; Chad; Chile; China (Taiwan); Colombia; Congo, Dem. Rep.; Costa Rica; Costa d'Ivoire; Cyprus; Czechoslovakia;[5] Denmark; Dominican Republic; Ecuador; Egypt; El Salvador; Fiji; Finland; Gabon; the Gambia; German Democratic Republic; Federal Republic of Germany;[6] Ghana; Greece; Guatemala; Honduras; Hungary; Iceland; India; Indonesia; Iran; Iraq; Ireland; Israel; Italy; Ivory Coast; Jamaica; Japan; Jordan; Kenya; Korea; Kuwait; Laos; Lebanon; Liberia; Libya; Luxembourg; Madagascar; Malawi; Malaysia; Malta; Mauritania; Mauritius; Mexico; Mongolia; Morocco; Nepal; the Netherlands;[7] New Zealand; Nicaragua; Niger; Nigeria; Norway; Pakistan; Panama; Papua New Guinea; Peru; the Philippines; Poland; Romania; Rwanda; San Marino; Senegal; Seychelles; Sierra Leone; Singapore; Slovak Rep.; Slovenia; South Africa; Spain; Sri Lanka; Sudan; Swaziland; Sweden; Switzerland; Syria; Tanzania; Thailand; Togo; Tonga; Trinidad & Tobago; Tunisia; Turkey; Uganda; Ukraine; Union of Soviet Socialist Republics;[8] United Kingdom; United States of America; Uruguay; Venezuela; Western Samoa; Yemen (Aden); Yugoslavia;[9] Zaire; Zambia

Full Text

The Governments of the United States of America, the United Kingdom of Great Britain and Northern Ireland, and the Union of Soviet Socialist Republics, hereinafter referred to as the "Original Parties",

Proclaiming as their principal aim the speediest possible achievement of an agreement on general and complete disarmament under strict international

---

[5] *Id.*

[6] Including Land Berlin.

[7] Extended to the Netherlands Antilles.

[8] *See* Methodology, State Succession.

[9] *Id.*

control in accordance with the objectives of the United Nations which would put an end to the armaments race and eliminate the incentive to the production and testing of all kinds of weapons, including nuclear weapons,

Seeking to achieve the discontinuance of all test explosions of nuclear weapons for all time, determined to continue negotiations to this end, and desiring to put an end to the contamination of man's environment by radioactive substances,

Have agreed as follows:

Article I

1. Each of the Parties to this Treaty undertakes to prohibit, to prevent, and not to carry out any nuclear weapon test explosion, or any other nuclear explosion, at any place under its jurisdiction or control:

(a) in the atmosphere; beyond its limits, including outer space; or under water, including territorial waters or high seas; or

(b) in any other environment if such explosion causes radioactive debris to be present outside the territorial limits of the State under whose jurisdiction or control such explosion is conducted. It is understood in this connection that the provisions of this subparagraph are without prejudice to the conclusion of a treaty resulting in the permanent banning of all nuclear test explosions, including all such explosions underground, the conclusion of which, as the Parties have stated in the Preamble to this Treaty, they seek to achieve.

2. Each of the Parties to this Treaty undertakes furthermore to refrain from causing, encouraging, or in any way participating in, the carrying out of any nuclear weapon test explosion, or any other nuclear explosion, anywhere which would take place in any of the environments described, or have the effect referred to, in paragraph 1 of this Article.

Article II

1. Any Party may propose amendments to this Treaty. The text of any proposed amendment shall be submitted to the Depositary Governments which shall circulate it to all Parties to this Treaty. Thereafter, if requested to do so by one-third or more of the Parties, the Depositary Governments shall convene a conference, to which they shall invite all the Parties, to consider such amendment.

2. Any amendment to this Treaty must be approved by a majority of the votes of all the Parties to this Treaty, including the votes of all of the Original Parties. The amendment shall enter into force for all Parties upon the deposit of instruments of ratification by a majority of all the Parties, including the instruments of ratification of all of the Original Parties.

Article III

1. This Treaty shall be open to all States for signature. Any State which does not sign this Treaty before its entry into force in accordance with paragraph 3 of this Article may accede to it at any time.

2. This Treaty shall be subject to ratification by signatory States. Instruments of ratification and instruments of accession shall be deposited with the Governments of the Original Parties--the United States of America, the United Kingdom of Great

Britain and Northern Ireland, and the Union of Soviet Socialist Republics--which are hereby designated the Depositary Governments.

3. This Treaty shall enter into force after its ratification by all the Original Parties and the deposit of their instruments of ratification.

4. For States whose instruments of ratification or accession are deposited subsequent to the entry into force of this Treaty, it shall enter into force on the date of the deposit of their instruments of ratification or accession.

5. The Depositary Governments shall promptly inform all signatory and acceding States of the date of each signature, the date of deposit of each instrument of ratification of and accession to this Treaty, the date of its entry into force, and the date of receipt of any requests for conferences or other notices.

6. This Treaty shall be registered by the Depositary Governments pursuant to Article 102 of the Charter of the United Nations.

Article IV

This Treaty shall be of unlimited duration.

Each Party shall in exercising its national sovereignty have the right to withdraw from the Treaty if it decides that extraordinary events, related to the subject matter of this Treaty, have jeopardized the supreme interests of its country. It shall give notice of such withdrawal to all other Parties to the Treaty three months in advance.

Article V

This Treaty, of which the English and Russian texts are equally authentic, shall be deposited in the archives of the Depositary Governments. Duly certified copies of this Treaty shall be transmitted by the Depositary Governments to the Governments of the signatory and acceding States.

IN WITNESS WHEREOF the undersigned, duly authorized, have signed this Treaty.

DONE in triplicate at the city of Moscow the fifth day of August, one thousand nine hundred and sixty-three.

International Humanitarian Law and Arms Control Agreements 497

III-3. Treaty on Principles Governing the Activities of States in the Exploration and Use of Outer Space, Including the Moon and Other Celestial Bodies, *signed at Washington, London and Moscow*, 27 January 1967, 18 U.S.T. 2410, 610 U.N.T.S. 205, 6 I.L.M. 386, entered into force 10 October 1967; entered into force with respect to the United States 10 October 1967. Authentic Texts: Chinese, English, French, Russian, Spanish

Relevant Penal Characteristics & Penal Provisions

2. Implicit recognition of the penal nature of the act by establishing a duty to prohibit, prevent, prosecute, punish, or the like: Article IV

8. Establishment of a criminal jurisdictional basis: Articles I, II (excludes claim of national sovereignty)

Applicability
War & Peace

Control
Regulation & Prohibition

State Signatories

Afghanistan; Argentina; Australia; Austria; Belgium; Bolivia; Botswana; Brazil; Bulgaria; Burma; Burundi; Byelorussian Soviet Socialist Republic; Cameroon; Canada; Central African Republic; Chile; China (Taiwan); Colombia; the Congo (Kinshasa); Cyprus; Czechoslovakia;[1] Denmark; Dominican Republic; Ecuador; Egypt; El Salvador; Ethiopia; Finland; France; the Gambia; Federal Republic of Germany; German Democratic Republic; Ghana; Greece; Guyana; Haiti; the Holy See; Honduras; Hungary; Iceland; India; Indonesia; Iran; Iraq; Ireland; Israel; Italy; Jamaica; Japan; Jordan; Korea; Laos; Lebanon; Lesotho; Luxembourg; Malaysia; Mexico; Mongolia; Nepal; the Netherlands; New Zealand; Nicaragua; Niger; Norway; Pakistan; Panama; Peru; the Philippines; Poland; Romania; Rwanda; San Marino; Sierra Leone; Somalia; South Africa; Sweden; Switzerland; Thailand; Togo; Trinidad & Tobago; Tunisia; Turkey; Union of Soviet Socialist Republics;[2] United Arab Republic; United Kingdom; United States of America; Upper Volta; Uruguay; Venezuela; Vietnam; Yugoslavia[3]

---

[1] *See* Methodology, State Succession.

[2] *Id.*

[3] *Id.*

State Parties

Afghanistan; Algeria; Antigua & Barbuda; Argentina; Australia; Austria; the Bahamas; Bangladesh; Barbados; Belarus; Belgium; Benin; Brazil; Bulgaria; Brunei; Burma; Burkina Faso; Burma; Byelorussian Soviet Socialist Republic; Canada; Chile; China (Taiwan); Cyprus; Cuba; Czechoslovakia;[4] Denmark; Dominica; Dominican Republic; Ecuador; Egypt; El Salvador; Fiji; Finland; France; German Democratic Republic; Federal Republic of Germany;[5] Greece; Grenada; Guinea-Bissau; Hungary; Iceland; India; Iraq; Ireland; Israel; Italy; Jamaica; Japan; Kenya; Korea; Kuwait; Laos; Lebanon; Libya; Madagascar;[6] Mali; Mauritius; Mexico; Mongolia; Morocco; Nepal; the Netherlands;[7] New Zealand; Niger; Nigeria; Norway; Pakistan; Papua New Guinea; Peru; Poland; Romania; Russian Federation; St. Kitts & Nevis; St. Lucia; San Marino; Saudi Arabia; the Seychelles; Sierra Leone; Singapore; Slovak Rep.; Solomon Islands; South Africa; Spain; Sri Lanka; Sweden; Switzerland; Syria; Thailand; Togo; Tonga; Tunisia; Turkey; Uganda; Ukrainian Soviet Socialist Republic; Union of Soviet Socialist Republics;[8] United Kingdom;[9] United States of America; Upper Volta; Uruguay; Venezuela; Socialist Republic of Vietnam; Yemen (Aden); Zambia

Full Text

The States Parties to this Treaty,

Inspired by the great prospects opening up before mankind as a result of man's entry into outer space,

Recognizing the common interest of all mankind in the progress of the exploration and use of outer space for peaceful purposes,

Believing that the exploration and use of outer space should be carried on for the benefit of all peoples irrespective of the degree of their economic or scientific development,

---

[4] *Id.*

[5] Applicable to Land Berlin.

[6] With a statement.

[7] Extended to the Netherlands Antilles.

[8] *See* Methodology, State Succession.

[9] Extended to the territories under the territorial sovereignty of the United Kingdom, and to Brunei and St. Christopher-Nevis-Anguilla.

Desiring to contribute to broad international co-operation in the scientific as well as the legal aspects of the exploration and use of outer space for peaceful purposes,

Believing that such co-operation will contribute to the development of mutual understanding and to the strengthening of friendly relations between States and peoples,

Recalling resolution 1962 (XVIII), entitled "Declaration of Legal Principles Governing the Activities of States in the Exploration and Use of Outer Space," which was adopted unanimously by the United Nations General Assembly on 13 December 1963,

Recalling resolution 1884 (XVIII), calling upon States to refrain from placing in orbit around the Earth any objects carrying nuclear weapons or any other kinds of weapons of mass destruction or from installing such weapons on celestial bodies, which was adopted unanimously by the United Nations General Assembly on 17 October 1963,

Taking account of United Nations General Assembly resolution 110 (II) of 3 November 1947, which condemned propaganda designed or likely to provoke or encourage any threat to the peace, breach of the peace or act of aggression, and considering that the aforementioned resolution is applicable to outer space,

Convinced that a Treaty on Principles Governing the Activities of States in the Exploration and Use of Outer Space, including the Moon and Other Celestial Bodies, will further the Purposes and Principles of the Charter of the United Nations,

Have agreed on the following:

Article I

The exploration and use of outer space, including the moon and other celestial bodies, shall be carried out for the benefit and in the interests of all countries, irrespective of their degree of economic or scientific development, and shall be the province of all mankind.

Outer space, including the moon and other celestial bodies, shall be free for exploration and use by all States without discrimination of any kind, on a basis of equality and in accordance with international law, and there shall be free access to all areas of celestial bodies.

There shall be freedom of scientific investigation in outer space, including the moon and other celestial bodies, and States shall facilitate and encourage international co-operation in such investigation.

Article II
Outer space, including the moon and other celestial bodies, is not subject to national appropriation by claim of sovereignty, by means of use or occupation, or by any other means.

Article III
States Parties to the Treaty shall carry on activities in the exploration and use of outer space, including the moon and other celestial bodies, in accordance with international law, including the Charter of the United Nations, in the interest of maintaining international peace and security and promoting international co-operation and understanding.

Article IV
States Parties to the Treaty undertake not to place in orbit around the Earth any objects carrying nuclear weapons or any other kinds of weapons of mass destruction, install such weapons on celestial bodies, or station such weapons in outer space in any other manner.

The Moon and other celestial bodies shall be used by all States Parties to the Treaty exclusively for peaceful purposes. The establishment of military bases, installations and fortifications, the testing of any type of weapons and the conduct of military maneuvers on celestial bodies shall be forbidden. The use of military personnel for scientific research or for any other peaceful purposes shall not be prohibited. The use of any equipment or facility necessary for peaceful exploration of the Moon and other celestial bodies shall also not be prohibited.

Article V
States Parties to the Treaty shall regard astronauts as envoys of mankind in outer space and shall render to them all possible assistance in the event of accident, distress, or emergency landing on the territory of another State Party or on the high seas. When astronauts make such a landing, they shall be safely and promptly returned to the State of registry of their space vehicle.

In carrying on activities in outer space and on celestial bodies, the astronauts of one State Party shall render all possible assistance to the astronauts of other States Parties.

States Parties to the Treaty shall immediately inform the other States Parties to the Treaty or the Secretary-General of the United Nations of any phenomena they discover in outer space, including the Moon and other celestial bodies, which could constitute a danger to the life or health of astronauts.

Article VI
States Parties to the Treaty shall bear international responsibility for national activities in outer space, including the Moon and other celestial bodies, whether such activities are carried on by governmental agencies or by non-governmental entities, and for assuring that national activities are carried out in conformity with

the provisions set forth in the present Treaty. The activities of non-governmental entities in outer space, including the Moon and other celestial bodies, shall require authorization and continuing supervision by the appropriate State Party to the Treaty. When activities are carried on in outer space, including the Moon and other celestial bodies, by an international organization, responsibility for compliance with this Treaty shall be borne both by the international organization and by the States Parties to the Treaty participating in such organization.

Article VII

Each State Party to the Treaty that launches or procures the launching of an object into outer space, including the Moon and other celestial bodies, and each State Party from whose territory or facility an object is launched, is internationally liable for damage to another State Party to the Treaty or to its natural or juridical persons by such object or its component parts on the Earth, in air space or in outer space, including the Moon and other celestial bodies.

Article VIII

A State Party to the Treaty on whose registry an object launched into outer space is carried shall retain jurisdiction and control over such object, and over any personnel thereof, while in outer space or on a celestial body. Ownership of objects launched into outer space, including objects landed or constructed on a celestial body, and of their component parts, is not affected by their presence in outer space or on a celestial body or by their return to the Earth. Such objects or component parts found beyond the limits of the State Party to the Treaty on whose registry they are carried shall be returned to that State Party, which shall, upon request, furnish identifying data prior to their return.

Article IX

In the exploration and use of outer space, including the Moon and other celestial bodies, States Parties to the Treaty shall be guided by the principle of co-operation and mutual assistance and shall conduct all their activities in outer space, including the Moon and other celestial bodies, with due regard to the corresponding interests of all other States Parties to the Treaty. States Parties to the Treaty shall pursue studies of outer space, including the Moon and other celestial bodies, and conduct exploration of them so as to avoid their harmful contamination and also adverse changes in the environment of the Earth resulting from the introduction of extraterrestrial matter and, where necessary, shall adopt appropriate measures for this purpose. If a State Party to the Treaty has reason to believe that an activity or experiment planned by it or its nationals in outer space, including the Moon and other celestial bodies, would cause potentially harmful interference with activities of other States Parties in the peaceful exploration and use of outer space, including the Moon and other celestial bodies, it shall undertake appropriate international consultations before proceeding with any such activity or experiment. A State Party to the Treaty which has reason to believe that an activity or experiment planned by another State Party in outer space, including the Moon and other celestial bodies, would cause potentially harmful interference with activities in the peaceful exploration and use of outer space, including the Moon and other celestial bodies, may request consultation concerning the activity or experiment.

Article X

In order to promote international co-operation in the exploration and use of outer space, including the Moon and other celestial bodies, in conformity with the purposes of this Treaty, the States Parties to the Treaty shall consider on a basis of equality any requests by other States Parties to the Treaty to be afforded an opportunity to observe the flight of space objects launched by those States.
The nature of such an opportunity for observation and the conditions under which it could be afforded shall be determined by agreement between the States concerned.

Article XI

In order to promote international co-operation in the peaceful exploration and use of outer space, States Parties to the Treaty conducting activities in outer space, including the Moon and other celestial bodies, agree to inform the Secretary-General of the United Nations as well as the public and the international scientific community, to the greatest extent feasible and practicable, of the nature, conduct, locations and results of such activities. On receiving the said information, the Secretary-General of the United Nations should be prepared to disseminate it immediately and effectively.

Article XII

All stations, installations, equipment and space vehicles on the Moon and other celestial bodies shall be open to representatives of other States Parties to the Treaty on a basis of reciprocity. Such representatives shall give reasonable advance notice of a projected visit, in order that appropriate consultations may be held and that maximum precautions may be taken to assure safety and to avoid interference with normal operations in the facility to be visited.

Article XIII

The provisions of this Treaty shall apply to the activities of States Parties to the Treaty in the exploration and use of outer space, including the Moon and other celestial bodies, whether such activities are carried on by a single State Party to the Treaty or jointly with other States, including cases where they are carried on within the framework of international intergovernmental organizations.

Any practical questions arising in connection with activities carried on by international inter-governmental organizations in the exploration and use of outer space, including the Moon and other celestial bodies, shall be resolved by the States Parties to the Treaty either with the appropriate international organization or with one or more States members of that international organization, which are Parties to this Treaty.

Article XIV
1. This Treaty shall be open to all States for signature. Any State which does not sign this Treaty before its entry into force in accordance with paragraph 3 of this article may accede to it at any time.
2. This Treaty shall be subject to ratification by signatory States. Instruments of ratification and instruments of accession shall be deposited with the Governments of the United States of America, the United Kingdom of Great Britain and Northern Ireland and the Union of Soviet Socialist Republics, which are hereby designated the Depositary Governments.

3. This Treaty shall enter into force upon the deposit of instruments of ratification by five Governments including the Governments designated as Depositary Governments under this Treaty.

4. For States whose instruments of ratification or accession are deposited subsequent to the entry into force of this Treaty, it shall enter into force on the date of the deposit of their instruments of ratification or accession.

5. The Depositary Governments shall promptly inform all signatory and acceding States of the date of each signature, the date of deposit of each instrument of ratification of and accession to this Treaty, the date of its entry into force and other notices.

6. This Treaty shall be registered by the Depositary Governments pursuant to Article 102 of the Charter of the United Nations.

Article XV
Any State Party to the Treaty may propose amendments to this Treaty. Amendments shall enter into force for each State Party to the Treaty accepting the amendments upon their acceptance by a majority of the States Parties to the Treaty and thereafter for each remaining State Party to the Treaty on the date of acceptance by it.

Article XVI
Any State Party to the Treaty may give notice of its withdrawal from the Treaty one year after its entry into force by written notification to the Depositary Governments. Such withdrawal shall take effect one year from the date of receipt of this notification.

Article XVII
This Treaty, of which the English, Russian, French, Spanish and Chinese texts are equally authentic, shall be deposited in the archives of the Depositary Governments. Duly certified copies of this Treaty shall be transmitted by the Depositary Governments to the Governments of the signatory and acceding States.

IN WITNESS WHEREOF the undersigned, duly authorized, have signed this Treaty.

DONE in triplicate, at the cities of Washington, London and Moscow, this twenty-seventh day of January one thousand nine hundred sixty-seven.

III-4. Treaty on the Prohibition of the Emplacement of Nuclear Weapons and Other Weapons of Mass Destruction on the Sea-bed and the Ocean Floor and in the Subsoil Thereof, *signed at Washington, London and Moscow,* **11 February 1971, 23 U.S.T. 701, T.I.A.S. No. 7337, 955 U.N.T.S. 115, entered into force 18 May 1972; entered into force with respect to the United States 18 May 1972.** Authentic Texts: Chinese, English, French, Russian, Spanish

Relevant Penal Characteristic & Penal Provision

2. Implicit recognition of the penal nature of the act by establishing a duty to prohibit, prevent, prosecute, punish, or the like: Article I

Applicability
Peace

Control
Regulation & Prohibition

State Signatories

Afghanistan; Argentina; Australia; Austria; Belgium; Bolivia; Botswana; Brazil; Bulgaria; Burma; Burundi; Canada; Central African Republic; China; Colombia; Costa Rica; Cyprus; Czechoslovakia;[1] Dahomey; Denmark; Dominican Republic; Equatorial Guinea; Ethiopia; Finland; the Gambia; Federal Republic of Germany; Ghana; Greece; Guatemala; Guinea; Honduras; Hungary; Iceland; Iran; Ireland; Italy; Jamaica; Japan; Jordan; the Khmer Republic; Korea; Laos; Lebanon; Lesotho; Liberia; Luxembourg; Malagasy Republic; Malaysia; Mali; Malta; Mauritius; Morocco; Nepal; the Netherlands; New Zealand; Nicaragua; Niger; Norway; Panama; Paraguay; Poland; Romania; Rwanda; Saudi Arabia; Senegal; Sierra Leone; Singapore; South Africa; Swaziland; Sweden; Switzerland; Tanzania; Togo; Tunisia; Turkey; Union of Soviet Socialist Republics;[2] United Kingdom; United States of America; Uruguay; Vietnam; Yugoslavia[3]

State Parties

Afghanistan; Algeria; Antigua & Barbuda; Argentina; Australia; Austria; Bahamas; Belgium; Belarus; Benin; Bosnia-Herzegovina; Botswana; Bulgaria; Brazil; Brunei; Byelorussian Soviet Socialist Republic; Canada;[4] Cape Verde; Central African Republic; China (Taiwan); the Congo; Cote d'Ivoire; Croatia; Cuba; Cyprus; Czechoslovakia;[5] Denmark; Dominica; Dominican Republic; Ethiopia; Finland; German Democratic Republic; Federal Republic of Germany;[6]

---

[1] *See* Methodology, "State Succession."
[2] *Id.*
[3] *Id.*
[4] With a declaration.
[5] *See* Methodology, State Succession.
[6] Applicable to West Berlin.

Ghana; Greece; Grenada; Guatemala; Guinea-Bissau; Hungary; Iceland; India;[7] Iran; Iraq; Ireland; Italy;[8] Ivory Coast; Jamaica; Japan; Jordan; Korea; Laos; Lesotho; Luxembourg; Liechtenstein; Malaysia; Malta; Mauritius; Mexico; Mongolia; Morocco; Nepal; the Netherlands;[9] New Zealand; Nicaragua; Niger; Norway; Panama; Philippines; Poland; Portugal; Qatar; Romania; Rwanda; St. Kitts and Nevis; St. Lucia; St. Vincent and the Grenadines; Sao Tome & Principe; Saudi Arabia; the Seychelles; Singapore; Slovak Rep.; Slovenia; Solomon Islands; South Africa; Swaziland; Sweden; Switzerland; Togo; Tunisia; Turkey; Ukrainian Soviet Socialist Republic; Union of Soviet Socialist Republics;[10] United Kingdom;[11] United States of America; Socialist Republic of Vietnam;[12] Yemen (Aden); Yugoslavia;[13] Zambia

Full Text

The States Parties to this Treaty,

Recognizing the common interest of mankind in the progress of the exploration and use of the seabed and the ocean floor for peaceful purposes, Considering that the prevention of a nuclear arms race on the seabed and the ocean floor serves the interests of maintaining world peace, reduces international tensions and strengthens friendly relations among States, Convinced that this Treaty constitutes a step towards the exclusion of the seabed, the ocean floor and the subsoil thereof from the arms race,

Convinced that this Treaty constitutes a step towards a Treaty on general and complete disarmament under strict and effective international control, and determined to continue negotiations to this end,

Convinced that this Treaty will further the purposes and principles of the Charter of the United Nations, in a manner consistent with the principles of international law and without infringing the freedoms of the high seas,

Have agreed as follows:

Article I

1. The States Parties to this Treaty undertake not to emplant or emplace on the seabed and the ocean floor and in the subsoil thereof beyond the outer limit of a seabed zone, as defined in article II, any nuclear weapons or any other types of weapons of mass destruction as well as structures, launching installations or any other facilities specifically designed for storing, testing or using such weapons.

---

[7] With a declaration.
[8] Id.
[9] Extended to the Netherlands Antilles.
[10] See Methodology, State Succession.
[11] Extended to Brunei, St. Christopher-Nevis-Anguilla, and territories under the territorial sovereignty of the United Kingdom.
[12] With a declaration.
[13] See Methodology, State Succession.

2. The undertakings of paragraph 1 of this article shall also apply to the seabed zone referred to in the same paragraph, except that within such seabed zone, they shall not apply either to the coastal State or to the seabed beneath its territorial waters.

3. The States Parties to this Treaty undertake not to assist, encourage or induce any State to carry out activities referred to in paragraph 1 of this article and not to participate in any other way in such actions.

Article II

For the purpose of this Treaty, the outer limit of the seabed zone referred to in article I shall be coterminous with the twelve-mile outer limit of the zone referred to in part II of the Convention on the Territorial Sea and the Contiguous Zone, signed at Geneva on April 29, 1958, and shall be measured in accordance with the provisions of part I, section II, of that Convention and in accordance with international law.

Article III

1. In order to promote the objectives of and insure compliance with the provisions of this Treaty, each State Party to the Treaty shall have the right to verify through observations the activities of other States Parties to the Treaty on the seabed and the ocean floor and in the subsoil thereof beyond the zone referred to in article I, provided that observation does not interfere with such activities.

2. If after such observation reasonable doubts remain concerning the fulfillment of the obligations assumed under the Treaty, the State Party having such doubts and the State Party that is responsible for the activities giving rise to the doubts shall consult with a view to removing the doubts. If the doubts persist, the State Party having such doubts shall notify the other States Parties, and the Parties concerned shall cooperate on such further procedures for verification as may be agreed, including appropriate inspection of objects, structures, installations or other facilities that reasonably may be expected to be of a kind described in article I. The Parties in the region of the activities, including any coastal State, and any other Party so requesting, shall be entitled to participate in such consultation and cooperation. After completion of the further procedures for verification, an appropriate report shall be circulated to other Parties by the Party that initiated such procedures.

3. If the State responsible for the activities giving rise to the reasonable doubts is not identifiable by observation of the object, structure, installation or other facility, the State Party having such doubts shall notify and make appropriate inquiries of States Parties in the region of the activities and of any other State Party. If it is ascertained through these inquiries that a particular State Party is responsible for the activities, that State Party shall consult and cooperate with other Parties as provided in paragraph 2 of this article. If the identity of the State responsible for the activities cannot be ascertained through these inquiries, then further verification procedures, including inspection, may be undertaken by the inquiring State Party,

which shall invite the participation of the Parties in the region of the activities, including any coastal State, and of any other Party desiring to cooperate.

4. If consultation and cooperation pursuant to paragraphs 2 and 3 of this article have not removed the doubts concerning the activities and there remains a serious question concerning fulfillment of the obligations assumed under this Treaty, a State Party may, in accordance with the provisions of the Charter of the United Nations, refer the matter to the Security Council, which may take action in accordance with the Charter.

5. Verification pursuant to this article may be undertaken by any State Party using its own means, or with the full or partial assistance of any other State Party, or through appropriate international procedures within the framework of the United Nations and in accordance with its Charter.

6. Verification activities pursuant to this Treaty shall not interfere with activities of other States Parties and shall be conducted with due regard for rights recognized under international law, including the freedoms of the high seas and the rights of coastal States with respect to the exploration and exploitation of their continental shelves.

Article IV

Nothing in this Treaty shall be interpreted as supporting or prejudicing the position of any State Party with respect to existing international conventions, including the 1958 Convention on the Territorial Sea and the Contiguous Zone, or with respect to rights or claims which such State Party may assert, or with respect to recognition or non-recognition of rights or claims asserted by any other State, related to waters off its coasts, including, inter alia, territorial seas and contiguous zones, or to the seabed and the ocean floor, including continental shelves.

Article V

The Parties to this Treaty undertake to continue negotiations in good faith concerning further measures in the field of disarmament for the prevention of an arms race on the seabed, the ocean floor and the subsoil thereof.

Article VI

Any State Party may propose amendments to this Treaty. Amendments shall enter into force for each State Party accepting the amendments upon their acceptance by a majority of the States Parties to the Treaty and, thereafter, for each remaining State Party on the date of acceptance by it.

Article VII

Five years after the entry into force of this Treaty, a conference of Parties to the Treaty shall be held at Geneva, Switzerland, in order to review the operation of this Treaty with a view to assuring that the purposes of the preamble and the provisions of the Treaty are being realized. Such review shall take into account any relevant technological developments. The review conference shall determine, in accordance with the views of a majority of those Parties attending, whether and when an additional review conference shall be convened.

Article VIII

Each State Party to this Treaty shall in exercising its national sovereignty have the right to withdraw from this Treaty if it decides that extraordinary events related to the subject matter of this Treaty have jeopardized the supreme interests of its country. It shall give notice of such withdrawal to all other States Parties to the Treaty and to the United Nations Security Council three months in advance. Such notice shall include a statement of the extraordinary events it considers to have jeopardized its supreme interests.

Article IX

The provisions of this Treaty shall in no way affect the obligations assumed by States Parties to the Treaty under international instruments establishing zones free from nuclear weapons.

Article X

1. This Treaty shall be open for signature to all States. Any State which does not sign the Treaty before its entry into force in accordance with paragraph 3 of this article may accede to it at any time.

2. This Treaty shall be subject to ratification by signatory States. Instruments of ratification and of accession shall be deposited with the Governments of the United States of America, the United Kingdom of Great Britain and Northern Ireland, and the Union of Soviet Socialist Republics, which are hereby designated the Depositary Governments.

3. This Treaty shall enter into force after the deposit of instruments of ratification by twenty-two Governments, including the Governments designated as Depositary Governments of this Treaty.

4. For states whose instruments of ratification or accession are deposited after the entry into force of this Treaty, it shall enter into force on the date of the deposit of their instruments of ratification or accession.

5. The Depositary Governments shall promptly inform the Governments of all signatory and acceding States of the date of each signature, of the date of deposit of each instrument of ratification or of accession, of the date of the entry into force of this Treaty, and of the receipt of other notices.

6. This Treaty shall be registered by the Depositary Governments pursuant to Article 102 of the Charter of the United Nations.

Article XI

This Treaty, the English, Russian, French, Spanish and Chinese texts of which are equally authentic, shall be deposited in the archives of the Depositary Governments. Duly certified copies of this Treaty shall be transmitted by the Depositary Governments to the Governments of the States signatory and acceding thereto.

IN WITNESS WHEREOF the undersigned, being duly authorized thereto, have signed this Treaty.

DONE in triplicate, at the cities of Washington, London and Moscow, this eleventh day of February, one thousand nine hundred seventy-one.

III-5. Agreement Governing the Activities of States on the Moon and Other Celestial Bodies, *opened for signature at New York,* **5 December 1979, 1363 U.N.T.S. 3, 18 I.L.M. 1434, entered into force 11 July 1984.**

Relevant Penal Characteristics & Penal Provisions
2. Implicit recognition of the penal nature of the act by establishing a duty to prohibit, prevent, prosecute, punish, or the like: Article 2; Article 3, Sections 2,3,4; & Article 4

Applicability
War & Peace

Control
Regulation & Prohibition

State Signatories
Austria; Chile; France; Guatemala; India; Morocco; the Netherlands; Peru; the Philippines; Romania; Urugauy

State Parties
Australia; Austria; Chile; Mexico; Morocco; the Netherlands; Pakistan; the Philippines; Uruguay

Reservations upon Signature, Accession or Ratification
France

Relevant Text

Article 2
All activities on the moon, including its exploration and use, shall be carried out in accordance with international law, in particular the Charter of the United Nations, and taking into account the Declaration on Principles of International Law Concerning Friendly Relations and Co-operation among States in accordance with the Charter of the United Nations, adopted by the General Assembly on 24 October 1970, in the interests of maintaining international peace and security and promoting international co-operation and mutual understanding, and with due regard to the corresponding interests of all other States Parties.

Article 3
1. The moon shall be used by all States Parties exclusively for peaceful purposes.
2. Any threat or use of force or any other hostile act or threat of hostile act on the moon is prohibited. It is likewise prohibited to use the moon in order to

commit any such act or to engage in any such threat in relation to the earth, the moon, spacecraft, the personnel of spacecraft or man-made space objects.

3. States Parties shall not place in orbit around or other trajectory to or around the moon object carrying nuclear weapons or any other kinds of weapons of mass destruction or place or use such weapons on or in the moon.

4. The establishment of military bases, installations, and fortifications, the testing of any type of weapons and the conduct of military manoeuvres on the moon shall be forbidden. The use of military personnel for scientific research or for any other peaceful purposes shall not be prohibited. The use of any equipment or facility necessary for peaceful exploration and use of the moon shall also not be prohibited.

Article 4

1. The exploration and use of the moon shall be the province of all mankind and shall be carried out for the benefit and in the interests of all countries, irrespective of their degree of economic or scientific development. Due regard shall be paid to the interests of present and future generations as well as to the need to promote higher standards of living and conditions of economic and social progress and development in accordance with the Charter of the United Nations.

2. States Parties shall be guided by the principle of co-operation and mutual assistance in all their activities concerning the exploration and use of the moon. International co-operation in pursuance of this Agreement should be as wide as possible and may take place on a multilateral basis, on a bilateral basis or through international intergovernmental organizations.

CHAPTER IV

REGIONAL NUCLEAR FREE ZONES AGREEMENTS

INTRODUCTION

Chapter IV includes seven regional nuclear free zones agreements. The regions covered are Latin America, Africa, South East Asia, and the South Pacific. The earliest agreement is from 1968 with the Treaty for the Prohibition of Nuclear Weapons in Latin America (Treaty of Tlatelolco), which also has two Additional Protocols included. The most recent regional nuclear free zone agreement is the 1996 African Nuclear Free Zone Treaty (Treaty of Pelindaba), which is accompanied by the Cairo Declaration of 1996. It is significant to note that these were signed after the mid-1960's. These dates suggest a continued trend toward a paradigm and strategy of regionalism in the domain of international security.

These instruments are not deemed part of international humanitarian law, and they are not necessarily part of "arms control" agreements. They are therefore in a category of their own. They do not contain penal characteristics and the violation of their terms raises only the prospect of international civil adjudication. It can be said that violations of such agreements constitute a breach of the Principles of State Responsibility elaborated by the ILC.

The relevance of these agreements is that, taken in *pari material* with developments on the use of nuclear weapons (see Chapter II, particularly instrument II-8 at p. 435), leads to the conclusion that an emerging custom bans not only the "first use" of nuclear weapons, but also their possession.

IV-1(a). Treaty for the Prohibition of Nuclear Weapons in Latin America [Treaty of Tlatelolco] (Inter-American), *opened for signature at Mexico City,* **14 February 1967, 22 U.S.T. 762, 634 U.N.T.S. 281, 6 I.L.M. 521, entered into force 22 April 1968. Authentic Texts: Chinese, English, French, Portuguese, Russian, Spanish**

Relevant Penal Characteristics & Penal Provisions
2. Implicit recognition of the penal nature of the act by establishing a duty to prohibit, prevent, prosecute, punish, or the like: Article 1

Applicability
War & Peace

Control
Regulation & Prohibition

State Signatories
Argentina; the Bahamas; Barbados; Bolivia; Brazil; Chile; Colombia; Costa Rica; Dominican Republic; Ecuador; El Salvador; Grenada; Guatemala; Haiti; Honduras; Jamaica; Mexico; Nicaragua; Panama; Paraguay; Peru; Suriname; Trinidad & Tobago; Uruguay; Venezuela

State Parties
Argentina; the Bahamas; Barbados; Bolivia; Brazil; Chile; Colombia; Costa Rica; Dominican Republic; Ecuador; El Salvador; Grenada; Guatemala; Haiti; Honduras; Jamaica; Mexico; Nicaragua; Panama; Paraguay; Peru; Suriname; Trinidad & Tobago; Uruguay; Venezuela

Full Text
Preamble

In the name of their peoples and faithfully interpreting their desires and aspirations, the Governments of the States which sign the Treaty for the Prohibition of Nuclear Weapons in Latin America,

Desiring to contribute, so far as lies in their power, towards ending the armaments race, especially in the field of nuclear weapons, and towards strengthening a world at peace, based on the sovereign equality of States, mutual respect and good neighbourliness,

Recalling that the United Nations General Assembly, in its Resolution 808 (IX), adopted unanimously as one of the three points of a coordinated programme of disarmament "the total prohibition of the use and manufacture of nuclear weapons and weapons of mass destruction of every type,"

Recalling that military denuclearized zones are not an end in themselves but rather a means for achieving general and complete disarmament at a later stage,

Recalling United Nations General Assembly Resolution 1911 (XVIII), which established that the measures that should be agreed upon for the denuclearization of Latin America should be taken "in the light of the principles of the Charter of the United Nations and of regional agreements,"

Recalling United Nations General Assembly Resolution 2028 (XX), which established the principle of an acceptable balance of mutual responsibilities and duties for the nuclear and non-nuclear powers, and

Recalling that the Charter of the Organization of American States proclaims that it is an essential purpose of the Organization to strengthen the peace and security of the hemisphere,

Convinced:

That the incalculable destructive power of nuclear weapons has made it imperative that the legal prohibition of war should be strictly observed in practice if the survival of civilization and of mankind itself is to be assured,

That nuclear weapons, whose terrible effects are suffered, indiscriminately and inexorably, by military forces and civilian population alike, constitute, through the persistence of the radioactivity they release, an attack on the integrity of the human species and ultimately may even render the whole earth uninhabitable,

That general and complete disarmament under effective international control is a vital matter which all the peoples of the world equally demand,

That the proliferation of nuclear weapons, which seems inevitable unless States, in the exercise of their sovereign rights, impose restrictions on themselves in order to prevent it, would make any agreement on disarmament enormously difficult and would increase the danger of the outbreak of a nuclear conflagration,

That the establishment of militarily denuclearized zones is closely linked with the maintenance of peace and security in the respective regions,

That the military denuclearization of vast geographical zones, adopted by the sovereign decision of the States comprised therein, will exercise a beneficial influence on other regions where similar conditions exist,

That the privileged situation of the signatory States, whose territories are wholly free from nuclear weapons, imposes upon them the inescapable duty of preserving that situation both in their own interest and for the good of mankind,

That the existence of nuclear weapons in any country of Latin America would make it a target for possible nuclear attacks and would inevitably set off, throughout the region, a ruinous race in nuclear weapons which would involve the unjustifiable diversion, for warlike purposes, of the limited resources required for economic and social development,

That the foregoing reasons, together with the traditional peace-loving outlook of Latin America, give rise to an inescapable necessity that nuclear energy should be used in that region exclusively for peaceful purposes, and that the Latin American countries should use their right to the greatest and most equitable possible access to this new source of energy in order to expedite the economic and social development of their peoples,

Convinced finally:

That the military denuclearization of Latin America -- being understood to mean the undertaking entered into internationally in this Treaty to keep their territories forever free from nuclear weapons -- will constitute a measure which will spare their peoples from the squandering of their limited resources on nuclear armaments and will protect them against possible nuclear attacks on their territories, and will also constitute a significant contribution towards preventing the proliferation of nuclear weapons and a powerful factor for general and complete disarmament, and

That Latin America, faithful to its tradition of universality, must not only endeavour to banish from its homelands the scourge of a nuclear war, but must also strive to promote the well-being and advancement of its peoples, at the same time co-operating in the fulfillment of the ideals of mankind, that is to say, in the consolidation of a permanent peace based on equal rights, economic fairness and social justice for all, in accordance with the principles and purposes set forth in the Charter of the United Nations and in the Charter of the Organization of American States.

Have agreed as follows:

Obligations
Article 1
1. The Contracting Parties hereby undertake to use exclusively for peaceful purposes the nuclear material and facilities which are under their jurisdiction, and to prohibit and prevent in their respective territories:
(a) The testing, use, manufacture, production or acquisition by any means whatsoever of any nuclear weapons, by the Parties themselves, directly or indirectly, on behalf of anyone else or in any other way, and
(b) The receipt, storage, installation, deployment and any form of possession of any nuclear weapons, directly or indirectly, by the Parties themselves, by anyone on their behalf or in any other way.
2. The Contracting Parties also undertake to refrain from engaging in, encouraging or authorizing, directly or indirectly, or in any way participating in the testing, use, manufacture, production, possession or control of any nuclear weapon.

Definition of the Contracting Parties
Article 2
For the purposes of this Treaty, the Contracting Parties are those for whom the Treaty is in force.

Definition of territory
Article 3
For the purposes of this Treaty, the term "territory" shall include the territorial sea, air space and any other space over which the State exercises sovereignty in accordance with its own legislation.

Zone of application
Article 4
1. The zone of application of this Treaty is the whole of the territories for which the Treaty is in force.
2. Upon fulfillment of the requirements of article 28, paragraph 1, the zone of application of this Treaty shall also be that which is situated in the western

hemisphere within the following limits (except the continental part of the territory of the United States of America and its territorial waters): starting at a point located at 35 north latitude, 75 west longitude; from this point directly southward to a point at 30 north latitude, 75 west longitude; from there, directly eastward to a point at 30 north latitude, 50 west longitude; from there, along a loxodromic line to a point at 5 north latitude, 20 west longitude; from there directly southward to a point 60 south latitude, 20 west longitude; from there, directly westward to a point at 60 south latitude, 115 west longitude; from there, directly northward to a point at 0 latitude, 115 west longitude; from there, along a loxodromic line to a point at 35 north latitude, 150 west longitude; from there, directly eastward to a point at 35 north latitude, 75 west longitude.

Definition of nuclear weapons
Article 5
For the purposes of this Treaty, a nuclear weapon is any device which is capable of releasing nuclear energy in an uncontrolled manner and which has a group of characteristics that are appropriate for use for warlike purposes. An instrument that may be used for the transport or propulsion of the device is not included in this definition if it is separable from the device and not an indivisible part thereof.

Meeting of signatories
Article 6
At the request of any of the signatory States or if the Agency established by article 7 should so decide, a meeting of all the signatories may be convoked to consider in common questions which may affect the very essence of this instrument, including possible amendments to it. In either case, the meeting will be convoked by the General Secretary.

Organization
Article 7
1. In order to ensure compliance with the obligations of this Treaty, the Contracting Parties hereby establish an international organization to be known as the "Agency for the Prohibition of Nuclear Weapons in Latin America," hereinafter referred to as "the Agency." Only the Contracting Parties shall be affected by its decisions.
2. The Agency shall be responsible for the holding of periodic or extraordinary consultations among Member States on matters relating to the purposes, measures and procedures set forth in this Treaty and to the supervision of compliance with the obligations arising therefrom.
3. The Contracting Parties agree to extend to the Agency full and prompt cooperation in accordance with the provisions of this Treaty, of any agreements they may conclude with the Agency and of any agreements the Agency may conclude with any other international organization or body.
4. The headquarters of the Agency shall be in Mexico City.

Organs
Article 8
1. There are hereby established as principal organs of the Agency a General Conference, a Council and a Secretariat.
2. Such subsidiary organs as are considered necessary by the General Conference may be established within the purview of this Treaty.

The General Conference
Article 9
1. The General Conference, the supreme organ of the Agency, shall be composed of all the Contracting Parties; it shall hold regular sessions every two years, and may also hold special sessions whenever this Treaty so provides or, in the opinion of the Council, the circumstances so require.
2. The General Conference:
(a) May consider and decide on any matters or questions covered by this Treaty, within the limits thereof, including those referring to powers and functions of any organ provided for in this Treaty.
(b) Shall establish procedures for the control system to ensure observance of this Treaty in accordance with its provisions.
(c) Shall elect the Members of the Council and the General Secretary.
(d) May remove the General Secretary from office if the proper functioning of the Agency so requires.
(e) Shall receive and consider the biennial and special reports submitted by the Council and the General Secretary.
(f) Shall initiate and consider studies designed to facilitate the optimum fulfillment of the aims of this Treaty, without prejudice to the power of the General Secretary independently to carry out similar studies for submission to and consideration by the Conference.
(g) Shall be the organ competent to authorize the conclusion of agreements with Governments and other international organizations and bodies.
3. The General Conference shall adopt the Agencys budget and fix the scale of financial contributions to be paid by Member States, taking into account the systems and criteria used for the same purpose by the United Nations.
4. The General Conference shall elect its officers for each session and may establish such subsidiary organs as it deems necessary for the performance of its functions.
5. Each Member of the Agency shall have one vote. The decisions of the General Conference shall be taken by a two-thirds majority of the Members present and voting in the case of matters relating to the control system and measures referred to in article 20, the admission of new Members, the election or removal of the General Secretary, adoption of the budget and matters related thereto. Decisions on other matters, as well as procedural questions and also determination of which questions must be decided by a two-thirds majority, shall be taken by a simple majority of the Members present and voting.
6. The General Conference shall adopt its own rules of procedure.

The Council
Article 10
1. The Council shall be composed of five Members of the Agency elected by the General Conference from among the Contracting Parties, due account being taken of equitable geographic distribution.
2. The Members of the Council shall be elected for a term of four years. However, in the first election three will be elected for two years. Outgoing Members may not be reelected for the following period unless the limited number of States for which the Treaty is in force so requires.
3. Each Member of the Council shall have one representative.
4. The Council shall be so organized as to be able to function continuously.
5. In addition to the functions conferred upon it by this Treaty and to those which may be assigned to it by the General Conference, the Council shall, through the General Secretary, ensure the proper operation of the control system in accordance with the provisions of this Treaty and with the decisions adopted by the General Conference.
6. The Council shall submit an annual report on its work to the General Conference as well as such special reports as it deems necessary or which the General Conference requests of it.
7. The Council shall elect its officers for each session.
8. The decisions of the Council shall be taken by a simple majority of its Members present and voting.
9. The Council shall adopt its own rules of procedure.

The Secretariat
Article 11
1. The Secretariat shall consist of a General Secretary, who shall be the chief administrative officer of the Agency, and of such staff as the Agency may require. The term of office of the General Secretary shall be four years and he may be re-elected for a single additional term. The General Secretary may not be a national of the country in which the Agency has its headquarters. In case the office of General Secretary becomes vacant, a new election shall be held to fill the office for the remainder of the term.
2. The staff of the Secretariat shall be appointed by the General Secretary, in accordance with rules laid down by the General Conference.
3. In addition to the functions conferred upon him by this Treaty and to those which may be assigned to him by the General Conference, the General Secretary shall ensure, as provided by article 10, paragraph 5, the proper operation of the control system established by this Treaty, in accordance with the provisions of the Treaty and the decisions taken by the General Conference.
4. The General Secretary shall act in that capacity in all meetings of the General Conference and of the Council and shall make an annual report to both bodies on the work of the Agency and any special reports requested by the General Conference or the Council or which the General Secretary may deem desirable.
5. The General Secretary shall establish the procedures for distributing to all Contracting Parties information received by the Agency from governmental

sources and such information from non-governmental sources as may be of interest to the Agency.

6. In the performance of their duties the General Secretary and the staff shall not seek or receive instructions from any Government or from any other authority external to the Agency and shall refrain from any action which might reflect on their position as international officials responsible only to the Agency; subject to their responsibility to the Agency, they shall not disclose any industrial secrets or other confidential information coming to their knowledge by reason of their official duties in the Agency.

7. Each of the Contracting Parties undertakes to respect the exclusively international character of the responsibilities of the General Secretary and the staff and not to seek to influence them in the discharge of their responsibilities.

Control system
Article 12
1. For the purpose of verifying compliance with the obligations entered into by the Contracting Parties in accordance with article 1, a control system shall be established which shall be put into effect in accordance with the provisions of articles 13-18 of this Treaty.
2. The control system shall be used in particular for the purpose of verifying:
(a) That devices, services and facilities intended for peaceful uses of nuclear energy are not used in the testing or manufacture of nuclear weapons,
(b) That none of the activities prohibited in article 1 of this Treaty are carried out in the territory of the Contracting Parties with nuclear materials or weapons introduced from abroad, and
(c) That explosions for peaceful purposes are compatible with article 18 of this Treaty.

IAEA safeguards
Article 13
Each Contracting Party shall negotiate multilateral or bilateral agreements with the International Atomic Energy Agency for the application of its safeguards to its nuclear activities. Each Contracting Party shall initiate negotiations within a period of 180 days after the date of the deposit of its instrument of ratification of this Treaty. These agreements shall enter into force, for each Party, not later than eighteen months after the date of the initiation of such negotiations except in case of unforeseen circumstances or *force majeure*.

Reports of the Parties
Article 14
1. The Contracting Parties shall submit to the Agency and to the International Atomic Energy Agency, for their information, semi-annual reports stating that no activity prohibited under this Treaty has occurred in their respective territories.
2. The Contracting Parties shall simultaneously transmit to the Agency a copy of any report they may submit to the International Atomic Energy Agency which

relates to matters that are the subject of this Treaty and to the application of safeguards.

3. The Contracting Parties shall also transmit to the Organization of American States, for its information, any reports that may be of interest to it, in accordance with the obligations established by the Inter-American System.

Special reports requested by the General Secretary
Article 15
1. With the authorization of the Council, the General Secretary may request any of the Contracting Parties to provide the Agency with complementary or supplementary information regarding any event or circumstance connected with compliance with this Treaty, explaining his reasons. The Contracting Parties undertake to co-operate promptly and fully with the General Secretary.
2. The General Secretary shall inform the Council and the Contracting Parties forthwith of such requests and of the respective replies.

Special inspections
Article 16
1. The International Atomic Energy Agency and the Council established by this Treaty have the power of carrying out special inspections in the following cases:
(a) In the case of the International Atomic Energy Agency, in accordance with the agreements referred to in article 13 of this Treaty;
(b) In the case of the Council:
(i) When so requested, the reasons for the request being stated, by any Party which suspects that some activity prohibited by this Treaty has been carried out or is about to be carried out, either in the territory of any other Party or in any other place on such latter Party's behalf, the Council shall immediately arrange for such an inspection in accordance with article 10, paragraph 5.
(ii) When requested by any Party which has been suspected of or charged with having violated this Treaty, the Council shall immediately arrange for the special inspection requested in accordance with article 10, paragraph 5.
The above requests will be made to the Council through the General Secretary.
2. The costs and expenses of any special inspection carried out under paragraph 1, sub-paragraph (b), sections (i) and (ii) of this article shall be borne by the requesting Party or Parties, except where the Council concludes on the basis of the report on the special inspection that, in view of the circumstances existing in the case, such costs and expenses should be borne by the agency.
3. The General Conference shall formulate the procedures for the organization and execution of the special inspections carried out in accordance with paragraph 1, sub-paragraph (b), sections (i) and (ii) of this article.
4. The Contracting Parties undertake to grant the inspectors carrying out such special inspections full and free access to all places and all information which may be necessary for the performance of their duties and which are directly and intimately connected with the suspicion of violation of this Treaty. If so requested by the authorities of the Contracting Party in whose territory the inspection is carried out, the inspectors designated by the General Conference shall be

accompanied by representatives of said authorities, provided that this does not in any way delay or hinder the work of the inspectors.
5. The Council shall immediately transmit to all the Parties, through the General Secretary, a copy of any report resulting from special inspections.
6. Similarly, the Council shall send through the General Secretary to the Secretary-General of the United Nations, for transmission to the United Nations Security Council and General Assembly, and to the Council of the Organization of American States, for its information, a copy of any report resulting from any special inspection carried out in accordance with paragraph 1, sub-paragraph (b), sections (i) and (ii) of this article.
7. The Council may decide, or any Contracting Party may request, the convening of a special session of the General Conference for the purpose of considering the reports resulting from any special inspection. In such a case, the General Secretary shall take immediate steps to convene the special session requested.
8. The General Conference, convened in special session under this article, may make recommendations to the Contracting Parties and submit reports to the Secretary-General of the United Nations to be transmitted to the United Nations Security Council and the General Assembly.

Use of nuclear energy for peaceful purposes
Article 17
Nothing in the provisions of this Treaty shall prejudice the rights of the Contracting Parties, in conformity with this Treaty, to use nuclear energy for peaceful purposes, in particular for their economic development and social progress.

Explosions for peaceful purposes
Article 18
1. The Contracting Parties may carry out explosions of nuclear devices for peaceful purposes -- including explosions which involve devices similar to those used in nuclear weapons -- or collaborate with third parties for the same purpose, provided that they do so in accordance with the provisions of this article and the other articles of the Treaty, particularly articles 1 and 5.
2. Contracting Parties intending to carry out, or to cooperate in carrying out, such an explosion shall notify the Agency and the International Atomic Energy Agency, as far in advance as the circumstances require, of the date of the explosion and shall at the same time provide the following information:
(a) The nature of the nuclear device and the source from which it was obtained,
(b) The place and purpose of the planned explosion,
(c) The procedures which will be followed in order to comply with paragraph 3 of this article,
(d) The expected force of the device, and
(e) The fullest possible information on any possible radioactive fall-out that may result from the explosion or explosions, and measures which will be taken to avoid danger to the population, flora, fauna and territories of any other Party or Parties.
3. The General Secretary and the technical personnel designated by the Council and the International Atomic Energy Agency may observe all the preparations,

including the explosion of the device, and shall have unrestricted access to any area in the vicinity of the site of the explosion in order to ascertain whether the device and the procedures followed during the explosion are in conformity with the information supplied under paragraph 2 of this article and the other provisions of this Treaty.
4. The Contracting Parties may accept the collaboration of third parties for the purpose set forth in paragraph 1 of the present article, in accordance with paragraphs 2 and 3 thereof.

Relations with other international organizations
Article 19
1. The Agency may conclude such agreements with the International Atomic Energy Agency as are authorized by the General Conference and as it considers likely to facilitate the efficient operation of the control system established by this Treaty.
2. The Agency may also enter into relations with any international organization or body, especially any which may be established in the future to supervise disarmament or measures for the control of armaments in any part of the world.
3. The Contracting Parties may, if they see fit, request the advice of the International American Nuclear Energy Commission on all technical matters connected with the application of this Treaty with which the Commission is competent to deal under its Statute.

Measures in the event of violation of the Treaty
Article 20
1. The General Conference shall take note of all cases in which, in its opinion, any Contracting Party is not complying fully with its obligations under this Treaty and shall draw the matter to the attention of the Party concerned, making such recommendations as it deems appropriate.
2. If, in its opinion, such non-compliance constitutes a violation of this Treaty which might endanger peace and security, the General Conference shall report thereon simultaneously to the United Nations Security Council and the General Assembly through the Secretary-General of the United Nations, and to the Council of the Organization of American States. The General Conference shall likewise report to the International Atomic Energy Agency for such purposes as are relevant in accordance with its Statute.

United Nations and Organization of American States
Article 21
None of the provisions of this Treaty shall be construed as impairing the rights and obligations of the Parties under the Charter of the United Nations or, in the case of States Members of the Organization of American States, under existing regional treaties.

Privileges and immunities
Article 22
1. The Agency shall enjoy in the territory of each of the Contracting Parties such legal capacity and such privileges and immunities as may be necessary for the exercise of its functions and the fulfillment of its purposes.
2. Representatives of the Contracting Parties accredited to the Agency and officials of the Agency shall similarly enjoy such privileges and immunities as are necessary for the performance of their functions.
3. The Agency may conclude agreements with the Contracting Parties with a view to determining the details of the application of paragraphs 1 and 2 of this article.

Notification of other agreements
Article 23
Once this Treaty has entered into force, the Secretariat shall be notified immediately of any international agreement concluded by any of the Contracting Parties on matters with which this Treaty is concerned; the Secretariat shall register it and notify the other Contracting Parties.

Settlement of disputes
Article 24
Unless the Parties concerned agree on another mode of peaceful settlement, any question or dispute concerning the interpretation or application of this Treaty which is not settled shall be referred to the International Court of Justice with the prior consent of the Parties to the controversy.

Signature
Article 25
1. This Treaty shall be open indefinitely for signature by:
   (a) All the Latin American Republics, and

   (b) All other sovereign States situated in their entirety south of latitude 35° north in the western hemisphere; and,

   (c) except as provided in paragraph 2 of this article, all such States which become sovereign, when they have been admitted by the General Conference.

2. The General Conference shall not take any decision regarding the admission of a political entity part or all of whose territory is the subject, prior to the date when this Treaty is opened for signature, of a dispute or claim between an extra-continental country and one or more Latin American States, so long as the dispute has not been settled by peaceful means.

Ratification and deposit
Article 26
1. This Treaty shall be subject to ratification by signatory States in accordance with their respective constitutional procedures.
2. This Treaty and the instruments of ratification shall be deposited with the Government of the Mexican United States, which is hereby designated the Depositary Government.
3. The Depositary Government shall send certified copies of this Treaty to the Governments of signatory States and shall notify them of the deposit of each instrument of ratification.

Reservations
Article 27
This Treaty shall not be subject to reservations.

Entry into force
Article 28
1. Subject to the provisions of paragraph 2 of this article, this Treaty shall enter into force among the States that have ratified it as soon as the following requirements have been met:
(a) Deposit of the instruments of ratification of this Treaty with the Depositary Government by the Governments of the States mentioned in article 25 which are in existence on the date when this Treaty is opened for signature and which are not affected by the provisions of article 25, paragraph 2;
(b) Signature and ratification of Additional Protocol I annexed to this Treaty by all extra-continental or continental States having *de jure* or *de facto* international responsibility for territories situated in the zone of application of the Treaty;
(c) Signature and ratification of the Additional Protocol II annexed to this Treaty by all powers possessing nuclear weapons;
(d) Conclusion of bilateral or multilateral agreements on the application of Safeguards System of the International Atomic Energy Agency in accordance with article 13 of this Treaty.
2. All signatory States shall have the imprescriptible right to waive, wholly or in part, the requirements laid down in the preceding paragraph. They may do so by means of a declaration which shall be annexed to their respective instrument of ratification and which may be formulated at the time of deposit of the instrument or subsequently. For those States which exercise this right, this Treaty shall enter into force upon deposit of the declaration, or as soon as those requirements have been met which have not been expressly waived.
3. As soon as this Treaty has entered into force in accordance with this provisions of paragraph 2 for eleven States, the Depositary Government shall convene a preliminary meeting of those States in order that the Agency may be set up and commence its work.
4. After the entry into force of this Treaty for all the countries of the zone, the rise of a new power possessing nuclear weapons shall have the effect of suspending the execution of this Treaty for those countries which have ratified it without waiving

requirements of paragraph 1, sub-paragraph (c) of this article, and which request such suspension; the Treaty shall remain suspended until the new power, on its own initiative or upon request by the General Conference, ratifies the annexed Additional Protocol II.

Amendments
Article 29
1. Any Contracting Party may propose amendments to this Treaty and shall submit its proposals to the Council through the General Secretary, who shall transmit them to all the other Contracting Parties and, in addition, to all other signatories in accordance with article 6. The Council, through the General Secretary, shall immediately following the meeting of signatories convene a special session of the General Conference to examine the proposals made, for the adoption of which a two-thirds majority of the Contracting Parties present and voting shall be required.
2. Amendments adopted shall enter into force as soon as the requirements set forth in article 28 of this Treaty have been complied with.

Duration and denunciation
Article 30
1. This Treaty shall be of a permanent nature and shall remain in force indefinitely, but any Party may denounce it by notifying the General Secretary of the Agency if, in the opinion of the denouncing State, there have arisen or may arise circumstances connected with the content of this Treaty or of the annexed Additional Protocols I and II which affect its supreme interests or the peace and security of one or more Contracting Parties.
2. The denunciation shall take effect three months after the delivery to the General Secretary of the Agency of the notification by the Government of the signatory State concerned. The General Secretary shall immediately communicate such notification to the other Contracting Parties and to the Secretary-General of the United Nations for the information of the United Nations Security Council and the General Assembly. He shall also communicate it to the Secretary-General of the Organization of American States.

Authentic texts and registration
Article 31
This Treaty, of which the Spanish, Chinese, English, French, Portuguese and Russian texts are equally authentic, shall be registered by the Depositary Government in accordance with article 102 of the United Nations Charter. The Depositary Government shall notify the Secretary-General of the United Nations of the signatures, ratification and amendments relating to this Treaty and shall communicate them to the Secretary-General of the Organization of American States for its information.

Transitional Article

Denunciation of the declaration referred to article 28, paragraph 2, shall be subject to the same procedures as the denunciation of this Treaty, except that it will take effect on the date of delivery of the respective notification.

IN WITNESS WHEREOF the undersigned Plenipotentiaries, having deposited their full powers, found in good and due form, sign this Treaty on behalf of their respective Governments.

DONE at Mexico, Distrito Federal, on the Fourteenth day of February, one thousand nine hundred and sixty-seven.

IV-1(b). Additional Protocol I to the Treaty for the Prohibition of Nuclear Weapons in Latin America [Treaty of Tlatelolco] (Inter-American), done at Mexico City, 14 February 1967, T.I.A.S. No. 10147, 634 U.N.T.S. 362, 28 I.L.M. 1405, entered into force with respect to the United States 23 November 1981. Authentic Texts: Chinese, English, French, Portuguese, Russian, Spanish

Relevant Penal Characteristics & Penal Provisions
None

Applicability
Peace

Control
Regulate & Prohibit

State Signatories
France; the Netherlands; United Kingdom, United States of America

State Parties
the Netherlands;[1] United Kingdom;[2] United States of America[3]

Full Text
The undersigned Plenipotentiaries, furnished with full powers by their respective Governments, *Convinced* that the Treaty for the Prohibition of Nuclear Weapons in Latin America, negotiated and signed in accordance with the recommendations of the General Assembly of the United Nations in Resolution 1911 (XVIII) of 27 November 1963, represents an important step towards ensuring the non-proliferation of nuclear weapons, *Aware* that the non-proliferation of nuclear weapons is not an end in itself but, rather, a means of achieving general and complete disarmament at a later stage, and *Desiring* to contribute, so far as lies in their power, towards ending the armaments race, especially in the field of nuclear

---

[1] With a statement(s).
[2] Applicable to Anguilla, British Virgin Islands, the Caymen Islands, the Falkland Islands, Montserrat, and the Turks and Caicos Islands.
[3] With an understanding and declarations.

weapons, and towards strengthening a world at peace, based on mutual respect and sovereign equality of States, *Have agreed as follows:*

Article 1. To undertake to apply the statute of denuclearization in respect of warlike purposes as defined in articles 1, 3, 5 and 13 of the Treaty for the Prohibition of Nuclear Weapons in Latin America in territories for which, de jure or de facto, they are internationally responsible and which lie within the limits of the geographical zone established in that Treaty.

Article 2. The duration of this Protocol shall be the same as that of the Treaty for the Prohibition of Nuclear Weapons in Latin America of which this Protocol is an annex, and the provisions regarding ratification and denunciation contained in the Treaty shall be applicable to it.

Article 3. This Protocol shall enter into force, for the States which have ratified it, on the date of the deposit of their respective instruments of ratification.

IN WITNESS WHEREOF the undersigned Plenipotentiaries, having deposited their full powers, found in good and due form, sign this Protocol on behalf of their respective Governments.

International Humanitarian Law and Arms Control Agreements 531

IV-1(c). Additional Protocol II to the Treaty of 14 February 1967 for the Prohibition of Nuclear Weapons in Latin America [Treaty of Tlatelolco] (Inter-American), *done at Mexico City*, 14 February 1967, 22 U.S.T. 754, 634 U.N.T.S. 364, 28 I.L.M. 1413, entered into force with respect to the United States 12 May 1971. Authentic Texts: Chinese, English, French, Portuguese, Russian, Spanish

Relevant Penal Characteristics & Penal Provisions
None

Application
Peace

Control
Regulation & Prohibition

State Signatories
China; France; Union of Soviet Socialist Republics;[1] United Kingdom; United States of America

State Parties
China;[2] France;[3] Union of Soviet Socialist Republics;[4] United Kingdom;[5] United States of America[6]

Full Text
The undersigned Plenipotentiaries, furnished with full powers by their respective Governments,

Convinced that the Treaty for the Prohibition of Nuclear Weapons in Latin America, negotiated and signed in accordance with the recommendations of the General Assembly of the United Nations in Resolution 1911 (XVIII) of 27 November 1963, represents an important step towards ensuring the non-proliferation of nuclear weapons,

Aware that the non-proliferation of nuclear weapons is not an end in itself but, rather, a means of achieving general and complete disarmament at a later stage, and

Desiring to contribute, so far as lies in their power, towards ending the armaments race, especially in the field of nuclear weapons, and towards promoting

---

[1] *See* Methodology, State Succession.
[2] With a statement.
[3] *Id.*
[4] *Id. See* Methodology, State Succession.
[5] With a declaration. Applicable to Anguilla, British Virgin Islands, the Cayman Islands, the Falkland Islands, Montserrat, and the Turks and Caicos Islands.
[6] With understandings and declarations.

and strengthening a world at peace, based on mutual respect and sovereign equality of States,

Have agreed as follows:

Article 1. The statute of denuclearization of Latin America in respect or warlike purposes, as defined, delimited and set forth in the Treaty for the Prohibition of Nuclear Weapons in Latin America of which this instrument is an annex, shall be fully respected by the Parties to this Protocol in all its express aims and provisions.

Article 2. The Governments represented by the undersigned Plenipotentiaries undertake, therefore, not to contribute in any way to the performance of acts involving a violation of the obligations of article 1 of the Treaty in the territories to which the Treaty applies in accordance with article 4 thereof.

Article 3. The Governments represented by the undersigned Plenipotentiaries also undertake not to use or threaten to use nuclear weapons against the Contracting Parties of the Treaty for the Prohibition of Nuclear Weapons in Latin America.

Article 4. The duration of this Protocol shall be the same as that of the Treaty for the Prohibition of Nuclear Weapons in Latin America of which this protocol is an annex, and the definitions of territory and nuclear weapons set forth in articles 3 and 5 of the Treaty shall be applicable to this Protocol, as well as the provisions regarding ratification, reservations, denunciation, authentic texts and registration contained in articles 26, 27, 30 and 31 of the Treaty.

Article 5. This Protocol shall enter into force, for the States which have ratified it, on the date of the deposit of their respective instruments of ratification.

IN WITNESS WHEREOF the undersigned Plenipotentiaries, having deposited their full powers, found in good and due form, sign this Additional Protocol on behalf of their respective Governments.

IV-2. South Pacific Nuclear-Free Zone Treaty [Treaty of Rarotonga],
signed at Rarotonga, Cook Islands, **6 August 1985, 24 I.L.M. 1440.**

Relevant Penal Characteristics & Penal Provisions

2. Implicit recognition of the penal nature of the act by establishing a duty to prohibit, prevent, prosecute, punish, or the like: Article 5; Article 6; & Article 7

Application
Peace

Control
Prohibition

State Signatories
Australia; Cook Islands; Fiji; Kiribati; New Zealand; Niue; Papua New Guinea

Full Text

PREAMBLE

The Parties to this Treaty,

United in their commitment to a world at peace;

Gravely concerned that the continuing nuclear arms race presents the risk of nuclear war which would have devastating consequences for all people;

Convinced that all countries have an obligation to make every effort to achieve the goal of eliminating nuclear weapons, the terror which they hold for humankind and the threat which they pose to life on earth;

Believing that regional arms control measures can contribute to global efforts to reverse the nuclear arms race and promote the national security of each country in the region and the common security of all;

Determined to ensure, so far as lies within their power, that the bounty and beauty of the land and sea in their region shall remain the heritage of their peoples and their descendants in perpetuity to be enjoyed by all in peace;

Reaffirming the importance of the Treaty on the Non-Proliferation of Nuclear Weapons (NPT) in preventing the proliferation of nuclear weapons and in contributing to world security;

Noting, in particular, that Article VII of the NPT recognizes the right of any group of States to conclude regional treaties in order to assure the total absence of nuclear weapons in their respective territories;

Noting that the prohibitions of emplantation and emplacement of nuclear weapons on the seabed and the ocean floor and in the subsoil thereof contained in the Treaty on the Prohibition of the Emplacement of Nuclear Weapons and Other Weapons of Mass Destruction on the Seabed and the Ocean Floor and in the Subsoil Thereof apply in the South Pacific;

Noting also that the prohibition of testing of nuclear weapons in the atmosphere or under water, including territorial waters or high seas, contained in the Treaty Banning Nuclear Weapon Tests in the Atmosphere, in Outer Space and Under Water applies in the South Pacific;

Determined to keep the region free of environmental pollution by radioactive wastes and other radioactive matter;

Guided by the decision of the Fifteenth South Pacific Forum at Tuvalu that a nuclear free zone should be established in the region at the earliest possible opportunity in accordance with the principles set out in the communique of that meeting;

Have agreed as follows:

ARTICLE 1 USAGE OF TERMS

For the purposes of this Treaty and its Protocols:

(a) "South Pacific Nuclear Free Zone" means the areas described in Annex 1 as illustrated by the map attached to that Annex;

(b) "territory" means internal waters, territorial sea and archipelagic waters, the seabed and subsoil beneath, the land territory and the airspace above them;

(c) "nuclear explosive device" means any nuclear weapon or other explosive device capable of releasing nuclear energy, irrespective of the purpose for which it could be used. The term includes such a weapon or device in unassembled and partly assembled forms, but does not include the means of transport or delivery of such a weapon or device if separable from and not an indivisible part of it;

(d) "stationing" means emplantation, emplacement, transportation on land or inland waters, stockpiling, storage, installation and deployment.

ARTICLE 2 APPLICATION OF THE TREATY

1. Except where otherwise specified, this Treaty and its Protocols shall apply to territory within the South Pacific Nuclear Free Zone.

2. Nothing in this Treaty shall prejudice or in any way affect the rights, or the exercise of the rights, of any State under international law with regard to freedom of the seas.

ARTICLE 3 RENUNCIATION OF NUCLEAR EXPLOSIVE DEVICES

Each Party undertakes:

(a) not to manufacture or otherwise acquire, possess or have control over any nuclear explosive device by any means anywhere inside or outside the South Pacific Nuclear Free Zone;

(b) not to seek or receive any assistance in the manufacture or acquisition of any nuclear explosive device;

(c) not to take any action to assist or encourage the manufacture or acquisition of any nuclear explosive device by any State.

ARTICLE 4 PEACEFUL NUCLEAR ACTIVITIES
Each Party undertakes:

(a) not to provide source or special fissionable material, or equipment or material especially designed or prepared for the processing, use or production of special fissionable material for peaceful purposes to:

(i) any non-nuclear-weapon State unless subject to the safeguards required by Article III.1 of the NPT, or

(ii) any nuclear-weapon State unless subject to applicable safeguards agreements with the International Atomic Energy Agency (IAEA).

Any such provisions shall be in accordance with strict non-proliferation measures to provide assurance of exclusively peaceful non-explosive use;

(b) to support the continued effectiveness of the international non-proliferation system based on the NPT and the IAEA safeguards system.

ARTICLE 5 PREVENTION OF STATIONING OF NUCLEAR EXPLOSIVE DEVICES

1. Each Party undertakes to prevent in its territory the stationing of any nuclear explosive device.

2. Each Party in the exercise of its sovereign rights remains free to decide for itself whether to allow visits by foreign ships and aircraft to its ports and airfields, transit of its airspace by foreign aircraft, and navigation by foreign ships in its territorial sea or archipelagic waters in a manner not covered by the rights of innocent passage, archipelagic sea lane passage or transit passage of straits.

ARTICLE 6 PREVENTION OF TESTING OF NUCLEAR EXPLOSIVE DEVICES
Each Party undertakes:

(a) to prevent in its territory the testing of any nuclear explosive device;

(b) not to take any action to assist or encourage the testing of any nuclear explosive device by any State.

ARTICLE 7 PREVENTION OF DUMPING
1. Each Party undertakes:

(a) not to dump radioactive wastes and other radioactive matter at sea anywhere within the South Pacific Nuclear Free Zone.

(b) to prevent the dumping of radioactive wastes and other radioactive matter by anyone in its territorial sea;

(c) not to take any action to assist or encourage the dumping by anyone of radioactive wastes and other radioactive matter at sea anywhere within the South Pacific Nuclear Free Zone;

(d) to support the conclusion as soon as possible of the proposed Convention relating to the protection of the natural resources and environment of the South Pacific region and its Protocol for the prevention of pollution of the South Pacific region by dumping, with the aim of precluding dumping at sea of radioactive wastes and other radioactive matter by anyone anywhere in the region.

2. Paragraphs l(a) and l(b) of this Article shall not apply to areas of the South Pacific Nuclear Free Zone in respect of which such a Convention and Protocol have entered into force.

ARTICLE 8 CONTROL SYSTEM

1. The Parties hereby establish a control system for the purpose of verifying compliance with their obligations under this Treaty.

2. The control system shall comprise:

(a) reports and exchange of information as provided for in Article 9;

(b) consultations as provided for in Article 10 and Annex 4 (1);

(c) the application to peaceful nuclear activities of safeguards by the IAEA as provided for in Annex 2;

(d) a complaints procedure as provided for in Annex 4.

ARTICLE 9 REPORTS AND EXCHANGES OF INFORMATION
1. Each Party shall report to the Director of the South Pacific Bureau for Economic Co-operation (the Director) as soon as possible any significant event within its jurisdiction affecting the implementation of this Treaty. The Director shall circulate such reports promptly to all Parties.

2. The Parties shall endeavour to keep each other informed on matters arising under or in relation to this Treaty. They may exchange information by communicating it to the Director, who shall circulate it to all Parties.

3. The Director shall report annually to the South Pacific Forum on the status of

this Treaty and matters arising under or in relation to it, incorporating reports and communications made under paragraphs 1 and 2 of this Article and matters arising under Articles 8(2)(d) and 10 and Annex 2(4).

ARTICLE 10 CONSULTATIONS AND REVIEW
Without prejudice to the conduct of consultations among Parties by other means, the Director, at the request of any Party, shall convene a meeting of the Consultative Committee established by Annex 3 for consultation and co-operation on any matter arising in relation to this Treaty or for reviewing its operation.

ARTICLE 11 AMENDMENT
The Consultative Committee shall consider proposals for amendment of the provisions of this Treaty proposed by any Party and circulated by the Director to all Parties not less than three months prior to the convening of the Consultative Committee for this purpose. Any proposal agreed upon by consensus by the Consultative Committee shall be communicated to the Director who shall circulate it for acceptance to all Parties. An amendment shall enter into force thirty days after receipt by the depositary of acceptances from all Parties.

ARTICLE 12 SIGNATURE AND RATIFICATION
1. This Treaty shall be open for signature by any Member of the South Pacific Forum.

2. This Treaty shall be subject to ratification. Instruments of ratification shall be deposited with the Director who is hereby designated depositary of this Treaty and its Protocols.

3. If a Member of the South Pacific Forum whose territory is outside the South Pacific Nuclear Free Zone becomes a Party to this Treaty, Annex 1 shall be deemed to be amended so far as is required to enclose at least the territory of that Party within the boundaries of the South Pacific Nuclear Free Zone. The delineation of any area added pursuant to this paragraph shall be approved by the South Pacific Forum.

ARTICLE 13 WITHDRAWAL
1. This Treaty is of a permanent nature and shall remain in force indefinitely, provided that in the event of a violation by any Party of a provision of this Treaty essential to the achievement of the objectives of the Treaty or of the spirit of the Treaty, every other Party shall have the right to withdraw from the Treaty.

2. Withdrawal shall be effected by giving notice twelve months in advance to the Director who shall circulate such notice to all other Parties.

ARTICLE 14 RESERVATIONS
This Treaty shall not be subject to reservations.

ARTICLE 15 ENTRY INTO FORCE
1. This Treaty shall enter into force on the date of deposit of the eighth instrument of ratification.

2. For a signatory which ratifies this Treaty after the date of deposit of the eighth instrument of ratification, the Treaty shall enter into force on the date of deposit of its instrument of ratification.

ARTICLE 16 DEPOSITARY FUNCTIONS

The depositary shall register this Treaty and its Protocols pursuant to Article 102 of the Charter of the United Nations and shall transmit certified copies of the Treaty and its Protocols to all Members of the South Pacific Forum and all States eligible to become Party to the Protocols to the Treaty and shall notify them of signatures and ratifications of the Treaty and its Protocols.

IN WITNESS WHEREOF the undersigned, being duly authorized by their Governments, have signed this Treaty.

DONE at Rarotonga, this sixth day of August, One thousand nine hundred and eighty-five, in a single original in the English language.

ANNEX 1 SOUTH PACIFIC NUCLEAR FREE ZONE A. The area bounded by a line:

(1) commencing at the point of intersection of the Equator by the maritime boundary between Indonesia and Papua New Guinea;

(2) running thence northerly along that maritime boundary to its intersection by the outer limit of the exclusive economic zone of Papua New Guinea;

(3) thence generally north-easterly, easterly and south-easterly along that outer limit to its intersection by the Equator;

(4) thence east along the Equator to its intersection by the meridian of Longitude 163 degrees East;

(5) thence north along that meridian to its intersection by the parallel of Latitude 3 degrees North;

(6) thence east along that parallel to its intersection by the meridian of Longitude 171 degrees East;

(7) thence north along that meridian to its intersection by the parallel of Latitude 4 degrees North;

(8) thence east along that parallel to its intersection by the meridian of Longitude 180 degrees East;

(9) thence south along that meridian to its intersection by the Equator;

(10) thence east along the Equator to its intersection by the meridian of Longitude 165 degrees West;

(11) thence north along that meridian to its intersection by the parallel of Latitude 5 degrees 30 minutes North;

(12) thence east along that parallel to its intersection by the meridian of Longitude 154 degrees West;

(13) thence south along that meridian to its intersection by the Equator;

(14) thence east along the Equator to its intersection by the meridian of Longitude 115 degrees West;

(15) thence south along that meridian to its intersection by the parallel of Latitude 60 degrees South;

(16) thence west along that parallel to its intersection by the meridian of Longitude 115 degrees East;

(17) thence north along that meridian to its southernmost intersection by the outer limit of the territorial sea of Australia;

(18) thence generally northerly and easterly along the outer limit of the territorial sea of Australia to its intersection by the meridian of Longitude 136 degrees 45 minutes East;

(19) thence north-easterly along the geodesic to the point of Latitude 10 degrees 50 minutes South, Longitude 139 degrees 12 minutes East;

(20) thence north-easterly along the maritime boundary between Indonesia and Papua New Guinea to where it joins the land border between those two countries;

(21) thence generally northerly along that land border to where it joins the maritime boundary between Indonesia and Papua New Guinea, on the northern coastline of Papua New Guinea; and

(22) thence generally northerly along that boundary to the point of commencement.

B. The areas within the outer limits of the territorial seas of all Australian islands lying westward of the area described in paragraph A and north of Latitude 60 degrees South, provided that any such areas shall cease to be part of the South Pacific Nuclear Free Zone upon receipt by the depositary of written notice from the Government of Australia stating that the areas have become subject to another treaty having an object and purpose substantially the same as that of this Treaty.

(illustrative map not included) ANNEX 2 IAEA SAFEGUARDS

1. The safeguards referred to in Article 8 shall in respect of each Party be applied by the IAEA as set forth in an agreement negotiated and concluded with the IAEA on all source or special fissionable material in all peaceful nuclear activities within the territory of the Party, under its jurisdiction or carried out under its control anywhere.

2. The agreement referred to in paragraph 1 shall be, or shall be equivalent in its scope and effect to, an agreement required in connection with the NPT on the basis of the material reproduced in document INFCIRC/153 (Corrected) of the IAEA. Each Party shall take all appropriate steps to ensure that such an agreement is in force for it not later than 18 months after the date of entry into force for that Party of this Treaty.

3. For the purposes of this Treaty, the safeguards referred to in paragraph 1 shall have as their purpose the verification of the non-diversion of nuclear material from peaceful nuclear activities to nuclear explosive devices.

4. Each Party agrees upon the request of any other Party to transmit to that Party and to the Director for the information of all Parties a copy of the overall conclusions of the most recent report by the IAEA on its inspection activities in the territory of the Party concerned, and to advise the Director promptly of any subsequent findings of the Board of Governors of the IAEA in relation to those conclusions for the information of all Parties.

ANNEX 3 CONSULTATIVE COMMITTEE

1. There is hereby established a Consultative Committee which shall be convened by the Director from time to time pursuant to Articles 10 and 11 and Annex 4 (2). The Consultative Committee shall be constituted of representatives of the Parties, each Party being entitled to appoint one representative who may be accompanied by advisers. Unless otherwise agreed, the Consultative Committee shall be chaired at any given meeting by the representative of the Party which last hosted the meeting of Heads of Government of Members of the South Pacific Forum. A quorum shall be constituted by representatives of half the Parties. Subject to the provisions of Article 11, decisions of the Consultative Committee shall be taken by consensus or, failing consensus, by a two-thirds majority of those present and voting. The Consultative Committee shall, adopt such other rules of procedure as it sees fit.

2. The costs of the Consultative Committee, including the costs of special inspections pursuant to Annex 4, shall be borne by the South Pacific Bureau for Economic Co-operation. It may seek special funding should this be required.

ANNEX 4 COMPLAINTS PROCEDURE

1. A Party which considers that there are grounds for a complaint that another Party is in breach of its obligations under this Treaty shall, before bringing such a

complaint to the Director, bring the subject matter of the complaint to the attention of the Party complained of and shall allow the latter reasonable opportunity to provide it with an explanation and to resolve the matter.

2. If the matter is not so resolved, the complainant Party may bring the complaint to the Director with a request that the Consultative Committee be convened to consider it. Complaints shall be supported by an account of evidence of breach of obligations known to the complainant Party. Upon receipt of a complaint the Director shall convene the Consultative Committee as quickly as possible to consider it.

3. The Consultative Committee, taking account of efforts made under paragraph 1, shall afford the Party complained of a reasonable opportunity to provide it with an explanation of the matter.

4. If, after considering any explanation given to it by the representatives of the Party complained of, the Consultative Committee decides that there is sufficient substance in the complaint to warrant a special inspection in the territory of that Party or elsewhere, the Consultative Committee shall direct that such special inspection be made as quickly as possible by a special inspection team of three suitably qualified special inspectors appointed by the Consultative Committee in consultation with the complained of and complainant Parties, provided that no national of either Party shall serve on the special inspection team. If so requested by the Party complained of, the special inspection team shall be accompanied by representatives of that Party. Neither the right of consultation on the appointment of special inspectors, nor the right to accompany special inspectors, shall delay the work of the special inspection team.

5. In making a special inspection, special inspectors shall be subject to the direction only of the Consultative Committee and shall comply with such directives concerning tasks, objectives, confidentiality and procedures as may be decided upon by it. Directives shall take account of the legitimate interests of the Party complained of in complying with its other international obligations and commitments and shall not duplicate safeguards procedures to be undertaken by the IAEA pursuant to agreements referred to in Annex 2 (1). The special inspectors shall discharge their duties with due respect for the laws of the Party complained of.

6. Each Party shall give to special inspectors full and free access to all information and places within its territory which may be relevant to enable the special inspectors to implement the directives given to them by the Consultative Committee.

7. The Party complained of shall take all appropriate steps to facilitate the special inspection, and shall grant to special inspectors privileges and immunities necessary for the performance of their functions, including inviolability for all papers and documents and immunity from arrest, detention and legal process for

acts done and words spoken and written, for the purpose of the special inspection.

8. The special inspectors shall report in writing as quickly as possible to the Consultative Committee, outlining their activities, setting out relevant facts and information as ascertained by them, with supporting evidence and documentation as appropriate, and stating their conclusions. The Consultative Committee shall report fully to all Members of the South Pacific Forum, giving its decision as to whether the Party complained of is in breach of its obligations under this Treaty.

9. If the Consultative Committee has decided that the Party complained of is in breach of its obligations under this Treaty, or that the above provisions have not been complied with, or at any time at the request of either the complainant or complained of Party, the Parties shall meet promptly at a meeting of the South Pacific Forum.

PROTOCOL 1 The Parties to this Protocol

Noting the South Pacific Nuclear Free Zone Treaty (the Treaty)

Have agreed as follows:

ARTICLE 1

Each Party undertakes to apply, in respect of the territories for which it is internationally responsible situated within the South Pacific Nuclear Free Zone, the prohibitions contained in Articles 3, 5 and 6, insofar as they related to the manufacture, stationing and testing of any nuclear explosive device within those territories, and the safeguards specified in Article 8(2)(c) and Annex 2 of the Treaty.

ARTICLE 2

Each Party may, by written notification to the depositary, indicate its acceptance from the date of such notification of any alteration to its obligation under this Protocol brought about by the entry into force of an amendment to the Treaty pursuant to Article 11 of the Treaty.

ARTICLE 3

This Protocol shall be open for signature by the French Republic, the United Kingdom of Great Britain and Northern Ireland and the United States of America.

ARTICLE 4

This Protocol shall be subject to ratification.

ARTICLE 5

This Protocol is of a permanent nature and shall remain in force indefinitely, provided that each Party shall, in exercising its national sovereignty, have the right to withdraw from this Protocol if it decides that extraordinary events, related to the subject matter of this Protocol, have jeopardized its supreme interests. It shall give notice of such withdrawal to the depositary three months in advance. Such notice shall include a statement of the extraordinary events it regards as having jeopardized its supreme interests.

ARTICLE 6

This Protocol shall enter into force for each State on the date of its deposit with the depositary of its instrument of ratification.

IN WITNESS WHEREOF the undersigned, being duly authorized by their Governments, have signed this Protocol.

DONE at Suva, this eighth day of August, one thousand nine hundred and eighty-six, in a single original in the English language.

PROTOCOL 2 The Parties to this Protocol

Noting the South Pacific Nuclear Free Zone Treaty (the Treaty)

Have agreed as follows:

ARTICLE 1 Each Party undertakes not to use or threaten to use any nuclear explosive device against:

(a) Parties to the Treaty; or

(b) Any territory within the South Pacific Nuclear Free Zone for which a State that has become a Party to Protocol 1 is internationally responsible.

ARTICLE 2 Each Party undertakes not to contribute to any act of a Party to the Treaty which constitutes a violation of the Treaty, or to any act of another Party to a Protocol which constitutes a violation of a Protocol.

ARTICLE 3

Each Party may, by written notification to the depositary, indicate its acceptance from the date of such notification of any alteration to its obligation under this Protocol brought about by the entry into force of an amendment to the Treaty pursuant to Article 11 of the Treaty or by the extension of the South Pacific Nuclear Free Zone pursuant to Article 12(3) of the Treaty.

ARTICLE 4

This Protocol shall be open for signature by the French Republic, the People's Republic of China, the Union of Soviet Socialist Republics, the United Kingdom of

Great Britain and Northern Ireland and the United States of America.

ARTICLE 5

This Protocol shall be subject to ratification.

ARTICLE 6

This Protocol is of a permanent nature and shall remain in force indefinitely, provided that each Party shall, in exercising its national sovereignty, have the right to withdraw from this Protocol if it decides that extraordinary events, related to the subject matter of this Protocol, have jeopardized its supreme interests. It shall give notice of such withdrawal to the depositary three months in advance. Such notice shall include a statement of the extraordinary events it regards as having jeopardized its supreme interests.

ARTICLE 7

This Protocol shall enter into force for each State on the date of its deposit with the depositary of its instrument of ratification.

IN WITNESS WHEREOF the undersigned, being duly authorized by their Governments, have signed this Protocol.

DONE at Suva, this eighth day of August, one thousand nine hundred and eighty-six, in a single original in the English language.

PROTOCOL 3 The Parties to this Protocol

Noting the South Pacific Nuclear Free Zone Treaty (the Treaty)

Have agreed as follows:

ARTICLE 1

Each Party undertakes not to test any nuclear explosive device anywhere within the South Pacific Nuclear Free Zone.

ARTICLE 2

Each Party may, by written notification to the depositary, indicate its acceptance from the date of such notification of any alteration to its obligation under this Protocol brought about by the entry into force of an amendment to the Treaty pursuant to Article 11 of the Treaty or by the extension of the South Pacific Nuclear Free Zone pursuant to Article 12(3) of the Treaty.

ARTICLE 3

This Protocol shall be open for signature by the French Republic, the People's Republic of China, the Union of Soviet Socialist Republics, the United Kingdom of Great Britain and Northern Ireland and the United States of America.

ARTICLE 4

This Protocol shall be subject to ratification.

ARTICLE 5

This Protocol is of a permanent nature and shall remain in force indefinitely, provided that each Party shall, in exercising its national sovereignty, have the right to withdraw from this Protocol if it decides that extraordinary events, related to the subject matter of this Protocol, have jeopardized its supreme interests. It shall give notice of such withdrawal to the depositary three months in advance. Such notice shall include a statement of the extraordinary events it regards as having jeopardized its supreme interests.

ARTICLE 6

This Protocol shall enter into force for each State on the date of its deposit with the depositary of its instrument of ratification.

IN WITNESS WHEREOF the undersigned, being duly authorized by their Governments, have signed this Protocol.

DONE at Suva, this eighth day of August, one thousand nine hundred and eighty-six, in a single original in the English language.

IV-3. Treaty on Southeast Asia Nuclear Weapon-Free Zone, *signed at Bangkok,* 15 December 1995, 35 I.L.M. 635.

Relevant Penal Characteristics & Provisions

2. Implicit recognition of the penal nature of the act by establishing a duty to prohibit, prevent, prosecute, punish, or the like: Article 3

Applicability
War & Peace

Control
Prohibition

State Signatories
Brunei; Darussalam; Cambodia; Indonesia; Laos; Malaysia; Philippines; Singapore; Thailand; Vietnam

Full Text
The States Parties to this Treaty:
DESIRING to contribute to the realization of the purposes and principles of the Charter of the United Nations;
DETERMINED to take concrete action which will contribute to the progress towards general and complete disarmament of nuclear weapons, and to the promotion of international peace and security;
REAFFIRMING the desire of the Southeast Asian States to maintain peace and stability in the region in the spirit of peaceful coexistence and mutual understanding and cooperation as enunciated in various communiques, declarations and other legal instruments;
RECALLING the Declaration on the Zone of Peace, Freedom and Neutrality (ZOPFAN) signed in Kuala Lumpur on 27 November 1971 and the Programme of Action on ZOPFAN adopted at the 26th ASEAN Ministerial Meeting in Singapore in July 1993;
CONVINCED that the establishment of a Southeast Asia Nuclear Weapon-Free Zone, as an essential component of the ZOPPAN, will contribute towards strengthening the security of States within the Zone and towards enhancing international peace and security as a whole;
REAFFIRMING the importance of the Treaty on the Non-Proliferation of Nuclear Weapons (NPT) in preventing the proliferation of nuclear weapons and in contributing towards international peace and security;
RECALLING Article VII of the NPT which recognizes the right of any group of States to conclude regional treaties in order to assume the total absence of nuclear weapons in their respective territories;
RECALLING the Final Document of the Tenth Special Session of the United Nations General Assembly which encourages the establishment of nuclear weapon-free zones;

RECALLING the Principles and Objectives for Nuclear Non-Proliferation and Disarmament, adopted at the 1995 Review and Extension Conference of the Parties to the NPT, that the cooperation of all the nuclear-weapon States and their respect and support for the relevant protocols is important for the maximum effectiveness of this nuclear weapon-free zone treaty and its relevant protocols.
DETERMINED to protect the region from environmental pollution and the hazards posed by radioactive wastes and other radioactive material;
HAVE AGREED as follows:
Article 1
USE OF TERMS
For the purposes of this Treaty and its Protocol:
(a) "Southeast Asia Nuclear Weapon-Free Zone", hereinafter referred to as the "Zone", means the area comprising the territories of all States in Southeast Asia, namely, Brunei, Darussalam, Cambodia, Indonesia, Laos, Malaysia, Myanmar, Philippines, Singapore, Thailand and Vietnam, and their respective continental shelves and Exclusive Economic Zones (EEZ);
(b) "territory" means the land territory, internal waters, territorial sea, archipelagic waters, the seabed and the sub-soil thereof and the airspace above them;
(c) "nuclear weapon" means any explosive device capable of releasing nuclear energy in an uncontrolled manner but does not include the means of transport or delivery of such device if separable from and not an indivisible part thereof;
(d) "station" means to deploy, emplace, implant, install, stockpile or store;
(e) "radioactive material" means material that contains radionuclides above clearance or exemption levels recommended by the International Atomic Energy Agency (IAEA);
(f) "radioactive wastes" means material that contains or is contaminated with radionuclides at concentrations or activities greater than clearance levels recommended by the IAEA and for which no use is foreseen; and
(g) "dumping" means
    (i) any deliberate disposal at sea, including seabed and subsoil insertion, of radioactive wastes or other matter from vessels, aircraft, platforms or other man-made structures at sea, and
    (ii) any deliberate disposal at sea, including seabed and subsoil insertion, of vessels, aircraft, platforms or other man-made structures at sea, containing radioactive material, but does not include the disposal of wastes or other matter incidental to, or derived from the normal operations of vessels, aircraft, platforms or other man-made structures at sea and their equipment, other than wastes or other matter transported by or to vessels, aircraft, platforms or other man-made structures at sea, operating for the purpose of disposal of such matter or derived from the treatment of such wastes or other matter on such vessels, aircraft, platforms or structures.

Article 2
APPLICATION OF THE TREATY
1. This Treaty and its Protocol shall apply to the territories, continental selves, and EEZ of the States Parties within the Zone in which the Treaty is in force.
2. Nothing in this Treaty shall prejudice the rights or the exercise of these rights by any State under the provisions of the United Nations Convention on the Law of the Sea of 1982, in particular with regard to freedom of the high seas, rights of innocent passage, archipelagic sea lanes passage or transit passage of ships and aircraft, and consistent with the Charter of the United Nations.

Article 3
BASIC UNDERTAKINGS
1. Each State Party undertakes not to, anywhere inside or outside the Zone:
   (a) develop, manufacture or otherwise acquire, possess or have control over nuclear weapons;
   (b) station or transport nuclear weapons by any means; or
   (c) test or use nuclear weapons.
2. Each State Party also undertakes not to allow, in its territory, any other State to:
   (a) develop, manufacture or otherwise acquire, possess or have control over nuclear weapons;
   (b) station nuclear weapons; or
   (c) test or use nuclear weapons.
3. Each State Party also undertake not to:
   (a) dump at sea or discharge into the atmosphere anywhere within the Zone any radioactive material or wastes;
   (b) dispose radioactive material or wastes on land in the territory of or under the jurisdiction of other States except as stipulated in Paragraph 2 (e) of Article 4; or
   (c) allow, within its territory, any other State to dump at sea or discharge into the atmosphere any radioactive material or wastes.

4. Each State Party undertakes not to :
   (a) seek or receive any assistance in the Commission of any act in violation of the provisions of Paragraphs 1, 2 and 3 of this Article; or

   (b) take any action to assist or encourage the Commission of any act in violation of the provisions of Paragraphs 1, 2 and 3 of this Article.

Article 4
USE OF NUCLEAR ENERGY FOR PEACEFUL PURPOSES
1. Nothing in this Treaty shall prejudice the right of the States Parties to use nuclear energy, in particular for their economic development and social progress.
2. Each State Party therefore undertakes:
   (a) to use exclusively for peaceful purposes nuclear material and facilities which are within its territory and areas under its jurisdiction and control;

(b) prior to embarking on its peaceful nuclear energy programme, to subject its programme to rigorous nuclear safety assessment conforming to guidelines and standards recommended by the IAEA for the protection of health and minimization of danger to life and property in accordance with Paragraph 6 of Article III of the Statute of the IAEA;
(c) upon request, to make available to another State Party the assessment except information relating to personal data, information protected by intellectual property rights or by industrial or commercial confidentiality, and information relating to national security;
(d) to support the continued effectiveness of the international non-proliferation system based on the Treaty on the Non-Proliferation of Nuclear Weapons (NPT) and the IAEA safeguard system; and
(e) to dispose radioactive wastes and other radioactive material in accordance with IAEA standards and procedures on land within its territory or on land within the territory of another State which has consented to such disposal.

3. Each State Party further undertakes not to provide source or special fissionable material, or equipment or material especially designed or prepared for the processing, use or production of special fissionable material to :
(a) any non-nuclear-weapon State except under conditions subject to the safeguards required by Paragraph 1 of Article III of the NPT; or
(b) any nuclear-weapon State except in conformity with applicable safeguards agreements with the IAEA.

Article 5
IAEA SAFEGUARDS
Each State Party which has not done so shall conclude an agreement with the IAEA for the application of full scope safeguards to its peaceful nuclear activities not later than eighteen months after the entry into force for that State Party of the Treaty.

Article 6
EARLY NOTIFICATION OF A NUCLEAR ACCIDENT
Each State Party which has not acceded to the Convention on Early Notification of a Nuclear Accident shall endeavour to do so.

Article 7
FOREIGN SHIPS AND AIRCRAFT
Each State Party, on being notified, may decide for itself whether to allow visits by foreign ships and aircraft to its ports and airfields, transit of its airspace by foreign aircraft, and navigation by foreign ships through its territorial sea or archipelagic waters and overflight of foreign aircraft above those waters in a manner not governed by the rights of innocent passage, archipelagic sea lanes passage or transit passage.

Article 8
ESTABLISHMENT OF THE COMMISSION FOR THE
SOUTHEAST ASIA NUCLEAR WEAPON-FREE ZONE

1. There is hereby established a Commission for the Southeast Asia Nuclear Weapon-Free Zone, hereinafter referred to as the "Commission".
2. All States Parties are ipso facto members of the Commission. Each State Party shall be represented by its Foreign Minister or his representative accompanied by alternates and advisers.
3. The function of the Commission shall be to oversee the implementation of this Treaty and ensure compliance with its provisions.
4. The Commission shall meet as and when necessary in accordance with the provisions of this Treaty including upon the request of any State Party. As far as possible, the Commission shall meet in conjunction with the ASEAN Ministerial Meeting.
5. At the beginning of each meeting, the Commission shall elect its Chairman and such other officers as may be required. They shall hold office until a new Chairman and other officers are elected at the next meeting.
6. Unless otherwise provided for in this Treaty, two-thirds of the members of the Commission shall be present to constitute a quorum.
7. Each member of the Commission shall have one vote.
8. Except as provided for in this Treaty, decisions of the Commission shall be taken by consensus or, failing consensus, by a two-thirds majority of the members present and voting.
9. The Commission shall, by consensus, agree upon and adopt rules of procedure for itself as well as financial rules governing its funding and that of its subsidiary organs.

Article 9
THE EXECUTIVE COMMITTEE

1. There is hereby established, as a subsidiary organ of the Commission, the Executive Committee.
2. The Executive Committee shall be composed of all States Parties to this Treaty. Each State Party shall be represented by one senior official as its representative, who may be accompanied by alternates and advisers.
3. The functions of the Executive Committee shall be to:
    (a) ensure the proper operation of verification measures in accordance with the provisions on the control system as stipulated in Article 10;
    (b) consider and decide on requests for clarification and for a fact-finding mission;
    (c) set up a fact-finding mission in accordance with the Annex of this Treaty;
    (d) consider and decide on the findings of a fact finding mission and report to the Commission;
    (e) request the Commission to convene a meeting when appropriate and necessary;

(f) conclude such agreements with the IAEA or other international organizations as referred to in Article 18 on behalf of the Commission after being duly authorized to do so by the Commission; and

(g) carry out such other tasks as may, from time to time, be assigned by the Commission.

4. The Executive Committee shall meet as and when necessary for the efficient exercise of its functions. As far as possible, the Executive Committee shall meet in conjunction with the ASEAN Senior Officials Meeting.

5. The Chairman of the Executive Committee shall be the representative of the Chairman of the Commission. Any submission or communication made by a State Party to the Chairman of the Executive Committee shall be disseminated to the other members of the Executive Committee.

6. Two-thirds of the members of the Executive Committee shall be present to constitute a quorum.

7. Each member of the Executive Committee shall have one vote.

8. Decisions of the Executive Committee shall be taken by consensus or, failing consensus, by a two-thirds majority of the members present and voting.

Article 10
CONTROL SYSTEM

1. There is hereby established a control system for the purpose of verifying compliance with the obligations of the States Parties under this Treaty.

2. The Control System shall comprise:

    (a) the IAEA safeguards system as provided for in Article 5;

    (b) report and exchange of information as provided for in Article 11;

    (c) request for clarification as provided for in Article 12; and

    (d) request and procedures for a fact-finding mission as provided for in Article 13.

Article 11
REPORT AND EXCHANGE OF INFORMATION

1. Each State Party shall submit reports to the Executive Committee on any significant event within its territory and areas under its jurisdiction and control affecting the implementation of this Treaty.

2. The States Parties may exchange information on matters arising under or in relation to this Treaty.

Article 12
REQUEST FOR CLARIFICATION

1. Each State Party shall have the right to request another State Party for clarification concerning any situation which may be considered ambiguous or which may give rise to doubts about the compliance of that State Party with this Treaty. It shall inform the Executive Committee of such a request. The requested State Party shall duly respond by providing without delay the necessary

information and inform the Executive Committee of its reply to the requesting State Party.
2. Each State Party shall have the right to request the Executive Committee to seek clarification for another State Party concerning any situation which may be considered ambiguous or which may give rise to doubts about compliance of that State Party with this Treaty. Upon receipt of such a request, the Executive Committee shall consult the State Party from which clarification is sought for the purpose of obtaining the clarification requested.

Article 13
REQUEST FOR A FACT-FINDING MISSION
A State Party shall have the right to request the Executive Committee to send a fact-finding mission to another State Party in order to clarify and resolve a situation which may be considered ambiguous or which may give rise to doubts about compliance with the provisions of this Treaty, in accordance with the procedure contained in the Annex to this Treaty.

Article 14
REMEDIAL MEASURES
1. In case the Executive Committee decide in accordance with the Annex that there is a breach of this Treaty by a State Party, that State Party shall, within a reasonable time, take all steps necessary to bring itself in full compliance with this Treaty and shall promptly inform the Executive Committee of the action taken or proposed to be taken by it.
2. Where a State Party fails or refuses to comply with the provisions of Paragraph 1 of this Article, the Executive Committee shall request the Commission to convene a meeting in accordance with the provisions of Paragraph 3(e) of Article 9.
3. At the meeting convened pursuant to Paragraph 2 of this Article, the Commission shall consider the emergent situation and shall decide on any measure it deems appropriate to cope with the situation, including the submission of the matter to the IAEA and, where the situation might endanger international peace and security, the Security Council and the General Assembly of the United Nations.
4. In the event of breach of the Protocol attached to this Treaty by a State Party to the Protocol, the Executive Committee shall convene a special meeting of the Commission to decide on appropriate measures to be taken.

Article 15
SIGNATURE, RATIFICATION, ACCESSION, DEPOSIT AND REGISTRATION
1. This Treaty shall be open for signature by all States in Southeast Asia, namely, Brunei, Darussalam, Cambodia, Indonesia, Laos, Malaysia, Myanmar, Philippines, Singapore, Thailand and Vietnam.
2. This Treaty shall be subject to ratification in accordance with the constitutional procedure of the signatory states. The instruments of ratification shall be deposited

with the Government of the Kingdom of Thailand which is hereby designated as the Depositary State.
3. This Treaty shall be open for accession. The instruments of accession shall be deposited with the Depositary State.
4. The Depositary State shall inform the other States Parties to this Treaty on the deposit of instruments of ratification or accession.
5. The Depositary State shall register this Treaty and its Protocol pursuant to Article 102 of the Charter of the United Nations.

Article 16
ENTRY INTO FORCE
1. This Treaty shall enter into force on the date of the deposit of the seventh instrument of ratification and/or accession.
2. For States which ratify or accede to this Treaty after the date of the seventh instrument of ratification or accession, the Treaty shall enter into force on the date of deposit of its instrument of ratification or accession.

Article 17
RESERVATIONS
This Treaty shall not be subject to reservations.

Article 18
RELATIONS WITH OTHER
INTERNATIONAL ORGANIZATIONS
The Commission may conclude such agreements with the IAEA or other international organizations as it considers likely to facilitate the efficient operation of the control system established by this Treaty.

Article 19
AMENDMENTS
1. Any State Party may propose amendments to this Treaty and its Protocol and shall submit its proposals to the Executive Committee, which shall transmit them to all the other States Parties. The Executive Committee shall immediately request the Commission to convene a meeting to examine the proposed amendments. The quorum required for such a meeting shall be all the members of the Commission. Any amendment shall be adopted by a consensus decision of the Commission.
2. Amendments adopted shall enter into force 30 days after the receipt by the Depositary State of the seventh instrument of acceptance from the States Parties.

Article 20
REVIEW
Ten years after this Treaty enters into force, a meeting of the Commission shall be convened for the purpose of reviewing the operation of the Treaty. A meeting of the Commission for the same purpose may also be convened at anytime thereafter if there is consensus among all its members.

Article 21
SETTLEMENT OF DISPUTES
Any dispute arising from the interpretation of the provisions of this Treaty shall be settled by peaceful means as may be agreed upon by the States Parties to the dispute. If within one month, the parties to the dispute are unable to achieve a peaceful settlement of the dispute by negotiation, mediation, enquiry or conciliation, any of the parties concerned shall, with the prior consent of the other parties concerned, refer the dispute to arbitration or to the International Court of Justice.

Article 22
DURATION AND WITHDRAWAL
1. This Treaty shall remain in force indefinitely.
2. In the event of a breach by any State Party of this Treaty essential to the achievement of the objectives of the Treaty, every other State Party shall have the right to withdraw from the Treaty.
3. Withdrawal under Paragraph 2 of Article 22, shall be effected by giving notice twelve months in advance to the members of the Commission.
IN WITNESS WHEREOF, the undersigned have signed this Treaty.
DONE at Bangkok, this fifteenth day of December, one thousand nine hundred and ninety-five, in one original in the English language.

ANNEX
to the Treaty on the Southeast Asia Nuclear-Weapon-Free Zone

PROCEDURE FOR A FACT-FINDING MISSION
1. The State Party requesting a fact-finding mission as provided in Article 13, hereinafter referred to as the "requesting State", shall submit the request to the Executive Committee specifying the following:
    (a) the doubts or concerns and the reasons for such doubts or concerns;
    (b) the location in which the situation which gives rise to doubts has allegedly occurred;
    (c) the relevant provisions of the Treaty about which doubts of compliance have arisen; and
    (d) any other relevant information.
2. Upon receipt of a request for a fact-finding mission, the Executive Committee shall:
    (a) immediately inform the State Party to which the fact-finding mission is requested to be sent, hereinafter referred to as the "receiving State", about the receipt of the request; and
    (b) not later than 3 weeks after receiving the request, decide if the request complies with the provisions of Paragraph 1 and whether or not it is frivolous,

abusive or clearly beyond the scope of the Treaty. Neither the requesting nor receiving State Party shall participate in such decisions.

3. In case the Executive Committee decides that the request does not comply with the provisions of Paragraph 1, or that it is frivolous, abusive or clearly beyond the scope of the Treaty, it shall take no further action on the request and inform the requesting State and the receiving State accordingly.

4. In the event that the Executive Committee decide that the request complies with the provisions of Paragraph 1, and that it is not frivolous, abusive or clearly beyond the scope of the Treaty, it shall immediately forward the request for a fact-finding mission to the receiving State, indicating, inter alia, the proposed date for sending the mission. The proposed date shall not be later that 3 weeks from the time the receiving State receives the request for a fact-finding mission. The Executive Committee shall also immediately set up a fact-finding mission consisting of 3 inspectors from the IAEA who are neither nationals of the requesting nor receiving State.

5. The receiving State shall comply with the request for a fact-finding mission referred to in Paragraph 4. It shall cooperate with the Executive Committee in order to facilitate the effective functioning of the fact-finding mission, inter alia, by promptly providing unimpeded access of the fact-finding mission to the location in question. The receiving State shall accord to the members of the fact-finding mission such privileges and immunities as are necessary for them to exercise their functions effectively, including inviolability of all papers and documents and immunity from arrest, detention and legal process for acts done and words spoken for the purpose of the mission.

6. The receiving State shall have the right to take measures to protect sensitive installations and to prevent disclosures of confidential information and data not related to this Treaty.

7. The fact-finding mission, in the discharge of its functions, shall:
   (a) respect the laws and regulations of the receiving State;
   (b) refrain from activities inconsistent with the objectives and purposes of this Treaty;
   (c) submit preliminary or interim reports to the Executive Committee; and
   (d) complete its task without undue delay and shall submit its final report to the Executive Committee within a reasonable time upon completion of its work.

8. The Executive Committee shall :
   (a) consider the reports submitted by the fact-finding mission and reach a decision on whether or not there is a breach of the Treaty;
   (b) immediately communicate its decision to the requesting State and the receiving State, and
   (c) present a full report on its decision to the Commission.

9. In the event that the receiving State refuses to comply with the request for a fact-finding mission in accordance with Paragraph 4, the requesting State through the Executive Committee shall have the right to request for a meeting of the Commission. The Executive Committee shall immediately request the Commission to convene a meeting in accordance with Paragraph 3 (e) of Article 9.

PROTOCOL
TO THE TREATY ON THE SOUTHEAST ASIA NUCLEAR WEAPON-FREE ZONE

The States Parties to this Protocol,

DESIRING to contribute to efforts towards achieving general and complete disarmament of nuclear weapons, and thereby ensuring international peace and security, including in Southeast Asia;

NOTING the Treaty on the Southeast Asia Nuclear Weapon-Free Zone;

HAVE AGREED as follows:

Article 1
Each State Party undertakes to respect the Treaty on the Southeast Asia Nuclear Weapon-Free Zone, hereinafter referred to as the "Treaty", and not to contribute to any act which constitutes a violation of the Treaty or its Protocol by States Parties to them.

Article 2
Each State Party undertakes not to use or threaten to use nuclear weapons against any State Party to the Treaty. It further undertakes not to use or threaten to use nuclear weapons within the Southeast Asia Nuclear Weapon-Free Zone.

Article 3
This Protocol shall be open for signature by the People's Republic of China, France, the Russian Federation, the United Kingdom of Great Britain and Northern Ireland and the United States of America.

Article 4
Each State Party undertakes, by written notification to the Depositary State, to indicate its acceptance or otherwise of any alteration to its obligation under the Protocol that may be brought about by the entry into force of an amendment to the Treaty pursuant to Article 19 thereof.

Article 5
This Protocol is of a permanent nature and shall remain in force indefinitely, provided that each State Party shall, in exercising its national sovereignty, have the right to withdraw from this Protocol if it decides that extraordinary events, related to the subject-matter of this Protocol, have jeopardized its supreme national interests. It shall give notice of such withdrawal to the Depositary State twelve months in advance. Such notice shall include a statement of the extraordinary events it regards as having jeopardized its supreme national interests.

Article 6
This Protocol shall be subject to ratification.

Article 7
This Protocol shall enter into force for each State Party on the date of its deposit of its instrument of ratification with the Depositary State. The Depositary State shall inform the other States Parties to the Treaty and to this Protocol on the deposit of instruments of ratification.

IN WITNESS WHEREOF the undersigned, being duly authorized by their Governments, have signed this Protocol.

DONE at Bangkok this fifteenth day of December, one thousand nine hundred and ninety-five, in one original in the English language.

IV-4(a). African Nuclear-Weapon-Free Zone Treaty [Treaty of Pelindaba], signed at Addis Ababa, June 21-23, 1996, 35 I.L.M. 698.

Relevant Penal Characteristics & Penal Provisions
2. Implicit recognition of the penal nature of the act by establishing a duty to prohibit, prevent, prosecute, punish, or the like: Article 3; Article 4(1); & Article 5

Applicability
Peace

Control
Prohibition

State Signatories
Algeria; Angola; Benin; Burkina Faso; Burundi; Cameroon; Cape Verde; Central African Republic; Chad; Comoros; Côte D'Ivoire; Djibouti; Egypt; Eritrea; Ethiopia; Gambia; Ghana; Guinea; Guinea-Bissau; Kenya; Lesotho; Libya; Malawi; Mali; Mauritania; Mauritius; Morocco; Mozambique; Namibia; Niger; Nigeria; Rwanda; Senegal; Sierra Leone; South Africa; The Sudan; Swaziland; Tanzania; Togo; Tunisia; Uganda; Zaire; Zambia; Zimbabwe

Full Text

The Parties to this Treaty,

Guided by the Declaration on the Denuclearization of Africa, adopted by the Assembly of Heads of State and Government of the Organization of African Unity (hereinafter referred to as OAU) at its first ordinary session, held at Cairo from 17 to 21 July 1964 (AHG/Res. 11(I)), in which they solemnly declared their readiness to undertake, through an international agreement to be concluded under United Nations auspices, not to manufacture or acquire control of nuclear weapons,

Guided also, by the resolutions of the fifty-fourth and fifty-sixth ordinary sessions of the Council of Ministers of OAU, held at Abuja from 27 May to 1 June 1991 and at Dakar from 22 to 28 June 1992 respectively (CM/Res.1342 (LIV) and CM/Res.1395 (LVI)), which affirmed that the evolution of the international situation was conducive to the implementation of the Cairo Declaration, as well as the relevant provisions of the 1986 OAU Declaration on Security, Disarmament and Development,

Recalling United Nations General Assembly resolution 3472 B (XXX) of 11 December 1975, in which it considered nuclear-weapon-free zones one of the most effective means for preventing the proliferation, both horizontal and vertical, of nuclear weapons,

Convinced of the need to take all steps in achieving the ultimate goal of a world entirely free of nuclear weapons, as well as of the obligations of all States to contribute to this end,

Convinced also that the African nuclear-weapon-free zone will constitute an important step towards strengthening the non-proliferation regime, promoting cooperation in the peaceful uses of nuclear energy, promoting general and complete disarmament and enhancing regional and international peace and security,

Aware that regional disarmament measures contribute to global disarmament efforts,

Believing that the African nuclear-weapon-free zone will protect African States against possible nuclear attacks on their territories,

Noting with satisfaction existing NWFZs and recognizing that the establishment of other NWFZs, especially in the Middle East, would enhance the security of States Parties to the African NWFZ,

Reaffirming the importance of the Treaty on the Non-Proliferation of Nuclear Weapons (hereinafter referred to as the NPT) and the need for the implementation of all its provisions,

Desirous of taking advantage of article IV of the NPT, which recognizes the inalienable right of all States Parties to develop research on, production and use of nuclear energy for peaceful purposes without discrimination and to facilitate the fullest possible exchange of equipment, materials and scientific and technological information for such purposes,

Determined to promote regional cooperation for the development and practical application of nuclear energy for peaceful purposes in the interest of sustainable social and economic development of the African continent,

Determined to keep Africa free of environmental pollution by radioactive wastes and other radioactive matter,

Welcoming the cooperation of all States and governmental and non-governmental organizations for the attainment of these objectives,

Have decided by this treaty to establish the African NWFZ and hereby agree as follows:

Article 1 DEFINITION/USAGE OF TERMS

For the purpose of this Treaty and its Protocols:

(a) "African nuclear-weapon-free zone" means the territory of the continent of Africa, islands States members of OAU and all islands considered by the Organization of African Unity in its resolutions to be part of Africa;

(b) "Territory" means the land territory, internal waters, territorial seas and archipelagic waters and the airspace above them as well as the sea bed and subsoil beneath;

(c) "Nuclear explosive device" means any nuclear weapon or other explosive device capable of releasing nuclear energy, irrespective of the purpose for which it could be used. The term includes such a weapon or device in unassembled and partly assembled forms, but does not include the means of transport or delivery of such a weapon or device if separable from and not an indivisible part of it;

(d) "Stationing" means implantation, emplacement, transport on land or inland waters, stockpiling, storage, installation and deployment;

(e) "Nuclear installation" means a nuclear-power reactor, a nuclear research reactor, a critical facility, a conversion plant, a fabrication plant, a reprocessing plant, an isotope separation plant, a separate storage installation and any other installation or location in or at which fresh or irradiated nuclear material or significant quantities of radioactive materials are present;

(f) "Nuclear material" means any source material or special fissionable material as defined in Article XX of the Statute of the International Atomic Energy Agency (IAEA) and as amended from time to time by the IAEA.

Article 2 APPLICATION OF THE TREATY

1. Except where otherwise specified, this Treaty and its Protocols shall apply to the territory within the African nuclear-weapon-free zone, as illustrated in the map in annex I.

2. Nothing in this Treaty shall prejudice or in any way affect the rights, or the exercise of the rights, of any State under international law with regard to freedom of the seas.

Article 3 RENUNCIATION OF NUCLEAR EXPLOSIVE DEVICES

Each Party undertakes:

(a) Not to conduct research on, develop, manufacture, stockpile or otherwise acquire, possess or have control over any nuclear explosive device by any means anywhere;

(b) Not to seek or receive any assistance in the research on, development, manufacture, stockpiling or acquisition, or possession of any nuclear explosive device;

(c) Not to take any action to assist or encourage the research on, development, manufacture, stockpiling or acquisition, or possession of any nuclear explosive device.

Article 4 PREVENTION OF STATIONING OF NUCLEAR EXPLOSIVE DEVICES

1. Each Party undertakes to prohibit, in its territory, the stationing of any nuclear explosive device.

2. Without prejudice to the purposes and objectives of the treaty, each party in the exercise of its sovereign rights remains free to decide for itself whether to allow visits by foreign ships and aircraft to its ports and airfields, transit of its airspace by foreign aircraft, and navigation by foreign ships in its territorial sea or archipelagic waters in a manner not covered by the rights of innocent passage, archipelagic sea lane passage or transit passage of straits.

Article 5 PROHIBITION OF TESTING OF NUCLEAR EXPLOSIVE DEVICES

Each Party undertakes:

Not to test any nuclear explosive device;

To prohibit in its territory the testing of any nuclear explosive device;

Not to assist or encourage the testing of any nuclear explosive device by any State anywhere.

Article 6 DECLARATION, DISMANTLING, DESTRUCTION OR CONVERSION OF NUCLEAR
EXPLOSIVE DEVICES AND THE FACILITIES FOR THEIR MANUFACTURE

Each Party undertakes:

(a) To declare any capability for the manufacture of nuclear explosive devices;

(b) To dismantle and destroy any nuclear explosive device that it has manufactured prior to the coming into force of this Treaty;

(c) To destroy facilities for the manufacture of nuclear explosive devices or, where possible, to convert them to peaceful uses;

(d) To permit the International Atomic Energy Agency (hereinafter referred to as IAEA) and the Commission established in article 12 to verify the processes of dismantling and destruction of the nuclear explosive devices, as well as the destruction or conversion of the facilities for their production.

Article 7 PROHIBITION OF DUMPING OF RADIOACTIVE WASTES

Each Party undertakes:

(a) To effectively implement or to use as guidelines the measures contained in the Bamako Convention on the Ban of the Import into Africa and Control of Transboundary Movement and Management of Hazardous Wastes within Africa in so far as it is relevant to radioactive waste;

(b) Not to take any action to assist or encourage the dumping of radioactive wastes and other radioactive matter anywhere within the African nuclear-weapon-free zone.

Article 8 PEACEFUL NUCLEAR ACTIVITIES

1. Nothing in this Treaty shall be interpreted as to prevent the use of nuclear science and technology for peaceful purposes.

2. As part of their efforts to strengthen their security, stability and development, the Parties undertake to promote individually and collectively the use of nuclear science and technology for economic and social development. To this end they undertake to establish and strengthen mechanisms for cooperation at the bilateral, subregional and regional levels.

3. Parties are encouraged to make use of the programme of assistance available in IAEA and, in this connection, to strengthen cooperation under the African Regional Cooperation Agreement for Research, Training and Development Related to Nuclear Science and Technology (hereinafter referred to as AFRA).

Article 9 VERIFICATION OF PEACEFUL USES

Each Party undertakes:

To conduct all activities for the peaceful use of nuclear energy under strict non-proliferation measures to provide assurance of exclusively peaceful uses;

(b) To conclude a comprehensive safeguards agreement with IAEA for the purpose of verifying compliance with the undertakings in subparagraph (a) of this article;

(c) Not to provide source or special fissionable material, or equipment or material especially designed or prepared for the processing, use or production of special fissionable material for peaceful purposes of any non-nuclear-weapon State unless subject to a comprehensive safeguards agreement concluded with IAEA.

Article 10 PHYSICAL PROTECTION OF NUCLEAR MATERIALS AND FACILITIES

Each Party undertakes to maintain the highest standards of security and effective physical protection of nuclear materials, facilities and equipment to prevent theft or unauthorized use and handling. To that end each Party, *inter alia*, undertakes to apply measures of physical protection equivalent to those provided for in the Convention on Physical Protection of Nuclear Material and in recommendations and guidelines developed by IAEA for that purpose.

Article 11 PROHIBITION OF ARMED ATTACK ON NUCLEAR INSTALLATIONS

Each Party undertakes not to take, or assist, or encourage any action aimed at an armed attack by conventional or other means against nuclear installations in the African nuclear-weapon-free zone.

Article 12 MECHANISM FOR COMPLIANCE

1. For the purpose of ensuring compliance with their undertakings under this Treaty, the Parties agree to establish the African Commission on Nuclear Energy (hereafter referred to as the Commission) as set out in annex III.

2. The Commission shall be responsible *inter alia* for:

(a) Collating the reports and the exchange of information as provided for in article 13;

(b) Arranging consultations as provided for in annex IV, as well as convening conferences of Parties on the concurrence of simple majority of State Parties on any matter arising from the implementation of the Treaty;

(c) Reviewing the application to peaceful nuclear activities of safeguards by IAEA as elaborated in annex II;

(d) Bringing into effect the complaints procedure elaborated in annex IV;

(e) Encouraging regional and subregional programmes for cooperation in the peaceful uses of nuclear science and technology;

(f) Promoting international cooperation with extra-zonal States for the peaceful uses of nuclear science and technology.

3. The Commission shall meet in ordinary session once a year, and may meet in extraordinary session as may be required by the complaints and settlement of disputes procedure in annex IV.

Article 13 REPORT AND EXCHANGES OF INFORMATION

1. Each Party shall submit an annual report to the Commission on its nuclear activities as well as other matters relating to the Treaty, in accordance with the format for reporting to be developed by the Commission.

2. Each Party shall promptly report to the Commission any significant event affecting the implementation of the Treaty.

3. The Commission shall request the IAEA to provide it with an annual report on the activities of AFRA.

Article 14 CONFERENCE OF PARTIES

1. A Conference of all Parties to the Treaty shall be convened by the Depositary as soon as possible after the entry into force of the Treaty to, *inter alia*, elect members of the commission and determine its headquarters. Further conferences of State Parties shall be held as necessary and at least every two years, and convened in accordance with paragraph 2 (b) of Article 12.

2. The Conference of all Parties to the Treaty shall adopt the Commission's budget and a scale of assessment to be paid by the State Parties.

Article 15 INTERPRETATION OF THE TREATY

Any dispute arising out of the interpretation of the Treaty shall be settled by negotiation, by recourse to the Commission or another procedure agreed to by the Parties, which may include recourse to an arbitral panel or to the International Court of Justice.

Article 16 RESERVATIONS

This Treaty shall not be subject to reservations.

Article 17 DURATION

This Treaty shall be of unlimited duration and shall remain in force indefinitely.

Article 18 SIGNATURE, RATIFICATION AND ENTRY INTO FORCE

1. It shall enter into force on the date of deposit of the twenty-eighth instrument of

2. For a signatory that ratifies this Treaty after the date of the deposit of the twenty-eighth instrument of ratification, it shall enter into force for that signatory on the date of deposit of its instrument of ratification.

Article 19 AMENDMENTS

1. Any amendments to the Treaty proposed by a Party shall be submitted to the Commission, which shall circulate it to all Parties.

2. Decision on the adoption of such an amendment shall be taken by a two-thirds majority of the Parties either through written communication to the Commission or through a conference of Parties convened upon the concurrence of a simple majority.

3. An amendment so adopted shall enter into force for all Parties after receipt by the Depositary of the instrument of ratification by the majority of Parties.

Article 20 WITHDRAWAL

1. Each Party shall, in exercising its national sovereignty, have the right to withdraw from this Treaty if it decides that extraordinary events, related to the subject-matter of this Treaty, have jeopardized its supreme interests.

2. Withdrawal shall be effected by a Party giving notice, which includes a statement of the extraordinary events it regards as having jeopardized its supreme interest, twelve months in advance to the Depositary. The Depositary shall

circulate such notice to all other Parties.

Article 21 DEPOSITARY FUNCTIONS

1. This Treaty, of which the Arabic, English, French and Portuguese texts are equally authentic, shall be deposited with the Secretary-General of OAU, who is hereby designated as Depositary of the Treaty.

2. The Depositary shall:

(a) Receive instruments of ratification;

(b) Register this Treaty and its Protocols pursuant to Article 102 of the Charter of the United Nations;

(c) Transmit certified copies of the Treaty and its Protocols to all States in the African nuclear-weapon-free zone and to all States eligible to become Party to the Protocols to the Treaty, and shall notify them of signatures and ratification of the Treaty and its Protocols.

Article 22 STATUS OF THE ANNEXES
The annexes form an integral part of this Treaty. Any reference to this Treaty includes the annexes.

In witness whereof the undersigned, being duly authorized by their Governments, have signed this Treaty.

IV-4(b). Cairo Declaration, June 1996; Adopted on the occasion of the signing of the African Nuclear-Weapon-Free Zone Treaty (the Treaty of Pelindaba) Cairo, 11 April 1996. General Distr. English; Original: Arabic

Relevant Penal Characeristics & Penal Provisions
None

Full Text

Adopted on the occasion of the signature of the African Nuclear-Weapon-Free Zone Treaty (the Treaty of Pelindaba), at Cairo on 11 April 1996 The African States signatories of the African Nuclear-Weapon Free-Zone Treaty (the Treaty of Pelindaba), meeting at Cairo on 11 April 1996,

Recalling the Declaration on the Denuclearization of Africa adopted by the Assembly of Heads of State and Government of the Organization of African Unity at its first ordinary session, held at Cairo in 1964,

Recalling also the adoption by the Assembly of Heads of State and Government of the Organization of African Unity at its thirty-first ordinary session, held at Addis Ababa from 26 to 28 June 1995, of the final text of the Treaty,

Recalling further United Nations General Assembly resolution 50/78 of 12 December 1995, by which the Assembly welcomed the adoption of the African leaders of the final text of the Treaty,

Recognizing the valuable contribution that the establishment of nuclear-weapon-free zones in Latin America and the Caribbean, South Pacific and South-East Asia have made to the process of nuclear non-proliferation,

Stressing the importance of promoting regional and international cooperation for the development of nuclear energy for peaceful purposes in the interest of sustainable social and economic development of the African continent,

Solemnly declare that the signing of the Treaty further consolidates global efforts towards the non-proliferation of nuclear weapons including the objectives of the Treaty on the Non-Proliferation of Nuclear Weapons (NPT) and is a highly significant contribution to the enhancement of international peace and security;

Invite the African States to ratify the Treaty as soon as possible so that it can enter into force without delay;

Call upon the nuclear-weapon States as well as the States contemplated in Protocol III to sign and ratify the relevant protocols to the Treaty as soon as possible;

Emphasize that the establishment of nuclear-weapon-free zones, especially in regions of tension, such as the Middle East, on the basis of arrangements freely arrived at among the States of the regions concerned, enhances global and regional peace and security;

Call upon all those States who have not yet done so to adhere to the NPT;

Call upon the nuclear-weapon States to actively pursue the goal of a nuclear-weapon-free world as embodied in Article VI of the NPT, through the urgent negotiation of agreements with effective measures of verification towards the complete elimination of nuclear weapons at the earliest possible time;

Decide that the first session of the Conference of the States Parties to the Treaty shall be held not later than one year after its entry into force, and endorse the establishment of the headquarters of the African Commission on Nuclear Energy in South Africa;

Request the Secretary-General of the United Nations, in accordance with resolution 50/78, adopted by the United Nations General Assembly on 12 December 1995, to provide the necessary assistance in 1996 in order to achieve the aims of the present declaration.

CHAPTER V

MIDDLE EAST ARMS CONTROL AND SECURITY AGREEMENTS

INTRODUCTION

The Middle East region has yet to develop a comprehensive arms control regime. From the 1948 UN Security Council Resolution on Palestine to the 1999 Protocol Concerning Safe Passage Between the West Bank and Gaza Strip, the evolution of arms control in that region has been ad hoc. But the prospects of generalized peace in the region may exist, particularly after bilateral agreements have been completed between Israel and all its Arab neighbors. At that time, the possibility for a multilateral regional security regime, which also eliminates weapons of mass destruction, will have arrived.

As can be seen in the instruments that are listed below, arms control provisions in Middle Eastern agreements are generally secondary to the issues of military, political, and security issues including: terrorism; refugees; safe passage; transfer of political authority; and economic issues. The agreements involving Egypt, Israel, Jordan, and Lebanon deal with the security arrangements. However, the 1994 Treaty of Peace Between the State of Israel and the Hashemite Kingdom of Jordan has provisions that are exceptional in that they deal with non-conventional weapons, and call for a regional weapons of mass destruction free zone in the Middle East. These bilateral agreements can form the basis for a future regional agreement.

V-1. United Nations Security Council Resolution 50, U.N. SCOR, May 29, 1948, U.N. Doc. S/801, 50 (1948).

Full Text

The Security Council,
Desiring to bring about a cessation of hostilities in Palestine without prejudice to the rights, claims and position of either Arabs or Jews,

1. Calls upon all Governments and authorities concerned to order cessation of all acts of ammed force for a period of four weeks;

2. Calls upon all Governments and authorities concerned to undertake that they will not introduce fighting personnel into Palestine, Egypt, Iraq, Lebanon Saudi Arabia, Syria, Transjordan and Yemen during the cease-fire;

3. Calls upon all Governments and authorities concerned, should men of military age be introduced into countries or territories under their control, to undertake not to mobilize or submit them to military training during the cease-fire;

4. Calls upon all Governments and authorities concerned to refrain from importing or exporting war material. into or to Palestine, Egypt, Iraq, Lebanon, Saudi Arabia, Syria, Transjordan or Yemen during the cease-fire;

5. Urges all Governments and authorities concerned to take every possible precaution for the protection of the Holy Places and of the City of Jerusalem, including access to all shrines and sanctuaries for the purpose of worship by those who have an established tight to visit and worship at them;

6. Instructs the United Nations Mediator in Palestine, in concert with the Truce Commission, to supervise the observance of the above provisions, and decides that they shall be provided with a sufficient number of military observers;

7. Instructs the United Nations Mediator to make contact with all parties as soon as the cease-fire is in force with a view to carding out his functions as determined by the General Assembly;

8. Calls upon all concerned to give the greatest possible assistance to the United Nations Mediator;

9. Instructs the United Nations Mediator to make a weekly report to the Security Council during the cease-fire;

10. Invites the States members of the Arab League and the Jewish and Arab authorities in Palestine to communicate their acceptance of the resolution to the Security Council not later than 6 p.m. New York standard time on 1 June 1948;

11. Decides that it the prevent resolution is rejected by either party or by both, or If, having been accepted, it is subsequently repudiated or violated, the situation in Palestine will be reconsidered with a view to action under Chapter VII of the Charter of the United Nations;

12. Calls upon all Governments to take all possible steps to assist in the implementation of this resolution.

V-2. Agreement for the Demilitarization of Mount Scopus Area (July 7, 1948)

Full Text

It is hereby jointly agreed that

1. The area as delineated on the attached map will be assigned to the United Nations protection until hostilities cease or a new agreement is entered upon. It shall include the areas designated as Hadassah Hospital, Hebrew University, Augusta Victoria and the Arab village of Issawiya. The United Nations agrees to become a signatory to this document by representation through the Senior Observer in the Jerusalem area and the Chairman of the Truce Commission. It therefore accepts responsibility for the security of this area as described herewith.

2. There shall be a no-man's-land location extending for approximately 200 yards along the main road between Augusta Victoria and Hebrew University buildings, with suitable checkposts established at each end. Other check posts will be established on the perimeter of the zone under protection, and all parties agree that access desired should be sought along the main road via the United Nations check posts as established by the United Nations Commander. All other attempts at entry will be considered as unlawful invasion and treated accordingly.

3. In their respective areas armed Arab and Jewish civilian police will be placed on duty under the United Nations Commander. The United Nations flag will fly on the main buildings. All military personnel of both sides will be withdrawn this day, together with their equipment and such other supplies as are not required by the United Nations Commander.

4. The United Nations will arrange that both parties receive adequate supplies of food and water. Replacements of necessary personnel in residence on Mount Scopus will be scheduled by the United Nations Commander in consultation with each party in respect of its area. The United Nations undertakes to limit the population on Mount Scopus to those individuals needed for its operation, plus the present population of the village of Issawiya. No additions will be made to the village population except by agreement of both parties. The intitial personnel roster of civilian police in the Jewish section shall not exceed a total of 85. The civilian personnel attached thereto shall not exceed a total of 40.

5. It is hereby agreed by both parties that the area is not to be used as a base for military operations, not will it be attacked or unlawfully entered upon.

6. In the event that the Arab Legion withdraws from the area, the United Nations Commander is to be given sufficient advance notice in writing in order that satisfactory arrangements may be made to substitute for this protocol another agreement.

V-3. Egyptian-Israeli General Armistice Agreement, February 24, 1949
<http://metalab.unc.edu/sullivan/docs?Sinail.html>.

State Signatories
Egypt; Israel

State Parties
Egypt; Israel

Full Text

Preamble

The Parties to the present Agreement, responding to the Security Council resolution of 16 November 1948 calling upon them, as a further provisional measure under Article 40 of the Charter of the United Nations and in order to facilitate the transition from the present truce to permanent peace in Palestine, to negotiate an Armistice; having decided to enter into negotiations under United Nations Chairmanship concerning the implementation of the Security Council resolutions of 4 and 16 November 1948; (2) and having appointed representatives empowered to negotiate and conclude an Armistice Agreement;

The undersigned representatives, in the full authority entrusted to them by their respective Governments, have agreed upon the following provisions:

Article I

With a view to promoting the return to permanent peace in Palestine and in recognition of the importance in this regard of mutual assurances concerning the future military operations of the Parties, the following principles, which shall be fully observed by both Parties during the Armistice, are hereby affirmed:

1. The injunction of the Security Council against resort to military force in the settlement of the Palestine question shall henceforth be scrupulously respected by both Parties.

2. No aggressive action by the armed forces land, sea, or air of either Party shall be undertaken, planned, or threatened against the people or the armed forces of the other; it being understood that the use of the term "planned" in this context has no bearing on normal staff planning as generally practiced in military organizations.

3. The right of each Party to its security and freedom from fear of attack by the armed forces of the other shall be fully respected.

4. The establishment of an armistice between the armed forces of the two Parties is accepted as an indispensable step toward the liquidation of armed conflict and the restoration of peace in Palestine.

Article II

1. In pursuance of the foregoing principles and of the resolutions of the Security Council of 4 and 16 November 1948, a general armistice between the armed forces of the two Parties-land, sea and air-is hereby established.

2. No element of the land, sea or air military or paramilitary forces of either Party, including non-regular forces, shall commit any warlike or hostile act against the military or paramilitary forces of the other Party, or against civilians in territory under the control of that Party; or shall advance beyond or pass over for any purpose whatsoever the Armistice Demarcation Line set forth in Article VI of this Agreement except as provided in Article III of this Agreement; and elsewhere shall not violate the international frontier; or enter into or pass through the air space of the other Party or through the waters within three miles of the coastline of the other Party.

Article III

1. In pursuance of the Security Council's resolution of 4 November 1948, and with a view to the implementation of the Security Council's resolution of 16 November 1948, the Egyptian Military Forces in the AL FALUJA area shall be withdrawn.

2. This withdrawal shall begin on the day after that which follows the signing of this Agreement, at 0500 hours GMT, and shall be beyond the Egypt-Palestine frontier.

3. The withdrawal shall be under the supervision of the United Nations and in accordance with the Plan of Withdrawal set forth in Annex I (3) to this Agreement.

Article IV

With specific reference to the implementation of the resolutions of the Security Council of 4 and 16 November 1948, the following principles and purposes are affirmed:

1. The principle that no military or political advantage should be gained under the truce ordered by the Security Council is recognized.

2. It is also recognized that the basic purposes and spirit of the Armistice would not be served by the restoration of previously held military positions, changes from those now held other than as specifically provided for in this Agreement, or by the advance of the military forces of either side beyond positions held at the time this Armistice Agreement is signed.

3. It is further recognized that rights, claims or interests of a nonmilitary character in the area of Palestine covered by this Agreement may be asserted by either Party, and that these, by mutual agreement being excluded from the Armistice negotiations, shall be, at the discretion of the Parties, the subject of later settlement. It is emphasized that it is not the purpose of this Agreement to establish, to recognize, to strengthen, or to weaken or nullify, in any way, any territorial, custodial or other rights, claims or interests which may be asserted by either Party in the area of Palestine or any part or locality thereof covered by this Agreement, whether such asserted rights, claims or interests derive from Security Council resolutions, including the resolution of 4 November 1948 and the Memorandum of 13 November 1948 (4) for its implementation, or from any other source. The provisions of this Agreement are dictated exclusively by military considerations and are valid only for the period of the Armistice.

Article V

1. The line described in Article VI of this Agreement shall be designated as the Armistice Demarcation Line and is delineated in pursuance of the purpose and intent of the resolutions of the Security Council of 4 and 16 November 1948.

2. The Armistice Demarcation Line is not to be construed in any sense as a political or territorial boundary, and is delineated without prejudice to rights, claims and positions of either Party to the Armistice as regards ultimate settlement of the Palestine question.

3. The basic purpose of the Armistice Demarcation Line is to delineate the line beyond which the armed forces of the respective Parties shall not move except as provided in Article III of this Agreement.

4. Rules and regulations of the armed forces of the Parties, which prohibit civilians from crossing the fighting lines or entering the area between the lines, shall remain in effect after the signing of this Agreement with application to the Armistice Demarcation Line defined in Article VI.

Article VI

1. In the GAZA-RAFAH area the Armistice Demarcation Line shall be as delineated in paragraph 2.B (i) of the Memorandum of 13 November 1948 on the

implementation of the Security Council resolution of 4 November 1948, namely by a line from the coast at the mouth of the Wadi Hasi in an easterly direction through Deir Suneid and across the Gaza-Al Majdal Highway to a point 3 kilometres east of the Highway, then in a southerly direction parallel to the Gaza-Al Madjal [Majdal] Highway, and continuing thus to the Egyptian frontier.

2. Within this line Egyptian forces shall nowhere advance beyond their present positions, and this shall include Beit Hanun and its surrounding area from which Israeli forces shall be withdrawn to north of the Armistice Demarcation Line, and any other positions within the line delineated in paragraph 1 which shall be evacuated by Israeli forces as set forth in paragraph 3.

3. Israeli outposts, each limited to platoon strength, may be maintained in this area at the following points: Deir Suneid, on the north side of the Wadi (MR 10751090); 700 SW of Sa'ad (MR 10500982); Sulphur Quarries (MR 09870924); Tall-Jamma (MR 09720887); and KH AL Ma'in (MR 09320821).
The Israeli outpost maintained at the Cemetery (MR 08160723) shall be evacuated on the day after that which follows the signing of this Agreement. The Israeli outpost at Hill 79 (MR 10451017) shall be evacuated not later than four weeks following the day on which this Agreement is signed. Following the evacuation of the above outposts, new Israeli outposts may be established at MR 08360700, and at a point due east of Hill 79 east of the Armistice Demarcation Line.

4. In the BETHLEHEM-HEBRON area, wherever positions are held by Egyptian forces, the provisions of this Agreement shall apply to the forces of both Parties in each such locality, except that the demarcation of the Armistice Line and reciprocal arrangements for withdrawal and reduction of forces shall be undertaken in such manner as may be decided by the Parties, at such time as an Armistice Agreement may be concluded covering military forces in that area other than those of the Parties to this Agreement, or sooner at the will of the Parties.

Article VII

1. It is recognized by the Parties to this Agreement that in certain sectors of the total area involved, the proximity of the forces of a third party not covered by this Agreement makes impractical the full application of all provisions of the Agreement to such sectors. For this reason alone, therefore, and pending the conclusion of an Armistice Agreement in place of the existing truce with that third party, the provisions of this Agreement relating to reciprocal reduction and withdrawal of forces shall apply only to the western front and not to the eastern front.

2. The areas comprising the western and eastern fronts shall be as defined

International Humanitarian Law and Arms Control Agreements 579

by the United Nations Chief of Staff of the Truce Supervision Organization, on the basis of the deployment of forces against each other and past military activity or the future possibility thereof in the area. This definition of the western and eastern fronts is set forth in Annex II (5) of this Agreement.

3. In the area of the western front under Egyptian control, Egyptian defensive forces only may be maintained. All other Egyptian forces shall be withdrawn from this area to a point or points no further east than El Arish-Abou Aoueigila.

4. In the area of the western front under Israeli control, Israeli defensive forces only, which shall be based on the settlements, may be maintained. All other Israeli forces shall be withdrawn from this area to a point or points north of the line delineated in paragraph 2.A of the Memorandum of 13 November 1948 on the implementation of the resolution of the Security Council of 4 November 1948.

5. The defensive forces referred to in paragraphs 3 and 4 above shall be as defined in Annex III to this Agreement.

Article VIII

1. The area comprising the village of El Auja and vicinity, as defined in paragraph 2 of this Article, shall be demilitarized, and both Egyptian and Israeli armed forces shall be totally excluded therefrom. The Chairman of the Mixed Armistice Commission established in Article X of this Agreement and United Nations Observers attached to the Commission shall be responsible for ensuring the full implementation of this provision.

2. The area thus demilitarized shall be as follows: From a point on the Egypt-Palestine frontier five (5) kilometres north-west of the intersection of the Rafah-El Auja road and the frontier (MR 08750468), south-east to Khashm El Mamdud (MR 09650414), thence south-east to Hill 405 (MR 10780285), thence south-west to a point on the Egypt-Palestine frontier five (5) kilometres southeast of the intersection of the old railway tracks and the frontier (MR 09950145), thence returning north-west along the Egypt-Palestine frontier to the point of origin.

3. On the Egyptian side of the frontier, facing the El Auja area, no Egyptian defensive positions shall be closer to El Auja than El Qouseima and Abou Aoueigila.

4. The road Taba-Qouseima-Auja shall not be employed by any military forces whatsoever for the purpose of entering Palestine.

5. The movement of armed forces of either Party to this Agreement into any part of the area defined in paragraph 2 of this Article, for any purpose, or failure by either Party to respect or fulfil any of the other provisions of this Article, when confirmed by the United Nations representatives, shall constitute a flagrant violation of this Agreement.

Article IX

All prisoners of war detained by either Party to this Agreement and belonging to the armed forces, regular or irregular, of the other Party shall be exchanged as follows:

1. The exchange of prisoners of war shall be under United Nations supervision and control throughout. The exchange shall begin within ten days after the signing of this Agreement and shall be completed not later than twenty-one days following. Upon the signing of this Agreement, the Chairman of the Mixed Armistice Commission established in Article X of this Agreement, in consultation with the appropriate military authorities of the Parties, shall formulate a plan for the exchange of prisoners of war within the above period, defining the date and places of exchange and all other relevant details.

2. Prisoners of war against whom a penal prosecution may be pending, as well as those sentenced for crime or other offence, shall be included in this exchange of prisoners.

3. All articles of personal use, valuables, letters, documents, identification marks, and other personal effects of whatever nature, belonging to prisoners of war who are being exchanged, shall be returned to them, or, if they have escaped or died, to the Party to whose armed forces they belonged.

4. All matters not specifically regulated in this Agreement shall be decided in accordance with the principles laid down in the International Convention relating to the Treatment of Prisoners of War, signed at Geneva on 27 July 1929.

5. The Mixed Armistice Commission established in Article X of this Agreement shall assume responsibility for locating missing persons, whether military or civilian, within the areas controlled by each Party, to facilitate their expeditious exchange. Each Party undertakes to extend to the Commission full co-operation and assistance in the discharge of this function.

Article X

1. The execution of the provisions of this Agreement shall be supervised by a Mixed Armistice Commission composed of seven members, of whom each Party

International Humanitarian Law and Arms Control Agreements 581

to this Agreement shall designate three, and whose Chairman shall be the United Nations Chief of Staff of the Truce Supervision Organization or a senior officer from the Observer personnel of that Organization designated by him following consultation with both Parties to this Agreement.

2. The Mixed Armistice Commission shall maintain its headquarters at El Auja, and shall hold its meetings at such places and at such times as it may deem necessary for the effective conduct of its work.

3. The Mixed Armistice Commission shall be convened in its first meeting by the United Nations Chief of Staff of the Truce Supervision Organization not later than one week following the signing of this Agreement.

4. Decisions of the Mixed Armistice Commission, to the extent possible, shall be based on the principle of unanimity. In the absence of unanimity, decisions shall be taken by a majority vote of the members of the Commission present and voting. On questions of principle, appeal shall lie to [sic] a Special Committee, composed of the United Nations Chief of Staff of the Truce Supervision Organization and one member each of the Egyptian and Israeli Delegations to the Armistice Conference at Rhodes or some other senior officer, whose decisions on all such questions shall be final. If no appeal against a decision of the Commission is filed within one week from the date of said decision, that decision shall be taken as final. Appeals to the Special Committee shall be presented to the United Nations Chief of Staff of the Truce Supervision Organization, who shall convene the Committee at the earliest possible date.

5. The Mixed Armistice Commission shall formulate its own rules of procedure. Meetings shall be held only after due notice to the members by the Chairman. The quorum for its meetings shall be a majority of its members.

6. The Commission shall be empowered to employ Observers, who may be from among the military organizations of the Parties or from the military personnel of the United Nations Truce Supervision Organization, or from both, in such numbers as may be considered essential to the performance of its functions. In the event United Nations Observers should be so employed, they shall remain under the command of the United Nations Chief of Staff of the Truce Supervision Organization. Assignments of a general or special nature given to United Nations Observers attached to the Mixed Armistice Commission shall be subject to approval by the United Nations Chief of Staff or his designated representative on the Commission, whichever s serving as Chairman.

7. Claims or complaints presented by either Party relating to the application of this Agreement shall be referred immediately to the Mixed Armistice Commission through its Chairman. The Commission shall take such action on all

such claims or complaints by means of its observation and investigation machinery as it may deem appropriate, with a view to equitable and mutually satisfactory settlement.

8. Where interpretation of the meaning of a particular provision of this Agreement is at issue, the Commission's interpretation shall prevail, subject to the right of appeal as provided in paragraph 4. The Commission, in its discretion and as the need arises, may from time to time recommend to the Parties modifications in the provisions of this Agreement.

9. The Mixed Armistice Commission shall submit to both Parties reports on its activities as frequently as it may consider necessary. A copy of each such report shall be presented to the Secretary-General of the United Nations for transmission to the appropriate organ or agency of the United Nations.

10. Members of the Commission and its Observers shall be accorded such freedom of movement and access in the areas covered by this Agreement as the Commission may determine to be necessary, provided that when such decisions of the Commission are reached by a majority vote United Nations Observers only shall be employed.

11. The expenses of the Commission, other than those relating to United Nations Observers, shall be apportioned in equal shares between the two Parties to this Agreement.

Article XI

No provision of this Agreement shall in any way prejudice the rights, claims and positions of either Party hereto in the ultimate peaceful settlement of the Palestine question.

Article XII

1. The present Agreement is not subject to ratification and shall come into force immediately upon being signed.

2. This Agreement having been negotiated and concluded in pursuance of the resolution of the Security Council of 16 November 1948 calling for the establishment of an armistice in order to eliminate the threat to the peace in Palestine and to facilitate the transition from the present truce to permanent peace in Palestine, shall remain in force until a peaceful settlement between the Parties is achieved, except as provided in paragraph 3 of this Article.

3. The Parties to this Agreement may, by mutual consent, revise this

Agreement or any of its provisions, or may suspend its application, other than Articles I and II, at any time. In the absence of mutual agreement and after this Agreement has been in effect for one year from the date of its signing, either of the Parties may call upon the Secretary-General of the United Nations to convoke a conference of representatives of the two Parties for the purpose of reviewing, revising or suspending any of the provisions of this Agreement other than Articles I and II. Participation in such conference shall be obligatory upon the Parties.

4. If the conference provided for in paragraph 3 of this Article does not result in an agreed solution of a point in dispute, either Party may bring the matter before the Security Council of the United Nations for the relief sought on the grounds that this Agreement has been concluded in pursuance of Security Council action toward the end of achieving peace in Palestine.

5. This Agreement supersedes the Egyptian-Israeli General Cease-Fire Agreement entered into by the Parties on 24 January 1949.

6. This Agreement is signed in quintuplicate, of which one copy shall be retained by each Party, two copies communicated to the Secretary-General of the United Nations for transmission to the Security Council and to the United Nations Conciliation Commission on Palestine, and one copy to the Acting Mediator on Palestine.

IN FAITH WHEREOF the undersigned representatives of the Contracting Parties have signed hereafter, in the presence of the United Nations Acting Mediator on Palestine and the United Nations Chief of Staff of the Truce Supervision Organization.

DONE at Rhodes, Island of Rhodes, Greece, on the twenty-fourth of February nineteen forty-nine.

International Humanitarian Law and Arms Control Agreements 585

V-4. Separation of Forces Agreement Between Israel and Syria, May 31, 1974
<http://www.israel.org/mfa/go.asp?MFAH00pw0>.

State Parties
Israel; Syria

State Signatories
Israel; Syria

Full Text

A. Israel and Syria will scrupulously observe the cease-fire on land, sea and air and will refrain from all military actions against each other, from the time of the signing of the document, in implementation of United Nations Security Council resolution 338 dated October 22, 1973.

B. The military forces of Israel and Syria will be separated in accordance with the following principles:

1. All Israeli military forces will be west of the line designated as Line A on the map attached hereto, except in the Kuneitra area, where they will be west of line A-1.
2. All territory east of Line A will be under Syrian administration, and the Syrian civilians will return to this territory.
3. The area between Line A and the Line designated, as Line B on the attached map will be an area of separation. In this area will be stationed the United Nations Disengagement Observer Force established in accordance with the accompanying protocol.
4. All Syrian military forces will be east of the line designated as Line B on the attached map.
5. There will be two equal areas of limitation in armament and forces, one west of Line A and one east of Line B as agreed upon.
6. Air forces of the two sides will be permitted to operate up to their respective lines without interference from the other side.

C. In the area between Line A and Line A-1 on the attached map there shall be no military forces.

D. This agreement and the attached map will be signed by the military representatives of Israel and Syria in Geneva not later than May 31, 1974, in the Egyptian Israeli military working group of the Geneva Peace Conference under the aegis of the United Nations, after that group has been joined by a Syrian military representative, and with the participation of representatives of the United States and the Soviet Union. The precise delineation of a detailed map and a plan for the implementation of the disengagement of forces will be worked by military representatives of Israel and Syria in the Egyptian-Israeli military working group, who will agree on the stages of this process. The military working group described above will state their work for this purpose in Geneva under the aegis of the United Nations within 24 hours after the signing of this agreement. They will complete this task within five days. Disengagement will begin within 24 hours after the completion of the task of the military working group. The process of disengagement will be completed not later than twenty days after it begins.

E. The provisions of paragraph A, B, and C shall be inspected by personnel of the United Nations Disengagement Observer Force under this agreement.

F. Within 24 hours after the signing of this agreement in Geneva all wounded prisoners of war which each side holds of the other as certified by the ICRC will be repatriated. The morning after the completion of the task of the military working group, all remaining prisoners of war will be repatriated.

G. The bodies of all dead soldiers held by either side will be returned for burial in their respective countries within 10 days after the signing of this agreement.

H. This agreement is not a peace agreement. It is a step toward a just and durable peace on the basis of Security Council Resolution 338 dated October 22, 1973.

V-5. Separation of Forces Agreement Between Israel and Egypt, January 18, 1974, <http://metalab.unc.edu/sullivan/docs?Sinail.html>.

State Signatories
Egypt; Israel

State Parties
Egypt; Israel

Full Text

A. Egypt and Israel will scrupulously observe the cease-fire on land, sea, and air called for by the U.N. Security Council and will refrain from the time of the signing of this document from all military or para-military actions against each other.

B. The military forces of Egypt and Israel will be separated in accordance with the following principles:

1. All Egyptian forces on the east side of the Canal will be deployed west of the line designated as Line A on the attached map. All Israeli forces, including those west of the Suez Canal and the Bitter Lakes, will be deployed east of the line designated as Line B on the attached map.

2. The area between the Egyptian and Israeli lines will be a zone of disengagement in which the United Nations Emergency Force (UNEF) will be stationed. The UNEF will continue to consist of units from countries that are not permanent members of the Security Council.

3. The area between the Egyptian line and the Suez Canal will be limited in armament and forces.

4. The area between the Israeli line (Line B on the attached map) and the line designated as Line C on the attached map, which runs along the western base of the mountains where the Gidi and Mitla Passes are located, will be limited in armament and forces.

5. The limitations referred to in paragraphs 3 and 4 will be inspected by UNEF. Existing procedures of the UNEF, including the attaching of Egyptian and Israel liaison officers to UNEF, will be continued.

6. Air forces of the two sides will be permitted to operate up to their respective lines without interference from the other side.

C. The detailed implementation of the disengagement of forces will be worded out by military representatives of Egypt and Israel, who will agree on the stages of this process. These representatives will meet no later that 48 hours after the signature of this agreement at Kilometre 101 under the aegis of the United Nations for this purpose. They will complete this task within five days. Disengagement will begin within 48 hours after the completion of the word of the military representatives and in no event later than seven days after the signature of this agreement . The process of disengagement will be completed not later than 40 days after it begins.

D. This agreement is not regarded by Egypt and Israel as a final peace agreement. It constitutes a first step toward a final, just and durable peace according to the provisions of Security Council Resolution 338 and within the framework of the Geneva Conference.

V-6. Interim Agreement Between Israel and Egypt, September 1, 1975, <http://metalab.unc.edu/sullivan/docs?Sinail.html>.

State Signatories
Egypt; Israel

State Parties
Egypt; Israel

Full Text

The Government of the Arab Republic of Egypt and the Government of Israel have agreed that:

Article I

The conflict between them and in the Middle East shall not be resolved by military force but by peaceful means.

The Agreement concluded by the parties on 18 January 1974, within the framework of the Geneva Peace Conference, constituted a first step towards a just and durable peace according to the provisions of Security Council Resolution 338 of 22 October 1973.

They are determined to reach a final and just peace settlement by means of negotiations called for by Security Council Resolution 338, this Agreement being a significant step towards that end.

Article II

The parties hereby undertake not to resort to the threat or use of force or military blockade against each other.

Article III

The parties shall continue scrupulously to observe the cease-fire on land, sea and air and to refrain from all military or para-military actions against each other. The parties also confirm that the obligations contained in the annex and, when concluded, the Protocol shall be an integral part of this Agreement.

Article IV

A. The military forces of the parties shall be deployed in accordance with the following principles:

(1) All Israel forces shall be deployed east of the lines designated as lined J and M on attached map.

(2) All Egyptian forces shall be deployed west of the line designated as line E on the attached map.

(3) The area between the lines designated on the attached map as lines E and F and the area between the lines designated on the attached map as lines J and K shall be limited in armament and forces.

(4) The limitations on armament and forces in the areas described by paragraph (3) above shall be agreed as described in the attached annex.

(5) The zone between the lines designated on the attached map as lines E and J will be a buffer zone. In this zone the United Nations Emergency Force will continue to perform its functions as under the Egyptian-Israeli Agreement of 18 January 1974.

(6) In the area south from line E and west from line M, as defined on the attached map, there will be no military forces, as specified in the attached annex.

B. The details concerning the new lines, the redeployment of the forces and its timing, the limitation on armaments and forces, aerial reconnaissance, the operation of the early warning and surveillance installations and the use of the roads, the United Nations functions and other arrangements will all be in accordance with the provisions of the annex and map which are an integral part of this Agreement and of the protocol which is to result from negotiations pursuant to the annex and which, when concluded, shall become an integral part of this Agreement.

Article V

The United Nations Emergency Force is essential and shall continue its functions and its mandate shall be extended annually.

Article VI

The parties hereby establish a joint commission for the duration of this Agreement. It will function under the aegis of the chief co-ordinator of the United Nations peace-keeping missions in the Middle East in order to consider any problem arising from this Agreement and to assist the United Nations Emergency Force in the execution of its mandate. The joint commission shall function in accordance with procedures established in the Protocol.

Article VII

Non-military cargoes destined for or coming from Israel shall be permitted through the Suez Canal.

Article VIII

This Agreement is regarded by the parties as a significant step toward a just and lasting peace. It is not a final peace agreement.

The parties shall continue their efforts to negotiate a final peace agreement within the framework of the Geneva peace conference in accordance with Security Council Resolution 338.

Article IX

This Agreement shall enter into force upon signature of the Protocol and remain in force until superseded by a new agreement.

ANNEX TO THE EGYPT-ISRAEL AGREEMENT

Within five days after the signature of the Egypt-Israel Agreement, representatives of the two parties shall meet in the military working group of the Middle East peace conference at Geneva to begin preparation of a detailed Protocol for the implementation of the Agreement. The working group will complete the Protocol within two weeks. In order to facilitate preparation of the Protocol and implementation of the agreement, and to assist in maintaining the scrupulous observance of the cease-fire and other elements of the Agreement, the two parties have agreed on the following
principles, which are integral part of the Agreement, as guidelines for the working group.

1. DEFINITIONS OF LINES AND AREA

The deployment lines, areas of limited forces and armaments, buffer zones, the area south from line E and west from line M, other designated areas, road sections for common use and other features referred to in article IV of the Agreement shall be indicated on the attached map (1:100,000 - United States edition).

2. BUFFER ZONES

(A) Access to the buffer zones will be controlled by the United Nations Emergency Force, according to procedures to be worked out by the working group and the United Nations Emergency Force.

(B) Aircraft of either party will be permitted to fly freely up to the forward line of the party. Reconnaissance aircraft of either party may fly up to the middle line of the buffer zone between E and J on an agreed schedule.

(C) In the buffer zone, between lines E and J, there will be established under article IV of the Agreement an early warning system entrusted to United States civilian personnel as detailed in a separate proposal, which is a part of this Agreement.

(D) Authorized personnel shall have access to the buffer zone for transit to and from the early warning system; the manner in which this is carried out shall be worked out by the working group and the United Nations Emergency Force.

3. AREA SOUTH OF LINE E AND WEST OF LINE M

(A) In this area, the United Nations Emergency Force will assure that there are no military or para-military forces of any kind, military fortifications and military installations; it will establish checkpoints and have the freedom of movement necessary to perform this function.

(B) Egyptian civilians and third country civilian oil field personnel shall have the right to enter, exit from, work and live in the above indicated area, except for buffer zones 2A, 2B and the United Nations posts. Egyptian civilian police shall be allowed in the area to perform normal civil police functions among the civilian population in such number and with such weapons and equipment as shall be provided for in the Protocol.

(C) Entry to and exit from the area, by land, by air or by sea, shall be only through United Nations Emergency Force checkpoints. The United Nations Emergency Force shall also establish checkpoints along the road, the dividing line and at either points, with the precise locations and number to be included in the Protocol.

(D) Access to the airspace and the coastal area shall be limited to unarmed Egyptian civilian vessels and unarmed civilian helicopters and transport planes involved in the civilian activities of the areas agreed by the working group.

(E) Israel undertakes to leave intact all currently existing civilian installations and infrastructures.

(F) Procedures for use of the common sections of the coastal road along the Gulf of Suez shall be determined by the working group and detailed in the Protocol.

4. AERIAL SURVEILLANCE

There shall be a continuation of aerial reconnaissance missions by the United States over the areas covered by the Agreement (the area between lines F and K), following the same procedures already in practice. The missions will ordinarily be carried out at a frequency of one mission every 7 - 10 days, with either party or the United Nations Emergency Force empowered to request an earlier mission. The United States Government will make the mission results available expeditiously to Israel, Egypt and the chief coordinator of the United Nations peace-keeping missions in the Middle East.

5. LIMITATION OF FORCES AND ARMAMENTS

(A) Within the areas of limited forces and armaments (the areas between lines J and K and lines E and F) the major limitation shall be as follows:

(1) Eight (8) standard infantry battalions.

(2) Seventy-five (75) tanks.

(3) Seventy-two (72) artillery pieces, including heavy mortars (i.e. with caliber larger than 120 mm.), whose range shall not exceed twelve (12) km.

(4) The total number of personnel shall not exceed eight thousand (8,000).

(5) Both parties agree not to station or locate in the area weapons which can reach the line of the other side.

(6) Both parties agree that in the areas between line A (of the disengagement agreement of 18 January 1974) and line E they will construct no new fortifications or installations for forces of a size greater than that agreed herein.

(B) The major limitations beyond the areas of limited forces and armament will be:

(1) Neither side will station nor locate any weapon in areas from which they can reach the other line.

(2) The parties will not place any anti-aircraft missiles within an area of ten (10) kilometers east of line K and west of line F, respectively.

(C) The United Nations Emergency Force will conduct inspections in order to ensure the maintenance of the agreed limitations within these areas.

6. PROCESS OF IMPLEMENTATION

The detailed implementation and timing of the redeployment of forces, turnover of oil fields, and other arrangements called for by the Agreement, annex and Protocol shall be determined by the working group, which will agree on the stages of this process, including the phased movement of Egyptian troops to line E and Israeli troops to line J. The first phase will be the transfer of the oil fields and installations to Egypt. This process will begin within two weeks from the signature of the

Protocol with the introduction of the necessary technicians, and it will be completed no later than eight weeks after it begins. The detail of the phasing will be worked out in the military working group.

PROPOSAL

In connection with the early warning system referred to in article IV of the Agreement between Egypt and Israel concluded on this date and as an integral part of that Agreement (hereafter referred to as the basic Agreement), the United States proposes the following:

1. The early warning system to be established in accordance with article IV in the area shown on the map attached to the basic agreement will be entrusted to the United States. It shall have the following elements:

A. There shall be two surveillance stations to provide strategic early warning, one operated by Egyptian and one operated by Israeli personnel. Their locations are shown on map attached to the basic Agreement. Each station shall be manned by not more than 250 technical and administrative personnel. They shall perform the functions of visual and electronic surveillance only within their stations.

B. In support of these stations, to provide tactical early warning and to verify access to them, three watch stations shall be established by the United States in the Mitla and Giddi Passes as will be shown on the map attached to the basic Agreement. These stations shall be operated by United States civilian personnel. In support of these stations, there shall be established three unmanned electronic sensor fields at both ends of each Pass and in the general vicinity of each station and the roads leading to and from those stations.

2. The United States civilian personnel shall perform the following duties in connection with the operation and maintenance of these stations:

A. At the two surveillance stations described in paragraph 1A above, United States civilian personnel will verify that nature of the operations of the stations and all movement into and out of each station and will immediately report any detected divergency from its authorized role of visual and electronic surveillance to the parties to the basic Agreement and to the United Nations Emergency Force.

B. At each watch station described in paragraph B above, the United States civilian personnel will immediately report to the parties of the basic Agreement and to the United Nations Emergency Force any movement of armed forces, other than the United Nations Emergency Force, into either Pass and any observed preparations for such movement.

C. The total number of United States civilian personnel assigned to functions under this proposal shall not exceed 200. Only civilian personnel shall be assigned to functions under this proposal.

3. No arms shall be maintained at the stations and other facilities covered by this proposal, except for small arms required for their protection.

4. The United States personnel serving the early warning system shall be allowed to move freely within the area of the system.

5. The United States and its personnel shall be entitled to have such support facilities as are reasonably necessary to perform their functions.

6. The United States personnel shall be immune from local criminal, civil, tax and customs jurisdiction and may be accorded any other specific privileges and immunities provided for in the United Nations Emergency Force Agreement of 13 February 1957.

7. The United States affirms that it will continue to perform the functions described above for the duration of the basic Agreement.

8. Notwithstanding any other provision of this proposal, the United States may withdraw its personnel only if it concludes that their safety is jeopardized or that continuation of their role is no longer necessary. In the latter case the parties to the basic Agreement will be informed in advance in order to give them the opportunity to make alternative arrangements. If both parties to the basic Agreement request the United States to conclude its role under this proposal. the United States will consider such requests conclusive.

9. Technical problems including the location of the watch stations will be worked out through consultation with the United States.

Signed, Henry A. Kissinger Secretary of State

V-7. Camp David Accords, September 17, 1978,
<http://metalab.unc.edu/sullivan/docs?Sinail.html>.

State Signatories
Egypt; Israel

State Parties
Egypt; Israel

Full Text

The Framework for Peace in the Middle East

Muhammad Anwar Al-Sadat, President of the Arab Republic of Egypt, and Menachem Begin, Prime Minister of Israel, met with Jimmy Carter, President of the United States of America, at Camp David from September 5 to September 17, 1978, and have agreed on the following framework for peace in the Middle East. They invite other parties to the Arab-Israel conflict to adhere to it.

Preamble

The search for peace in the Middle East must be guided by the following:

The agreed basis for a peaceful settlement of the conflict between Israel and its neighbors is United Nations Security Council Resolution 242, in all its parts.

After four wars during 30 years, despite intensive human efforts, the Middle East, which is the cradle of civilization and the birthplace of three great religions, does not enjoy the blessings of peace. The people of the Middle East yearn for peace so that the vast human and natural resources of the region can be turned to the pursuits of peace and so that this area can become a model for coexistence and cooperation among nations.

The historic initiative of President Sadat in visiting Jerusalem and the reception accorded to him by the parliament, government and people of Israel, and the reciprocal visit of Prime Minister Begin to Ismailia, the peace proposals made by both leaders, as well as the warm reception of these missions by the peoples of both countries, have created an unprecedented opportunity for peace which must not be lost if this generation and future generations are to be spared the tragedies of war.

The provisions of the Charter of the United Nations and the other accepted norms of international law and legitimacy now provide accepted standards for the conduct of relations among all states. To achieve a relationship of peace, in the spirit of Article 2 of the United Nations Charter, future negotiations between Israel and any neighbor prepared to negotiate peace and security with it are necessary for the purpose of carrying out all the provisions and principles of Resolutions 242 and 338.

Peace requires respect for the sovereignty, territorial integrity and political independence of every state in the area and their right to live in peace within secure and recognized boundaries free from threats or acts of force. Progress toward that goal can accelerate movement toward a new era of reconciliation in the Middle East marked by cooperation in promoting economic development, in maintaining stability and in assuring security.

Security is enhanced by a relationship of peace and by cooperation between nations which enjoy normal relations. In addition, under the terms of peace treaties, the parties can, on the basis of reciprocity, agree to special security arrangements such as demilitarized zones, limited armaments areas, early warning stations, the presence of international forces, liaison, agreed measures for monitoring and other arrangements that they agree are useful.

Framework

Taking these factors into account, the parties are determined to reach a just, comprehensive, and durable settlement of the Middle East conflict through the conclusion of peace treaties based on Security Council resolutions 242 and 338 in all their parts. Their purpose is to achieve peace and good neighborly relations. They recognize that for peace to endure, it must involve all those who have been most deeply affected by the conflict. They therefore agree that this framework, as appropriate, is intended by them to constitute a basis for peace not only between Egypt and Israel, but also between Israel and each of its other neighbors which is prepared to negotiate peace with Israel on this basis. With that objective in mind, they have agreed to proceed as follows:

West Bank and Gaza

Egypt, Israel, Jordan and the representatives of the Palestinian people should participate in negotiations on the resolution of the Palestinian problem in all its aspects. To achieve that objective, negotiations relating to the West Bank and Gaza should proceed in three stages:

Egypt and Israel agree that, in order to ensure a peaceful and orderly transfer of authority, and taking into account the security concerns of all the parties, there should be transitional arrangements for the West Bank and Gaza for a period not exceeding five years. In order to provide full autonomy to the inhabitants, under these arrangements the Israeli military government and its civilian administration will be withdrawn as soon as a self-governing authority has been freely elected by the inhabitants of these areas to replace the existing military government. To negotiate the details of a transitional arrangement, Jordan will be invited to join the negotiations on the basis of this framework. These new arrangements should give due consideration both to the principle of self-government by the inhabitants of these territories and to the legitimate security concerns of the parties involved. Egypt, Israel, and Jordan will agree on the modalities for establishing elected self-governing authority in the West Bank and Gaza. The delegations of Egypt and Jordan may include Palestinians from the West Bank and Gaza or other Palestinians as mutually agreed. The parties will negotiate an agreement which will define the powers and responsibilities of the self-governing authority to be exercised in the West Bank and Gaza. A withdrawal of Israeli armed forces will take place and there will be a redeployment of the remaining Israeli forces into specified security locations. The agreement will also include arrangements for assuring internal and external security and public order. A strong local police force will be established, which may include Jordanian citizens. In addition, Israeli and Jordanian forces will participate in joint patrols and in the manning of control posts to assure the security of the borders.

When the self-governing authority (administrative council) in the West Bank and Gaza is established and inaugurated, the transitional period of five years will begin. As soon as possible, but not later than the third year after the beginning of the transitional period, negotiations will take place to determine the final status of the West Bank and Gaza and its relationship with its neighbors and to conclude a peace treaty between Israel and Jordan by the end of the transitional period. These negotiations will be conducted among Egypt, Israel, Jordan and the elected representatives of the inhabitants of the West Bank and Gaza. Two separate but related committees will be convened, one committee, consisting of representatives of the four parties which will negotiate and agree on the final status of the West Bank and Gaza, and its relationship with its neighbors, and the second committee, consisting of representatives of Israel and representatives of Jordan to be joined by the elected representatives of the inhabitants of the West Bank and Gaza, to negotiate the peace treaty between Israel and Jordan, taking into account the agreement reached in the final status of the West Bank and Gaza. The negotiations shall be based on all the provisions and principles of UN Security Council Resolution 242. The negotiations will resolve, among other matters, the location of the boundaries and the nature of the security arrangements. The solution from the negotiations must also recognize the legitimate right of the Palestinian peoples and their just requirements. In this way, the Palestinians will participate in the determination of their own future through:

The negotiations among Egypt, Israel, Jordan and the representatives of the inhabitants of the West Bank and Gaza to agree on the final status of the West Bank and Gaza and other outstanding issues by the end of the transitional period.

Submitting their agreements to a vote by the elected representatives of the inhabitants of the West Bank and Gaza. Providing for the elected representatives of the inhabitants of the West Bank and Gaza to decide how they shall govern themselves consistent with the provisions of their agreement.

Participating as stated above in the work of the committee negotiating the peace treaty between Israel and Jordan.

All necessary measures will be taken and provisions made to assure the security of Israel and its neighbors during the transitional period and beyond. To assist in providing such security, a strong local police force will be constituted by the self-governing authority. It will be composed of inhabitants of the West Bank and Gaza. The police will maintain liaison on internal security matters with the designated Israeli, Jordanian, and Egyptian officers.

During the transitional period, representatives of Egypt, Israel, Jordan, and the self-governing authority will constitute a continuing committee to decide by agreement on the modalities of admission of persons displaced from the West Bank and Gaza in 1967, together with necessary measures to prevent disruption and disorder. Other matters of common concern may also be dealt with by this committee. Egypt and Israel will work with each other and with other interested parties to establish agreed procedures for a prompt, just and permanent implementation of the resolution of the refugee problem.

Egypt-Israel

Egypt-Israel undertake not to resort to the threat or the use of force to settle disputes. Any disputes shall be settled by peaceful means in accordance with the provisions of Article 33 of the U.N. Charter.

In order to achieve peace between them, the parties agree to negotiate in good faith with a goal of concluding within three months from the signing of the Framework a peace treaty between them while inviting the other parties to the conflict to proceed simultaneously to negotiate and conclude similar peace treaties with a view the achieving a comprehensive peace in the area. The Framework for the Conclusion of a Peace Treaty between Egypt and Israel will govern the peace negotiations between them. The parties will agree on the modalities and the timetable for the implementation of their obligations under the treaty.

Associated Principles

Egypt and Israel state that the principles and provisions described below should apply to peace treaties between Israel and each of its neighbors - Egypt, Jordan, Syria and Lebanon. Signatories shall establish among themselves relationships normal to states at peace with one another. To this end, they should undertake to abide by all the provisions of the U.N. Charter. Steps to be taken in this respect include:

full recognition;

abolishing economic boycotts;

guaranteeing that under their jurisdiction the citizens of the other parties shall enjoy the protection of the due process of law.

Signatories should explore possibilities for economic development in the context of final peace treaties, with the objective of contributing to the atmosphere of peace, cooperation and friendship which is their common goal.

Claims commissions may be established for the mutual settlement of all financial claims. The United States shall be invited to participated in the talks on matters related to the modalities of the implementation of the agreements and working out the timetable for the carrying out of the obligations of the parties.

The United Nations Security Council shall be requested to endorse the peace treaties and ensure that their provisions shall not be violated. The permanent members of the Security Council shall be requested to underwrite the peace treaties and ensure respect or the provisions. They shall be requested to conform their policies an actions with the undertaking contained in this Framework.

For the Government of Israel: Menachem Begin For the Government of the Arab Republic of Egypt Muhammed Anwar al-Sadat

Witnessed by Jimmy Carter, President of the United States of America

Framework for the Conclusion of a Peace Treaty between Egypt and Israel

In order to achieve peace between them, Israel and Egypt agree to negotiate in good faith with a goal of concluding within three months of the signing of this framework a peace treaty between them: It is agreed that:

The site of the negotiations will be under a United Nations flag at a location or locations to be mutually agreed.

All of the principles of U.N. Resolution 242 will apply in this resolution of the dispute between Israel and Egypt.

Unless otherwise mutually agreed, terms of the peace treaty will be implemented between two and three years after the peace treaty is signed.

The following matters are agreed between the parties:

the full exercise of Egyptian sovereignty up to the internationally recognized border between Egypt and mandated Palestine;

the withdrawal of Israeli armed forces from the Sinai;

the use of airfields left by the Israelis near al-Arish, Rafah, Ras en-Naqb, and Sharm el-Sheikh for civilian purposes only, including possible commercial use only by all nations;

the right of free passage by ships of Israel through the Gulf of Suez and the Suez Canal on the basis of the Constantinople Convention of 1888 applying to all nations; the Strait of Tiran and Gulf of Aqaba are international waterways to be open to all nations for unimpeded and nonsuspendable freedom of navigation and overflight;

the construction of a highway between the Sinai and Jordan near Eilat with guaranteed free and peaceful passage by Egypt and Jordan; and the stationing of military forces listed below.

Stationing of Forces

No more than one division (mechanized or infantry) of Egyptian armed forces will be stationed within an area lying approximately 50 km. (30 miles) east of the Gulf of Suez and the Suez Canal. Only United Nations forces and civil police equipped with light weapons to perform normal police functions will be stationed within an area lying west of the international border and the Gulf of Aqaba, varying in width from 20 km. (12 miles) to 40 km. (24 miles).

In the area within 3 km. (1.8 miles) east of the international border there will be Israeli limited military forces not to exceed four infantry battalions and United Nations observers.

Border patrol units not to exceed three battalions will supplement the civil police in maintaining order in the area not included above.

The exact demarcation of the above areas will be as decided during the peace negotiations. Early warning stations may exist to insure compliance with the terms of the agreement.

United Nations forces will be stationed:

in part of the area in the Sinai lying within about 20 km. of the Mediterranean Sea and adjacent to the international border, and in the Sharm el-Sheikh area to insure freedom of passage through the Strait of Tiran; and these forces will not be removed unless such removal is approved by the Security Council of the United Nations with a unanimous vote of the five permanent members.

After a peace treaty is signed, and after the interim withdrawal is complete, normal relations will be established between Egypt and Israel, including full recognition, including diplomatic, economic and cultural relations; termination of economic boycotts and barriers to the free movement of goods and people; and mutual protection of citizens by the due process of law.

Interim Withdrawal

Between three months and nine months after the signing of the peace treaty, all Israeli forces will withdraw east of a line extending from a point east of El-Arish to Ras Muhammad, the exact location of this line to be determined by mutual agreement.

For the Government of the Arab Republic of Egypt: Muhammed Anwar al-Sadat

For the Government of Israel: Menachem Begin

Witnessed by: Jimmy Carter, President of the United States of America

V-8. Peace Treaty Between Israel and Egypt, March 26, 1979,
<http://metalab.unc.edu/sullivan/docs?Sinail.html>.

State Signatories
Egypt; Israel

State Parties
Egypt; Israel

Full Text

The Government of the Arab Republic of Egypt and the Government of the State of Israel;

PREAMBLE

Convinced of the urgent necessity of the establishment of a just, comprehensive and lasting peace in the Middle East in accordance with Security Council Resolutions 242 and 338;

Reaffirming their adherence to the "Framework for Peace in the Middle East Agreed at Camp David," dated September 17, 1978;

Noting that the aforementioned Framework as appropriate is intended to constitute a basis for peace not only between Egypt and Israel but also between Israel and each of its other Arab neighbors which is prepared to negotiate peace with it on this basis;

Desiring to bring to an end the state of war between them and to establish a peace in which every state in the area can live in security;

Convinced that the conclusion of a Treaty of Peace between Egypt and Israel is an important step in the search for comprehensive peace in the area and for the attainment of settlement of the Arab- Israeli conflict in all its aspects;

Inviting the other Arab parties to this dispute to join the peace process with Israel guided by and based on the principles of the aforementioned Framework;

Desiring as well to develop friendly relations and cooperation between themselves in accordance with the United Nations Charter and the principles of international law governing international relations in times of peace;

Agree to the following provisions in the free exercise of their sovereignty, in order to implement the "Framework for the Conclusion of a Peace Treaty Between Egypt and Israel";

Article I

The state of war between the Parties will be terminated and peace will be established between them upon the exchange of instruments of ratification of this Treaty. Israel will withdraw all its armed forces and civilians from the Sinai behind the international boundary between Egypt and mandated Palestine, as provided in the annexed protocol (Annex I), and Egypt will resume the exercise of its full sovereignty over the Sinai. Upon completion of the interim withdrawal provided for in Annex I, the parties will establish normal and friendly relations, in accordance with Article III (3).

Article II

The permanent boundary between Egypt and Israel is the recognized international boundary between Egypt and the former mandated territory of Palestine, as shown on the map at Annex II, without prejudice to the issue of the status of the Gaza Strip. The Parties recognize this boundary as inviolable. Each will respect the territorial integrity of the other, including their territorial waters and airspace.

Article III

The Parties will apply between them the provisions of the Charter of the United Nations and the principles of international law governing relations among states in times of peace. In particular: They recognize and will respect each other's sovereignty, territorial integrity and political independence; They recognize and will respect each other's right to live in peace within their secure and recognized boundaries; They will refrain from the threat or use of force, directly or indirectly, against each other and will settle all disputes between them by peaceful means. Each Party undertakes to ensure that acts or threats of belligerency, hostility, or violence do not originate from and are not committed from within its territory, or by any forces subject to its control or by any other forces stationed on its territory, against the population, citizens or property of the other Party. Each Party also undertakes to refrain from organizing, instigating, inciting, assisting or participating in acts or threats of belligerency, hostility, subversion or violence against the other Party, anywhere, and undertakes to ensure that perpetrators of such acts are brought to justice. The Parties agree that the normal relationship established between them will include full recognition, diplomatic, economic and cultural relations, termination of economic boycotts and discriminatory barriers to the free movement of people and goods, and will guarantee the mutual enjoyment by citizens of the due process of law. The process by which they undertake to achieve such a relationship parallel to the implementation of other provisions of this Treaty is set out in the annexed protocol (Annex III).

Article IV
In order to provide maximum security for both Parties on the basis of reciprocity, agreed security arrangements will be established including limited force zones in Egyptian and Israeli territory, and United Nations forces and observers, described in detail as to nature and timing in Annex I, and other security arrangements the parties may agree upon. The Parties agree to the stationing of United Nations personnel in areas described in Annex I. The Parties agree not to request withdrawal of the United Nations personnel and that these personnel will not be removed unless such removal is approved by the Security Council of the United Nations, with the affirmative vote of the five Permanent Members, unless the Parties otherwise agree. A Joint Commission will be established to facilitate the implementation of the Treaty, as provided for in Annex I. The security arrangements provided for in paragraphs 1 and 2 of this Article may at the request of either party be reviewed and amended by mutual agreement of the Parties.

Article V
Ships of Israel, and cargoes destined for or coming from Israel, shall enjoy the right of free passage through the Suez Canal and its approaches through the Gulf of Suez and the Mediterranean Sea on the basis of the Constantinople Convention of 1888, applying to all nations, Israeli nationals, vessels and cargoes, as well as persons, vessels and cargoes destined for or coming from Israel, shall be accorded non-discriminatory treatment in all matters connected with usage of the canal. The Parties consider the Strait of Tiran and the Gulf of Aqaba to be international waterways open to all nations for unimpeded and non-suspendable freedom of navigation and overflight. The parties will respect each other's right to navigation and overflight for access to either country through the Strait of Tiran and the Gulf of Aqaba.

Article VI
This Treaty does not affect and shall not be interpreted as affecting in any way the rights and obligations of the Parties under the Charter of the United Nations. The Parties undertake to fulfill in good faith their obligations under this Treaty, without regard to action or inaction of any other party and independently of any instrument external to this Treaty. They further undertake to take all the necessary measures for the application in their relations of the provisions of the multilateral conventions to which they are parties, including the submission of appropriate notification to the Secretary General of the United Nations and other depositaries of such conventions. The Parties undertake not to enter into any obligation in conflict with this Treaty. Subject to Article 103 of the United Nations Charter in the event of a conflict between the obligation of the Parties under the present Treaty and any of their other obligations, the obligations under this Treaty will be

binding and implemented.

Article VII
Disputes arising out of the application or interpretation of this Treaty shall be resolved by negotiations. Any such disputes which cannot be settled by negotiations shall be resolved by conciliation or submitted to arbitration.

Article VIII
The Parties agree to establish a claims commission for the mutual settlement of all financial claims.

Article IX
This Treaty shall enter into force upon exchange of instruments of ratification. This Treaty supersedes the Agreement between Egypt and Israel of September, 1975. All protocols, annexes, and maps attached to this Treaty shall be regarded as an integral part hereof. The Treaty shall be communicated to the Secretary General of the United Nations for registration in accordance with the provisions of Article 102 of the Charter of the United Nations.

Annex I Protocol Concerning Israeli Withdrawal and Security Agreements

Article I
Concept of Withdrawal Israel will complete withdrawal of all its armed forces and civilians from the Sinai not later than three years from the date of exchange of instruments of ratification of this Treaty. To ensure the mutual security of the Parties, the implementation of phased withdrawal will be accompanied by the military measures and establishment of zones set out in this Annex and in Map 1, hereinafter referred to as "the Zones." The withdrawal from the Sinai will be accomplished in two phases: The interim withdrawal behind the line from east of El-Arish to Ras Mohammed as delineated on Map 2 within nine months from the date of exchange of instruments of ratification of this Treaty. The final withdrawal from the Sinai behind the international boundary not later than three years from the date of exchange of instruments of ratification of this Treaty. A Joint Commission will be formed immediately after the exchange of instruments of ratification of this Treaty in order to supervise and coordinate movements and schedules during the withdrawal, and to adjust plans and timetables as necessary within the limits established by paragraph 3, above. Details relating to the Joint Commission are set out in Article IV of the attached Appendix. The Joint Commission will be dissolved upon completion of final Israeli withdrawal from the Sinai.

Article II
Determination of Final Lines and Zones In order to provide maximum security for both Parties after the final withdrawal, the lines and the Zones delineated on Map 1 are to be established and organized as follows:

Zone A
Zone A is bounded on the east by line A (red line) and on the west by the Suez Canal and the east coast of the Gulf of Suez, as shown on Map 1. An Egyptian armed force of one mechanized infantry division and its military installations, and field fortifications, will be in this Zone. The main elements of that Division will consist of: Three mechanized infantry brigades. One armed brigade. Seven field artillery battalions including up to 126 artillery pieces. Seven anti-aircraft artillery battalions including individual surface-to-air missiles and up to 126 anti-aircraft guns of 37 mm and above. Up to 230 tanks. Up to 480 armored personnel vehicles of all types. Up to a total of twenty-two thousand personnel.

Zone B
Zone B is bounded by line B (green line) on the east and by line A (red line) on the west, as shown on Map 1. Egyptian border units of four battalions equipped with light weapons and wheeled vehicles will provide security and supplement the civil police in maintaining order in Zone B. The main elements in the four Border Battalions will consist of up to a total of four thousand personnel. Land based, short range, low power, coastal warning points of the border patrol units may be established on the coast of this Zone. There will be in Zone B field fortifications and military installations for the four border battalions.

Zone C
Zone C is bounded by line B (green line) on the west and the International Boundary and the Gulf of Aqaba on the east, as shown on Map 1. Only United Nations forces and Egyptian civil police will be stationed in Zone C. The Egyptian civil police armed with light weapons will perform normal police functions within this Zone. The United Nations Force will be deployed within Zone C and perform its functions as defined in Article VI of this annex. The United Nations Force will be stationed mainly in camps located within the following stationing areas shown on Map 1, and will establish its precise locations after consultations with Egypt: In that part of the area in the Sinai lying within about 20 Km. of the Mediterranean Sea and adjacent to the International Boundary. In the Sharm el Sheikh area. Zone D Zone D is bounded by line D (blue line) on the east and the international boundary on the west, as shown on Map 1. In this Zone there will be an Israeli limited force of four infantry battalions, their military installations, and field fortifications, and United Nations observers. The Israeli forces in Zone D will not include tanks, artillery and anti-aircraft missiles except individual surface-to-air missiles. The main elements of the four Israeli infantry battalions will consist of up to 180 armored personnel vehicles of all types and up to a total of four thousand personnel. Access across the international boundary shall only be permitted through entry check points designated by each Party and under its control. Such access shall be in accordance with laws and regulations of each country. Only those field fortifications, military installations, forces, and weapons specifically

permitted by this Annex shall be in the Zones.

Article III Aerial Military Regime
Flights of combat aircraft and reconnaissance flights of Egypt and Israel shall take place only over Zones A and D, respectively. Only unarmed, non-combat aircraft of Egypt and Israel will be stationed in Zones A and D, respectively. Only Egyptian unarmed transport aircraft will take off and land in Zone B and up to eight such aircraft may be maintained in Zone B. The Egyptian border unit may be equipped with unarmed helicopters to perform their functions in Zone B. The Egyptian civil police may be equipped with unarmed police helicopters to perform normal police functions in Zone C. Only civilian airfields maybe built in the Zones. Without prejudice to the provisions of this Treaty, only those military aerial activities specifically permitted by this Annex shall be allowed in the Zones and the airspace above their territorial waters.

Article IV Naval Regime
Egypt and Israel may base and operate naval vessels along the coasts of Zones A and D, respectively. Egyptian coast guard boats, lightly armed, may be stationed and operate in the territorial waters of Zone B to assist the border units in performing their functions in this Zone. Egyptian civil police equipped with light boats, lightly armed, shall perform normal police functions within the territorial waters of Zone C. Nothing in this Annex shall be considered as derogating from the right of innocent passage of the naval vessels of either party. Only civilian maritime ports and installations may be built in the Zones. Without prejudice to the provisions of this Treaty, only those naval activities specifically permitted by this Annex shall be allowed in the Zones and in their territorial waters.

Article V Early Warning Systems
Egypt and Israel may establish and operate early warning systems only in Zones A and D respectively.

Article VI United Nations Operations
The Parties will request the United Nations to provide forces and observers to supervise the implementation of this Annex and employ their best efforts to prevent any violation of its terms. With respect to these United Nations forces and observers, as appropriate, the Parties agree to request the following arrangements: Operation of check points, reconnaissance patrols, and observation posts along the international boundary and line B, and within Zone C. Periodic verification of the implementation of the provisions of this Annex will be carried out not less than twice a month unless otherwise agreed by the Parties. Additional verifications within 48 hours after the receipt of a request from either Party. Ensuring the freedom of navigation through the Strait of Tiran in accordance with Article V of the Treaty of Peace.

The arrangements described in this article for each zone will be implemented in zones A, B, and C by the United Nations Force and in Zone D by the United Nations Observers. United Nations verification teams shall be accompanied by liaison officers of the respective Party. The United Nations Force and observers will report their findings to both Parties. The United Nations Force and Observers operating in the Zones will enjoy freedom of movement and other facilities necessary for the performance of their tasks. The United Nations Force and Observers are not empowered to authorize the crossing of the international boundary. The Parties shall agree on the nations from which the United Nations Force and Observers will be drawn. They "ill be drawn from nations other than those which are permanent members of the United Nations Security Council. The Parties agree that the United Nations should make those command arrangements that will best assure the effective implementation of its responsibilities.

Article VII Liaison System
Upon dissolution of the Joint Commission, a liaison system between the Parties will be established. This liaison system is intended to provide an effective method to assess progress in the implementation of obligations under the present Annex and to resolve any problem that may arise in the course of implementation, and refer other unresolved matters to the higher military authorities of the two countries respectively for consideration. It is also intended to prevent situations resulting from errors or misinterpretation on the part of either Party. An Egyptian liaison office will be established in the city of El-Arish and an Israeli liaison office will be established in the city of Beer-Sheba. Each office will be headed by and officer of the respective country, and assisted by a number of officers. A direct telephone link between the two offices will be set up and also direct telephone lines with the United Nations command will be maintained by both offices.

Article VIII Respect for War Memorials
Each Party undertakes to preserve in good condition the War Memorials erected in the memory of soldiers of the other Party, namely those erected by Egypt in Israel, and shall permit access to such monuments.

Article IX Interim Arrangements
The withdrawal of Israeli armed forces and civilians behind the interim withdrawal line, and the conduct of the forces of the Parties and the United Nations prior to the final withdrawal, will be governed by the attached Appendix and Map 2.

Appendix to Annex I Organization of Movements in the Sinai

Article I Principles of Withdrawal
The withdrawal of Israeli armed forces and civilians from the Sinai will be accomplished in two phases as described in Article I of Annex I. The description

and timing of the withdrawal are included in this Appendix. The Joint Commission will develop and present to the Chief Coordinator of the United Nations forces in the Middle East the details of these phases not later than one month before the initiation of each phase of withdrawal. Both parties agree on the following principles for the sequences of military movements. Notwithstanding the provisions of Article IX, paragraph 2, of this Treaty, until Israeli armed forces complete withdrawal from the current J and M Lines established by the Egyptian-Israeli Agreement of September 1975, hereinafter referred to as the 1975 Agreement, up to the interim withdrawal line, all military arrangements existing under that Agreement will remain in effect, except those military arrangements otherwise provided for in this Appendix. As Israeli armed forces withdraw, United Nations forces will immediately enter the evacuated areas to establish interim and temporary buffer zones as shown on Maps 2 and 3, respectively, for the purpose of maintaining a separation of forces. United Nations forces' deployment will precede the movement of any other personnel into these areas. Within a period of seven days after Israeli armed forces have evacuated any area located in Zone A, units of Egyptian armed forces shall deploy in accordance with the provisions of Article II of this Appendix. Within a period of seven days after Israeli armed forces have evacuated any area located in Zones A or B, Egyptian border units shall deploy in accordance with the provisions of Article II of this Appendix, and will function in accordance with the provisions of Article II of Annex I. Egyptian civil police will enter evacuated areas immediately after the United Nations forces to perform normal police functions. Egyptian naval units shall deploy in the Gulf of Suez in accordance with the provisions of Article II of this Appendix. Except those movements mentioned above, deployments of Egyptian armed forces and the activities covered in Annex I will be offered in the evacuated areas when Israeli armed forces have completed their withdrawal behind the interim withdrawal line.

Article II Subphases of the Withdrawal to the Interim Withdrawal Line
The withdrawal to the interim withdrawal line will be accomplished in subphases as described in this Article and as shown on Map 3. Each subphase will be completed within the indicated number of months from the date of the exchange of instruments of ratification of this Treaty: First subphase: within two months, Israeli armed forces will withdraw from the area of El Arish, including the town of El Arish and its airfield, shown as Area I on Map 3. Second subphase: within three months, Israeli armed forces will withdraw from the area between line M of the 1975 Agreement and line A, shown as Area II on Map 3. Third subphase: within five months, Israeli armed forces will withdraw from the area east and south of Area II, shown as Area III on Map 3. Fourth subphase: within seven months, Israeli armed forces will withdraw from the area of El Tor- Ras El Kenisa, shown as Area IV on Map 3. Fifth subphase: Within nine months, Israeli armed forces will withdraw from the remaining areas west of the interim withdrawal line, including the areas of Santa Katrina and the areas east of the Giddi and Mitla passes, shown as Area V on Map 3, thereby completing Israeli

withdrawal behind the interim withdrawal line. Egyptian forces will deploy in the areas evacuated by Israeli armed forces as follows: Up to one-third of the Egyptian armed forces in the Sinai in accordance with the 1975 Agreement will deploy in the portions of Zone A lying within Area I, until the completion of interim withdrawal. Thereafter, Egyptian armed forces as described Article II of Annex I will be deployed in Zone A up to the limits of the interim zone. The Egyptian naval activity in accordance with Article IV of Annex I will commence along the coasts of areas I, III and IV, upon completion of the second, third, and fourth subphases, respectively. Of the Egyptian border units described in Article II of Annex I, upon completion of the first subphase one battalion will be deployed in Area I. A second battalion will deployed in Area II upon completion of the second subphase. A third battalion will deployed in Area III upon completion of the third subphase. The second and third battalions mentioned above may also be deployed in any of the subsequently evacuated areas of the southern Sinai. United Nations forces in Buffer Zone I of the 1976 Agreement will redeploy enable the deployment of Egyptian forces described above upon the completion of the subphase, but will otherwise continue to function in accordance with the provisions of that Agreement in the remainder of that zone until the completion of interim withdrawal, as indicated in Article I of this Appendix. Israeli convoys may use the roads south and east of the main road junction east of El Arish to evacuate Israeli forces up to the completion of interim withdrawal. These convoys will proceed in daylight upon four hours notice to the Egyptian liaison group and United Nations forces, will be escorted by United Nations forces, and will be in accordance with schedules coordinated by the Joint Commission. An Egyptian liaison officer will accompany convoys to assure uninterrupted movement. The Joint Commission may approve other arrangements for convoys.

Article III United Nations Forces The Parties shall request that United Nations forces be deployed as necessary to perform the functions described in the Appendix up to the time of completion of final Israeli withdrawal. For that purpose, the Parties agree to the redeployment of the United Nations Emergency Force. United Nations forces will supervise the implementation of this Appendix and will employ their best efforts to prevent any violation of its terms. When United Nations forces deploy in accordance with the provisions of Article and II of this Appendix, they will perform the functions of verification in limited force zones in accordance with Article VI of Annex I, and will establish check points, reconnaissance patrols, and observation posts in the temporary buffer zones described in Article II above. Other functions of the United Nations forces which concern the interim buffer zone are described in Article V of this Appendix.

Article IV Joint Commission and Liaison
The Joint Commission referred to in Article IV of this Treaty will function from

the date of exchange of instruments of ratification of this Treaty up to the date of completion of final Israeli withdrawal from the Sinai. The Joint Commission will be composed of representatives of each Party headed by senior officers. This Commission shall invite a representative of the United Nations when discussing subjects concerning the United Nations, or when either Party requests United Nations presence. Decisions of the Joint Commission will be reached by agreement of Egypt and Israel. The Joint Commission will supervise the implementation of the arrangements described in Annex I and this Appendix. To this end, and by agreement of both Parties, it will: coordinate military movements described in this Appendix and supervise their implementation; address and seek to resolve any problem arising out of the implementation of Annex I and this Appendix, and discuss any violations reported by the United Nations Force and Observers and refer to the Governments of Egypt and Israel any unresolved problems; assist the United Nations Force and Observers in the execution of their mandates, and deal with the timetables of the periodic verification when referred to it by the Parties as provided for in Annex I and this Appendix; organize the demarcation of the international boundary and all lines and zones described in Annex I and this Appendix; supervise the handing over of the main installations in the Sinai from Israel to Egypt; agree on necessary arrangements for finding and returning missing bodies of Egyptian and Israeli soldiers; organize the setting up and operation of entry check points along the El Arish-Ras Mohammed line in accordance with the provisions of Article 4 of Annex III; conduct its operations through the use of joint liaison teams consisting of one Israeli representative and one Egyptian representative, provided from a standing Liaison Group, which will conduct activities as directed by the Joint Commission; provide liaison and coordination to the United Nations command implementing provisions of the Treaty, and, through the joint liaison teams, maintain local coordination and cooperation with the United Nations Force stationed in specific areas or United Nations Observers monitoring specific areas for any assistance as needed; discuss any other matters which the Parties by agreement may place before it. Meetings of the Joint Commission shall be held at least once a month. In the event that either Party of the Command of the United Nations Force requests a specific meeting, it will be convened within 24 hours. The Joint Committee will meet in the buffer zone until the completion of the interim withdrawal and in El Arish and Beer-Sheba alternately afterwards. The first meeting will be held not later than two weeks after the entry into force of this Treaty.

Article V Definition of the Interim Buffer Zone and Its Activities

An interim buffer zone, by which the United Nations Force will effect a separation of Egyptian and Israeli elements, will be established west of and adjacent to the interim withdrawal line as shown on Map 2 after implementation of Israeli withdrawal and deployment behind the interim withdrawal line. Egyptian civil police equipped with light weapons will perform normal police functions within this zone. The United Nations Force will operate check points, reconnaissance patrols, and observation posts within the interim buffer zone in order to ensure compliance with the terms of this Article. In accordance with arrangements agreed upon by both Parties and to be coordinated by the Joint Commission, Israeli personnel will operate military technical installations at four specific locations shown on Map 2 and designated as T1 (map central coordinate 57163940), T2 (map central coordinate 59351541), T3 (map central coordinate 5933-1527), and T4 (map central coordinate 61130979) under the following principles: The technical installations shall be manned by technical and administrative personnel equipped with small arms required for their protection (revolvers, rifles, sub-machine guns, light machine guns, hand grenades, and ammunition), as follows: T1 - up to 150 personnel T2 and T3 - up to 350 personnel T4 - up to 200 personnel Israeli personnel will not carry weapons outside the sites, except officers who may carry personal weapons. Only a third party agreed to by Egypt and Israel will enter and conduct inspections within the perimeters of technical installations in the buffer zone. The third party will conduct inspections in a random manner at least once a month. The inspections will verify the nature of the operation of the installations and the weapons and personnel therein. The third party will immediately report to the Parties any divergence from an installation's visual and electronic surveillance or communications role. Supply of the installations, visits for technical and administrative purposes, and replacement of personnel and equipment situated in the sites, may occur uninterruptedly from the United Nations check points to the perimeter of the technical installations, after checking and being escorted by only the United Nations forces. Israel will be permitted to introduce into its technical installations items required for the proper functioning of the installations and personnel. As determined by the Joint Commission, Israel will be permitted to Maintain in its installations fire-fighting and general maintenance equipment as well as wheeled administrative vehicles and mobile engineering equipment necessary for the maintenance of the sites. All vehicles shall be unarmed. Within the sites and in the buffer zone, maintain roads, water lines, and communications cables which serve the site. At each of the three installation locations (T1, T2 and T3, and T4), this maintenance may be performed with up to two unarmed wheeled vehicles and by up to twelve unarmed personnel with only necessary equipment, including heavy engineering equipment if needed. This maintenance may be performed three times a week, except for special problems, and only after giving the United Nations four hours notice. The teams will be escorted by the United Nations. Movement to and from the technical installations will take place only during daylight hours. Access to, and exit from, the technical installations shall be as follows: T1: Through a United Nations check point, and via the road between Abu Aweigila and the intersection of the Abu Aweigila road and the Gebel Libni road (at Km. 161), as shown on Map 2. T2 and T3: through a United Nations checkpoint and via the road constructed across the buffer zone to Gebel Katrina, as shown on Map 2. T2, T3, and T4: via helicopters flying within a corridor at the times, and according to a flight profile, agreed to by the Joint Commission. The helicopters will be checked by the United Nations Force at landing sites outside the perimeter of the installations. Israel will inform the United Nations Force at least one hour in advance of each intended movement to and from the installations. Israel shall be entitled to evacuate sick and wounded and summon medical experts and medical teams at any time after giving immediate notice to the United Nations Force. The details of the above principles and all other matters in this Article requiring coordination by the Parties will be handled by the Joint Commission. These technical installations will be withdrawn when Israeli forces withdraw from the interim withdrawal line, or at a time agreed by the parties.

Article VI Disposition of Installations and Military Barriers

Disposition of installations and military barriers will be determined by the Parties in accordance with the following guidelines: Up to three weeks before Israeli withdrawal from any area, the Joint Commission will arrange for Israeli and Egyptian liaison and technical teams to conduct a joint inspection of all appropriate installations to agree upon condition of structures and articles which will be transferred to Egyptian control and to arrange for such transfer. Israel will declare, at that time, its plans for disposition of installations and articles within the installations. Israel undertakes to transfer to Egypt all agreed infrastructures, utilities, and installations intact, inter alia, airfields, roads, pumping stations, and ports. Israel will present to Egypt the information necessary for the maintenance and operation of the facilities. Egyptian technical teams will be permitted to observe and familiarize themselves with the operation of these facilities for a period of up to two weeks prior to transfer. When Israel relinquishes Israeli military water points near El Arish and El Tor, Egyptian technical teams will assume control of those installations and ancillary equipment in accordance with an orderly transfer process arranged beforehand by the Joint Commission. Egypt undertakes to continue to make available at all water supply points the normal quantity of currently available water up to the time Israel withdraws behind the international boundary, unless otherwise agreed in the Joint Commission. Israel will make its best effort to remove or destroy all military barriers, including obstacles and minefields, in the areas and adjacent waters from which it withdraws, according to the following concept: Military barriers will be cleared first from areas near populations, roads and major installations and utilities. For those obstacles and minefields which cannot be removed or destroyed prior to Israeli withdrawal, Israel will provide detailed maps to Egypt and the United Nations through the Joint Commission not later than 15 days before entry of United Nations forces into the affected areas. Egyptian engineers will enter those areas after United Nations forces enter to conduct barrier clearance operations in accordance with Egyptian plans to be submitted prior to implementation.

Article VII Surveillance Activities

Aerial surveillance activities during the withdrawal will be carried out as follows: Both Parties request the United States to continue airborne surveillance flights in accordance with previous agreements until the completion of final Israeli withdrawal. Flight profiles will cover the Limited Forces Zones to monitor the limitations on forces and armaments, and to determine that Israeli armed forces have withdrawn from the areas described in Article II of Annex I, Article II of this Appendix, and Maps 2 and 3, and that these forces thereafter remain behind their lines. Special inspection flights may be flown at the request of either Party or of the United Nations. Only the main elements in the military organizations of each Party, as described in Annex I and in this Appendix, will be reported. Both Parties request the United States operated Sinai Field Mission to continue its operations in accordance with previous agreements until completion of the Israeli withdrawal from the area east of the Giddi and Mitla Passes. Thereafter, the Mission will be terminated.

Article VIII Exercise of Egyptian Sovereignty
Egypt will resume the exercise of its full sovereignty over evacuated parts of the Sinai upon Israeli withdrawal as provided for in Article I of this Treaty.

ANNEX II Map of Israel-Egypt International Boundary

ANNEX III Protocol Concerning Relations of the Parties

Article 1 Diplomatic and Consular Relations
The Parties agree to establish diplomatic and consular relations and to exchange ambassadors upon completion of the interim withdrawal.

Article 2 Economic and Trade Relations
The Parties agree to remove all discriminatory barriers to normal economic relations and to terminate economic boycotts of each other upon completion of the interim withdrawal. As soon as possible, and not later than six months after the completion of the interim withdrawal, the Parties will enter negotiations with a view to concluding an agreement on trade and commerce for the purpose of promoting beneficial economic relations.

Article 3 Cultural Relations
The Parties agree to establish normal cultural relations following completion of the interim withdrawal. They agree on the desirability of cultural exchanges in all fields, and shall, as soon as possible and not later than six months after completion of the interim withdrawal, enter into negotiations with a view to concluding a cultural agreement for this purpose.

Article 4 Freedom of Movement
Upon completion of the interim withdrawal, each Party will permit the free

movement of the nationals and vehicles of the other into and within its territory according to the general rules applicable to nationals and vehicles of other states. Neither Party will impose discriminatory restrictions on the free movement of persons and vehicles from its territory to the territory of the other. Mutual unimpeded access to places of religious and historical significance will be provided on a non-discriminatory basis.

Article 5 Cooperation for Development and Good Neighborly Relations
The Parties recognize a mutuality of interest in good neighbourly relations and agree to consider means to promote such relations. The Parties will cooperate in promoting peace, stability and development in their region. Each agrees toconsider proposals the other may wish to make to this end. The Parties shall seek to foster mutual understanding and tolerance and will, accordingly, abstain from hostile propaganda against each other.

Article 6 Transportation and Telecommunications
The Parties recognize as applicable to each other the rights, privileges and obligations provided for by the aviation agreements to which they are both party, particularly by the Convention on International Civil Aviation, 1944 ("The Chicago Convention") and the International Air Services Transit Agreement, 1944. Upon completion of the interim withdrawal any declaration of national emergency by a party under Article 89 of the Chicago Convention will not be applied to the other party on a discriminatory basis. Egypt agrees that the use of airfields left by Israel near El-Arish, Rafah, Ras El-Nagb and Sharm El-Sheikh shall be for civilian purposes only, including possible commercial use by all nations. As soon as possible and not later than six months after the completion of the interim withdrawal, the Parties shall enter into negotiations for the purpose of concluding a civil aviation agreement. The Parties will reopen and maintain roads and railways between their countries and will consider further road and rail links. The Parties further agree that a highway will be constructed and maintained between Egypt, Israel and Jordan near Eilat with guaranteed free and peaceful passage of persons, vehicles and goods between Egypt and Jordan, without prejudice to their sovereignty over that part of the highway which falls within their respective territory. Upon completion of the interim withdrawal, normal postal, telephone, telex, data facsimile, wireless and cable communications and television relay services by cable, radio and satellite shall be established between the two Parties in accordance with all relevant international conventions and regulations. Upon completion of the interim withdrawal, each Party shall grant normal access to its ports for vessels and cargoes of the other, as well as vessels and cargoes destined for or coming from the other. Such access will be granted on the same conditions generally applicable to vessels and cargoes of other nations. Article 5 of the Treaty of Peace will be implemented upon the exchange of instruments of ratification of the aforementioned treaty.

Article 7 Enjoyment of Human Rights
The Parties affirm their commitment to respect and observe human rights and fundamental freedoms for all, and they will promote these rights and freedoms in accordance with the United Nations Charter.

Article 8 Territorial Seas
Without prejudice to the provisions of Article 5 of the Treaty of Peace each Party recognizes the right of the vessels of the other Party to innocent passage through its territorial sea in accordance with the rules of international law.

AGREED MINUTES

Article I Egypt's resumption of the exercise of full sovereignty over the Sinai provided for in paragraph 2 of Article I shall occur with regard to each area upon Israel's withdrawal from the area. Article IV It is agreed between the parties that the review provided for in Article IV (4) will be undertaken when requested by either party, commencing within three months of such a request, but that any amendment can be made only by mutual agreement of both parties. Article V The second sentence of paragraph 2 of Article V shall not be construed as limiting the first sentence of that paragraph. The foregoing is not to be construed as contravening the second sentence of paragraph 2 of Article V, which reads as follows: "The Parties will respect each other's right to navigation and overflight for access to either country through the Strait of Tiran and the Gulf of Aqaba." Article VI (2) The provisions of Article VI shall not be construed in contradiction to the provisions of the framework for peace in the Middle East agreed at Camp David. The foregoing is not to be construed as contravening the provisions of Article VI (2) of the Treaty, which reads as follows: "The Parties undertake to fulfill in good faith their obligations under this Treaty, without regard to action of any other Party and independently of any instrument external to this Treaty." Article VI (5) It is agreed by the Parties that there is no assertion that this Treaty prevails over other Treaties or agreements or that other Treaties or agreements prevail over this Treaty. The foregoing is not to be construed as contravening the provisions of Article VI (5) of the Treaty, which reads as follows: "Subject to Article 103 of the United Nations Charter, in the event of a conflict between the obligations of the Parties under the present Treaty and any of their other obligations, the obligation under this Treaty will be binding and implemented." Annex I Article VI, Paragraph 8, of Annex I provides as follows: "The Parties shall agree on the nations from which the United Nations forces and observers will be drawn. They will be drawn from nations other than those which are permanent members of the United Nations Security Council." The Parties have agreed as follows: "With respect to the provisions of paragraph 8, Article VI, of Annex 1, if no agreement is reached between the Parties, they will accept or support a U.S. proposal concerning the composition of the United Nations force and observers."

Annex III
The Treaty of Peace and Annex III thereto provide for establishing normal economic relations between the Parties. In accordance herewith, it is agreed that such relations will include normal commercial sales of oil by Egypt to Israel, and that Israel shall be fully entitled to make bids for Egyptian-origin oil not needed for Egyptian domestic oil consumption, and Egypt and its oil concessionaires will entertain bids made by Israel, on the same basis and terms as apply to other bidders for such oil.

For the Government of Israel For the Government of the Arab Republic of Egypt Witnessed by: Jimmy Carter President of the United States of America

V-9. Treaty of Peace Between The State of Israel and The Hashemite Kingdom of Jordan (1994).
<http://metalab.unc.edu/sullivan/docs?Sinail.html>.

Authentic Texts: Hebrew, Arabic, English

State Signatories
Israel; Jordan

State Parties
Israel; Jordan

Full Text

Preamble
The Government of the State of Israel and the Government of the Hashemite Kingdom of Jordan:
Bearing in mind the Washington Declaration, signed by them on 25th July, 1994, and which they are both committed to honour:
Aiming at the achievement of a just, lasting and comprehensive peace in the Middle East based on Security Council resolutions 242 and 338 in all their aspects:
Bearing in mind the importance of maintaining and strengthening peace based on freedom, equality, justice and respect for fundamental human rights, thereby overcoming psychological barriers and promoting human dignity:
Reaffirming their faith in the purposes and principles of the Charter of the United Nations and recognising their right and obligation to live in peace with each other as well as with all states, within secure and recognised boundaries:
Desiring to develop friendly relations and co-operation between them in accordance with the principles of international law governing international relations in time of peace:
Desiring as well to ensure lasting security for both their States and in particular to avoid threats and the use of force between them:
Bearing in mind that in their Washington Declaration of 25th July, 1994, they declared the termination of the state of belligerency between them:
Deciding to establish peace between them in accordance with this Treaty of Peace:
Have agreed as follows:

Article 1 - Establishment of Peace
Peace is hereby established between the State of Israel and the Hashemite Kingdom of Jordan (the "Parties") effective from the exchange of the instruments of ratification of this Treaty.

Article 2 - General Principles
The Parties will apply between them the provisions of the Charter of the United Nations and the principles of international law governing relations among states in time of peace. In particular:

1. They recognise and will respect each other's sovereignty, territorial integrity and political independence;
2. They recognise and will respect each other's right to live in peace within secure and recognised boundaries;
3. They will develop good neighbourly relations of co-operation between them to ensure lasting security, will refrain from the threat or use of force against each other and will settle all disputes between them by peaceful means;
4. They respect and recognise the sovereignty, territorial integrity and political independence of every state in the region;
5. They respect and recognise the pivotal role of human development and dignity in regional and bilateral relationships;
6. They further believe that within their control, involuntary movements of persons in such a way as to adversely prejudice the security of either Party should not be permitted.

Article 3 - International Boundary
1. The international boundary between Israel and Jordan is delimited with reference to the boundary definition under the Mandate as is shown in Annex I (a), on the mapping materials attached thereto and coordinates specified therein.
2. The boundary, as set out in Annex I (a), is the permanent, secure and recognised international boundary between Israel and Jordan, without prejudice to the status of any territories that came under Israeli military government control in 1967.
3. The Parties recognise the international boundary, as well as each other's territory, territorial waters and airspace, as inviolable, and will respect and comply with them.
4. The demarcation of the boundary will take place as set forth in Appendix (I) to Annex I and will be concluded not later than 9 months after the signing of the Treaty.
5. It is agreed that where the boundary follows a river, in the event of natural changes in the course of the flow of the river as described in Annex I (a), the boundary shall follow the new course of the flow. In the event of any other changes the boundary shall not be affected unless otherwise agreed.
6. Immediately upon the exchange of the instruments of ratification of this Treaty, each Party will deploy on its side of the international boundary as defined in Annex I (a).
7. The Parties shall, upon the signature of the Treaty, enter into negotiations to conclude, within 9 months, an agreement on the delimitation of their maritime boundary in the Gulf of Aqaba.
8. Taking into account the special circumstances of the Naharayim Baqura area, which is under Jordanian sovereignty, with Israeli private ownership rights, the Parties agree to apply the provisions set out in Annex I (b).
9. With respect to the Zofar Al-Ghamr area, the provisions set out in Annex I (c) will apply.

Article 4 - Security
1. a. Both Parties, acknowledging that mutual understanding and cooperation in security-related matters will form a significant part of their relations and will

further enhance the security of the region, take upon themselves to base their security relations on mutual trust, advancement of joint interests and co-operation, and to aim towards a regional framework of partnership in peace.

b. Towards that goal, the Parties recognise the achievements of the European Community and European Union in the development of the Conference on Security and Co-operation in Europe (CSCE) and commit themselves to the creation, in the Middle East, of a Conference on Security and Co-operation in the Middle East (CSCME).

This commitment entails the adoption of regional models of security successfully implemented in the post World War era (along the lines of the Helsinki Process) culminating in a regional zone of security and stability.

2. The obligations referred to in this Article are without prejudice to the inherent right of self-defence in accordance with the United Nations Charter.

3. The Parties undertake, in accordance with the provisions of this Article, the following:

a. to refrain from the threat or use of force or weapons, conventional, non-conventional or of any other kind, against each other, or of other actions or activities that adversely affect the security of the other Party;

b. to refrain from organising, instigating, inciting, assisting or participating in acts or threats of belligerency, hostility, subversion or violence against the other Party;

c. to take necessary and effective measures to ensure that acts or threats of belligerency, hostility, subversion or violence against the other Party do not originate from, and are not committed within, through or over their territory (hereinafter the term "territory" includes the airspace and territorial waters).

4. Consistent with the era of peace and with the efforts to build regional security and to avoid and prevent aggression and violence, the Parties further agree to refrain from the following:

a. joining or in any way assisting, promoting or co-operating with any coalition, organisation or alliance with a military or security character with a third party, the objectives or activities of which include launching aggression or other acts of military hostility against the other Party, in contravention of the provisions of the present Treaty;

b. allowing the entry, stationing and operating on their territory, or through it, of military forces, personnel or materiel of a third party, in circumstances which may adversely prejudice the security of the other Party.

5. Both Parties will take necessary and effective measures, and will co-operate in combating terrorism of all kinds. The Parties undertake:

a. to take necessary and effective measures to prevent acts of terrorism, subversion or violence from being carried out from their territory or through it and to take necessary and effective measures to combat such activities and all their perpetrators;

b. without prejudice to the basic rights of freedom of expression and association, to take necessary and effective measures to prevent the entry, presence and operation in their territory of any group or organisation, and their

infrastructure, which threatens the security of the other Party by the use of, or incitement to the use of, violent means;
   c. to co-operate in preventing and combating cross-boundary infiltrations.
6. Any question as to the implementation of this Article will be dealt with through a mechanism of consultations which will include a liaison system, verification, supervision, and where necessary, other mechanisms, and higher level consultations. The details of the mechanism of consultations will be contained in an agreement to be concluded by the Parties within 3 months of the exchange of the instruments of ratification of this Treaty.
7. The Parties undertake to work as a matter of priority, and as soon as possible in the context of the Multilateral Working Group on Arms Control and Regional Security, and jointly, towards the following:
   a. the creation in the Middle East of a region free from hostile alliances and coalitions;
   b. the creation of a Middle East free from weapons of mass destruction, both conventional and non-conventional, in the context of a comprehensive, lasting and stable peace, characterised by the renunciation of the use of force, and by reconciliation and goodwill.

Article 5 - Diplomatic and Other Bilateral Relations
1. The Parties agree to establish full diplomatic and consular relations and to exchange resident ambassadors within one month of the exchange of the instruments of ratification of this Treaty.
2. The Parties agree that the normal relationship between them will further include economic and cultural relations.

Article 6 - Water
With the view to achieving a comprehensive and lasting settlement of all the water problems between them:
1. The Parties agree mutually to recognise the rightful allocations of both of them in Jordan River and Yarmouk River waters and Araba Arava ground water in accordance with the agreed acceptable principles, quantities and quality as set out in Annex II, which shall be fully respected and complied with.
2. The Parties, recognising the necessity to find a practical, just and agreed solution to their water problems and with the view that the subject of water can form the basis for the advancement of co-operation between them, jointly undertake to ensure that the management and development of their water resources do not, in any way, harm the water resources of the other Party.
3. The Parties recognise that their water resources are not sufficient to meet their needs. More water should be supplied for their use through various methods, including projects of regional and international co-operation.
4. In light of paragraph 3 of this Article, with the understanding that co-operation in water-related subjects would be to the benefit of both Parties, and will help alleviate their water shortages, and that water issues along their entire boundary must be dealt with in their totality, including the possibility of trans-boundary water transfers, the Parties agree to search for ways to alleviate water shortages and to co-operate in the following fields:

a. development of existing and new water resources, increasing the water availability, including cooperation on a regional basis as appropriate, and minimising wastage of water resources through the chain of their uses;
b. prevention of contamination of water resources;
c. mutual assistance in the alleviation of water shortages;
d. transfer of information and joint research and development in water-related subjects, and review of the potentials for enhancement of water resources development and use.
5. The implementation of both Parties' undertakings under this Article is detailed in Annex II.

Article 7 - Economic Relations
1. Viewing economic development and prosperity as pillars of peace, security and harmonious relations between states, peoples and individual human beings, the Parties, taking note of understandings reached between them, affirm their mutual desire to promote economic co-operation between them, as well as within the framework of wider regional economic co-operation.
2. In order to accomplish this goal, the Parties agree to the following:
a. to remove all discriminatory barriers to normal economic relations, to terminate economic boycotts directed at the other Party, and to co-operate in terminating boycotts against either Party by third parties:
b. recognising that the principle of free and unimpeded flow of goods and services should guide their relations, the Parties will enter into negotiations with a view to concluding agreements on economic co-operation, including trade and the establishment of a free trade area or areas, investment, banking, industrial co-operation and labour, for the purpose of promoting beneficial economic relations, based on principles to be agreed upon, as well as on human development considerations on a regional basis. These negotiations will be concluded no later than 6 months from the exchange of the instruments of ratification of this Treaty;
c. to co-operate bilaterally, as well as in multilateral forums, towards the promotion of their respective economies and of their neighbourly economic relations with other regional parties.

Article 8 - Refugees and Displaced Persons
1. Recognising the massive human problems caused to both Parties by the conflict in the Middle East, as well as the contribution made by them towards the alleviation of human suffering, the Parties will seek to further alleviate those problems arising on a bilateral level.
2. Recognising that the above human problems caused by the conflict in the Middle East cannot be fully resolved on the bilateral level, the Parties will seek to resolve them in appropriate forums, in accordance with international law, including the following:
a. in the case of displaced persons, in a quadripartite committee together with Egypt and the Palestinians;
b. in the case of refugees;
i. in the framework of the Multilateral Working Group on Refugees.

ii. in negotiations, in a framework to be agreed, bilateral or otherwise, in conjunction with and at the same time as the permanent status negotiations pertaining to the Territories referred to in Article 3 of this Treaty;

c. through the implementation of agreed United Nations programmes and other agreed international economic programmes concerning refugees and displaced persons, including assistance to their settlement.

Article 9 - Places of Historical and Religious Significance and Interfaith Relations

1. Each Party will provide freedom of access to places of religious and historical significance.
2. In this regard, in accordance with the Washington Declaration, Israel respects the present special role of the Hashemite Kingdom of Jordan in Muslim Holy shrines in Jerusalem. When negotiations on the permanent status will take place, Israel will give high priority to the Jordanian historic role in these shrines.
3. The Parties will act together to promote interfaith relations among the three monotheistic religions, with the aim of working towards religious understanding, moral commitment, freedom of religious worship, and tolerance and peace.

Article 10 - Cultural and Scientific Exchanges

The Parties, wishing to remove biases developed through periods of conflict, recognise the desirability of cultural and scientific exchanges in all fields, and agree to establish normal cultural relations between them. Thus, they shall, as soon as possible and not later than 9 months from the exchange of the instruments of ratification of this Treaty, conclude the negotiations on cultural and scientific agreements.

Article 11 - Mutual Understanding and Good Neighbourly Relations

1. The Parties will seek to foster mutual understanding and tolerance based on shared historic values, and accordingly undertake:

a. to abstain from hostile or discriminatory propaganda against each other, and to take all possible legal and administrative measures to prevent the dissemination of such propaganda by any organisation or individual present in the territory of either Party;

b. as soon as possible, and not later than 3 months from the exchange of the instruments of ratification of this Treaty, to repeal all adverse or discriminatory references and expressions of hostility in their respective legislation;

c. to refrain in all government publications from any such references or expressions;

d. to ensure mutual enjoyment by each other's citizens of due process of law within their respective legal systems and before their courts.

2. Paragraph 1 (a) of this Article is without prejudice to the right to freedom of expression as contained in the International Covenant on Civil and Political Rights.
3. A joint committee shall be formed to examine incidents where one Party claims there has been a violation of this Article.

Article 12 - Combating Crime and Drugs

The Parties will co-operate in combating crime, with an emphasis on smuggling, and will take all necessary measures to combat and prevent such activities as the production of, as well as the trafficking in illicit drugs, and will bring to trial perpetrators of such acts. In this regard, they take note of the understandings reached between them in the above spheres, in accordance with Annex III and undertake to conclude all relevant agreements not later than 9 months from the date of the exchange of the instruments of ratification of this Treaty.

Article 13 - Transportation and Roads
Taking note of the progress already made in the area of transportation, the Parties recognise the mutuality of interest in good neighbourly relations in the area of transportation and agree to the following means to promote relations between them in this sphere:
1. Each party will permit the free movement of nationals and vehicles of the other into and within its territory according to the general rules applicable to nationals and vehicles of other states. Neither Party will impose discriminatory taxes or restrictions on the free movement of persons and vehicles from its territory to the territory of the other.
2. The Parties will open and maintain roads and border-crossings between their countries and will consider further road and rail links between them.
3. The Parties will continue their negotiations concerning mutual transportation agreements in the above and other areas, such as joint projects, traffic safety, transport standards and norms, licensing of vehicles, land passages, shipment of goods and cargo, and meteorology, to be concluded not later than 6 months from the exchange of the instruments of ratification of this Treaty.
4. The Parties agree to continue their negotiations for a highway to be constructed and maintained between Egypt, Israel and Jordan near Eilat.

Article 14 - Freedom of Navigation and Access to Ports
1. Without prejudice to the provisions of paragraph 3, each Party recognises the right of the vessels of the other Party to innocent passage through its territorial waters in accordance with the rules of international law.
2. Each Party will grant normal access to its ports for vessels and cargoes of the other, as well as vessels and cargoes destined for or coming from the other Party. Such access will be granted on the same conditions as generally applicable to vessels and cargoes of other nations.
3. The Parties consider the Strait of Tiran and the Gulf of Aqaba to be international waterways open to all nations for unimpeded and non-suspendable freedom of navigation and overflight. The Parties will respect each other's right to navigation and overflight for access to either Party through the Strait of Tiran and the Gulf of Aqaba.

Article 15 - Civil Aviation
1. The Parties recognise as applicable to each other the rights, privileges and obligations provided for by the multilateral aviation agreements to which they are both party, particularly by the 1944 Convention on International Civil Aviation

(the Chicago Convention) and the 1944 International Air Services Transit Agreement.
2. Any declaration of national emergency by a Party under Article 89 of the Chicago Convention will not be applied to the other Party on a discriminatory basis.
3. The Parties take note of the negotiations on the international air corridor to be opened between them in accordance with the Washington Declaration. In addition, the Parties shall, upon ratification of this Treaty, enter into negotiations for the purpose of concluding a Civil Aviation Agreement. All the above negotiations are to be concluded not later than 6 months from the exchange of the instruments of ratification of this Treaty.

Article 16 - Posts and Telecommunications
The Parties take note of the opening between them, in accordance with the Washington Declaration, of direct telephone and facsimile lines. Postal links, the negotiations on which having been concluded, will be activated upon the signature of this Treaty. The Parties further agree that normal wireless and cable communications and television relay services by cable, radio and satellite, will be established between them, in accordance with all relevant international conventions and regulations. The negotiations on these subjects will be concluded not later than 9 months from the exchange of the instruments of ratification of this Treaty.

Article 17 - Tourism
The Parties affirm their mutual desire to promote co-operation between them in the field of tourism. In order to accomplish this goal, the Parties - taking note of the understandings reached between them concerning tourism - agree to negotiate, as soon as possible, and to conclude not later than 3 months from the exchange of the instruments of ratification of this Treaty, an agreement to facilitate and encourage mutual tourism and tourism from third countries.

Article 18 - Environment
The Parties will co-operate in matters relating to the environment, a sphere to which they attach great importance, including conservation of nature and prevention of pollution, as set forth in Annex IV. They will negotiate an agreement on the above, to be concluded not later than 6 months from the exchange of the instruments of ratification of this Treaty.

Article 19 - Energy
1. The Parties will co-operate in the development of energy resources, including the development of energy related projects such as the utilisation of solar energy.
2. The Parties, having concluded their negotiations on the interconnecting of their electric grids in the Eilat-Aqaba area, will implement the interconnecting upon the signature of this Treaty. The Parties view this step as a part of a wider binational and regional concept. They agree to continue their negotiations as soon as possible to widen the scope of their interconnected grids.
3. The Parties will conclude the relevant agreements in the field of energy within 6 months from the date of exchange of the instruments of ratification of this Treaty.

Article 20 - Rift Valley Development

The Parties attach great importance to the integrated development of the Jordan Rift Valley area, including joint projects in the economic, environmental, energy-related and tourism fields. Taking note of the Terms of Reference developed in the framework of the Trilateral Israel-Jordan-US Economic Committee towards the Jordan Rift Valley Development Master Plan, they will vigorously continue their efforts towards the completion of planning and towards implementation.

Article 21 - Health

The Parties will co-operate in the area of health and shall negotiate with a view to the conclusion of an agreement within 9 months of the exchange of the instruments of ratification of this Treaty.

Article 22 - Agriculture

The Parties will co-operate in the areas of agriculture, including veterinary services, plant protection, biotechnology and marketing, and shall negotiate with a view to the conclusion of an agreement within 6 months from the date of the exchange of instruments of ratification of this Treaty.

Article 23 - Aqaba and Eilat

The Parties agree to enter into negotiations, as soon as possible, and not later than one month from the exchange of the instruments of ratification of this Treaty, on arrangements that would enable the joint development of the towns of Aqaba and Eilat with regard to such matters, inter alia, as joint tourism development, joint customs posts, free trade zone, co-operation in aviation, prevention of pollution, maritime matters, police, customs and health co-operation. The Parties will conclude all relevant agreements within 9 months from the exchange of instruments of ratification of the Treaty.

Article 24 - Claims

The Parties agree to establish a claims commission for the mutual settlement of all financial claims.

Article 25 - Rights and Obligations

1. This Treaty does not affect and shall not be interpreted as affecting, in any way, the rights and obligations of the Parties under the Charter of the United Nations.
2. The Parties undertake to fulfil in good faith their obligations under this Treaty, without regard to action or inaction of any other party and independently of any instrument inconsistent with this Treaty. For the purposes of this paragraph, each Party represents to the other that in its opinion and interpretation there is no inconsistency between their existing treaty obligations and this Treaty.
3. They further undertake to take all the necessary measures for the application in their relations of the provisions of the multilateral conventions to which they are parties, including the submission of appropriate notification to the Secretary General of the United Nations and other depositories of such conventions.
4. Both Parties will also take all the necessary steps to abolish all pejorative references to the other Party, in multilateral conventions to which they are parties, to the extent that such references exist.

5. The Parties undertake not to enter into any obligation in conflict with this Treaty.
6. Subject to Article 103 of the United Nations Charter, in the event of a conflict between the obligations of the Parties under the present Treaty and any of their other obligations, the obligations under this Treaty will be binding and implemented.

Article 26 - Legislation
Within 3 months of the exchange of the instruments of ratification of this Treaty, the Parties undertake to enact any legislation necessary in order to implement the Treaty, and to terminate any international commitments and to repeal any legislation that is inconsistent with the Treaty.

Article 27 - Ratification and Annexes
1. This Treaty shall be ratified by both Parties in conformity with their respective national procedures. It shall enter into force on the exchange of the instruments of ratification.
2. The Annexes, Appendices, and other attachments to this Treaty shall be considered integral parts thereof.

Article 28 - Interim Measures
The Parties will apply, in certain spheres, to be agreed upon, interim measures pending the conclusion of the relevant agreements in accordance with this Treaty, as stipulated in Annex V.

Article 29 - Settlement of Disputes
1. Disputes arising out of the application or interpretation of this Treaty shall be resolved by negotiations.
2. Any such disputes which cannot be settled by negotiations shall be resolved by conciliation or submitted to arbitration.

Article 30 - Registration
This Treaty shall be transmitted to the Secretary General of the United Nations for registration in accordance with the provisions of Article 102 of the Charter of the United Nations.
Done at the Arava Araba Crossing Point this day Heshvan 21st, 5755, Jumada Al-Ula, 21st, 1415 which corresponds to 26th October, 1994 in the Hebrew, Arabic and English languages, all texts being equally authentic. In case of divergence of interpretation the English text shall prevail.

V-10. **Israeli-Palestinian Interim Agreement on the West Bank and the Gaza Strip, Washington, D.C., September 28, 1995,** <http://www.israel-mfa.gov.il/peace/iaannex1.html>.

Parties
Israel; Palestine Liberation Organization

Full Text

The Government of the State of Israel and the Palestine Liberation Organization (hereinafter "the PLO"), the representative of the Palestinian people;

PREAMBLE

WITHIN the framework of the Middle East peace process initiated at Madrid in October 1991;

REAFFIRMING their determination to put an end to decades of confrontation and to live in peaceful coexistence, mutual dignity and security, while recognizing their mutual legitimate and political rights;

REAFFIRMING their desire to achieve a just, lasting and comprehensive peace settlement and historic reconciliation through the agreed political process;

RECOGNIZING that the peace process and the new era that it has created, as well as the new relationship established between the two Parties as described above, are irreversible, and the determination of the two Parties to maintain, sustain and continue the peace process;

RECOGNIZING that the aim of the Israeli-Palestinian negotiations within the current Middle East peace process is, among other things, to establish a Palestinian Interim Self-Government Authority, i.e. the elected Council (hereinafter "the Council" or "the Palestinian Council"), and the elected Ra'ees of the Executive Authority, for the Palestinian people in the West Bank and the Gaza Strip, for a transitional period not exceeding five years from the date of signing the Agreement on the Gaza Strip and the Jericho Area (hereinafter "the Gaza-Jericho Agreement") on May 4, 1994, leading to a permanent settlement based on Security Council Resolutions 242 and 338;

REAFFIRMING their understanding that the interim self-government arrangements contained in this Agreement are an integral part of the whole peace process, that the negotiations on the permanent status, that will start as soon as possible but not later than May 4, 1996, will lead to the implementation of Security Council Resolutions 242 and 338, and that the Interim Agreement shall settle all the issues of the interim period and that no such issues will be deferred to the agenda of the permanent status negotiations;

REAFFIRMING their adherence to the mutual recognition and commitments expressed in the letters dated September 9, 1993, signed by and exchanged between the Prime Minister of Israel and the Chairman of the PLO;

DESIROUS of putting into effect the Declaration of Principles on Interim Self-Government Arrangements signed at Washington, D.C. on September 13, 1993, and the Agreed Minutes thereto (hereinafter "the DOP") and in particular Article III and Annex I concerning the holding of direct, free and general political elections for the Council and the Ra'ees of the Executive Authority in order that the Palestinian people in the West Bank, Jerusalem and the Gaza Strip may democratically elect accountable representatives;

RECOGNIZING that these elections will constitute a significant interim preparatory step toward the realization of the legitimate rights of the Palestinian people and their just requirements and will provide a democratic basis for the establishment of Palestinian institutions;

REAFFIRMING their mutual commitment to act, in accordance with this Agreement, immediately, efficiently and effectively against acts or threats of terrorism, violence or incitement, whether committed by Palestinians or Israelis;

FOLLOWING the Gaza-Jericho Agreement; the Agreement on Preparatory Transfer of Powers and Responsibilities signed at Erez on August 29, 1994 (hereinafter "the Preparatory Transfer Agreement"); and the Protocol on Further Transfer of Powers and Responsibilities signed at Cairo on August 27, 1995 (hereinafter "the Further Transfer Protocol"); which three agreements will be superseded by this Agreement;

HEREBY AGREE as follows:

CHAPTER I - THE COUNCIL

ARTICLE I
Transfer of Authority

1. Israel shall transfer powers and responsibilities as specified in this Agreement from the Israeli military government and its Civil Administration to the Council in accordance with this Agreement. Israel shall continue to exercise powers and responsibilities not so transferred.

2. Pending the inauguration of the Council, the powers and responsibilities transferred to the Council shall be exercised by the Palestinian Authority established in accordance with the Gaza-Jericho Agreement, which shall also have all the rights, liabilities and obligations to be assumed by the Council in this regard. Accordingly, the term "Council" throughout this Agreement shall, pending the inauguration of the Council, be construed as meaning the Palestinian Authority.

3. The transfer of powers and responsibilities to the police force established by the Palestinian Council in accordance with Article XIV below (hereinafter "the Palestinian Police") shall be accomplished in a phased manner, as detailed in this Agreement and in the Protocol concerning Redeployment and Security Arrangements attached as Annex I to this Agreement (hereinafter "Annex I").

4. As regards the transfer and assumption of authority in civil spheres, powers and responsibilities shall be transferred and assumed as set out in the Protocol Concerning Civil Affairs attached as Annex III to this Agreement (hereinafter "Annex III").

5. After the inauguration of the Council, the Civil Administration in the West Bank will be dissolved, and the Israeli military government shall be withdrawn. The withdrawal of the military government shall not prevent it from exercising the powers and responsibilities not transferred to the Council.

6. A Joint Civil Affairs Coordination and Cooperation Committee (hereinafter "the CAC"), Joint Regional Civil Affairs Subcommittees, one for the Gaza Strip and the other for the West Bank, and District Civil Liaison Offices in the West Bank shall be established in order to provide for coordination and

cooperation in civil affairs between the Council and Israel, as detailed in Annex III.

7. The offices of the Council, and the offices of its Ra'ees and its Executive Authority and other committees, shall be located in areas under Palestinian territorial jurisdiction in the West Bank and the Gaza Strip.

ARTICLE II
Elections

1. In order that the Palestinian people of the West Bank and the Gaza Strip may govern themselves according to democratic principles, direct, free and general political elections will be held for the Council and the Ra'ees of the Executive Authority of the Council in accordance with the provisions set out in the Protocol concerning Elections attached as Annex II to this Agreement (hereinafter "Annex II").

2. These elections will constitute a significant interim preparatory step towards the realization of the legitimate rights of the Palestinian people and their just requirements and will provide a democratic basis for the establishment of Palestinian institutions.

3. Palestinians of Jerusalem who live there may participate in the election process in accordance with the provisions contained in this Article and in Article VI of Annex II (Election Arrangements concerning Jerusalem).

4. The elections shall be called by the Chairman of the Palestinian Authority immediately following the signing of this Agreement to take place at the earliest practicable date following the redeployment of Israeli forces in accordance with Annex I, and consistent with the requirements of the election timetable as provided in Annex II, the Election Law and the Election Regulations, as defined in Article I of Annex II.

ARTICLE III
Structure of the Palestinian Council

1. The Palestinian Council and the Ra'ees of the Executive Authority of the Council constitute the Palestinian Interim Self-Government Authority, which will be elected by the Palestinian people of the West Bank, Jerusalem and the Gaza Strip for the transitional period agreed in Article I of the DOP.

2. The Council shall possess both legislative power and executive power, in accordance with Articles VII and IX of the DOP. The Council shall carry out and be responsible for all the legislative and executive powers and

responsibilities transferred to it under this Agreement. The exercise of legislative powers shall be in accordance with Article XVIII of this Agreement (Legislative Powers of the Council).

3. The Council and the Ra'ees of the Executive Authority of the Council shall be directly and simultaneously elected by the Palestinian people of the West Bank, Jerusalem and the Gaza Strip, in accordance with the provisions of this Agreement and the Election Law and Regulations, which shall not be contrary to the provisions of this Agreement.

4. The Council and the Ra'ees of the Executive Authority of the Council shall be elected for a transitional period not exceeding five years from the signing of the Gaza-Jericho Agreement on May 4, 1994.

5. Immediately upon its inauguration, the Council will elect from among its members a Speaker. The Speaker will preside over the meetings of the Council, administer the Council and its committees, decide on the agenda of each meeting, and lay before the Council proposals for voting and declare their results.

6. The jurisdiction of the Council shall be as determined in Article XVII of this Agreement (Jurisdiction).

7. The organization, structure and functioning of the Council shall be in accordance with this Agreement and the Basic Law for the Palestinian Interim Self-government Authority, which Law shall be adopted by the Council. The Basic Law and any regulations made under it shall not be contrary to the provisions of this Agreement.

8. The Council shall be responsible under its executive powers for the offices, services and departments transferred to it and may establish, within its jurisdiction, ministries and subordinate bodies, as necessary for the fulfillment of its responsibilities.

9. The Speaker will present for the Council's approval proposed internal procedures that will regulate, among other things, the decision-making processes of the Council.

ARTICLE IV
Size of the Council

The Palestinian Council shall be composed of 82 representatives and the Ra'ees of the Executive Authority, who will be directly and simultaneously elected by the Palestinian people of the West Bank, Jerusalem and the Gaza Strip.

ARTICLE V
The Executive Authority of the Council

1. The Council will have a committee that will exercise the executive authority of the Council, formed in accordance with paragraph 4 below (hereinafter "the Executive Authority").

2. The Executive Authority shall be bestowed with the executive authority of the Council and will exercise it on behalf of the Council. It shall determine its own internal procedures and decision making processes.

3. The Council will publish the names of the members of the Executive Authority immediately upon their initial appointment and subsequent to any changes.

4. a. The Ra'ees of the Executive Authority shall be an ex officio member of the Executive Authority.

b. All of the other members of the Executive Authority, except as provided in subparagraph c. below, shall be members of the Council, chosen and proposed to the Council by the Ra'ees of the Executive Authority and approved by the Council.

c. The Ra'ees of the Executive Authority shall have the right to appoint some persons, in number not exceeding twenty percent of the total membership of the Executive Authority, who are not members of the Council, to exercise executive authority and participate in government tasks. Such appointed members may not vote in meetings of the Council.

d. Non-elected members of the Executive Authority must have a valid address in an area under the jurisdiction of the Council.

ARTICLE VI
Other Committees of the Council

1. The Council may form small committees to simplify the proceedings of the Council and to assist in controlling the activity of its Executive Authority.

2. Each committee shall establish its own decision-making processes within the general framework of the organization and structure of the Council.

ARTICLE VII
Open Government

1. All meetings of the Council and of its committees, other than the Executive Authority, shall be open to the public, except upon a resolution of the Council or the relevant committee on the grounds of security, or commercial or personal confidentiality.

2. Participation in the deliberations of the Council, its committees and the Executive Authority shall be limited to their respective members only. Experts may be invited to such meetings to address specific issues on an ad hoc basis.

ARTICLE VIII
Judicial Review

Any person or organization affected by any act or decision of the Ra'ees of the Executive Authority of the Council or of any member of the Executive Authority, who believes that such act or decision exceeds the authority of the Ra'ees or of such member, or is otherwise incorrect in law or procedure, may apply to the relevant Palestinian Court of Justice for a review of such activity or decision.

ARTICLE IX
Powers and Responsibilities of the Council

1. Subject to the provisions of this Agreement, the Council will, within its jurisdiction, have legislative powers as set out in Article XVIII of this Agreement, as well as executive powers.

2. The executive power of the Palestinian Council shall extend to all matters within its jurisdiction under this Agreement or any future agreement that may be reached between the two Parties during the interim period. It shall include the power to formulate and conduct Palestinian policies and to supervise their implementation, to issue any rule or regulation under powers given in approved legislation and administrative decisions necessary for the realization of Palestinian self-government, the power to employ staff, sue and be sued and conclude contracts, and the power to keep and administer registers and records of the population, and issue certificates, licenses and documents.

3. The Palestinian Council's executive decisions and acts shall be consistent with the provisions of this Agreement.

4. The Palestinian Council may adopt all necessary measures in order to enforce the law and any of its decisions, and bring proceedings before the Palestinian courts and tribunals.

5. a. In accordance with the DOP, the Council will not have powers and responsibilities in the sphere of foreign relations, which sphere includes the establishment abroad of embassies, consulates or other types of foreign missions and posts or permitting their establishment in the West Bank or the Gaza Strip, the appointment of or admission of diplomatic and consular staff, and the exercise of diplomatic functions.

b. Notwithstanding the provisions of this paragraph, the PLO may conduct negotiations and sign agreements with states or international organizations for the benefit of the Council in the following cases only:

(1) economic agreements, as specifically provided in Annex V of this Agreement:

(2) agreements with donor countries for the purpose of implementing arrangements for the provision of assistance to the Council,

(3) agreements for the purpose of implementing the regional development plans detailed in Annex IV of the DOP or in agreements entered into in the framework of the multilateral negotiations, and

(4) cultural, scientific and educational agreements. Dealings between the Council and representatives of foreign states and international organizations, as well as the establishment in the West Bank and the Gaza Strip of representative offices other than those described in subparagraph 5.a above, for the purpose of implementing the agreements referred to in subparagraph 5.b above, shall not be considered foreign relations.

6. Subject to the provisions of this Agreement, the Council shall, within its jurisdiction, have an independent judicial system composed of independent Palestinian courts and tribunals.

CHAPTER 2 - REDEPLOYMENT AND SECURITY ARRANGEMENTS

ARTICLE X
Redeployment of Israeli Military Forces

1. The first phase of the Israeli military forces redeployment will cover populated areas in the West Bank - cities, towns, villages, refugee camps and hamlets - as set out in Annex I, and will be completed prior to the eve of the Palestinian elections, i. e., 22 days before the day of the elections.

2. Further redeployments of Israeli military forces to specified military locations will commence after the inauguration of the Council and will be gradually implemented commensurate with the assumption of responsibility for public order and internal security by the Palestinian Police, to be completed within 18 months from the date of the inauguration of the Council as detailed in Articles XI (Land) and XIII (Security), below and in Annex I.

3. The Palestinian Police shall be deployed and shall assume responsibility for public order and internal security for Palestinians in a phased manner in accordance with XIII (Security) below and Annex I.

4. Israel shall continue to carry the responsibility for external security, as well as the responsibility for overall security of Israelis for the purpose of safeguarding their internal security and public order.

5. For the purpose of this Agreement, "Israeli military forces" includes Israel Police and other Israeli security forces.

ARTICLE XI
Land

1. The two sides view the West Bank and the Gaza Strip as a single territorial unit, the integrity and status of which will be preserved during the interim period.

2. The two sides agree that West Bank and Gaza Strip territory, except for issues that will be negotiated in the permanent status negotiations, will come under the jurisdiction of the Palestinian Council in a phased manner, to be completed within 18 months from the date of the inauguration of the Council, as specified below:

a. Land in populated areas (Areas A and B), including government and Al Waqf land, will come under the jurisdiction of the Council during the first phase of redeployment.

b. All civil powers and responsibilities, including planning and zoning, in Areas A and B, set out in Annex III, will be transferred to and assumed by the Council during the first phase of redeployment.

c. In Area C, during the first phase of redeployment Israel will transfer to the Council civil powers and responsibilities not relating to territory, as set out in Annex III.

d. The further redeployments of Israeli military forces to specified military locations will be gradually implemented in accordance with the DOP in three phases, each to take place after an interval of six months, after the inauguration of the Council, to be completed within 18 months from the date of the inauguration of the Council.

e. During the further redeployment phases to be completed within 18 months from the date of the inauguration of the Council, powers and responsibilities relating to territory will be transferred gradually to Palestinian jurisdiction that will cover West Bank and Gaza Strip territory, except for the issues that will be negotiated in the permanent status negotiations.

f. The specified military locations referred to in Article X, paragraph 2 above will be determined in the further redeployment phases, within the specified time-frame ending not later than 18 months from the date of the inauguration of the Council, and will be negotiated in the permanent status negotiations.

3. For the purpose of this Agreement and until the completion of the first phase of the further redeployments:

a. "Area A" means the populated areas delineated by a red line and shaded in brown on attached map No. 1;

b. "Area B" means the populated areas delineated by a red line and shaded in yellow on attached map No. 1, and the built-up area of the hamlets listed in Appendix 6 to Annex I, and

c. "Area C" means areas of the West Bank outside Areas A and B, which, except for the issues that will be negotiated in the permanent status negotiations, will be gradually transferred to Palestinian jurisdiction in accordance with this Agreement.

ARTICLE XII
Arrangements for Security and Public Order

1. In order to guarantee public order and internal security for the Palestinians of the West Bank and the Gaza Strip, the Council shall establish a strong police force as set out in Article XIV below. Israel shall continue to carry the responsibility for defense against external threats, including the responsibility for protecting the Egyptian and Jordanian borders, and for defense against external threats from the sea and from the air, as well as the responsibility for overall security of Israelis and Settlements, for the purpose of safeguarding their internal security and public order, and will have all the powers to take the steps necessary to meet this responsibility.

2. Agreed security arrangements and coordination mechanisms are specified in Annex I.

3. A Joint Coordination and Cooperation Committee for Mutual Security Purposes (hereinafter "the JSC"), as well as Joint Regional Security Committees (hereinafter "RSCs") and Joint District Coordination Offices (hereinafter "DCOs"), are hereby established as provided for in Annex I.

4. The security arrangements provided for in this Agreement and in Annex I may be reviewed at the request of either Party and may be amended by mutual agreement of the Parties. Specific review arrangements are included in Annex I.

5. For the purpose of this Agreement, "the Settlements" means, in the West Bank the settlements in Area C; and in the Gaza Strip, the Gush Katif and Erez settlement areas, as well as the other settlements in the Gaza Strip, as shown on attached map No. 2.

ARTICLE XIII
Security

1. The Council will, upon completion of the redeployment of Israeli military forces in each district, as set out in Appendix 1 to Annex I, assume the powers and responsibilities for internal security and public order in Area A in that district.

2. a. There will be a complete redeployment of Israeli military forces from Area B. Israel will transfer to the Council and the Council will assume responsibility for public order for Palestinians. Israel shall have the overriding responsibility for security for the purpose of protecting Israelis and confronting the threat of terrorism.

b. In Area B the Palestinian Police shall assume the responsibility for public order for Palestinians and shall be deployed in order to accommodate the Palestinian needs and requirements in the following manner:

(1) The Palestinian Police shall establish 25 police stations and posts in towns, villages, and other places listed in Appendix 2 to Annex I and as delineated on map No. 3. The West Bank RSC may agree on the establishment of additional police stations and posts, if required.

(2) The Palestinian Police shall be responsible for handling public order incidents in which only Palestinians are involved.

(3) The Palestinian Police shall operate freely in populated places where police stations and posts are located, as set out in paragraph b(1) above.

(4) While the movement of uniformed Palestinian policemen in Area B outside places where there is a Palestinian police station or post will be carried out after coordination and confirmation through the relevant DCO, three months after the completion of redeployment from Area B, the DCOs may decide that movement of Palestinian policemen from the police stations in Area B to Palestinian towns and villages in Area B on roads that are used only by Palestinian traffic will take place after notifying the DCO.

(5) The coordination of such planned movement prior to confirmation through the relevant DCO shall include a scheduled plan, including the number of policemen, as well as the type and number of weapons and vehicles intended to take part. It shall also include details of arrangements for ensuring continued coordination through appropriate communication links, the exact schedule of movement to the area of the planned operation, including the destination and routes thereto, its proposed duration and the schedule for returning to the police station or post.

The Israeli side of the DCO will provide the Palestinian side with its response, following a request for movement of policemen in accordance with this paragraph, in normal or routine cases within one day and in emergency cases no later than 2 hours.

(6) The Palestinian Police and the Israeli military forces will conduct joint security activities on the main roads as set out in Annex I.

(7) The Palestinian Police will notify the West Bank RSC of the names of the policemen, number plates of police vehicles and serial numbers of weapons, with respect to each police station and post in Area B.

(8) Further redeployments from Area C and transfer of internal security responsibility to the Palestinian Police in Areas B and C will be carried out in three phases, each to take place after an interval of six months, to be completed 18 months after the inauguration of the Council, except for the issues of permanent status negotiations and of Israel's overall responsibility for Israelis and borders.

(9) The procedures detailed in this paragraph will be reviewed within six months of the completion of the first phase of redeployment.

ARTICLE XIV
The Palestinian Police

1. The Council shall establish a strong police force. The duties, functions, structure, deployment and composition of the Palestinian Police, together with provisions regarding its equipment and operation, as well as rules of conduct, are set out in Annex I.

2. The Palestinian police force established under the Gaza-Jericho Agreement will be fully integrated into the Palestinian Police and will be subject to the provisions of this Agreement.

3. Except for the Palestinian Police and the Israeli military forces, no other armed forces shall be established or operate in the West Bank and the Gaza Strip.

4. Except for the arms, ammunition and equipment of the Palestinian Police described in Annex I, and those of the Israeli military forces, no organization, group or individual in the West Bank and the Gaza Strip shall manufacture, sell, acquire, possess, import or otherwise introduce into the West Bank or the Gaza Strip any firearms, ammunition, weapons, explosives, gunpowder or any related equipment, unless otherwise provided for in Annex I.

ARTICLE XV
Prevention of Hostile Acts

1. Both sides shall take all measures necessary in order to prevent acts of terrorism, crime and hostilities directed against each other, against individuals falling under the other's authority and against their property and shall take legal measures against offenders.

2. Specific provisions for the implementation of this Article are set out in Annex I.

ARTICLE XVI
Confidence Building Measures

With a view to fostering a positive and supportive public atmosphere to accompany the implementation of this Agreement, to establish a solid basis of mutual trust and good faith, and in order to facilitate the anticipated cooperation and new relations between the two peoples, both Parties agree to carry out confidence building measures as detailed herewith:

1. Israel will release or turn over to the Palestinian side, Palestinian detainees and prisoners, residents of the West Bank and the Gaza Strip. The first stage of release of these prisoners and detainees will take place on the signing of this Agreement and the second stage will take place prior to the date of the elections. There will be a third stage of release of detainees and prisoners. Detainees and prisoners will be released from among categories detailed in Annex VII (Release of Palestinian Prisoners and Detainees). Those released will be free to return to their homes in the West Bank and the Gaza Strip.

2. Palestinians who have maintained contact with the Israeli authorities will not be subjected to acts of harassment, violence, retribution or prosecution. Appropriate ongoing measures will be taken, in coordination with Israel, in order to ensure their protection.

3. Palestinians from abroad whose entry into the West Bank and the Gaza Strip is approved pursuant to this Agreement, and to whom the provisions of this Article are applicable, will not be prosecuted for offenses committed prior to September 13, 1993.

CHAPTER 3 - LEGAL AFFAIRS

ARTICLE XVII
Jurisdiction

1. In accordance with the DOP, the jurisdiction of the Council will cover West Bank and Gaza Strip territory as a single territorial unit, except for:

a. issues that will be negotiated in the permanent status negotiations: Jerusalem, settlements, specified military locations, Palestinian refugees, borders, foreign relations and Israelis; and

b. powers and responsibilities not transferred to the Council.

2. Accordingly, the authority of the Council encompasses all matters that fall within its territorial, functional and personal jurisdiction, as follows:

a. The territorial jurisdiction of the Council shall encompass Gaza Strip territory, except for the Settlements and the Military Installation Area shown on map No. 2, and West Bank territory, except for Area C which, except for the issues that will be negotiated in the permanent status negotiations, will be gradually transferred to Palestinian jurisdiction in three phases, each to take place after an interval of six months, to be completed 18 months after the inauguration of the Council. At this time, the jurisdiction of the Council will cover West Bank and Gaza Strip territory, except for the issues that will be negotiated in the permanent status negotiations.

Territorial jurisdiction includes land, subsoil and territorial waters, in accordance with the provisions of this Agreement.

b. The functional jurisdiction of the Council extends to all powers and responsibilities transferred to the Council, as specified in this Agreement or in any future agreements that may be reached between the Parties during the interim period.

c. The territorial and functional jurisdiction of the Council will apply to all persons, except for Israelis, unless otherwise provided in this Agreement.

d. Notwithstanding subparagraph a. above, the Council shall have functional jurisdiction in Area C, as detailed in Article IV of Annex III.

3. The Council has, within its authority, legislative, executive and judicial powers and responsibilities, as provided for in this Agreement.

4. a. Israel, through its military government, has the authority over areas that are not under the territorial jurisdiction of the Council, powers and responsibilities not transferred to the Council and Israelis.

b. To this end, the Israeli military government shall retain the necessary legislative, judicial and executive powers and responsibilities, in accordance with international law. This provision shall not derogate from Israel's applicable legislation over Israelis in personam.

5. The exercise of authority with regard to the electromagnetic sphere and air space shall be in accordance with the provisions of this Agreement.

6. Without derogating from the provisions of this Article, legal arrangements detailed in the Protocol Concerning Legal Matters attached as Annex IV to this Agreement (hereinafter "Annex IV") shall be observed. Israel and the Council may negotiate further legal arrangements.

7. Israel and the Council shall cooperate on matters of legal assistance in criminal and civil matters through a legal committee (hereinafter "the Legal Committee"), hereby established.

8. The Council's jurisdiction will extend gradually to cover West Bank and Gaza Strip territory, except for the issues to be negotiated in the permanent status negotiations, through a series of redeployments of the Israeli military forces. The first phase of the redeployment of Israeli military forces will cover populated areas in the West Bank - cities, towns, refugee camps and hamlets, as set out in Annex I - and will be completed prior to the eve of the Palestinian elections, i.e. 22 days before the day of the elections. Further redeployments of Israeli military forces to specified military locations will commence immediately upon the inauguration of the Council and will be effected in three phases, each to take place after an interval of six months, to be concluded no later than eighteen months from the date of the inauguration of the Council.

ARTICLE XVIII
Legislative Powers of the Council

1. For the purposes of this Article, legislation shall mean any primary and secondary legislation, including basic laws, laws, regulations and other legislative acts.

2. The Council has the power, within its jurisdiction as defined in Article XVII of this Agreement, to adopt legislation.

3. While the primary legislative power shall lie in the hands of the Council as a whole, the Ra'ees of the Executive Authority of the Council shall have the following legislative powers

a. the power to initiate legislation or to present proposed legislation to the Council;

b. the power to promulgate legislation adopted by the Council; and

c. the power to issue secondary legislation, including regulations, relating to any matters specified and within the scope laid down in any primary legislation adopted by the Council.

4. a. Legislation, including legislation which amends or abrogates existing laws or military orders, which exceeds the jurisdiction of the Council or which is otherwise inconsistent with the provisions of the DOP, this Agreement, or of any other agreement that may be reached between the two sides during the interim period, shall have no effect and shall be void ab initio.

b. The Ra'ees of the Executive Authority of the Council shall not promulgate legislation adopted by the Council if such legislation falls under the provisions of this paragraph.

5. All legislation shall be communicated to the Israeli side of the Legal Committee.

6. Without derogating from the provisions of paragraph 4 above, the Israeli side of the Legal Committee may refer for the attention of the Committee any legislation regarding which Israel considers the provisions of paragraph 4 apply, in order to discuss issues arising from such legislation. The Legal Committee will consider the legislation referred to it at the earliest opportunity.

ARTICLE XIX
Human Rights and the Rule of Law

Israel and the Council shall exercise their powers and responsibilities pursuant to this Agreement with due regard to internationally-accepted norms and principles of human rights and the rule of law.

ARTICLE XX
Rights, Liabilities and Obligations

1. a. The transfer of powers and responsibilities from the Israeli military government and its civil administration to the Council, as detailed in Annex III, includes all related rights, liabilities and obligations arising with regard to acts or omissions which occurred prior to such transfer. Israel will cease to bear any financial responsibility regarding such acts or omissions and the Council will bear all financial responsibility for these and for its own functioning.

b. Any financial claim made in this regard against Israel will be referred to the Council.

c. Israel shall provide the Council with the information it has regarding pending and anticipated claims brought before any court or tribunal against Israel in this regard.

d. Where legal proceedings are brought in respect of such a claim, Israel will notify the Council and enable it to participate in defending the claim and raise any arguments on its behalf.

e. In the event that an award is made against Israel by any court or tribunal in respect of such a claim, the Council shall immediately reimburse Israel the full amount of the award.

f. Without prejudice to the above, where a court or tribunal hearing such a claim finds that liability rests solely with an employee or agent who acted beyond the scope of the powers assigned to him or her, unlawfully or with willful malfeasance, the Council shall not bear financial responsibility.

2. a. Notwithstanding the provisions of paragraphs 1.d through 1.f above, each side may take the necessary measures, including promulgation of legislation, in order to ensure that such claims by Palestinians including pending claims in which the hearing of evidence has not yet begun, are brought only before Palestinian courts or tribunals in the West Bank and the Gaza Strip, and are not brought before or heard by Israeli courts or tribunals.

b. Where a new claim has been brought before a Palestinian court or tribunal subsequent to the dismissal of the claim pursuant to subparagraph a. above, the Council shall defend it and, in accordance with subparagraph 1.a above, in the event that an award is made for the plaintiff, shall pay the amount of the award.

c. The Legal Committee shall agree on arrangements for the transfer of all materials and information needed to enable the Palestinian courts or tribunals to hear such claims as referred to in subparagraph b. above, and, when necessary, for the provision of legal assistance by Israel to the Council in defending such claims.

3. The transfer of authority in itself shall not affect rights, liabilities and obligations of any person or legal entity, in existence at the date of signing of this Agreement.

4. The Council, upon its inauguration, will assume all the rights, liabilities and obligations of the Palestinian Authority.

5. For the purpose of this Agreement, "Israelis" also includes Israeli statutory agencies and corporations registered in Israel.

ARTICLE XXI
Settlement of Differences and Disputes

Any difference relating to the application of this Agreement shall be referred to the appropriate coordination and cooperation mechanism established under this Agreement. The provisions of Article XV of the DOP shall apply to any such difference which is not settled through the appropriate coordination and cooperation mechanism, namely:

1. Disputes arising out of the application or interpretation of this Agreement or any related agreements pertaining to the interim period shall be settled through the Liaison Committee.

2. Disputes which cannot be settled by negotiations may be settled by a mechanism of conciliation to be agreed between the Parties.

3. The Parties may agree to submit to arbitration disputes relating to the interim period, which cannot be settled through conciliation. To this end, upon the agreement of both Parties, the Parties will establish an Arbitration Committee.

CHAPTER 4 - COOPERATION

ARTICLE XXII
Relations between Israel and the Council

1. Israel and the Council shall seek to foster mutual understanding and tolerance and shall accordingly abstain from incitement, including hostile propaganda, against each other and, without derogating from the principle of freedom of expression, shall take legal measures to prevent such incitement by any organizations, groups or individuals within their jurisdiction.

2. Israel and the Council will ensure that their respective educational systems contribute to the peace between the Israeli and Palestinian peoples and to peace in the entire region, and will refrain from the introduction of any motifs that could adversely affect the process of reconciliation.

3. Without derogating from the other provisions of this Agreement, Israel and the Council shall cooperate in combating criminal activity which may affect both sides, including offenses related to trafficking in illegal drugs and psychotropic substances, smuggling, and offenses against property, including offenses related to vehicles.

ARTICLE XXIII
Cooperation with Regard to Transfer of Powers and Responsibilities

In order to ensure a smooth, peaceful and orderly transfer of powers and responsibilities, the two sides will cooperate with regard to the transfer of security powers and responsibilities in accordance with the provisions of Annex I, and the transfer of civil powers and responsibilities in accordance with the provisions of Annex III.

ARTICLE XXIV
Economic Relations

The economic relations between the two sides are set out in the Protocol on Economic Relations signed in Paris on April 29, 1994, and the Appendices thereto, and the Supplement to the Protocol on Economic Relations all attached as Annex V, and will be governed by the relevant provisions of this Agreement and its Annexes.

ARTICLE XXV
Cooperation Programs

1. The Parties agree to establish a mechanism to develop programs of cooperation between them. Details of such cooperation are set out in Annex VI.

2. A Standing Cooperation Committee to deal with issues arising in the context of this cooperation is hereby established as provided for in Annex VI.

ARTICLE XXVI
The Joint Israeli-Palestinian Liaison Committee

1. The Liaison Committee established pursuant to Article X of the DOP shall ensure the smooth implementation of this Agreement. It shall deal with issues requiring coordination, other issues of common interest and disputes.

2. The Liaison Committee shall be composed of an equal number of members from each Party. It may add other technicians and experts as necessary.

3. The Liaison Committee shall adopt its rules of procedures, including the frequency and place or places of its meetings.

4. The Liaison Committee shall reach its decisions by agreement.

5. The Liaison Committee shall establish a subcommittee that will monitor and steer the implementation of this Agreement (hereinafter "the Monitoring and Steering Committee"). It will function as follows:

a. The Monitoring and Steering Committee will, on an ongoing basis, monitor the implementation of this Agreement, with a view to enhancing the cooperation and fostering the peaceful relations between the two sides.

b. The Monitoring and Steering Committee will steer the activities of the various joint committees established in this Agreement (the JSC, the CAC, the Legal Committee, the Joint Economic Committee and the Standing Cooperation

Committee) concerning the ongoing implementation of the Agreement, and will report to the Liaison Committee.

c. The Monitoring and Steering Committee will be composed of the heads of the various committees mentioned above.

d. The two heads of the Monitoring and Steering Committee will establish its rules of procedures, including the frequency and places of its meetings.

ARTICLE XXVII
Liaison and Cooperation with Jordan and Egypt

1. Pursuant to Article XII of the DOP, the two Parties have invited the Governments of Jordan and Egypt to participate in establishing further liaison and cooperation arrangements between the Government of Israel and the Palestinian representatives on the one hand, and the Governments of Jordan and Egypt on the other hand, to promote cooperation between them. As part of these arrangements a Continuing Committee has been constituted and has commenced its deliberations.

2. The Continuing Committee shall decide by agreement on the modalities of admission of persons displaced from the West Bank and the Gaza Strip in 1967, together with necessary measures to prevent disruption and disorder.

3. The Continuing Committee shall also deal with other matters of common concern.

ARTICLE XXVIII
Missing Persons

1. Israel and the Council shall cooperate by providing each other with all necessary assistance in the conduct of searches for missing persons and bodies of persons which have not been recovered, as well as by providing information about missing persons.

2. The PLO undertakes to cooperate with Israel and to assist it in its efforts to locate and to return to Israel Israeli soldiers who are missing in action and the bodies of soldiers which have not been recovered.

CHAPTER 5 - MISCELLANEOUS PROVISIONS

ARTICLE XXIX
Safe Passage between the West Bank and the Gaza Strip

Arrangements for safe passage of persons and transportation between the West Bank and the Gaza Strip are set out in Annex I.

ARTICLE XXX
Passages

Arrangements for coordination between Israel and the Council regarding passage to and from Egypt and Jordan, as well as any other agreed international crossings, are set out in Annex I.

ARTICLE XXXI
Final Clauses

1. This Agreement shall enter into force on the date of its signing.

2. The Gaza-Jericho Agreement, except for Article XX (Confidence-Building Measures), the Preparatory Transfer Agreement and the Further Transfer Protocol will be superseded by this Agreement.

3. The Council, upon its inauguration, shall replace the Palestinian Authority and shall assume all the undertakings and obligations of the Palestinian Authority under the Gaza-Jericho Agreement, the Preparatory Transfer Agreement, and the Further Transfer Protocol.

4. The two sides shall pass all necessary legislation to implement this Agreement.

5. Permanent status negotiations will commence as soon as possible, but not later than May 4, 1996, between the Parties. It is understood that these negotiations shall cover remaining issues, including: Jerusalem, refugees, settlements, security arrangements, borders, relations and cooperation with other neighbors, and other issues of common interest.

6. Nothing in this Agreement shall prejudice or preempt the outcome of the negotiations on the permanent status to be conducted pursuant to the DOP. Neither Party shall be deemed, by virtue of having entered into this Agreement, to have renounced or waived any of its existing rights, claims or positions.

7. Neither side shall initiate or take any step that will change the status of the West Bank and the Gaza Strip pending the outcome of the permanent status negotiations.

8. The two Parties view the West Bank and the Gaza Strip as a single territorial unit, the integrity and status of which will be preserved during the interim period.

9. The PLO undertakes that, within two months of the date of the inauguration of the Council, the Palestinian National Council will convene and formally approve the necessary changes in regard to the Palestinian Covenant, as undertaken in the letters signed by the Chairman of the PLO and addressed to the Prime Minister of Israel, dated September 9, 1993 and May 4, 1994.

10. Pursuant to Annex I, Article IX of this Agreement, Israel confirms that the permanent checkpoints on the roads leading to and from the Jericho Area (except those related to the access road leading from Mousa Alami to the Allenby Bridge) will be removed upon the completion of the first phase of redeployment.

11. Prisoners who, pursuant to the Gaza Jericho Agreement, were turned over to the Palestinian Authority on the condition that they remain in the Jericho Area for the remainder of their sentence, will be free to return to their homes in the West Bank and the Gaza Strip upon the completion of the first phase of redeployment.

12. As regards relations between Israel and the PLO, and without derogating from the commitments contained in the letters signed by and exchanged between the Prime Minister of Israel and the Chairman of the PLO, dated September 9, 1993 and May 4, 1994, the two sides will apply between them the provisions contained in Article XXII, paragraph 1, with the necessary changes.

13. a. The Preamble to this Agreement, and all Annexes, Appendices and maps attached hereto, shall constitute an integral part hereof.

b. The Parties agree that the maps attached to the Gaza-Jericho Agreement as:

a. map No. 1 (The Gaza Strip), an exact copy of which is attached to this Agreement as map No. (in this Agreement "map No. 2");

b. map No. 4 (Deployment of Palestinian Police in the Gaza Strip), an exact copy of which is attached to this Agreement as map No. 5 (in this Agreement "map No. 5"); and

c. map No. 6 (Maritime Activity Zones), an exact copy of which is attached to this Agreement as map No. 8 (in this Agreement "map No. 8"; are an integral part hereof and will remain in effect for the duration of this Agreement.

14. While the Jeftlik area will come under the functional and personal jurisdiction of the Council in the first phase of redeployment, the area's transfer to the territorial jurisdiction of the Council will be considered by the Israeli side in the first phase of the further redeployment phases.

International Humanitarian Law and Arms Control Agreements

V-11. Israel-Lebanon Ceasefire Understanding (1996),
<http://www.israel-mfa.gov.il/peace/ceasefir.html>.

Full Text

Following is the text of the "understanding" reached on Friday, April 26, 1996, for the cease-fire in Lebanon:

The United States understands that after discussions with the governments of Israel and Lebanon, and in consultation with Syria, Lebanon and Israel will ensure the following:

    1 Armed groups in Lebanon will not carry out attacks by Katyusha rockets or by any kind of weapon into Israel.

    2.Israel and those cooperating with it will not fire any kind of weapon at civilians or civilian targets in Lebanon.

    3.Beyond this, the two parties commit to ensuring that under no circumstances will civilians be the target of attack and that civilian populated areas and industrial and electrical installations will not be used as launching grounds for attacks.

    4.Without violating this understanding, nothing herein shall preclude any party from exercising the right of self-defense.

    A Monitoring Group is established consisting of the United States, France, Syria, Lebanon and Israel. Its task will be to monitor the application of the understanding stated above. Complaints will be submitted to the Monitoring Group.

    In the event of a claimed violation of the understanding, the party submitting the complaint will do so within 24 hours. Procedures for dealing with the complaints will be set by the Monitoring Group.

    The United States will also organize a Consultative Group, to consist of France, the European Union, Russia and other interested parties, for the purpose of assisting in the reconstruction needs of Lebanon.

    It is recognized that the understanding to bring the current crisis between Lebanon and Israel to an end cannot substitute for a permanent solution. The United States understands the importance of achieving a comprehensive peace in the region. Toward this end, the United States proposes the resumption of negotiations between Syria and Israel and between Lebanon and Israel at a time to be agreed upon, with the objective of reaching comprehensive peace.

The United States understands that it is desirable that these negotiations be conducted in a climate of stability and tranquility.

This understanding will be announced simultaneously at 1800 hours, April 26, 1996, in all countries concerned.

The time set for implementation is 0400 hours, April 27, 1996.

International Humanitarian Law and Arms Control Agreements 657

V-12. Protocol Concerning the Redeployment in Hebron, January 17, 1997, <http://www.israel-mfa.gov.il/peace.html>.

Full Text

In accordance with the provisions of the Interim Agreement and in particular of Article VII of Annex I to the Interim Agreement, both Parties have agreed on this Protocol for the implementation of the redeployment in Hebron.

Security Arrangements Regarding Redeployment in Hebron

1. Redeployment in Hebron

The redeployment of Israeli Military Forces in Hebron will be carried out in accordance with the Interim Agreement and this Protocol. This redeployment will be completed not later than ten days from the signing of this Protocol. During these ten days both sides will exert every possible effort to prevent friction and any action that would prevent the redeployment. This redeployment shall constitute full implementation of the provisions of the Interim Agreement with regard to the City of Hebron unless otherwise provided for in Article VII of Annex I to the Interim Agreement.

2. Security Powers and Responsibilities

a.
1. The Palestinian Police will assume responsibilities in Area H-1 similar to those in other cities in the West Bank; and

2. Israel will retain all powers and responsibilities for internal security and public order in Area H-2. In addition, Israel will continue to carry the responsibility for overall security of Israelis.

b. In this context both sides reaffirm their commitment to honor the relevant security provisions of the Interim Agreement, including the provisions regarding Arrangements for Security and Public Order (Article XII of the Interim Agreement); Prevention of Hostile Acts (Article XV the Interim Agreement); Security Policy for the Prevention of Terrorism and Violence (Article II of Annex I to the Interim Agreement); Guidelines for Hebron (Article VII of Annex I to the Interim Agreement); and Rules of Conduct in Mutual Security Matters (Article XI of Annex I to the Interim Agreement).

3. Agreed Security Arrangements

a. With a view to ensuring mutual security and stability in the City of Hebron, special security arrangements will apply adjacent to the areas under the security responsibility of Israel, in Area H-1, in the area between the Palestinian Police checkpoints delineated on the map attached to this Protocol as Appendix 1 (hereinafter referred to as "the attached map") and the areas under the security responsibility of Israel.

b. The purpose of the abovementioned checkpoints will be to enable the Palestinian Police, exercising their responsibilities under the Interim Agreement, to prevent entry of armed persons and demonstrators or other people threatening security and public order, into the abovementioned area.

4. Joint Security Measures

a. The DCO will establish a sub-office in the City of Hebron as indicated on the attached map.

b. JMU will operate in Area H-2 to handle incidents that involve Palestinians only. The JMU movement will be detailed on the attached map. The DCO will coordinate the JMU movement and activity.

c. As part of the security arrangements in the area adjacent to the areas under the security responsibility of Israel, as defined above, Joint Mobile Units will be operating in this area, with special focus on the following places:

    1. Abu Sneinah
    2. Harat A-Sheikh
    3. Sha'aba
    4. The high ground overlooking new Route No. 35.

d. Two Joint Patrols will function in Area H-1:

1. a Joint Patrol which will operate on the road from Ras e-Jura to the north of the Dura junction via E-Salaam Road, as indicated on the attached map; and

2. a Joint Patrol which will operate on existing Route No. 35, including the eastern part of existing Route No. 35, as indicated on the attached map.

e. The Palestinian and Israeli side of the Joint Mobile Units in the City of Hebron will be armed with equivalent types of weapons (Mini-Ingraham submachine guns for the Palestinian side and short M16s for the Israeli side).

f. With a view to dealing with the special security situation in the City of Hebron, a Joint Coordination Center (hereinafter the "JCC") headed by senior officers of both sides, will be established in the of the JCC will be to coordinate the joint security measures in the City of Hebron. The JCC will be guided by all the relevant provisions of the Interim Agreement, including Annex I and this Protocol. In his context, each side will notify the JCC of demonstrations and actions taken in respect of such demonstrations, and of any security activity, close to the areas under the responsibility of the other side, including in the area defined in Article 3(a) above. The JCC shall be informed of activities in accordance with Article 5(d)(3) of this Protocol.

5. The Palestinian Police

a. Palestinian police stations or posts will be established in Area H-1, manned by a total of up to 400 policemen, equipped with 20 vehicles and armed with 200 pistols, and 100 rifles for the protection of the police stations.

b. Four designated Rapid Response Teams (RRTs) will be established and stationed in Area H-1, one in each of the police stations, as delineated on the attached map. The main task of the RRTs will be to handle special security cases. Each RRT shall be comprised of up to 16 members.

c. The above mentioned rifles will be designated for the exclusive use of the RRTs, to handle special cases.

d.
1. The Palestinian Police shall operate freely in Area H-1.

2. Activities of the RRTs armed with rifles in the Agreed Adjacent Area, as defined in Appendix 2, shall require the agreement of the JCC.

3. The RRTs will use the rifles in the rest of Area H-1 to fulfil their above mentioned tasks.

e. The Palestinian Police will ensure that all Palestinian policemen, prior to their deployment in order to verify their suitability for service, taking into account the sensitivity of the area.

6. Holy Sites

a. Paragraphs 2 and 3(a) of Article 32 of Appendix 1 to Annex III of the Interim Agreement will be applicable to the following Holy Sites in Area H-1:

1. The Cave of Othniel Ben Knaz/El-Khalil;
2. Elonei Mamre/Haram Er-Rameh;
3. Eshel Avraham/Balotat Ibrahim; and
4. Maayan Sarah/Ein Sarah.

b. The Palestinian Police will be responsible for the protection of the above Jewish Holy Sites. Without derogating from the above responsibility of the Palestinian Police, visits to the above Holy Sites by worshippers or other visitors shall be accompanied by a Joint Mobile Unit, which will ensure free, unimpeded and secure access to the Holy Sites, as well as their peaceful use.

7. Normalization of Life in the Old City

a. Both sides reiterate their commitment to maintain normal life throughout the City of Hebron and to prevent any provocation or friction that may affect the normal life in the city.

b. In this context, both sides are committed to take all steps and measures necessary for the normalization of life in Hebron, including:

1. The wholesale market - Hasbahe - will be opened as a retail market in which goods will be sold directly to consumers from within the existing shops.

2. The movement of vehicles on the Shuhada Road will be gradually returned, within 4 months, to the same situation which existed prior to February 1994.

8. The Imara

The Imara will be turned over to the Palestinian side upon the completion of the redeployment and will become the headquarters of the Palestinian Police in the City of Hebron.

9. City of Hebron

Both sides reiterate their commitment to the unity of the City of Hebron, and their understanding that the division of security responsibility will not divide the city. In this context, and without derogating from the security powers and responsibilities of either side, both sides share the mutual goal that movement of people, goods and vehicles within and in and out of the city will be smooth and normal, without obstacles or barriers.

Civil Arrangements Regarding the Redeployment in Hebron

10. Transfer of Civil Powers and Responsibilities

a. The transfer of civil powers and responsibilities that have yet to be transferred to the Palestinian side in the city of Hebron (12 spheres) in accordance with Article VII of Annex I to the Interim Agreement shall be conducted concurrently with the beginning of the redeployment of Israeli military forces in Hebron.

b. In Area H-2, the civil powers and responsibilities will be transferred to the Palestinian side, except for those relating to Israelis and their property, which shall continue to be exercised by the Israeli Military Government.

11. Planning, Zoning and Building

a. The two parties are equally committed to preserve and protect the historic character of the city in a way which does not harm or change that character in any part of the city.

b. The Palestinian side has informed the Israeli side that in exercising its powers and responsibilities, taking into account the existing municipal regulations, it has undertaken to implement the following provisions:

1. Proposed construction of buildings above two floors (6 meters) within 50 meters of the external boundaries of the locations specified in the list attached to this Protocol as Appendix 3 (hereinafter referred to as "the attached list") will be coordinated through the DCL.

2. Proposed construction of buildings above three floors (9 meters) between 50 and 100 meters of the external boundaries of the locations specified in the attached list will be coordinated through the DCL.

3. Proposed construction of non-residential, non-commercial buildings within 100 meters of the external boundaries of the locations specified in the attached list that are designed for uses that may adversely affect the environment (such as industrial factories) or buildings and institutions in which

more that 50 persons are expected to gather together will be coordinated through the DCL.

4. Proposed construction of buildings above two floors (6 meters) within 50 meters from each side of the road specified in the attached list will be coordinated through the DCL.

5. The necessary enforcement measures will be taken to ensure compliance on the ground with the preceding provisions.

6. This Article does not apply to existing buildings or to new construction or renovation for which fully approved permits were issued by the Municipality prior to January 15th, 1997.

12. Infrastructure

a. The Palestinian side shall inform the Israeli side, through the DCL, 48 hours in advance of any anticipated activity regarding infrastructure which may disturb the regular flow of traffic on roads in Area H-2 or which may affect infrastructure (such as water, sewage, electricity and communications) serving Area H-2.

b. The Israeli side may request, through the DCL, that the Municipality carry out works regarding the roads or other infrastructure required for the well being of the Israelis in Area H-2. If the Israeli side offers to cover the costs of these works, the Palestinian side will ensure that these works are carried out as a top priority.

c. The above does not prejudice the provisions of the Interim Agreement regarding the access to infrastructure, facilities and installations located in the city of Hebron, such as the electricity grid.

13. Transportation

The Palestinian side shall have the power to determine bus stops, traffic arrangements and traffic signalization in the city of Hebron. Traffic signalization, traffic arrangements and the location of bus stops in Area H-2 will remain as they are on the date of the redeployment in Hebron. Any subsequent change in these arrangements in Area H-2 will be done in cooperation between the two sides in the transportation sub-committee.

14. Municipal Inspectors

a. In accordance with paragraph 4.c of Article VII of Annex I of the Interim Agreement, plainclothes unarmed municipal inspectors will operate in Area H-2. The number of these inspectors shall not exceed 50.

b. The inspectors shall carry official identification cards with a photograph issued by the Municipality.

c. The Palestinian side may request the assistance of the Israel Police, through the DCL of Hebron, in order to carry out its enforcement activities in Area H-2.

15. Location of Offices of the Palestinian Council

The Palestinian side, when operating new offices in Area H-2, will take into consideration the need to avoid provocation and friction. Where establishing such offices might affect public order or security the two sides will cooperate to find a suitable solution.

16. Municipal Services

In accordance with paragraph 5 of Article VII of Annex I of the Interim Agreement, municipal services shall be provided regularly and continuously to all parts of the city of Hebron, at the same quality and cost. The cost shall be determined by the Palestinian side with respect to work done and materials consumed, without discrimination.

Miscellaneous

17. Temporary International Presence

There will be a Temporary International Presence in Hebron (TIPH). Both sides will agree on the modalities of the TIPH, including the number of its members and its area of operation.

18. Annex I

Nothing in this Protocol will derogate from the security powers and responsibilities of either side in accordance with Annex I to the Interim Agreement.

19. Attached Appendices

The appendices attached to this Protocol shall constitute an integral part hereof.

Done at Jerusalem, this 17th day of January 1997.

D. Shomrom
_____

For the Government of
the State of Israel

S. Erakat
_____

For the PLO

Appendix 1

Hebron Redeployment Map (469 KB)

Appendix 2
(Article 5)

Agreed Adjacent Area

The Agreed Adjacent Area ("AAA") shall include the following:

1. An area defined by a line commencing from AAA Reference Point (RP) 100, proceeding along old Route No. 35 until RP 101, continuing by a straight line to RP 102, and from there connected by a straight line to RP 103.

2. An area defined by a line commencing at RP 104, following a straight line to RP 105, from there following a line immediately westward of checkpoints 4, 5, 6, 8, 9, 10, 11, 12 and 13, and from there connected by a straight line to RP 106.

3. An area defined by a line connecting RPs 107 and 108, passing immediately northward of checkpoint 15.

Appendix 3
(Article 12)

List of Locations

The area of Al Haram Al Ibrahimi/the Tomb of the Patriarchs (including the military and police installations in its vicinity)
Al Hisba/Abraham Avinu
Osama School/Beit Romano (including the military location in its vicinity)
Al Daboya/Beit Hadasseh
Jabla Al Rahama/Tel Rumeida
The Jewish Cemeteries
Dir Al Arbein/the Tomb of Ruth and Yishai
Tel Al Jaabra/Givaat Avot Neighborhood (including the police station in its vicinity)
The Road connecting Al Haram Al Ibrahimi/the Tomb of the Patriarchs and Qiryat Arba

International Humanitarian Law and Arms Control Agreements 667

V-13. The Wye River Memorandum, October 23, 1998,
<http://www.israel.org/mfa/go.asp?MFAH00pq0>.

Parties
Israel and Palestine Liberation Organization

Full Text

The following are steps to facilitate implementation of the Interim Agreement on the West Bank and Gaza Strip of September 28, 1995 (the "Interim Agreement") and other related agreements including the Note for the Record of January 17, 1997 (hereinafter referred to as "the prior agreements") so that the Israeli and Palestinian sides can more effectively carry out their reciprocal responsibilities, including those relating to further redeployments and security respectively. These steps are to be carried out in a parallel phased approach in accordance with this Memorandum and the attached time line. They are subject to the relevant terms and conditions of the prior agreements and do not supersede their other requirements.

I. FURTHER REDEPLOYMENTS

A. Phase One and Two Further Redeployments

1. Pursuant to the Interim Agreement and subsequent agreements, the Israeli side's implementation of the first and second F.R.D. will consist of the transfer to the Palestinian side of 13% from Area C as follows:

1% to Area (A)

12% to Area (B)

The Palestinian side has informed that it will allocate an area/areas amounting to 3% from the above Area (B) to be designated as Green Areas and/or Nature Reserves. The Palestinian side has further informed that they will act according to the established scientific standards, and that therefore there will be no changes in the status of these areas, without prejudice to the rights of the existing inhabitants in these areas including Bedouins; while these standards do not allow new construction in these areas, existing roads and buildings may be maintained.

The Israeli side will retain in these Green Areas/Nature Reserves the overriding security responsibility for the purpose of protecting Israelis and confronting the threat of terrorism. Activities and movements of the Palestinian Police forces may be carried out after coordination and confirmation; the Israeli side will respond to such requests expeditiously.

2. As part of the foregoing implementation of the first and second F.R.D., 14.2% from Area (B) will become Area (A).

B. Third Phase of Further Redeployments

With regard to the terms of the Interim Agreement and of Secretary Christopher's letters to the two sides of January 17, 1997 relating to the further redeployment process, there will be a committee to address this question. The United States will be briefed regularly.

II. SECURITY

In the provisions on security arrangements of the Interim Agreement, the Palestinian side agreed to take all measures necessary in order to prevent acts of terrorism, crime and hostilities directed against the Israeli side, against individuals falling under the Israeli side's authority and against their property, just as the Israeli side agreed to take all measures necessary in order to prevent acts of terrorism, crime and individuals falling under the Palestinian side's authority and against their property. The two sides also agreed to take legal measures against offenders within their jurisdiction and to prevent incitement against each other by any organizations, groups or individuals within their jurisdiction.

Both sides recognize that it is in their vital interests to combat terrorism and fight violence in accordance with Annex I of the Interim Agreement and the Note for the Record. They also recognize that the struggle against terror and violence must be comprehensive in that it deals with terrorists, the terror support structure, and the environment conducive to the support of terror. It must be continuous and constant over a long-term, in that there can be no pauses in the work against terrorists and their structure. It must be cooperative in that no effort can be fully effective without Israeli-Palestinian cooperation and the continuous exchange of information, concepts, and actions.

Pursuant to the prior agreements, the Palestinian side's implementation of its responsibilities for security, security cooperation, and other issues will be as detailed below during the time periods specified in the attached time line:

A. Security Actions

1. Outlawing and Combating Terrorist Organizations

a. The Palestinian side will make known its policy of zero tolerance for terror and violence against both sides.

b. A work plan developed by the Palestinian side will be shared with the U.S. and thereafter implementation will begin immediately to ensure the systematic and effective combat of terrorist organizations and their infrastructure.

c. In addition to the bilateral Israeli-Palestinian security cooperation, a U.S.-Palestinian committee will meet biweekly to review the steps being taken to eliminate terrorist cells and the support structure that plans, finances, supplies and abets terror. In these meetings, the Palestinian side will inform the U.S. fully of the actions it has taken to outlaw all organizations (or wings of organizations, as appropriate) of a military, terrorist or violent character and their support structure and to prevent them from operating in areas under its jurisdiction.

d. The Palestinian side will apprehend the specific individuals suspected of perpetrating acts of violence and terror for the purpose of further investigation, and prosecution and punishment of all persons involved in acts of violence and terror.

e. A U.S.-Palestinian committee will meet to review and evaluate information pertinent to the decisions on prosecution, punishment or other legal measures which affect the status of individuals suspected of abetting or perpetrating acts of violence and terror.

2. Prohibiting Illegal Weapons

a. The Palestinian side will ensure an effective legal framework is in place to criminalize, in conformity with the prior agreements, any importation, manufacturing or unlicensed sale, acquisition or possession of firearms, ammunition or weapons in areas under Palestinian jurisdiction.

b. In addition, the Palestinian side will establish and vigorously and continuously implement a systematic program for the collection and appropriate handling of all such illegal items in accordance with the prior agreements. The U.S. has agreed to assist in carrying out this program.

c. A U.S.-Palestinian-Israeli committee will be established to assist and enhance cooperation in preventing the smuggling or other unauthorized introduction of weapons or explosive materials into areas under Palestinian jurisdiction.

3. Preventing Incitement

a. Drawing on relevant international practice and pursuant to Article XXII (1) of the Interim Agreement and the Note for the Record, the Palestinian side will issue a decree prohibiting all forms of incitement to violence or terror, and establishing mechanisms for acting systematically against all expressions or threats of violence or terror. This decree will be comparable to the existing Israeli legislation which deals with the same subject.

b. A U.S.-Palestinian-Israeli committee will meet on a regular basis to monitor cases of possible incitement to violence or terror and to make recommendations and reports on how to prevent such incitement. The Israeli, Palestinian and U.S. sides will each appoint a media specialist, a law enforcement representative, an educational specialist and a current or former elected official to the committee.

B. Security Cooperation

The two sides agree that their security cooperation will be based on a spirit of partnership and will include, among other things, the following steps:

1. Bilateral Cooperation

There will be full bilateral security cooperation between the two sides which will be continuous, intensive and comprehensive.

2. Forensic Cooperation

There will be an exchange of forensic expertise, training, and other assistance.

3. Trilateral Committee

In addition to the bilateral Israeli-Palestinian security cooperation, a high-ranking U.S.-Palestinian-Israeli committee will meet as required and not less than biweekly to assess current threats, deal with any impediments to effective security cooperation and coordination and address the steps being taken to combat terror and terrorist organizations. The committee will also serve as a forum to address the issue of external support for terror. In these meetings, the Palestinian side will fully inform the members of the committee of the results of its investigations concerning terrorist suspects already in custody and the participants will exchange additional relevant information. The committee will report regularly to the leaders of the two sides on the status of cooperation, the results of the meetings and its recommendations.

C. Other Issues

1. Palestinian Police Force

a. The Palestinian side will provide a list of its policemen to the Israeli side in conformity with the prior agreements.

b. Should the Palestinian side request technical assistance, the U.S. has indicated its willingness to help meet these needs in cooperation with other donors.

c. The Monitoring and Steering Committee will, as part of its functions, monitor the implementation of this provision and brief the U.S.

2. PLO Charter

The Executive Committee of the Palestine Liberation Organization and the Palestinian Central Council will reaffirm the letter of 22 January 1998 from PLO Chairman Yasir Arafat to President Clinton concerning the nullification of the Palestinian National Charter provisions that are inconsistent with the letters exchanged between the PLO and the Government of Israel on 9/10 September 1993. PLO Chairman Arafat, the Speaker of the Palestine National Council, and the Speaker of the Palestinian Council will invite the members of the PNC, as well as the members of the Central Council, the Council, and the Palestinian Heads of Ministries to a meeting to be addressed by President Clinton to reaffirm their support for the peace process and the aforementioned decisions of the Executive Committee and the Central Council.

3. Legal Assistance in Criminal Matters

Among other forms of legal assistance in criminal matters, the requests for arrest and transfer of suspects and defendants pursuant to Article II (7) of Annex IV of the Interim Agreement will be submitted (or resubmitted) through the mechanism of the Joint Israeli-Palestinian Legal Committee and will be responded to in conformity with Article II (7) (f) of Annex IV of the Interim Agreement within the twelve week period. Requests submitted after the eighth week will be responded to in conformity with Article II (7) (f) within four weeks of their submission. The U.S. has been requested by the sides to report on a regular basis on the steps being taken to respond to the above requests.

4. Human Rights and the Rule of Law

Pursuant to Article XI (1) of Annex I of the Interim Agreement, and without derogating from the above, the Palestinian Police will exercise powers and responsibilities to implement this Memorandum with due regard to internationally accepted norms of human rights and the rule of law, and will be guided by the need to protect the public, respect human dignity, and avoid harassment.

III. INTERIM COMMITTEES AND ECONOMIC ISSUES

1. The Israeli and Palestinian sides reaffirm their commitment to enhancing their relationship and agree on the need actively to promote economic development in the West Bank and Gaza. In this regard, the parties agree to continue or to reactivate all standing committees established by the Interim Agreement, including the Monitoring and Steering Committee, the Joint Economic Committee (JEC), the Civil Affairs Committee (CAC), the Legal Committee, and the Standing Cooperation Committee.

2. The Israeli and Palestinian sides have agreed on arrangements which will permit the timely opening of the Gaza Industrial Estate. They also have concluded a "Protocol Regarding the Establishment and Operation of the International Airport in the Gaza Strip During the Interim Period."

3. Both sides will renew negotiations on Safe Passage immediately. As regards the southern route, the sides will make best efforts to conclude the agreement within a week of the entry into force of this Memorandum. Operation of the southern route will start as soon as possible thereafter. As regards the northern route, negotiations will continue with the goal of reaching agreement as soon as possible. Implementation will take place expeditiously thereafter.

4. The Israeli and Palestinian sides acknowledge the great importance of the Port of Gaza for the development of the Palestinian economy, and the expansion of Palestinian trade. They commit themselves to proceeding without delay to conclude an agreement to allow the construction and operation of the port in accordance with the prior agreements. The Israeli-Palestinian Committee will reactivate its work immediately with a goal of concluding the protocol within sixty days, which will allow commencement of the construction of the port.

5. The two sides recognize that unresolved legal issues adversely affect the relationship between the two peoples. They therefore will accelerate efforts through the Legal Committee to address outstanding legal issues and to implement solutions to these issues in the shortest possible period. The Palestinian side will provide to the Israeli side copies of all of its laws in effect.

6. The Israeli and Palestinian sides also will launch a strategic economic dialogue to enhance their economic relationship. They will establish within the framework of the JEC an Ad Hoc Committee for this purpose. The committee will review the following four issues: (1) Israeli purchase taxes; (2) cooperation in combating vehicle theft; (3) dealing with unpaid Palestinian debts; and (4) the impact of Israeli standards as barriers to trade and the expansion of the A1 and A2 lists. The committee will submit an interim report within three weeks of the entry into force of this Memorandum, and within six weeks will submit its conclusions and recommendations to be implemented.

7. The two sides agree on the importance of continued international donor assistance to facilitate implementation by both sides of agreements reached. They also recognize the need for enhanced donor support for economic development in the West Bank and Gaza. They agree to jointly approach the donor community to organize a Ministerial Conference before the end of 1998 to seek pledges for enhanced levels of assistance.

IV. PERMANENT STATUS NEGOTIATIONS

The two sides will immediately resume permanent status negotiations on an accelerated basis and will make a determined effort to achieve the mutual goal of reaching an agreement by May 4, 1999. The negotiations will be continuous and without interruption. The U.S. has expressed its willingness to facilitate these negotiations.

V. UNILATERAL ACTIONS

Recognizing the necessity to create a positive environment for the negotiations, neither side shall initiate or take any step that will change the status of the West Bank and the Gaza Strip in accordance with the Interim Agreement.

ATTACHMENT: Time Line

This Memorandum will enter into force ten days from the date of signature.

Done at Washington, D.C. this 23d day of October 1998.

For the Government of the State of Israel:
Benjamin Netanyahu

For the PLO:
Yassir Arafat

Witnessed by:
William J. Clinton
The United States of America

TIME LINE

Note: Parenthetical references below are to paragraphs in "The Wye River Memorandum" to which this time line is an integral attachment. Topics not included in the time line follow the schedule provided for in the text of the Memorandum.

1. Upon Entry into Force of the Memorandum:

Third further redeployment committee starts (I (B))
Palestinian security work plan shared with the U.S. (II (A) (1) (b))
Full bilateral security cooperation (II (B) (1))
Trilateral security cooperation committee starts (II (B) (3))
Interim committees resume and continue; Ad Hoc Economic Committee starts (III)
Accelerated permanent status negotiations start (IV)

2. Entry into Force - Week 2:

Security work plan implementation begins (II (A) (1) (b)); (II (A) (1) (c)) committee starts
Illegal weapons framework in place (II (A) (2) (a));
Palestinian implementation report (II (A) (2) (b))
Anti-incitement committee starts (II (A) (3) (b)); decree issued (II (A) (3) (a))
PLO Executive Committee reaffirms Charter letter (II (C) (2))
Stage 1 of F.R.D. implementation: 2% C to B, 7.1% B to A. Israeli officials acquaint their Palestinian counterparts as required with areas; F.R.D. carried out; report on F.R.D. implementation (I(A))

3. Week 2-6:

Palestinian Central Council reaffirms Charter letter (weeks two to four) (II (C) (2))
PNC and other PLO organizations reaffirm Charter letter (weeks four to six) (II (C) (2))
Establishment of weapons collection program (II (A) (2)

(b)) and collection stage (II (A) (2) (c)); committee starts and reports on activities.
Anti-incitement committee report (II (A) (3) (b))
Ad Hoc Economic Committee: interim report at week three; final report at week six (III)
Policemen list (II (C) (1) (a)); Monitoring and Steering Committee review starts (II (C) (1) (c)
Stage 2 of F.R.D. implementation: 5% C to B. Israeli officials acquaint their Palestinian counterparts as required with areas; F.R.D. carried out; report on F.R.D. implementation (I (A))

4. Week 6-12:

Weapons collection stage II (A) (2) (b); II (A) (2) (c) committee report on its activities.
Anti-incitement committee report (II (A) (3) (b))
Monitoring and Steering Committee briefs U.S. on policemen list (II (C) (1) (c))
Stage 3 of F.R.D. implementation: 5% C to B, 1% C to A, 7.1% B to A. Israeli officials acquaint Palestinian counterparts as required with areas; F.R.D. carried out; report on F.R.D. implementation (I (A))

5. After Week 12:

Activities described in the Memorandum continue as appropriate and if necessary, including:

Trilateral security cooperation committee (II (B)(3))
(II (A) (1) (c)) committee
(II (A) (1) (e)) committee
Anti-incitement committee (II (A) (3) (b))
Third Phase F.R.D. Committee (I (B))
Interim Committees (III)
Accelerated permanent status negotiations (IV)

V-14. **The Sharm el-Sheikh Memorandum on Implementation Timeline of Outstanding Commitments of Agreements Signed and the Resumption of Permanent Status Negotiations (1999),** <http://www.israel.org/mfa/go.asp?MFAH00pq0>.

Parties
Israel and Palestine Liberation Organization

Full Text
The Government of the State of Israel ("GOI") and the Palestine Liberation Organization ("PLO") commit themselves to full and mutual implementation of the Interim Agreement and all other agreements concluded between them since September 1993 (hereinafter "the prior agreements"), and all outstanding commitments emanating from the prior agreements. Without derogating from the other requirements of the prior agreements, the two Sides have agreed as follows:

1. Permanent Status negotiations:

a. In the context of the implementation of the prior agreements, the two Sides will resume the Permanent Status negotiations in an accelerated manner and will make a determined effort to achieve their mutual goal of reaching a Permanent Status Agreement based on the agreed agenda i.e. the specific issues reserved for Permanent Status negotiators and other issues of common interest.

b. The two Sides reaffirm their understanding that the negotiations on the Permanent Status will lead to the implementation of Security Council Resolutions 242 and 338;

c. The two Sides will make a determined effort to conclude a Framework Agreement on all Permanent Status issues in five months from the resumption of the Permanent Status negotiations;

d. The two Sides will conclude a comprehensive agreement on all Permanent Status issues within one year from the resumption of the Permanent Status negotiations;

e. Permanent Status negotiations will resume after the implementation of the first stage of release of prisoners and the second stage of the First and Second Further Redeployments and not later than September 13, 1999. In the Wye River Memorandum, the United States has expressed its willingness to facilitate these negotiations.

2. Phase One and Phase Two of the Further Redeployments

The Israeli Side undertakes the following with regard to Phase One and Phase Two of the Further Redeployments:

a. On September 5, 1999, to transfer 7% from Area C to Area B;

b. On November 15, 1999, to transfer 2% from Area B to Area A and 3% from Area C to Area B;

c. On January 20, 2000, to transfer 1% from Area C to Area A, and 5.1% from Area B to Area A.

3. Release of Prisoners

a. The two Sides shall establish a joint committee that shall follow-up on matters related to release of Palestinian prisoners.

b. The Government of Israel shall release Palestinian and other prisoners who committed their offences prior to September 13, 1993, and were arrested prior to May 4, 1994. The Joint Committee shall agree on the names of those who will be released in the first two stages. Those lists shall be recommended to the relevant Authorities through the Monitoring and Steering Committee;

c. The first stage of release of prisoners shall be carried out on September 5, 1999 and shall consist of 200 prisoners. The second stage of release of prisoners shall be carried out on October 8, 1999 and shall consist of 150 prisoners;

d. The joint committee shall recommend further lists of names to be released to the relevant Authorities through the Monitoring and Steering Committee;

e. The Israeli side will aim to release Palestinian prisoners before next Ramadan.

4. Committees

a. The Third Further Redeployment Committee shall commence its activities not later than September 13, 1999;

b. The Monitoring and Steering Committee, all Interim Committees (i.e. CAC, JEC, JSC, legal committee, people to people), as well as Wye River Memorandum committees shall resume and/or continue their activity, as the case may be, not later than September 13, 1999. The Monitoring and Steering

Committee will have on its agenda, inter alia, the Year 2000, Donor/PA projects in Area C, and the issue of industrial estates;

c. The Continuing Committee on displaced persons shall resume its activity on October 1, 1999 (Article XXVII, Interim Agreement);

d. Not later than October 30, 1999, the two Sides will implement the recommendations of the Ad-hoc Economic Committee (article III-6, WRM).

5. Safe Passage

a. The operation of the Southern Route of the Safe Passage for the movement of persons, vehicles, and goods will start on October 1, 1999 (Annex I, Article X, Interim Agreement) in accordance with the details of operation, which will be provided for in the Safe Passage Protocol that will be concluded by the two Sides not later than September 30, 1999;

b. The two Sides will agree on the specific location of the crossing point of the Northern Route of the Safe Passage as specified in Annex I, Article X, provision c-4, in the Interim Agreement not later than October 5, 1999;

c. The Safe Passage Protocol applied to the Southern Route of the Safe Passage shall apply to the Northern Route of the Safe Passage with relevant agreed modifications;

d. Upon the agreement on the location of the crossing point of the Northern Route of the Safe Passage, construction of the needed facilities and related procedures shall commence and shall be ongoing. At the same time, temporary facilities will be established for the operation of the Northern Route not later than four months from the agreement on the specific location of the crossing-point;

e. In between the operation of the Southern crossing point of the Safe Passage and the Northern crossing point of the Safe Passage, Israel will facilitate arrangements for the movement between the West Bank and the Gaza Strip, using non-Safe Passage routes other than the Southern Route of the Safe Passage;

f. The location of the crossing points shall be without prejudice to the Permanent Status negotiations (Annex I, Article X, provision e, Interim Agreement).

6. Gaza Sea Port

The two Sides have agreed on the following principles to facilitate and enable the construction works of the Gaza Sea Port. The principles shall not prejudice or preempt the outcome of negotiations on the Permanent Status:

a. The Israeli Side agrees that the Palestinian Side shall commence construction works in and related to the Gaza Sea Port on October 1, 1999;

b. The two Sides agree that the Gaza Sea Port will not be operated in any way before reaching a joint Sea Port protocol on all aspects of operating the Port, including security;

c. The Gaza Sea Port is a special case, like the Gaza Airport, being situated in an area under the responsibility of the Palestinian Side and serving as an international passage. Therefore, until the conclusion of a joint Sea Port Protocol, all activities and arrangements relating to the construction of the Port shall be in accordance with the provisions of the Interim Agreement, especially those relating to international passages, as adapted in the Gaza Airport Protocol;

d. The construction shall ensure adequate provision for effective security and customs inspection of people and goods, as well as the establishment of a designated checking area in the Port;

e. In this context, the Israeli side will facilitate on an on-going basis the works related to the construction of the Gaza Sea Port, including the movement in and out of the Port of vessels, equipment, resources, and material required for the construction of the Port;

f. The two Sides will coordinate such works, including the designs and movement, through a joint mechanism.

7. Hebron Issues

a. The Shuhada Road in Hebron shall be opened for the movement of Palestinian vehicles in two phases. The first phase has been carried out, and the second phase shall be carried out not later than October 30, 1999;

b. The wholesale market Hasbahe will be opened not later than November 1, 1999, in accordance with arrangements which will be agreed upon by the two sides;

c. A high level Joint Liaison Committee will convene not later than September 13, 1999 to review the situation in the Tomb of the Patriarchs / Al

Haram Al Ibrahimi (Annex I, Article VII, Interim Agreement and as per the January 15, 1998 US Minute of Discussion).

8. Security

a. The two Sides will, in accordance with the prior agreements, act to ensure the immediate, efficient and effective handling of any incident involving a threat or act of terrorism, violence or incitement, whether committed by Palestinians or Israelis. To this end, they will cooperate in the exchange of information and coordinate policies and activities. Each side shall immediately and effectively respond to the occurrence or anticipated occurrence of an act of terrorism, violence or incitement and shall take all necessary measures to prevent such an occurrence;

b. Pursuant to the prior agreements, the Palestinian side undertakes to implement its responsibilities for security, security cooperation, on-going obligations and other issues emanating from the prior agreements, including, in particular, the following obligations emanating from the Wye River Memorandum:

1. continuation of the program for the collection of the illegal weapons, including reports;
2. apprehension of suspects, including reports;
3. forwarding of the list of Palestinian policemen to the Israeli Side not later than September 13, 1999;
4. beginning of the review of the list by the Monitoring and Steering Committee not later than October 15, 1999.

9. The two Sides call upon the international donor community to enhance its commitment and financial support to the Palestinian economic development and the Israeli-Palestinian peace process.

10. Recognizing the necessity to create a positive environment for the negotiations, neither side shall initiate or take any step that will change the status of the West Bank and the Gaza Strip in accordance with the Interim Agreement.

11. Obligations pertaining to dates, which occur on holidays or Saturdays, shall be carried out on the first subsequent working day.

This memorandum will enter into force one week from the date of its signature.1

1999.
Made and signed in Sharm el-Sheikh this fourth day of September

For the Government of the State of Israel
For the PLO

Witnessed by
For the Arab Republic of Egypt
For the United States of America
For the Hashemite Kingdom of Jordan

1. It is understood that, for technical reasons, implementation of Article 2-a and the first stage mentioned in Article 3-c will be carried out within a week from the signing of this Memorandum.

V-15. Protocol Concerning Safe Passage Between the West Bank and the Gaza Strip, October 5, 1999, <http://www.israel.org/mfa/go.asp?MFAH00pq0>.

Parties
Israel and Palestine Liberation Organization

Full Text

1. Preamble

A. Pursuant to the Wye River Memorandum of October 23, 1998 and the Sharm el-Sheikh Memorandum on Implementation Timeline of Outstanding Commitments of Agreements Signed and the Resumption of Permanent Status Negotiations of September 4, 1999; and

In accordance with the Israeli-Palestinian Interim Agreement on the West Bank and the Gaza Strip, signed in Washington, D.C. on September 28, 1995 (hereinafter "the Agreement"); and

With a view to implement Article X and the other related provisions of Annex I to the Agreement "Protocol Concerning Redeployment and Security Arrangements" (hereinafter "Annex I"), both sides hereby agree to the following "Protocol Concerning Safe Passage between the West Bank and the Gaza Strip" (hereinafter the "Protocol").

B. This Protocol establishes the modalities for the use of safe passage. The arrangements set out in this Protocol are subject to the Agreement and are not in any way intended to derogate from any of its provisions, including, inter alia, the provisions of the Agreement regarding passage between the West Bank and Israel, between the Gaza Strip and Israel and between the West Bank and the Gaza Strip.

C. This Protocol may be amended by a decision of both sides.

D. This Protocol will come into force upon the signing thereof by both parties.

E. This Preamble is an integral part of this Protocol.

2. General Provisions

A. Article X of Annex I, and the attached map No. 6 delineate two routes through which Israel will make safe passage available.

B.

1. Israel will ensure safe passage for persons and transportation during daylight hours (from sunrise to sunset) or as otherwise agreed, but in any event not less than 10 hours a day.

2. Travelers will be required to commence their journey as follows,

   i. one and a half hours for travelers using private vehicles and taxis;
   ii. two hours for commercial traffic and buses, before sunset on the day of the journey.

C.

1. Safe passage will be effected by means of privately owned road vehicles and public transportation, as detailed in paragraph 5 below.

2. Safe passage shall be via the following designated crossing points:

   i. the Erez crossing point (for persons and vehicles only);
   ii. the Karni crossing point (Commercial) (for goods only);
   iii. the Tarkumya crossing point (for persons, vehicles and goods); and
   iv. an additional crossing point around Mevo Horon.

D.

1. The safe passage arrangements will not be available on Yom Kippur, Israel's Memorial Day and Israel's Independence Day.

2. Both sides may make special arrangements for other designated days, as agreed between them.

E. Israel shall signpost the safe passage routes clearly and shall take all necessary measures to ensure smooth movement while preserving safety and security on the route or routes in use on any specific day.

F. Except as provided in paragraph 3.H.2 below, the use of safe passage by residents of the West Bank and the Gaza Strip does not afford them license to be present in Israel except along the safe passage routes designated for their use.

G. Israel may, for security or safety reasons, temporarily halt the operation of a safe passage route or modify the passage arrangements while ensuring that one of the routes is kept open for safe passage. Notice of such temporary closure or modification shall be given to the Palestinian side, through agreed channels, as far in advance as the circumstances will allow.

H. Israel may deny the use of its territory for safe passage by persons who have seriously or repeatedly violated the safe passage provisions detailed in this Protocol or in the Agreement. Israel will notify the Palestinian side, through agreed channels, of any decision to deny the use of its territory as a result of such violations. The notification shall include details of the violations giving rise to the denial. The individual in question shall have the right to request, through the Palestinian side, that Israel reconsider its decision.

I. Nothing in this Protocol will be construed as derogating from Israel's right to apply inspection measures necessary for ensuring security and safety at the crossing points of the safe passage. Maximum efforts will be made to maintain the dignity of persons using safe passage and to implement inspection measures relying heavily on brief and modern procedures.

J. Israel shall notify the Palestinian side of incidents involving persons using safe passage routes through the agreed channels.

K. It is understood that the safe passage shall be operated on a cost-reimbursement basis, in accordance with an agreement on the modalities to be reached in the Joint Economic Committee.

L. Israel shall be compensated for damages incurred by Israel, Israelis or their property as a result of the use of safe passage, in accordance with an agreement on the modalities to be reached in the Joint Economic Committee.

3. Use of Safe Passage

A. Residents of the West Bank and the Gaza Strip wishing to make use of safe passage shall arrive with a safe passage card at the safe passage terminal at one of the crossing points specified at paragraph 2.C.2 above, where they will identify themselves by means of identification documents as mentioned in paragraph 6, Article 28, Appendix 1, Annex III to the Agreement.

B. After identification at the terminal, and after the validity check of the safe passage card, travelers will be issued with safe passage slips subject to the provisions of this Protocol and the Agreement, except for persons provided for in paragraph 2.H above and paragraph 6 below.

C.

1. The Palestinian side shall transfer to the Israeli side all applications for safe passage cards, after initial Palestinian security approval. The applications shall be in accordance with the agreed procedures (including the submission of all required information as well as two updated photographs).

2. The Israeli side shall respond to the applications within two working days. It is agreed that in all cases in which the photographs submitted with the application do not match the Israeli database, or in which the photograph of the individual does not appear in the Israeli database, the application shall not be processed and shall be returned to the Palestinian side.

3. Safe passage cards shall be issued in the relevant Israeli District Civil Liaison Office (DCL) in the West Bank or in the Regional Civil Affairs Subcommittee (RCAC) in the Gaza Strip.

4. On-duty Palestinian policemen and minors under age 14, traveling in accordance with the provisions of paragraphs 7 and 3.I below, respectively, shall not be required to receive a safe passage card for the use of safe passage.

5. Men over 50 and women shall generally receive their safe passage cards through the Palestinian side, except for special cases. The Israeli side will make all efforts to minimize such exceptions.

6. In light of the special nature of the safe passage, those persons whose applications for safe passage have been approved shall receive from the Israeli side their safe passage cards at the Israeli side of the District Palestinian liaison officer shall be present throughout all stages of this process. Receipt of the safe passage card shall be contingent on the individual being definitively identified by the Israeli side, using the best available methods (including, in the near future, biometric information), as agreed upon by the two sides.

D. A safe passage card shall be valid for one year for multiple two-way journeys on the safe passage routes. Travelers can only use safe passage within the operation time as provided for in paragraphs 2.B.1 and 2.B.2 above.

International Humanitarian Law and Arms Control Agreements 687

E. Upon completion of the journey, the safe passage slips and safe passage stickers shall be returned to the Israeli authorities at the destination crossing point.

F. Residents of the West Bank and the Gaza Strip in possession of permits enabling them to enter Israel will be able to use these permits as safe passage cards, subject to the conditions of such permits and to the modalities set out in this Protocol.

G.

1. Individual safe passage slips will be issued and stamped by the Israeli authorities at the crossing points, with the time of departure from the crossing point and the estimated time of arrival (hereinafter "the designated time").

2. The designated time shall enable completion of the journey within a reasonable time.

H.

1. Persons and vehicles using safe passage under these arrangements shall neither break their journey nor depart from the designated routes, and shall complete the passage within the designated time, unless a delay is caused by a medical emergency or a technical breakdown.

2. Notwithstanding paragraph 3.H.1 above, in the case of a medical emergency, travelers may drive directly to the nearest hospital or first aid station. Such travelers will be required to report the incident to the relevant authorities at the destination crossing point as soon as circumstances allow.

3. In the case of a technical breakdown, travelers must remain on the safe passage route with their vehicles until the arrival of the Israeli police and follow their instructions. In addition, travelers may stop another vehicle using safe passage and request the driver to inform the authorities at the destination crossing point of the case.

I.

1.
 a. Minors under the age of 16 who are accompanied by a parent and registered in the identity card of that parent will not be required to carry individual safe passage cards.

b. Such minors shall identify themselves via the identity card of the accompanying parent.

2.

a. Minors who are not accompanied by a parent may also use safe passage without carrying a safe passage card provided that:

    i. they are under the age of 14; and
    ii. they are accompanied by an adult (18 or over).

b. Such minors shall identify themselves by means of a birth certificate or a certified copy of the parent's identity card in which they are registered.

J. Persons and vehicles shall not carry explosives, firearms or other weapons or ammunition except for special cases that may be agreed by both sides. Transportation of dangerous substances shall be in accordance with the provisions of the Agreement.

4. Use of Safe Passage Routes by Visitors from Abroad

A. Provisions of the Agreement and this Protocol regarding the use of safe passage will apply to visitors to the West Bank and the Gaza Strip from abroad, without derogating from the provisions of the Agreement concerning visitors.

B. Visitors will identify themselves by means of: (i) valid visitors' permits; and (ii) passports or travel documents when using the safe passage.

5. Use of Vehicles on Safe Passage Routes

A.

1. Residents of the West Bank and the Gaza Strip wishing to use their privately owned vehicles to travel along the safe passage shall apply for a vehicle safe passage permit through the Palestinian side. The Israeli side shall respond to such applications within five working days. Such applications shall include the identification documents referred to in paragraph 3.A above; safe passage cards or permits enabling them entry into Israel; valid drivers' licenses; valid vehicle licenses; and valid insurance policies. The vehicle safe passage permits shall be issued in the relevant Israeli DCL in the West Bank or in the RCAC in the Gaza Strip and transferred to the Palestinian side.

2. In addition to the above, the two sides may agree on specific categories or persons who may use a vehicle not owned by them. Such categories include, inter alia: (i) persons employed by the Palestinian Authority driving a vehicle owned by the Palestinian Authority; (ii) persons employed by a private company driving a vehicle owned by the private company; and (iii) taxi drivers (only one designated driver per taxi). In such cases, in addition to all other requirements of this Protocol, the person shall be required to possess and submit a written permit signed by the Palestinian side and by the vehicle-owner authorizing that person's use of the vehicle for safe passage.

B.

1. On the day of the journey, the drivers will arrive at the safe passage terminal at the departure crossing point with their vehicle safe passage permits; safe passage cards or permits enabling them entry into Israel; identity cards; valid drivers' licenses; valid vehicle licenses; valid insurance policies; and, if applicable, the permit referred to in paragraph 5.A.2 above. After identification, and after the validity check of the vehicle safe passage permit, drivers will be issued with an individual safe passage slip and a safe passage sticker, to be displayed on the right-hand side of the front windshield of the vehicle.

2. The names of all passengers traveling in the vehicle shall be listed on a separate document to be attached to the driver's safe passage slip.

3. Persons listed as travelers in a particular vehicle must remain with the vehicle for the full duration of their safe passage journey, except for the medical emergencies provided for in paragraph 3.H.2 above.

C. Residents of the West Bank or the Gaza Strip in possession of valid permits enabling them to enter Israel with their vehicles, will be able to use these permits as vehicle safe passage permits, subject to the conditions of such permits and to the modalities set out in this Protocol.

D.

1.Vehicle safe passage permits shall be valid for not less than three months from the date of issuance, for multiple two-way journeys.

2.Certain persons who are acceptable to both sides will be issued vehicle safe passage permits, the validity of which shall be for more than the period specified in paragraph 5.D.1 above and up to one year. Such permits shall be issued provided that the Joint Civil Affairs Coordination and Cooperation

Committee (CAC) had applied for them through the relevant DCL in the West Bank or the RCAC in the Gaza Strip.

E. All vehicles used by residents of the West Bank and the Gaza Strip for the purpose of traveling via safe passage must have valid licensing in accordance with Article 38, Appendix 1, Annex III to the Agreement and at least valid compulsory insurance policies, in accordance with Article 19, Appendix 1, Annex III to the Agreement, and Article XI, Annex V to the Agreement.

F. All vehicles used for the purpose of safe passage shall meet Israeli standards and applicable Israeli law.

G.

1. "Sterile" public transportation vehicles shall operate between Tarkumya and Erez crossing points.

2. The public transportation vehicles will be designated for the purpose of safe passage only.

3. The public transportation vehicles as well as their drivers should be acceptable to both sides.

H. In special emergency related cases, to be handled through agreed channels, safe passage may be used by privately owned vehicles without having submitted an application in advance.

6. Use of Safe Passage by Persons Denied Entry into Israel

A. Persons who are denied entry into Israel will use safe passage by means of shuttle buses which will he escorted by Israeli security forces vehicles, and which will operate from 7:00 AM to 2:00 PM on Mondays and Wednesdays of every week.

B. Applications by persons denied entry into Israel to use the safe passage must be submitted to, and agreed upon, at least five working days prior to the planned journey.

C. Cases of persons denied entry into Israel whose applications to use safe passage are not agreed upon shall be discussed in the agreed channels.

D.

1. Persons denied entry into Israel who have used the safe passage will be able to return that same day to their original point of departure via the mechanism established in paragraph 6.A above.

2. Persons denied entry into Israel and who have used the safe passage will be able to return to their original point of departure by shuttle bus within two weeks following the date of departure with notification through the agreed channels at least 1 working day prior to the planned journey.

3. Persons denied entry into Israel and who have stayed for a period in excess of that specified in paragraph 6.D.2 above, will be required to submit applications as provided for in paragraph 6.B above.

E.

1. The aforementioned shuttle buses shall have Palestinian registration and shall be driven by Palestinian residents.

2. The aforementioned shuttle buses as well as their drivers should be acceptable to both sides.

7. Passage of Palestinian Police

A. In accordance with paragraph 2.g, Article X of Annex I, uniformed and plainclothes Palestinian policemen required to use the safe passage so as to perform their duty in the West Bank and the Gaza Strip, or Palestinian policemen other than in instances covered by paragraph 7.E below, using privately owned vehicles, official vehicles or other means of transportation, will be able to use the safe passage after the Palestinian police has submitted an application and after that application was approved, through the relevant DCO two working days prior to the planned journey.

B. Palestinian policemen provided for in paragraph 7.A above and Palestinian police vehicles and equipment moving between the West Bank and the Gaza Strip via safe passage shall be escorted by Israeli security forces vehicles.

C. When in safe passage, the weapons of the Palestinian policemen will be handed over to the Israeli police and placed in a closed trailer affixed to the Israel police vehicle. A Palestinian policeman may travel in the aforementioned Israeli police vehicle. The vehicle shall be driven by a member of the Israeli police.

Upon completion of the safe passage journey the weapons shall be handed over to the Palestinian officer in charge in the DCO.

D. Cases of usage of safe passage by Palestinian policemen requiring special attention and arrangements will be dealt with and coordinated through the Joint Coordination and Cooperation Committee for Mutual Security Purposes (JSC).

E. The provisions set out in this Protocol and in the Agreement relating to regular persons will apply to Palestinian policemen using safe passage when off duty. Such policemen may only use safe passage when unarmed and out of uniform.

8. Use of Safe Passage for Commercial Traffic

A. Goods transferred to or from the Gaza Strip via the safe passage will enter or leave the Gaza Strip through the Karni (Commercial) crossing point.

B. Commercial vehicles carrying goods from the West Bank to the Gaza Strip via safe passage will travel along the relevant safe passage route as far as the Yad Mordechai Junction, and from there branch off to Karni as indicated on Map No. 6 (attached to the Agreement). Commercial vehicles carrying goods from the Gaza Strip to the West Bank will follow the same routes in reverse.

C. All provisions of this Protocol and the Agreement relating to use of vehicles on safe passage routes shall apply to the use of commercial vehicles.

D. The provisions in this paragraph 8 shall not prejudice any other mechanism established in the Agreement, or based on the Agreement, with respect to passage of goods.

E. Further details concerning commercial traffic will be agreed upon in a special sub-committee in the CAC. Until decided otherwise, the current arrangements adopted by the CAC concerning commercial traffic shall remain in effect.

9. Future Meetings for Improving Operation of the Safe Passage

A Continuing Safe Passage Committee shall meet regularly to supervise the implementation of this Protocol and to discuss ways to improve the safe passage operation, as agreed between both sides.

10. Use of Safe Passage by the Ra'ees of the Executive Authority

Arrangements for the use of safe passage by the Ra'ees of the Executive Authority shall be discussed in a special sub-committee through the JSC.

11. Final Clauses

A. Consistent with paragraph 6, Article XXXI of the Agreement, the arrangements included in this Protocol are without prejudice to the permanent status negotiations.

B. There shall be a Liaison Bureau at agreed locations close to each of the safe passage crossing points. In addition, the Palestinian side shall establish coordination points at agreed locations on the roads leading to the crossing points. The function of the coordination points shall be to ensure the smooth and orderly movement of persons and vehicles to the crossing points, in accordance with their capacity.

C. In between the operation of the Southern crossing point of the safe passage and the Northern crossing point of the safe passage, Israel will facilitate arrangements for the movement between the West Bank and the Gaza Strip, using non-safe passage routes other than the Southern route of the safe passage.

Done at Jerusalem, this 5th day of October, 1999.

V-16. **Establishment of a Nuclear-Weapon-Free Zone in the Region of the Middle East, United Nations General Assembly,** Distr. GENERAL A/RES/54/51 7 January 2000 Fifty-fourth session Agenda item 73 Resolution Adopted By the General Assembly [*on the report of the First Committee (A/54/560)*].

Full Text

The General Assembly,

Recalling its resolutions 3263 (XXIX) of 9 December 1974, 3474 (XXX) of 11 December 1975, 31/71 of 10 December 1976, 32/82 of 12 December 1977, 33/64 of 14 December 1978, 34/77 of 11 December 1979, 35/147 of 12 December 1980, 36/87 A and B of 9 December 1981, 37/75 of 9 December 1982, 38/64 of 15 December 1983, 39/54 of 12 December 1984, 40/82 of 12 December 1985, 41/48 of 3 December 1986, 42/28 of 30 November 1987, 43/65 of 7 December 1988, 44/108 of 15 December 1989, 45/52 of 4 December 1990, 46/30 of 6 December 1991, 47/48 of 9 December 1992, 48/71 of 16 December 1993, 49/71 of 15 December 1994, 50/66 of 12 December 1995, 51/41 of 10 December 1996, 52/34 of 9 December 1997 and 53/74 of 4 December 1998 on the establishment of a nuclear-weapon-free zone in the region of the Middle East,

Recalling also the recommendations for the establishment of such a zone in the Middle East consistent with paragraphs 60 to 63, and in particular paragraph 63 (*d*), of the Final Document of the Tenth Special Session of the General Assembly,

Emphasizing the basic provisions of the above-mentioned resolutions, which call upon all parties directly concerned to consider taking the practical and urgent steps required for the implementation of the proposal to establish a nuclear-weapon-free zone in the region of the Middle East and, pending and during the establishment of such a zone, to declare solemnly that they will refrain, on a reciprocal basis, from producing, acquiring or in any other way possessing nuclear weapons and nuclear explosive devices and from permitting the stationing of nuclear weapons on their territory by any third party, to agree to place their nuclear facilities under International Atomic Energy Agency safeguards and to declare their support for the establishment of the zone and to deposit such declarations with the Security Council for consideration, as appropriate,

Reaffirming the inalienable right of all States to acquire and develop nuclear energy for peaceful purposes,

Emphasizing the need for appropriate measures on the question of the prohibition of military attacks on nuclear facilities,

Bearing in mind the consensus reached by the General Assembly since its thirty-fifth session that the establishment of a nuclear-weapon-free zone in the Middle East would greatly enhance international peace and security,

Desirous of building on that consensus so that substantial progress can be made towards establishing a nuclear-weapon-free zone in the Middle East,

Welcoming all initiatives leading to general and complete disarmament, including in the region of the Middle East, and in particular on the establishment therein of a zone free of weapons of mass destruction, including nuclear weapons,

Noting the peace negotiations in the Middle East, which should be of a comprehensive nature and represent an appropriate framework for the peaceful settlement of contentious issues in the region,

Recognizing the importance of credible regional security, including the establishment of a mutually verifiable nuclear-weapon-free zone,

Emphasizing the essential role of the United Nations in the establishment of a mutually verifiable nuclear-weapon-free zone,

Having examined the report of the Secretary-General on the implementation of General Assembly resolution 53/74,
1. *Urges* all parties directly concerned to consider seriously taking the practical and urgent steps required for the implementation of the proposal to establish a nuclear-weapon-free zone in the region of the Middle East in accordance with the relevant resolutions of the General Assembly, and, as a means of promoting this objective, invites the countries concerned to adhere to the Treaty on the Non-Proliferation of Nuclear Weapons;

2.*Calls upon* all countries of the region that have not done so, pending the establishment of the zone, to agree to place all their nuclear activities under International Atomic Energy Agency safeguards;

3. *Takes note* of resolution GC(43)/RES/23, adopted on 1 October 1999 by the General Conference of the International Atomic Energy Agency at its forty-third regular session, concerning the application of Agency safeguards in the Middle East;

4. *Notes* the importance of the ongoing bilateral Middle East peace negotiations and the activities of the multilateral Working Group on Arms Control and Regional Security in promoting mutual confidence and security in the Middle East, including the establishment of a nuclear-weapon-free zone;

5. *Invites* all countries of the region, pending the establishment of a nuclear-weapon-free zone in the region of the Middle East, to declare their support for

establishing such a zone, consistent with paragraph 63 (*d*) of the Final Document of the Tenth Special Session of the General Assembly, and to deposit those declarations with the Security Council;

6. *Also invites* those countries, pending the establishment of the zone, not to develop, produce, test or otherwise acquire nuclear weapons or permit the stationing on their territories, or territories under their control, of nuclear weapons or nuclear explosive devices;

7. *Invites* the nuclear-weapon States and all other States to render their assistance in the establishment of the zone and at the same time to refrain from any action that runs counter to both the letter and the spirit of the present resolution;

8. *Takes note* of the report of the Secretary-General;

9. *Invites* all parties to consider the appropriate means that may contribute towards the goal of general and complete disarmament and the establishment of a zone free of weapons of mass destruction in the region of the Middle East;

10. *Requests* the Secretary-General to continue to pursue consultations with the States of the region and other concerned States, in accordance with paragraph 7 of resolution 46/30 and taking into account the evolving situation in the region, and to seek from those States their views on the measures outlined in chapters III and IV of the study annexed to his report or other relevant measures, in order to move towards the establishment of a nuclear-weapon-free zone in the Middle East;

11. *Also requests* the Secretary-General to submit to the General Assembly at its fifty-fifth session a report on the implementation of the present resolution;

12. *Decides* to include in the provisional agenda of its fifty-fifth session the item entitled "Establishment of a nuclear-weapon-free zone in the region of the Middle East".

69th plenary meeting
1 December 1999
A/45/435.

CHAPTER VI

EUROPEAN ARMS CONTROL AND SECURITY AGREEMENTS

INTRODUCTION

Chapter VI pertains to a classic arms control category. It includes the 1990 Conventional Armed Forces in Europe (CFE) Treaty, and the Addendum to the Treaty. The Treaty limits five categories of weapons: tanks, artillery, armored combat vehicles, combat helicopters, and attack aircraft. The agreement applies among NATO members and former Warsaw Pact members. By way of the Tashkent Agreement, the Russian Federation and the Ukraine acknowledged as successor states the responsibilities originally agreed to by the Soviet Union. Also, in 1992 the Russian Federation announced that it would be successor state to all treaties formerly binding on the Union of Soviet Socialist Republics.

International Humanitarian Law and Arms Control Agreements 701

VI-1. Conventional Armed Forces in Europe (CFE) Treaty, November 10, 1990; done at Paris, November 19, 1990, 30 I.L.M. 6 (1991). Authentic Texts: English, French, German, Italian, Russian and Spanish.

State Parties

Armenia; Azerbaijan; Belarus; The Kingdom of Belgium; the Republic of Bulgaria; Canada; the Czech and Slovak Federal Republic; the Kingdom of Denmark; Georgia; the French Republic; the Federal Republic of Germany, Greece; the Republic of Hungary; the Republic of Iceland; the Italian Republic; Kazakhstan; the Grand Duchy of Luxembourg; Moldovia; the Kingdom of the Netherlands; the Kingdom of Norway; the Republic of Poland; the Portuguese Republic, Romania; Russian Federation; Slovak Republic; the Kingdom of Spain, the Republic of Turkey; Ukraine; the United Kingdom of Great Britain and Northern Ireland; the United States of America

With Reservation
Turkey

Full Text

The Kingdom of Belgium, the Republic of Bulgaria, Canada, the Czech and Slovak Federal Republic, the Kingdom of Denmark, the French Republic, the Federal Republic of Germany, the Hellenic Republic, the Republic of Hungary, the Republic of Iceland, the Italian Republic, the Grand Duchy of Luxembourg, the Kingdom of the Netherlands, the Kingdom of Norway, the Republic of Poland, the Portuguese Republic, Romania, the Kingdom of Spain, the Republic of Turkey, the Union of Soviet Socialist Republics, the United Kingdom of Great Britain and Northern Ireland and the United States of America, hereinafter referred to as the States Parties,

Guided by the Mandate for Negotiation on Conventional Armed Forces in Europe of January 10, 1989, and having conducted this negotiation in Vienna beginning on March 9, 1989,

Guided by the objectives and the purposes of the Conference on Security and Cooperation in Europe, within the framework of which the negotiation of this Treaty was conducted,

Recalling their obligation to refrain in their mutual relations, as well as in their international relations in general, from the threat or use of force against the territorial integrity or political independence of any State, or in any other manner inconsistent with the purposes and principles of the Charter of the United Nations, Conscious of the need to prevent any military conflict in Europe,
Conscious of the common responsibility which they all have for seeking to achieve greater stability and security in Europe,

Striving to replace military confrontation with a new pattern of security relations among all the States Parties based on peaceful cooperation and thereby to contribute to overcoming the division of Europe,

Committed to the objectives of establishing a secure and stable balance of conventional armed forces in Europe at lower levels than heretofore, of eliminating disparities prejudicial to stability and security and of eliminating, as a matter of high priority, the capability for launching surprise attack and for initiating large-scale offensive action in Europe,

Recalling that they signed or acceded to the Treaty of Brussels of 1948, the Treaty of Washington of 1949 or the Treaty of Warsaw of 1955 and that they have the right to be or not to be a party to treaties of alliance,

Committed to the objective of ensuring that the numbers of conventional armaments and equipment limited by the Treaty within the area of application of this Treaty do not exceed 40,000 battle tanks, 60,000 armoured combat vehicles, 40,000 pieces of artillery, 13,600 combat aircraft and 4,000 attack helicopters, Affirming that this Treaty is not intended to affect adversely the security interests of any State,

Affirming their commitment to continue the conventional arms control process including negotiations, taking into account future requirements for European stability and security in the light of political developments in Europe,
Have agreed as follows:

Article I
1. Each State Party shall carry out the obligations set forth in this Treaty in accordance with its provisions, including those obligations relating to the following five categories of conventional armed forces: battle tanks, armoured combat vehicles, artillery, combat aircraft and combat helicopters.

2. Each State Party also shall carry out the other measures set forth in this Treaty designed to ensure security and stability both during the period of reduction of conventional armed forces and after the completion of reductions.

3. This Treaty incorporates the Protocol on Existing Types of Conventional Armaments and Equipment, hereinafter referred to as the Protocol on Existing Types, with an Annex thereto; the Protocol on Procedures Governing the Reclassification of Specific Models or Versions of Combat-Capable Trainer Aircraft Into Unarmed Trainer Aircraft, hereinafter referred to as the Protocol on Aircraft Reclassification; the Protocol on Procedures Governing the Reduction of Conventional Armaments and Equipment Limited by the Treaty on Conventional Armed Forces in Europe, hereinafter referred to as the Protocol on Reduction; the Protocol on Procedures Governing the Categorization of Combat Helicopters and the Recategorization of Multi-Purpose Attack Helicopters, hereinafter referred to

as the Protocol on Helicopter Recategorization; the Protocol on Notification and Exchange of Information, hereinafter referred to as the Protocol on Information Exchange, with an Annex on the Format for the Exchange of Information, hereinafter referred to as the Annex on Format; the Protocol on Inspection; the Protocol on the Joint Consultative Group; and the Protocol on the Provisional Application of Certain Provisions of the Treaty on Conventional Armed Forces in Europe, hereinafter referred to as the Protocol on Provisional Application. Each of these documents constitutes an integral part of this Treaty.

Article II
For the purposes of this Treaty:

(A) The term "group of States Parties" means the group of States Parties that signed the Treaty of Warsaw* of 1955 consisting of the Republic of Bulgaria, the Czech and Slovak Federal Republic, the Republic of Hungary, the Republic of Poland, Romania and the Union of Soviet Socialist Republics, or the group of States Parties that signed or acceded to the Treaty of Brussels** of 1948 or the Treaty of Washington*** of 1949 consisting of the Kingdom of Belgium, Canada, the Kingdom of Denmark, the French Republic, the Federal Republic of Germany, the Hellenic Republic, the Republic of Iceland, the Italian Republic, the Grand Duchy of Luxembourg, the Kingdom of the Netherlands, the Kingdom of Norway, the Portuguese Republic, the Kingdom of Spain, the Republic of Turkey, the United Kingdom of Great Britain and Northern Ireland and the United States of America.

(B) The term "area of application" means the entire land territory of the States Parties in Europe from the Atlantic Ocean to the Ural Mountains, which includes all the European island territories of the States Parties, including the Faroe Islands of the Kingdom of Denmark, Svalbard including Bear Island of the Kingdom of Norway, the islands of Azores and Madeira of the Portuguese Republic, the Canary Islands of the Kingdom of Spain and Franz Josef Land and Novaya Zemlya of the Union of Soviet Socialist Republics. In the case of the Union of Soviet Socialist Republics, the area of application includes all territory lying west of the Ural River and the Caspian Sea. In the case of the Republic of Turkey, the area of application includes the territory of the Republic of Turkey north and west of a line extending from the point of intersection of the Turkish border with the 39th parallel to Muradiye, Patnos, Karayazi, Tekman, Kemaliye, Feke, Ceyhan, Dogankent, Gozne and thence to the sea.

(C) The term "battle tank" means a self-propelled armoured fighting vehicle, capable of heavy firepower, primarily of a high muzzle velocity direct fire main gun necessary to engage armoured and other targets, with high cross-country mobility, with a high level of self-protection, and which is not designed and equipped primarily to transport combat troops. Such armoured vehicles serve as the principal weapon system of ground-force tank and other armoured formations. Battle tanks are tracked armoured fighting vehicles which weigh at least 16.5

metric tonnes unladen weight and which are armed with a 360-degree traverse gun of at least 75 millimeters calibre. In addition, any wheeled armoured fighting vehicles entering into service which meet all the other criteria stated above shall also be deemed battle tanks.

(D) The term "armoured combat vehicle" means a self-propelled vehicle with armoured protection and cross-country capability. Armoured combat vehicles include armoured personnel carriers, armoured infantry fighting vehicles and heavy armament combat vehicles.

The term "armoured personnel carrier" means an armoured combat vehicle which is designed and equipped to transport a combat infantry squad and which, as a rule, is armed with an integral or organic weapon of less than 20 millimeters calibre.

The term "armoured infantry fighting vehicle"means an armoured combat vehicle which is designed and equipped primarily to transport a combat infantry squad, which normally provides the capability for the troops to deliver fire from inside the vehicle under armoured protection, and which is armed with an integral or organic cannon of at least 20 millimeters calibre and sometimes an antitank missile launcher. Armoured infantry fighting vehicles serve as the principal weapon system of armoured infantry or mechanized infantry or motorized infantry formations and units of ground forces.

The term "heavy armament combat vehicle" means an armoured combat vehicle with an integral or organic direct fire gun of at least 75 millimeters calibre, weighing at least 6.0 metric tonnes unladen weight, which does not fall within the definitions of an armoured personnel carrier, or an armoured infantry fighting vehicle or a battle tank.

(E) The term "unladen weight" means the weight of a vehicle excluding the weight of ammunition; fuel, oil and lubricants; removable reactive amour; spare parts, tools and accessories; removable snorkeling equipment; and crew and their personal kit.

(F) The term "artillery" means large calibre systems capable of engaging ground targets by delivering primarily indirect fire. Such artillery systems provide the essential indirect fire support to combined arms formations.

Large calibre artillery systems are guns, howitzers, artillery pieces combining the characteristics of guns and howitzers, mortars and multiple launch rocket systems with a calibre of 100 millimeters and above. In addition, any future large calibre direct fire system which has a secondary effective indirect fire capability shall be counted against the artillery ceilings.

(G) The term "stationed conventional armed forces" means conventional armed forces of a State Party that are stationed within the area of application on the territory of another State Party.

(H) The term "designated permanent storage site" means a place with a clearly defined physical boundary containing conventional armaments and equipment limited by the Treaty, which are counted within overall ceilings but which are not subject to limitations on conventional armaments and equipment limited by the Treaty in active units.

(I) The term "armoured vehicle launched bridge" means a self-propelled armoured transporter-launcher vehicle capable of carrying and, through built-in mechanisms, of emplacing and retrieving a bridge structure. Such a vehicle with a bridge structure operates as an integrated system.

(J) The term "conventional armaments and equipment limited by the Treaty" means battle tanks, armoured combat vehicles, artillery, combat aircraft and attack helicopters subject to the numerical limitations set forth in Articles IV, V and VI.

(K) The term "combat aircraft" means a fixed-wing or variable-geometry wing aircraft armed and equipped to engage targets by employing guided missiles, unguided rockets, bombs, guns, cannons, or other weapons of destruction, as well as any model or version of such an aircraft which performs other military functions such as reconnaissance or electronic warfare.
The term "combat aircraft" does not include primary trainer aircraft.

(L) The term "combat helicopter" means a rotary wing aircraft armed and equipped to engage targets or equipped to perform other military functions. The term "combat helicopter" comprises attack helicopters and combat support helicopters. The term "combat helicopter" does not include unarmed transport helicopters.

(M) The term "attack helicopter" means a combat helicopter equipped to employ anti-armour, air-to-ground, or air-to-air guided weapons and equipped with an integrated fire control and aiming system for these weapons. The term "attack helicopter" comprises specialized attack helicopters and multi-purpose attack helicopters.

(N) The term "specialized attack helicopter" means an attack helicopter that is designed primarily to employ guided weapons.

(O) The term "multi-purpose attack helicopter" means an attack helicopter designed to perform multiple military functions and equipped to employ guided weapons.

(P) The term "combat support helicopter" means a combat helicopter which does not fulfill the requirements to qualify as an attack helicopter and which may be equipped with a variety of self-defense and area suppression weapons, such as guns, cannons and unguided rockets, bombs or cluster bombs, or which may be equipped to perform other military functions.

(Q) The term "conventional armaments and equipment subject to the Treaty" means battle tanks, armoured combat vehicles, artillery, combat aircraft, primary trainer aircraft, unarmed trainer aircraft, combat helicopters, unarmed transport helicopters, armoured vehicle launched bridges, armoured personnel carrier look-alikes and armoured infantry fighting vehicle look-alikes subject to information exchange in accordance with the Protocol on Information Exchange.

(R) The term "in service," as it applies to conventional armed forces and conventional armaments and equipment, means battle tanks, armoured combat vehicles, artillery, combat aircraft, primary trainer aircraft, unarmed trainer aircraft, combat helicopters, unarmed transport helicopters, armoured vehicle launched bridges, armoured personnel carrier look-alikes and armoured infantry fighting vehicle look-alikes that are within the area of application, except for those that are held by organizations designed and structured to perform in peacetime internal security functions or that meet any of the exceptions set forth in Article III.

(S) The terms "armoured personnel carrier look-alike" and "armoured infantry fighting vehicle look-alike" mean an armoured vehicle based on the same chassis as, and externally similar to, an armoured personnel carrier or armoured infantry fighting vehicle, respectively, which does not have a cannon or gun of 20 millimeters calibre or greater and which has been constructed or modified in such a way as not to permit the transportation of a combat infantry squad. Taking into account the provisions of the Geneva Convention "For the Amelioration of the Conditions of the Wounded and Sick in Armed Forces in the Field" of 12 August 1949 that confer a special status on ambulances, armoured personnel carrier ambulances shall not be deemed armoured combat vehicles or armoured personnel carrier look-alikes.

(T) The term "reduction site" means a clearly designated location where the reduction of conventional armaments and equipment limited by the Treaty in accordance with Article VIII takes place.

(U) The term "reduction liability" means the number in each category of conventional armaments and equipment limited by the Treaty that a State Party commits itself to reduce during the period of 40 months following the entry into force of this Treaty in order to ensure compliance with Article VII.

2. Existing types of conventional armaments and equipment subject to the Treaty are listed in the Protocol on Existing Types. The lists of existing types shall be periodically updated in accordance with Article XVI, paragraph 2, subparagraph (D) and Section IV of the Protocol on Existing Types. Such updates to the existing types lists shall not be deemed amendments to this Treaty.

3. The existing types of combat helicopters listed in the Protocol on Existing Types shall be categorized in accordance with Section I of the Protocol on Helicopter Recategorization.

Article III
1. For the purposes of this Treaty, the States Parties shall apply the following counting rules: All battle tanks, armoured combat vehicles, artillery, combat aircraft and attack helicopters, as defined in Article II, within the area of application shall be subject to the numerical limitations and other provisions set forth in Articles IV, V and VI, with the exception of those which in a manner consistent with a State Party's normal practices:

(A) are in the process of manufacture, including manufacturing-related testing;
(B) are used exclusively for the purposes of research and development;
(C) belong to historical collections;
(D) are awaiting disposal, having been decommissioned from service in accordance with the provisions of Article IX;
(E) are awaiting, or are being refurbished for, export or re-export and are temporarily retained within the area of application. Such battle tanks, armoured combat vehicles, artillery, combat aircraft and attack helicopters shall be located elsewhere than at sites declared under the terms of Section V of the Protocol on Information Exchange or at no more than 10 such declared sites which shall have been notified in the previous year's annual information exchange. In the latter case, they shall be separately distinguishable from conventional armaments and equipment limited by the Treaty;
(F) are, in the case of armoured personnel carriers, armoured infantry fighting vehicles, heavy armament combat vehicles or multi-purpose attack helicopters, held by organizations designed and structured to perform in peacetime internal security functions; or
(G) are in transit through the area of application from a location outside the area of application to a final destination outside the area of application, and are in the area of application for no longer than a total of seven days.

2. If, in respect of any such battle tanks, armoured combat vehicles, artillery, combat aircraft or attack helicopters, the notification of which is required under Section IV of the Protocol on Information Exchange, a State Party notifies an unusually high number in more than two successive annual information exchanges, it shall explain the reasons in the Joint Consultative Group, if so requested.

Article IV
1. Within the area of application, as defined in Article II, each State Party shall limit and, as necessary, reduce its battle tanks, armoured combat vehicles, artillery, combat aircraft and attack helicopters so that, 40 months after entry into force of this Treaty and thereafter, for the group of States Parties to which it belongs, as defined in Article II, the aggregate numbers do not exceed:

(A) 20,000 battle tanks, of which no more than 16,500 shall be in active units;
(B) 30,000 armoured combat vehicles, of which no more than 27,300 shall be in active units. Of the 30,000 armoured combat vehicles, no more than 18,000 shall be armoured infantry fighting vehicles and heavy armament combat vehicles; of

armoured infantry fighting vehicles and heavy armament combat vehicles, no more than 1,500 shall be heavy armament combat vehicles;
(C) 20,000 pieces of artillery, of which no more than 17,000 shall be in active units;
(D) 6,800 combat aircraft; and
(E) 2,000 attack helicopters.

Battle tanks, armoured combat vehicles and artillery not in active units shall be placed in designated permanent storage sites, as defined in Article II, and shall be located only in the area described in paragraph 2 of this Article. Such designated permanent storage sites may also be located in that part of the territory of the Union of Soviet Socialist Republics comprising the Odessa Military District and the southern part of the Leningrad Military District. In the Odessa Military District, no more than 400 battle tanks and no more than 500 pieces of artillery may be thus stored. In the southern part of the Leningrad Military District, no more than 600 battle tanks, no more than 800 armoured combat vehicles, including no more than 300 armoured combat vehicles of any type with the remaining number consisting of armoured personnel carriers, and no more than 400 pieces of artillery may be thus stored. The southern part of the Leningrad Military District is understood to mean the territory within that military district south of the line East-West 60 degrees 15 minutes northern latitude.

2. Within the area consisting of the entire land territory in Europe, which includes all the European island territories, of the Kingdom of Belgium, the Czech and Slovak Federal Republic, the Kingdom of Denmark including the Faroe Islands, the French Republic, the Federal Republic of Germany, the Republic of Hungary, the Italian Republic, the Grand Duchy of Luxembourg, the Kingdom of the Netherlands, the Republic of Poland, the Portuguese Republic including the islands of Azores and Madeira, the Kingdom of Spain including the Canary Islands, the United Kingdom of Great Britain and Northern Ireland and that part of the territory of the Union of Soviet Socialist Republics west of the Ural Mountains comprising the Baltic, Byelorussian, Carpathian, Kiev, Moscow and Volga-Ural Military Districts, each State Party shall limit and, as necessary, reduce its battle tanks, armoured combat vehicles and artillery so that, 40 months after entry into force of this Treaty and thereafter, for the group of States Parties to which it belongs the aggregate numbers do not exceed:

(A) 15,300 battle tanks, of which no more than 11,800 shall be in active units; (B) 24,100 armoured combat vehicles, of which no more than 21,400 shall be in active units; and
(C) 14,000 pieces of artillery, of which no more than 11,000 shall be in active units.

3. Within the area consisting of the entire land territory in Europe, which includes all the European island territories, of the Kingdom of Belgium, the Czech and Slovak Federal Republic, the Kingdom of Denmark including the Faroe Islands,

the French Republic, the Federal Republic of Germany, the Republic of Hungary, the Italian Republic, the Grand Duchy of Luxembourg, the Kingdom of the Netherlands, the Republic of Poland, the United Kingdom of Great Britain and Northern Ireland and that part of the territory of the Union of Soviet Socialist Republics comprising the Baltic, Byelorussian, Carpathian and Kiev Military Districts, each State Party shall limit and, as necessary, reduce its battle tanks, armoured combat vehicles and artillery so that, 40 months after entry into force of this Treaty and thereafter, for the group of States Parties to which it belongs the aggregate numbers in active units do not exceed: </P><DIR>

(A) 10,300 battle tanks;
(B) 19,260 armoured combat vehicles; and
(C) 9,100 pieces of artillery; and
(D) in the Kiev Military District, the aggregate numbers in active units and designated permanent storage sites together shall not exceed:

(1) 2,250 battle tanks;
(2) 2,500 armoured combat vehicles; and
(3) 1,500 pieces of artillery.

4. Within the area consisting of the entire land territory in Europe, which includes all the European island territories, of the Kingdom of Belgium, the Czech and Slovak Federal Republic, the Federal Republic of Germany, the Republic of Hungary, the Grand Duchy of Luxembourg, the Kingdom of the Netherlands and the Republic of Poland, each State Party shall limit and, as necessary, reduce its battle tanks, armoured combat vehicles and artillery so that, 40 months after entry into force of this Treaty and thereafter, for the group of States Parties to which it belongs the aggregate numbers in active units do not exceed:

(A) 7,500 battle tanks;
(B) 11,250 armoured combat vehicles; and
(C) 5,000 pieces of artillery.

5. States Parties belonging to the same group of States Parties may locate battle tanks, armoured combat vehicles and artillery in active units in each of the areas described in this Article and Article V, paragraph 1, subparagraph (A) up to the numerical limitations applying in that area, consistent with the maximum levels for holdings notified pursuant to Article VII and provided that no State Party stations conventional armed forces on the territory of another State Party without the agreement of that State Party.

6. If a group of States Parties' aggregate numbers of battle tanks, armoured combat vehicles and artillery in active units within the area described in paragraph 4 of this Article are less than the numerical limitations set forth in paragraph 4 of this Article, and provided that no State Party is thereby prevented from reaching its

maximum levels for holdings notified in accordance with Article VII, paragraphs 2, 3 and 5, then amounts equal to the difference between the aggregate numbers in each of the categories of battle tanks, armoured combat vehicles and artillery and the specified numerical limitations for that area may be located by States Parties belonging to that group of States Parties in the area described in paragraph 3 of this Article, consistent with the numerical limitations specified in paragraph 3 of this Article.

Article V
1. To ensure that the security of each State Party is not affected adversely at any stage:

(A) within the area consisting of the entire land territory in Europe, which includes all the European island territories, of the Republic of Bulgaria, the Hellenic Republic, the Republic of Iceland, the Kingdom of Norway, Romania, the part of the Republic of Turkey within the area of application and that part of the Union of Soviet Socialist Republics comprising the Leningrad, Odessa, Transcaucasus and North Caucasus Military Districts, each State Party shall limit and, as necessary, reduce its battle tanks, armoured combat vehicles and artillery so that, 40 months after entry into force of this Treaty and thereafter, for the group of States Parties to which it belongs the aggregate numbers in active units do not exceed the difference between the overall numerical limitations set forth in Article IV, paragraph 1 and those in Article IV, paragraph 2, that is:

(1) 4,700 battle tanks;
(2) 5,900 armoured combat vehicles; and
(3) 6,000 pieces of artillery;

(B) notwithstanding the numerical limitations set forth in subparagraph (A) of this paragraph, a State Party or States Parties may on a temporary basis deploy into the territory belonging to the members of the same group of States Parties within the area described in subparagraph (A) of this paragraph additional aggregate numbers in active units for each group of States Parties not to exceed:

(1) 459 battle tanks;
(2) 723 armoured combat vehicles; and
(3) 420 pieces of artillery; and

(C) provided that for each group of States Parties no more than one-third of each of these additional aggregate numbers shall be deployed to any State Party with territory within the area described in subparagraph (A) of this paragraph, that is:

(1) 153 battle tanks;
(2) 241 armoured combat vehicles; and
(3) 140 pieces of artillery.

2. Notification shall be provided to all other States Parties no later than at the start of the deployment by the State Party or States Parties conducting the deployment and by the recipient State Party or States Parties, specifying the total number in each category of battle tanks, armoured combat vehicles and artillery deployed. Notification also shall be provided to all other States Parties by the State Party or States Parties conducting the deployment and by the recipient State Party or States Parties within 30 days of the withdrawal of those battle tanks, armoured combat vehicles and artillery that were temporarily deployed.

Article VI
With the objective of ensuring that no single State Party possesses more than approximately one-third of the conventional armaments and equipment limited by the Treaty within the area of application, each State Party shall limit and, as necessary, reduce its battle tanks, armoured combat vehicles, artillery, combat aircraft and attack helicopters so that, 40 months after entry into force of this Treaty and thereafter, the numbers within the area of application for that State Party do not exceed:

(A) 13,300 battle tanks;
(B) 20,000 armoured combat vehicles;
(C) 13,700 pieces of artillery;
(D) 5,150 combat aircraft; and
(E) 1,500 attack helicopters.

Article VII
1. In order that the limitations set forth in Articles IV, V and VI are not exceeded, no State Party shall exceed, from 40 months after entry into force of this Treaty, the maximum levels which it has previously agreed upon within its group of States Parties, in accordance with paragraph 7 of this Article, for its holdings of conventional armaments and equipment limited by the Treaty and of which it has provided notification pursuant to the provisions of this Article.

2. Each State Party shall provide at the signature of this Treaty notification to all other States Parties of the maximum levels for its holdings of conventional armaments and equipment limited by the Treaty. The notification of the maximum levels for holdings of conventional armaments and equipment limited by the Treaty provided by each State Party at the signature of this Treaty shall remain valid until the date specified in a subsequent notification pursuant to paragraph 3 of this Article.

3. In accordance with the limitations set forth in Articles IV, V and VI, each State Party shall have the right to change the maximum levels for its holdings of conventional armaments and equipment limited by the Treaty. Any change in the maximum levels for holdings of a State Party shall be notified by that State Party to all other States Parties at least 90 days in advance of the date, specified in the

notification, on which such a change takes effect. In order not to exceed any of the limitations set forth in Articles IV and V, any increase in the maximum levels for holdings of a State Party that would otherwise cause those limitations to be exceeded shall be preceded or accompanied by a corresponding reduction in the previously notified maximum levels for holdings of conventional armaments and equipment limited by the Treaty of one or more States Parties belonging to the same group of States Parties. The notification of a change in the maximum levels for holdings shall remain valid from the date specified in the notification until the date specified in a subsequent notification of change pursuant to this paragraph.

4. Each notification required pursuant to paragraph 2 or 3 of this Article for armoured combat vehicles shall also include maximum levels for the holdings of armoured infantry fighting vehicles and heavy armament combat vehicles of the State Party providing the notification.

5. Ninety days before expiration of the 40-month period of reductions set forth in Article VIII and subsequently at the time of any notification of a change pursuant to paragraph 3 of this Article, each State Party shall provide notification of the maximum levels for its holdings of battle tanks, armoured combat vehicles and artillery with respect to each of the areas described in Article IV, paragraphs 2 to 4 and Article V, paragraph 1, subparagraph (A).

6. A decrease in the numbers of conventional armaments and equipment limited by the Treaty held by a State Party and subject to notification pursuant to the Protocol on Information Exchange shall by itself confer no right on any other State Party to increase the maximum levels for its holdings subject to notification pursuant to this Article.

7. It shall be the responsibility solely of each individual State Party to ensure that the maximum levels for its holdings notified pursuant to the provisions of this Article are not exceeded. States Parties belonging to the same group of States Parties shall consult in order to ensure that the maximum levels for holdings notified pursuant to the provisions of this Article, taken together as appropriate, do not exceed the limitations set forth in Articles IV, V and VI.

Article VIII
1. The numerical limitations set forth in Articles IV, V and VI shall be achieved only by means of reduction in accordance with the Protocol on Reduction, the Protocol on Helicopter Recategorization, the Protocol on Aircraft Reclassification, the Footnote to Section I, paragraph 2, subparagraph (A) of the Protocol on Existing Types and the Protocol on Inspection.

2. The categories of conventional armaments and equipment subject to reductions are battle tanks, armoured combat vehicles, artillery, combat aircraft and attack helicopters. The specific types are listed in the Protocol on Existing Types.

(A) Battle tanks and armoured combat vehicles shall be reduced by destruction, conversion for non-military purposes, placement on static display, use as ground targets, or, in the case of armoured personnel carriers, modification in accordance with the Footnote to Section I, paragraph 2, subparagraph (A) of the Protocol on Existing Types.
(B) Artillery shall be reduced by destruction or placement on static display, or, in the case of self-propelled artillery, by use as ground targets.
(C) Combat aircraft shall be reduced by destruction, placement on static display, use for ground instructional purposes, or, in the case of specific models or versions of combat-capable trainer aircraft, reclassification into unarmed trainer aircraft.
(D) Specialized attack helicopters shall be reduced by destruction, placement on static display, or use for ground instructional purposes.
(E) Multi-purpose attack helicopters shall be reduced by destruction, placement on static display, use for ground instructional purposes, or recategorization.

3. Conventional armaments and equipment limited by the Treaty shall be deemed to be reduced upon execution of the procedures set forth in the Protocols listed in paragraph 1 of this Article and upon notification as required by these Protocols. Armaments and equipment so reduced shall no longer be counted against the numerical limitations set forth in Articles IV, V and VI.

4. Reductions shall be effected in three phases and completed no later than 40 months after entry into force of this Treaty, so that:

(A) by the end of the first reduction phase, that is, no later than 16 months after entry into force of this Treaty, each State Party shall have ensured that at least 25 percent of its total reduction liability in each of the categories of conventional armaments and equipment limited by the Treaty has been reduced;
(B) by the end of the second reduction phase, that is, no later than 28 months after entry into force of this Treaty, each State Party shall have ensured that at least 60 percent of its total reduction liability in each of the categories of conventional armaments and equipment limited by the Treaty has been reduced;
(C) by the end of the third reduction phase, that is, no later than 40 months after entry into force of this Treaty, each State Party shall have reduced its total reduction liability in each of the categories of conventional armaments and equipment limited by the Treaty. States Parties carrying out conversion for non-military purposes shall have ensured that the conversion of all battle tanks in accordance with Section VIII of the Protocol on Reduction shall have been completed by the end of the third reduction phase; and
(D) armoured combat vehicles deemed reduced by reason of having been partially destroyed in accordance with Section VIII, paragraph 6 of the Protocol on Reduction shall have been fully converted for non-military purposes, or destroyed in accordance with Section IV of the Protocol on Reduction, no later than 64 months after entry into force of this Treaty.

5. Conventional armaments and equipment limited by the Treaty to be reduced shall have been declared present within the area of application in the exchange of information at signature of this Treaty.

6. No later than 30 days after entry into force of this Treaty, each State Party shall provide notification to all other States Parties of its reduction liability.

7. Except as provided for in paragraph 8 of this Article, a State Party's reduction liability in each category shall be no less than the difference between its holdings notified, in accordance with the Protocol on Information Exchange, at signature or effective upon entry into force of this Treaty, whichever is the greater, and the maximum levels for holdings it notified pursuant to Article VII.

8. Any subsequent revision of a State Party's holdings notified pursuant to the Protocol on Information Exchange or of its maximum levels for holdings notified pursuant to Article VII shall be reflected by a notified adjustment to its reduction liability. Any notification of a decrease in a State Party's reduction liability shall be preceded or accompanied by either a notification of a corresponding increase in holdings not exceeding the maximum levels for holdings notified pursuant to Article VII by one or more States Parties belonging to the same group of States Parties, or a notification of a corresponding increase in the reduction liability of one or more such States Parties.

9. Upon entry into force of this Treaty, each State Party shall notify all other States Parties, in accordance with the Protocol on Information Exchange, of the locations of its reduction sites, including those where the final conversion of battle tanks and armoured combat vehicles for non-military purposes will be carried out.

10. Each State Party shall have the right to designate as many reduction sites as it wishes, to revise without restriction its designation of such sites and to carry out reduction and final conversion simultaneously at a maximum of 20 sites. States Parties shall have the right to share or co-locate reduction sites by mutual agreement.

11. Notwithstanding paragraph 10 of this Article, during the baseline validation period, that is, the interval between entry into force of this Treaty and 120 days after entry into force of this Treaty, reduction shall be carried out simultaneously at no more than two reduction sites for each State Party.

12. Reduction of conventional armaments and equipment limited by the Treaty shall be carried out at reduction sites, unless otherwise specified in the Protocols listed in paragraph 1 of this Article, within the area of application.

13. The reduction process, including the results of the conversion of conventional armaments and equipment limited by the Treaty for non-military purposes both during the reduction period and in the 24 months following the reduction period,

shall be subject to inspection, without right of refusal, in accordance with the Protocol on Inspection.

Article IX
1. Other than removal from service in accordance with the provisions of Article VIII, battle tanks, armoured combat vehicles, artillery, combat aircraft and attack helicopters within the area of application shall be removed from service only by decommissioning, provided that:

(A) such conventional armaments and equipment limited by the Treaty are decommissioned and awaiting disposal at no more than eight sites which shall be notified as declared sites in accordance with the Protocol on Information Exchange and shall be identified in such notifications as holding areas for decommissioned conventional armaments and equipment limited by the Treaty. If sites containing conventional armaments and equipment limited by the Treaty decommissioned from service also contain any other conventional armaments and equipment subject to the Treaty, the decommissioned conventional armaments and equipment limited by the Treaty shall be separately distinguishable; and </P>
(B) the numbers of such decommissioned conventional armaments and equipment limited by the Treaty do not exceed, in the case of any individual State Party, one percent of its notified holdings of conventional armaments and equipment limited by the Treaty, or a total of 250, whichever is greater, of which no more than 200 shall be battle tanks, armoured combat vehicles and pieces of artillery, and no more than 50 shall be attack helicopters and combat aircraft.

2. Notification of decommissioning shall include the number and type of conventional armaments and equipment limited by the Treaty decommissioned and the location of decommissioning and shall be provided to all other States Parties in accordance with Section IX, paragraph 1, subparagraph (B) of the Protocol on Information Exchange.

Article X
1. Designated permanent storage sites shall be notified in accordance with the Protocol on Information Exchange to all other States Parties by the State Party to which the conventional armaments and equipment limited by the Treaty contained at designated permanent storage sites belong. The notification shall include the designation and location, including geographic coordinates, of designated permanent storage sites and the numbers by type of each category of its conventional armaments and equipment limited by the Treaty at each such storage site.

2. Designated permanent storage sites shall contain only facilities appropriate for the storage and maintenance of armaments and equipment (e.g., warehouses, garages, workshops and associated stores as well as other support accommodation). Designated permanent storage sites shall not contain firing ranges or training areas associated with conventional armaments and equipment limited by the Treaty.

Designated permanent storage sites shall contain only armaments and equipment belonging to the conventional armed forces of a State Party.

3. Each designated permanent storage site shall have a clearly defined physical boundary that shall consist of a continuous perimeter fence at least 1.5 meters in height. The perimeter fence shall have no more than three gates providing the sole means of entrance and exit for armaments and equipment.

4. Conventional armaments and equipment limited by the Treaty located within designated permanent storage sites shall be counted as conventional armaments and equipment limited by the Treaty not in active units, including when they are temporarily removed in accordance with paragraphs 7, 8, 9 and 10 of this Article. Conventional armaments and equipment limited by the Treaty in storage other than in designated permanent storage sites shall be counted as conventional armaments and equipment limited by the Treaty in active units.

5. Active units or formations shall not be located within designated permanent storage sites, except as provided for in paragraph 6 of this Article.

6. Only personnel associated with the security or operation of designated permanent storage sites, or the maintenance of the armaments and equipment stored therein, shall be located within the designated permanent storage sites.

7. For the purpose of maintenance, repair or modification of conventional armaments and equipment limited by the Treaty located within designated permanent storage sites, each State Party shall have the right, without prior notification, to remove from and retain outside designated permanent storage sites simultaneously up to 10 percent, rounded up to the nearest even whole number, of the notified holdings of each category of conventional armaments and equipment limited by the Treaty in each designated permanent storage site, or 10 items of the conventional armaments and equipment limited by the Treaty in each category in each designated permanent storage site, whichever is less. </P>

8. Except as provided for in paragraph 7 of this Article, no State Party shall remove conventional armaments and equipment limited by the Treaty from designated permanent storage sites unless notification has been provided to all other States Parties at least 42 days in advance of such removal. Notification shall be given by the State Party to which the conventional armaments and equipment limited by the Treaty belong. Such notification shall specify:

(A) the location of the designated permanent storage site from which conventional armaments and equipment limited by the Treaty are to be removed and the numbers by type of conventional armaments and equipment limited by the Treaty of each category to be removed;
(B) the dates of removal and return of conventional armaments and equipment limited by the Treaty; and

(C) the intended location and use of conventional armaments and equipment limited by the Treaty while outside the designated permanent storage site.

9. Except as provided for in paragraph 7 of this Article, the aggregate numbers of conventional armaments and equipment limited by the Treaty removed from and retained outside designated permanent storage sites by States Parties belonging to the same group of States Parties shall at no time exceed the following levels:

(A) 550 battle tanks;
(B) 1,000 armoured combat vehicles; and
(C) 300 pieces of artillery.

10. Conventional armaments and equipment limited by the Treaty removed from designated permanent storage sites pursuant to paragraphs 8 and 9 of this Article shall be returned to designated permanent storage sites no later than 42 days after their removal, except for those items of conventional armaments and equipment limited by the Treaty removed for industrial rebuild. Such items shall be returned to designated permanent storage sites immediately on completion of the rebuild.

11. Each State Party shall have the right to replace conventional armaments and equipment limited by the Treaty located in designated permanent storage sites. Each State Party shall notify all other States Parties, at the beginning of replacement, of the number, location, type and disposition of conventional armaments and equipment limited by the Treaty being replaced.

Article XI

1. Each State Party shall limit its armoured vehicle launched bridges so that, 40 months after entry into force of this Treaty and thereafter, for the group of States Parties to which it belongs the aggregate number of armoured vehicle launched bridges in active units within the area of application does not exceed 740.

2. All armoured vehicle launched bridges within the area of application in excess of the aggregate number specified in paragraph 1 of this Article for each group of States Parties shall be placed in designated permanent storage sites, as defined in Article II. When armoured vehicle launched bridges are placed in a designated permanent storage site, either on their own or together with conventional armaments and equipment limited by the Treaty, Article X, paragraphs 1 to 6 shall apply to armoured vehicle launched bridges as well as to conventional armaments and equipment limited by the Treaty. Armoured vehicle launched bridges placed in designated permanent storage sites shall not be considered as being in active units.

3. Except as provided for in paragraph 6 of this Article, armoured vehicle launched bridges may be removed, subject to the provisions of paragraphs 4 and 5 of this Article, from designated permanent storage sites only after notification has been provided to all other States Parties at least 42 days prior to such removal. This notification shall specify:

(A) the locations of the designated permanent storage sites from which armoured vehicle launched bridges are to be removed and the numbers of armoured vehicle launched bridges to be removed from each such site;
(B) the dates of removal of armoured vehicle launched bridges from and return to designated permanent storage sites; and
(C) the intended use of armoured vehicle launched bridges during the period of their removal from designated permanent storage sites.

4. Except as provided for in paragraph 6 of this Article, armoured vehicle launched bridges removed from designated permanent storage sites shall be returned to them no later than 42 days after the actual date of removal.

5. The aggregate number of armoured vehicle launched bridges removed from and retained outside of designated permanent storage sites by each group of States Parties shall not exceed 50 at any one time.

6. States Parties shall have the right, for the purpose of maintenance or modification, to remove and have outside of designated permanent storage sites simultaneously up to 10 percent, rounded up to the nearest even whole number, of their notified holdings of armoured vehicle launched bridges in each designated permanent storage site, or 10 armoured vehicle launched bridges from each designated permanent storage site, whichever is less.

7. In the event of natural disasters involving flooding or damage to permanent bridges, States Parties shall have the right to withdraw armoured vehicle launched bridges from designated permanent storage sites. Notification to all other States Parties of such withdrawals shall be given at the time of withdrawal.

Article XII
1. Armoured infantry fighting vehicles held by organizations of a State Party designed and structured to perform in peacetime internal security functions, which are not structured and organized for ground combat against an external enemy, are not limited by this Treaty. The foregoing notwithstanding, in order to enhance the implementation of this Treaty and to provide assurance that the number of such armaments held by such organizations shall not be used to circumvent the provisions of this Treaty, any such armaments in excess of 1,000 armoured infantry fighting vehicles assigned by a State Party to organizations designed and structured to perform in peacetime internal security functions shall constitute a portion of the permitted levels specified in Articles IV, V and VI. No more than 600 such armoured infantry fighting vehicles of a State Party, assigned to such organizations, may be located in that part of the area of application described in Article V, paragraph 1, subparagraph (A). Each State Party shall further ensure that such organizations refrain from the acquisition of combat capabilities in excess of those necessary for meeting internal security requirements.

2. A State Party that intends to reassign battle tanks, armoured infantry fighting vehicles, artillery, combat aircraft, attack helicopters and armoured vehicle launched bridges in service with its conventional armed forces to any organization of that State Party not a part of its conventional armed forces shall notify all other States Parties no later than the date such reassignment takes effect. Such notification shall specify the effective date of the reassignment, the date such equipment is physically transferred, as well as the numbers, by type, of the conventional armaments and equipment limited by the Treaty being reassigned.

Article XIII
1. For the purpose of ensuring verification of compliance with the provisions of this Treaty, each State Party shall provide notifications and exchange information pertaining to its conventional armaments and equipment in accordance with the Protocol on Information Exchange.

2. Such notifications and exchange of information shall be provided in accordance with Article XVII.

3. Each State Party shall be responsible for its own information; receipt of such information and of notifications shall not imply validation or acceptance of the information provided.

Article XIV
1. For the purpose of ensuring verification of compliance with the provisions of this Treaty, each State Party shall have the right to conduct, and the obligation to accept, within the area of application, inspections in accordance with the provisions of the Protocol on Inspection.

2. The purpose of such inspections shall be:

(A) to verify, on the basis of the information provided pursuant to the Protocol on Information Exchange, the compliance of States Parties with the numerical limitations set forth in Articles IV, V and VI;
(B) to monitor the process of reduction of battle tanks, armoured combat vehicles, artillery, combat aircraft and attack helicopters carried out at reduction sites in accordance with Article VIII and the Protocol on Reduction; and
(C) to monitor the certification of recategorized multi-purpose attack helicopters and reclassified combat-capable trainer aircraft carried out in accordance with the Protocol on Helicopter Recategorization and the Protocol on Aircraft Reclassification, respectively.

3. No State Party shall exercise the rights set forth in paragraphs 1 and 2 of this Article in respect of States Parties which belong to the group of States Parties to which it belongs in order to elude the objectives of the verification regime.

4. In the case of an inspection conducted jointly by more than one State Party, one of them shall be responsible for the execution of the provisions of this Treaty.

5. The number of inspections pursuant to Sections VII and VIII of the Protocol on Inspection which each State Party shall have the right to conduct and the obligation to accept during each specified time period shall be determined in accordance with the provisions of Section II of that Protocol.

6. Upon completion of the 120-day residual level validation period, each State Party shall have the right to conduct, and each State Party with territory within the area of application shall have the obligation to accept, an agreed number of aerial inspections within the area of application. Such agreed numbers and other applicable provisions shall be developed during negotiations referred to in Article XVIII.

Article XV
1. For the purpose of ensuring verification of compliance with the provisions of this Treaty, a State Party shall have the right to use, in addition to the procedures referred to in Article XIV, national or multinational technical means of verification at its disposal in a manner consistent with generally recognized principles of international law.

2. A State Party shall not interfere with national or multinational technical means of verification of another State Party operating in accordance with paragraph 1 of this Article.

3. A State Party shall not use concealment measures that impede verification of compliance with the provisions of this Treaty by national or multinational technical means of verification of another State Party operating in accordance with paragraph 1 of this Article. This obligation does not apply to cover or concealment practices associated with normal personnel training, maintenance or operations involving conventional armaments and equipment limited by the Treaty.

Article XVI
1. To promote the objectives and implementation of the provisions of this Treaty, the States Parties hereby establish a Joint Consultative Group. </P>

2. Within the framework of the Joint Consultative Group, the States Parties shall:

(A) address questions relating to compliance with or possible circumvention of the provisions of this Treaty;
(B) seek to resolve ambiguities and differences of interpretation that may become apparent in the way this Treaty is implemented;
(C) consider and, if possible, agree on measures to enhance the viability and effectiveness of this Treaty;

(D) update the lists contained in the Protocol on Existing Types, as required by Article II, paragraph 2;
(E) resolve technical questions in order to seek common practices among the States Parties in the way this Treaty is implemented;
(F) work out or revise, as necessary, rules of procedure, working methods, the scale of distribution of expenses of the Joint Consultative Group and of conferences convened under this Treaty and the distribution of costs of inspections between or among States Parties;
(G) consider and work out appropriate measures to ensure that information obtained through exchanges of information among the States Parties or as a result of inspections pursuant to this Treaty is used solely for the purposes of this Treaty, taking into account the particular requirements of each State Party in respect of safeguarding information which that State Party specifies as being sensitive;
(H) consider, upon the request of any State Party, any matter that a State Party wishes to propose for examination by any conference to be convened in accordance with Article XXI; such consideration shall not prejudice the right of any State Party to resort to the procedures set forth in Article XXI; and
(I) consider matters of dispute arising out of the implementation of this Treaty.

3. Each State Party shall have the right to raise before the Joint Consultative Group, and have placed on its agenda, any issue relating to this Treaty.

4. The Joint Consultative Group shall take decisions or make recommendations by consensus. Consensus shall be understood to mean the absence of any objection by any representative of a State Party to the taking of a decision or the making of a recommendation.

5. The Joint Consultative Group may propose amendments to this Treaty for consideration and confirmation in accordance with Article XX. The Joint Consultative Group may also agree on improvements to the viability and effectiveness of this Treaty, consistent with its provisions. Unless such improvements relate only to minor matters of an administrative or technical nature, they shall be subject to consideration and confirmation in accordance with Article XX before they can take effect.

6. Nothing in this Article shall be deemed to prohibit or restrict any State Party from requesting information from or undertaking consultations with other States Parties on matters relating to this Treaty and its implementation in channels or fora other than the Joint Consultative Group.

7. The Joint Consultative Group shall follow the procedures set forth in the Protocol on the Joint Consultative Group.

Article XVII
The States Parties shall transmit information and notifications required by this Treaty in written form. They shall use diplomatic channels or other official

channels designated by them, including in particular a communications network to be established by a separate arrangement.

Article XVIII
1. The States Parties, after signature of this Treaty, shall continue the negotiations on conventional armed forces with the same Mandate and with the goal of building on this Treaty.

2. The objective for these negotiations shall be to conclude an agreement on additional measures aimed at further strengthening security and stability in Europe, and pursuant to the Mandate, including measures to limit the personnel strength of their conventional armed forces within the area of application.

3. The States Parties shall seek to conclude these negotiations no later than the follow-up meeting of the Conference on Security and Cooperation in Europe to be held in Helsinki in 1992.

Article XIX
1. This Treaty shall be of unlimited duration. It may be supplemented by a further treaty.

2. Each State Party shall, in exercising its national sovereignty, have the right to withdraw from this Treaty if it decides that extraordinary events related to the subject matter of this Treaty have jeopardized its supreme interests. A State Party intending to withdraw shall give notice of its decision to do so to the Depositary and to all other States Parties. Such notice shall be given at least 150 days prior to the intended withdrawal from this Treaty. It shall include a statement of the extraordinary events the State Party regards as having jeopardized its supreme interests.

3. Each State Party shall, in particular, in exercising its national sovereignty, have the right to withdraw from this Treaty if another State Party increases its holdings in battle tanks, armoured combat vehicles, artillery, combat aircraft or attack helicopters, as defined in Article II, which are outside the scope of the limitations of this Treaty, in such proportions as to pose an obvious threat to the balance of forces within the area of application.

Article XX
1. Any State Party may propose amendments to this Treaty. The text of a proposed amendment shall be submitted to the Depositary, which shall circulate it to all the States Parties.

2. If an amendment is approved by all the States Parties, it shall enter into force in accordance with the procedures set forth in Article XXII governing the entry into force of this Treaty.

Article XXI

1. Forty-six months after entry into force of this Treaty, and at five-year intervals thereafter, the Depositary shall convene a conference of the States Parties to conduct a review of the operation of this Treaty.

2. The Depositary shall convene an extraordinary conference of the States Parties, if requested to do so by any State Party which considers that exceptional circumstances relating to this Treaty have arisen, in particular, in the event that a State Party has announced its intention to leave its group of States Parties or to join the other group of States Parties, as defined in Article II, paragraph 1, subparagraph (A). In order to enable the other States Parties to prepare for this conference, the request shall include the reason why that State Party deems an extraordinary conference to be necessary. The conference shall consider the circumstances set forth in the request and their effect on the operation of this Treaty. The conference shall open no later than 15 days after receipt of the request and, unless it decides otherwise, shall last no longer than three weeks.

3. The Depositary shall convene a conference of the States Parties to consider an amendment proposed pursuant to Article XX, if requested to do so by three or more States Parties. Such a conference shall open no later than 21 days after receipt of the necessary requests.

4. In the event that a State Party gives notice of its decision to withdraw from this Treaty pursuant to Article XIX, the Depositary shall convene a conference of the States Parties which shall open no later than 21 days after receipt of the notice of withdrawal in order to consider questions relating to the withdrawal from this Treaty.

Article XXII

1. This Treaty shall be subject to ratification by each State Party in accordance with its constitutional procedures. Instruments of ratification shall be deposited with the Government of the Kingdom of the Netherlands, hereby designated the Depositary.

2. This Treaty shall enter into force 10 days after instruments of ratification have been deposited by all States Parties listed in the Preamble.

3. The Depositary shall promptly inform all States Parties of:

(A) the deposit of each instrument of ratification;
(B) the entry into force of this Treaty;
(C) any withdrawal in accordance with Article XIX and its effective date;
(D) the text of any amendment proposed in accordance with Article XX;
(E) the entry into force of any amendment to this Treaty;
(F) any request to convene a conference in accordance with Article XXI;
(G) the convening of a conference pursuant to Article XXI; and

(H) any other matter of which the Depositary is required by this Treaty to inform the States Parties.

4. This Treaty shall be registered by the Depositary pursuant to Article 102 of the Charter of the United Nations.

Article XXIII
The original of this Treaty, of which the English, French, German, Italian, Russian and Spanish texts are equally authentic, shall be deposited in the archives of the Depositary. Duly certified copies of this Treaty shall be transmitted by the Depositary to all the States Parties.

---

* The Treaty of Friendship, Cooperation and Mutual Assistance signed in Warsaw, 14 May 1955
** The Treaty of Economic, Social and Cultural Collaboration and Collective Self-Defense signed in Brussels, 17 March 1948
*** The North Atlantic Treaty signed in Washington, 4 April 1949

VI-2. Addendum to the Treaty on Conventional Armed Forces in Europe, Final Document of the First Conference to Review the Operation of the Treaty on Conventional Armed Forces in Europe and the Concluding Act of the Negotiation on Personnel Strength, Vienna, 15-31 May 1996,
<http://www.state.gov/www/global/arms/bureau_np/treaties_np.htm>
Authentic Texts: English, French, German, Italian, Russian and Spanish.

State Parties

The Republic of Armenia, the Azerbaijan Republic, the Republic of Belarus, the Kingdom of Belgium, the Republic of Bulgaria, Canada, the Czech Republic, the Kingdom of Denmark, the French Republic, Georgia, the Federal Republic of Germany, the Hellenic Republic, the Republic of Hungary, the Republic of Iceland, the Italian Republic, the Republic of Kazakstan, the Grand Duchy of Luxembourg, the Republic of Moldova, the Kingdom of the Netherlands, the Kingdom of Norway, the Republic of Poland, the Portuguese Republic, Romania, the Russian Federation, the Slovak Republic, the Kingdom of Spain, the Republic of Turkey, Ukraine, the United Kingdom of Great Britain and Northern Ireland and the United States of America

Full Text

The Republic of Armenia, the Azerbaijan Republic, the Republic of Belarus, the Kingdom of Belgium, the Republic of Bulgaria, Canada, the Czech Republic, the Kingdom of Denmark, the French Republic, Georgia, the Federal Republic of Germany, the Hellenic Republic, the Republic of Hungary, the Republic of Iceland, the Italian Republic, the Republic of Kazakstan, the Grand Duchy of Luxembourg, the Republic of Moldova, the Kingdom of the Netherlands, the Kingdom of Norway, the Republic of Poland, the Portuguese Republic, Romania, the Russian Federation, the Slovak Republic, the Kingdom of Spain, the Republic of Turkey, Ukraine, the United Kingdom of Great Britain and Northern Ireland and the United States of America, which are the States Parties to the Treaty on Conventional Armed Forces in Europe of 19 November 1990, hereinafter referred to as the States Parties,

Fulfilling the obligation set forth in Article XXI, paragraph 1, of the Treaty on Conventional Armed Forces in Europe, hereinafter referred to as the Treaty, to conduct a review of the operation of the Treaty, and thereby taking into account the Final Documents of the Extraordinary Conferences of the States Parties of 10 July 1992 in Helsinki and 13 November 1992 in Vienna,
Acting in accordance with the provision of Section VII, paragraph 3, of the Concluding Act of the Negotiation on Personnel Strength of Conventional Armed Forces in Europe of 10 July 1992, hereinafter referred to as the Concluding Act,

Recalling the results of the Extraordinary Conferences held thus far,
Reaffirming all the decisions of the Joint Consultative Group made thus far,
Having met at the First Review Conference, chaired by the Kingdom of the Netherlands, from 15 to 31 May 1996 in Vienna,
Have adopted the following:

I. INTRODUCTION

1. The States Parties reaffirm the fundamental role of the Treaty as a cornerstone of European security and their adherence to its goals and objectives. It is in their common interest to preserve the integrity of the Treaty and the Concluding Act as well as the predictability and transparency they have created. The States Parties reaffirm their determination to fulfil in good faith all obligations and commitments arising from the Treaty and its associated documents. Bearing that in mind, they commit themselves to enhance the viability and effectiveness of the Treaty.

2. The negotiation, conclusion and implementation of the Treaty and the Concluding Act, as well as the ratification of the Treaty, took place in times of change during which the European security environment evolved significantly. The Warsaw Treaty Organization has ceased to exist. New States have emerged and became States Parties to the Treaty. At the same time, new risks and challenges to security have come to the fore. As a result of common efforts of the States Parties, the Treaty and the Concluding Act have remained vital stabilizing factors in this period of transition and contributed to its peaceful unfolding.

3. The States Parties stress that security and stability in Europe are vitally underpinned by the continuation and enhancement of robust arms control measures. Recognizing the evolution of the European political and security environment, the States Parties are resolved to continue the conventional arms control process, including through the enhancement of the viability and effectiveness of the Treaty. They see this as a common responsibility.

4. The States Parties recognize that the Treaty and the Concluding Act are essential contributions to the achievement of the goals and purposes of the Organization for Security and Co-operation in Europe (OSCE), in particular the promotion of confidence, stability and security in an undivided Europe. In that context, they stress the importance of the development of a common and comprehensive security model for Europe for the twenty-first century, of the implementation of the Treaty on Open Skies and of the ongoing security dialogue and negotiations in the Forum for Security Co-operation.

II. REVIEW OF THE OPERATION OF THE TREATY AND THE CONCLUDING ACT

5. The States Parties note with satisfaction that more than 58,000 pieces of conventional armaments and equipment have been reduced, and that the overall

holdings of conventional armaments and equipment within the area of application are substantially lower than the limits set in the Treaty.
More than 2,500 inspections have taken place. A permanent system for regular and routine exchange of Treaty notifications and other information has been developed. The Joint Consultative Group has been firmly established and has demonstrated its utility and importance as the ongoing Treaty forum.
With regard to the Concluding Act, the States Parties note with satisfaction that the personnel strength of conventional armed forces in the area of application was reduced by 1.2 million persons.

6. The States Parties note that the Treaty established a high degree of transparency in military relations through its comprehensive system for exchange of information and for verification. Together with the extensive reductions of conventional armaments and equipment, this has led to greater predictability and confidence in security relations. The Treaty has also nurtured the development of new patterns of co-operation in Europe and provides a basis for stability and enhanced security in Europe at substantially lower levels of conventional armaments and equipment than heretofore. Although risks and challenges still exist in some parts of Europe, the capability for launching surprise attack and the danger of large-scale offensive action in Europe as a whole have been diminished substantially. Nevertheless, the achievement of the goals of the Treaty in the whole area of its application requires continuous efforts by the States Parties.

7. The States Parties reaffirm the continued relevance of the basic structures of the Treaty, including the principle of zonal limitations, as embodied in Articles IV and V of the Treaty. In this respect, and in line with the Decision of the Joint Consultative Group of 17 November 1995, the States Parties have agreed on a Document, which is contained in Annex A, reflecting a combination of measures agreed in co-operative fashion and acceptable to all Parties to the Treaty.

8. The States Parties regret that not all reduction obligations pursuant to the Treaty have been met. They stress the necessity to complete as soon as possible reductions of conventional armaments and equipment limited by the Treaty (TLE) in accordance with obligations under the Treaty. They note with satisfaction the reiterated commitment of those States Parties which still have to complete reductions to comply with the provisions of the Treaty and its associated documents. All States Parties express their readiness to follow this process to its completion in accordance with the provisions of the Treaty. In this context, being aware of difficulties which have delayed the completion of reductions, they take positive note of efforts undertaken in order to meet fully obligations under the Treaty.

9. The States Parties express their concern with serious difficulties of some States Parties to comply fully, within their territory, with the provisions of the Treaty and its related documents due to TLE unaccounted for and uncontrolled within the

Treaty. This situation adversely affects the operation of the Treaty and complicates its implementation.

They stress the need to reach as soon as possible relevant political solutions and to elaborate necessary measures to enable the implementation of the Treaty in accordance with its provisions.

They express their readiness to address the issue of this TLE in the Joint Consultative Group, including the ways and means to facilitate the resolution of this issue.

10. The States Parties have adopted the understandings and agreed interpretations with regard to implementation and ways and means to improve the viability and effectiveness of the Treaty as specified in Annex B of this Final Document.

11. The States Parties have agreed that the implementation issues contained in Annex C of this Final Document require further consideration and resolution in the Joint Consultative Group.

12. The States Parties reaffirm the arrangements regarding Article XII reached at the Extraordinary Conference in Oslo in 1992.

They understand that for successor States that had become States Parties by 1992, paragraph 2 of the Article XII part of the Oslo arrangement should be read as: 'In particular, no State Party will increase within the area of application its holdings of armoured infantry fighting vehicles held by organizations designed and structured to perform in peacetime internal security functions above that aggregate number held by such organizations at the time of signature of the Treaty, as notified on their territory pursuant to the information exchange as of November 19, 1990.'

They agree to work further on the issue of Article XII in the Joint Consultative Group, taking into account the proposals made at the Review Conference.

13. The States Parties stressed the importance of full and continuous respect for the provisions of Article IV, paragraph 5, in the context of maintaining the viability of the Treaty, as well as for the sovereignty of the States Parties involved.

The States Parties noted that, in certain instances, bilateral agreements are under negotiation -- or in the process of ratification or implementation -- which relate to the provisions of Article IV, paragraph 5. The States Parties expressed their support for early and positive results of the ongoing process.

The States Parties consider that the importance of the Article IV provisions on stationing forces should be recognized in the context of the process foreseen in Section III of this Final Document.

14. In the context of the process foreseen in Section III of this Final Document, the States Parties will examine different interpretations of temporary deployments so as to ensure that these temporary deployments do not become indefinite.

15. The States Parties recall that, according to Article II, paragraph 2, of the Treaty, the lists of existing types contained in the Protocol on Existing Types of

International Humanitarian Law and Arms Control Agreements 729

Conventional Armaments and Equipment (POET) shall be updated periodically by the Joint Consultative Group in accordance with Section IV of the POET. However, it has not been updated since the Treaty's conclusion.
The States Parties instruct their delegations to the Joint Consultative Group to update the POET. They further agreed that:
* any inaccuracies should be corrected, including by removal of types, models and versions of conventional armaments and equipment that do not meet Treaty criteria;
* the Joint Consultative Group should consider if a yearly update of the lists would be appropriate;
* the Joint Consultative Group should consider an electronic version of the lists in all official languages.

16. The States Parties also discussed the topics contained in Annex D of this Final Document.

17. The States Parties welcome the statement of the representative of the Russian Federation to promote the implementation of the statement of the representative of the Union of Soviet Socialist Republics in the Joint Consultative Group on 14 June 1991 in Vienna. The text of the Russian statement is given in Annex E of this Final Document.

18. The States Parties recommend that, in view of the issues that have been referred to the Joint Consultative Group, most effective use is made of the provisions of Article XVI and the Protocol on the Joint Consultative Group in order to allow the Joint Consultative Group to address all those issues in a proper manner.

III. FUTURE WORK ON THE TREATY

19. In view of Sections I and II of this Final Document, the States Parties instruct their delegations to the Joint Consultative Group to expand upon their work in accordance with Article XVI of the Treaty. Taking fresh impetus from this Review Conference, they will immediately start a thorough process aimed at improving the operation of the Treaty in a changing environment and, through that, the security of each State Party, irrespective of whether it belongs to a politico-military alliance. As part of this process, the States Parties will consider measures and adaptations with the aim of promoting the objectives of the Treaty and of enhancing its viability and effectiveness, including but not limited to the consideration of proposals already made to that effect. The character of this process should be such as to permit the Treaty to sustain its key role in the European security architecture. Its scope and parameters should be defined as a matter of priority.

20. Until the entry into force of such measures and adaptations, the States Parties will observe all provisions of the Treaty and its associated documents.

21. The States Parties will consider a progress report on the intermediate results of this process at the time of the OSCE Lisbon Summit. That report will, inter alia, include recommendations on the way ahead.
*****

In accordance with Article XXI, paragraph 1, the States parties look forward to gathering again in five years' time at the Second Conference to Review the Operation of the Treaty on Conventional Armed Forces in Europe.
This Final Document, together with its Annexes A, B, C, D and E, which are integral to it, having been drawn up in all the official languages of the Organization for Security and Co-operation in Europe, shall be deposited with the Government of the Kingdom of the Netherlands, as the designated Depositary for the Treaty, which shall circulate copies of this Final Document to all States Parties.

Annex A:
Document agreed among the States Parties to the Treaty on
Conventional Armed Forces in Europe of November 19, 1990
The 30 States Parties to the Treaty on Conventional Armed Forces in Europe of November 19, 1990, hereinafter referred to as the Treaty,
Have agreed as follows:

I

1. Each State Party shall, taking into account the clarification set forth in this Document relating to the area described in Article V, subparagraph 1(A), of the Treaty and taking into account the understandings on flexibility set forth in this Document, comply fully with the numerical limitations set forth in the Treaty, including Article V thereof, no later than 31 May 1999.
2. Paragraph 1 of this Section shall be understood as not giving any State Party, which was in compliance with the numerical limitations set forth in the Treaty, including Article V thereof, as of 1 January 1996, the right to exceed any of the numerical limitations set forth in the Treaty.
3. Pursuant to the Decision of the Joint Consultative Group of 17 November 1995, the States Parties shall co-operate to the maximum extent possible to ensure the full implementation of the provisions of this Document.

II

1. Within the area described in Article V, subparagraph 1(A), of the Treaty, as understood by the Union of Soviet Socialist Republics at the time the Treaty was signed, Russian Federation shall limit its battle tanks, armoured combat vehicles, and artillery so that, no later than 31 May 1999 and thereafter, the aggregate numbers do not exceed:
(A) 1,800 battle tanks;
(B) 3,700 armoured combat vehicles, of which no more than 552 shall be located within the Astrakhan oblast; no more than 552 shall be located within the

Volgograd oblast; no more than 310 shall be located within the eastern part of the Rostov oblast described in Section III, paragraph 1, of this Document; and no more than 600 shall be located within the Pskov oblast; and
(C) 2,400 pieces of artillery.

2. Within the Odessa oblast, Ukraine shall limit its battle tanks, armoured combat vehicles, and artillery so that, upon provisional application of this Document and thereafter, the aggregate numbers do not exceed:
(A) 400 battle tanks;
(B) 400 armoured combat vehicles; and
(C) 350 pieces of artillery.

3. Upon provisional application of this Document and until 31 May 1999, the Russian Federation shall limit its battle tanks, armoured combat vehicles, and artillery, within the area described in Article V, subparagraph 1(A), of the Treaty, as understood by the Union of Soviet Socialist Republics at the time the Treaty was signed, so that the aggregate numbers do not exceed:
(A) 1,897 battle tanks;
(B) 4,397 armoured combat vehicles; and
(C) 2,422 pieces of artillery.

III

1. For the purposes of this Document and the Treaty, the following territory, as constituted on 1 January 1996, of the Russian Federation shall be deemed to be located in the area described in Article IV, paragraph 2, of the Treaty rather than in the area described in Article V, subparagraph 1(A), of the Treaty: the Pskov oblast; the Volgograd oblast; the Astrakhan oblast; that part of the Rostov oblast east of the line extending from Kushchevskaya to Volgodonsk to the Volgograd oblast border, including Volgodonsk; and Kushchevskaya and a narrow corridor in Krasnodar kray leading to Kushchevskaya.

2. For the purposes of this Document and the Treaty, the territory of the Odessa oblast, as constituted on 1 January 1996, of Ukraine shall be deemed to be located in the area described in Article IV, paragraph 3, of the Treaty rather than in the area described in Article V, subparagraph 1(A), of the Treaty.

IV

1. The States Parties shall, during the period before 31 May 1999, examine the Treaty provisions on designated permanent storage sites so as to allow all battle tanks, armoured combat vehicles, and artillery in designated permanent storage sites, including those subject to regional numerical limitations, to be located with active units.

2. The Russian Federation shall have the right to utilize to the maximum extent possible the provisions of the Treaty on temporary deployment of battle tanks, armoured combat vehicles, and artillery within its territory and outside its territory. Such temporary deployments on the territory of other States Parties shall be achieved by means of free negotiations and with full respect for the sovereignty of the States Parties involved.

3. The Russian Federation shall have the right to utilize, to the maximum extent possible, reallocation, in accordance with existing agreements, of the current quotas for battle tanks, armoured combat vehicles, and artillery established by the Agreement on the Principles and Procedures for the Implementation of the Treaty on Conventional Armed Forces in Europe, done at Tashkent on 15 May 1992. Such reallocations shall be achieved by means of free negotiations and with full respect for the sovereignty of the States Parties involved.

4. The Russian Federation shall count against the numerical limitations established in the Treaty and paragraph 1 of Section II of this Document any armoured combat vehicles listed as 'to be removed' in its information exchange of 1 January 1996 that are not so removed by 31 May 1999.

V

1. In addition to the annual information exchange provided pursuant to Section VII, subparagraph 1(C), of the Protocol on Notification and Exchange of Information, the Russian Federation shall provide information equal to that reported in the annual information exchange on the area described in Article V, subparagraph 1(A), of the Treaty, as understood by the Union of Soviet Socialist Republics at the time the Treaty was signed, upon provisional application of this Document and every six months after the annual information exchange. In the case of Kuskchevskaya, the Russian Federation shall provide such additional information every three months after the annual information exchange.

2. Upon provisional application of this Document, Ukraine shall provide 'F21' notifications for its holdings within the Odessa oblast on the basis of changes of five, rather than ten, per cent or more in assigned holdings.

3. Subject to paragraphs 5 and 6 of this Section, the Russian Federation shall, upon provisional application of this Document, accept each year, in addition to its passive declared site inspection quota established pursuant to Section II, subparagraph 10(D), of the Protocol on Inspection, up to a total of 10 supplementary declared site inspections, conducted in accordance with the Protocol on Inspection, at objects of verification:
(A) located within the Pskov oblast; the Volgograd oblast; the Astrakhan oblast; that part of the Rostov oblast east of the line extending from Kushchevskaya to Volgodonsk to the Volgograd oblast border, including Volgodonsk; and Kuskchevskaya and a narrow corridor in Kasnodar kray leading to Kushchevskaya;

(B) containing conventional armaments and equipment limited by the Treaty designated by the Russian Federation in its annual information exchange of 1 January 1996 as 'to be removed', until such time that a declared site inspection confirms that such equipment has been removed.

4. Subject to paragraphs 5 and 6 of this Section, Ukraine shall, upon provisional application of this Document, accept each year, in addition to its passive declared site inspection quota established pursuant to Section II, subparagraph 10(D), of the Protocol on Inspection, up to a total of one supplementary declared site inspection, conducted in accordance with the Protocol on Inspection, at objects of verification located within the Odessa oblast.

5. The number of supplementary declared site inspections conducted at objects of verification pursuant to paragraph 3 or 4 of this Section shall not exceed the number of declared site passive quota inspections, established in accordance with Section II, subparagraph 10(D), of the Protocol on Inspection, conducted at those objects of verification in the course of the same year.

6. All supplementary declared site inspections conducted pursuant to paragraph 3 or 4 of this Section:
(A) shall be carried out at the cost of the inspecting State Party, consistent with prevailing commercial rates; and
(B) at the discretion of the inspecting State Party, shall be conducted either as a sequential inspection or as a separate inspection.

VI

1. This Document shall enter into force upon receipt by the Depositary of notification of confirmation of approval by all States Parties. Section II, paragraphs 2 and 3, Section IV and Section V of this Document are hereby provisionally applied as of 31 May 1996 through 15 December 1996. If this Document does not enter into force by 15 December 1996, then it shall be reviewed by the States Parties.

2. This Document, in all six official languages of the Treaty, shall be deposited with the Government of the Kingdom of the Netherlands, as the designated Depositary for the Treaty, which shall circulate copies of this Document to all States Parties.

Annex B:
Understandings and agreed interpretations with regard to implementation and ways and means to improve the viability and effectiveness of the Treaty

1. The States Parties stress the need to ensure that relevant Government authorities charged with Treaty implementation fulfil all the obligations of the Decision of the Joint Consultative Group on the cost of inspections dated 23 May 1995.

2. The States Parties agree that, pursuant to the Protocol on Inspection, Section VII, paragraph 1,
(a) in case an inspected State Party or the State Party exercising the rights and obligations of the inspected State Party delays an inspection on grounds of force majeure, it shall, in written form, explain the reasons for this delay in detail;
This should take place as follows:
* if force majeure is declared prior to the arrival of the inspection team, through the answer to the relevant notifications;
* if force majeure is declared after the arrival of the inspection team at the point of entry, the explanation should be presented as soon as possible, through diplomatic channels or other officials channels.
(b) in case of such a delay due to force majeure, the provisions of Section XI, paragraph 2, of the Protocol on Inspection shall apply.

3. Each State Party shall provide to all other States Parties annually, but not later than 15 December, the complete updated list of inspectors and transport crew members. In case of additions to the list of inspectors and transport crew members, the State Party shall provide the complete updated list, highlighting the additions.

4. Each State Party with territory in the area of application shall provide to all other States Parties during the annual exchange of information the standing diplomatic clearance numbers for their aviation transportation means for the subsequent calendar year.

5. Each State Party shall provide to all other States Parties during the annual exchange of information the list of its officially recognized holidays for the subsequent calendar year.

6. The State Party whose inspection team intends to transit the territory of another State Party prior to concluding the inspection should inform the transited State(s) Party (Parties) about the estimated time of transit, cross-border points and transportation means to be used by the inspection team, as well as a list of inspectors and drivers with passport numbers.

7. The States Parties agree that a specified area may contain declared sites of their own and stationed forces; but all declared sites within a specified area are excluded from an inspection of the specified area (inspections in accordance with Section VIII of the Protocol on Inspection) as they can be inspected only in accordance with Section VII of the Protocol on Inspection.

8. The States Parties agree to send the notification of the intent to inspect simultaneously to the host and the stationing States Parties, if the inspecting State intends to conduct a sequential inspection which involves stationed forces.

9. Where appropriate and with the agreement of the State Party on whose territory an inspection is to be carried out in respect of conventional armaments and equipment limited by the Treaty of a stationing State Party, the stationing State Party shall assist the host nation in the provision of security protection to both the inspection team and the escort team for the duration of the inspection.

10. Notifications of changes of 10 per cent of holdings:
* The States Parties agree that, pursuant to Section VIII, subparagraph 1(B), of the Protocol on Notification and Exchange of Information, the most recent update of information on holdings will always constitute the basis for any subsequent change to be notified under this paragraph.
* The notification of any change of 10 per cent or more shall be given no later than five days after such change occurs. The time period of five days is understood as being five working days.

11. The States Parties agree to notify.
* Any changes in the designation of formations or units pursuant to Sections I, III and V of the Protocol on Notification and Exchange of Information, at least 42 days in advance;
* Any closures of objects of verification within the last month pursuant to Section V of the Protocol on Notification and Exchange of Information, on the fifteenth of each month;
* Any creation of, or relocation of, an object of verification at least 42 days in advance.

12. The States Parties agree that, in addition to the requirements for the submission of information and notifications as prescribed in Article XVII of the Treaty and in paragraph 1 of the Annex on the Format for the Exchange of Information to the Protocol on Notification and Exchange of Information, they will endeavour to supplement the annual exchange of information pursuant to the aforementioned Protocol in written form by an electronic data version on diskette in the agreed format, the written form remaining the official version.

13. Each State Party should notify to all other States Parties its passive declared site inspection quota coincident with each annual exchange of information provided pursuant to the Protocol on Notification and Exchange of Information, Section VII, subparagraph 1(C).

Annex C:
Implementation issues requiring further consideration and resolution in the Joint Consultative Group

1. Introducing of common procedures governing flights of the aviation transportation means with the inspection team.

2. Point of entry/exit.

3. Immunity of the transportation means of an inspection team.

4. Formulation of principles for the elaboration of declared site diagrams, including the possibility of a more precise formulation/interpretation of the term 'routinely'.

5. Equipment to be used during inspections.

6. Rules on photography.

7. Calendar year/possibility of synchronization with implementation year.

8. Financing of the inspections.

9. Common understanding of the obligation pursuant to the Protocol on Notification and Exchange of Information, Section VIII, subparagraph 1(B).

10. Review and updating of the Treaty Notification Formats to ensure their continued viability.

11. The issue of TLE which has left, on a temporary basis, without reassignment, the normal peacetime locations, for commitments under the auspices of the United Nations or the Organization for Security and Co-operation in Europe.

12. The question whether, with reference to the Protocol on Notification and Exchange of Information, Section I, paragraph 1, all units and formations holding equipment subject to the Treaty, including depots, bases, and designated permanent storage sites, should be notified in both Charts I and III.

13. Disposal of TLE in excess of reduction liabilities and disposal of decommissioned TLE.

14. Rounding of passive inspection quotas.

15. Enhanced transparency measures on ambulances built on the chassis of ACVs or APC look-alikes as listed in the Protocol on Existing Types of Conventional Armaments and Equipment.

Annex D:
Topics that have been discussed during the Review Conference of the Treaty on Conventional Armed Forces in Europe

1. Article II: Definitions of:
'group of States Parties';
'area of application';
'accession of other OSCE States Parties';

'designated permanent storage site';
'armoured vehicle launched bridge';
'combat aircraft',
and the Protocol on Existing Types of Conventional Armaments and Equipment.

2. Article III:
Export of equipment;
Transparency concerning TLE assigned to Internal Security Forces;
United peacekeeping force proposal.

3. Article IV:
Approach to limitations and maximum levels of holdings;
Stationing forces on the territory of another State Party.

4. Article V:
Implementation;
Temporary deployments;
Stationed forces.

5. Article VI:
Sufficiency rule.

6. Article X:
Removal from designated permanent storage sites.

7. Article XI:
Implementation;
Limits;
Removals from storage.

8. Article XII:
Armoured infantry fighting vehicles held by Internal Security Forces (pursuant to Oslo Final Document, 5 June 1992);
Transparency;
Needs of those States which joined the Treaty in 1992;
Criteria concerning Internal Security Force levels.

9. Article XIV:
Aerial inspections.

10. Article XVI:
Future role of the Joint Consultative Group;
Duration of sessions of the Joint Consultative Group.

11. Article XVIII:
Follow-up negotiations;

Modalities;
Proposal for a Supplementary Agreement.

12. Miscellaneous
United peacekeeping force proposal;
Exceptional circumstances;
Joint Consultative Group dialogue on a Treaty support fund.

CHAPTER VII

BILATERAL NUCLEAR WEAPONS CONTROL AGREEMENTS BETWEEN THE UNITED STATES OF AMERICA AND THE UNION OF SOVIET SOCIALIST REPUBLICS AND ITS SUCCESSOR STATES

INTRODUCTION

Chapter VII includes six bilateral nuclear weapons control agreements between the United States and the Union of Soviet Socialist Republics. The first agreement is the 1972 Treaty Between the United States of America and the Union of Soviet Socialist Republics on the Limitation of Anti-Ballistic Missile Systems (ABM Treaty). The last agreement included is the 1974 Treaty Between the United States of America and the Union of Soviet Socialist Republics on the Limitation of Underground Nuclear Weapon Tests (Threshold Test Ban Treaty, TTBT), and the 1990 Protocol to the Treaty.

On May 23, 1992, Belarus, Kazakhstan, Russian Federation, and Ukraine signed the Lisbon Protocol, which established them as legally bound successor states to the Soviet Union's START I Treaty obligation. In addition Belarus, Kazakhstan, and Ukraine committed in the Lisbon Protocol to accede to the Nuclear Non-Proliferation Treaty (NPT) as non-nuclear weapons states.[1]

The United States, Russian Federation, Belarus, Kazakhstan, and Ukraine signed two sets of strategic arms control agreements on September 26, 1997, advancing commitments made during the March 1997 Clinton-Yeltsin Helsinki Summit. Secretary of State Albright and Foreign Ministers Primakov, Antonovich, Tokayev, and Udovendo of the Russian Federation, Belarus, Kazakhstan, and Ukraine, respectively, signed a Memorandum of Understanding providing for succession to the ABM Treaty. In addition, Representatives of the US and Russian Federation exchanged legally binding letters codifying the Helsinki Summit commitment to the progress of START II agenda.[2]

In January 1992, the Ministry of Foreign Affairs of the Russian Federation issued the following statement indicating state succession:

---

[1] http://www.state.gov/www/global/ar...ets/wmd/nuclear/start2/abmtmd.html

[2] http://www.state.gov/www/global/ar...ets/wmd/nuclear/start2/abmtmd.html

739

The Ministry of Foreign Affairs of the Russian Federation presents its compliments to the Heads of Diplomatic Representations in Moscow and has the honour to request them to inform their Governments about the following.

The Russian Federation continues to perform the rights and fulfill the obligations following from the international agreements signed by the Union of the Soviet Socialist Republics.

Accordingly the Government of the Russian Federation shall perform the functions of a depository in conformity with the corresponding multilateral agreements instead of the Government of the USSR.

Therefore, the Ministry kindly requests to consider the Russian Federation as a Party to all international agreements in force instead of the USSR.

The Ministry avails itself of this opportunity to renew to the Heads of Diplomatic Representations the assurances of its highest consideration.

       Moscow, January 13, 1992

  As classic arms control agreements, particularly bilateral ones, their breach by any party only raises the possibility of an action before the ICJ for breach of treaty. Their relevance, however, is that they support the emerging custom applicable to the elimination of nuclear weapons. (See Chapters III, IV, V, and VI.)

VII-1. Treaty Between the United States of America and the Union of Soviet Socialist Republics on the Limitation of Anti-Ballistic Missile Systems (ABM Treaty), 3 October 1972, [Signed at Moscow May 26, 1972; Ratification advised by U.S. Senate August 3, 1972; Ratified by U.S. President September 30, 1972; Proclaimed by U.S. President October 3, 1972; Instruments of ratification exchanged October 3, 1972; Entered into force October 3, 1972]. Authentic Texts: English, Russian.

Applicability
Peace

Control
Prohibit

State Signatories
Union of Soviet Socialist Republics[1]; United States of America

State Parties
Union of Soviet Socialist Republics[2]; United States of America

Full Text

The United States of America and the Union of Soviet Socialist Republics, hereinafter referred to as the Parties, Proceeding from the premise that nuclear war would have devastating consequences for all mankind,
Considering that effective measures to limit anti-ballistic missile systems would be a substantial factor in curbing the race in strategic offensive arms and would lead to a decrease in the risk of outbreak of war involving nuclear weapons,
Proceeding from the premise that the limitation of anti-ballistic missile systems, as well as certain agreed measures with respect to the limitation of strategic offensive arms, would contribute to the creation of more favorable conditions for further negotiations on limiting strategic arms,

Mindful of their obligations under Article VI of the Treaty on the Non-Proliferation of Nuclear Weapons,

Declaring their intention to achieve at the earliest possible date the cessation of the nuclear arms race and to take effective measures toward reductions in strategic arms, nuclear disarmament, and general and complete disarmament,

---

[1] See Methodology, "State Succession."
[2] *Id.*

Desiring to contribute to the relaxation of international tension and the strengthening of trust between States,

Have agreed as follows:

Article I

1. Each Party undertakes to limit anti-ballistic missile (ABM) systems and to adopt other measures in accordance with the provisions of this Treaty.

2. Each Party undertakes not to deploy ABM systems for a defense of the territory of its country and not to provide a base for such a defense, and not to deploy ABM systems for defense of an individual region except as provided for in Article III of this Treaty.

Article II

1. For the purpose of this Treaty an ABM system is a system to counter strategic ballistic missiles or their elements in flight trajectory, currently consisting of:

(a) ABM interceptor missiles, which are interceptor missiles constructed and deployed for an ABM role, or of a type tested in an ABM mode;

(b) ABM launchers, which are launchers constructed and deployed for launching ABM interceptor missiles; and

(c) ABM radars, which are radars constructed and deployed for an ABM role, or of a type tested in an ABM mode.

2. The ABM system components listed in paragraph 1 of this Article include those which are:

(a) operational;

(b) under construction;

(c) undergoing testing;

(d) undergoing overhaul, repair or conversion; or

(e) mothballed.

Article III

Each Party undertakes not to deploy ABM systems or their components except that:

(a) within one ABM system deployment area having a radius of one hundred and fifty kilometers and centered on the Partys national capital, a Party may deploy:
(1) no more than one hundred ABM launchers and no more than one hundred ABM interceptor missiles at launch sites, and
(2) ABM radars within no more than six ABM radar complexes, the area of each complex being circular and having a diameter of no more than three kilometers; and

(b) within one ABM system deployment area having a radius of one hundred and fifty kilometers and containing ICBM silo launchers, a Party may deploy: (1) no more than one hundred ABM launchers and no more than one hundred ABM interceptor missiles at launch sites,
(2) two large phased-array ABM radars comparable in potential to corresponding ABM radars operational or under construction on the date of signature of the Treaty in an ABM system deployment area containing ICBM silo launchers, and (3) no more than eighteen ABM radars each having a potential less than the potential of the smaller of the above-mentioned two large phased-array ABM radars.

Article IV

The limitations provided for in Article III shall not apply to ABM systems or their components used for development or testing, and located within current or additionally agreed test ranges. Each Party may have no more than a total of fifteen ABM launchers at test ranges.

Article V

1. Each Party undertakes not to develop, test, or deploy ABM systems or components which are sea-based, air-based, space based, or mobile land-based.

2. Each Party undertakes not to develop, test or deploy ABM launchers for launching more than one ABM interceptor missile at a time from each launcher, not to modify deployed launchers to provide them with such a capacity, not to develop, test, or deploy automatic or semi-automatic or other similar systems for rapid reload of ABM launchers.

Article VI

To enhance assurance of the effectiveness of the limitations on ABM systems and their components provided by the Treaty, each Party undertakes:

(a) not to give missiles, launchers, or radars, other than ABM interceptor missiles, ABM launchers, or ABM radars, capabilities to counter strategic ballistic missiles or their elements in flight trajectory, and not to test them in an ABM mode; and

(b) not to deploy in the future radars for early warning of strategic ballistic missile attack except at locations along the periphery of its national territory and oriented outward.

Article VII

Subject to the provisions of this Treaty, modernization and replacement of ABM systems or their components may be carried out.

Article VIII

ABM systems or their components in excess of the numbers or outside the areas specified in this Treaty, as well as ABM systems or their components prohibited by this Treaty, shall be destroyed or dismantled under agreed procedures within the shortest possible agreed period of time.

Article IX

To assure the viability and effectiveness of this Treaty, each Party undertakes not to transfer to other States, and not to deploy outside its national territory, ABM systems or their components limited by this Treaty.

Article X

Each Party undertakes not to assume any international obligations which would conflict with this Treaty.

Article XI

The Parties undertake to continue active negotiations for limitations on strategic offensive arms.

Article XII

1. For the purpose of providing assurance or compliance with the provisions of this Treaty, each Party shall use national technical means of verification at its disposal in a manner consistent with generally recognized principles of international law.

2. Each Party undertakes not to interfere with the national technical means of verification of the other Party operating in accordance with paragraph 1 of this Article.

3. Each Party undertakes not to use deliberate concealment measures which impede verification by national technical means of compliance with the provisions of this Treaty. This obligation shall not require changes in current construction, assembly, conversion, or overhaul practices.

Article XIII

1. To promote the objectives and implementation of the provisions of this Treaty, the Parties shall establish promptly a Standing Consultative Commission, within the framework of which they will:

(a) consider questions concerning compliance with the obligations assumed and related situations which may be considered ambiguous;

(b) provide on a voluntary basis such information as either Party considers necessary to assure confidence in compliance with the obligations assumed;

(c) consider questions involving unintended interference with national technical means of verification;

(d) consider possible changes in the strategic situation which have a bearing on the provisions of this Treaty;

(e) agree upon procedures and dates for destruction or dismantling of ABM systems or their components in cases provided for by the provisions of this Treaty;

(f) consider, as appropriate, possible proposals for further increasing the viability of this Treaty;
including proposals for amendments in accordance with the provisions of this Treaty;

(g) consider, as appropriate, proposals for further measures aimed at limiting strategic arms.

2. The Parties through consultation shall establish, and may amend as appropriate, Regulations for the Standing Consultative Commission governing procedures, composition and other relevant matters.

Article XIV

1. Each Party may propose amendments to this Treaty. Agreed amendments shall enter into force in accordance with the procedures governing the entry into force of this Treaty.

2. Five years after entry into force of this Treaty, and at five-year intervals thereafter, the Parties shall together conduct a review of this Treaty.

Article XV

1. This Treaty shall be of unlimited duration.

2. Each Party shall, in exercising its national sovereignty, have the right to withdraw from this Treaty if it decides that extraordinary events related to the subject matter of this Treaty have jeopardized its supreme interests. It shall give notice of its decision to the other Party six months prior to withdrawal from the Treaty. Such notice shall include a statement of the extraordinary events the notifying Party regards as having jeopardized its supreme interests.

Article XVI

1. This Treaty shall be subject to ratification in accordance with the constitutional procedures of each Party.
The Treaty shall enter into force on the day of the exchange of instruments of ratification.

2. This Treaty shall be registered pursuant to Article 102 of the Charter of the United Nations.

DONE at Moscow on May 26, 1972, in two copies, each in the English and Russian languages, both texts being equally authentic.

FOR THE UNITED STATES OF AMERICA:
RICHARD NIXON
President of the United States of America

FOR THE UNION OF SOVIET SOCIALIST REPUBLICS:
L. I. BREZHNEV
General Secretary of the Central Committee of the CPSU

VII-2. Treaty Between the United States of America and the Union of Soviet Socialist Republics on the Limitation of Strategic Offensive Arms (SALT II), signed at Vienna, June 18, 1979. Authentic Texts: English, Russian.

Applicability
Peace

Control
Prohibit

State Signatories
Union of Soviet Socialist Republics[1]; United States of America

State Parties
Union of Soviet Socialist Republics[2]; United States of America

Full Text

The United States of America and the Union of Soviet Socialist Republics, hereinafter referred to as the Parties,

Conscious that nuclear war would have devastating consequences for all mankind,

Proceeding from the Basic Principles of Relations Between the United States of America and the Union of Soviet Socialist Republics of May 29, 1972,

Attaching particular significance to the limitation of strategic arms and determined to continue their efforts begun with the Treaty on the Limitation of Anti-Ballistic Missile Systems and the Interim Agreement on Certain Measures with Respect to the Limitation of Strategic Offensive Arms, of May 26, 1972,

Convinced that the additional measures limiting strategic offensive arms provided for in this Treaty will contribute to the improvement of relations between the Parties, help to reduce the risk of outbreak of nuclear war and strengthen international peace and security,

Mindful of their obligations under Article VI of the Treaty on the Non-Proliferation of Nuclear Weapons,

Guided by the principle of equality and equal security,

---

[1] See Methodology, "State Succession."
[2] *Id.*

Recognizing that the strengthening of strategic stability meets the interests of the Parties and the interests of international security,

Reaffirming their desire to take measures for the further limitation and for the further reduction of strategic arms, having in mind the goal of achieving general and complete disarmament,

Declaring their intention to undertake in the near future negotiations further to limit and further to reduce strategic offensive arms,

Have agreed as follows:

Article I

Each Party undertakes, in accordance with the provisions of this Treaty, to limit strategic offensive arms quantitatively and qualitatively, to exercise restraint in the development of new types of strategic offensive arms, and to adopt other measures provided for in this Treaty.

Article II

For the purposes of this Treaty:

1. Intercontinental ballistic missile (ICBM) launchers are land-based launchers of ballistic missiles capable of a range in excess of the shortest distance between the northeastern border of the continental part of the territory of the United States of America and the northwestern border of the continental part of the territory of the Union of Soviet
Socialist Republics, that is, a range in excess of 5,500 kilometers.

* The text of the SALT II Treaty and Protocol, as signed in Vienna, is accompanied by a set of Agreed Statements and Common Understandings, also signed by President Carter and General Secretary Brezhnev, which is prefaced as follows:

In connection with the Treaty Between the United States of America and the Union of Soviet Socialist Republics on the Limitation of Strategic Offensive Arms, the Parties have agreed on the following Agreed Statements and Common Understandings undertaken on behalf of the Government of the United States and the Government of the Union of Soviet Socialist Republics:

As an aid to the reader, the texts of the Agreed Statements and Common Understandings are beneath the articles of the Treaty or Protocol to which they pertain.

First Agreed Statement. The term "intercontinental ballistic missile launchers," as defined in paragraph 1 of Article II of the Treaty, includes all launchers which have been developed and tested for launching ICBMs. If a launcher has been developed and tested for launching an ICBM, all launchers of that type shall be considered to have been developed and tested for launching ICBMs.

First Common Understanding. If a launcher contains or launches an ICBM, that launcher shall be considered to have been developed and tested for launching ICBMs.

Second Common Understanding. If a launcher has been developed and tested for launching an ICBM, all launchers of that type, except for ICBM test and training launchers, shall be included in the aggregate numbers of strategic offensive arms provided for in Article III of the Treaty, pursuant to the provisions of Article VI of the Treaty.

Third Common Understanding. The one hundred and seventy-seven former Atlas and Titan I ICBM launchers of the United States of America, which are no longer operational and are partially dismantled, shall not be considered as subject to the limitations provided for in the Treaty.

Second Agreed Statement. After the date on which the Protocol ceases to be in force, mobile ICBM launchers shall be subject to the relevant limitations provided for in the Treaty which are applicable to ICBM launchers, unless the Parties agree that mobile ICBM launchers shall not be deployed after that date.

2. Submarine-launched ballistic missile (SLBM) launchers are launchers of ballistic missiles installed on any nuclear-powered submarine or launchers of modern ballistic missiles installed on any submarine, regardless of its type.

Agreed Statement. Modern submarine-launched ballistic missiles are: for the United States of America, missiles installed in all nuclear-powered submarines; for the Union of Soviet Socialist Republics, missiles of the type installed in nuclear-powered submarines made operational since 1965; and for both Parties, submarine-launched ballistic missiles first flight-tested since 1965 and installed in any submarine, regardless of its type.

3. Heavy bombers are considered to be:

(a) currently, for the United States of America, bombers of the B-52 and B-1 types, and for the Union of Soviet Socialist Republics, bombers of the Tupolev-95 and Myasishchev types;

(b) in the future, types of bombers which can carry out the mission of a heavy bomber in a manner similar or superior to that of bombers listed in subparagraph (a) above;

(c) types of bombers equipped for cruise missiles capable of a range in excess of 600 kilometers; and

(d) types of bombers equipped for ASBMs.

First Agreed Statement. The term "bombers," as used in paragraph 3 of Article II and other provisions of the Treaty, means airplanes of types initially constructed to be equipped for bombs or missiles.

Second Agreed Statement. The Parties shall notify each other on a case-by-case basis in the Standing Consultative Commission of inclusion of types of bombers as heavy bombers pursuant to the provisions of paragraph 3 of Article II of the Treaty; in this connection the Parties shall hold consultations, as appropriate, consistent with the provisions of paragraph 2 of Article XVII of the Treaty.

Third Agreed Statement. The criteria the Parties shall use to make case-by-case determinations of which types of bombers in the future can carry out the mission of a heavy bomber in a manner similar or superior to that of current heavy bombers, as referred to in subparagraph 3(b) of Article II of the Treaty, shall be agreed upon in the Standing Consultative Commission.

Fourth Agreed Statement. Having agreed that every bomber of a type included in paragraph 3 of Article II of the Treaty is to be considered a heavy bomber, the Parties further agree that:

(a) airplanes which otherwise would be bombers of a heavy bomber type shall not be considered to be bombers of a heavy bomber type if they have functionally related observable differences which indicate that they cannot perform the mission of a heavy bomber;

(b) airplanes which otherwise would be bombers of a type equipped for cruise missiles capable of a range in excess of 600 kilometers shall not be considered to be bombers of a type equipped for cruise missiles capable of a range in excess of 600 kilometers if they have functionally related observable differences which indicate that they cannot perform the mission of a bomber equipped for cruise missiles capable of a range in excess of 600 kilometers, except that heavy bombers of current types, as designated in subparagraph 3(a) of Article II of the Treaty, which otherwise would be of a type equipped for cruise missiles capable of a range in excess of 600 kilometers shall not be considered to be heavy bombers of a type equipped for cruise missiles capable of a range in excess of 600 kilometers if they are distinguishable on the basis of externally observable differences from heavy bombers of a type equipped for cruise missiles capable of a range in excess of 600 kilometers; and

(c) airplanes which otherwise would be bombers of a type equipped for ASBMs shall not be considered to be bombers of a type equipped for ASBMs if they have functionally related observable differences which indicate that they cannot perform the mission of a bomber equipped for ASBMs, except that heavy bombers of current types, as designated in subparagraph 3(a) of Article II of the Treaty, which otherwise would be of a type equipped for ASBMs shall not be considered to be heavy bombers of a type equipped for ASBMs if they are distinguishable on the basis of externally observable differences from heavy bombers of a type equipped for ASBMs.

First Common Understanding. Functionally related observable differences are differences in the observable features of airplanes which indicate whether or not these airplanes can perform the mission of a heavy bomber, or whether or not they can perform the mission of a bomber equipped for cruise missiles capable of a range in excess of 600 kilometers or whether or not they can perform the mission of a bomber equipped for ASBMs. Functionally related observable differences shall be verifiable by national technical means. To this end, the Parties may take, as appropriate, cooperative measures contributing to the effectiveness of verification by national technical means.

Fifth Agreed Statement. Tupolev-142 airplanes in their current configuration, that is, in the configuration for anti-submarine warfare, are considered to be airplanes of a type different from types of heavy bombers referred to in subparagraph 3(a) of Article II of the Treaty and not subject to the Fourth Agreed Statement to paragraph 3 of Article II of the Treaty. This Agreed Statement does not preclude improvement of Tupolev-142 airplanes as an anti-submarine system, and does not prejudice or set a precedent for designation in the future of types of airplanes as heavy bombers pursuant to subparagraph 3(b) of Article II of the Treaty or for application of the Fourth Agreed Statement to paragraph 3 of Article II of the Treaty to such airplanes.

Second Common Understanding. Not later than six months after entry into force of the Treaty the Union of Soviet Socialist Republics will give its thirty-one Myasishchev airplanes used as tankers in existence as of the date of signature of the Treaty functionally related observable differences which indicate that they cannot perform the mission of a heavy bomber.

Third Common Understanding. The designations by the United States of America and by the Union of Soviet Socialist Republics for heavy bombers referred to in subparagraph 3(a) of Article II of the Treaty correspond in the following manner:

Heavy bombers of the types designated by the United States of America as the B-52 and the B-1 are known to the Union of Soviet Socialist Republics by the same designations;

Heavy bombers of the type designated by the Union of Soviet Socialist Republics as the Tupolev-95 are known to the United States of America as heavy bombers of the Bear type; and

Heavy bombers of the type designated by the Union of Soviet Socialist Republics as the Myasishchev are known to the United States of America as heavy bombers of the Bison type.

4. Air-to-surface ballistic missiles (ASBMs) are any such missiles capable of a range in excess of 600 kilometers and installed in an aircraft or on its external mountings.

5. Launchers of ICBMs and SLBMs equipped with multiple independently targetable reentry vehicles (MIRVs) are launchers of the types developed and tested for launching ICBMs or SLBMs equipped with MIRVs.

First Agreed Statement. If a launcher has been developed and tested for launching an ICBM or an SLBM equipped with MIRVs, all launchers of that type shall be considered to have been developed and tested for launching ICBMs or SLBMs equipped with MIRVs.

First Common Understanding. If a launcher contains or launches an ICBM or an SLBM equipped with MIRVs, that launcher shall be considered to have been developed and tested for launching ICBMs or SLBMs equipped with MIRVs.

Second Common Understanding. If a launcher has been developed and tested for launching an ICBM or an SLBM equipped with MIRVs, all launchers of that type, except for ICBM and SLBM test and training launchers, shall be included in the corresponding aggregate numbers provided for in Article V of the Treaty, pursuant to the provisions of Article VI of the Treaty.

Second Agreed Statement. ICBMs and SLBMs equipped with MIRVs are ICBMs and SLBMs of the types which have been flight-tested with two or more independently targetable reentry vehicles, regardless of whether or not they have also been flight-tested with a single reentry vehicle or with multiple reentry vehicles which are not independently targetable. As of the date of signature of the Treaty, such ICBMs and SLBMs are: for the United States of America, Minuteman III ICBMs, Poseidon C-3 SLBMs, and Trident C-4 SLBMs; and for the Union of Soviet Socialist Republics, RS-16, RS-18, RS-20 ICBMs and RSM-50 SLBMs.

International Humanitarian Law and Arms Control Agreements   753

Each Party will notify the other Party in the Standing Consultative Commission on a case-by-case basis of the designation of the one new type of light ICBM, if equipped with MIRVs, permitted pursuant to paragraph 9 of Article IV of the Treaty when first flight-tested; of designations of additional types of SLBMs equipped with MIRVs when first installed on a submarine; and of designations of types of ASBMs equipped with MIRVs when first flight-tested.

Third Common Understanding. The designations by the United States of America and by the Union of Soviet Socialist Republics for ICBMs and SLBMs equipped with MIRVs correspond in the following manner:

   -- Missiles of the type designated by the United States of America as the Minuteman III and known to the Union of Soviet Socialist Republics by the same designation, a light ICBM that has been flight-tested with multiple independently targetable reentry vehicles;

   -- Missiles of the types designated by the United States of America as the Poseidon C-3 and known to the Union of Soviet Socialist Republics by the same designation, an SLBM that was first flight-tested in 1968 and that has been flight-tested with multiple independently targetable reentry vehicles;

   -- Missiles of the type designated by the United States of America as the Trident C-4 and known to the Union of Soviet Socialist Republics by the same designation, an SLBM that was first flight-tested in 1977 and that has been flight-tested with multiple independently targetable reentry vehicles;

   -- Missiles of the type designated by the Union of Soviet Socialist Republics as the RS-16 and known to the United States of America as the SS-17, a light ICBM that has been flight-tested with a single reentry vehicle and with multiple independently targetable reentry vehicles;

   -- Missiles of the type designated by the Union of Soviet Socialist Republics as the RS-18 and known to the United States of America as the SS-19, the heaviest in terms of launch-weight and throw weight of light ICBMs, which has been flight-tested with a single reentry vehicle and with multiple independently targetable reentry vehicles;

   -- Missiles of the type designated by the Union of Soviet Socialist Republics as the RS-20 and known to the United States of America as the SS-18, the heaviest in terms of launch-weight and throw-weight of heavy ICBMs, which has been flight-tested with a single reentry vehicle and with multiple independently targetable reentry vehicles;

   -- Missiles of the type designated by the Union of Soviet Socialist Republics as the RSM-50 and known to the United States of America as the SS-N-18, an SLBM that has been flight-tested with a single reentry vehicle and with multiple independently targetable reentry vehicles.

Third Agreed Statement. Reentry vehicles are independently targetable:

(a) if, after separation from the booster, maneuvering and targeting of the reentry vehicles to separate aim points along trajectories which are unrelated to each other are accomplished by means of devices which are installed in a self-contained dispensing mechanism or on the reentry vehicles, and which are based on the use of electronic or other computers in combination with devices using jet engines, including rocket engines, or aerodynamic systems;

(b) if maneuvering and targeting of the reentry vehicles to separate aim points along trajectories which are unrelated to each other are accomplished by means of other devices which may be developed in the future.

Fourth Common Understanding. For the purposes of this Treaty, all ICBM launchers in the Derazhnya and Pervomaysk areas in the Union of Soviet Socialist Republics are included in the aggregate numbers provided for in Article V of the Treaty.

Fifth Common Understanding. If ICBM or SLBM launchers are converted, constructed or undergo significant changes to their principal observable structural design features after entry into force of the Treaty, any such launchers which are launchers of missiles equipped with MIRVs shall be distinguishable from launchers of missiles not equipped with MIRVs, and any such launchers which are launchers of missiles not equipped with MIRVs shall be distinguishable from launchers of missiles equipped with MIRVs, on the basis of externally observable design features of the launchers. Submarines with launchers of SLBMs equipped with MIRVs shall be distinguishable from submarines with launchers of SLBMs not equipped with MIRVs on the basis of externally observable design features of the submarines.

This Common Understanding does not require changes to launcher conversion or construction programs, or to programs including significant changes to the principal observable structural design features of launchers, underway as of the date of signature of the Treaty.

6. ASBMs equipped with MIRVs are ASBMs of the types which have been flight-tested with MIRVs.

First Agreed Statement. ASBMs of the types which have been flight-tested with MIRVs are all ASBMs of the types which have been flight-tested with two or more independently targetable reentry vehicles, regardless of whether or not they have also been flight-tested with a single reentry vehicle or with multiple reentry vehicles which are not independently targetable.

Second Agreed Statement. Reentry vehicles are independently targetable:

(a) if, after separation from the booster, maneuvering and targeting of the reentry vehicles to separate aim points along trajectories which are unrelated to each other are accomplished by means of devices which are installed in a self-contained dispensing mechanism or on the reentry vehicles, and which are based on the use of electronic or other computers in combination with devices using jet engines, including rocket engines, or aerodynamic systems;

(b) if maneuvering and targeting of the reentry vehicles to separate aim points along trajectories which are unrelated to each other are accomplished by means of other devices which may be developed in the future.

7. Heavy ICBMs are ICBMs which have a launch-weight greater or a throw-weight greater than that of the heaviest, in terms of either launch-weight or throw-weight, respectively, of the light ICBMs deployed by either Party as of the date of signature of this Treaty.

First Agreed Statement. The launch-weight of an ICBM is the weight of the fully loaded missile itself at the time of launch.

Second Agreed Statement. The throw-weight of an ICBM is the sum of the weight of:

(a) its reentry vehicle or reentry vehicles;

(b) any self-contained dispensing mechanisms or other appropriate devices for targeting one reentry vehicle, or for releasing or for dispensing and targeting two or more reentry vehicles; and

(c) its penetration aids, including devices for their release.

Common Understanding. The term "other appropriate devices," as used in the definition of the throw weight of an ICBM in the Second Agreed Statement to paragraph 7 of Article II of the Treaty, means any devices for dispensing and targeting two or more reentry vehicles; and any devices for releasing two or more reentry vehicles or for targeting one reentry vehicle, which cannot provide their reentry vehicles or reentry vehicle with additional velocity of more than 1,000 meters per second.

8. Cruise missiles are unmanned, self-propelled, guided, weapon-delivery vehicles which sustain flight through the use of aerodynamic lift over most of their flight path and which are flight-tested from or deployed on aircraft, that is, air-launched cruise missiles, or such vehicles which are referred to as cruise missiles in subparagraph 1(b) of Article IX.

First Agreed Statement. If a cruise missile is capable of a range in excess of 600 kilometers, all cruise missiles of that type shall be considered to be cruise missiles capable of a range in excess of 600 kilometers.

First Common Understanding. If a cruise missile has been flight-tested to a range in excess of 600 kilometers, it shall be considered to be a cruise missile capable of a range in excess of 600 kilometers.

Second Common Understanding. Cruise missiles not capable of a range in excess of 600 kilo-meters shall not be considered to be of a type capable of a range in excess of 600 kilometers if they are distinguishable on the basis of externally observable design features from cruise missiles of types capable of a range in excess of 600 kilometers.

Second Agreed Statement. The range of which a cruise missile is capable is the maximum distance which can be covered by the missile in its standard design mode flying until fuel exhaustion, determined by projecting its flight path onto the Earths sphere from the point of launch to the point of impact.

Third Agreed Statement. If an unmanned, self-propelled, guided vehicle which sustains flight through the use of aerodynamic lift over most of its flight path has been flight-tested or deployed for weapon delivery, all vehicles of that type shall be considered to be weapon-delivery vehicles.

Third Common Understanding. Unmanned, self-propelled, guided vehicles which sustain flight through the use of aerodynamic lift over most of their flight path and are not weapon-delivery vehicles, that is, unarmed, pilotless, guided vehicles, shall not be considered to be cruise missiles if such vehicles are distinguishable from cruise missiles on the basis of externally observable design features.

Fourth Common Understanding. Neither Party shall convert unarmed, pilotless, guided vehicles into cruise missiles capable of a range in excess of 600 kilometers, nor shall either Party convert cruise missiles capable of a range in excess of 600 kilometers into unarmed, pilotless, guided vehicles.

Fifth Common Understanding. Neither Party has plans during the term of the Treaty to flight-test from or deploy on aircraft unarmed, pilotless, guided vehicles which are capable of a range in excess of 600 kilometers. In the future, should a Party have such plans, that Party will provide notification thereof to the other Party well in advance of such flight-testing or deployment. This Common Understanding does not apply to target drones.

Article III

1. Upon entry into force of this Treaty, each Party undertakes to limit ICBM launchers, SLBM launchers, heavy bombers, and ASBMs to an aggregate number not to exceed 2,400.

International Humanitarian Law and Arms Control Agreements 757

2. Each Party undertakes to limit, from January 1, 1981, strategic offensive arms referred to in paragraph 1 of this Article to an aggregate number not to exceed 2,250, and to initiate reductions of those arms which as of that date would be in excess of this aggregate number.

3. Within the aggregate numbers provided for in paragraphs 1 and 2 of this Article and subject to the provisions of this Treaty, each Party has the right to determine the composition of these aggregates.

4. For each bomber of a type equipped for ASBMs, the aggregate numbers provided for in paragraphs 1 and 2 of this Article shall include the maximum number of such missiles for which a bomber of that type is equipped for one operational mission.

5. A heavy bomber equipped only for ASBMs shall not itself be included in the aggregate numbers provided for in paragraphs 1 and 2 of this Article.

6. Reductions of the numbers of strategic offensive arms required to comply with the provisions of paragraphs 1 and 2 of this Article shall be carried out as provided for in Article XI.

Article IV

1. Each Party undertakes not to start construction of additional fixed ICBM launchers.

2. Each Party undertakes not to relocate fixed ICBM launchers.

3. Each Party undertakes not to convert launchers of light ICBMs, or of ICBMs of older types deployed prior to 1964, into launchers of heavy ICBMs of types deployed after that time.

4. Each Party undertakes in the process of modernization and replacement of ICBM silo launchers not to increase the original internal volume of an ICBM silo launcher by more than thirty-two percent. Within this limit each Party has the right to determine whether such an increase will be made through an increase in the original diameter or in the original depth of an ICBM silo launcher, or in both of these dimensions.

Agreed Statement. The word "original" in paragraph 4 of Article IV of the Treaty refers to the internal dimensions of an ICBM silo launcher, including its internal volume, as of May 26, 1972, or as of the date on which such launcher becomes operational, whichever is later.

Common Understanding. The obligations provided for in paragraph 4 of Article IV of the Treaty and in the Agreed Statement thereto mean that the original diameter or the original depth of an ICBM silo launcher may not be increased by an amount greater than that which would result in an increase in the original internal volume of the ICBM silo launcher by thirty-two percent solely through an increase in one of these dimensions.

5. Each Party undertakes:

(a) not to supply ICBM launcher deployment areas with intercontinental ballistic missiles in excess of a number consistent with normal deployment, maintenance, training, and replacement requirements;

(b) not to provide storage facilities for or to store ICBMs in excess of normal deployment requirements at launch sites of ICBM launchers;

(c) not to develop, test, or deploy systems for rapid reload of ICBM launchers.

Agreed Statement. The term "normal deployment requirements," as used in paragraph 5 of Article IV of the Treaty, means the deployment of one missile at each ICBM launcher.

6. Subject to the provisions of this Treaty, each Party undertakes not to have under construction at any time strategic offensive arms referred to in paragraph 1 of Article III in excess of numbers consistent with a normal construction schedule.

Common Understanding. A normal construction schedule, in paragraph 6 of Article IV of the Treaty, is understood to be one consistent with the past or present construction practices of each Party.

7. Each Party undertakes not to develop, test, or deploy ICBMs which have a launch-weight greater or a throw-weight greater than that of the heaviest, in terms of either launch-weight or throw-weight, respectively, of the heavy ICBMs deployed by either Party as of the date of signature of this Treaty.

First Agreed Statement. The launch-weight of an ICBM is the weight of the fully loaded missile itself at the time of launch.

Second Agreed Statement. The throw-weight of an ICBM is the sum of the weight of:

(a) its reentry vehicle or reentry vehicles;

(b) any self-contained dispensing mechanisms or other appropriate devices for targeting one reentry vehicle, or for releasing or for dispensing and targeting two or more reentry vehicles; and

International Humanitarian Law and Arms Control Agreements 759

(c) its penetration aids, including devices for their release.

Common Understanding. The term "other appropriate devices," as used in the definition of the throw-weight of an ICBM in the Second Agreed Statement to paragraph 7 of Article IV of the Treaty, means any devices for dispensing and targeting two or more reentry vehicles; and any devices for releasing two or more reentry vehicles or for targeting one reentry vehicle, which cannot provide their reentry vehicles or reentry vehicle with additional velocity or more than 1,000 meters per second.

8. Each Party undertakes not to convert land-based launchers of ballistic missiles which are not ICBMs into launchers for launching ICBMs, and not to test them for this purpose.

Common Understanding. During the term of the Treaty, the Union of Soviet Socialist Republics will not produce, test, or deploy ICBMs of the type designated by the Union of Soviet Socialist Republics as the RS-14 and known to the United States of America as the SS-16, a light ICBM first flight-tested after 1970 and flight-tested only with a single reentry vehicle; this Common Understanding also means that the Union of Soviet Socialist Republics will not produce the third stage of that missile, the reentry vehicle of that missile, or the appropriate device for targeting the reentry vehicle of that missile.

9. Each Party undertakes not to flight-test or deploy new types of ICBMs, that is, types of ICBMs not flight-tested as of May 1, 1979, except that each Party may flight-test and deploy one new type of light ICBM.

First Agreed Statement. The term "new types of ICBMs," as used in paragraph 9 of Article IV of the Treaty, refers to any ICBM which is different from those ICBMs flight-tested as of May 1, 1979 in any one or more of the following respects:

(a) the number of stages, the length, the largest diameter, the launch-weight, or the throw-weight, of the missile;

(b) the type of propellant (that is, liquid or solid) of any of its stages.

First Common Understanding. As used in the First Agreed Statement to paragraph 9 of Article IV of the Treaty, the term "different," referring to the length, the diameter, the launch-weight, and the throw-weight of the missile, means a difference in excess of five percent.

Second Agreed Statement. Every ICBM of the one new type of light ICBM permitted to each Party pursuant to paragraph 9 of Article IV of the Treaty shall have the same number of stages and the same type of propellant (that is, liquid or solid) of each stage as the first ICBM of the one new type of light ICBM launched by that Party. In addition, after the twenty-fifth launch of an ICBM of that type, or after the last launch before deployment begins of ICBMs of that type, whichever occurs earlier, ICBMs of the one new type of light ICBM permitted to that Party shall not be different in any one or more of the following respects: the length, the largest diameter, the launch-weight, or the throw-weight, of the missile.

A Party which launches ICBMs of the one new type of light ICBM permitted pursuant to paragraph 9 of Article IV of the Treaty shall promptly notify the other Party of the date of the first launch and of the date of either the twenty-fifth or the last launch before deployment begins of ICBMs of that type, whichever occurs earlier.

Second Common Understanding. As used in the Second Agreed Statement to paragraph 9 of Article IV of the Treaty, the term "different," referring to the length, the diameter, the launch-weight, and the throw-weight, of the missile, means a difference in excess of five percent from the value established for each of the above parameters as of the twenty-fifth launch or as of the last launch before deployment begins, whichever occurs earlier. The values demonstrated in each of the above parameters during the last twelve of the twenty-five launches or during the last twelve launches before deployment begins, whichever twelve launches occur earlier, shall not vary by more than ten percent from any other of the corresponding values demonstrated during those twelve launches.

Third Common Understanding. The limitations with respect to launch-weight and throw-weight, provided for in the First Agreed Statement and the First Common Understanding to paragraph 9 of Article IV of the Treaty, do not preclude the flight-testing or the deployment of ICBMs with fewer reentry vehicles, or fewer penetration aids, or both, than the maximum number of reentry vehicles and the maximum number of penetration aids with which ICBMs of that type have been flight-tested as of May 1, 1979, even if this results in a decrease in launch-weight or in throw-weight in excess of five percent.

In addition to the aforementioned cases, those limitations do not preclude a decrease in launch-weight or in throw-weight in excess of five percent, in the case of the flight-testing or the deployment of ICBMs with a lesser quantity of propellant, including the propellant of a self-contained dispensing mechanism or other appropriate device, than the maximum quantity of propellant, including the propellant of a self-contained dispensing mechanism or other appropriate device, with which ICBMs of that type have been flight-tested as of May 1, 1979, provided that such an ICBM is at the same time flight-tested or deployed with fewer reentry vehicles, or fewer penetration aids, or both, than the maximum number of reentry vehicles and the maximum number of penetration aids with which ICBMs of that type have been flight-tested as of May 1, 1979, and the decrease in launch-weight and throw-weight in such cases results only from the reduction in the number of reentry vehicles, or penetration aids, or both, and the reduction in the quantity of propellant.

Fourth Common Understanding. The limitations with respect to launch-weight and throw-weight, provided for in the Second Agreed Statement and the Second Common Understanding to paragraph 9 of Article IV of the Treaty, do not preclude the flight-testing or the deployment of ICBMs of the one new type of light ICBM permitted to each Party pursuant to paragraph 9 of Article IV of the Treaty with fewer reentry vehicles, or fewer penetration aids, or both, than the maximum number of reentry vehicles and the maximum number of penetration aids with which ICBMs of that type have been flight-tested, even if this results in a decrease in launch-weight or in throw-weight in excess of five percent.

In addition to the aforementioned cases, those limitations do not preclude a decrease in launch-weight or in throw-weight in excess of five percent, in the case of the flight-testing or the deployment of ICBMs of that type with a lesser quantity of propellant, including the propellant of a self-contained dispensing mechanism or other appropriate device, than the maximum quantity of propellant, including the propellant of a self-contained dispensing mechanism or other appropriate device, with which ICBMs of that type have been flight-tested, provided that such an ICBM is at the same time flight-tested or deployed with fewer reentry vehicles, or fewer penetration aids, or both, than the maximum number of reentry vehicles and the maximum number of penetration aids with which ICBMs of that type have been flight-tested, and the decrease in launch-weight and throw-weight in such cases results only from the reduction in the number of reentry vehicles, or penetration aids, or both, and the reduction in the quantity of propellant.

10. Each Party undertakes not to flight-test or deploy ICBMs of a type flight-tested as of May 1, 1979 with a number of reentry vehicles greater than the maximum number of reentry vehicles with which an ICBM of that type has been flight-tested as of that date.

First Agreed Statement. The following types of ICBMs and SLBMs equipped with MIRVs have been flight-tested with the maximum number of reentry vehicles set forth below:

For the United States of America

*ICBMs of the Minuteman III type -- Seven reentry vehicles;

*SLBMs of the Poseidon C-3 type -- Fourteen reentry vehicles;

*SLBMs of the Trident C-4 type -- Seven reentry vehicles.

For the Union of Soviet Socialist Republics

*ICBMs of the RS-16 type -- Four reentry vehicles;

*ICBMs of the RS-18 type -- Six reentry vehicles;

*ICBMs of the RS-20 type -- Ten reentry vehicles;

*SLBMs of the RSM-50 type -- Seven reentry vehicles.

Common Understanding. Minuteman III ICBMs of the United States of America have been deployed with no more than three reentry vehicles. During the term of the Treaty, the United States of America has no plans to and will not flight-test or deploy missiles of this type with more than three reentry vehicles.

Second Agreed Statement. During the flight-testing of any ICBM, SLBM, or ASBM after May 1, 1979, the number of procedures for releasing or for dispensing may not exceed the maximum number of reentry vehicles established for missiles of corresponding types as provided for in paragraphs 10, 11, 12, and 13 of Article IV of the Treaty. In this Agreed Statement "procedures for releasing or for dispensing" are understood to mean maneuvers of a missile associated with targeting and releasing or dispensing its reentry vehicles to aim points, whether or not a reentry vehicle is actually released or dispensed. Procedures for releasing anti-missile defense penetration aids will not be considered to be procedures for releasing or for dispensing a reentry vehicle so long as the procedures for releasing anti-missile defense penetration aids differ from those for releasing or for dispensing reentry vehicles.

Third Agreed Statement. Each Party undertakes:

(a) not to flight-test or deploy ICBMs equipped with multiple reentry vehicles, of a type flight-tested as of May 1, 1979, with reentry vehicles the weight of any of which is less than the weight of the lightest of those reentry vehicles with which an ICBM of that type has been flight-tested as of that date;

(b) not to flight-test or deploy ICBMs equipped with a single reentry vehicle and without an appropriate device for targeting a reentry vehicle, of a type flight-tested as of May 1, 1979, with a reentry vehicle the weight of which is less than the weight of the lightest reentry vehicle on an ICBM of a type equipped with MIRVs and flight-tested by that Party as of May 1, 1979; and

(c) not to flight-test or deploy ICBMs equipped with a single reentry vehicle and with an appropriate device for targeting a reentry vehicle, of a type flight-tested as of May 1, 1979, with a reentry vehicle the weight
of which is less than fifty percent of the throw-weight of that ICBM.

11. Each Party undertakes not to flight-test or deploy ICBMs of the one new type permitted pursuant to paragraph 9 of this Article with a number of reentry vehicles greater than the maximum number of reentry vehicles with

which an ICBM of either Party has been flight-tested as of May 1, 1979, that is, ten.

First Agreed Statement. Each Party undertakes not to flight-test or deploy the one new type of light ICBM permitted to each Party pursuant to paragraph 9 of Article IV of the Treaty with a number of reentry vehicles greater than the maximum number of reentry vehicles with which an ICBM of that type has been flight-tested as of the twenty-fifth launch or the last launch before deployment begins of ICBMs of that type, whichever occurs earlier.

Second Agreed Statement. During the flight-testing of any ICBM, SLBM, or ASBM after May 1, 1979 the number of procedures for releasing or for dispensing may not exceed the maximum number of reentry vehicles established for missiles of corresponding types as provided for in paragraphs 10, 11, 12, and 13 of Article IV of the Treaty. In this Agreed Statement "procedures for releasing or for dispensing" are understood to mean maneuvers of a missile associated with targeting and releasing or dispensing its reentry vehicles to aim points, whether or not a reentry vehicle is actually released or dispensed. Procedures for releasing anti-missile defense penetration aids will not be considered to be procedures for releasing or for dispensing a reentry vehicle so long as the procedures for releasing anti-missile defense penetration aids differ from those for releasing or for dispensing reentry vehicles.

12. Each Party undertakes not to flight-test or deploy SLBMs with a number of reentry vehicles greater than the maximum number of reentry vehicles with which an SLBM of either Party has been flight-tested as of May 1, 1979, that is, fourteen.

First Agreed Statement. The following types of ICBMs and SLBMs equipped with MIRVs have been flight-tested with the maximum number of reentry vehicles set forth below:

For the United States of America

*ICBMs of the Minuteman III type -- Seven reentry vehicles;

*SLBMs of the Poseidon C-3 type -- Fourteen reentry vehicles;

*SLBMs of the Trident C-4 type -- Seven reentry vehicles.

For the Union of Soviet Socialist Republics

*ICBMs of the RS-16 type -- Four reentry vehicles;

*ICBMs of the RS-18 type -- Six reentry vehicles;

*ICBMs of the RS-20 type -- Ten reentry vehicles;

*SLBMs of the RSM-50 type -- Seven reentry vehicles.

Second Agreed Statement. During the flight-testing of any ICBM, SLBM, or ASBM after May 1, 1979 the number of procedures for releasing or for dispensing may not exceed the maximum number of reentry vehicles established for missiles of corresponding types as provided for in paragraphs 10, 11, 12, and 13 of Article IV of the Treaty. In this Agreed Statement "procedures for releasing or dispensing" are understood to mean maneuvers of a missile associated with targeting and releasing or dispensing its reentry vehicles to aim points, whether or not a reentry vehicle is actually released or dispensed. Procedures for releasing anti-missile defense penetration aids will not be considered to be procedures for releasing or for dispensing a reentry vehicle so long as the procedures for releasing anti-missile defense penetration aids differ from those for releasing or for dispensing reentry vehicles.

13. Each Party undertakes not to flight-test or deploy ASBMs with a number of reentry vehicles greater than the maximum number of reentry vehicles with which an ICBM of either Party has been flight-tested as of May 1, 1979, that is, ten.

Agreed Statement. During the flight-testing of any ICBM, SLBM, or ASBM after May 1, 1979 the number of procedures for releasing or for dispensing may not exceed the maximum number of reentry vehicles established for missiles of corresponding types as provided for in paragraphs 10, 11, 12, and 13 of Article IV of the Treaty. In this Agreed Statement "procedures for releasing or for dispensing" are understood to mean maneuvers of a missile associated with targeting and releasing or dispensing its reentry vehicles to aim points, whether or not a reentry vehicle is actually released or dispensed. Procedures for releasing anti-missile defense penetration aids will not be considered to be procedures for releasing or for dispensing a reentry vehicle so long as the procedures for releasing anti-missile defense penetration aids differ from those for releasing or for dispensing reentry vehicles.

14. Each Party undertakes not to deploy at any one time on heavy bombers equipped for cruise missiles capable of a range in excess of 600 kilometers a number of such cruise missiles which exceeds the product of 28 and the number of such heavy bombers.

First Agreed Statement. For the purposes of the limitation provided for in paragraph 14 of Article IV of the Treaty, there shall be considered to be deployed on each heavy bomber of a type equipped for cruise missiles capable of a range in excess of 600 kilometers the maximum number of such missiles for which any bomber of that type is equipped for one operational mission.

Second Agreed Statement. During the term of the Treaty no bomber of the B-52 or B-1 types of the United States of America and no bomber of the Tupolev-95 or Myasishchev types of the Union of Soviet Socialist Republics will be equipped for more than twenty cruise missiles capable of a range in excess of 600 kilometers.

Article V

1. Within the aggregate numbers provided for in paragraphs 1 and 2 of Article III, each Party undertakes to limit launchers of ICBMs and SLBMs equipped with MIRVs, ASBMs equipped with MIRVs, and heavy bombers equipped for cruise missiles capable of a range in excess of 600 kilometers to an aggregate number not to exceed 1,320,455.

2. Within the aggregate number provided for in paragraph 1 of this Article, each Party undertakes to limit launchers of ICBMs and SLBMs equipped with MIRVs, and ASBMs equipped with MIRVs to an aggregate number not to exceed 1,200.

3. Within the aggregate number provided for in paragraph 2 of this Article, each Party undertakes to limit launchers of ICBMs equipped with MIRVs to an aggregate number not to exceed 820.

4. For each bomber of a type equipped for ASBMs equipped with MIRVs, the aggregate numbers provided for in paragraphs 1 and 2 of this Article shall include the maximum number of ASBMs for which a bomber of that type is equipped for one operational mission.

Agreed Statement. If a bomber is equipped for ASBMs equipped with MIRVs, all bombers of that type shall be considered to be equipped for ASBMs equipped with MIRVs.

5. Within the aggregate numbers provided for in paragraphs 1, 2, and 3 of this Article and subject to the provisions of this Treaty, each Party has the right to determine the composition of these aggregates.

Article VI

1. The limitations provided for in this Treaty shall apply to those arms which are:

(a) operational;

(b) in the final stage of construction;

(c) in reserve, in storage, or mothballed;

(d) undergoing overhaul, repair, modernization, or conversion.

2. Those arms in the final stage of construction are:

(a) SLBM launchers on submarines which have begun sea trials;

(b) ASBMs after a bomber of a type equipped for such missiles has been brought out of the shop, plant, or other facility where its final assembly or conversion for the purpose of equipping it for such missiles has been performed;

(c) other strategic offensive arms which are finally assembled in a shop, plant, or other facility after they have been brought out of the shop, plant, or other facility where their final assembly has been performed.

3. ICBM and SLBM launchers of a type not subject to the limitation provided for in Article V, which undergo conversion into launchers of a type subject to that limitation, shall become subject to that limitation as follows:

(a) fixed ICBM launchers when work on their conversion reaches the stage which first definitely indicates that they are being so converted;

(b) SLBM launchers on a submarine when that submarine first goes to sea after their conversion has been performed.

Agreed Statement. The procedures referred to in paragraph 7 of Article VI of the Treaty shall include procedures determining the manner in which mobile ICBM launchers of a type not subject to the limitation provided for in Article V of the Treaty, which undergo conversion into launchers of a type subject to that limitation, shall become subject to that limitation, unless the Parties agree that mobile ICBM launchers shall not be deployed after the date on which the Protocol ceases to be in force.

4. ASBMs on a bomber which undergoes conversion from a bomber of a type equipped for ASBMs which are not subject to the limitation provided for in Article V into a bomber of a type equipped for ASBMs which are subject to that limitation shall become subject to that limitation when the bomber is brought out of the shop, plant, or other facility where such conversion has been performed.

5. A heavy bomber of a type not subject to the limitation provided for in paragraph 1 of Article V shall become subject to that limitation when it is brought out of the shop, plant, or other facility where it has been converted into a heavy bomber of a type equipped for cruise missiles capable of a range in excess of 600 kilometers. A bomber of a type not subject to the limitation provided for in paragraph 1 or 2 of Article III shall become subject to that limitation and to the limitation provided for in paragraph 1 of Article V when it is brought out of the shop, plant, or other facility where it has been converted into a bomber of a type equipped for cruise missiles capable of a range in excess of 600 kilometers.

6. The arms subject to the limitations provided for in this Treaty shall continue to be subject to these limitations until they are dismantled, are destroyed, or otherwise cease to be subject to these limitations under procedures to be agreed upon.

Agreed Statement. The procedures for removal of strategic offensive arms from the aggregate numbers provided for in the Treaty, which are referred to in paragraph 6 of Article VI of the Treaty, and which are to be agreed upon in the Standing Consultative Commission, shall include:

(a) procedures for removal from the aggregate numbers, provided for in Article V of the Treaty, of ICBM and SLBM launchers which are being converted from launchers of a type subject to the limitation provided for in Article V of the Treaty, into launchers of a type not subject to that limitation;

(b) procedures for removal from the aggregate numbers, provided for in Articles III and V of the Treaty, of bombers which are being converted from bombers of a type subject to the limitations provided for in Article III of the Treaty or in Articles III and V of the Treaty into airplanes or bombers of a type not so subject.

Common Understanding. The procedures referred to in subparagraph (b) of the Agreed Statement to paragraph 6 of Article VI of the Treaty for removal of bombers from the aggregate numbers provided for in Articles III and V of the Treaty shall be based upon the existence of functionally related observable differences which indicate whether or not they can perform the mission of a heavy bomber, or whether or not they can perform the mission of a bomber equipped for cruise missiles capable of a range in excess of 600 kilometers.

7. In accordance with the provisions of Article XVII, the Parties will agree in the Standing Consultative Commission upon procedures to implement the provisions of this Article.

Article VII

1. The limitations provided for in Article III shall not apply to ICBM and SLBM test and training launchers or to space vehicle launchers for exploration and use of outer space. ICBM and SLBM test and training launchers are ICBM and SLBM launchers used only for testing or training.

Common Understanding. The term "testing," as used in Article VII of the Treaty, includes research and development.

2. The Parties agree that:

(a) there shall be no significant increase in the number of ICBM or SLBM test and training launchers or in the number of such launchers of heavy ICBMs;

(b) construction or conversion of ICBM launchers at test ranges shall be undertaken only for purposes of testing and training;

(c) there shall be no conversion of ICBM test and training launchers or of space vehicle launchers into ICBM launchers subject to the limitations provided for in Article III.

First Agreed Statement. The term "significant increase," as used in subparagraph 2(a) of Article VII of the Treaty, means an increase of fifteen percent or more. Any new ICBM test and training launchers which replace ICBM test and training launchers at test ranges will be located only at test ranges.

Second Agreed Statement. Current test ranges where ICBMs are tested are located: for the United States of America, near Santa Maria, California, and at Cape Canaveral, Florida; and for the Union of Soviet Socialist Republics, in the areas of Tyura-Tam and Plesetskaya. In the future, each Party shall provide notification in the Standing Consultative Commission of the location of any other test range used by that Party to test ICBMs.

First Common Understanding. At test ranges where ICBMs are tested, other arms, including those not limited by the Treaty, may also be tested.

Second Common Understanding. Of the eighteen launchers of fractional orbital missiles at the test range where ICBMs are tested in the area of Tyura-Tam, twelve launchers shall be dismantled or destroyed and six launchers may be converted to launchers for testing missiles undergoing modernization.

Dismantling or destruction of the twelve launchers shall begin upon entry into force of the Treaty and shall be completed within eight months, under procedures for dismantling or destruction of these launchers to be agreed upon in the Standing Consultative Commission. These twelve launchers shall not be replaced.

Conversion of the six launchers may be carried out after entry into force of the Treaty. After entry into force of the Treaty, fractional orbital missiles shall be removed and shall be destroyed pursuant to the provisions of subparagraph 1(c) of Article IX and of Article XI of the Treaty and shall not be replaced by other missiles, except in the case of conversion of these six launchers for testing missiles undergoing modernization. After removal of the fractional orbital missiles, and prior to such conversion, any activities associated with these launchers shall be limited to normal maintenance requirements for launchers in which missiles are not deployed. These six launchers shall be subject to the provisions of Article VII of the Treaty and, if converted, to the provisions of the Fifth Common Understanding to paragraph 5 of Article II of the Treaty.

Article VIII

1. Each Party undertakes not to flight-test cruise missiles capable of a range in excess of 600 kilometers or ASBMs from aircraft other than bombers or to convert such aircraft into aircraft equipped for such missiles.

Agreed Statement. For purposes of testing only, each Party has the right, through initial construction or, as an exception to the provisions of paragraph 1 of Article VIII of the Treaty, by conversion, to equip for cruise missiles capable of a range in excess of 600 kilometers or for ASBMs no more than sixteen airplanes, including airplanes which are prototypes of bombers equipped for such missiles. Each Party also has the right, as an exception to the provisions of paragraph 1 of Article VIII of the Treaty, to flight-test from such airplanes cruise missiles capable of a range in excess of 600 kilometers and, after the date on which the Protocol ceases to be in force, to flight-test ASBMs from such airplanes as well, unless the Parties agree that they will not flight-test ASBMs after that date. The limitations provided for in Article III of the Treaty shall not apply to such airplanes. The aforementioned airplanes may include only:

(a) airplanes other than bombers which, as an exception to the provisions of paragraph 1 of Article VIII of the Treaty, have been converted into airplanes equipped for cruise missiles capable of a range in excess of 600 kilometers or for ASBMs;

(b) airplanes considered to be heavy bombers pursuant to subparagraph 3(c) or 3(d) of Article II of the Treaty; and

(c) airplanes other than heavy bombers which, prior to March 7, 1979, were used for testing cruise missiles capable of a range in excess of 600 kilometers.

The airplanes referred to in subparagraphs (a) and (b) of this Agreed Statement shall be distinguishable on the basis of functionally related observable differences from airplanes which otherwise would be of the same type but cannot perform the mission of a bomber equipped for cruise missiles capable of a range in excess of 600 kilometers or for ASBMs.

The airplanes referred to in subparagraph (c) of this Agreed Statement shall not be used for testing cruise missiles capable of a range in excess of 600 kilometers after the expiration of a six-month period from the date of entry into force of the Treaty, unless by the expiration of that period they are distinguishable on the basis of functionally related observable differences from airplanes which otherwise would be of the same type but cannot perform the mission of a bomber equipped for cruise missiles capable of a range in excess of 600 kilometers.

First Common Understanding. The term "testing," as used in the Agreed Statement to paragraph 1 of Article VIII of the Treaty, includes research and development.

Second Common Understanding. The Parties shall notify each other in the Standing Consultative Commission of the number of airplanes, according to type, used for testing pursuant to the Agreed Statement to paragraph 1 of Article VIII of the Treaty. Such notification shall be provided at the first regular session of the Standing Consultative Commission held after an airplane has been used for such testing.

Third Common Understanding. None of the sixteen airplanes referred to in the Agreed Statement to paragraph 1 of Article VIII of the Treaty may be replaced, except in the event of the involuntary destruction of any such airplane or in the case of the dismantling or destruction of any such airplane. The procedures for such replacement and for removal of any such airplane from that number, in case of its conversion, shall be agreed upon in the Standing Consultative Commission.

2. Each Party undertakes not to convert aircraft other than bombers into aircraft which can carry out the mission of a heavy bomber as referred to in subparagraph 3(b) of Article II.

Article IX

1. Each Party undertakes not to develop, test, or deploy:

(a) ballistic missiles capable of a range in excess of 600 kilometers for installation on waterborne vehicles other than submarines, or launchers of such missiles;

Common Understanding to subparagraph (a). The obligations provided for in subparagraph 1(a) of Article IX of the Treaty do not affect current practices for transporting ballistic missiles.

(b) fixed ballistic or cruise missile launchers for emplacement on the ocean floor, on the seabed, or on the beds of internal waters and inland waters, or in the subsoil thereof, or mobile launchers of such missiles, which move only in contact with the ocean floor, the seabed, or the beds of internal waters and inland waters, or missiles for such launchers;

Agreed Statement to subparagraph (b). The obligations provided for in subparagraph 1(b) of Article IX of the Treaty shall apply to all areas of the ocean floor and the seabed, including the seabed zone referred to in Articles I and II of the 1971 Treaty on the Prohibition of the Emplacement of Nuclear Weapons and Other Weapons of Mass Destruction on the Seabed and the Ocean Floor and in the Subsoil Thereof.

(c) systems for placing into Earth orbit nuclear weapons or any other kind of weapons of mass destruction, including fractional orbital missiles;

International Humanitarian Law and Arms Control Agreements 771

Common Understanding to subparagraph (c). The provisions of subparagraph 1(c) of Article IX of the Treaty do not require the dismantling or destruction of any existing launchers of either Party.

(d) mobile launchers of heavy ICBMs;

(e) SLBMs which have a launch-weight greater or a throw-weight greater than that of the heaviest, in terms of either launch-weight or throw-weight, respectively, of the light ICBMs deployed by either Party as of the date of signature of this Treaty, or launchers of such SLBMs; or

(f) ASBMs which have a launch-weight greater or a throw-weight greater than that of the heaviest, in terms of either launch-weight or throw-weight, respectively, of the light ICBMs deployed by either Party as of the date of signature of this Treaty.

First Agreed Statement to subparagraphs (e) and (f). The launch-weight of an SLBM or of an ASBM is the weight of the fully loaded missile itself at the time of launch.

Second Agreed Statement to subparagraphs (e) and (f). The throw-weight of an SLBM or of an ASBM is the sum of the weight of:

(a) its reentry vehicle or reentry vehicles;

(b) any self-contained dispensing mechanisms or other appropriate devices for targeting one reentry vehicle, or for releasing or for dispensing and targeting two or more reentry vehicles; and

(c) its penetration aids, including devices for their release.

Common Understanding to subparagraphs (e) and (f). The term "other appropriate devices," as used in the definition of the throw-weight of an SLBM or of an ASBM in the Second Agreed Statement to subparagraphs 1(e) and (f) of Article IX of the Treaty, means any devices for dispensing and targeting two or more reentry vehicles; and any devices for releasing two or more reentry vehicles or for targeting one reentry vehicle, which cannot provide their reentry vehicles or reentry vehicle with additional velocity of more than 1,000 meters per second.

2. Each Party undertakes not to flight-test from aircraft cruise missiles capable of a range in excess of 600 kilometers which are equipped with multiple independently targetable warheads and not to deploy such cruise missiles on aircraft.

Agreed Statement. Warheads of a cruise missile are independently targetable if maneuvering or targeting of the warheads to separate aim points along ballistic trajectories or any other flight paths, which are unrelated to each other, is accomplished during a flight of a cruise missile.

Article X

Subject to the provisions of this Treaty, modernization and replacement of strategic offensive arms may be carried out.

Article XI

1. Strategic offensive arms which would be in excess of the aggregate numbers provided for in this Treaty as well as strategic offensive arms prohibited by this Treaty shall be dismantled or destroyed under procedures to be agreed upon in the Standing Consultative Commission.

2. Dismantling or destruction of strategic offensive arms which would be in excess of the aggregate number provided for in paragraph 1 of Article III shall begin on the date of the entry into force of this Treaty and shall be completed within the following periods from that date: four months for ICBM launchers; six months for SLBM launchers; and three months for heavy bombers.

3. Dismantling or destruction of strategic offensive arms which would be in excess of the aggregate number provided for in paragraph 2 of Article III shall be initiated no later than January 1, 1981, shall be carried out throughout the ensuing twelve-month period, and shall be completed no later than December 31, 1981.

4. Dismantling or destruction of strategic offensive arms prohibited by this Treaty shall be completed within the shortest possible agreed period of time, but not later than six months after the entry into force of this Treaty.

Article XII

In order to ensure the viability and effectiveness of this Treaty, each Party undertakes not to circumvent the provisions of this Treaty, through any other state or states, or in any other manner.

Article XIII

Each Party undertakes not to assume any international obligations which would conflict with this Treaty.

Article XIV

The Parties undertake to begin, promptly after the entry into force of this Treaty, active negotiations with the objective of achieving, as soon as possible, agreement on further measures for the limitation and reduction of strategic arms. It is also the objective of the Parties to conclude well in advance of 1985 an agreement limiting strategic offensive arms to replace this Treaty upon its expiration.

Article XV

1. For the purpose of providing assurance of compliance with the provisions of this Treaty, each Party shall use national technical means of verification at its disposal in a manner consistent with generally recognized principles of international law.

2. Each party undertakes not to interfere with the national technical means of verification of the other Party operating in accordance with paragraph 1 of this Article.

3. Each Party undertakes not to use deliberate concealment measures which impede verification by national technical means of compliance with the provisions of this Treaty. This obligation shall not require changes in current construction, assembly, conversion, or overhaul practices.

First Agreed Statement. Deliberate concealment measures, as referred to in paragraph 3 of Article XV of the Treaty, are measures carried out deliberately to hinder or deliberately to impede verification by national technical means of compliance with the provisions of the Treaty.

Second Agreed Statement. The obligation not to use deliberate concealment measures, provided for in paragraph 3 of Article XV of the Treaty, does not preclude the testing of anti-missile defense penetration aids.

First Common Understanding. The provisions of paragraph 3 of Article XV of the Treaty and the First Agreed Statement thereto apply to all provisions of the Treaty, including provisions associated with testing. In this
connection, the obligation not to use deliberate concealment measures associated with testing, including those measures aimed at concealing the association between ICBMs and launchers during testing.

Second Common Understanding. Each Party is free to use various methods of transmitting telemetric information during testing, including its encryption, except that, in accordance with the provisions of paragraph 3 of Article XV of the Treaty, neither Party shall engage in deliberate denial of telemetric information, such as through the use of telemetry encryption, whenever such denial impedes verification of compliance with the provisions of the Treaty.

Third Common Understanding. In addition to the obligations provided for in paragraph 3 of Article XV of the Treaty, no shelters which impede verification by national technical means of compliance with the provisions of the Treaty shall be used over ICBM silo launchers.

Article XVI

1. Each Party undertakes, before conducting each planned ICBM launch, to notify the other Party well in advance on a case-by-case basis that such a launch will occur, except for single ICBM launches from test ranges or from ICBM launcher deployment areas, which are not planned to extend beyond its national territory.

First Common Understanding. ICBM launches to which the obligations provided for in Article XVI of the Treaty apply, include, among others, those ICBM launches for which advance notification is required pursuant to the provisions of the Agreement on Measures to Reduce the Risk of Outbreak of Nuclear War Between the United States of America and the Union of Soviet Socialist Republics, signed September 30, 1971, and the Agreement Between the Government of the United States of America and the Government of the Union of Soviet Socialist Republics on the Prevention of Incidents On and Over the High Seas, signed May 25, 1972. Nothing in Article XVI of the Treaty is intended to inhibit advance notification, on a voluntary basis, of any ICBM launches not subject to its provisions, the advance notification of which would enhance confidence between the Parties.

Second Common Understanding. A multiple ICBM launch conducted by a Party, as distinct from single ICBM launches referred to in Article XVI of the Treaty, is a launch which would result in two or more of its ICBMs being in flight at the same time.

Third Common Understanding. The test ranges referred to in Article XVI of the Treaty are those covered by the Second Agreed Statement to paragraph 2 of Article VII of the Treaty.

2. The Parties shall agree in the Standing Consultative Commission upon procedures to implement the provisions of this Article.

Article XVII

1. To promote the objectives and implementation of the provisions of this Treaty, the Parties shall use the Standing Consultative Commission established by the Memorandum of Understanding Between the Government of the United States of America and the Government of the Union of Soviet Socialist Republics Regarding the Establishment of a Standing Consultative Commission of December 21, 1972.

2. Within the framework of the Standing Consultative Commission, with respect to this Treaty, the Parties will:

(a) consider questions concerning compliance with the obligations assumed and related situations which may be considered ambiguous;

(b) provide on a voluntary basis such information as either Party considers necessary to assure confidence in compliance with the obligations assumed;

(c) consider questions involving unintended interference with national technical means of verification, and questions involving unintended impeding of verification by national technical means of compliance with the provisions of this Treaty;

(d) consider possible changes in the strategic situation which have a bearing on the provisions of this Treaty;

(e) agree upon procedures for replacement, conversion, and dismantling or destruction, of strategic offensive arms in cases provided for in the provisions of this Treaty and upon procedures for removal of such arms from the aggregate numbers when they otherwise cease to be subject to the limitations provided for in this Treaty, and at regular sessions of the Standing Consultative Commission, notify each other in accordance with the aforementioned procedures, at least twice annually, of actions completed and those in process;

(f) consider, as appropriate, possible proposals for further increasing the viability of this Treaty, including proposals for amendments in accordance with the provisions of this Treaty;

(g) consider, as appropriate, proposals for further measures limiting strategic offensive arms.

3. In the Standing Consultative Commission the Parties shall maintain by category the agreed data base on the numbers of strategic offensive arms established by the Memorandum of Understanding Between the United States of America and the Union of Soviet Socialist Republics Regarding the Establishment of a Data Base on the Numbers of Strategic Offensive Arms of June 18, 1979.

Agreed Statement. In order to maintain the agreed data base on the numbers of strategic offensive arms subject to the limitations provided for in the Treaty in accordance with paragraph 3 of Article XVII of the Treaty, at each regular session of the Standing Consultative Commission the Parties will notify each other of and consider changes in those numbers in the following categories: launchers of ICBMs; fixed launchers of ICBMs; launchers of ICBMs equipped with MIRVs; launchers of SLBMs; launchers of SLBMs equipped with MIRVs; heavy bombers; heavy bombers equipped for cruise missiles capable of a range in excess of 600 kilometers; heavy bombers equipped only for ASBMs; ASBMs; and ASBMs equipped with MIRVs.

Article XVIII

Each Party may propose amendments to this Treaty. Agreed amendments shall enter into force in accordance with the procedures governing the entry into force of this Treaty.

Article XIX

1. This Treaty shall be subject to ratification in accordance with the constitutional procedures of each Party. This Treaty shall enter into force on the day of the exchange of instruments of ratification and shall remain in force through December 31, 1985, unless replaced earlier by an agreement further limiting strategic offensive arms.

2. This Treaty shall be registered pursuant to Article 102 of the Charter of the United Nations.

3. Each Party shall, in exercising its national sovereignty, have the right to withdraw from this Treaty if it decides that extraordinary events related to the subject matter of this Treaty have jeopardized its supreme interests. It shall give notice of its decision to the other Party six months prior to withdrawal from the Treaty. Such notice shall include a statement of the extraordinary events the notifying Party regards as having jeopardized its supreme interests.

DONE at Vienna on June 18, 1979, in two copies, each in the English and Russian languages, both texts being equally authentic.

FOR THE UNITED STATES OF AMERICA:
JIMMY CARTER
President of the United States of America

FOR THE UNION OF SOVIET SOCIALIST REPUBLICS:
L. BREZHNEV
General Secretary of the CPSU, Chairman of the Presidium of the Supreme Soviet of the USSR

VII-3. Protocol to the Treaty Between the United States of America and the Union of Soviet Socialist Republics on the Limitation of Strategic Offensive Arms.

State Signatories
Union of Soviet Socialist Republics[1]; United States of America

State Parties
Union of Soviet Socialist Republics[2]; United States of America

Full Text

The United States of America and the Union of Soviet Socialist Republics, hereinafter referred to as the Parties,

Having agreed on limitations on strategic offensive arms in the Treaty,

Having agreed on additional limitations for the period during which this Protocol remains in force, as follows:

Article I

Each Party undertakes not to deploy mobile ICBM launchers or to flight-test ICBMs for such launchers.

Article II

1. Each Party undertakes not to deploy cruise missiles capable of a range in excess of 600kilometers on sea-based launchers or on land-based launchers.

2. Each Party undertakes not to flight-test cruise missiles capable of a range in excess of 600kilometers which are equipped with multiple independently targetable warheads from sea-based launchers or from land-based launchers.

Agreed Statement. Warheads of a cruise missile are independently targetable if maneuvering or targeting of the warheads to separate aim points along ballistic trajectories or any other flight paths, which are unrelated to each other, is accomplished during a flight of a cruise missile.

3. For the purposes of this Protocol, cruise missiles are unmanned, self-propelled, guided, weapon-delivery vehicles which sustain flight through the use of aerodynamic lift over most of their flight path and which are flight-tested from or

---

[1] See Methodology, "State Succession."
[2] *Id.*

deployed on sea-based or land-based launchers, that is, sea-launched cruise missiles and ground-launched cruise missiles, respectively.

First Agreed Statement. If a cruise missile is capable of a range in excess of 600 kilometers, all cruise missiles of that type shall be considered to be cruise missiles capable of a range in excess of 600 kilometers.

First Common Understanding. If a cruise missile has been flight-tested to a range in excess of 600 kilometers, it shall be considered to be a cruise missile capable of a range in excess of 600 kilometers.

Second Common Understanding. Cruise missiles not capable of a range in excess of 600 kilometers shall not be considered to be of a type capable of a range in excess of 600 kilometers if they are distinguishable on the basis of externally observable design features from cruise missiles of types capable of a range in excess of 600 kilometers.

Second Agreed Statement. The range of which a cruise missile is capable is the maximum distance which can be covered by the missile in its standard design mode flying until fuel exhaustion, determined by projecting its flight path onto the Earths sphere from the point of launch to the point of impact.

Third Agreed Statement. If an unmanned, self-propelled, guided vehicle which sustains flight through the use of aerodynamic lift over most of its flight path has been flight-tested or deployed for weapon delivery, all vehicles of that type shall be considered to be weapon-delivery vehicles.

Third Common Understanding. Unmanned, self-propelled, guided vehicles which sustain flight through the use of aerodynamic lift over most of their flight path and are not weapon-delivery vehicles, that is, unarmed, pilotless, guided vehicles, shall not be considered tobe cruise missiles if such vehicles are distinguishable from cruise missiles on the basis of externally observable design features.

Fourth Common Understanding. Neither Party shall convert unarmed, pilotless, guided vehicles into cruise missiles capable of a range in excess of 600 kilometers, nor shall either Party convert cruise missiles capable of a range in excess of 600 kilometers into unarmed, pilotless, guided vehicles.

Fifth Common Understanding. Neither Party has plans during the term of the Protocol to flight-test from or deploy on sea-based or land-based launchers unarmed, pilotless, guided vehicles which are capable of a range in excess of 600 kilometers. In the future, should a Party have such plans, that Party will provide notification thereof to the other Party well in advance of such flight-testing or deployment. This Common Understanding does not apply to target drones.

Article III

Each Party undertakes not to flight-test or deploy ASBMs.

Article IV

This Protocol shall be considered an integral part of the Treaty. It shall enter into force on the day of the entry into force of the Treaty and shall remain in force through December 31, 1981,unless replaced earlier by an agreement on further measures limiting strategic offensive arms.

DONE at Vienna on June 18, 1979, in two copies, each in the English and Russian languages, both texts being equally authentic.

FOR THE UNITED STATES OF AMERICA:
JIMMY CARTER
President of the United States of America

FOR THE UNION OF SOVIET SOCIALIST REPUBLICS:
L. BREZHNEV
General Secretary of the CPSU, Chairman of the Presidium of the Supreme Soviet of the USSR

VII-4. **Treaty Between the United States of America and the Union of Soviet Socialist Republics on the Elimination of Intermediate-Range and Short-Range Missiles, 1 June 1979 [Signed at Washington December 8, 1987; Ratification advised by U.S. Senate May 27, 1988; Instruments of ratification exchanged June 1, 1988; Entered into force June 1, 1988; Proclaimed by U.S. President December 27, 1988. Authentic Texts: English, Russian.**

Applicability
Peace

Control
Prohibit

State Signatories
Union of Soviet Socialist Republics[1]; United States of America

State Parties
Union of Soviet Socialist Republics[2]; United States of America

Full Text

The United States of America and the Union of Soviet Socialist Republics, hereinafter referred to as the Parties,

Conscious that nuclear war would have devastating consequences for all mankind,

Guided by the objective of strengthening strategic stability,

Convinced that the measures set forth in this Treaty will help to reduce the risk of outbreak of war and strengthen international peace and security, and

Mindful of their obligations under Article VI of the Treaty on the Non-Proliferation of Nuclear Weapons,

Have agreed as follows:

Article I

In accordance with the provisions of this Treaty which includes the Memorandum of Understanding and Protocols which form an integral part thereof, each Party

---

[1] See Methodology, "State Succession."
[2] *Id.*

shall eliminate its intermediate-range and shorter-range missiles, not have such systems thereafter, and carry out the other obligations set forth in this Treaty.

Article II

For the purposes of this Treaty:

1. The term "ballistic missile" means a missile that has a ballistic trajectory over most of its flight path. The term "ground-launched ballistic missile (GLBM)" means a ground-launched ballistic missile that is a weapon-delivery vehicle.

2. The term "cruise missile" means an unmanned, self-propelled vehicle that sustains flight through the use of aerodynamic lift over most of its flight path. The term "ground-launched cruise missile (GLCM)" means a ground-launched cruise missile that is a weapon-delivery vehicle.

3. The term "GLBM launcher" means a fixed launcher or a mobile land-based transporter-erector-launcher mechanism for launching a GLBM.

4. The term "GLCM launcher" means a fixed launcher or a mobile land-based transporter-erector-launcher mechanism for launching a GLCM.

5. The term "intermediate-range missile" means a GLBM or a GLCM having a range capability in excess of 1000 kilometers but not in excess of 5500 kilometers.

6. The term "shorter-range missile" means a GLBM or a GLCM having a range capability equal to or in excess of 500 kilometers but not in excess of 1000 kilometers.

7. The term "deployment area" means a designated area within which intermediate-range missiles and launchers of such missiles may operate and within which one or more missile operating bases are located.

8. The term "missile operating base" means:

(a) in the case of intermediate-range missiles, a complex of facilities, located within a deployment area, at which intermediate-range missiles and launchers of such missiles normally operate, in which support structures associated with such missiles and launchers are also located and in which support equipment associated with such missiles and launchers is normally located; and

(b) in the case of shorter-range missiles, a complex of facilities, located any place, at which shorter-range missiles and launchers of such missiles normally operate and in which support equipment associated with such missiles and launchers is normally located.

9. The term "missile support facility," as regards intermediate-range or shorter-range missiles and launchers of such missiles, means a missile production facility or a launcher production facility, a missile repair facility or a launcher repair facility, a training facility, a missile storage facility or a launcher storage facility, a test range, or an elimination facility as those terms are defined in the Memorandum of Understanding.

10. The term "transit" means movement, notified in accordance with paragraph 5(f) of Article IX of this Treaty, of an intermediate-range missile or a launcher of such a missile between missile support facilities, between such a facility and a deployment area or between deployment areas, or of a shorter-range missile or a launcher of such a missile from a missile support facility or a missile operating base to an elimination facility.

11. The term "deployed missile" means an intermediate-range missile located within a deployment area or a shorter-range missile located at a missile operating base.

12. The term "non-deployed missile" means an intermediate-range missile located outside a deployment area or a shorter-range missile located outside a missile operating base.

13. The term "deployed launcher" means a launcher of an intermediate-range missile located within a deployment area or a launcher of a shorter-range missile located at a missile operating base.

14. The term "non-deployed launcher" means a launcher of an intermediate-range missile located outside a deployment area or a launcher of a shorter-range missile located outside a missile operating base.

15. The term "basing country" means a country other than the United States of America or the Union of Soviet Socialist Republics on whose territory intermediate-range or shorter-range missiles of the Parties, launchers of such missiles or support structures associated with such missiles and launchers were located at any time after November 1, 1987. Missiles or launchers in transit are not considered to be "located."

Article III

1. For the purposes of this Treaty, existing types of intermediate-range missiles are:

(a) for the United States of America, missiles of the types designated by the United States of America as the Pershing II and the BGM-109G, which are known to the Union of Soviet Socialist Republics by the same designations; and

(b) for the Union of Soviet Socialist Republics, missiles of the types designated by the Union of Soviet Socialist Republics as the RSD-10, the R-12 and the R-14, which are known to the United States of America as the SS-20, the SS-4 and the SS-5, respectively.

2. For the purposes of this Treaty, existing types of shorter-range missiles are:

(a) for the United States of America, missiles of the type designated by the United States of America as the Pershing IA, which is known to the Union of Soviet Socialist Republics by the same designation; and

(b) for the Union of Soviet Socialist Republics, missiles of the types designated by the Union of Soviet Socialist Republics as the OTR-22 and the OTR-23, which are known to the United States of America as the SS-12 and the SS-23, respectively.

Article IV

1. Each Party shall eliminate all its intermediate-range missiles and launchers of such missiles, and all support structures and support equipment of the categories listed in the Memorandum of Understanding associated with such missiles and launchers, so that no later than three years after entry into force of this Treaty and thereafter no such missiles, launchers, support structures or support equipment shall be possessed by either Party.

2. To implement paragraph 1 of this Article, upon entry into force of this Treaty, both Parties shall begin and continue throughout the duration of each phase, the reduction of all types of their deployed and non-deployed intermediate-range missiles and deployed and non-deployed launchers of such missiles and support structures and support equipment associated with such missiles and launchers in accordance with the provisions of this Treaty. These reductions shall be implemented in two phases so that:

(a) by the end of the first phase, that is, no later than 29 months after entry into force of this Treaty:

(i) the number of deployed launchers of intermediate-range missiles for each Party shall not exceed the number of launchers that are capable of carrying or containing at one time missiles considered by the Parties to carry 171 warheads;

(ii) the number of deployed intermediate-range missiles for each Party shall not exceed the number of such missiles considered by the Parties to carry 180 warheads;

(iii) the aggregate number of deployed and non-deployed launchers of intermediate-range missiles for each Party shall not exceed the number of launchers that are capable of carrying or containing at one time missiles considered by the Parties to carry 200 warheads;

(iv) the aggregate number of deployed and non-deployed intermediate-range missiles for each Party shall not exceed the number of such missiles considered by the Parties to carry 200 warheads; and

(v) the ratio of the aggregate number of deployed and non-deployed intermediate-range GLBMs of existing types for each Party to the aggregate number of deployed and non-deployed intermediate-range missiles of existing types possessed by that Party shall not exceed the ratio of such intermediate-range GLBMs to such intermediate-range missiles for that Party as of November 1, 1987, as set forth in the Memorandum of Understanding; and

(b) by the end of the second phase, that is, no later than three years after entry into force of this Treaty, all intermediate-range missiles of each Party, launchers of such missiles and all support structures and support equipment of the categories listed in the Memorandum of Understanding associated with such missiles and launchers, shall be eliminated.

Article V

1. Each Party shall eliminate all its shorter-range missiles and launchers of such missiles, and all support equipment of the categories listed in the Memorandum of Understanding associated with such missiles and launchers, so that no later than 18 months after entry into force of this Treaty and thereafter no such missiles, launchers or support equipment shall be possessed by either Party.

2. No later than 90 days after entry into force of this Treaty, each Party shall complete the removal of all its deployed shorter-range missiles and deployed and non-deployed launchers of such missiles to elimination facilities and shall retain them at those locations until they are eliminated in accordance with the procedures set forth in the Protocol on Elimination. No later than 12 months after entry into force of this Treaty, each Party shall complete the removal of all its non-deployed shorter-range missiles to elimination facilities and shall retain them at those locations until they are eliminated in accordance with the procedures set forth in the Protocol on Elimination.

3. Shorter-range missiles and launchers of such missiles shall not be located at the same elimination facility. Such facilities shall be separated by no less than 1000 kilometers.

Article VI

1. Upon entry into force of this Treaty and thereafter, neither Party shall:

(a) produce or flight-test any intermediate-range missiles or produce any stages of such missiles or any launchers of such missiles; or

(b) produce, flight-test or launch any shorter-range missiles or produce any stages of such missiles or any launchers of such missiles.

2. Notwithstanding paragraph 1 of this Article, each Party shall have the right to produce a type of GLBM not limited by this Treaty which uses a stage which is outwardly similar to, but not interchangeable with, a stage of an existing type of intermediate-range GLBM having more than one stage, providing that that Party does not produce any other stage which is outwardly similar to, but not interchangeable with, any other stage of an existing type of intermediate-range GLBM.

Article VII

For the purposes of this Treaty:

1. If a ballistic missile or a cruise missile has been flight-tested or deployed for weapon delivery, all missiles of that type shall be considered to be weapon-delivery vehicles.

2. If a GLBM or GLCM is an intermediate-range missile, all GLBMs or GLCMs of that type shall be considered to be intermediate-range missiles. If a GLBM or GLCM is a shorter-range missile, all GLBMs or GLCMs of that type shall be considered to be shorter-range missiles.

3. If a GLBM is of a type developed and tested solely to intercept and counter objects not located on the surface of the earth, it shall not be considered to be a missile to which the limitations of this Treaty apply.

4. The range capability of a GLBM not listed in Article III of this Treaty shall be considered to be the maximum range to which it has been tested. The range capability of a GLCM not listed in Article III of this Treaty shall be considered to be the maximum distance which can be covered by the missile in its standard design mode flying until fuel exhaustion, determined by projecting its flight path onto the earths sphere from the point of launch to the point of impact. GLBMs or GLCMs that have a range capability equal to or in excess of 500 kilometers but not in excess of 1000 kilometers shall be considered to be shorter-range missiles. GLBMs or GLCMs that have a range capability in excess of 1000 kilometers but not in excess of 5500 kilometers shall be considered to be intermediate-range missiles.

5. The maximum number of warheads an existing type of intermediate-range missile or shorter-range missile carries shall be considered to be the number listed for missiles of that type in the Memorandum of Understanding.

6. Each GLBM or GLCM shall be considered to carry the maximum number of warheads listed for a GLBM or GLCM of the type in the Memorandum of Understanding.

7. If a launcher has been tested for launching a GLBM or a GLCM, all launchers of that type shall be considered to have been tested for launching GLBMs or GLCMs.

8. If a launcher has contained or launched a particular type of GLBM or GLCM, all launchers of that type shall be considered to be launchers of that type of GLBM or GLCM .

9. The number of missiles each launcher of an existing type of intermediate-range missile or shorter-range missile shall be considered to be capable of carrying or containing at one time is the number listed for launchers of missiles of that type in the Memorandum of Understanding.

10. Except in the case of elimination in accordance with the procedures set forth in the Protocol on Elimination, the following shall apply:

(a) for GLBMs which are stored or moved in separate stages, the longest stage of an intermediate-range or shorter-range GLBM shall be counted as a complete missile;

(b) for GLBMs which are not stored or moved in separate stages, a canister of the type used in the launch of an intermediate-range GLBM, unless a Party proves to the satisfaction of the other Party that it does not contain such a missile, or an assembled intermediate-range or shorter-range GLBM, shall be counted as a complete missile; and

(c) for GLCMs, the airframe of an intermediate-range or shorter-range GLCM shall be counted as a complete missile.

11. A ballistic missile which is not a missile to be used in a ground-based mode shall not be considered to be a GLBM if it is test-launched at a test site from a fixed land-based launcher which is used solely for test purposes and which is distinguishable from GLBM launchers. A cruise missile which is not a missile to be used in a ground-based mode shall not be considered to be a GLCM if it is test-launched at a test site from a fixed land-based launcher which is used solely for test purposes and which is distinguishable from GLCM launchers.

12. Each Party shall have the right to produce and use for booster systems, which might otherwise be considered to be intermediate-range or shorter-range missiles, only existing types of booster stages for such booster systems. Launches of such booster systems shall not be considered to be flight-testing of intermediate-range or shorter-range missiles provided that:

(a) stages used in such booster systems are different from stages used in those missiles listed as existing types of intermediate-range or shorter-range missiles in Article III of this Treaty;

(b) such booster systems are used only for research and development purposes to test objects other than the booster systems themselves;

(c) the aggregate number of launchers for such booster systems shall not exceed 35 for each Party at any one time; and

(d) the launchers for such booster systems are fixed, emplaced above ground and located only at research and development launch sites which are specified in the Memorandum of Understanding.

Research and development launch sites shall not be subject to inspection pursuant to Article XI of this Treaty.

Article VIII

1. All intermediate-range missiles and launchers of such missiles shall be located in deployment areas, at missile support facilities or shall be in transit. Intermediate-range missiles or launchers of such missiles shall not be located elsewhere.

2. Stages of intermediate-range missiles shall be located in deployment areas, at missile support facilities or moving between deployment areas, between missile support facilities or between missile support facilities and deployment areas.

3. Until their removal to elimination facilities as required by paragraph 2 of Article V of this Treaty, all shorter-range missiles and launchers of such missiles shall be located at missile operating bases, at missile support facilities or shall be in transit. Shorter-range missiles or launchers of such missiles shall not be located elsewhere.

4. Transit of a missile or launcher subject to the provisions of this Treaty shall be completed within 25 days.

5. All deployment areas, missile operating bases and missile support facilities are specified in the Memorandum of Understanding or in subsequent updates of data pursuant to paragraphs 3, 5(a) or 5(b) of Article IX of this Treaty. Neither Party shall increase the number of, or change the location or boundaries of, deployment areas, missile operating bases or missile support facilities, except for elimination facilities, from those set forth in the Memorandum of Understanding. A missile support facility shall not be considered to be part of a deployment area even though it may be located within the geographic boundaries of a deployment area.

International Humanitarian Law and Arms Control Agreements 789

6. Beginning 30 days after entry into force of this Treaty, neither Party shall locate intermediate-range or shorter-range missiles, including stages of such missiles, or launchers of such missiles at missile production facilities, launcher production facilities or test ranges listed in the Memorandum of Understanding.

7. Neither Party shall locate any intermediate-range or shorter-range missiles at training facilities.

8. A non-deployed intermediate-range or shorter-range missile shall not be carried on or contained within a launcher of such a type of missile, except as required for maintenance conducted at repair facilities or for elimination by means of launching conducted at elimination facilities.

9. Training missiles and training launchers for intermediate-range or shorter-range missiles shall be subject to the same locational restrictions as are set forth for intermediate-range and shorter-range missiles and launchers of such missiles in paragraphs 1 and 3 of this Article.

Article IX

1. The Memorandum of Understanding contains categories of data relevant to obligations undertaken with regard to this Treaty and lists all intermediate-range and shorter-range missiles, launchers of such missiles, and support structures and support equipment associated with such missiles and launchers, possessed by the Parties as of November 1, 1987. Updates of that data and notifications required by this Article shall be provided according to the categories of data contained in the Memorandum of Understanding.

2. The Parties shall update that data and provide the notifications required by this Treaty through the Nuclear Risk Reduction Centers, established pursuant to the Agreement Between the United States of America and the Union of Soviet Socialist Republics on the Establishment of Nuclear Risk Reduction Centers of September 15, 1987.

3. No later than 30 days after entry into force of this Treaty, each Party shall provide the other Party with updated data, as of the date of entry into force of this Treaty, for all categories of data contained in the Memorandum of Understanding.

4. No later than 30 days after the end of each six-month interval following the entry into force of this Treaty, each Party shall provide updated data for all categories of data contained in the Memorandum of Understanding by informing the other Party of all changes, completed and in process, in that data, which have occurred during the six-month interval since the preceding data exchange, and the net effect of those changes.

5. Upon entry into force of this Treaty and thereafter, each Party shall provide the following notifications to the other Party:

(a) notification, no less than 30 days in advance, of the scheduled date of the elimination of a specific deployment area, missile operating base or missile support facility;

(b) notification, no less than 30 days in advance, of changes in the number or location of elimination facilities, including the location and scheduled date of each change;

(c) notification, except with respect to launches of intermediate-range missiles for the purpose of their elimination, no less than 30 days in advance, of the scheduled date of the initiation of the elimination of intermediate-range and shorter-range missiles, and stages of such missiles, and launchers of such missiles and support structures and support equipment associated with such missiles and launchers, including:

(i) the number and type of items of missile systems to be eliminated;

(ii) the elimination site;

(iii) for intermediate-range missiles, the location from which such missiles, launchers of such missiles and support equipment associated with such missiles and launchers are moved to the elimination facility; and

(iv) except in the case of support structures, the point of entry to be used by an inspection team conducting an inspection pursuant to paragraph 7 of Article XI of this Treaty and the estimated time of departure of an inspection team from the point of entry to the elimination facility;

(d) notification, no less than ten days in advance, of the scheduled date of the launch, or the scheduled date of the initiation of a series of launches, of intermediate-range missiles for the purpose of their elimination, including:

(i) the type of missiles to be eliminated;

(ii) the location of the launch, or, if elimination is by a series of launches, the location of such launches and the number of launches in the series;

(iii) the point of entry to be used by an inspection team conducting an inspection pursuant to paragraph 7 of Article XI of this Treaty; and

(iv) the estimated time of departure of an inspection team from the point of entry to the elimination facility;

(e) notification, no later than 48 hours after they occur, of changes in the number of intermediate-range and shorter-range missiles, launchers of such missiles and support structures and support equipment associated with such missiles and launchers resulting from elimination as described in the Protocol on Elimination, including:

(i) the number and type of items of a missile system which were eliminated; and

(ii) the date and location of such elimination; and

(f) notification of transit of intermediate-range or shorter-range missiles or launchers of such missiles, or the movement of training missiles or training launchers for such intermediate-range and shorter-range missiles, no later than 48 hours after it has been completed, including:

(i) the number of missiles or launchers;

(ii) the points, dates, and times of departure and arrival;

(iii) the mode of transport; and

(iv) the location and time at that location at least once every four days during the period of transit.

6. Upon entry into force of this Treaty and thereafter, each Party shall notify the other Party, no less than ten days in advance, of the scheduled date and location of the launch of a research and development booster system as described in paragraph 12 of Article VII of this Treaty.

Article X

1. Each Party shall eliminate its intermediate-range and shorter-range missiles and launchers of such missiles and support structures and support equipment associated with such missiles and launchers in accordance with the procedures set forth in the Protocol on Elimination.

2. Verification by on-site inspection of the elimination of items of missile systems specified in the Protocol on Elimination shall be carried out in accordance with Article XI of this Treaty, the Protocol on Elimination and the Protocol on Inspection.

3. When a Party removes its intermediate-range missiles, launchers of such missiles and support equipment associated with such missiles and launchers from deployment areas to elimination facilities for the purpose of their elimination, it shall do so in complete deployed organizational units. For the United States of

America, these units shall be Pershing II batteries and BGM-109G flights. For the Union of Soviet Socialist Republics, these units shall be SS-20 regiments composed of two or three battalions.

4. Elimination of intermediate-range and shorter-range missiles and launchers of such missiles and support equipment associated with such missiles and launchers shall be carried out at the facilities that are specified in the Memorandum of Understanding or notified in accordance with paragraph 5(b) of Article IX of this Treaty, unless eliminated in accordance with Sections IV or V of the Protocol on Elimination. Support structures, associated with the missiles and launchers subject to this Treaty, that are subject to elimination shall be eliminated in situ.

5. Each Party shall have the right, during the first six months after entry into force of this Treaty, to eliminate by means of launching no more than 100 of its intermediate-range missiles.

6. Intermediate-range and shorter-range missiles which have been tested prior to entry into force of this Treaty, but never deployed, and which are not existing types of intermediate-range or shorter-range missiles listed in Article III of this Treaty, and launchers of such missiles, shall be eliminated within six months after entry into force of this Treaty in accordance with the procedures set forth in the Protocol on Elimination. Such missiles are:

(a) for the United States of America, missiles of the type designated by the United States of America as the Pershing IB, which is known to the Union of Soviet Socialist Republics by the same designation; and

(b) for the Union of Soviet Socialist Republics, missiles of the type designated by the Union of Soviet Socialist Republics as the RK-55, which is known to the United States of America as the SSC-X-4.

7. Intermediate-range and shorter-range missiles and launchers of such missiles and support structures and support equipment associated with such missiles and launchers shall be considered to be eliminated after completion of the procedures set forth in the Protocol on Elimination and upon the notification provided for in paragraph 5(e) of Article IX of this Treaty.

8. Each Party shall eliminate its deployment areas, missile operating bases and missile support facilities. A Party shall notify the other Party pursuant to paragraph 5(a) of Article IX of this Treaty once the conditions set forth below are fulfilled:

(a) all intermediate-range and shorter-range missiles, launchers of such missiles and support equipment associated with such missiles and launchers located there have been removed;

International Humanitarian Law and Arms Control Agreements 793

(b) all support structures associated with such missiles and launchers located there have been eliminated; and

(c) all activity related to production, flight-testing, training, repair, storage or deployment of such missiles and launchers has ceased there.

Such deployment areas, missile operating bases and missile support facilities shall be considered to be eliminated either when they have been inspected pursuant to paragraph 4 of Article XI of this Treaty or when 60 days have elapsed since the date of the scheduled elimination which was notified pursuant to paragraph 5(a) of Article IX of this Treaty. A deployment area, missile operating base or missile support facility listed in the Memorandum of Understanding that met the above conditions prior to entry into force of this Treaty, and is not included in the initial data exchange pursuant to paragraph 3 of Article IX of this Treaty, shall be considered to be eliminated.

9. If a Party intends to convert a missile operating base listed in the Memorandum of Understanding for use as a base associated with GLBM or GLCM systems not subject to this Treaty, then that Party shall notify the other Party, no less than 30 days in advance of the scheduled date of the initiation of the conversion, of the scheduled date and the purpose for which the base will be converted.

Article XI

1. For the purpose of ensuring verification of compliance with the provisions of this Treaty, each Party shall have the right to conduct on-site inspections. The Parties shall implement on-site inspections in accordance with this Article, the Protocol on Inspection and the Protocol on Elimination.

2. Each Party shall have the right to conduct inspections provided for by this Article both within the territory of the other Party and within the territories of basing countries.

3. Beginning 30 days after entry into force of this Treaty, each Party shall have the right to conduct inspections at all missile operating bases and missile support facilities specified in the Memorandum of Understanding other than missile production facilities, and at all elimination facilities included in the initial data update required by paragraph 3 of Article IX of this Treaty. These inspections shall be completed no later than 90 days after entry into force of this Treaty. The purpose of these inspections shall be to verify the number of missiles, launchers, support structures and support equipment and other data, as of the date of entry into force of this Treaty, provided pursuant to paragraph 3 of Article IX of this Treaty.

4. Each Party shall have the right to conduct inspections to verify the elimination, notified pursuant to paragraph 5(a) of Article IX of this Treaty, of missile operating

bases and missile support facilities other than missile production facilities, which are thus no longer subject to inspections pursuant to paragraph 5(a) of this Article. Such an inspection shall be carried out within 60 days after the scheduled date of the elimination of that facility. If a Party conducts an inspection at a particular facility pursuant to paragraph 3 of this Article after the scheduled date of the elimination of that facility, then no additional inspection of that facility pursuant to this paragraph shall be permitted.

5. Each Party shall have the right to conduct inspections pursuant to this paragraph for 13 years after entry into force of this Treaty. Each Party shall have the right to conduct 20 such inspections per calendar year during the first three years after entry into force of this Treaty, 15 such inspections per calendar year during the subsequent five years, and ten such inspections per calendar year during the last five years. Neither Party shall use more than half of its total number of these inspections per calendar year within the territory of any one basing country. Each Party shall have the right to conduct:

(a) inspections, beginning 90 days after entry into force of this Treaty, of missile operating bases and missile support facilities other than elimination facilities and missile production facilities, to ascertain, according to the categories of data specified in the Memorandum of Understanding, the numbers of missiles, launchers, support structures and support equipment located at each missile operating base or missile support facility at the time of the inspection; and

(b) inspections of former missile operating bases and former missile support facilities eliminated pursuant to paragraph 8 of Article X of this Treaty other than former missile production facilities.

6. Beginning 30 days after entry into force of this Treaty, each Party shall have the right, for 13 years after entry into force of this Treaty, to inspect by means of continuous monitoring:

(a) the portals of any facility of the other Party at which the final assembly of a GLBM using stages, any of which is outwardly similar to a stage of a solid-propellant GLBM listed in Article III of this Treaty, is accomplished; or

(b) if a Party has no such facility, the portals of an agreed former missile production facility at which existing types of intermediate-range or shorter-range GLBMs were produced.

The Party whose facility is to be inspected pursuant to this paragraph shall ensure that the other Party is able to establish a permanent continuous monitoring system at that facility within six months after entry into force of this Treaty or within six months of initiation of the process of final assembly described in subparagraph (a). If, after the end of the second year after entry into force of this Treaty, neither Party conducts the process of final assembly described in subparagraph (a) for a period of 12 consecutive months, then neither Party shall have the right to inspect by means of continuous monitoring any missile production facility of the other Party unless the process of final assembly as described in subparagraph (a) is initiated again. Upon entry into force of this Treaty, the facilities to be inspected by continuous monitoring shall be: in accordance with subparagraph (b), for the United States of America, Hercules Plant Number 1, at Magna, Utah; in accordance with subparagraph (a), for the Union of Soviet Socialist Republics, the Votkinsk Machine Building Plant, Udmurt Autonomous Soviet Socialist Republic, Russian Soviet Federative Socialist Republic.

7. Each Party shall conduct inspections of the process of elimination, including elimination of intermediate-range missiles by means of launching, of intermediate-range and shorter-range missiles and launchers of such missiles and support equipment associated with such missiles and launchers carried out at elimination facilities in accordance with Article X of this Treaty and the Protocol on Elimination. Inspectors conducting inspections provided for in this paragraph shall determine that the processes specified for the elimination of the missiles, launchers and support equipment have been completed.

8. Each Party shall have the right to conduct inspections to confirm the completion of the process of elimination of intermediate-range and shorter range missiles and launchers of such missiles and support equipment associated with such missiles and launchers eliminated pursuant to Section V of the Protocol on Elimination, and of training missiles, training missile stages, training launch canisters and training launchers eliminated pursuant to Sections II, IV and V of the Protocol on Elimination.

Article XII

1. For the purpose of ensuring verification of compliance with the provisions of this Treaty, each Party shall use national technical means of verification at its disposal in a manner consistent with generally recognized principles of international law.

2. Neither Party shall:

(a) interfere with national technical means of verification of the other Party operating in accordance with paragraph 1 of this Article; or

(b) use concealment measures which impede verification of compliance with the provisions of this Treaty by national technical means of verification carried out in accordance with paragraph 1 of this Article. This obligation does not apply to cover or concealment practices, within a deployment area, associated with normal training, maintenance and operations, including the use of environmental shelters to protect missiles and launchers.

3. To enhance observation by national technical means of verification, each Party shall have the right until a Treaty between the Parties reducing and limiting strategic offensive arms enters into force, but in any event for no more than three years after entry into force of this Treaty, to request the implementation of cooperative measures at deployment bases for road-mobile GLBMs with a range capability in excess of 5500 kilometers, which are not former missile operating bases eliminated pursuant to paragraph 8 of Article X of this Treaty. The Party making such a request shall inform the other Party of the deployment base at which cooperative measures shall be implemented. The Party whose base is to be observed shall carry out the following cooperative measures:

(a) no later than six hours after such a request, the Party shall have opened the roofs of all fixed structures for launchers located at the base, removed completely all missiles on launchers from such fixed structures for launchers and displayed such missiles on launchers in the open without using concealment measures; and

(b) the Party shall leave the roofs open and the missiles on launchers in place until twelve hours have elapsed from the time of the receipt of a request for such an observation.

Each Party shall have the right to make six such requests per calendar year. Only one deployment base shall be subject to these cooperative measures at any one time.

Article XIII

1. To promote the objectives and implementation of the provisions of this Treaty, the Parties hereby establish the Special Verification Commission. The Parties agree that, if either Party so requests, they shall meet within the framework of the Special Verification Commission to:

(a) resolve questions relating to compliance with the obligations assumed; and

(b) agree upon such measures as may be necessary to improve the viability and effectiveness of this Treaty.

2. The Parties shall use the Nuclear Risk Reduction Centers, which provide for continuous communication between the Parties, to:

(a) exchange data and provide notifications as required by paragraphs 3, 4, 5 and 6 of Article IX of this Treaty and the Protocol on Elimination;

(b) provide and receive the information required by paragraph 9 of Article X of this Treaty;

(c) provide and receive notifications of inspections as required by Article XI of this Treaty and the Protocol on Inspection; and

(d) provide and receive requests for cooperative measures as provided for in paragraph 3 of Article XII of this Treaty.

Article XIV

The Parties shall comply with this Treaty and shall not assume any international obligations or undertakings which would conflict with its provisions.

Article XV

1. This Treaty shall be of unlimited duration.
2. Each Party shall, in exercising its national sovereignty, have the right to withdraw from this Treaty if it decides that extraordinary events related to the subject matter of this Treaty have jeopardized its supreme interests. It shall give notice of its decision to withdraw to the other Party six months prior to withdrawal from this Treaty. Such notice shall include a statement of the extraordinary events the notifying Party regards as having jeopardized its supreme interests.

Article XVI

Each Party may propose amendments to this Treaty. Agreed amendments shall enter into force in accordance with the procedures set forth in Article XVII governing the entry into force of this Treaty.

Article XVII

1. This Treaty, including the Memorandum of Understanding and Protocols, which form an integral part thereof, shall be subject to ratification in accordance with the constitutional procedures of each Party. This Treaty shall enter into force on the date of the exchange of instruments of ratification.

2. This Treaty shall be registered pursuant to Article 102 of the Charter of the United Nations.

DONE at Washington on December 8, 1987, in two copies, each in the English and Russian languages, both texts being equally authentic.

VII-5. **Treaty Between the United States of America and the Union of Soviet Socialist Republics on the Limitation of Underground Nuclear Weapons Tests (Threshold Test Ban Treaty, TTBT), 11 December 1990, [Signed at Moscow July 3, 1974; Ratified December 8, 1990; Entered into force December 11, 1990], 13 I.L.M. 967. Authentic Texts: English, Russian.**

Relevant Penal Characteristics & Penal Provision
2. Implicit recognition of the penal nature of the act by establishing a duty to prohibit, prevent, prosecute, punish, or the like: Article I.

Applicability
Peace

Control
Prohibit

State Signatories
Union of Soviet Socialist Republics[1]; United States of America

State Parties
Union of Soviet Socialist Republics[2]; United States of America

Full Text

The United States of America and the Union of Soviet Socialist Republics, hereinafter referred to as the Parties,

Declaring their intention to achieve at the earliest possible date the cessation of the nuclear arms race and to take effective measures toward reductions in strategic arms, nuclear disarmament, and general and complete disarmament under strict and effective international control,

Recalling the determination expressed by the Parties to the 1963 Treaty Banning Nuclear Weapon Tests in the Atmosphere, in Outer Space and Under Water in its Preamble to seek to achieve the discontinuance of all test explosions of nuclear weapons for all time, and to continue negotiations to this end,

Noting that the adoption of measures for the further limitation of underground nuclear weapon tests would contribute to the achievement of these objectives and

---

[1] See Methodology, "State Succession."
[2] *Id.*

would meet the interests of strengthening peace and the further relaxation of international tension,

Reaffirming their adherence to the objectives and principles of the Treaty Banning Nuclear Weapon Tests in the Atmosphere, in Outer Space and Under Water and of the Treaty on the Non-Proliferation of Nuclear Weapons,

Have agreed as follows:

Article I

1. Each Party undertakes to prohibit, to prevent, and not to carry out any underground nuclear weapon test having a yield exceeding 150 kilotons at any place under its jurisdiction or control, beginning March 31, 1976.

2. Each Party shall limit the number of its underground nuclear weapon tests to a minimum.

3. The Parties shall continue their negotiations with a view toward achieving a solution to the problem of the cessation of all underground nuclear weapon tests.

Article II

1. For the purpose of providing assurance of compliance with the provisions of this Treaty, each Party shall use national technical means of verification at its disposal in a manner consistent with the generally recognized principles of international law.

2. Each Party undertakes not to interfere with the national technical means of verification of the other Party operating in accordance with paragraph 1 of this Article.

3. To promote the objectives and implementation of the provisions of this Treaty the Parties shall, as necessary, consult with each other, make inquiries and furnish information in response to such inquiries.

Article III

The provisions of this Treaty do not extend to underground nuclear explosions carried out by the Parties for peaceful purposes. Underground nuclear explosions for peaceful purposes shall be governed by an agreement which is to be negotiated and concluded by the Parties at the earliest possible time.

Article IV

This Treaty shall be subject to ratification in accordance with the constitutional procedures of each Party. This Treaty shall enter into force on the day of the exchange of instruments of ratification.

Article V

1. This Treaty shall remain in force for a period of five years. Unless replaced earlier by an agreement in implementation of the objectives specified in paragraph 3 of Article I of this Treaty, it shall be extended for successive five-year periods unless either Party notifies the other of its termination no later than six months prior to the expiration of the Treaty. Before the expiration of this period the Parties may, as necessary, hold consultations to consider the situation relevant to the substance of this Treaty and to introduce possible amendments to the text of the Treaty.

2. Each Party shall, in exercising its national sovereignty, have the right to withdraw from this Treaty if it decides that extraordinary events related to the subject matter of this Treaty have jeopardized its supreme interests. It shall give notice of its decision to the other Party six months prior to withdrawal from this Treaty. Such notice shall include a statement of the extraordinary events the notifying Party regards as having jeopardized its supreme interests.

3. This Treaty shall be registered pursuant to Article 102 of the Charter of the United Nations.

DONE at Moscow on July 3, 1974, in duplicate, in the English and Russian languages, both texts being equally authentic.

FOR THE UNITED STATES OF AMERICA:
RICHARD NIXON
The President of the United States of America

FOR THE UNION OF SOVIET SOCIALIST REPUBLICS:
L. BREZHNEV
General Secretary of the Central Committee of the CPSU

VII-6. Protocol to the Treaty of July 3, 1974, Between the United States of America and the Union of Soviet Socialist Republics on the Limitation of Underground Nuclear Weapons Tests, s*igned at Washington*, **June 1, 1990; entered into force December 11, 1990.**

Applicability
Peace

Control
Regulate

State Signatories
Union of Soviet Socialist Republics[1]; United States of America

State Parties
Union of Soviet Socialist Republics[2]; United States of America

Full Text

The United States of America and the Union of Soviet Socialist Republics, hereinafter referred to as the Parties,

Having agreed to limit underground nuclear weapon tests,

Have agreed as follows:

1. For the Purpose of ensuring verification of compliance with the obligations of the Parties under the Treaty by national technical means, the Parties shall, on the basis of reciprocity, exchange the following data:

    a. The geographic coordinates of the boundaries of each test site and of the boundaries of the geophysically distinct testing areas therein.

    b. Information on the geology of the testing areas of the sites (the rock characteristics of geological formations and the basic physical properties of the rock, i.e., density, seismic velocity, water saturation, porosity and the depth of water table).

---

[1] See Methodology, "State Succession."
[2] *Id.*

c. The geographic coordinates of underground nuclear weapon tests, after they have been conducted.

d. Yield, date, time, depth and coordinates for two nuclear weapon tests for calibration purposes from each geophysically distinct testing area where underground nuclear weapon tests have been and are to be conducted.

In this connection the yield of such explosions for calibration purposes should be as near as possible to the limit defined in Article I of the Treaty and not less than one-tenth of that limit. In the case of testing areas where data are not available on two tests for calibration purposes, the data pertaining to one such test shall be exchanged, if available, and the data pertaining to the second test shall be exchanged as soon as possible after the second test having a yield in the above-mentioned range. The provisions of this Protocol shall not require the Parties to conduct tests solely for calibration purposes.

2. The Parties agree that the exchange of data pursuant to subparagraphs a, b, and d of paragraph 1 shall be carried out simultaneously with the exchange of instruments of ratification of the Treaty, as provided in Article IV of the Treaty, having in mind that the Parties shall, on the basis of reciprocity, afford each other the opportunity to familiarize themselves with these data before the exchange of instruments of ratification.

3. Should a Party specify a new test site or testing area after the entry into force of the Treaty, the data called for by subparagraphs a and b of paragraph 1 shall be transmitted to the other Party in advance of use of that site or area. The data called for by subparagraph d of paragraph 1 shall also be transmitted in advance of use of that site or area if they are available; if they are not available, they shall be transmitted as soon as possible after they have been obtained by the transmitting Party.

4. The Parties agree that the test sites of each Party shall be located at places under its jurisdiction or control and that all nuclear weapon tests shall be conducted solely within the testing areas specified in accordance with paragraph 1.

5. For the purposes of the Treaty, all underground nuclear explosions at the specified test sites shall be considered nuclear weapon tests and shall be subject to all the provisions of the Treaty relating to nuclear weapon tests. The provisions of Article III of the Treaty apply to all underground nuclear explosions conducted outside of the specified test sites, and only to such explosions.

This Protocol shall be considered an integral part of the Treaty.

DONE at Moscow on July 3, 1974.

FOR THE UNITED STATES OF AMERICA:
RICHARD M. NIXON
The President of the United States of America

FOR THE UNION OF SOVIET SOCIALIST REPUBLICS:
L. BREZHNEV
General Secretary of the Central Committee of the CPSU

CHAPTER VIII

THE MISSILE TECHNOLOGY CONTROL REGIME (MTCR)[1]

INTRODUCTION

The Missile Technology Control Regime (MTCR) is an informal and voluntary association of countries which share the goals of nonproliferation of unmanned delivery systems for weapons of mass destruction, and which seek to coordinate national export licensing efforts aimed at preventing their proliferation. The G-7 countries formed the Missile Technology Control Regime in 1987 to restrict the proliferation of nuclear-capable missiles and related technology. The original participants in the Regime were Canada, West Germany, France, Italy, Japan, the United Kingdom and the United States. Since 1987, twenty-five additional countries have become MTCR Partners (members).

The current twenty-nine members of the MTCR are Argentina, Australia, Austria, Belgium, Brazil, Canada, Denmark, Finland, France, Germany, Greece, Hungary, Iceland, Ireland, Italy, Japan, Luxembourg, Netherlands, New Zealand, Norway, Portugal, Russia, South Africa, Spain, Sweden, Switzerland, Turkey, United Kingdom, and the United States of America.

The MTCR is not a treaty. The "Regime" consists of a common export policy (MTCR Guidelines) applied to a common list (MTCR Annex) of controlled items, including virtually all equipment and technology needed or missile development, production, and operation. These multilateral export controls are implemented by each Partner in accordance with its national legislation. The MTCR is the only multilateral arrangement dealing with ballistic and cruise missile and other WMD delivery vehicle systems or related equipment, material and technology.

The MTCR Guidelines restrict transfers of missiles -- and technology related to missiles -- capable of delivering a payload of at least 500kg to a distance of at least 300 km. The original (1987) Guidelines restricted transfers of nuclear-capable missiles and related technology. However, in January 1993, the MTCR Partners extended the Guidelines to cover delivery systems capable of carrying all

---

[1] The following overview is excerpted with modifications from the U.S. Department of State, Bureau of Nonproliferation website on the MTCR at
<http://www.state.gov/www/global/arms/np/mtcr/questions.html > and is dated 2/8/00.

types of weapons of mass destruction (chemical and biological weapons, as well as nuclear).

The MTCR Annex of controlled items is divided into two sections:

Category I Annex items -- complete missile systems, as well as major subsystems (e.g., rocket stages, engines, guidance sets, and re-entry vehicles) -- *carry a strong presumption of denial* and are rarely licensed for export. In effect, they are not exported at all to countries of proliferation concern. Transfers of production facilities for Category I items are prohibited absolutely.

Category II Annex items -- other missile related components-- can be licensed as long as they are not destined for an end-use that could contribute to the development of a missile of MTCR range/payload capability.

The regime rests on adherence to common export policy guidelines (the MTCR guidelines) applied to an integral common list of controlled items(the MTCR equipment and technology annex) (copies of these are available to interested non-partners). Partners have equal standing in the regime. All MTCR decisions are taken by consensus.

The MTCR does not take export licensing decisions as a group. Rather, individual partners are responsible for implementing the guidelines and annex on the basis of sovereign national discretion and in accordance with national legislation and practice. Partners regularly exchange information about relevant national export licensing issues in the context of the regime's overall aims. Partner countries exercise restraint in the consideration of all transfers of items contained in the MTCR equipment and technology annex. All such transfers are considered on a case-by-case basis.

The relevance of this voluntary control regime is that it paves the way for a worldwide legal control regime on weapons of mass destruction and the delivery capabilities that can be used in connection with these weapons. Thus, the elimination of weapons of mass destruction must necessarily lead to the control of delivery systems in order to be fully effective.

VIII-1. Guidelines for Sensitive Missile-Relevant Transfers, January 7, 1993, <http://www.state.gov/www/global/arms/treaties/mtcr_anx.html>.

Applicability

Peace

Control

Regulate and Prohibit

Member Partners

Argentina; Australia; Austria; Belgium; Brazil; Canada; Denmark; Finland; France; Germany; Greece; Hungary; Iceland; Ireland; Italy; Japan; Luxembourg; Netherlands; New Zealand; Norway; Portugal; Russia; South Africa; Spain; Sweden; Switzerland; Turkey; United Kingdom; United States

Full Text

1. The purpose of these Guidelines is to limit the risks of proliferation of weapons of mass destruction (i.e. nuclear, chemical and biological weapons), by controlling transfers that could make a contribution to delivery systems (other than manned aircraft) for such weapons. The Guidelines are not designed to impede national space programs or international cooperation in such programs as long as such programs could not contribute to delivery systems for weapons of mass destruction. These Guidelines, including the attached Annex, form the basis for controlling transfers to any destination beyond the Government's jurisdiction or control of all delivery systems (other than manned aircraft) capable of delivering weapons of mass destruction, and of equipment and technology relevant to missiles whose performance in terms of payload and range exceeds stated parameters. Restraint will be exercised in the consideration of all transfers of items contained within the Annex and all such transfers will be considered on a case-by-case basis. The Government will implement the Guidelines in accordance with national legislation.

2. The Annex consists of two categories of items, which term includes equipment and technology. Category I items, all of which are in Annex Items 1 and 2, are those items of greatest sensitivity. If a Category I item is included in a system, that system will also be considered as Category I, except when the incorporated item cannot be separated, removed or duplicated. Particular restraint will be exercised in the consideration of Category I transfers regardless of their purpose, and there will be a strong presumption to deny such transfers. Particular restraint will also be

exercised in the consideration of transfers of any items in the Annex, or of any missiles (whether or not in the Annex), if the Government judges, on the basis of all available, persuasive information, evaluated according to factors including those in paragraph 3, that they are intended to be used for the delivery of weapons of mass destruction, and there will be a strong presumption to deny such transfers. Until further notice, the transfer of Category I production facilities will not be authorized. The transfer of other Category I items will be authorized only on rare occasions and where the Government (A) obtains binding government-to-government undertakings embodying the assurances from the recipient government called for in paragraph 5 of these Guidelines and (B) assumes responsibility for taking all steps necessary to ensure that the item is put only to its stated end-use. It is understood that the decision to transfer remains the sole and sovereign judgment of the United States Government.

3. In the evaluation of transfer applications for Annex items, the following factors will be taken into account:

A. Concerns about the proliferation of weapons of mass destruction;

B. The capabilities and objectives of the missile and space programs of the recipient state;

C. The significance of the transfer in terms of the potential development of delivery systems (other than manned aircraft) for weapons of mass destruction;

D. The assessment of the end-use of the transfers, including the relevant assurances of the recipient states referred to in sub-paragraphs 5.A and 5.B below;

E. The applicability of relevant multilateral agreements.

4. The transfer of design and production technology directly associated with any items in the Annex will be subject to as great a degree of scrutiny and control as will the equipment itself, to the extent permitted by national legislation.

5. Where the transfer could contribute to a delivery system for weapons of mass destruction, the Government will authorize transfers of items in the Annex only on receipt of appropriate assurances from the government of the recipient state that:

A. The items will be used only for the purpose stated and that such use will not be modified nor the items modified or replicated without the prior consent of the United States Government;

B. Neither the items nor replicas nor derivatives thereof will be retransferred without the consent of the United States Government.

6. In furtherance of the effective operation of the Guidelines, the United States Government will, as necessary and appropriate, exchange relevant information with other governments applying the same Guidelines.

7. The adherence of all States to these Guidelines in the interest of international peace and security would be welcome.

International Humanitarian Law and Arms Control Agreements 813

VIII-2. Missile Technology Control Regime (MTCR) Equipment and Technology Annex 11 JUNE 1996, <http://www.state.gov/www/global/arms/treaties/mtcr_anx.html>.

Full Text

1. INTRODUCTION

(a) This Annex consists of two categories of items, which term includes equipment and "technology". Category I items, all of which are in Annex items 1 and 2, are those items of greatest sensitivity. If a Category I item is included in a system, that system will also be considered as Category I, except when the incorporated item cannot be separated, removed or duplicated. Category II items are those items in the Annex not designated Category I.

(b) The transfer of "technology" directly associated any items in the Annex will be subject to as great a degree of scrutiny and control as will the equipment itself, to the extent permitted by national legislation. The approval of any Annex item for export also authorizes the export to the same end user of the minimum technology required for the installation, operation, maintenance, and repair of the item.

(c) In reviewing the proposed applications for transfers of complete rocket and unmanned air vehicle systems described in Items 1 and 19, and of equipment or technology which is listed in the Technical Annex, for potential use in such systems, the Government will take account of the ability to trade off range and payload.

2. DEFINITIONS

For the purpose of this Annex, the following definitions apply:

(a) "Development" is related to all phases prior to "production" such as:

- design
- design research
- design analysis
- design concepts
- assembly and testing of prototypes
- pilot production schemes

o   design data

o   process of transforming design data into a product

o   configuration design

o   integration design

o   layouts

(b) A "microcircuit" is defined as a device in which a number of passive and/or active elements are considered as indivisibly associated on or within a continuous structure to perform the function of a circuit.

(c) "Production" means all production phases such as:

o   production engineering

o   manufacture

o   integration

o   assembly (mounting)

o   inspection

o   testing

o   quality assurance

(d) "Production equipment" means tooling, templates, jigs, mandrels, moulds, dies, fixtures, alignment mechanisms, test equipment, other machinery and components therefor, limited to those specially designed or modified for "development" or for one or more phases of "production".

(e) "Production facilities" means equipment and specially designed software therefor integrated into installations for "development" or for one or more phases of "production".

(f) "Radiation Hardened" means that the component or equipment is designed or rated to withstand radiation levels which meet or exceed a total irradiation dose of 5×10^5 rads (Si).

(g) "Technology" means specific information which is required for the "development", "production" or "use" of a product. The information may take the form of "technical data" or "technical assistance".

(1) "Technical assistance" may take forms such as:

- instruction
- skills
- training
- working knowledge
- consulting services

(2) "Technical data" may take forms such as:

- blueprints
- plans
- diagrams
- models
- formulae
- engineering designs and specifications
- manuals and instructions written or recorded on other media or devices such as:

  -- disk

  -- tape

  -- read-only memories

NOTE:

This definition of technology does not include technology "in the public domain" nor "basic scientific research".

(i) "In the public domain" as it applies to this Annex means technology which has been made available without restrictions upon its further dissemination. (Copyright restrictions do not remove technology from being "in the public domain".)

(ii) "Basic scientific research" means experimental or theoretical work undertaken principally to acquire new knowledge of the fundamental principles of phenomena and observable facts, not primarily directed towards a specific practical aim or objective.

(h) "Use" means:

- operation
- installation (including on-site installation)
- maintenance
- repair
- overhaul
- refurbishing

3. TERMINOLOGY

Where the following terms appear in the text, they are to be understood according to the explanations below:

(a) "Specially Designed" describes equipment, parts, components or software which, as a result of "development", have unique properties that distinguish them for certain predetermined purposes. For example, a piece of equipment that is "specially designed" for use in a missile will only be considered so if it has no other function or use. Similarly, a piece of manufacturing equipment that is "specially designed" to produce a certain type of component will only be considered such if it is not capable of producing other types of components.

(b) "Designed or Modified" describes equipment, parts, components or software which, as a result of "development," or modification, have specified properties that make them fit for a particular application. "Designed or Modified" equipment, parts, components or software can be used for other applications. For example, a titanium coated pump designed for a missile may be used with corrosive fluids other than propellants.

(c) "Usable In" or "Capable Of" describes equipment, parts, components or software which are suitable for a particular purpose. There is no need for the equipment, parts, components or software to have been configured, modified or specified for the particular purpose. For example, any military specification memory circuit would be "capable of" operation in a guidance system.

ITEM 1- CATEGORY I

Complete rocket systems (including ballistic missile systems, space launch vehicles and sounding rockets) and unmanned air vehicle systems (including cruise missile systems, target drones and reconnaissance drones) capable of delivering at least a 500 kg payload to a range of at least 300 km as well as the specially designed "production facilities" for these systems.

ITEM 2 - CATEGORY I

Complete subsystems usable in the systems in Item 1, as follows, as well as the specially designed "production facilities" and "production equipment" therefor:

(a) Individual rocket stages;

(b) Reentry vehicles, and equipment designed or modified therefor, as follows, except as provided in Note (1) below for those designed for non-weapon payloads:

(1) Heat shields and components thereof fabricated of ceramic or ablative materials;

(2) Heat sinks and components thereof fabricated of light-weight, high heat capacity materials;

(3) Electronic equipment specially designed for reentry vehicles;

(c) Solid or liquid propellant rocket engines, having a total impulse capacity of 1.1×10^6 N-sec (2.5×10^5 lb-sec) or greater;

(d) "Guidance sets" capable of achieving system accuracy of 3.33 percent or less of the range (e.g. a CEP of 10 km or less at a range of 300 km), except as provided in Note (1) below for those designed for missiles with a range under 300 km or manned aircraft;

(e) Thrust vector control sub-systems, except as provided in Note (1) below for those designed for rocket systems that do not exceed the range/payload capability of Item 1;

(f) Weapon or warhead safing, arming, fuzing, and firing mechanisms, except as provided in Note (1) below for those designed for systems other than those in Item 1.

Notes to Item 2:

(1) The exceptions in (b), (d), (e) and (f) above may be treated as Category II if the subsystem is exported subject to end use statements and quantity limits appropriate for the excepted end use stated above.

(2) CEP (circle of equal probability) is a measure of accuracy; and defined as the radius of the circle centered at the target, at a specific range, in which 50 percent of the payloads impact.

(3) A "guidance set" integrates the process of measuring and computing a vehicle's position and velocity (i.e. navigation) with that of computing and sending commands to the vehicle's flight control systems to correct the trajectory.

(4) Examples of methods of achieving thrust vector control which are covered by (e) include:

    a. Flexible nozzle;

    b. Fluid or secondary gas injection;

    c. Movable engine or nozzle;

    d. Deflection of exhaust gas stream (jet vanes or probes); or

    e. Use of thrust tabs.

ITEM 3 - CATEGORY II

Propulsion components and equipment usable in the systems in Item 1, as follows, as well as the specially designed "production facilities" and "production equipment" therefor, and flow-forming machines specified in Note (1):

    (a) Lightweight turbojet and turbofan engines (including turbocompound engines) that are small and fuel efficient;

    (b) Ramjet/scramjet/pulse jet/combined cycle engines, including devices to regulate combustion, and specially designed components therefor;

    (c) Rocket motor cases, "interior lining", "insulation" and nozzles therefor;

    (d) Staging mechanisms, separation mechanisms, and interstages therefor;

    (e) Liquid and slurry propellant (including oxidizers) control systems, and specially designed components therefor, designed or modified to operate

International Humanitarian Law and Arms Control Agreements 819

in vibration environments of more than 10 g RMS between 20 Hz and 2,000 Hz.

(f) Hybrid rocket motors and specially designed component therefor.

Notes to Item 3:

(1) Flow-forming machines, and specially designed components and specially designed software therefor, which:

(a) according to the manufacturer's technical specification, can be equipped with numerical control units or a computer control, even when not equipped with such units at delivery, and

(b) with more than two axes which can be coordinated simultaneously for contouring control

Technical Note:

Machines combining the function of spin-forming and flow-forming are for the purpose of this item regarded as flow-forming machines.

This item does not include machines that are not usable in the production of propulsion components and equipments (e.g. motor cases) for systems in Item 1.

(2) (a) The only engines covered in subitem (a) above, are the following:

(1)Engines having both of the following characteristics:

(a)Maximum thrust value greater than 1000N (achieved un-installed) excluding civil certified engines with a maximum thrust value greater than 8,890N (achieved un-installed), and

(b)Specific fuel consumption of 0.13kg/N/hr or less (at sea level static and standard conditions); or

(2)Engines designed or modified for systems in Item 1, regardless of thrust or specific fuel consumption.

(b)Item 3(a) engines may be exported as part of a manned aircraft or in quantities appropriate for replacement parts for manned aircraft.

(3) In Item 3(c), "interior lining" suited for the bond interface between the solid propellant and the case or insulating liner is usually a liquid polymer based

dispersion of refractory or insulating materials. e.g., carbon filled HTPB or other polymer with added curing agents to be sprayed or screeded over a case interior.

(4) In Item 3(c), "insulation" intended to be applied to the components of a rocket motor, i.e., the case, nozzle inlets, case closures, includes cured or semi-cured compounded rubber sheet stock containing an insulating or refractory material. It may also be incorporated as stress relief boots or flaps.

(5) The only servo valves and pumps covered in (e) above, are the following:

    a. Servo valves designed for flow rates of 24 litres per minute or greater, at an absolute pressure of 7,000 kPa (1,000 psi) or greater, that have an actuator response time of less than 100 msec;

    b. Pumps, for liquid propellants, with shaft speeds equal to or greater than 8,000 RPM or with discharge pressures equal to or greater than 7,000 kPa (1,000 psi).

(6) Item 3(e) systems and components may be exported as part of a satellite.

ITEM 4 - CATEGORY II

Propellants and constituent chemicals for propellants as follows:

    (a) Composite Propellants

        (1) Composite and composite modified double base propellants;

    (b) Fuel Substances

        (1) Hydrazine with concentration of more than 70 percent and its derivatives including monomethylhydrazine (MMH);

        (2) Unsymmetric dimethylhydrazine (UDMH);

        (3) Spherical aluminum powder with particles of uniform diameter of less than 500×10^{-6} m (500 micrometer) and an aluminum content of 97 percent by weight or greater;

        (4) Metal with particle sizes less than 500×10^{-6} m (500 micrometer), whether spherical, atomized, spheroidal, flaked or ground, consisting of 97 percent by weight or more of the following: beryllium, boron, magnesium, zirconium, and alloys of these;

(5) High energy density materials such as boron slurry, having an energy density of 40 x 10^6 J/kg or greater.

(c) Oxidizers/Fuels

(1) Perchlorates, chlorates, or chromates mixed with powdered metels or other high energy fuel components.

(d) Oxidizer Substances

(1) Liquid

(a) Dinitrogen tetroxide;

(b) Nitrogen dioxide/dinitrogen tetroxide;

(c) Dinitrogen pentoxide;

(d) Inhibited Red Fuming Nitric Acid (IRFNA);

(e) Compounds composed of flourine and one or more of other halogens, oxygen or nitrogen.

(2) Solid

(a) Ammonium perchlorate;

(b) Ammonium Dinitramide (ADN);

(c) Nitro-amines (cyclotctramethylene-tetranitramine (HMX), cyclotrimethylene-trinitramine (RDX);

(e) Polymeric Substances

(1) Carboxl-terminated polybutadiene (CTPB)

(2) Hydroxy-terminated polybutadiene (HTPB)

(3) Glycidyl azide polymer (GAP)

(4) Polybutadiene-acrylic acid (PBAA)

(5) Polybutadiene-adrylic acid-acrylonitrile (PBAN).

(f) Other Propellant Additives and Agents

(1) Bonding Agents

(a) Tris (1-(2-methyl)aziridinyl phosphine oxide (MAPO);

(b) Trimesoyl-1(2-ethyl)aziridine (HX-868,BITA);

(c) "Tepanol" (HX-878), reaction product of tetraethylenepentramine, acrylonitrile and glycidol;

(d) "Tepan" (HX-879), reaction product of tetraethylenepentamine and acrylonitrile;

(e) Polyfunctional aziridine amides with isophthalic, trimesic, isocyanuric, or trimethyladipic backbone and also having a 2-methyl or 2-ethyl aziridine group (HX-752, HX-874 and HX-77)

(2) Curing Agents and Catalysts

(a) Triphenyl Bismuth (TPB);

(3) Burning Rate Modifiers

(a) Catocene;

(b) N-butyl-ferrocene;

(c) Butacene;

(d) Other ferrocene derivatives;

(e) Carboranes, decarboranes; pentaboranes and derivatives thereof;

(4) Nitrate Esters and Nitrated Plasticizers

(a) Triethylene glycol dinitrate (TEGDN);

(b) Trimethylolethane trinitrate (TMETN);

(c) 1,2,4-Butanetriol trinitrate (BTTN);

(d) Diethylene glycol dinitrate (DEGDN);

(5) Stabilizers, as follows

(a) 2-Nitrodiphenylamine;

(b) N-methyl-p-nitroaniline

ITEM 5 - CATEGORY II

Production technology, or "production equipment" (including its specially designed components) for:

(a) Production, handling or acceptance testing of liquid propellants or propellant constituents described in Item 4.

(b) Production, handling, mixing, curing, casting, pressing, machining, extruding or acceptance testing of solid propellants or propellant constituents described in Item 4.

Notes to Item 5:

(1) Batch mixers or continuous mixers covered by (b) above, both with provision for mixing under vacuum in the range of zero to 13.326 kPa and with temperature control capability of the mixing chamber, are the following:

Batch mixers having:

a. A total volumetric capacity of 110 litres (30 gallons) or more; and

b. At least one mixing/kneading shaft mounted off centre.

Continuous mixers having:

a. Two or more mixing/kneading shafts; and

b. Capability to open the mixing chamber.

(2) The following equipment is included in (b) above:

a. Equipment for the production of atomized or spherica metallic powder in a controlled environment;

b. Fluid energy mills for grinding or milling ammonium perchlorate, RDX or HMX.

ITEM 6 - CATEGORY II

Equipment, "technical-data" and procedures for the production of structural composites usable in the systems in Item 1 as follows and specially designed components, and accessories and specially designed software therefor:

(a) Filament winding machines of which the motions for positioning, wrapping and winding fibers can be coordinated and programmed in three or more axes, designed to fabricate composite structures or laminates from fibrous or filamentary materials, and coordinating and programming controls;

(b) Tape-laying machines of which the motions for positioning and laying tape and sheets can be coordinated and programmed in two or more axes, designed for the manufacture of composite airframes and missile structures;

(c) Multi-directional, multi-dimensional weaving machines or interlacing machines, including adapters and modification kits for weaving, interlacing or braiding fibres to manufacture composite structures except textile machinery not modified for the above end uses;

(d) Equipment designed or modified for the production of fibrous or filamentary materials as follows:

(1) Equipment for converting polymeric fibres (such as polyacrylonitrile, rayon or polycarbosilane) including special provision to strain the fibre during heating;

(2) Equipment for the vapor deposition of elements or compounds on heated filament substrates; and

(3) Equipment for the wet-spinning of refractory ceramics (such as aluminium oxide);

(e) Equipment designed or modified for special fibre surface treatment or for producing prepregs and preforms.

(f) "Technical data" (including processing conditions) and procedures for the regulation of temperature, pressures or atmosphere in autoclaves or hydroclaves when used for the production of composites or partially processed composites.

Note to Item 6:

(1) Examples of components and accessories for the machines covered by this entry are: moulds, mandrels, dies, fixtures and tooling for the preform pressing, curing, casting, sintering or bonding of composite structures, laminates and manufactures thereof.

(2) Equipment covered by sub item (e) includes but is not limited to rollers, tension stretchers, coating equipment cutting equipment and clicker dies.

ITEM 7 - CATEGORY II

Pyrolytic deposition and densification equipment and "technology" as follows:

(a) "Technology" for producing pyrolytically derived materials formed on a mould, mandrel or other substrate from precursor gases which decompose in the 1,300 degrees C to 2,900 degrees C temperature range at pressures of 130 Pa (1 mm Hg) to 20 kPa (150 mm Hg) including technology for the composition of precursor gases, flow-rates and process control schedules and parameters;

(b) Specially designed nozzles for the above processes;

(c) Equipment and process controls, and specially designed software therefor, designed or modified for densification and pyrolysis of structural composite rocket nozzles and reentry vehicle nose tips.

Notes to Item 7:

(1) Equipment included under (c) above are isostatic presses having all of the following characteristics:

a. Maximum working pressure of 69 MPa (10,000 psi) or greater;

b. Designed to achieve and maintain a controlled thermal environment of 600 degrees C or greater; and

c. Possessing a chamber cavity with an inside diameter of 254 mm (10 inches) or greater.

(2) Equipment included under (c) above are chemical vapour deposition furnaces designed or modified for the densification of carbon-carbon composites.

ITEM 8 - CATEGORY II

Structural materials usable in the system in Item 1, as follows:

(a) Composite structures, laminates, and manufactures thereof, specially designed for use in the systems in Item 1 and the subsystems in Item 2, and resin impregnated fibre prepregs and metal coated fibre preforms therefor, made either with organic matrix or metal matrix utilizing fibrous or filamentary reinforcements having a specific tensile strength greater than 7.62×10^4 m (3×10^6 inches) and a specific modulus greater than 3.18×10^6 m (1.25×10^8 inches);

(b) Resaturated pyrolized (i.e. carbon-carbon) materials designed for rocket systems;

(c) Fine grain recrystallized bulk graphites (with a bulk density of at least 1.72 g/cc measured at 15 degrees C and having a particle size of 100×10^{-6} m (100 microns) or less), pyrolytic, or fibrous reinforced graphites usable for rocket nozzles and reentry vehicle nose tips;

(d) Ceramic composite materials (dielectric constant less than 6 at frequencies from 100 Hz to 10,000 MHz) for use in missile radomes, and bulk machinable silicon-carbide reinforced unfired ceramic usable for nose tips;

(e) Tungsten, molybdenum and alloys of these metals in the form of uniform spherical or atomized particles of 500 micrometer diameter or less with a purity of 97 percent or higher for fabrication of rocket motor components; i.e. heat shields, nozzle substrates, nozzle throats and thrust vector control surfaces;

(f) Maraging steels (steels generally characterized by high Nickel, very low carbon content and the use of substitutional elements or precipitates to produce age-hardening) having an Ultimate Tensile Strength of 1.5×10^9 Pa or greater, measured at 20 C.

Notes to Item 8:

(1) Maraging steels are only covered by 8(f) above for the purpose of this Annex in the form of sheet, plate or tubing with a wall or plate thickness equal to or less than 5.0 mm (0.2 inch).

(2) The only resin impregnated fibre prepregs specified in (a) above are those using resins with a glass transition temperature (T_g), after cure, exceeding 145°C as determined by ASTM D4065 or national equivalents.

ITEM 9 - CATEGORY II

Instrumentation, navigation and direction finding equipment and systems, and associated production and test equipment as follows; and specially designed components and software therefor:

(a) Integrated flight instrument systems, which include gyrostabilizers or automatic pilots and integration software therefor, designed or modified for use in the systems in Item 1;

(b) Gyro-astro compasses and other devices which derive position or orientation by means of automatically tracking celestial bodies or satellites;

(c) Accelerometers with a threshold of 0.05 g or less, or a linearity error within 0.25 percent of full scale output, or both, which are designed for use in inertial navigation systems or in guidance systems of all types;

(d) All types of gyros usable in the systems in Item 1, with a rated drift rate stability of less than 0.5 degree (1 sigma or rms) per hour in a 1 g environment;

(e) Continuous output accelerometers or gyros of any type, specified to function at acceleration levels greater than 100 g;

(f) Inertial or other equipment using accelerometers described by subitems (c) or (e) above or gyros described by subitems (d) or (e) above, and systems incorporating such equipment, and specially designed integration software therefor;

(g) Specially designed test, calibration, and alignment equipment, and "production equipment" for the above, including the following:

    (1) For laser gyro equipment, the following equipment used to characterize mirrors, having the threshold accuracy shown or better:

        (i) Scatterometer (10 ppm);

        (ii) Reflectometer (50 ppm);

        (iii) Profilometer (5 Angstroms).

    (2) For other inertial equipment:

        (i) Inertial Measurement Unit (IMU Module) Tester;

(ii) IMU Platform Tester;

(iii) IMU Stable Element Handling Fixture;

(iv) IMU Platform Balance fixture;

(v) Gyro Tuning Test Station;

(vi) Gyro Dynamic Balance Station;

(vii) Gyro Run-In/Motor Test Station;

(viii) Gyro Evacuation and Filling Station;

(ix) Centrifuge Fixture for Gyro Bearings;

(x) Accelerometer Axis Align Station;

(xi) Accelerometer Test Station.

Notes to Item 9:

(1) Items (a) through (f) may be exported as part of a manned aircraft, satellite, land vehicle or marine vessel or in quantities appropriate for replacement parts for such applications.

(2) In sub-item (d):

a. Drift rate is defined as the time rate of output deviation from the desired output. It consists of random and systematic components and is expressed as an equivalent angular displacement per unit time with respect to inertial space.

b. Stability is defined as standard deviation (1 sigma) of the variation of a particular parameter from its calibrated value measured under stable temperature conditions. This can be expressed as a function of time.

(3) Accelerometers which are specially designed and developed as MWD (Measurement While Drilling) Sensors for use in downhole well service operations are not specified in Item 9(c).

ITEM 10 - CATEGORY II

Flight control systems and "technology" as follows; designed or modified for the systems in Item 1 as well as the specially designed test, calibration, and alignment equipment therefor:

> (a) Hydraulic, mechanical, electro-optical, or electro-mechanical flight control systems (including fly-by-wire systems);
>
> (b) Attitude control equipment;
>
> (c) Design technology for integration of air vehicle fuselage, propulsion system and lifting control surfaces to optimize aerodynamic performance throughout the flight regime of an unmanned air vehicle;
>
> (d) Design technology for integration of the flight control, guidance, and propulsion data into a flight management system for optimization of rocket system trajectory.

Note of Item 10:

Items (a) and (b) may be exported as part of a manned aircraft or satellite or in quantities appropriate for replacement parts for manned aircraft.

ITEM 11 - CATEGORY II

Avionics equipment, "technology" and components as follows; designed or modified for use in the systems in Item 1, and specially designed software therefor:

> (a) Radar and laser radar systems, including altimeters;
>
> (b) Passive sensors for determining bearings to specific electromagnetic sources (direction finding equipment) or terrain characteristics;
>
> (c) Global Positioning System (GPS) or similar satellite receivers;
>
>> (1) Capable of providing navigation information under the following operational conditions;
>>
>>> (i) At speeds in excess of 515 m/sec (1,000 nautical miles/hour); and
>>>
>>> (ii) At altitudes in excess of 18 km (60,000 feet); or
>>
>> (2) Designed or modified for use with unmanned air vehicles covered by Item 1.

(d) Electronic assemblies and components specially designed for military use and operation at temperatures in excess of 125 degrees C.

(e) Design technology for protection of avionics and electrical subsystems against electromagnetic pulse (EMP) and electromagnetic interference (EMI) hazards from external sources, as follows:

(1) Design technology for shielding systems;

(2) Design technology for the configuration of hardened electrical circuits and subsystems;

(3) Determination of hardening criteria for the above.

Notes to Item 11:

(1) Item 11 equipment may be exported as part of a manned aircraft or satellite or in quantities appropriate for replacement parts for manned aircraft.

(2) Examples of equipment included in this Item:

a. Terrain contour mapping equipment;

b. Scene mapping and correlation (both digital and analogue) equipment;

c. Doppler navigation radar equipment;

d. Passive interferometer equipment;

e. Imaging sensor equipment (both active and passive);

(3) In subitem (a), laser radar systems embody specialized transmission, scanning, receiving and signal processing techniques for utilization of lasers for echo ranging, direction finding and discrimination of targets by location, radial speed and body reflection characteristics.

ITEM 12 - CATEGORY II

Launch support equipment, facilities and software for the systems in Item 1, as follows:

(a) Apparatus and devices designed or modified for the handling, control, activation and launching of the systems in Item 1;

(b) Vehicles designed or modified for the transport, handling, control, activation and launching of the systems in Item 1;

International Humanitarian Law and Arms Control Agreements 831

(c) Gravity meters (gravimeters), gravity gradiometers, and specially designed components therefor, designed or modified for airborne or marine use, and having a static or operational accuracy of 7×10^{-6} m/sec^2 (0.7 milligal) or better, with a time to steady-state registration of two minutes or less;

(d) Telemetering and telecontrol equipment usable for unmanned air vehicles or rocket systems,

(e) Precision tracking systems:

>(1) Tracking systems which use a code translator installed on the rocket or unmanned air vehicle in conjunction with either surface or airborne references or navigation satellite systems to provide real-time measurements of in-flight position and velocity;
>
>(2) Range instrumentation radars including associated optical/infrared trackers and the specially designed software therefor with all of the following capabilities:
>
>>(i) an angular resolution better than 3 milli-radians (0.5 mils);
>>
>>(ii) a range of 30 km or greater with a range resolution better than 10 metres RMS;
>>
>>(iii) a velocity resolution better than 3 metres per second.
>
>(3) Software which processes post-flight, recorded data, enabling determination of vehicle position throughout its flight path.

ITEM 13 - CATEGORY II

Analogue computers, digital computers, or digital differential analyzers designed or modified for use in the systems in Item 1, having either of the following characteristics:

(a) Rated for continuous operation at temperatures from below minus 45 degrees C to above plus 55 degrees C; or

(b) Designed as ruggedized or "radiation hardened".

Note to Item 13:

Item 13 equipment may be exported as part of a manned aircraft or satellite or in quantities appropriate for replacement parts for manned aircraft.

ITEM 14 - CATEGORY II

Analogue-to-digital converters, usable in the systems in Item 1, having either of the following characteristics:

(a) Designed to meet military specifications for ruggedized equipment; or,

(b) Designed or modified for military use; and being one of the following types:

1) Analogue-to-digital converter "microcircuits", which are "radiation-hardened" or have all of the following characteristics:

i) Having a resolution of 8 bits or more;

ii) Rated for operation in the temperature range from below minus 54 degrees C to above plus 125 degrees C; and

iii) Hermetically sealed.

2) Electrical input type analogue-to-digital converter printed circuit boards or modules, with all of the following characteristics:

i) Having a resolution of 8 bits or more;

ii) Rated for operation in the temperature range from below minus 45 degrees C to above plus 55 degrees C; and

iii) Incorporating "microcircuits" listed in (1), above.

ITEM 15 - CATEGORY II

Test facilities and test equipment usable for the systems in Item 1 and Item 2 as follows; and specially designed software therefor:

(a) Vibration test systems and components therefor, the following:

(1) Vibration test systems employing feedback or closed loop techniques and incorporating a digital controller, capable of vibrating a system at 10g RMS or more over the entire range 20 Hz to 2000 Hz and imparting forces of 50kN (11,250 lbs), measured 'bare table', or greater;

(2) Digital controllers, combined with specially designed vibration test software, with a real-time bandwidth greater than 5 kHz and designed for use with vibration test systems in (1) above;

(3) Vibration thrusters (shaker units), with or without associated amplifiers, capable of imparting a force of 50 kN (11,250 lbs), measured 'bare table', or greater, and usable in vibration test systems (1) above;

(4) Test piece support structures and electronic units designed to combine multiple shaker units into a complete shaker system capable of providing an effective combined force of 50 kN, measured 'bare table', or greater, and usable in vibration test systems in (1) above.

(b) Wind-tunnels for speeds of Mach 0.9 or more;

(c) Test benches/stands which have the capacity to handle solid or liquid propellant rockets or rocket motors of more than 90 kN (20,000 lbs) of thrust, or which are capable of simultaneously measuring the three axial thrust components;

(d) Environmental chambers and anechoic chambers capable of simulating the following flight conditions:

(1) Altitude of 15,000 meters or greater; or

(2) Temperature of at least minus 50 degrees C to plus 125 degrees C; and either

(3) Vibration environments of 10 g RMS or greater between 20 Hz and 2,000 Hz imparting forces of 5 kN or greater, for environmental chambers; or

(4) Acoustic environments at an overall sound pressure level of 140 dB or greater (referenced to 2×10^{-5} N per square metre) or with a rated power output of 4 kilowatts or greater, for anechoic chambers.

(e) Accelerators capable of delivering electromagnetic radiation produced by "bremsstrahlung" from accelerated electrons of 2 MeV or greater, and systems containing those accelerators.

Note: The above equipment does not include that specially designed for medical purposes.

Note to Item 15(a):

The term "digital control" refers to equipment, the functions of which are, partly or entirely, automatically controlled by stored and digitally coded electrical signals.

ITEM 16 - CATEGORY II

Specially designed software, or specially designed software with related specially designed hybrid (combined analogue/digital) computers, for modelling, simulation, or design integration of the systems in Item 1 and Item 2.

Note to Item 16:

The modelling includes in particular the aerodynamic and thermodynamic analysis of the systems.

ITEM 17 - CATEGORY II

Materials, devices, and specially designed software for reduced observables such as radar reflectivity, ultraviolet/infrared signatures and acoustic signatures (i.e. stealth technology), for applications usable for the systems in Item 1 or Item 2, for example:

(a) Structural materials and coatings specially designed for reduced radar reflectivity;

(b) Coatings, including paints, specially designed for reduced or tailored reflectivity or emissivity in the microwave, infrared or ultraviolet spectra, except when specially used for thermal control of satellites;

(c) Specially designed software or databases for analysis of signature reduction;

(d) Specially designed radar cross section measurement systems.

ITEM 18 - CATEGORY II

Devices for use in protecting rocket systems and unmanned air vehicles against nuclear effects (e.g. Electromagnetic Pulse (EMP), X-rays, combined blast and thermal effects), and usable for the systems in Item 1, as follows:

(a) "Radiation Hardened" "microcircuits" and detectors.

(b) Radomes designed to withstand a combined thermal shock greater than 100 cal/sq cm accompanied by a peak over pressure of greater than 50 kPa (7 pounds per square inch).

Note to Item 18 (a):

A detector is defined as a mechanical, electrical, optical or chemical device that automatically identifies and records, or registers a stimulus such as an environmental change in pressure or temperature, an electrical or electromagnetic signal or radiation from a radioactive material.

ITEM 19 - CATEGORY II

Complete rocket systems (including ballistic missile systems, space launch vehicles and sounding rockets) and unmanned air vehicles (including cruise missile systems, target drones and reconnaissance drones), not covered in Item 1, capable of a maximum range equal or superior to 300 km.

ITEM 20 - CATEGORY II

Complete subsystems as follows, usable in systems in Item 19, but not in systems in Item 1, as well as specially designed "production facilities" and "production equipment" therefor:

(a) Individual rocket stages

(b) Solid or liquid propellant rocket engines, having a total impulse capacity of 8.41×10^5 Ns (1.91×10^5 lb.s) or greater, but less than 1.1×10^6 Ns (2.5×10^5 lb.s).

CONCLUSION

Throughout history, different civilizations devised their own approaches to the conduct of war, how they would treat combatants and non-combatants, and the property of those whose territory they may occupy. In some cases, the origin of these limitations can be found in Divine Books such as, the New Testament, Torah, and Qur'an. In other civilizations, these ideas have emerged from philosophers and wise statesmen. Regardless of whether the source was humanistic or merely pragmatic policy, a commonality emerged amongst diverse civilizations. The goal was always the same: the humanization of armed conflict, reduction of harm, and protection of certain persons and targets. These different ideas from various civilizations and times represent commonly shared values, and, most importantly, they demonstrate that the concepts of humanism are part of social values commonly shared by the world community because they reflect fundamental human values.

The humanization of war emerged as legal doctrine and norms in the modern era through the Hague Conventions and Geneva Conventions. As the predecessor to the 1907 Hague Convention, the 1899 Hague Convention was the first comprehensive international instrument to develop rules derived from the customary practices of states in time of war.[1] At that time, it went even further when it stated that in cases not covered by specific regulations:

Populations and belligerents remain under the protection and empire of the Principles of international law, as they result from the usages established between civilized nations, from the laws of humanity, and the requirements of the public conscience.[2]

Te basis for such protection of the principles of international law was a consequence of the principles established in the Preamble to the 1899 and 1907 Hague Conventions:

It has not been found possible at present to concert regulations covering all the circumstances which arise in practice. On the other hand, the High Contracting Parties clearly do not intend that unforeseen cases should, in the absence of a written undertaking, be left to the arbitrary judgment of military

---

[1] The 1874 Declaration of Brussels also developed rules derived from the customary laws of war, but it never entered into force. Project of an International Declaration Concerning the Laws and Customs of War (Declaration of Brussels), Brussels Conference on the Laws and Customs of War, Aug. 27, 1874.

[2] 1899 Hague Convention With Respect to the Laws and Customs of War on Land, July 29, 1899, 32 Stat. 1803, T.S. No. 403, 26 MARTENS (ser. 2) 949, *reprinted in* 1 AM. J. INT'L L. 129 (1907) (Supp.) at ¶ 9 of the Pmbl.

commanders. Until a more complete code of law of war has been issued, the High Contracting parties deem it expedient to declare that, in cases not included in the Regulations adopted by them, the inhabitants and the belligerents remain under the protection and the rule of the principles of the law of nations, as they result from the usages established among civilized peoples, from the laws of humanity, and the dictates of the public conscience. [3]

This language embodies the well-known Martens clause,[4] which permits the resort to "general principles" as a means of interpreting provisions in international instruments and to fill gaps in conventional textual language.[5] This is particularly useful when dealing with the legal aspects of arms control. For example, Judge Shahabuddeen in his dissenting opinion to the International Court of Justice's

---

[3] 1907 Hague Convention Respecting the Laws and Customs of War on Land, Oct. 18, 1907, 36 Stat. 2277, T.S. No. 539, 3 MARTENS (ser. 3) 461, *reprinted in* 2 AM. J. INT'L L. 90 (1908) (Supp.), 1 FRIEDMAN 308, 1 BEVANS 631at ¶ ¶ 6-8 of the Pmbl. (emphasis added).

[4] The Martens Clause is named after Fyodor Martens, the Russian diplomat and jurist who drafted it. A similar formula appears in each of the 1949 Geneva Conventions and in the 1977 Protocols. *See* First Geneva Convention for the Amelioration of the Condition of the Wounded and Sick in Armed Forces in the Field, 75 U.N.T.S. 31, 6 U.S.T. 3114, T.I.A.S. No. 3362 at art. 63(4); Second Geneva Convention of 1949 for the Amelioration of the Condition of Wounded, Sick, and Shipwrecked Members of the Armed Forces at Sea, 75 U.N.T.S. 85, 6 U.S.T. 3217, T.I.A.S. No. 3363 at art. 62(4); Third Geneva Convention of 1949 relative to the Treatment of Prisoners of War, 75 U.N.T.S. 135, 6 U.S.T. 3316, T.I.A.S. No. 3364 at art. 142(4); Fourth Geneva Convention of 1949 relative to the Protection of Civilian Persons in Time of War, U.N.T.S. 287, 6 U.S.T. 3516, T.I.A.S. No. 3365 at art. 158(4); Protocol I, *supra* note72, at art. 1(2); Protocol Additional to Geneva Convention of Aug. 12, 1949, and Relating to the Protection of Victims of Non-International Armed Conflicts, *opened for signature*, Dec. 12, 1977, U.N. Doc. A/32/144 AnnexII, *reprinted in* 16 I.L.M. 1391 at pmbl. [hereinafter Protocol II]; PABLO BENVENUTI, *La Clausola Martens e la Tradizione Classica del Diritto Naturale nella Codificazione del Conflicts Armati, in* SCRITTI DEGLI ALLIEVI IN MEMORIA DI GUISEPPE BARILE 173 (1995).

[5] *See* M. Cherif Bassiouni, *A Functional Approach to "General Principles of International Law*,*"* 11 MICH J. INT'L L. 768 (1990). The same formulation of the Hague Conventions has been used in the latest international instrument on the humanitarian law of armed conflicts, Protocol I states in Article 1:

In cases not covered by this Protocol or by other international agreements, civilians and combatants remain under the protection and authority of the principles of international law derived from established custom, from the principles of humanity and from the dictates of public conscience. (emphasis added).

1977 Protocol Additional to Geneva Conventions of August 12, 1949, and Relating to the Protection of Victims of International Conflicts, *open for signature* Dec. 12, 1977, U.N. Doc. A/32/144 Annex I, *reprinted in* 16 I.L.M. 1391 (1977); 72 AM. J. INT'L L. 457 (1977) [hereinafter Protocol I] at art. 1. *See also* Waldemar A. Solf, *Protection of Civilians Against the Effects of Hostilities Under Customary International Law and Under Protocol I*, 1 AM. U.J. INT'L L. & POL'Y 117 (1986).

Advisory Opinion on the *Legality of the Threat or Use of Nuclear Weapons* argued that:

> In effect, the Martens Clause provided authority for treating principles of humanity and the dictates of public conscience as principles of international law, leaving the precise content of the standard implied by these principles of international law to be ascertained in the light of changing conditions, inclusive of changes in the means and methods of warfare . . . . Thus, the Martens Clause provided its own self-sufficient and conclusive authority for the proposition that there were already in existence principles of international law under which considerations of humanity could themselves exert legal force to govern military conduct in cases in which no relevant rule was provided by conventional law.[6]

A corollary to the general principles contained in the preamble of the 1899 and 1907 Conventions is the limitation contained in Article 22 of the Hague Regulations in these two Conventions which provides for another general norm that "*the right of belligerents to adopt means of injuring the enemy is not unlimited.*"[7]

In time, the values reflected in the Hague Conventions and the norms embodied in the Regulations became part of other conventions. Efforts to control the use of weapons gave rise to a humanistic doctrine, founded on three distinct yet related concepts. They are: 1) weapons should not cause unnecessary pain and suffering to combatants, 2) their use should be proportional to a reasonable military objective, and 3) weapons should not be used in a manner that is indiscriminate so as to prevent their harming of protected persons and targets. The principle of unnecessary pain and suffering can automatically and entirely prohibit certain weapons or it can prohibit a particular use of the weapon. In contrast, the principles of discrimination and proportionality only limit the use of certain permissible weapons.

The evolution of the concept of unnecessary pain and suffering finds its application in few treaties; however, it has successfully served as the foundation for contemporary norms, which prohibit the use of weapons that have such an effect. It may well be said that this concept started in 1139 when the Second Lateran Council prohibited the use of the crossbow and the harquebus as weapons that cause "unnecessary pain and suffering" and were, therefore, deemed inhumane and consequently, barred from use in war. Later, in 1868, the St. Petersburg

---

[6] Legality of Threat Or Use of Nuclear Weapons, 1996 ICJ Rep. 226, 406; *see also* Thomas Meron, *The Martens Clause, Principles of Humanity, and the Dictates of Public Conscience in* 94 AM. J. INT'L L. 1 (2000).

[7] Protocol 1, *supra* note 5, at Article 35(1) which parallels the Hague Conventions' general norm on the implicit limitation on the "methods" of war. That article states "*in any armed conflict, the right of the parties to the conflict to choose methods or means of warfare is not unlimited.*" (emphasis added).

Declaration, found on page 85, for the same reason, prohibited the use of explosive and fulminating projectiles. Then, in 1907, the Hague Convention prohibited the use of weapons that cause unnecessary pain and suffering.

The Geneva Conventions of 1949 advanced the concept in different ways, but did not build upon the basis established in the 1907 Hague Convention. In fact, the Geneva Conventions of 1949 steered away from dealing with weapons, focusing instead on protected persons and targets. It was not until 1977 that Additional Protocol I dealt with the consequences of weapons use.

This dual track of customary and conventional law strengthened legal norms pertaining to the elimination of weapons causing unnecessary pain and suffering, weapons that are indiscriminate in the destruction and harm they cause, and weapons which are not used in a proportional manner. This includes the most obvious weapons, namely those of mass destruction, and also other types of weapons considered conventional weapons, such as incendiary bombs, blinding laser weapons and land mines. Efforts to ban the latter have been evidenced by the following conventions and protocols: the 1980 Convention on Prohibitions and Restrictions on the Use of Certain Conventional Weapons Which May be Deemed to be Excessively Injurious or to have Indiscriminate Effects found at page 217; Protocol on Non-Detectable Fragments to the Convention on Prohibitions or Restrictions on the Use of Certain Conventional Weapons [Protocol I] at page 225; Protocol on Prohibitions or Restrictions on the Use of Mines, Booby-Traps, and Other Devices to the Conventions on Prohibitions or Restrictions on the Use of Certain Conventional Weapons [Protocol II] at page 227; Protocol on Prohibitions or Restrictions on the Use of Incendiary Weapons to the Convention on Prohibitions or Restrictions on the Use of Certain Conventional Weapons [Protocol III] at page 247; and Protocol on Blinding Laser Weapons [Protocol IV] at page 251. Regrettably, major powers possessing these capabilities are reluctant to give them up.

The separate evolution of "Hague Law" and "Geneva Law," has resulted in different regimes of weapons. Within the customary law track, we have seen the development of some thirty-four multilateral conventions that seek in different ways to eliminate or regulate the use of different types of weapons. This situation has created, to say the least, a hodgepodge of different legal instruments with different control regimes, varying degrees of effectiveness and a wide-range of state-parties. Above all, this approach created a great deal of uncertainly as to what is or is not part of binding customary international law. Since most of these conventional control regimes have few enforcement mechanisms, their breaches can only be deemed accountable if they rise to the level of a violation of customary international law, or fall under the norms of the Geneva Conventions.

The importance of developing and enforcing clear international norms has been made even more pressing given the fact that existing rules have been breached with impunity in the past few decades. Examples include Iraq's use of chemical weapons during the 1980-88 Iran-Iraq war, and the indiscriminate use of anti-personnel landmines, causing a large number of casualties to civilians both during and after various conflicts.[8]

Other modalities of weapons control have also developed outside the context of the law of armed conflicts, and largely outside the context of traditional legal regimes, through the field of arms control, which provide different categories of control mechanisms. These categories include multilateral and bilateral agreements on arms reduction, and regional and bilateral agreements on peace or security, which contain provisions pertaining to weapons control.

Unlike the law of armed conflicts whose principal protagonists have been international and military jurists, the field of arms control has been dominated by political scientists and military strategists. Consequently, the methodological differences between these professional disciplines necessarily resulted in two different fields, which, though overlapping in part, are nonetheless separate. The essential reason for this separation is that the law of armed conflicts is premised on humanistic values, though by no means excluding pragmatic considerations, while the field of arms control shuns these humanistic values, though by no means excluding them. Arms control rests almost entirely on pragmatic considerations, the least of which is not power-relations. The need to bridge these fields is, therefore, a task in progress.

The eight chapters of this book represent five different categories, which reflect different legal techniques. The first is reflected in general treaties on international humanitarian law, specific treaties on the prohibition of the use of certain weapons, and norms and rules that emerged from the customary practice of states. These are covered in Chapter I, with a total of forty-two instruments, starting with the St. Petersburg Declaration of 1868, found at page 85, and ending with the 1998 United Nations International Convention for the Suppression of Terrorist Bombings at page 259. This approach represents a traditional legal technique which is based on international law, and has developed into what is now called the field of international humanitarian law.

The second category, covered in Chapter II and Chapter VI with a total of fourteen instruments, focuses on the regulation, control and prohibition of weapons of mass destruction. The earliest of these is the 1925 Protocol for the Prohibition of the Use in War of Asphyxiating, Poisonous or Other Gases, and of Bacteriological Methods of Warfare, which can be found at page 357. The most recent instrument compiled in this book is the 1998 Draft Convention on Nuclear Terrorism, found at page 433. Unlike the first category, these treaties place the burden upon states to eliminate or limit the manufacture or stockpiling of certain weapons. As such it is an obligation of states undertaken voluntarily which does not in itself establish individual criminal responsibility as could arise from violations in the first category. Furthermore, unlike the first category, which is largely premised on humanistic values and humane considerations, the second

---

[8] *Strategic Survey* (International Institute for Strategic Studies), 1999/2000, at 34; ILARIA BOLTIGLIERO, 120 MILLION LANDMINES DEVELOPED WORLD WIDE: FACT OR FICTION? (2000).

category is essentially based on military and political interests of the states who have entered into these agreements.

The third category, covered in Chapter III, deals with the prohibition of emplacement of weapons in certain areas. There are five instruments in this category, starting with the 1959 Antarctic Treaty at page 485 and ending with the 1979 Agreement Governing the Activities of States on the Moon and Other Celestial Bodies at page 511. The concern of the world community in these treaties relates to the protection of certain environments such as outer space, the under water seabed, and Antarctica. However, unlike arms control agreements, these types of treaties rise to the level of customary international law and would therefore be binding upon non-signatory states. But, like the second category, these treaties do not provide for individual criminal responsibility in the event of a breach of treaty obligations.

The fourth category consisting of regional peace agreements that contain provisions on arms control is covered in Chapter IV, Chapter V, and Chapter VI. There are twenty-five instruments in this category. They represent the undertakings between states, designed to enhance peace and security, and they do not provide for individual criminal responsibility. Also, like the second category, these treaties are based on military and political security interests of states.

The fifth category, in Chapter VIII, includes voluntary regulations concerning the export or transfer of technology. For example, the 1996 Missile Technology Control Regime at page 813, developed by the G-8, is intended to pave the way for a worldwide legal control regime on weapons of mass destruction and the delivery capabilities that are commonly used in connection with these weapons. It is a logical sequel to the elimination of weapons of mass destruction that the control of delivery systems be effective.

The penal characteristics identified in some of these treaties are relevant to the development of international criminal law. For example, penal characteristic 2, which is the implicit recognition of the penal nature of the act by establishing a duty to prohibit, prevent, prosecute, punish, or the like, is by far the most commonly found in the documents examined. This suggests that since the Lieber Code of 1863 to the present, the method of creating international criminal law with respect to arms control has been through the implicit recognition of the penal nature of the given act, based on an agreed upon duty to prohibit, prevent, punish, prosecute, or the like. In total, there are forty-one multilateral instruments that utilize penal characteristic 2 (implicit recognition of the penal nature of the act by establishing a duty to prohibit, prevent, prosecute, punish, or the like) to achieve the particular arms control objective. Moreover, practically all of the agreements include penal characteristic 2 as well as other penal provisions, as reflected in Chart A found at page 67..

In the past decade there have been signs of a new trend towards explicit criminalization as the preferred mode of international arms control. Two significant documents in this regard are the Convention on the Prohibition of the Development, Production, Stockpiling and Use of Chemical Weapons and on Their Destruction (1993), located in Chapter II at page 385, and the United Nations

International Convention for the Suppression of Terrorist Bombings (1998), found in Chapter I at page 259. Both of these documents criminalize certain aspects of the proscribed conduct.

A second trend that has developed is that of peacetime arms control. Starting mainly in the Cold War era of the 1960's a number of international agreements were drawn up to achieve such varied goals as the creation of nuclear free zones, banning nuclear weapons tests in outer space,[9] and the control of production of certain schedules of chemical weapons. In total, there are thirty-six instruments that control arms during peacetime. Of these, only eight were pre-1940 agreements. Five bilateral nuclear weapons control agreements between the United States and the former Soviet Union represent this trend, as does the 1996 Missile Technology Control Regime included in Chapter VIII at page 813. The majority of pre-1940 agreements were concerned with arms control during wartime.

A third development has been international legal cooperation by way of mutual legal assistance provisions. There are at least four recent agreements that include penal characteristic 7 (duty or right to cooperate in prosecution, punishment) as reflected in Chart A located on page 67. Of these the most recent two agreements have provisions for mutual legal assistance in criminal matters. These are the Convention on the Prohibition of the Development, Production, Stockpiling and Use of Chemical Weapons and on Their Destruction (1993) at page 385, and the United Nations International Convention for the Suppression of Terrorist Bombings (1998) at page 259. Perhaps it is no coincidence that these two agreements reflect each of the emerging trends in arms control. Indeed, the three developments of explicit criminalization, peacetime arms control, and mutual legal assistance are directly in concert with the growing interconnection of international security arrangements.

Despite a long history of humanitarian law and arms control, the international legal community has yet to develop a comprehensive convention that clarifies the norm with respect to weapons of mass destruction. While the 1993 Convention on the Prohibition of the Development, Production, Stockpiling and Use of Chemical Weapons and on Their Destruction, at page 385, provides for the criminalization of some violations, the 1972 Convention on the Prohibition of the Development, Production and Stockpiling of Bacteriological (Biological) and Toxin Weapons and on Their Destruction, located in Chapter II at page 379, does not. Similarly, the 1996 International Court of Justice Advisory Opinion on the Legality of Threat Or Use of Nuclear Weapons, included in Chapter II at 443, merely holds that a first strike or a strike other than one in self-defense is prohibited. A clear and comprehensive norm is necessary in order to enhance compliance with the norm, increase the possibility to prosecute violations of the norm, increase accountability, engender deterrence, and ultimately reduce harm.

As mentioned earlier, the instruments contained in this book have never been compiled and published. This is largely due to the fact that these instruments are a

---

[9] See CHARLES J. MOXLEY, JR., NUCLEAR WEAPONS AND INTERNATIONAL LAW IN THE POST COLD WAR WORLD (2000). See also VED P. NANDA AND DAVID KRIEGER, NUCLEAR WEAPONS AND THE WORLD COURT (1998).

product of competing legal techniques developed from different professional categories, namely international and military jurists, and political scientists and military strategists.

Thus the field of weapons control is divided between international humanitarian law and arms control and disarmament, operating rather independently of one another even though their overall goal is the same—the limitation of the harmful effects of warfare. Hopefully this book will be a contribution to the rapprochement between these two disciplines, and above all it will be a contribution to greater prospects for limitations on the use of weapons in time of war and in time of peace, in order to achieve not only humanization of armed conflicts but also as a way of enhancing peace and security.